READINGS IN THE THEORY

OF

INCOME DISTRIBUTION

The Series of Republished
Articles on Economics

Volume III

Selection Committee For This Volume

WILLIAM FELLNER

BERNARD F. HALEY

*The participation of the American Economic Association in the
presentation of this series consists in the appointment of a
committee to determine the subjects of the volumes and of special
committees to select the articles for each volume.*

READINGS IN THE THEORY

OF

INCOME DISTRIBUTION

Selected by a Committee of

THE AMERICAN ECONOMIC ASSOCIATION

RICHARD D. IRWIN, INC.

HOMEWOOD, ILLINOIS

1951

PREFACE

The Blakiston Series of Republished Articles on Economics* is designed to make accessible in its successive volumes the most useful articles and essays in the various fields of economic analysis and policy. By an agreement between The Blakiston Company and the American Economic Association, the Company, during an initial experimental term, will undertake the publication of an annual volume devoted to a subject chosen by a standing committee of the Association and edited by a special committee of experts on that subject. The favorable reception of the first two volumes in the series has encouraged the publishers to continue the venture despite technical and editorial difficulties entailed by the war and reconversion periods.

Primarily, the Series is oriented toward the tuition of senior and graduate university students; but there is also the hope that professional economists will find it a useful means of keeping abreast of developments in fields other than their own. Thus the Series may help to lessen the intellectual provincialism of specialists, which, it is said, threatens them with having nothing in common—not even an education. Furthermore, despite the aridity which economists seem to cherish, and despite their affection of technical jargon and even of terminological monsters called up for the occasion, the intelligent layman will in general be able to find his way successfully through these collections, to his lasting benefit if not delight.

It should go without saying that the editorial committees desire not only to acquaint the reader with doctrines common to many or all of the scholars in the field, with the contentious issues, and with the more interesting idiosyncrasies of certain writers, but also to do all this without bias in the selection of content.

Editorial responsibility for the present volume was borne by Professor Bernard Haley until the pressure of duties in the Depart-

---

*Since 1952 this series has been published by Richard D. Irwin, Inc., and is now known as The Series of Republished Articles on Economics.

ment of State interfered. Thereupon Professor William Fellner took over the undertaking and carried it through to actual publication. Readers of the volume will find it profitable to begin with the explanatory introduction written by these editors. As with the earlier volumes in this Series, a helpful role was played by Professor Fritz Machlup, adviser on economic publications to The Blakiston Company.

It is contemplated that the fourth volume reproduce articles in the field of international economic theory and policy. Suggestions relative to that volume, or regarding the character of future volumes, are welcome; they may be addressed to Professor James Washington Bell, American Economic Association, Evanston, Illinois.

HOWARD S. ELLIS.

Chairman, General Committee on

Republications.

BERKELEY, CALIFORNIA
March, 1946.

INTRODUCTION

The present state of the theory of income distribution is generally considered unsatisfactory, and it is rightly so considered. However, important elements of a theory are recognizable. Some of these elements, such as the marginal productivity theory, are comparatively well developed, while others are in their initial stages or are as yet no more than tentative suggestions.

There exists a reasonable degree of consensus concerning the validity of the proposition that, on the assumptions underlying the profit-maximization axiom, the demand functions for factors of production are marginal value product (or marginal revenue product) functions. The qualifications to which this proposition is subject relate to cases in which it is impossible to speak of a demand function for factors (as under monopsony) or in which the demand function is discontinuous and therefore nonexistent for certain ranges. The relationship between marginal productivity and the demand for factors constitutes the main link between the theory of production and that of distribution. It seemed appropriate, therefore, to include in this volume a general section concerned with those areas of the theory of production from which the various concepts of marginal productivity have been developed.

The incompleteness of the marginal productivity theory as a theory of distribution manifests itself somewhat differently with respect to the various distributive shares. Consequently the volume contains no general section on these limitations and on the further analytical elements required for a satisfactory theory of distribution. Some discussion of these matters, however, is included under the separate headings corresponding to the "four distributive shares."

It was comparatively easy to select essays discussing those qualifications to the marginal productivity theory of wages which stem from discontinuities in the functions on the one hand, and from monopsony on the other. As far as a consistent general theory of wages is concerned, however, this leaves at least two further difficulties unresolved. In the first place, the marginal productivity theory is a theory of factor demand. A complete theory of factor prices (that is, of "distribution") must contain a theory of supply as well as of demand. Yet at present there exists no satisfactory theory of labor supply for the kind of economy in which we are living. If such a theory emerges, it will have to take into account the "institutional" circumstances determining the policies of labor unions. An article dealing with some of these circumstances was included in the volume, but it cannot of course be claimed that anything approaching a complete theory of labor supply is presented.

Aside from this deficiency in the available literature, it has become increasingly clear to economists that the demand for labor is interrelated with supply conditions and that no satisfactory analysis of this problem has so far been incorporated into the theory of wages. Even if we assume the wage claims of labor as given, instead of attempting to explain them by a theory of supply, we still should take account of the fact that the position of the marginal productivity functions depends on *what* the "given" level of the supply functions is for the economy as a whole and that the relationship between the demand side and the supply side of the labor market presumably is quite complex. The Keynesian assumption (in its extreme version) could be interpreted to maintain that shifts on the supply side typically produce shifts on the demand side of the size required to neutralize the original change (in all respects except those pertaining to the price level) and that therefore change in the general level of money wage rates produce no changes in real wage rates and in employment. Such an assumption probably is no more warranted than was the "orthodox" implication by which the interrelation between the supply side and the demand side, and with it the problem of effective demand, was disregarded (or at best was relegated to "business cycle theory," which was expected to live a more or less independent life). The sad fact is that the problem under consideration has not yet received an adequate treatment and that the theory of distribution will remain incomplete as long as it does not include an adequate treatment of this problem. The selection of readings here presented contains one of the well-known contributions to the problem of the relationship between changes in money wage rates and changes in real wage rates. This may start the reader along lines of thought pertaining to the problem just considered, but it obviously cannot be said to solve this problem. The problem remains unresolved— in this volume as in the available literature.

The more important contemporary interest theories are also not free from the weaknesses just considered in connection with wage theory but perhaps they may be said to suffer less from them. Most interest theories do include theories of supply, on the "real" level as well as on the "monetary" level. In other words, they include certain hypotheses concerning the main determinants of voluntary savings and—insofar as they go into the monetary aspects of the interest-rate mechanism—also concerning such further sources of capital supply as the creation of new money and dishoarding. The interrelation between capital supply (or the supply of funds for new investment) and the demand functions (marginal efficiency functions) in this case again is not particularly well integrated with the main body of the theories in question. However, in interest theory this problem has received some attention from the outset, and simplifying assumptions of an extreme character are less *en vogue* than in wage theory.

Differences of opinion exist on the nonmonetary level between the adherents of the time-period theories of capital (implying periodic disinvestment of capital) and those who favor deriving capital values from the *net* marginal productivity of capital (thereby implying perpetual maintenance when defining the quantity of capital). Both types of theory are "real" in the sense of being concerned mainly with the nature of the process of production and with the relationship between interest-rates and the capital stock. The "monetary" theories—such as the loanable funds theory, on the one hand, and the liquidity preference theory, on the other—

could be compatible with either type of "real" theory, and they usually focus attention on further determinants of "the" interest-rate. Readings expressing these different theories and analyzing the relationship between them are included in the volume and so is a well-known article discussing the problems of the interest-rate structure which lie behind the all too simple concept of "the" interest-rate.

The theory of profit and that of rent contain many controversial issues. So far as the concept of profit is concerned, difficulties arise from the lack of clarity of what constitutes the entrepreneurial function in the present institutional setting. One of the authors, whose views find expression in this volume, has shown on what assumptions these difficulties could be overcome, and he undertakes to develop a conceptually consistent theory of profit applicable to the mixed forms of enterprise in our present society. In another essay more skepticism is expressed concerning the possibility of over-coming the difficulties on assumptions that could be regarded as sufficiently realistic. The reader of this volume may get acquainted with both arguments and also with some of the older profit theories.

The selections on rent—which, like profit, overlaps the other distributive shares—are less suitable for giving even a sketchy picture of the present state of theory. The reason for this is that recent developments in rent theory have been integrated more closely with value theory than with distribution theory. Consequently, if a somewhat arbitrary line must be drawn between value theory and distribution theory, as must be the case for the present purpose, much of the literature incorporating newer developments in rent theory falls in the area beyond the line of demarcation. It is believed, however, that the two essays included here contribute to overcoming some of the difficulties inherent in the rent concept.

From the titles of the essays in the introductory section of this volume it will be obvious that an attempt has been made to include readings on the concept of national income and on some other concepts of the family to which the national income concept belongs. Before studying distribution, the student should of course ask the

·

question: the distribution of *what?* The introductory section is intended to be helpful in answering this question. It also contains a general essay on the problem of distribution and an article concerned with the problem of personal income distribution. Distribution theory in the usual sense relates mostly to functional income distribution, that is, to distribution as between different groups of the population performing different economic functions. Yet the nature of the personal income distribution pattern—the pattern of the distribution of aggregate income as between groups earning incomes of different sizes—also gives rise to problems of great significance. The article which deals with this problem discusses also the merits and limitations of alternative measures of inequality.

In the selection of articles for inclusion in the volume, an attempt has been made to give a tolerably rounded "presentation" of the field with which the volume is concerned. Much of what should go into an intermediate course on distribution theory can be taught by using these readings, provided they are supplemented with some care by observations of the instructor. It is fully realized by the editors, however, that the book will not by itself provide adequate reading material for such a course. An adequate textbook of selected readings for this purpose would have to include selections from books as well as of articles and essays, and it probably would have to contain an elaborate commentary by the editors. They have confined themselves to selecting for republication articles and essays which otherwise might not be easily accessible to students and to instructors of large classes and which, it is hoped, they will be able to use with profit.

The method of selection differed somewhat from that followed in the publication of the "Readings in Business Cycle Theory." The editors consulted approximately 30 professional economists who were known to have an interest in the theory of distribution. These economists were then requested to offer suggestions as to the articles and essays that should be considered for inclusion in the proposed volume. To the suggestions thus obtained the editors added their own, and then submitted the complete list to the same economists—who were regarded as the Selection Committee—for their comments and criticisms. Taking into account these comments and criticisms, the editors, or Co-Chairmen of the Selection Committee, then prepared the final list.

A substantial amount of clerical work involved in this procedure was performed by the Bureau of Business and Economic Research of the University of California. For this generous assistance we express our gratitude. We have received considerable help and valuable advice from Mr. Frank E. Norton, Jr. He is also the author of the bibliography at the close of the volume.

WILLIAM FELLNER,
BERNARD F. HALEY,
Co-Chairmen, Selection Committee

CONTENTS

INTEREST

PROFIT

RENT

CONCEPT OF INCOME AND DISTRIBUTION

1

NATIONAL INCOME*

By Simon S. Kuznets†

National income may be defined provisionally as the net total
of commodities and services (economic goods) produced by the
people comprising a nation; as the total of such goods received by
the nation's individual members in return for their assistance in
producing commodities and services; as the total of goods consumed
by these individuals out of the receipts thus earned; or, finally, as
the net total of desirable events enjoyed by the same individuals
in their double capacity as producers and consumers. Defined in
any one of these fashions national income is the end product of a
country's economic activity, reflecting the combined play of
economic forces and serving to appraise the prevailing economic
organization in terms of its returns.

Being thus a summary and appraisal notion rather than an
analytical entity, national income demands statistical measurement. It has been estimated in money terms over a number of
years for the principal countries of the world. A selected group of
such estimates is given in Table I. Specific measures of this type
seem at first glance to convey information of crucial importance.
Since the end product of each country's economic system is an
index of its producing power, income estimates furnish a comparison of the productivity of nations. Per capita income figures,
especially when adjusted for differences in purchasing power of
money, appear to measure the nation's economic welfare. A continuous series of annual estimates of total or per capita income
would reflect also the constancy of the income flow, another impor-

---

* *Encyclopaedia of the Social Sciences*, Volume XI, 1933, pages 205–224.
Reprinted by courtesy of The Macmillan Co. and the author.

† National Bureau of Economic Research.

CONCEPT OF INCOME AND DISTRIBUTION

TABLE I. TOTAL AND PER CAPITA INCOME ESTIMATES FOR VARIOUS COUNTRIES *

Country	Pre-war				Post-war			
	Year	Total Income (in $1,000,000)	Per Capita Income (in current dollars)	Per Capita Income (in 1913 dollars)	Year	Total Income (in $1,000,000)	Per Capita Income (in current dollars)	Per Capita Income (in 1913 dollars)
United States	1913	35,723	368	368	1928	89,419	749	541
Canada	1911	2,000	278	296	1928	5,938	604	401
United Kingdom	1911	9,840	234	250	1928	18,730	411	293
Germany	1913	11,934	178	178	1928	17,990	279	199
France	1913	6,387	161	161	1928	7,856	192	188
Belgium	1913	1,251	164	164	1924	1,438	187	135
Italy	1914	3,659	102	108	1928	4,944	121	96
Switzerland	1913	660	171	171	1924	1,131	289	178
Austria	1913	891	132	132	1927	940	141	152
Hungary	1913	1,366	64	64	1929	764	87	85
Spain	1914	2,149	105	94	1923	3,497	162	117
Russia	1913	7,216	52	52	1929	16,434	107	62
Japan	1913	1,156	22	22	1925	5,492	89	53
India †	1900-14	3,597	12	14	1921-22	6,496	20	13
Australia	1913-14	1,473	300	292	1927-28	3,165	504	304

* The total income of each country was converted into American dollars on the basis of the average rate of exchange of the corresponding year and divided by the population figure to give the per capita income in current dollars.   The total income of each country, expressed in its own currency, was deflated by the whole-sale price index for that country with 1913 as the base year, converted into American dollars on the basis of the rate of exchange in 1913 and divided by the population figure to give the per capita income in 1913 dollars. The quotations of exchange rates used are taken from J. R. Mood, "Handbook of Foreign Currency and Exchange," United States, Bureau of Foreign and Domestic Commerce, *Trade Promotion Series*, no. 102 (1930). Wholesale price indices are taken from W. C. Mitchell, "Index Numbers of Wholesale Prices," United States, Bureau of Labor Statistics, *Bulletin*, no. 284 (1921) and from Canada, Dominion Bureau of Statistics, *Prices and Price Indexes*, 1913-1931 (Ottawa 1932).

† Excludes income from personal services.

Source: For the United States: King, W. I., *The National Income and Its Purchasing Power*, National Bureau of Economic Research, Publication no. 15 (New York 1930).   For Canada: Coats, R. H., "National Wealth and Income of Canada" in *Monetary Times* for January 3, 1919, p. 19–21; Canada, Dominion Bureau of Statistics, *Canada Year Book* (Ottawa 1931).   For the United Kingdom: Bowley, A. L., and Stamp, J. C., *The National Income, 1924* (Oxford 1927); Clark, Colin G., *The National Income, 1924–1931* (London 1932).   For Germany: Germany, Statistisches Reichsamt, *Statistisches Jahrbuch für das Deutsche Reich* (Berlin 1931).   For France: Gide, Charles, and Oualid, W., *Le bilan de la guerre pour la France*, Carnegie Endowment for International Peace, Economic and Social History of the World War, French series (Paris 1931).   For Belgium: Baudhuin, F., *Le capital de la Belgique* (Louvain 1924), and *Finances belges: la stabilisation et ses conséquences* (2nd ed. Brussels 1928).   For Italy: Gini, Corrado, *A Comparison of the Wealth and National Income of Several Important Nations before and after the War* (Rome 1925); Meliadò, L., "Il reddito privato degli Italiani nel 1928" in *Metron*, vol. ix, no. 3–4 (1932) 251–321.   For Switzerland: Mori, P., "Das schweizerische Volkseinkommen" in *Zeit-*

tant criterion of economic welfare, and, if the series were long enough, would suggest whether the nation tended in the course of time to grow richer or poorer and how rapidly the change was taking place. Estimates of total income are also employed in ascertaining the proportions in which it is or may be divided among social classes, between the community and the individual, between consumption and capital accumulation, and the like. However used, figures like those given in Table I appear to be quite serviceable; they seem to measure in comparable units something quite definite and significant.

Further investigation reveals, however, that the clear and unequivocal character of such estimates is deceptive. Theoretical problems arise in defining the area of "nation"; in the choice of stage in the circulation of commodities and services at which income is to be segregated and measured; in the inclusion, exclusion and basis of evaluation of various commodities and services that are to be added into a national total. Finally, variations among estimates may arise from differences in the types of statistical data used and methods employed.

Problems in regard to the area covered by national income estimates are due to differences in the location of productive agencies and in the political allegiance and place of residence of their owners. We may thus distinguish productive agencies located within the boundaries of the given state (A) from those located outside (B); and among them, those owned by subjects of the state residing within its boundaries $(aA$ and $aB)$ or outside $(bA$ and $bB)$ from those owned by aliens residing within the given

schrift für schweizerische Statistik, vol. lxii (1926) 512–42. For Austria: Hertz, F. O., "Zahlungsbilanz und Lebensfähigkeit Österreichs," Verein für Sozialpolitik, Schriften, vol. clxvii (Munich 1925), and Kapitalbedarf, Kapitalbildung, und Volkseinkommen in Österreich (Vienna 1928). For Hungary: Fellner, F. von, "Das Volkseinkommen Österreichs und Ungarns" in Statistische Monatsschrift, n.s., vol. xxi (1916) 485–625, and "Le revenu national de la Hongrie actuelle" in Institut International de Statistique, Bulletin, vol. xxv, no. 3 (1931) 367–455. For Spain: Vandellós, J. A., "La richesse et le revenu de la péninsule ibérique" in Metron, vol. v no. 4 (1925) 151–86. For Russia: Kats, Vladimir, Narodny dokhod SSSR i ego raspredelenie (National income of the U.S.S.R. and its distribution) (Moscow 1932). For Japan: Mori, K., "The Estimate of the National Wealth and Income of Japan Proper" in Institut International de Statistique, Bulletin, vol. xxv, pt. ii (Tokyo 1931) p. 179–204. For India: Shah, K. T., and Khambata, K. J., Wealth and Taxable Capacity of India (Bombay 1924). For Australia: Sutcliffe, J. T., The National Dividend (Melbourne 1926); Wood, G. L., "Survey of Production and the National Income" in American Academy of Political and Social Science, Annals, vol. clviii (1931) 26–30.

state (cA and cB) or residing outside (dA and dB). The strictly political definition of the area of national income would then include aA, aB, bA and bB, and the purely territorial definition would include aA, bA, cA and dA. The definition used prevalently in national income estimates does not follow either the strict political or the territorial principle but that of residence of the owner of productive agencies, thus including aA, aB, cA and cB.

This definition conceives a nation as basically a group of residents within state boundaries and thus anchors national income to the material base of the economic system whose product is being measured. It is preferable, from the point of view of economic analysis, to the purely political definition of the area. But it departs from the territorial principle by including in national income receipts from capital invested abroad, by excluding payments on foreign capital functioning in the country and by counting into national income the earnings of shipping and other internationally operating agencies owned by the country's residents. The property principle is thus allowed to cut across the territorial base, implying the existence of normal conditions in the sphere of international trade and capital movements.

There remains a question as to the serviceability in economic analysis of area units, defined by state boundaries and supplemented by areas of net foreign investment and activity. In a political entity that happens to be a comparatively independent economic system, such as France, national income does measure the combined effect of related and integrated economic forces; but for economically dependent political entities, for instance, post-war Austria, national income ought to be studied in conjunction with the incomes of countries closely related; and a similar procedure appears advisable for a country with politically independent hinterlands. For many purposes the political unit approach, so prevalent in current statistical procedure, ought to be supplemented by a breakdown of national totals for some countries and a combination of national totals for other countries.

The preliminary definitions of national income given above distinguish income produced, received, consumed and enjoyed. The first three run in terms of commodities and services which are separable from the individual agents and capable of measurement in common units because of the leveling process of market valuation. The last runs in terms of subjective feelings, whose commensurability for various individuals is to be doubted and whose relation to the objectively perceptible economic goods is not, in the present state of knowledge, determined with sufficient precision to permit even purely qualitative economic analysis. Consequently the concept of income enjoyed has to be abandoned in favor of such cruder approximations as income received or consumed. The consideration of the level of subjective feelings is not, however, completely omitted; it is retained as a background of the analysis of national income at the measurable stages of circulation of goods and services and dictates some of the methods of detailed analysis.

As between income produced, received or consumed, the choice on theoretical grounds depends upon the function which the income concept is expected to perform, either as a summary or as an appraisal notion. If the national income concept is a summary of the play of economic forces, the choice depends upon an analysis of these forces indicating whether production, distribution or consumption is the stage at which the combined effects of the factors analyzed appear most clearly. And if income is an appraisal concept, the choice depends upon the basis of the appraisal: economic power as reflected in total productivity (income produced), individuals' potential welfare as expressed in the purchasing power of the incomes received or individuals' direct welfare as reflected in incomes consumed. In addition there is another, subordinate basis of choice: the quantitative definiteness of the national income total as revealed by statistical practise. In such practise the attempt is to provide a measure that could satisfy more than one purpose; and income produced, as the concept of the widest reference, seems at first most suitable. From this one can, by segregating savings of business units, measure income received by individuals and, by further subtraction of individual savings, obtain income consumed. But the shift from income produced to income received involves an estimate of savings of business units, which is clearly affected by the accounting procedure, may yield widely varying results in different times or different countries and is not likely at any given time or in any given country to reflect faithfully the value of commodities and services produced but not made available to individuals. Similarly, the further shift from income received to that consumed meets an obstacle in durable goods, for which the estimate of consumption for any given year can be made only on the basis of forecasting the future from the past life history of such commodities. These difficulties are more than statistical: they indicate that in current reality the most clear cut, general concept of national income is income received by individuals; and that the uninterrupted flow of commodities and services through the economic system is best arrested for the purpose of analysis and measurement at the point when the stream reaches the living individuals, after it leaves the productive units proper and before it has been diverted into the various channels of consumption. The discussion below of the contents of national income is carried on primarily in reference to income as received by individuals.

The inclusion, exclusion and evaluation of commodities and services that are to be added into a national total offer the widest range of theoretical problems. The modern economic system consists of individual units whose basic purpose is making a living; of purely business units whose main aim is the making of profits; and of social organizations whose primary purpose is to render service to society as a whole. Each of these groups contributes differently to the sum total of commodities and services produced and distributed, is motivated by forces of quite different nature and involves a different approach to income as an appraisal concept. In face of such diversity national income must be a single entity, reflecting the contributions of these various types of units and reducing them to a common unit of measurement. Since in the modern economic system it is the market, through its exchange of goods for money, that provides such a unifying mechanism, it is natural at first to identify national income with the sum total of money payments flowing to the individuals from the market. But such a simple definition immediately suggests a number of questions, arising from a conception of economic goods as having an existence and value independent of the changing market. These questions fall into three broad divisions: first, those relating to commodities and services to which there is no corresponding flow of money payments from the market to the individual; secondly, those relating to the exclusion of money payments to which no commodity or service corresponds, or to the adjustment of the money flow to reflect more properly the volume of economic goods involved; and, finally, those relating to the distinction between gross and net income.

Commodities and services to which no flow of money payments corresponds may be divided into three groups. The first consists of goods and services received in barter (as over against money exchange), such as farm rents paid in kind, food and board of farm workers, food, board and clothing of soldiers, sailors and all employees whose subsistence in whole or in part is supplied by the employer. From the point of view of the nation's productivity or welfare the omission of such bartered goods would obviously understate the total performance of the economic system. The second group consists of goods and services received gratis. The difficulty here is not the lack of monetary form but the absence of any specific productive service rendered by the recipient. In such cases, since no production of new economic goods takes place, it appears advisable to exclude the goods from the national income total. If an individual receives charity or a gift this is but a loss on the part of the donor (whose income has been recorded fully elsewhere); and to count the incomes of both donor and recipient involves either double counting or the consideration of the charity or gift recipient as a producer of service to the donor, an obviously far fetched conception. The problem becomes more complicated when such free flow of goods (or money) is directed not from individuals but from the business system, either directly or through such social agencies as the government or charitable foundations. Such free goods, whether in form of money or of commodities and services, must obviously be counted in somewhere in the national total. While their statistical estimate is difficult, their analytical and quantitative importance is appreciable and likely to grow in the future. The third type of commodities and services for which there is no corresponding money payment comprises those produced and consumed within the individual economic unit. Here the main problem lies in the segregation of economic from non-economic activity, since only a rigid line between the two will enable one to include in or exclude from national income such items as commodities produced as a hobby, services of durable goods used in the household or personal services of housewives and other members of the family. But there is no hard and fast rule by which economic activity can be distinguished from social and individual life in general. The importance of economic motives, the regularity of the activity, the relative proportion in which the resulting commodities and services usually appear on the market— all have to be considered. For the modern western economic system no doubt appears as to the propriety of including in national income commodities regularly produced and consumed within the household when they form a part of a larger total destined for the market, most conspicuously, for instance, the share of the farmers' produce retained for their own consumption. Similarly, the estimate of national income should include net services from houses owned and inhabited; but there is considerable doubt as to the propriety of including net services of other durable goods, such as automobiles, furniture or clothing; and more doubtful still is the inclusion of hobby products, for which moreover no statistical estimate of value can be made. Finally, there is general agreement among students of the problem as to the exclusion of housewives' services and services of other members of the family, in spite of the very large size of the items involved. It is recognized that these activities are motivated very largely by non-economic considerations and form much more a part of life in general than of professional economic activity proper.

Being conditioned by the institutional set up of the family and of economic society, the line between economic and non-economic activity shifts from country to country and from time to time. The statistical investigator can lend formal precision to his definition and measurement by extending the area of economic activity all the way through the individual household and thus abolishing non-economic areas. He will then estimate the values of all personal services rendered within the household and avoid the paradox, mentioned by Pigou, of a decline in national income resulting from a man marrying his housekeeper or that of the increase of national income because of the shift of women into industry during the World War. Such income concepts, however, achieve consistency at the expense of reality, for they disguise the basic, if shifting, line of difference between economic and non-economic areas existing in real life. The alternative is to adopt a narrower definition of economic activity and allow it to shift, the resulting income meas-urement reflecting changes in time or differences in space in the performance of an economic system with a slowly or rapidly shifting area. The exigencies of statistical work render the acceptance of the narrower definition of national income almost inevitable, but without a recognition of the limitations involved in its use any comparisons of national income across wide time intervals or between countries marked by essential differences in the relative scope of the economic system are highly misleading.

If not all commodities and services produced (or made avail-able to individuals) are reflected in money flow from the market to individuals, neither are all money payments to individuals a *bona fide* reflection of economic goods produced or distributed. Such identity is lacking first in the case of gratuitous money payments, i.e. gifts, charity and relief. Like the similar flow of commodities and services, these should be excluded from national income totals except in so far as they constitute indirect flow from the business system to the individuals and have therefore not been recorded elsewhere. Quite analogous is the second group of cases, those in which money payments come before or after the service is rendered; the essential element in both groups is the fact of a money flow to individuals without a corresponding return within a given period of time. Hence pensions, disbursements by business enterprises out of surplus or capital, withdrawals of accumulated interest on savings by individuals, all may be treated in the same way as charity or relief.   In so far as these payments flow directly or indirectly from the business system and have been deducted as expenses in arriving at net income, they should as a part of the national income produced be included at the point of receipt.   In so far as they are paid by the individuals themselves out of their past or present shares, from which no deduction has been or is made, the counting in of such payments constitutes duplication.   If for a given year the accumulated but not withdrawn interest on savings is counted into individual income, it cannot be counted again when such accumulated interest is withdrawn.   The principle has a similar application in cases of such savings schemes as insurance or building and loan funds.

A much wider range of questions arises with a departure from the market valuation scheme as such, of which the first step is an attempt to adjust for changes in the monetary unit itself (statistical deflation).   Of the numerous and intricate problems raised by this procedure only one need be mentioned here: the impossibility of getting price quotations for qualitatively uniform commodities over a range of time or from country to country.   Deflations, while necessary, are consequently at best crude approximations; they are the less reliable the longer the span of time they cover or the larger the differences in the countries compared.

Two further groups of amendments to the market scheme are suggested by economic theory: one based on distinguishing economic activities by the material nature of the results, the other distinguishing them by their organizational character.   The first relates activity to wealth.   Since wealth was originally conceived in material terms, only that labor was considered "productive" which resulted in material goods.   This definition excluded from productive activity all services and considered incomes from services not as primary but as derived shares.   While this point of view has proved inadequate, the distinction persists as a background to much current thought and retains its significance as a contrast which would be valid were our economic system to become again an economy of want rather than one of surplus.   In such eventuality commodities as a whole, in so far as they form directly the support of life, would be more important than most services.

The principle of material productivity survives also in the still current distinction between productive and unproductive loans of capital. Capital invested in manufacturing, mining, trade and similar occupations is supposed to be productive because it facilitates the adoption of more efficient methods of production and thus results in a greater excess of product over outlay. Hence interest payments on such capital investment represent *bona fide* incomes and are to be included in national income. But loans to consuming bodies, whether individuals or public, are unproductive since they are used for direct consumption, a utilization which by its very nature appears incapable of yielding an economically measurable surplus. Hence interest payments on such uses of capital are only a draft upon *bona fide* incomes. This distinction, however, seems to arise from a failure to carry through logically the whole treatment of interest on capital and is, in the case of individual consumers, contingent upon the acceptance of some form of the iron law of wages. Consumers are generally also producers, and loans to them may serve to raise or preserve earning capacity. Additional objections are made by many students to the inclusion in national income of interest payments on loans to a public body, like the government, because of the further doubt as to the productive character of governmental activity in general. But so far as governmental activity preserves and raises the productive character of the economic system, interest payments on government loans are of the same economic nature as interest payments on privately invested capital. The current paradox that an increase in government loans would, if payments on such loans are included in national income, serve to raise national income presents no puzzling aspects if it is realized that a rise in indebtedness of private industry would similarly raise the volume of national income.

At present a distinction more significant than that based on material productivity is the one between activities whose income yielding power is conditioned by the present organization of the economic system and those whose income yielding power would be retained or even augmented under a different social organization. The problem of services appears again here. The valuation of personal services sold on the free market is dependent upon the existing personal distribution of income—as manifested in the contrast between the emoluments of those who cater to the richer classes and the low rates at which a number of services are rendered to small income recipients. Should services be included at the high (or the low) prices which they fetch because of existing income distribution and thus be allowed to distort national income totals? The same question applies to commodities in which quality distinctions permit different pricing for various groups of income recipients. The problem may be generalized by recognizing that the extremely high or low valuation of some commodities and services is but a partial case of monopoly incomes, whether on the demand or on the supply side. Each investigator's economic philosophy will influence him either to acquiesce tacitly in the valuation within the current economic organization or to attempt some correction for its distorting influence. One might correct for the differences in valuation of the same commodities and services among the various income groups, just as one corrects for changes over time in the prices of identical commodities and services. One income group could then be adopted as a basic one (just as in the other comparisons some one year is taken as a base), and all commodities and services produced could be revalued at prices charged to this basic income group. The practical statistical difficulties of any such correction, however, are enormous, and it is rarely undertaken. Consequently a comparison of the absolute volume of national income among countries which differ greatly in the personal distribution of income and in the presence of monopolies, of so-called friction incomes, such as advertising, is likely to be misleading. Even for any one country comparisons of deflated income totals over a period of time are usually dangerous, in so far as the available price data reflect less adequately than do the income totals the change in the monopolistic areas of national economy.

The monopolistic aspect of some income categories assumes a particularly interesting form in the case of government, where the problem arises as to the valuation to be applied to services thus taken out of the area of free play of economic forces. The question whether government services are paid at prices warranted by the free play of forces in a competitive market is at bottom unanswerable, for the simple reason that if such play of free forces yielded an effective measure of those services the latter would probably have been left to private initiative. Consequently market valuation of government services as a whole cannot be made, not even for separate groups of services, except for some highly specific units. It can be established whether the compensation of a government stenographer or postal employee is higher or lower than that of a similarly trained and employed person in private service, but for larger groups of government services it is not the free market but the court of enlightened public opinion that can pass judgment as to the presence or absence of excessive compensation. In statistical practise in the United States and most other countries incomes paid to government employees are included in national income, with the recognition that their monetary value is the only available, while admittedly rough, approximation to the value of services these employees render; similarly, pensions for past services and interest payments on loans are included as the equivalent of past and present economic goods produced. Taxes paid by business units are deducted in arriving at the net income of these units, just as are all other business expenses. But taxes paid by individuals are not subtracted from individual incomes, on the assumption that the value of government services to individuals is equivalent to the amount of taxes which they pay and should thus be treated in the same fashion as the individuals' expenses on food, clothing and shelter. This assumption, as indicated above, may not be strictly true; and the resulting free incomes or losses to individuals (flowing from the business system via the government) should be included in national income.

There is, finally, the possibility of a complete abandonment of economic bases of valuation and the substitution of norms derived from other sciences. National income and individual incomes might be expressed in energy units, labor hour units or other standards. Theoretically feasible as such shifts may be, they are as yet not sufficiently developed to merit extended consideration. One distinction, however, is of some importance—that between wantability and usefulness. For it raises the question as to the inclusion in national income of the harmful commodities, like opium, and of other commodities or services that appear completely useless from the point of view of a physically and psychologically normal individual. Some practical aspects of this question are predetermined by the fact that with legal prohibition of certain commodities and services an adequate quantitative determination of their volume becomes almost impossible. On the other hand, data of income tax statistics often include receipts from illegal activities. Theoretically an attempt to make national income a gauge of scientifically determined, real welfare of the population involves an unwarranted optimism as to the validity of sciences concerning human nature. From another point of view, that of the nation's productivity, it should be recognized that the diversion of a certain part of the nation's resources to the production of what appear to be useless commodities is not irrevocable; the capacity of a nation to restrict its production of non-necessaries and increase the volume of necessaries depends largely upon the proportion of resources devoted to the former. It would be a highly misleading picture of comparative productivity of the two economic systems to compare only the output of necessary commodities and services in such countries as the United States and Soviet Russia.

The third group of problems in the determination of the specific contents of national income arises from the fact that during normal times, when a consideration of the future is of importance, the performance of the economic system is gauged not by the gross but by the net product, i.e. by the volumes of commodities and services remaining after the replacement of capital outlays; or, in terms of individual and corporate receipts, by the sum of incomes received after subtraction of expenses incurred.

The most important point in the distinction between gross and net is the contrast in procedure between property and labor incomes. In property incomes the net part is obtained after all capital outlays have been replaced and is thus a pure surplus. In labor incomes the procedure is quite different. Wage earners or salaried workers consume a part of their capital, viz. their working capacity, in the process of earning their income; and the replacement of this earning capacity can be accomplished only by consumption at a certain level of subsistence plus provision for complete replacement at the time when working capacity has dwindled to zero. Were we to proceed as in the case of property incomes, we should deduct from wages or salaries the living expenses plus provision for the future and count as net income only the residue, a procedure suggested by some economists (Loria). The actual practise, as is well known, differs materially from that suggested. True, in certain occupations specific professional expenses are deducted from gross revenue in the computation of net income; also the income tax laws, by setting exemption limits and by imposing lower rates on "earned" incomes, recognize that a certain part of labor income is not net. But by and large, in contrast to property revenues, in labor incomes the net is almost equal to the gross revenue received. This implies that the working capacity of individuals cannot be treated as a part of the property system; that therefore an outlay by an individual of his personal activity is a part of his general existence and the income he receives is a fund of subsistence and not a means of perpetuating the individual as a part of society's wealth. Hence distinguishing gross and net income of individuals from labor or personal services is a case of drawing a line between the area of the economic principle and the ways of life at large. As this line is drawn, so are the questions raised solved. For instance, what specific expenses should be allowed in arriving at an individual's net labor income? There is no precise answer, the general basis of determination being the importance to the individual's whole life of the object obtained as a result of expenses. If this importance is great, the outlay, like expenditures on living, cannot be imputed to the income getting activity proper and should not be subtracted. If, however, these expenses are bound up only with the income getting activity, they can and should be deducted. An interesting illustration is provided by the expenses of doctors, lawyers and other professional persons for their offices or tools, the outlays on which are obviously deductible, and for their education, the expenses for which are usually not deducted. Similar questions arise in connection with wage and salary earners in regard to such cases as the differential expenses incurred in order to live in proximity to place of work.

The segregation of the purely economic motives in expenses from the broad drives of human life is a difficult problem whose solution shifts from time to time and country to country. In the United States as in many other countries there is a tendency in the direction of extending the area of expenses allowable for deduction, as the result of a desire on the part of individuals to limit the base of taxable income. The same tendency to regard individuals more and more in the nature of capital is illustrated by the legal cases of compensation for injury. The exclusion of such payments as industrial compensation for injury from net income is inconsistent with the failure to allow for living and conservation expenses; this is also true of the exclusion of net returns (after subtraction of the past contribution of the recipient) from unemployment, sickness and other social types of insurance. For this reason statistical estimates tend to and should include industrial compensation for injury at the same time that they exclude insurance compensation for the destruction of a building by fire.

Since net income from property can be ascertained only by allowing for the restitution of property outlay, a question arises as to what changes in property should be included in income in order to keep property intact. Shifts in the value of property due to general causes may either be accidental in character, i.e. destruction of property by an earthquake or a sudden rise in the value of property which has survived such a calamity, or may stem from general changes in business conditions, usually manifesting themselves through a rise or fall in the general level of prices. Since national income is to be conceived as the end product of economic activity, measured as net addition of commodities and services, changes in property values arising from either of these two groups of causes are to be disregarded. But if the changes in property value are a reflection of changes in the surplus of gross revenue over expenses incurred plus a depreciation charge at secular rates, to include them with the change in such net income would obviously amount to double counting. The same objection would hold if the changes in property value are a reflection not of actual rise or decline in net income but of a forecast income shift. It is therefore only in the cases of changes in property value due to plowing back of income or actual impairment of property that, by definition, there takes place a conversion of income into property or property into income; it is only in such cases that net income cannot be confined to the surplus of gross revenue over expenses actually incurred plus a standard depreciation charge.

The consideration of the element of realization of changes in property value does not alter these conclusions. If a property has grown in value because of a general change in the level of prices and the property owner sells it, thus realizing a monetary gain, such gains are still to be excluded from national income; and if they are included in the estimate of national income in current money units, they ought to disappear in the deflation of these estimates by a properly constructed index of prices in which the prices of property are included. The consideration of the actual sale of property, however, suggests an additional source of changes in the value of property: an opening up of better marketing opportunities, due to the professional skill of the property sellers. Such changes take place in cases when buying and selling of property become a professional occupation; and in such cases incomes derived from the sale of property, i.e. from the change in the value of property because of the more skillful handling of it in the market, are to be counted as *bona fide* net incomes. But this is only another case of the plowing back into the property of certain currently produced services.

In actual statistical practise the inclusion or exclusion of such changes from net income from property is largely conditioned by the prevailing accounting procedure. For example, in a number of extractive industries the depletion of natural resources actually occurring is insufficiently taken care of by the accounting depletion rates, and in such cases net income as recorded by statistical practise contains large elements of gross income. In other industries deductions from current income for depreciation and obsolescence may exceed appreciably the actual destruction of property in the process of production; and it should be noted that the usual practise of relating depreciation and obsolescence charges to the original cost of equipment means, in the prevailing conditions of technical progress, a conservation of capital not at a constant but at a rising productive capacity. The practise of reporting inventories at cost or market, whichever is lower, means that in years of declining commodity prices the business units understate their net income by deducting losses on inventories. A correction in all such cases is rather difficult; and consequently the distinction between property and income, while theoretically feasible, is in actual statistical practise a reflection of the distinction made by current accounting procedure.

Of the numerous questions raised above in regard to the contents of national income some can be and have been answered unequivocally by the consensus of learned opinion; others are still in the zone of disputation; and still others, while yielding clear answers on theoretical grounds, fail of application because relevant data are lacking. Elements which are generally included in national income received are: wages, salaries, dividends, interest, net rents and royalties, net money receipts by entrepreneurs and independent providers of personal services—all flowing from legitimate pursuits; also commodity receipts of farmers and other self-contained producers; also the perquisites (such as food and board) of employees and receipts in kind of rent or interest. In order to pass from income realized by individuals to income produced the business savings of the individual and corporate business units and of social units should be added. Items which may still be considered in the doubtful zone are: free incomes to individuals from the business system, pensions, compensation for injury, returns from social insurance, hobby products and returns from incidental services, net services from durable goods used by owners, interest on government loans, the allowance for individuals' deductible expenses and, at a considerable remove, payments to government employees.   In some countries, e.g. India, certain estimates exclude payments for all personal services.   Finally, for the more deeply going problem of readjusting the market valuations practise lags far behind theory, even in the seemingly simple problem of correcting for changes in the value of the monetary unit.

National income estimates for various countries may differ not only because of the various ways in which the questions concerning doubtful items are answered but also because of differences in the statistical methods employed in arriving at such estimates.   These methods vary in their turn because of differences in available data. Such variation is perhaps greatest where the scarcity of statistical materials compels the application of an arbitrarily chosen coefficient to a statistical measure of only a small part of the total universe. Estimating procedures of this type offer no purely statistical problems and are usually unreliable, except when undertaken as an extrapolation based upon a long and extensive series of income estimates for other years or other areas.   Even where statistics cover a substantial proportion of the field, data are rarely available on all types of income yielding activity and do not always provide an undistorted picture of income flow.   Estimating methods may be distinguished according to the type of basic data used: production and trade statistics, income statistics and data on consumption and savings.

The commodity-service method attempts to measure national income as the net value of commodities and services produced, tracing them to their originating point in the industrial system. It utilizes the large body of production and trade statistics available in most of the principal countries of the world.   Such data permit a comparatively easy discrimination between payments and receipts that represent economic goods and services and those that do not reflect actual creation of new economic goods; for it is the tendency of production and trade statistics to cover only those branches of activity in which the genuinely economic character of the activity is firmly established.   Often such figures afford also an approximation to the physical volume of incomes.   The disadvantage of this method is the difficulty of guarding against duplications and omissions.   In production and trade statistics the full value of a good is usually recorded at each stage of its productive transformation from the point of origin to the sale of the final product. Even when "net value added" is segregated, as is the case in statistics for manufacturing in the United States, a large element of duplication still remains.   On the other hand, production and trade statistics are by their very nature better suited for the coverage of commodities than of services and, among commodities, for the measurement of basic materials of uniform quality than of finished goods of varying grades and brands; there is thus the danger of overlooking certain types of income yielding economic activities.

The incomes-received method derives the national total as a sum of net incomes received by individuals and business enterprises. It relies primarily upon the large volume of data gathered by income tax authorities and sometimes upon special studies relating to earnings of various occupational groups and to their family budgets.   At least in one country, Australia, data were obtained directly by means of a census.   The method of incomes received escapes the danger of duplications; and the resulting total, in so far as it is based largely on incomes of individuals, is consistent with the concept of national income as it is generally understood in a business economy.   The main disadvantage of the method is the deficiency in coverage.   All existing taxation systems exempt incomes below a certain range or of a certain type, and many of such non-taxable incomes are not even recorded; in the United States, for instance, more than half of the estimated national income is not reflected in income tax statistics.   The deficiency in coverage becomes less important as the exemption area narrows and disappears when an income census is taken.   But census taking is an expensive procedure and an income census develops defects of its own; the Australian census of 1915 was shown upon analysis to include a number of petty receipts whose economic nature was uncertain.   Even for the recorded incomes, tax (and income census) data do not provide a consistent quantitative picture. The statutory definition of income and the character of data requested vary from country to country and time to time. So does evasion of the tax by complete failure to report or by under-reporting incomes received. Moreover the character and statistical reliability of income tax data are not easily tested; these are available only in the form of summaries published by government bodies, to which they are merely a by-product of administrative activity.

The consumption-savings method, which registers income as it flows out of the individual economy, is used less extensively than the other methods, because it calls for data not generally available. No country has as yet continuous and reliable series on the volume of consumers' expenditures and savings, nor even such approximations as would be provided by data on the volume of retail trade or on consumers' budgets at various income levels. Such figures become available either through a greater development of trade, service and banking statistics, in which case the commodity-service method offers an easier way of arriving at total national income; or through a further study of the activity of individual households, which is both costly and unpractical because of resistance offered to the inquisitive statistician. At present the consumption-savings approach is used as a stop gap when industrial or income statistics are badly lacking; and data are available on individual savings, on apparent consumption of a number of consumers' goods and to some extent on household budgets. In the future, however, this method may come into greater prominence, for it is increasingly appreciated that a study of the various ways in which income is spent or saved is an essential aid in dealing with a number of pressing economic problems.

There is an obvious relation between the methods described above and national income at one or another stage of its circulation, but the correspondence is one of practical convenience rather than of logical necessity. Since the different stages of national income are closely related, it may be approached at any stage, that of income produced or received or consumed, and the resulting estimate adjusted for the succeeding or preceding stage. Therefore it is theoretically possible to measure the magnitude of income by any of the three methods suggested; the results should check, and such a check is most desirable. Practically, however, the more compelling reason for using more than one method is that because of paucity of data no single type of statistics is sufficient by itself for the purpose of arriving at a reliable national total, unless the investigator gives rein to imagination by employing "raising" or "correction" factors. Estimates utilizing several methods and types of data may be theoretically deficient, because the different constituent parts of the income measure are liable to errors of differing character and hence are not strictly comparable or addible; but the possible error thus involved would be much smaller than that due to a restriction of the estimate to one type of data with consequent extrapolation over a large field.

The allocation of national income by different categories is suggested by the questions formulated above as to the specific contents of the total; it arises in the statistical process of building up the total from estimates of its various component parts; and it is necessitated by the recognition that the mere total is not sufficiently illuminating for any of the purposes served by the concept and measurement. There is an obvious need for a breakdown of a national income estimate when the total refers to an economic system with widely differing regions; when the industrial constituents of the productive system change; when various types of income shift in importance; when the form of economic organization changes; and when the personal shares in the national total are unequal to a varying degree. The main types of allocation are: by economic regions, by industrial sources, by forms of economic organizations, by personal distribution according to size of income.

The need for a regional distribution of income totals has already been suggested. The problems raised by such a distribution are similar to those for the national total, but the gravity of some questions is increased in the smaller area units. For incomes conditioned by personal activity of recipients regional allocation may not be difficult, unless there is migration of such recipients across

regional boundaries.   Much graver problems appear in connection
with property incomes.   An enterprise may have its plant in one
region, sell its products to the country as a whole and pay its dividends and interest to individuals residing in various regions of the
country.   A regional allocation of property incomes produced or
paid out by such an enterprise offers obvious difficulties, problems
which have often been discussed by the courts in connection with
state taxation of corporations.   Up to the present regional allocation of national income has been carried through only to a limited
extent.   It requires a volume of data not easily available and a
clarity of concepts so far not attained in the existing income
literature.   But the increasing interest in regional similarities and
diversities of economic life may lead to a wider employment of such
distributions.

The distinction among the industrial sources of national income
is important because of differences among these fields of activity in
the character of work or life for the people employed; in stability,
either secular or cyclical, of net incomes derived from them; in the
importance of these industries in the general scale of human wants.
Such distributions carried through for one country at successive
dates or for various countries at the same date serve to indicate
changes in a country's industrial structure over a period of time or
structural differences between countries.   The distribution presented in Table II for the United States illustrates the type of
observation that is facilitated by such statistical measurements.

The dates at which various trends, such as those from agriculture to industry or trade, become observable differ from country to
country and occur earlier in older nations, such as the United
Kingdom or France, than in newer nations, such as the United
States or Australia.   Similarly, the exact rate at which shifts in the
industrial sources take place in the different countries will vary
because of differences in a host of natural and institutional determining factors, such as the availability of natural resources, the
class distribution of incomes and the extent of purposive control
exercised by society.   But with all such differences the decline in
the part of agriculture in the nations' end product; the rise, at first

TABLE II. DISTRIBUTION OF NATIONAL INCOME IN THE UNITED STATES BY INDUSTRIAL
SOURCES*

Year or Period	Total Income (in $1,000,000)	Percentages of Total					
		Agriculture	Mining	Manufacturing	Transportation and Public Utilities	Service and Trade	Government
1850	2,178.3	35.1	1.1	19.8	19.0	22.0	3.0
1860	3,596.7	30.3	1.7	22.1	20.1	22.4	3.4
1870	6,646.2	26.8	2.2	24.1	11.3	30.2	5.5
1880	7,343.8	20.1	3.0	24.4	12.7	34.1	5.6
1890	11,965.5	18.9	2.7	31.9	10.1	30.8	5.6
1900	17,417.7	21.2	3.4	29.2	9.3	31.6	5.3
1910	29,243.9	23.4	3.3	28.2	9.7	30.9	4.5
1910	29,805.0	19.2	3.2	28.7	10.2	33.9	4.8
1913–17	38,610.0	18.3	3.5	29.8	9.6	33.6	5.2
1913–17	36,652.0	17.2	3.5	28.0	9.4	36.2	5.6
1918–22	58,401.0	16.7	3.4	29.6	10.3	31.7	8.3
1923–27	71,891.0	11.7	3.2	27.8	9.5	40.5	7.2
1930†	72,141.0	8.0	2.3	26.4	10.0	44.3	9.0

* The three divisions of the table represent three different estimates which are not strictly comparable; the degree of disparity between them may be judged from the two sets of figures for 1910 and 1913–17. The first and second parts of the table—the figures for 1850–1910 and for 1910 to 1913–17—represent total income including business savings but excluding government rent and interest and miscellaneous income; the third part—the figures for 1913–17 to 1930—represents realized income exclusive of government rent and interest and miscellaneous income. The figures for 1913–17 to 1923–27 are annual averages for the corresponding five-year periods

† Preliminary figures.

Source: King, W. I., The Wealth and Income of the People of the United States (New York 1919); National Bureau of Economic Research, Income in the United States, 2 vols. (New York 1921–22) vol. ii, pt. i; King, W. I., The National Income and Its Purchasing Power. National Bureau of Economic Research, Publication no. 15 (New York 1930); an unpublished estimate by the National Bureau of Economic Research of national income for 1930.

rapid and then disappearing, in the relative contribution of mining and manufacturing; and the increase, especially marked in the United States during recent decades, of the share coming from service, trade, finance and government, are tendencies which appear as constituent elements of the growing capitalistic system of production and thus characterize all countries drawn into the path of its evolution. The figures resulting from the allocation of national income by industrial sources are thus measures which afford specific confirmation of the broad tendencies of industrial evolution observed otherwise by historians and economists; or of the broad differences, generally known, in the industrial constitution of various countries. The net contribution of such measurements lies only in refining and checking the generally held notions on these subjects. And when available annually they may aid in the study of the relative stability of income flows from various industrial sources, a problem on which the prevalent generalizations still need considerable testing.

There is a natural tendency to identify the industrial groupings, which are institutional categories, with the more analytically derived types of economic activity (extractive production, manufacturing production, distributive trading, finance, transportation and so on) and to infer that a shift in the relative importance of a given industrial source, such as personal service, trade and finance implies an identical shift in the extent of trading, financing and personal service activity. This, however, is not necessarily the case, for with changes or differences in the social division of labor the exact scope of activities subsumed under an identical industrial group may change or differ considerably. The manufacturers of the United States may have been distributing, financing and providing personal service to a greater extent (relatively to their purely manufacturing activity) several decades ago than they are doing now. The increase in the relative contribution to the national total shown by finance, trade and services may therefore be due partly to a shift of financing, distributing and service functions from manufacturing and other activities to a separate professional group. A similar lack of identity between industrial groupings and types of economic activity affects comparisons among various countries. Clearly the difficulty of inferences from allocations of national income by industrial sources is the greater the more specific such allocations are—even neglecting the fact that carrying industrial distinctions beyond a few major groups runs afoul of the absence of definite criteria as to what constitutes an industry or an industrial group.

It may be said that the general evolution of the industrial system is toward a more intensive division of labor, a greater specialization of functions and hence a closer identity of industrial groupings with types of economic activity; and that consequently the shifts in the relative shares of industrial sources tend to result in overestimation of the shifts in the relative importance of production versus transportation, transportation versus distribution and so forth. But such a general inference neglects two difficulties. The first is the existence of a counteracting tendency of vertical integration which complicates the proper allocation of single economic units; this difficulty may be enhanced by special factors, such as the allowance in the United States of consolidated income tax returns from corporations. In the second place, the difficulty of determining how far the division of labor has gone in the direction of segregating a new industrial division is especially disturbing, the best illustration being provided by the treatment of interest on loaned funds. If a bank receives interest payments on short term credits to a pig iron manufacturer, is this income produced by the banks or by the pig iron industry? The current statistical practise considers such incomes to be produced by the banking industry. But do banks produce the interest received by them on government securities? Are interest payments received by an individual on his railroad bond income produced by the individual or by the railroad? The current practise is to consider these interest payments as income produced or paid out by the government or the railroads, the basis of such decisions being the distinction between professional activity requiring skill and experience, as exemplified in a bank's commercial credit policy, and a non-professional activity of investment requiring no such qualifications. But the carrying through of such a distinction is beset by difficulties. Are the incomes of holding companies, insurance companies, savings banks, investment trusts and similar institutions, whose main source of income is equities in other concerns, to be counted as the product of insurance or the investment industry as such, or are they to be allocated to the industrial activities which constitute their primary origin? Such questions have arisen but seldom in statistical practise, mainly because of lack of data, but they will have to be faced in the near future.

For all these reasons the apparently precise results of distributions of national income totals by industrial sources must be interpreted with a great deal of caution, being an approximate reflection of only the broadest trends or differences, and need to be supplemented by allocations of the national total based on other criteria.

Forms of economic organization may be distinguished by types of the organized unit (individuals and corporations), by the general principle of organization (free competition, regulation and complete control) or by any of a number of basic elements. No matter how the form of economic organization is defined, the national economy of the last century and of the recent decades represents a combination of branches functioning under different forms of organizations. The distinction of the relative importance of the latter on the basis of shares of national income derived from activities organized upon different ruling principles is of considerable significance. But the difficulty of such distinction lies in the contrast between the absolute categories set up by analysis and the absence of such pure forms in reality. One could presumably formulate adequate definitions of free competition or of complete control; but to establish whether or not a given branch of activity is in a state of free competition is difficult, even with access to the internal records of the individual enterprises in the field. On the other hand, when the possibility of a clear distinction is given by formal criteria, e.g. corporate and non-corporate units, such criteria may not correspond to the essential meaning of the distinction. From the point of view of economic analysis the one-man corporations, which formally belong to the corporate field, are by the nature of their operation much more similar to individual businesses than to the giant, anonymous corporate units.

It is this difficulty that largely explains the failure of statistical study of national income to pay proper attention to the allocation by forms of organization. Such a breakdown takes place mostly in so far as it is coincident with allocation by industrial sources, a coincidence that is relevant since the technological differences among industrial divisions form a basic element which underlies differences in form of organization.   Thus the estimates presented in Table II permit one to draw inferences, from the relative growth of such corporation dominated industries as mining, manufacturing, transportation and finance, as to the growing share of national income paid out by corporations; and from the increasing share of government and public utilities in the total to draw inferences as to the growth of controlled areas of our economic system.   Further precision in the distribution by forms of organization is at present impossible because of lack of data.   But since such breakdowns are especially important in a national economy of a transitional type, when changes in organization are rapid and their effect has to be measured as a basis of economic prognosis or diagnosis, and since recent developments have stimulated changes in the relative areas of various principles of organization, the near future is likely to witness an increasing emphasis upon the allocation of national income by forms of organization.

The distribution of national income by forms of payment is an attempt to go beyond the industrial and organization groupings and to measure the current returns of such general productive factors as labor, capital and land.   The significant political and social conflicts that center about the relative share of these productive factors render a quantitative measurement and test supremely important.   An illustration of results obtained by such measurements for the United States is provided in Table III.

The difficulty of obtaining consistent estimates and hence of arriving at definite conclusions is shown in this table by the two sets of ratios for the year 1910.   Such inconsistencies make a comparison of the distribution for various countries impossible without a thorough reanalysis of the published data and some rather arbitrary adjustments.   But the broad trends in the United States over a period of time, as shown by Table III, can be said to be fairly typical of other industrial countries.   Wages and salaries appear to account for a slightly rising proportion of the national total; while entrepreneurial income, which is a combination of

TABLE III. DISTRIBUTION OF NATIONAL INCOME IN THE UNITED STATES BY FUNCTIONAL
SOURCES*

| Year | Total Income (in $1,000,000) | Percentages of Total | | | | | |
| | | Service Income | | | Property Income | | |
		Wages and Salaries	Enterpreneurial Income	Total	Rent	Interest and Dividends	Total
1850	2,178.3	36.4	44.7	81.1	7.3	11.6	18.9
1860	3,596.7	37.6	39.8	77.4	8.6	14.1	22.7
1870	6,646.2	49.2	31.9	81.1	6.6	12.3	18.9
1880	7,343.8	51.8	21.4	73.2	8.5	18.3	26.8
1890	11,965.5	54.0	24.8	78.8	7.3	13.9	21.2
1900	17,417.7	48.7	30.9	79.6	7.0	13.4	20.4
1910	29,243.9	48.9	28.9	77.7	7.7	14.7	22.4
1910	29,805.0	55.6					
1910	28,297.0	57.5	32.4†	89.9†		10.1	
1913–17	36,652.0	57.5	32.0†	89.5†		10.5	
1918-22	58,401.0	62.9	29.4†	92.3†		7.7	
1923–27	71,891.0	65.5	26.3†	91.8†		8.2	
1928	78,502.0	65.1	24.7†	89.8†		10.2	

* The three divisions of the table represent three different estimates, the degree of disparity between which
is indicated by the three sets of figures for 1910.   The first and second parts of the table—the figures for 1850–
1910 and the second set of figures for 1910—represent total income including business savings but excluding
government rent and interest and miscellaneous income; the third part—the figures for 1910-28—represents
realized income exclusive of government rent and interest and miscellaneous income.   The figures for 1913–17
to 1923–27 are annual averages for the corresponding five-year periods.
  † Includes rent.
  Source: The published sources specified in Table II.

wages or salaries, interest on capital invested, rent on land and
entrepreneurial profits, claims a markedly declining share of the
total.   The share of interest and dividends, the segregable elements
of pure property incomes, shows considerable stability during the
period covered.   Rather similar results are revealed for the United
Kingdom in the comparison of the years 1880 and 1913 by Bowley
and of later years by Colin Clark.   The movement of the same
shares in the years before the second half of the nineteenth century
is subject to conjecture.   Some students (Angelopoulos) suggest

that the early half of the nineteenth century was a period of a declining share of labor incomes; and the investigations of the founders of the Marxian school, indicating the same tendency, are well known. But the inferences for these earlier years can be based only upon a piecing together of the most variegated and detailed evidence, since the data do not permit a brief summary such as is provided in national income estimates for later years.

Such summary estimates, however, must be interpreted with the utmost degree of caution, if misleading inferences are to be avoided. Just as in the allocation of national income by industrial sources so also here there is a natural tendency to identify institutionally determined divisions with analytical categories. Wages and salaries tend to be identified with the theoretical category of labor income; and conclusions are often drawn as to the increase in labor's share of the national product from the rising percentage of wages and salaries in the total income. But such an inference is obviously misleading because of: first, the increasing relative weight of industrial branches in which the corporate form of organization predominates (e.g. the share of manufacturing increases while that of agriculture declines); and, secondly, the increasing weight within each industry of the corporate form of organization. As a result of both tendencies the share of labor payments, which has formerly been combined with other functional payments in the mixed category of entrepreneurial incomes, is increasingly segregated and goes to swell the relative weight of wages and salaries. There takes place here the same "purification" of categories that was suggested as occurring in the allocation of national income by industrial sources. The gradual breakdown of individual enterprises serves to increase the identity in the national totals of types of payments with economic functions, just as the intensification of the division of labor serves to raise the conformity of industrial grouping to types of economic activity.

It is for this reason that Table III combines entrepreneurial income with wages and salaries, to yield the estimate of labor and service income. This addition assumes that individual entrepreneurs (i.e. farmers, small traders and professional persons) obtain the bulk of their compensation in payment for their labor functions rather than as a return on capital or as entrepreneurial profits. This assumption granted, it is seen that the relative share of labor and services (earned income) in the national income of the United States has shown scarcely any increase during the past eighty years. And by the same token similar ratios in any other country for wages and salaries alone tend to underestimate the share of labor and services in the total income at any given moment of time and to reveal a trend in time that is more favorable than closer analysis would show.

Lack of identity between forms of payment actually distinguished and the theoretical categories of economic and social analysis stems not only from the existence of the mixed category of entrepreneurial incomes. Any one institutionally determined form of payment is not a "pure" income category. Thus wages and salaries are defined in economic analysis as a distributive share imputed to the working of a given productive factor, but the payments as registered by the statistician may include quasi-rent and other elements. In the United States salaries as reported by corporations are especially likely to include elements other than labor income, partly because in one-man corporations there is a tendency to report exaggerated salaries in order to reduce the net taxable profits shown, partly because in giant corporations the upper executive personnel wields such powers as to disqualify them from being characterized as employees or their compensation as payment for services. This particular tendency, unlike that of the reduction in the relative weight of entrepreneurial incomes, serves to widen the gap between the institutionally determined types of payment and the economic categories.

To those who conceive of individuals as the active and ultimate units and who do not accept the idea of the economic system as an organic whole it is the income received by every individual that is of importance. National income as a whole retains meaning only in so far as the national distribution by size of personal income shows tendencies toward stable patterns. But from any point of view such a frequency distribution is an indispensable complement of national income estimates if these are to throw any light on the welfare of the nation.   Welfare is an actuality only within the experience of every individual and varies materially with the size of a person's income.

The study of personal distribution of income has been rich in attempts at generalization and analytic interpretation.   The reason lies partly in the great theoretical interest which attaches to the whole problem of inequality of incomes as well as in the individualistic slant of theoretical economics after the classical school; and partly in the susceptibility of frequency distribution analysis to statistical generalizations, a property much less characteristic of the time series analyses involved in the other distributions.   Thus the past study of this type of breakdown of the national total, unlike that of the other types, has gone beyond a descriptive presentation of results in two directions: first, an attempt to establish a law as to the functional relationship between size of income and number of recipients; and, second, an attempt to summarize the distribution by a single measure of inequality of incomes.

In the first direction the basic point of departure is Pareto's law. This law, in its most dogmatic form, states that the distribution of incomes in the upper (income tax) ranges follows a straight line of the equation $\log N = \log A - \alpha \log x$, where x is income size, N is number of individuals having that income or larger, and A and α are constants to be found from the empirical statistics.   Moreover the constant α, the slope of the straight line, is approximately 1.5 in all countries and at all recent times; there is a strong suggestion that not only the upper range of the income distribution but the distribution through its entire length follows the same curve for all countries and at all times; and, because of the unchanging and unchangeable nature of the whole income frequency distribution, economic welfare can be increased only through an increase in the total amount of income.

The importance of such a law for major questions of economic theory and economic policy is obvious, and consequently the attention of economists and statisticians has been directed toward testing its validity.   As a result of such cumulative analysis (notably in the United States by F. R. Macaulay) it was established that Pareto's law is quite inadequate as a mathematical generalization; that because of the heterogeneity of the frequency distribution curve, due to the grouping together of incomes from various economic categories, it seems unlikely that any mathematical law describing the entire distribution will ever be formulated with satisfactory results; and, finally, that Pareto's conclusion that economic welfare can be increased only through increased production is based upon erroneous premises.   Other attempts to substitute for Pareto's curve a single curve with another mathematical expression have also been found unsatisfactory as methods of generalization, although recently a French student, R. Gibrat, using a modification of the normal curve of error, has obtained successful descriptions of a large number of frequency distributions of income.   The curve employed was of the equation $y = \pi^{-\frac{1}{2}}e^{-z^2}$ with $z = a \log (x - x_0) + b$, where y is the number of income recipients, x is variable size of incomes and $x_0 - x$ is a selected income constant.   The assumption in which this equation differs from the normal curve is that the effect of each of the numerous contributory factors is not independent but proportional to the effect of the others.

The more fruitful development in the direction of summarizing the inequality of incomes has yielded numerous measures, which fall easily into four groups: first, those derived from a specific type of mathematical equation and hence contingent upon the goodness of fit of the curve implied by the equation; second, measures of the mean deviation type, available in the statistical theory of frequency distributions and applicable, with varying reliability, to diverse types of distribution; third, measures of mean difference types; and, fourth, measures constructed upon definite theoretical criteria in regard to welfare equivalents of individual incomes.

In the first group three measures of inequality may be mentioned: first, the coefficient α, the slope of the straight line described by Pareto's law, has been employed as a measure of inequality.

The steeper the slope, i.e. the larger the numerical value of α, the smaller the inequality. Secondly, there is C. Gini's index of concentration, δ, derived from a different type of curve of the equation $\log N = \delta \log S - \log K$, where N is number of individuals whose income is above a certain size, S is sum of incomes, each greater than the certain size, and δ and K are the constants. In this equation N is a function of the sum of incomes greater than a certain size, rather than, as in Pareto's law, a function of that income size itself. The relationship between Pareto's and Gini's measure is expressed by equation $\delta = \alpha/(\alpha - 1)$. A third measure of inequality may be derived from the curve employed by Gibrat, being equal to $100/a$, where a is the constant in the equation $z = a \log (x - x_0) + b$.

Of the dispersion measures developed in the statistical theory of frequency distributions the average and the standard deviations suggest themselves as indices of inequality of incomes, both taken relatively to some average income, either the mode, median, arithmetic or geometric mean. The resulting relative measures of dispersion can be computed from a frequency distribution in which the class intervals of income size are taken in absolute figures or in logarithms. The advantage of the latter procedure arises from the fact that the positive skewness characterizing frequency distributions of income is reduced in taking the income variable in terms of logarithms, and that the representativeness both of the central tendency of the distribution and of the average or standard deviation is thereby raised.

The mean difference is computed as an arithmetic average of differences, taken without regard to sign, between all possible pairs of incomes. This measure, called the ratio of concentration by its originator, Gini, stands in definite relation to another, widely known measure of inequality, the Lorenz curve. In the latter cumulative percentages of total income are plotted along the horizontal axis; cumulative percentages of population, from poorest to richest, along the vertical axis; and the points of the curve are the intersections of the abscissae and ordinates thus obtained. In the Lorenz curve an equal distribution is represented by a straight line, equally inclined to both axes; empirical distributions of income usually appear as concave hyperbolae; and the existing inequality is measured by the area between these hyperbolae and the straight line. This area is equal to one half of the ratio of the mean difference to the arithmetic means of incomes.

Measures of inequality based upon functional relation between size of income and economic welfare usually assume that the welfare of different persons is additive; that the relation of income to welfare is the same for all members of the community; and that, for each individual, marginal economic welfare diminishes as income increases. But this last assumption is unfolded differently as preference is given to some specific welfare-income function. Thus according to Daniel Bernoulli the function is described by the equation: $w = dx/x$, where w is welfare and x the size of income. According to Dalton a more realistic hypothesis is expressed by the equation $w = dx/x^2$. According to Cramer (quoted by Alfred Marshall) welfare varies with the square root of income or, making it more general, $w = x^{1/n}$, when n is larger than 1. From each of these functions one can derive an index of inequality by comparing maximum aggregate welfare with actual aggregate welfare as shown by the empirical sample.

The choice of a measure of inequality may, on theoretical grounds, be based upon the conception of the measure as an index of statistical variability and hence utilize the customary statistical criteria of representativeness; or it may flow from an understanding of the measure as a summary of the welfare equivalents of income distribution and utilize corresponding tests. From the first point of view one tends to look skeptically upon Pareto's α and Gini's δ, based as they are upon curves fitted to cumulated variables; to consider the average and standard deviations as inadequate in themselves, unless taken for an income distribution that does not depart considerably from the normal type; and to consider the mean difference as subject to similar qualifications, in so far as it is shown (by Gini) that the mean difference is equal to the arithmetic mean of deviations from a median, weighted by the number of incomes plus one between the median and the given income. From the second point of view the choice hinges obviously upon an agreement as to the functional relation between welfare and income. But in default of that, the various measures of inequality, which are not based consciously upon a welfare-income relation, may be analyzed for the function which they imply; as a result some narrowing of the field of choice may be attained. Finally, in the selection of inequality measures for empirical application there is the additional factor of the influence of imperfections in data on the precision of the various measures. Those measures that may be best by the criteria of statistical representatives or theoretical adequacy may be the most susceptible to imperfections of statistical data.

The variety of methods devised to measure inequality of incomes illustrates the profusion of its aspects and suggests a high probability of divergent results from the analysis of one and the same set of data. Considering that this lack of agreement as to the precise aspect of inequality to be studied is accompanied by a comparative paucity of adequate data, one would expect to find few definitely promulgated conclusions as to trends or differences in inequality of incomes. One finds on the contrary a profusion of contradictory generalizations, which are too often obvious results of pressure to respond somehow to a problem so vital to social policy and prognosis. How divergent and withal unreliable such inferences are may be illustrated in the case of Prussia, one of the few countries for which data on personal distribution of incomes are available for some years back. From the figures for 1875, 1896, 1913 and 1919 Prokopovich concludes that the inequality of incomes is increasing, thus denying a contrary conclusion by Helfferich that no tendency toward a greater concentration of incomes is observable. From the data for 1896, 1914 and 1926 Angelopoulos infers that the inequality has diminished. And Gibrat, after inspecting the data for Prussia and some other countries, concludes that no definite trend in inequality can be established.

The absence of data as to personal distributions of income for lower income ranges and of data for one and the same country for

CHART I. LORENZ CURVES OF INCOME DISTRIBUTION AMONG INCOME RECIPIENTS,
SELECTED COUNTRIES

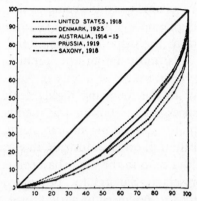

Scales: Percentage of income recipients, beginning with poorest, is indicated along the horizontal scale; percentage of total income is indicated along the vertical scale.

Source: Based on data derived from the following sources: Prokopovich, S. N., "The Distribution of National Income" in *Economic Journal*, vol. xxxvi (1926) 69–82, and *Narodny dokhod zapadno-evropeyskikh stran* (National income of west European countries) (Moscow 1930) ch. ii, sect. iii; National Bureau of Economic Research, *Income in the United States*, 2 vols. (New York 1921–22) vol. i.

CHART II. LORENZ CURVES OF INCOME DISTRIBUTION AMONG INCOME RECIPIENTS
IN SAXONY, SELECTED YEARS

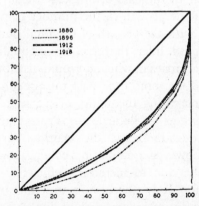

Scales: Percentage of income recipients, beginning with poorest, is indicated along the horizontal scale; percentage of total income is indicated along the vertical scale.

Source: Based on data adapted from Prokopovich, S. N., *Narodny dokhod zapadno-evropeyskikh stran* (National income of west European countries) (Moscow 1930) ch. ii, sect. iii.

successive years and the variations from country to country or
from year to year in the degree of coverage are but partly revealed
in Charts I and II. These assemble some of the various distributions available and give on the whole too favorable an illustration
of the kind of data at the disposal of those who attempt to deal
inductively with this most important problem. The various
studies which have been made, primarily of Austrian, Italian and
German data, lead to the following highly tentative suggestions
concerning differences and trends in the inequality of incomes.
First, income inequality among income recipients is less conspicuous in agricultural than in other industries, in rural than in urban
areas, in smaller cities than in the big urban centers (Austrian and
Prussian data—Bresciani, Savorgnan, Prokopovich). But since
average income tends to be lower in agricultural and rural areas,
the industrialization and urbanization of nations do not in themselves imply increasing inequality of incomes. As for the very
difficult international comparisons, one may only suggest that
inequality is less conspicuous in younger industrial countries
(United States) and in agricultural countries (Denmark, Norway)
than in the older industrial states (Prussia, Saxony, United Kingdom). In the second place, income inequality among income
recipients is greater in the case of property incomes than it is for
labor incomes. If the growth in the number of property owners
has not kept pace with the growth of the total number of income
recipients, one would infer that income inequality has grown.
Thirdly, in those countries in which personal distribution of income
has been measured for some time past the preponderance of evidence is toward increasing inequality of incomes among income
recipients. This seems to be true for Prussia and Saxony, for
Austria (for the decade before the World War, according to
Savorgnan, who, however, qualifies his conclusions by saying that
the change may be due to increasing efficiency of income tax
authorities) and for Italy (according to Gini and d'Addario).
Finally, the inequality of income among income recipients tends
to decline during years of depression and to rise during years of
business prosperity (Prokopovich, Gibrat).

As one increases the time range and attempts to compare income inequality characteristic of the capitalistic countries of the nineteenth and twentieth centuries with that for countries of precapitalistic times, even the slender foundation provided by the currently available statistical data disappears. Schmoller's suggestion in his communication in 1896 to the International Institute of Statistics that no marked change occurred in income distribution between the fifteenth and the nineteenth centuries is based upon too fragmentary a factual foundation to pass critical inspection. General historical knowledge would lead one to infer that numerically the income inequality must have been smaller in precapitalistic Europe than at present, if only for the reason that incomes were then absolutely lower and that the lower limit of incomes is more rigid than the upper. But this statement as such remains a conjecture, while its analytical interpretation, as to the implied welfare inequality, is all the more uncertain because of marked changes in absolute income, standards of living, organization of society and all other factors that affect the significance of a single aspect like income distribution.

Any analytical inferences, however, even if limited to the recent century and related to the more complete statistical data available at present, are made difficult by three considerations. First, all these studies refer to inequality of income among income recipients only and neglect perforce the number of persons capable and willing to earn incomes but unable to do so because of unemployment, legal limitations and other circumstances. The inclusion of these potential income recipients with zero incomes is likely to change considerably the differences in inequality of income distribution between industrial and agricultural, urban and rural areas; the trends in inequality with the passage of years; and especially the changes in the inequality of income distribution from years of prosperity to years of depression. Thus on the basis of 1918–30 data for the United States Morris A. Copeland suggests (in a paper presented at the 1932 meeting of the American Statistical Association) that a distribution among the entire population of money incomes, excluding profits from the sale of real estate and securities and other capital gains, tends to become more concentrated in years of depression and less concentrated in years of prosperity—a conclusion exactly opposite to that indicated above for the distribution of incomes among actual income recipients. Secondly, all studies tend to disregard the absolute size of incomes and study only relative inequality, although most of them note the positive correlation in time between size of average income and extent of inequality. But from the point of view of welfare, capital formation or any other analytic implication of a frequency distribution of income the absolute size of incomes involved is of material importance. Income inequality may decline during years of depression, but the welfare inequality may rise materially because of the general lowering of the absolute level of incomes. Similarly, inequality may be more conspicuous in one country than in another, but because of difference in the absolute size of income the capital forming power of the second country may be greater than that of the first; that is, assuming that inequality of distribution stimulates capital formation, a rather doubtful hypothesis. Thirdly, no personal distribution of income takes into account the costs incurred in obtaining the income and the needs it has to satisfy. The importance for any inferences as to welfare, savings, and so forth of establishing a net rather than a gross income distribution is obvious. From this point of view the treatment of labor and property incomes as if they were measured just by the amount received is of course a misleading distortion. And it is clearly important to have frequency distributions of income by families.

These difficulties are but different aspects of the same cardinal obstacle, which has been stressed before in connection with other types of allocation of national income: the disparity between the quantitatively available and measurable groups and the analytically clear cut categories to which they should correspond. It is highly doubtful that this disparity will ever be overcome completely; but progress in this direction will be made through a combination of groups based on more than one principle of division, through the collection of a more extensive body of data and through an evolution of a more definite consensus of scientific opinion as to the methods of quantitative analysis and their implications. Above all, the recognition of the gap between what can be and is measured and what ought to be measured is a necessary prerequisite of any further progress and a highly valuable antidote to those interpretations, all too common in national income literature, where the wish is the unrecognized father of the thought.

2

NATIONAL PRODUCT AND INCOME STATISTICS AS AN AID IN ECONOMIC PROBLEMS*

By Milton Gilbert and George Jaszi†

Since the Bureau of Foreign and Domestic Commerce began issuing current estimates of the gross national product many business men and economists have asked the Bureau about the meaning of, and need for, this new statistical data.

"Just as people were getting familiar with the idea of National Income," they say somewhat plaintively, "you come along with the Gross National Product and create a lot of confusion. What is it needed for? How does it differ from the national income and what advantage does it have in practical economic and business affairs?"

Such questions are answered in this article, describing the concept of the gross national product. Certain technical details have been omitted so as to focus attention on the central ideas involved.

As an introduction to both the meaning and uses of the gross national product concept, it is helpful to recall the economic problems of 1941. These presented the immediate occasion for compiling gross product statistics. The nation's rearmament program was in process of being stepped up month after month. As that program grew, two major problems confronted the policy-making officials both in Congress and the Administration, and they came to the technical economists and statisticians for facts and figures. The first of these was the question as to how large a rearmament program, or if need be a war effort, our economic system could provide. In other words, what the war potential was of the Ameri-

---

* *Dun's Review*, February, 1944, pages 9–11, 32–38. Reprinted by courtesy of the publisher and authors.

† Bureau of Foreign and Domestic Commerce, U.S. Department of Commerce.

can economy. The second was whether America would run into an inflationary situation and, if so, to what extent. Stated more explicitly, the problem was "were the people and their Government together trying to buy more goods than could be produced, and how much more?"

It is evident that certain statistical data were basic to getting even approximate answers to these questions. To begin with, it was essential to know the amount of goods and services currently being produced, if only as a means of approaching the possibilities of expanding production. But furthermore, some details of the various kinds of goods and services being produced had to be known to provide a basis for deciding what could be eliminated to free economic resources for armament production. In connection with the inflation problem the same data were needed, and, in addition, information on incomes and their disposition among consumption, taxes, and savings. Briefly stated, gross national product and income statistics are just such a statement of the various goods and services being produced, of the incomes generated, and of their disposal among various uses, as is essential in analyzing economic problems of this type.

A business audience easily will recognize the immense difficulty of formulating a war production program without this statistical background. It would be like bidding on a contract without knowing, let us say, the capacity of your plant or the financial facilities at the disposal of your business. It is significant that other countries felt the same need for statistical background material. During its months of greatest peril at the time of the "blitz," the British government set a small group of statisticians to work preparing the first official estimates of national product and national income. This was done because it was proving so difficult to organize the economy for war without these guideposts.

INCOME AND PRODUCT STATISTICS

The statistics on national income were the nearest thing to current information of this type on hand at the inception of our rearmament program. As readers of Charles L. Merwin's articles in *Dun's Review* (August and November 1942) will recall, national income is the sum of the earnings of the various factors of production for their participation in the productive process. A table of the national income for any year, say 1942, looks about like this:

	Billions
Total national income, 1942	$119.8
Salaries and wages	83.7
Net income of proprietors	20.1
Agricultural	9.7
Other business and professional	10.4
Interest and net rents	8.4
Corporate profits after taxes	7.6
Dividends	4.0
Undistributed profits	3.6

Clearly, this information was relevant for the purchasing power side of the picture. But it was not the whole story and consequently could not, by itself, be brought to bear effectively on the problems under discussion.

The first requirement, then, was to develop data on total current production. Since the problems at issue concerned the allocation of output and resources between Government and private uses, it was necessary to think of this total production as consisting of the output of the private business system plus the output of Government. A little reflection will show that the output of private business, exclusive of materials and business services used in the process of production, can be grouped according to its three major outlets as: goods and services sold to consumers; total capital goods sold to, or retained by, business; and products sold to Government. When the goods and services produced directly by Government, which most conveniently can be measured by the costs of the productive factors used by Government in their production, are added to the output of business one obtains the desired measure of total production.

Gross national product simply is the technical name of this measure of total production. It may be defined as the aggregate value of the current production of goods and services flowing to the Government, to consumers, and—for purposes of gross capital formation—to business.   In the breakdown in which it is currently published it looks about like the following table:

	Billions
Gross national product or expenditure, 1942...............	$151.7
Government production and purchases of goods and services.	61.7
War...	49.3
Non-war..	12.4
Private gross capital formation........................	8.0
Construction, machinery and equipment...............	8.0
Net change in business inventories...................	− .6
Other...	.6
Consumers' purchases of goods and services..............	82.0

It may not be clear immediately why it is permissible to break down a total, which refers to current production, into components that refer to sales or purchases, that is, why gross national product is the same thing as gross national expenditure.   The explanation lies in the fact that the change in business inventories, the balancing item which constitutes the difference between current sales and current production, is included in the total as a component of capital formation.

Another feature of the tabulation which requires comment is that capital formation is taken on a gross rather than a net basis—that is to say, replacements of existing equipment and construction as well as net additions to the stock of capital goods are included. The reason for this is twofold.

In the first place, gross capital formation was easier to estimate than net because of certain technical characteristics of the available sources of data.   These center around the fact that the estimates of new capital output must be derived from production data whereas the estimates of capital used up must be derived from financial records.   These two sources do not match at all well. As the statistics stand, the depreciation estimates cannot be subtracted from the gross capital formation to yield a meaningful estimate of net investment.   Although the statistical difficulties probably can and will be solved, there has not been time to solve them as yet.

Secondly, attention is focused on gross rather than on net capital formation because for many purposes it is the more important magnitude. When in connection with the war program, for instance, it had to be determined what volume of resources could be freed for war production by diminishing private capital formation, it was gross capital formation that was relevant. For, in the short run, resources could be made available not only by not adding to the stock of private capital, but also by not making certain ordinary replacements. A national product estimate which would have included only net capital formation would have concealed an important potential source of war output, and would have led to exaggerated notions of the necessary curtailment of consumers' goods. In many cases it is a lot easier to struggle along with old machinery and buildings than it is to have less food, clothing, or even amusements.

SUMMARY OF MAJOR TRANSACTIONS IN ECONOMY
Hypothetical figures in billions of dollars

I. Government		II. Business		III. Individuals	
Receipts	*Disposal of Receipts*	*Receipts*	*Disposal of Receipts*	*Receipts*	*Disposal of Receipts*
7. Business taxes....25	3. Purchases of products of business...50	1. Sales of consumer goods and services...80	5. Pay of factors of production..100	4. Pay received from Government..15	1. Purchases of consumers' goods and services..80
10. Personal taxes.....5	4. Pay of factors of production.....15	3. Sales of products to Government.....50	7. Business taxes.....25	5. Pay received from business.....100	10. Personal taxes.....5
	9. Transfer payments..5			9. Transfer payments..5	
12. Borrowing......40		2. Private gross capital fomation...5	6. Depreciation and other reserves ...6		11. Individual savings..35
			8. Undistributed profits.....4		
Total.......70	70	135	135	120	120

Relationship Illustrated

Since the national income is generated in the production of the national product, the reader probably is wondering what the relation of national income to gross national product is, and why the latter is so much larger than the former. It is necessary that this relation be understood if intelligent use is to be made of the statistics.

To clarify this relationship it is convenient to consider separately the two major components of gross national product, namely, Government product and private business output. So far as the direct contribution of the Government to gross national product is concerned, it is measured, as was mentioned earlier, by the costs for factors of production incurred by Government. Hence, it is exactly matched in national income by the income received by factors of production employed by the Government because national income is simply the earnings of all the factors of production utilized in the economy.

The relation between the rest of gross national product (sales of private business to Government, to consumers, and private gross capital formation) and the rest of national income (earnings of the factors of production employed by private business) can best be seen with the aid of the profit and loss statements of private business. If the profit and loss statements of all business firms are consolidated, current cost items that constitute purchases from other firms will cancel against corresponding receipt items in the accounts of the latter. For instance, raw materials sold by firm A to firm B will appear once as receipts in the accounts of firm A and once as a current cost in the accounts of firm B. The two entries will cancel out when the profit and loss statements are consolidated. Hence, on the receipt side, there will be left sales to consumers, to Government, and private gross capital formation. But this is exactly the remainder of national product for which we are trying to account in terms of incomes.

On the income and expense side, there will be left payments to factors of production (including dividends), depreciation and other reserves, taxes, and undistributed profits. These items will exhaust the list.   For current cost items with respect to purchases from other firms will have been eliminated in the process of consolidation.

This accounts for all the income and expense items that correspond to gross national product.   Assembling and rearranging them, we see that they equal the earnings of the factors of production as included in the national income with certain additions. These charges against business sales which are not included in the national income are depreciation and other reserves, and taxes paid or owing by business.   Thus, depreciation and similar charges plus business taxes constitute the two additions to national income needed to make it match gross national product.

Business taxes are of two main types: taxes that are treated as ordinary expenses in business accounting—principally sales taxes, excise and business property taxes, and so on—and corporation income and excess profits taxes which are deducted from income to determine the amounts available for dividends and undistributed profits.

The relation between national income and gross national product is illustrated by the following table:

	Billions
National income, 1942	$119.8
Plus: Business Taxes	24.0
Depreciation and other reserves	7.9
Equals: Gross national product or expenditure, 1942	151.7

USE OF INCOME

In tracing the income and expense flows that correspond to gross national product we incidentally have accounted for the manner in which private business as a whole disposes of its receipts since the income and expense side of the consolidated profit and loss account of private business is nothing more than a statement of the disposition of business receipts.   A corresponding statement of the accounts of individuals, essential to the analysis of the inflation problem, now may be developed.

To arrive at the income of individuals it is necessary to deduct undistributed corporate profits from national income, and to add transfer incomes (pensions, net social security payments, and relief) paid by Government to individuals.   The latter are excluded from national income on the grounds that they are not received for productive services, but they do represent currently received purchasing power to the individuals receiving them.   The sum total of individual incomes is used partly to buy consumer goods and services, and partly to pay personal taxes of various kinds such as income and estate taxes, personal property taxes, and licenses. The balance of incomes, not spent on consumption or paid in taxes, must constitute saving.   The following table of the disposition of individual income is the result of these calculations.

	Billions
National income, 1942.	$119.8
Add: Transfer payments.	2.6
Less: Corporate savings.	3.6
Contributions to social insurance funds.	3.3
Equals: Income payments to individuals.	115.5
Less: Taxes paid by individuals.	6.6
Equals: Disposable income of individuals.	108.8
Less: Consumer expenditures.	82.0
Equals: Net savings of individuals.	26.9

It may be noted that in developing statements on the receipts of businesses and individuals and their disposition, the data necessary for a similar statement for Government incidentally have been assembled.   On the one hand, there are the major categories of Government expenditures—pay of factors of production, purchases of goods and services from private business, and transfer payments. On the other hand, there are Government revenues—personal and business taxes.   The missing item needed to balance the expenditures and receipts sides of Government accounts is borrowing, or the Government deficit.

BIRD'S-EYE VIEWPOINT

In the course of constructing national product and income statistics, we have dealt with the basic aggregates required to give a summary view of the economic system in terms of the analytically important types of transactions, such transactions being shown in their interrelation to each other.   To think of the statistics in these terms—as a bird's-eye view of the economic system—is the most fruitful approach that can be taken in making use of national product and income data.

To show clearly that they constitute such a picture the data may be rearranged as in the summary table accompanying this article. The table, on page 48, has three double columns, one each for Government, business, and individuals, the three groups whose interplay determines the working of the economy. The left-hand side of each column shows the receipts of each group. The right-hand side shows the manner of their disposal.

The components of gross national product and income may be fitted into the columns of this table. To facilitate the task they are recapitulated in the order in which they were mentioned.

1. Consumer goods and services.
2. Private gross capital formation.
3. Products of private business sold to Government.
4. Pay of factors of production employed by Government.
5. Pay of factors of production employed by business (including dividends).
6. Depreciation and other reserves.
7. Business taxes.
8. Undistributed profits.
9. Transfer payments.
10. Personal taxes.
11. Individual savings.
12. Government borrowing.

Let us first enter items for which the interrelation between the three major accounts is most transparent, that is, those for which an entry in the left-hand side of one column is clearly matched by an entry in the right-hand side of another. Thus consumer goods and services, item 1, are put in the left-hand side of column II as a receipt of business. They also appear in the right-hand side of column III as an expenditure of individuals. Items 3, 4, 5, 7, 9, and 10 are handled similarly. This completes the items to which clear-cut counter-entries correspond.

Next the accounts of the Government are balanced by entering borrowing, 12, in the left-hand side of column I. The books of business are balanced by entering private gross capital formation, 2, in the left-hand side of column II and depreciation and other reserves, 6, and undistributed profits, 8, in the right-hand side. Finally, the accounts of individuals are balanced by entering individual savings, 11, in the right side of column III. We have balanced all the accounts, and fitted into the columns all the components discussed.

Examination of this table will show that it includes the aggregates necessary to give a complete summary of the economy in terms of its major transactions.   It is not surprising, therefore, that national product and income data form the basic statistical background and point of departure for the study of economic problems which affect the nation as a whole.   These statistics also can be looked upon as the first outline, as it were, of a detailed picture of the economy which can be much further refined.   For instance, consumer goods and services can be subdivided, showing the types of goods and services bought by consumers.   Gross capital formation similarly can be classified.   Government expenditures can be broken down, either by the type of products bought by the Government, or by the type of service provided to the community.

Income statistics, in turn, can be classified by distr butive shares, or by industrial origin, or by size of total income.   Taxes can be grouped in whatever manner seems most useful in the discussion of tax problems.   And savings can be broken down into currency, bank deposits, saving bank accounts, life insurance, bonds, stocks, and so on.

The filling in of all this information gives a more detailed view of the economy and considerably enhances its usefulness.   But no matter how the tables may be rearranged or what refinement of detail may be introduced, it is important to recognize clearly that the national income and national product are in essence neither more nor less than a summarization of the receipts and expenditures sides of the books of business, Government, and consumers. This means that the statistics are subject to the limitations of accounting practice but it also means that the various categories in the tables are essentially those used in, and hence significant for, practical business and economic affairs.

To have the income and product statistics presented in a set of interrelated tables, instead of having to collect them from a number of independent sources, facilitates quantitative comparisons between the various series.   It also is an inestimable aid to clarity of thinking.   The tables show how the various magnitudes are conceptually related to each other and indicate the legitimate comparisons and operations to which they can be put.   Two examples may be given in this connection.

COMMON FALLACIES

Prior to the presentation of the statistics as an interrelated set one of their most frequent misuses was somewhat as follows.   Economists would make a forecast of Government expenditures and of national income, in the light of the war program, and would deduct the former from the latter to estimate the amounts available for private capital formation and consumer expenditures.

The statistics as now presented should guard their users from this pitfall.   They show clearly that Government expenditures (including transfer payments), consumer expenditures, and private gross capital formation add up, not to national income, but to national income plus transfer payments plus depreciation and depletion charges plus business taxes.   Hence deduction of Government expenditures from national income to estimate the goods and services available for private use is an error which yields much too low a figure.

More subtle misuse of the statistics is made in connection with the savings data.   It recurs in infinite variations and constitutes one of the leading fallacies in the interpretation of the statistics. Only the variant that is most important at the present will be mentioned.   In discussions of fiscal policy the high level of savings often is adduced as proof that the danger of inflation is vastly overrated.   For, it is argued, the Government deficit is matched by a huge volume of savings, so that the net upward pressure on prices is negligible.

SAVINGS AND INFLATION

This argument is based upon a complete misconception of the nature of the statistics. As statistically measured, savings in excess of private gross capital formation always equal Government borrowing whether there is an inflation going on or not. This is revealed by an examination of the statistics as an interrelated set. Turning to the summary table, one sees that all the items above the first horizontal line cancel out. This is so, because they consist of a set of double entries. We also know that the column totals below the second horizontal line cancel out, since these were derived by balancing the left- and right-hand sides of the columns. Accordingly it follows that the items between the horizontal lines must be equal, that is, *Government borrowing plus private gross capital formation equals individual savings plus undistributed profits plus depreciation and other reserves.*

Since the summary table was derived without any assumptions regarding the presence or absence of an inflationary process, it follows that the above relation holds under all circumstances, and that it does not indicate a state of balance in the economic system.

This proof may leave the reader uneasy. "What," he may ask, "would happen if sufficient savings are not available and the Government prints money or borrows from the banks to cover the deficit? Will not the deficit exceed savings?" Suppose that in the situation depicted in the summary table the Government prints $10 billion of additional money and spends it on the products of private business. The Government deficit then will have increased by $10 billion. But the same $10 billion also appears as the receipts of private business and, provided that there is no change in other items, the undistributed profits of private business will rise by the same amount. Total savings will have increased exactly in the amount of the deficit, and the statistics will not indicate that new money has been created.

Suppose that the Government did not obtain more in goods from private business than it obtained prior to the increase in its expenditures, that is, that the additional $10 billion merely went to swell prices. Then we would have a clear case of inflation.

Or, to indicate another variation, suppose that private business did sell $10 billion worth of additional output to the Government so that there was no inflation in the prices paid by Government. Under conditions of full employment, this could be done, for instance, by cutting down the production of consumer goods. Given consumer demand, this would lead to a rise in the prices of consumer goods. Again an inflationary process would have occurred.

But in both instances the statistics would show total savings sufficient to cover the deficit. Thus to whatever inflationary strains and stresses the economic system may be subject, this will not be revealed by a deficiency of savings to cover the deficit.

ADEQUATE BASIS FOR PLANNING

A glance at the tables will show that they provide the basic information required as statistical background for analysis of the war potential and inflation problems mentioned at the outset of this article. Now, more than two years after these data were first used for these problems, it is apparent that they provided an adequate basis for making practical decisions—much more adequate than was supposed at the time. They enabled the Administration to set sights for the war production program consistent with the vast production potential of our economy and they provided the basis for determining the general character of the shift of industries from peace to war production required to attain that program. With the inflation problem too, the income and product statistics have made possible a continuing quantitative appraisal that has been of immeasurable value in mapping the details and timing of the anti-inflation program.

The thing to be stressed here, however, is that national product and income statistics are not only useful to Government but that they are equally useful to business. This is because they are absolutely fundamental to the analysis of the over-all economic and business situation, particularly with reference to its cyclical aspects. As is well known, the cylcical behavior of the economy as a whole is of major importance in assessing the prospects for any given industry, despite the fact that there are always peculiar circumstances which have to be taken into account.   Thus, the changes in prospect for business as a whole must be considered in deciding the production, pricing, purchasing, and selling policies which the individual business firm adopts.

Moreover, since the national product statistics provide a historical record of how the output of a particular type of commodity or service fluctuated with output as a whole, they also are useful to business in determining how a particular industry is likely to change with respect to total output in the future.   This is, of course, important in the regular month-to-month appraisal that business men must make of the changes in prospect for their business.   But it is important also with regard to longer range business planning as concerns questions of investment policy and plant expansion. This use of the gross product statistics is gaining wide acceptance at the present time in connection with business appraisal of postwar markets.   It is safe to say that most firms attempting to approach their post-war problems in quantitative terms are making use of the gross national product estimates.

3

DISTRIBUTION*

BY JOHN MAURICE CLARK †

The central problem of distribution in economic theory may be defined as the analysis of the forces which under free exchange govern the division of the product of industry between those who perform different functions or supply different factors. The shares may, however, be differently distinguished: according to the contractual arrangements under which the proceeds are received, according to the persons receiving them and according to the underlying functions or factors which constitute the sources of the incomes. Thus there are contractual distribution, personal distribution and functional distribution. Although these distinctions are generally made in economic textbooks and may be useful for didactic purposes, the main body of economic theory has for a long time concerned itself with functional distribution only.

While quantitative studies of distribution were early made in connection with estimates of the national income undertaken by such exponents of political arithmetic as Petty, they must be considered, as Cannan called them, "a statistical accident rather than a contribution to economic theory." The beginnings of abstract study of distribution were made by the physiocrats, who were the first to use the conception of a closed economy based on free exchange. But Quesnay and the other *économistes* were mainly interested in distribution between "sterile" and productive expenses; between handicrafts and trade, the sterile occupations, and agriculture, the only productive employment; and between consumption, replacement of capital and increase of capital. Land rent was the only true net product. Turgot thought that wages were

---

* *Encyclopaedia of the Social Sciences*, Volume V, 1931, pages 167–173. Reprinted by courtesy of The Macmillan Co. and the author.

† Columbia University.

based on subsistence and justified interest both on general grounds of natural liberty and as the necessary supply price of capital funds.

By the time of Adam Smith the wage system and the administration of land on a commercial basis were well established, but the typical organization of business managed directly by capitalist entrepreneurs did not lend itself to the distinction of the shares due to capital and management. Thus it was natural that Smith should have distinguished three shares: wages, rent and profits, the last including the earnings of capital.

These shares are treated as the "component parts of price": their natural levels govern the natural price, since the latter must be large enough to cover them. In harmony with this approach rent includes the rental value of land in the hands of the owner and contractual interest is almost neglected, being treated as something which, if paid, comes out of profits. Consistency might seem to require that wages be treated as the reward of labor whether hired or independent. But while this concept is mentioned, wages are in the main treated as a contractual payment. The three shares are viewed as the incomes of three fairly well marked classes: laborers, landowners and capitalist entrepreneurs.

The "natural levels" of these shares are described in a fairly empirical fashion, attention being paid both to the general levels of wages and profit and to the differences between different occupations. Some differences in wages tend to equalize the "real attractiveness" of different occupations, others not. Wages gravitate toward subsistence, but may be maintained indefinitely at a higher level by continued progress. Other shares are less satisfactorily explained.

With Malthus the subsistence theory of wages gained scientific support from his elaborately buttressed law of population. This theory was employed to demonstrate the helplessness of communist utopias based on equal distribution to raise the standard of living of the masses. Such leveling could only be a leveling downward. The law had more practical application, however, as a weapon against the prevailing poor laws with their indiscriminate outdoor relief, virtually resulting in an accepted system of subsidizing low wages.   This system, Malthus held, could end by absorbing all the income of the richer classes without raising that of the poor.   The latter, by their unchecked multiplication, were responsible for their own poverty.

With Ricardo value and distribution become the central problems of economics and are approached deductively.   Yet the three shares are still determined by different principles.   The Ricardian law of rent, credit for which must be shared with James Anderson, is the first great example of the marginal method, later to become the keystone of the entire Austrian system of economic theory. Rent proper is only that part of the payment to landlords which is due to the "original and indestructible qualities of the soil" as distinct from profit on capital improvements.   Since land is subject to diminishing returns and graded from better to poorer, the rent of a piece of land is the surplus of its total product, when cultivated with the proper quota of capital and labor, above the increment of product secured by a similar amount of labor and capital applied at the margin where this increment is smallest and yields no rent.

Wages are basically governed by subsistence according to the "iron law," with some slight allowance for rising standards of living. They are proximately governed by the ratio between population and the amount of circulating capital available for wage advances. This proposition constitutes the basis of the "wages fund" theory. With wages thus determined and rent fixed on a basis which excludes it from marginal costs of production, profits is a residuum.

The historical prospects afforded by this theory are based on the assumption of an inevitable increase in population.   With more mouths to feed, a larger amount of capital and labor is applied to fertile land and poorer soil is brought under cultivation; consequently the marginal yield of land declines.   It is to be anticipated therefore that rent will rise, wages will absorb an increasing portion of the remainder and profit will correspondingly decline.   When the point is reached at which further accumulation ceases, more workers cannot be supported and the "stationary state" is reached.

Senior traced the distributive shares other than rent to a basis in ultimate human sacrifices, the "abstinence" of the capitalist taking its place beside the toil of the worker. Senior follows the Ricardian treatment of rent and wages but considers that increases of fixed capital may increase profits by increasing productiveness. Although he notes the economic function of government in affording protection as a basis of economic action and states that distribution is affected by human institutions, he does not develop these principles but occupies himself with the "natural" Ricardian laws of distribution conceived without reference to alterable human institutions.

With John Stuart Mill the Ricardian scheme is built upon, but modified by, the infusion of social and institutional material. Mill stated that the laws of production "partake of the character of physical truths," while "the distribution of wealth is a matter of human institution solely"; and he took account of laws of property (including "property in abuses") and inheritance, systems of land tenure and customary practises as affecting rents and wages and the distribution of ownership. He noted the possibility of varying the scope of property rights, found that "sacredness does not belong in the same degree to landed property" as to property in movables and argued that "when land is not intended to be cultivated no good reason in general can be given for its being private property at all." He observed that personal shares in distribution overlapped the threefold scheme of rent, wages and profits, thus affording the basis for the distinction between personal and functional distribution. Mill displayed a humanitarian interest in the future of the laboring class but stressed the difficulties of permanently raising their standard of living. Originally committed to the wages fund doctrine, he made his famous recantation following Thornton's criticism. He improved upon his predecessors by making the rate of profit depend upon the cost of labor and by distinguishing in profits the elements of interest, insurance and wages of superintendence. Yet the theoretical underpinning of Mill's analysis of distribution is still the same as that of the other classical writers; rent is the surplus over marginal yield, wages are determined by the standard of living of the laboring people and profits absorb the residuum.

Among the contributions of the later writers in the classical tradition must be mentioned the doctrine of non-competing groups of Cairnes as applied particularly to wage recipients. Together with the wages fund doctrine, a partial rehabilitation of which he attempted, it suggested that in the numerous more or less segregated compartments of the economic system distribution is governed by relations of demand and supply. H. von Mangoldt's clear distinction between interest and profit and his treatment of rent as a surplus element which may be present in the other distributive shares were more integrally incorporated into distribution theory by Francis Walker. He distinguished between interest, which is due to abstinence, and profits, which are governed by the same principle as rent, and designated wages as the residual share while holding them governed by the wages fund principle.

The classical theories throw varied side lights on the interests of the different classes. Since with progress rents rose and profits fell, Smith considered the interests of landowners in harmony with those of society and those of capitalists opposed to progress. As rent signified to Ricardo an increasing impoverishment of society, his view of landowners and capitalists was the precise opposite of Smith's view. According to Smith labor produced all wealth and should in fairness be tolerably well provided for, while the shares of land and capital were deductions from the product of labor. On the other hand, capital was regarded, in a fashion characteristic of classical economics in general, as giving employment to labor, "setting it in motion"; and capitalist entrepreneurs were therefore considered the most progressive group in society. While the classical economists were personally humanitarian, this obviously finds little reflection in their theories of wages or of poverty.

The pessimistic trend of the classical economics was combated by Bastiat in France and by Henry C. Carey, founder of the "American school." Bastiat was an extreme individualist and Carey a believer in state action, but their views on distribution were alike. Both merged land value with capital, regarding it as the result of human improvements, and thought labor's share an increasing fraction of an increasing whole. Carey denied Ricardo's law of the trend from better to poorer lands.

While classical economists envisaged the division of society into classes and formulated principles in accordance with which national income is divided among them, the rigidity of their formulation precluded serious intellectual concern with the struggle among the classes for a larger share of the income. As to the justification of property and incomes based on property they were content with hypothetical history beginning with a primitive state of equality and tracing the accumulation of capital from savings made out of personal product. But their theories raised problems to which later thinkers offered a different answer, and which contained germs of doctrines that emphasized class antagonisms and class exploitation. A significant forerunner of the exploitation theorists, Sismondi, writing in the first quarter of the nineteenth century combated the hypothetical history of Smith, whom he followed in many matters of strict economic theory, with actual studies of the evolution of economic institutions, revealing much injustice and hardship in the development of property and of the content of property rights. He related distribution to overproduction in a theory strongly suggestive of the later views of John A. Hobson. The income from previous production pays for current production, and a lack of equilibrium may cause overproduction or underproduction. The share of profits and rent and the use made of it, in spending or saving, are important in determining whether or not an equilibrium can be maintained.

The first fully developed exploitation theory was given by Rodbertus, who built on the view that labor is the source of all wealth, the shares of the other factors being deductions from it which are to some extent justifiable. But he held that since the productivity of labor constantly increases and wages are limited by the iron law, labor's share is a decreasing one. The resulting inability to buy the whole product of industry explained the recurrence of overproduction and crises. Rodbertus, the Prussian landowner, was a liberal rather than a revolutionist; he proposed therefore a compromise system in which the decline of labor's share would be prevented without the abolition of the distributive shares accruing to property holders.

A more elaborate exploitation theory was developed by Karl

Marx, that many sided thinker who combined Ricardian theory with historical and institutional economics. His theory of wages and profits is not based like that of Rodbertus on the simpler expressions of Smith but is essentially an implacable carrying out of Ricardo's theory of value and distribution. The value of goods is the crystallization of the socially necessary labor time required for their production. The value of labor itself similarly determined is the labor time necessary to produce the worker's subsistence. If this represents half a day's work, the other half is appropriated by the employing capitalist as surplus value. Thus if the working day is long and the productivity of labor high, the capitalist wage system enables the capitalist to appropriate a part of the value the labor has produced and gives rise to a class struggle between labor and capital for the distribution of the surplus product. The ease with which appropriated surplus value may be accumulated and the competitive advantages of large scale production and capital investment lead to a concentration of economic power in the hands of a few and the proletarization of the small scale producer and independent artisan. In this process an "industrial reserve army" of unemployed is created which tends to depress the condition of the workers to a level of inevitably increasing misery.

The chief logical difficulty of this theory arises from the fact that prices do not follow the labor time formula, because the relationship between fixed capital and the outlay for wages varies with industry and period. This difficulty has never been satisfactorily dealt with, despite numerous attempts following the posthumous third volume of *Das Kapital*. But Marx' theory is not simply a logical construction. Marx also finds historical bases for existing inequality in many acts of expropriation through the long history of the class struggle. Some later exploitation theorists, notably Franz Oppenheimer, fixed upon one of these acts, the monopolization of land in the hands of private owners, as the taproot of exploitation incomes.

The marginal theories of distribution were developed after Marx; their bearing on the doctrines of Marxian socialism is so striking as to suggest that the challenge of Marxism acted as a stimulus to the search for more satisfactory explanations. They undermine the basis of Marxian surplus value doctrine by basing value on utility instead of on labor cost and furnish a substitute for all forms of exploitation doctrine, Marxian or other, in the theory that all factors of production are not only productive but receive rewards based on their assignable contributions to the joint product.

The great forerunner of marginalism was von Thünen. He broadened the concepts of diminishing and marginal productivity from the single case of land, which formed the basis of the Ricardian rent doctrine. He did not, however, consider the marginal productivity principle a satisfactory basis for distribution but developed a theory of the "natural" wage, which should be a mean proportional between subsistence of the laborer and total product, expressed in the celebrated formula: $\sqrt{AP}$.

The marginal theories, which reigned well nigh supreme among "orthodox" economists through the last quarter of the nineteenth century, insisted that value of products is not derived from costs but that costs, i.e. value of factors used, are derived from value of products. The problem of distribution is for that group of theories essentially a question of imputation; that is, of allocating the value of the product among the factors cooperating in its production. The methods by which this problem is solved vary with different writers. To Menger the per unit productive contribution of a factor is measured by the diminution of product resulting from the loss of a unit of the factor, while Wieser employed for the same purpose a system of simultaneous equations based on forms of production in which the factors were employed in different proportions. The marginal productivity theorists, notably J. B. Clark, equate the productivity of each unit of a factor to the addition made to the product by the marginal increment of this factor. One much neglected contribution is that of Stuart Wood (in American Economic Association, *Publications*, vol. iv, 1889, p. 5–35), who developed a form of productivity imputation based on competitive equivalence between labor and labor saving machinery at the margin of indifference. One point, obviously crucial to all marginal theories of distribution, is that the sum of the marginal contributions of productive factors must equal the total product. Wicksteed evolved a mathematical proof of this proposition but abandoned it on Edgeworth's criticism that the form of productivity function which it required was not plausible. This form of function was essentially static, involving no change in efficiency with change in scale of production.

The marginal theorists sensed a special problem in explaining the appropriation by the capitalists of interest on capital funds. Solutions were attempted by introducing a consideration relevant to the supply of capital funds, the tendency to discount future as compared with present goods. Böhm-Bawerk combined with this an explanation based on the "technical superiority" of present goods as means to the utilization of the more productive roundabout processes, thus introducing a productivity element into interest theories. On these matters he had a forerunner in John Rae. Among later writers Fetter rejected all productivity elements and based interest solely on time discount. Irving Fisher discussed the assimilation of personal marginal time discount rates to the market rate of interest by the process of borrowing and lending as well as the influence of the shape of the income stream on the effective desire of accumulation. Schumpeter relegated interest to the realm of dynamic phenomena.

Marginal theories assume the persistence of essentially static conditions; also their central formula concentrates on forces operating from the demand side, supply being taken for granted. Forces governing supply are thus left for separate treatment. Only the mathematical theorists, who expressed in one system of equations the conditions of equilibrium for both products and productive factors, are able to make one set of formulae take account, even though in a severely abstract form, of supply as well as demand conditions. Marginal theories recognize, however, the existence of some phenomena produced by dynamic conditions. Such are entrepreneurs' profits and losses and surplus returns yielded by productive equipment not reproducible within a short time (quasi-rent).

The marginal approach has the notable effect of making possible a homogeneous theory of distribution: at least on the demand side all shares are governed by an identical principle. This group of theories, therefore, offers less reason for distinguishing between the various factors of production. The differentiation between land and capital is no longer necessary; in fact, some writers have designated as rent the specific shares of any tangible factor, while they used interest to describe the same share as a percentage of investment or capital value. For the same reason this approach makes possible classification of productive factors into an indefinite number so long as they are susceptible of marginal analysis. The share of government—taxes—has, however, never been fully assimilated to this unitary scheme of explanation.

In the hedonistic form of the marginalist theory "product" meant a social gain, a creation of utility. With the general abandonment of utilitarian psychology and the striving for something more realistic than the "benevolent abstraction" of the static state it has seemed to some that the product which governs rewards must be defined as anything that commands a price, with no implications of a social character. The principle of marginal imputation is naturally still applicable, but the dynamic standpoint brings into view imperfect markets, bargaining handicaps, cases where the minimal dose is large, organic wholes like Davenport's three-legged stool—in short, numerous departures from pure marginal equilibrium, until the marginal method itself seems in danger of being discarded. Pigou, however, still uses it as a powerful weapon for tracing discrepancies between private acquisitive standards and the maximizing of the "social dividend."

Any static or equilibrium theory must recognize the existence of bargaining and the effect of unequal bargaining power in actual practise in causing departures from static standards as well as the importance of many social forces not included in the formulae of economic equilibrium. But most theories of this type tend either to dismiss the "higgling of the market" as a negligible disturbing element not capable or worthy of receiving scientific study or to consider that it operates within fairly narrow limits set by such strictly economic factors as productivity. Bargain theorists, on the other hand, regard these forces as so decisive that they tend to neglect the conditions of abstract equilibrium as not having sufficient force and reality, even as a point of departure for market variations, to repay serious analysis. They treat the market not as a passive machine whose function is limited to the registering of results rigidly predetermined by the independent forces of supply and demand but as an institution whose behavior may itself have some influence on the result.

Early anticipations of modern bargain theories may be found in Sismondi. The importance of non-economic factors is brought out very clearly in the writings of Dühring, who insisted that the phenomena of distribution are better explained by reference to forces of political compulsion than to economic laws. Elaborating on Dühring, Tugan-Baranovsky formulated what he calls a "social theory" of distribution. He maintained that the buyer and seller in the market for productive factors do not meet each other on the basis of equality and that the relations between them are basically conditioned by a number of non-economic factors, a situation which does not obtain in the market for final goods. This distinguishes the problem of distribution from that of value and price. Among American writers the effects of property and contract in their varying specific forms on production and distribution were traced at length by Ely and in a different way by Commons, while coercive elements in the economic system are stressed by Commons and R. L. Hale. In his "functional" theory of wages W. H. Hamilton translated the elements which are dealt with by the institutional and bargaining theories as well as by the equilibrium theories into a list of specific variables which influence the rate of wages.

In this group belong also a number of doctrines developed outside of the domain of strict theory. Such for instance is the view that trade unions bettering conditions in a limited field help unorganized labor by setting standards which will tend to spread rather than injure it by limiting access to the favored field and leaving other fields overcrowded. Another example is the theory of Sidney and Beatrice Webb that businesses paying wages too low to maintain labor in a state of efficiency are parasitic, laying the burden of necessary maintenance on other industries. Akin to this is the doctrine that a legally fixed minimum wage which the least efficient employers cannot pay is not necessarily a violation of economic law, since it merely hastens and strengthens the process of economic selection by transferring business and workers to more efficient employers.

The recent theories of high wages offer a peculiar reversal from the institutional point of view of some of the older doctrines. Thus the view that high wages may sustain themselves by causing increased productivity makes productivity the effect rather than the cause. Another example is found in the doctrine recently enunciated by the American Federation of Labor and adopted by progressive business men. In a fashion somewhat reminiscent of Rodbertus it regards high wages as essential to the prosperity of business: they offer the means of sustaining purchasing power necessary to absorb the output of modern mass production. This doctrine calls for the relaxation of exploitation in the sense of the nineteenth century exploitation theories, and assumes that business men may act in the interest of business as a whole rather than in the single interest of their own concern.

While distribution theories deal primarily with the forces which govern the division of the national product, inductive studies of income distribution aim in a majority of cases at the determination of the proportions in which income has been distributed among groups classified by size of income. The two types of study have therefore little in common except that generally labor incomes will be found in the lower income groups and property incomes in the upper. Even the national dividend in the two types of study is not exactly the same, since quantitative studies limit themselves as a rule to realized income only.

A number of quantitative studies have also been made of wages and profits in different industries and countries. Some of them, such as H. L. Moore's analysis of wages in France (*Laws of Wages*, New York 1911), have represented attempts at inductive verification of distribution theory. Others have had as their goal the ascertainment of trends in wages or profits.   The results of these studies in so far as they bear on the amount of income from labor relative to other shares do not corroborate earlier theories of either a general upward or a general downward tendency; they indicate rather a considerable degree of stability.

The quantitative studies most relevant to the purposes of this discussion are those differentiating national income by functional shares.   Such studies, few in number, have been undertaken only recently and the results obtained have not so far been very significant.   The chief difficulty with which such studies must contend is that the available material does not allow the segregation of income by abstract economic functions.   Thus American studies of farm incomes have habitually deducted 5 percent on the value of land and capital and reported the remainder as the farmer's labor income.   This remainder was usually astonishingly small.   But the rate of 5 percent appears arbitrary as applied to land, because in sections that were marked by rising land values farmers were buying land at prices representing much lower rates of capitalization, and were virtually taking part of their return in the appreciation of their investment so long as that appreciation continued.   In regions where a system of customary share tenancy or the cropper system prevails quantitative records of farm incomes inextricably merge rent, interest, wages and profits and make impossible any exact Ricardian adjustments.   Corporation reports furnish difficulties of their own, although the requirements of reporting income for taxation have to some extent standardized the form of the report.   The lack of uniform practise in accounting for capital makes the rate of return on investments a matter of estimate, and the practise of investing surplus funds in other industries makes the exact nature and the source of the income difficult to trace.

The limitations of such distribution studies are clearly exemplified in the estimates of national income made by the National Bureau of Economic Research in the United States.   These estimates make the best of the refractory material available, classifying it according to industrial groups and differentiating three functional shares: wages, salaries and income from entrepreneurship and property. The concept of income employed is that of "realized income," received by individuals from industry. This conception of income yields a highly significant figure but not the one figure most logically adapted to the requirements of all possible problems. Taxes paid by business are deducted; those paid by individuals are not. Corporate savings are left for separate estimate, with the result that in manufacturing, for example, wages and salaries averaged over 80 percent of the total realized income received by individuals from 1909 to 1925. For industrial groups as a whole from year to year amounts invested by the corporations are shown to have little or no relation to changes in the market values of the corporations as going concerns. This does not, of course, dispose of the question whether such investments have an effect in maintaining the values of the concerns over long periods.

The quantitative analysis of the functional distribution of income is still in its infancy. Improvements in data and developments in methods of analysis should yield in the future increasingly significant results.

4

A GRAPHICAL ANALYSIS OF PERSONAL INCOME DISTRIBUTION IN THE UNITED STATES*

BY MARY JEAN BOWMAN†

Interest in the various types of distribution of income in the United States has been snowballing in recent years as the relations between these distributions and economic processes are more fully recognized and as new data become available. At the same time the political significance of the various aspects of income distribution have become increasingly apparent. Income distributions of three distinct kinds have received increasing attention.

(1) Studies of national income and the composition of national product have involved extensive analyses of the value of output and of income payments according to the industry in which they originate. These studies are of interest not only as cross-section pictures of the structure of the economy, but also for the light they throw on the changing relative importance of different industrial sources of income (including government as a distinct category) with changing levels of business activity. Much of this work has been done in the Department of Commerce, which first published an analysis of this type in 1934.[1] This same study included a second type of analysis of income distribution, *i.e.*, by functional source.

(2) Functional distribution has been the focus of theoretical analysis in the classical tradition but has received only limited attention in empirical explorations. Since 1933, the Department

* *American Economic Review*, Volume XXXV, No. 4, September 1945, pages 607–628. Reprinted by courtesy of the publisher and author.

† Formerly, Bureau of Labor Statistics, U.S. Department of Labor.

[1] *National Income, 1929–32*, Sen. Doc. No. 124, 73rd Cong., 2nd sess. Dr. Simon Kuznets planned the study, supervised the estimates, and wrote the text.

of Commerce has maintained a continuous series of estimates of aggregate income payments accruing as wage and salary incomes, as entrepreneural incomes (including rents and royalties), as dividends and interest, and in other minor categories that have been reclassified from time to time. Although it is impossible to identify these (or any other statistical categories) with precisely defined theoretical concepts, the statistics provide rough approximations. The Department of Commerce series on income payments by "function" shows, among other things, that wage and salary incomes remained around 62 to 63 per cent of the aggregate of all incomes from 1929 to 1940, and that since that time they have increased, reaching 71 per cent in 1943. Income payments in the form of interest and dividends have meanwhile diminished in relative importance, gradually at first and more rapidly since 1940. This does not prove a redistribution in favor of wage earners, however, since corporate savings increased during this period.

(3) Distributions by recipients, or "personal income distributions," are at once the oldest and the newest field of statistical investigation of income distribution. Fifty years ago Italian statisticians were examining the size distributions of incomes of taxpayers, long before the federal income tax was established in the United States. Gradually we have added to our data and to our appreciation of the importance of the subject. Tax data have been supplemented as a source of information by large-scale expenditure studies in this country—notably the surveys conducted in 1935–36, 1941, and the first quarter of 1942. These have vastly increased our knowledge of the character of personal income distributions in the modal and lower income ranges, as well as providing data by households instead of taxpayers, and by various breakdowns of different population groups.[2] Special studies in Minnesota and Wisconsin in the late thirties contributed to techniques for collection of income data as well as to the body of facts concerning income distributions. The 1940 U.S. Census included questions

---

[2] In particular by family size, occupations, age, sex, and in the South, color.

concerning wage and salary incomes in 1939.   If present plans materialize, a sample personal income census may be taken this year as a part of the census program of basic economic statistics.

Interest in the distribution of personal incomes has many facets. One of the oldest is the relevance of such data for government fiscal planning, an interest that has taken on new coloring with the development of Keynesian and related analyses of unemployment and business activity.   Personal income distributions have also exceptional social, political, and ethical significance.

In view of the fact that the 1945 sample census may soon increase the detailed information available on personal income distribution among various sectors of the population of this country, this is an appropriate moment to examine the techniques by which these data may be most effectively summarized and their implications made clear.   A graphical analysis of selected aspects of the distribution of personal incomes has been undertaken in this article, in the hope that some improvements may be made in the presentation and interpretation of such data in the future.   Improved techniques of description of personal income distributions should facilitate also a better understanding of the relationships between income distributions by industry, by functional source, and by groups of income-receiving units (*i.e.*, "personal" distribution).

In the pages that follow several sets of data on income distributions in the United States will be used as examples to illustrate the advantages and limitations of different types of graphs and related statistics of income distribution.

I. Graphic Analysis of Consumer Incomes: 1935–36, 1941, and 1942

Income data for the United States for 1935–36, 1941, and 1942 have been used as the raw material for the first steps in this experiment with graphic analysis of personal income distributions.   These data have been plotted on several types of graphs.   The figures used on all graphs for the year 1935–36 are given in the table; other tables will be omitted in order to conserve space.

Pareto-type Chart

Pareto plotted on double logarithmic paper the number of income-receiving units with incomes equal to or exceeding each designated size of the income.   Income size is measured on the horizontal scale, number of income-receiving units on the vertical scale.   It is a cumulated curve, showing the number of income-receiving units with incomes of $100,000 and over, of $10,000 and over, of $1,000 and over, etc.

In Figure 1 the percentage of income-receiving units with incomes above each designated size is plotted on double logarithmic paper against the size of the income.   This differs from a standard Pareto chart only in the use of percentage instead of actual numerical figures for the number of consumer units; this procedure makes no change in the shape of the curve, but it puts all distributions on the same basis regardless of the size of the population involved. The 1941 and 1942 data are available up to the $10,000 income level; only the 1935–36 distribution carries details beyond that point.

What does this graph tell us?   First, it is evident that the curve begins to straighten out only at a point above $2,000 in each case, and some curvature continues to at least the $5,000 point.   This is to be expected since the Pareto formula was developed in the first place as a description only of the high income tail of the distribution.[3]   A considerable majority of consumer units had incomes below $2,000; more than 90 per cent had incomes below $5,000 in all three distributions.   A straight line is far from a perfect fit to the 1935–36 distribution even in the income range above

---

[3] Pareto suggested (in his *Cours d'économie politique*, Lausanne, 1897) the formula Log $N = K - \alpha \log x$, where x is the size of the individual's income and N is the number of income receivers having that income or larger.   It implies that plotting N against x on double-logarithmic paper gives a straight line with the slope α.   This formula was tested against data for the distribution of taxed incomes in many countries and at many times.   In contrast to the Gini and Lorenz methods, to be discussed subsequently, the Paretian formula takes no account of income aggregates.

DISTRIBUTION OF INCOME AMONG CONSUMER UNITS IN THE UNITED STATES, 1935–36

(1)	(2)	(3)	(4)	(5)	(6)	(7)	(8)	(9)
Income Class	No. of Consumer Units	% of Consumer Units	% of Consumer Units Cumulated from Low Incomes Upward	% of Consumer Units Cumulated from High Incomes Downward	Aggregate Income (in thousands)	% of Aggregate Income	% of Aggregate Income Cumulated from Low Incomes Upward	% of Aggregate Income Cumulate from High Incomes Downward
Under $ 250	2,123,534	5.38	5.38	100.00	$ 294,138	0.5	0.5	100.0
$ 250– 500	4,587,377	11.63	17.01	94.62	1,767,363	3.0	3.5	99.5
500– 750	5,771,960	14.64	31.65	82.99	3,615,653	6.1	9.6	96.5
750– 1,000	5,876,078	14.89	46.54	68.35	5,129,506	8.7	18.3	90.4
1,000– 1,250	4,990,995	12.67	59.21	53.46	5,589,111	9.4	27.7	81.7
1,250– 1,500	3,743,428	9.49	68.70	40.79	5,109,112	8.6	36.3	72.3
1,500– 1,750	2,889,904	7.32	76.02	31.30	4,660,793	7.9	44.2	63.7
1,750– 2,000	2,296,022	5.82	81.84	23.98	4,214,203	7.1	51.3	55.8
2,000– 2,250	1,704,535	4.32	86.16	18.16	3,602,861	6.1	57.4	48.7
2,250– 2,500	1,254,076	3.18	89.34	13.84	2,968,932	5.0	62.4	42.6
2,500– 3,000	1,475,474	3.73	93.07	10.66	4,004,774	6.8	69.2	37.6
3,000– 3,500	851,919	2.16	95.23	·6.93	2,735,487	4.6	73.8	30.8
3,500– 4,000	502,159	1.27	96.50	4.77	1,863,384	3.1	76.9	26.2
4,000– 4,500	286,053	0.72	97.22	3.50	1,202,826	2.0	78.9	23.1
4,500– 5,000	178,138	0.45	97.67	2.78	841,766	1.4	80.3	21.1
5,000– 7,500	380,266	0.96	98.63	2.33	2,244,406	3.8	84.1	19.7
7,500– 10,000	215,642	0.55	99.18	1.37	1,847,820	3.1	87.2	15.9
10,000– 15,000	152,682	0.38	99.56	.82	1,746,925	3.0	90.2	12.8
15,000– 20,000	67,923	0.17	99.73	.44	1,174,574	2.0	92.2	9.8
20,000– 25,000	39,825	0.10	99.83	.27	889,114	1.5	93.7	7.8
25,000– 30,000	25,583	0.06	99.89	.17	720,268	1.2	94.9	6.3
30,000– 40,000	17,959	0.05	99.94	.11	641,272	1.1	96.0	5.1
40,000– 50,000	8,340	0.02	99.96	.06	390,311	.7	96.7	4.0
50,000–100,000	13,041	0.03	99.99	.04	908,485	1.5	98.2	3.3
100,000 and over	5,387	0.01	100.00	.01	1,095,544	1.8	100.0	1.8
Total	39,458,300	100.00			59,258,628	100.0		

Source: U. S. National Resources Committee, *Consumer Incomes in the United States, 1935–36* (Washington: Govt. Printing Off., 1939). Data for Columns (2) and (6) are given on p. 189. All others were computed or this table.

$5,000. This graph, however, has certain uses regardless of the degree of fit to a Pareto equation.

It is possible to read off Figure 1 approximately the percent of income-receiving units with incomes above any given level. Conversion to percents makes it possible also to ascertain from the

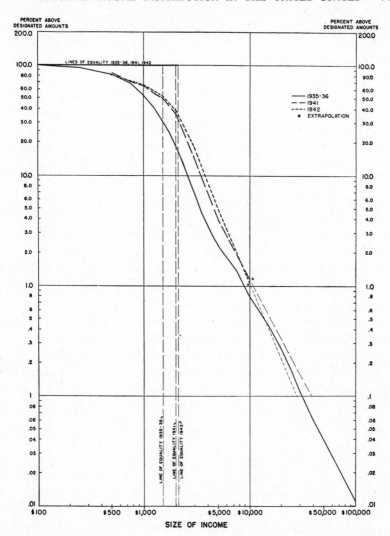

FIG. 1.   Pareto-type income curves; percent of consumer units with incomes above designated amounts, U. S. incomes, 1935–36, 1941 and 1942. (Source: 1935–36, see Table; 1941 and 1942, unpublished data of the U. S. Bureau of Labor Statistics.)

graph the relative importance of consumer units with income below any given level.   Thus, reading up the left-hand side of the graph, it is apparent that about 31.3 per cent of consumer units had incomes of $1,500 or more in 1935–36; and conversely, reading down the right-hand side of the graph, it is apparent that about 68.7 per cent of consumer units had incomes of $1,500 or less in 1935–36.   By replacing the percentage markings for each curve with the corresponding number of consuming units, an orthodox Pareto graph is obtained for each set of data.   It is then possible to read off the graph the actual number of consuming units in any given distribution that have incomes equal to or above any given level.   The emphasis, however, is on the upper 30 per cent of income receivers; and the most accurate readings from the graph are to be made for these higher income ranges.

There has been some confusion as to the meaning of the slope of a Pareto curve as an index of the degree of inequality in the distribution of incomes.   Pareto himself originally stated that the less the slope of the curve, the more equal the distribution.   Statisticians since that time have usually taken the opposite interpretation, though some argument on the point has persisted.   The difficulty arises in part from the fact that as an hypothetical income distribution approaches complete equality the plotted points approach a horizontal line up to the mean income and a vertical line at the mean.   These lines of perfect equality have been drawn in on Figure 1.

Is the approach to perfect equality then to be represented by an approach to a vertical or a horizontal position?   The answer depends on the section of the distribution under consideration.

As the lowest end of the income range is approached, all known income distributions plotted on a Pareto or a Pareto-type chart approach more closely to a horizontal position, close to the 100% mark.   This is in part a visual trick, due to the fact that the logarithmic scale telescopes the cases at the top of the graph and stretches those at the bottom; but it is due also to the fact that the frequency of income-receivers with the lowest incomes is small as compared to those with slightly greater incomes.   An income distribution that stays close to the 100 percent line up to an income level that is not far short of the arithmetic mean is necessarily a distribution in which the large mass of incomes are close to the mean; in such a distribution there will be a relatively sharp curvature on the Pareto chart in the income range around and just below the mean.   Such a distribution would generally be regarded as less "unequal" than one in which the curve drops far short of the mean, so that a large percent of income receivers have incomes considerably below the mean.   This interpretation is consistent with the Lorenz analysis, to be discussed subsequently.

For the part of an income distribution that may be adequately described by Pareto's formula, the answer is more precise.   The steeper the slope of the Pareto line, the less the dispersion in size of income within the Pareto range, that is, the less the "inequality" within that range.   This generalization would hold for the entire range of incomes if this range were adequately described by the Pareto formula; but in fact no known distribution of incomes fits this formula except for the high income tail, beginning well above the mean income.   The slope of the high income tail tells us little about the character of the rest of the distribution unless this tail begins at a level not far above the arithmetic mean income.[4]   This is one of the reasons why comparisons of the *Pareto-range* of different distributions by the use of Pareto's α (the slope of the curve in the section fitted by the Pareto formula) frequently give results in conflict with the ranking of these same income distributions *as a whole* on the basis of other measures of the degree of "inequality."

The forms of the three curves of Figure 1 may now be inter-

---

[4] If the Pareto formula adequately described the distribution of incomes from a level close to the mean, the slope of that part of the curve would carry some implications concerning the form of the distribution below the mean.   A very steep slope in a curve that cut the mean income at a point that included less than fifty percent of the cases, for example, would necessarily imply that income-receivers below the mean were heavily concentrated at a level not far short of the mean income.   By contrast, a curve with a very small slope, and cutting the mean at a point that included more than fifty percent of the cases would necessarily imply that income-receivers were to be found with high frequency receiving incomes far below the mean income.

preted in the light of these remarks. The distributions for 1941 and 1942 appear to be very much alike in form throughout the range for which data are available although the 1942 distribution drops a little more sharply in the high income range. The 1935–36 curve crosses the mean income for that year at a lower percentage point than those at which the 1941 and 1942 curves cut their respective means, suggesting greater inequality in the 1935–36 distribution. However, roughly the lowest twenty percent of families were eliminated at the same income level in all three distributions despite the higher mean income in the later years; this would suggest greater inequality in 1941–42 than in 1935–36. The extrapolations for the 1941 and 1942 data are too uncertain to justify any conclusions so far as the Pareto tails of the distributions are concerned. If they were taken at face value, it would appear that the 1941 distribution was the steepest, the least "unequal" in this range, the 1935–36 distribution next, and the 1942 distribution the most "unequal" at the top of the income scale.

One other feature of these modified Pareto graphs should be noted before turning to other graphic presentations. The percent of income receivers in any given income range may be read directly from the graph by subtracting the percent with incomes at or above the higher level, say $3,000, from the percent with incomes at or above the lower level, say $2,000. In the 1935–36 distribution, the graph shows approximately 7 per cent (to be exact, 6.93 per cent) of consumer units receiving incomes of $3,000 or more and roughly 18 per cent (*i.e.*, 18.16 per cent) with incomes of $2,000 or more. The difference, 11 per cent, must have received incomes between $2,000 and $3,000.

Finally, the fact that the three curves approach each other in the lower income levels indicates the differential effects of changes in the level of business activity on income receivers in different parts of the total income distribution.

Gini-type Chart

Corrado Gini's contributions to the mathematical analysis of personal income distributions are unfortunately not so well known as is Pareto's work; but as far back as 1908 Gini was working along similar lines. In contrast to Pareto, he took account not only of the numbers of incomes above given levels, but of the aggregate of incomes received by those above any given point.[5]

The lower part of Figure 2 is based on Gini's analysis, modified by the use of percents instead of absolute figures. It is like Figure 1 except that the percent of families has been plotted against the percent of *aggregate* income received, instead of against the size of the *individual* income. Income aggregates should be read from right to left. Thus in 1935–36 the highest one per cent of the income receivers had 15 per cent of the aggregate income, the highest 10 per cent had 34 per cent of the aggregate income, the highest 50 per cent had 80 per cent of the aggregate income, etc. The conversion of the actual figures into percents in no way changes the character of the distribution; but its meaning is more clearly shown, as is the relation between the Gini formula and the Lorenz approach, to be discussed below. It is immediately evident that the plotted points lie on a straight line except at the lowest income levels. The Gini formula describes the income distribution down to a much lower income level than is adequately described by a Pareto formula.[6]

The slope δ of the line in the Gini formula has been used, like Pareto's α, as an index of the degree of inequality in the distribution of incomes. Conversion of the original data into the percentage form makes possible a direct comparison between the distributions in relation to a single line of perfect equality. A perfectly equal

---

[5] For a concise discussion of Gini's formula and its relation to Pareto's formula, see Gini's paper delivered before the Cowles Commission in 1936, "On the Measure of Concentration with Especial Reference to Income and Wealth."

Gini uses the formula $\log N = p + \delta \log A_x$, where x is the size of an individual income, N is the number of income receivers with income of x or more, and A_x is the aggregate income above the level x.

[6] This is indeed not surprising, since the Gini line is one of those curiosities in statistics, the correlation of a thing with part of itself—in this case the sum of a set of numbers and a weighted sum of the same numbers. The Lorenz approach also involves such a relationship. (Furthermore, the Gini line, like the Pareto line and the Lorenz curve, involves an element of serial correlation.)

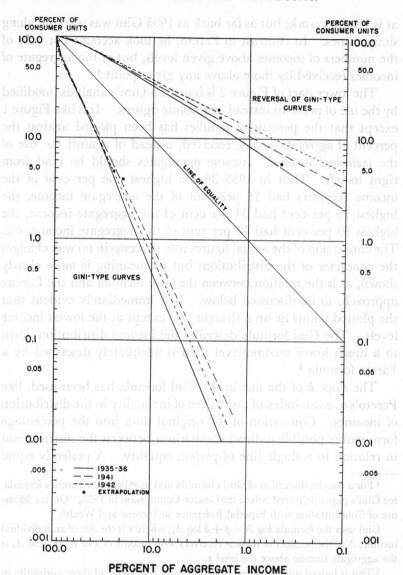

FIG. 2. Gini-type income curves and reversal of gini-type curves, U. S. incomes, 1935–36, 1941 and 1942. (Source: 1935–36, see Table; 1941 and 1942, unpublished data of the U. S. Bureau of Labor Statistics.)

income distribution would imply that any 10 per cent of the income receivers would have 10 per cent of the aggregate income, that any 20 per cent would have 20 per cent of the aggregate, etc. Such a distribution would be represented by a straight line drawn at a 45 degree angle. An approach to equality would involve an approach to this 45 degree line. According to this interpretation, the less the slope of the Gini curve, the more nearly equal the distribution of income would be. There is a clear distinction between the three curves of the lower section of Figure 2. The steepest slope, indicating the most unequal distribution, is shown by the 1935–36 data; the least slope by the 1942 distribution. The contrasts between 1935–36 and the other two years is more evident on this chart than in Figure 1, illustrating the greater sensitivity of Gini's δ.

Criticism of the Pareto Coefficient

In view of the extended discussions and disputes that have focused around the Pareto coefficient α, it is appropriate at this point to emphasize the already existing evidence as to its inferiority for the measurement of degrees of inequality.

The values found by Pareto for the slope of his line, α, were close to 1.5, and Pareto concluded that there was a similarity of income distributions in various countries and ages not only in the form of the distribution but also in the degree of "concentration" or "inequality." These conclusions have been taken very seriously by many of his followers down to the present day. H. T. Davis even goes so far as to explain the French Revolution on the basis of departures of the income distribution from the Pareto slope of 1.5.[7]

In 1933 Dwight Yntema ranked seven sets of income data according to the comparative degree of inequality of each series as shown by each of eight statistical measures of inequality.[8] On the

---

[7] Harold T. Davis, *The Analysis of Economic Time Series*, Cowles Commission for Research in Econ., Monog. No. 6 (Bloomington, Principia Press, 1941), chap. 9.

[8] "Measures of the Inequality in the Personal Distribution of Wealth or

combined grounds of sensitivity to differences between income distributions and stability under different groupings of class intervals for data from a given distribution Dr. Yntema selected as the "best" measures, first the mean deviation referred to the arithmetic mean, and then the coefficient of variation referred to the arithmetic mean and the coefficient of variation referred to the "standard attribute." He throws out the Pareto coefficient as both insensitive and unstable.[9] Yet this study of Yntema's seems to have had little effect in shaking the faith of Paretian devotees.

Gini's attack on Pareto, in a paper delivered before the Cowles Commission in 1936, should have been sufficient to dispel for all time the notion that Pareto has proven a given degree of inequality to be characteristic of even those distributions included in his investigations. And this same paper should certainly have caused users of the Paretian coefficient of inequality to pause and consider their procedures. In discussing his coefficient δ, Gini stated that: "As a matter of fact, a variation of δ between 2 and 6 means that one half of the total income is possessed by a fraction of the taxpayers that varies between $\frac{1}{4}$ and $\frac{1}{64}$. Pareto arrived at the opposite conclusion because of the very limited sensitiveness of α, which he did not perceive. In fact, he found values of α ranging from 1.9 (Prussia, 1852) to 1.1 (Hamburg, 1891). Theoretically these values would correspond to values of δ ranging from 2.6 to 8.6, and hence are far from justifying Pareto's conclusion about the similarity in the degree of concentration of income in various countries and ages."[10]

Income," *Jour. Am. Stat. Assoc.*, Vol. 28 (1933), p. 423.

Dr. Yntema compared the following measures: (1) Mean deviation referred to the arithmetic mean; (2) Mean difference referred to the arithmetic mean; (3) Coefficient of variation referred to the arithmetic mean; (4) Coefficient of variation referred to the "standard attribute"; (5) Mean deviation of logarithms taken from the arithmetic mean of the logarithms; (6) Standard deviation of logarithms; (7) Pareto's coefficient of inequality, α; (8) Gini's index of concentration δ. Gini's ratio of concentration was not included.

[9] *Ibid.*, p. 395.

[10] The paper cited above, "On the Measure of Concentration with Especial Reference to Income and Wealth." For a more detailed discussion of this point,

Reversal of the Gini Curve

We must not be too hasty, however, in accepting without qualification the Gini formula for description of the income distribution and his coefficient δ for the measurement of its "degree of inequality or concentration." Despite the fact that the Gini formula gives a better description of the modal range of the income distribution than is provided by the Pareto formula, it must still be recognized that the emphasis is on the behavior of the income distributions in the upper rather than the lower income levels. This is inherent in the double logarithmic treatment with cumulations from the top income groups toward the lower income levels. An experiment was therefore tried out on Figure 2, cumulating income receivers from the lower levels upward, and plotting these cumulated percents on the double logarithmic scale against the similarly cumulated aggregate incomes. Again a perfectly equal distribution would lie along a 45 degree line; but in this case the greater the departure from equality, the less is the slope of the line. The relationships between the income distributions are now exactly reversed. The 1935-36 distribution lies the closest to the line of equality; the 1942 distribution the farthest away. Viewed in terms of the character of the distribution at the lower end of the scale, it then appears that the 1935-36 distribution is the *less* unequal! Which conclusion are we to accept? The clear evidence of the lower part of the chart that the 1935-36 distribution is the most unequal, or the equally clear evidence of the upper half of the chart that it is the least unequal? The difficulty lies in the fact that one method of plotting emphasizes one part of the distribution, the other method the other part, and the two are not in this case mutually consistent. Both parts of the chart in fact tell the whole story, but the relationships are in each case obscured as the 100 per cent mark is approached. Whether the one conclusion or the other is to be accepted depends on the aspect of inequality that is regarded for any given purpose as the most significant.

---

see his article "Indici di concentrazione e di dipendenza," *Biblioteca dell'Economista*, 5 a serie, Vol. XX (1922), pp. 39–40.

Lorenz Curve and the "Concentration Ratio"

Although Pareto curves are probably the most commonly used for the description of income distributions in the upper income ranges, the Lorenz curve is undoubtedly the technique most commonly used to indicate differences in the degree of inequality of different income distributions.[11] It is a simple graphic device. The cumulated percents of aggregate income are plotted arithmetically against the cumulated percents of persons receiving that income. If income were evenly distributed this would give a diagonal straight line rising from the lower left-hand corner to the upper right-hand corner of the diagram. The convexity of the plotted curve toward the origin of the abscissa will be greater the greater the degree of inequality thus defined. This is in fact the relationship used in both parts of Figure 2, except that in Figure 2 the cumulated percents were plotted on a double logarithmic scale and the income aggregates were read from right to left. Figure 3 presents the same data plotted in a standard Lorenz distribution, on an arithmetic scale. It should not be surprising to find that the results conform closely to what is shown in both parts of Figure 2. Since the scale is arithmetic, neither end of the distribution is obscured, as in the two sets of cumulations on the logarithmic scales. Conclusions concerning the degree of inequality are again ambiguous, though the contrast between the forms of the distributions in the lower and in the upper income ranges is not so sharply emphasized as with the combined use of the Gini curve and its reversal in Figure 2.

Lorenz himself recognized the possible ambiguity in comparisons of income distributions when the curves intersect, as is the case in Figure 3. Gini turned his attention to this problem (as distinct from his logarithmic formula for the description of income distributions) in 1914. He then invented the "concentration ratio," a

---

[11] M. C. Lorenz, "Methods of Measuring the Concentration of Wealth," *Publications of the American Statistical Association*, Vol. 9 (New Series, 1905), pp. 209–19. The same idea was introduced almost simultaneously by Gini, Chatelain, and Seailles.

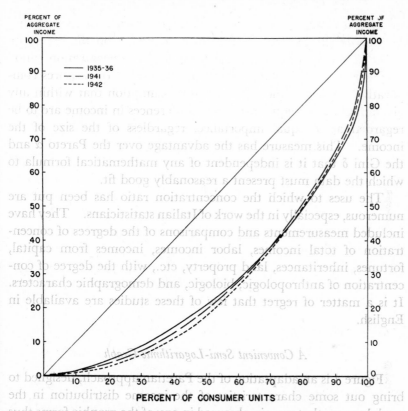

FIG. 3.   Lorenz curves, U. S. incomes, 1935-36, 1941 and 1942.   (Source: 1935-36, see Table; 1941 and 1942, unpublished data of the U. S. Bureau of Labor Statistics.)

measure that is based on the areas outlined on a Lorenz diagram. The "concentration ratio" is the ratio of the "area of concentration" shown by the Lorenz curve to the area of maximum possible concentration.[12]   This measure is the mean difference between the n

[12] The area of maximum concentration is the area that would be circumscribed by the Lorenz curve under the extreme condition that the total amount of income was possessed by only one individual.   Gini later elaborated his "ratio of concentration" to apply to cases in which the limit of maximum concentration was defined in other ways, and something less than complete equality was taken as the equalitarian limit.

incomes divided by twice the arithmetic average of the n terms. In view of the graphic analysis just completed on the preceding pages of this article, it is evident that the "concentration ratio" might be regarded as a compromise measure.   It measures comparative degrees of inequality on the assumption that within any given distribution equal arithmetic differences in income are to be regarded as of equal importance, regardless of the size of the income.   This measure has the advantage over the Pareto α and the Gini δ that it is independent of any mathematical formula to which the data must present a reasonably good fit.

The uses to which the concentration ratio has been put are numerous, especially in the work of Italian statisticians.   They have included measurements and comparisons of the degrees of concentration of total incomes, labor incomes, incomes from capital, fortunes, inheritances, land property, etc., with the degree of concentration of anthropologic, biologic, and demographic characters. It is a matter of regret that few of these studies are available in English.

A Convenient Semi-Logarithmic Graph

Figure 4 is an adaptation of the Paretian approach, designed to bring out some characteristics of the income distribution in the modal ranges that remain obscured in any of the graphic forms thus far used.   The number of persons with income above designated levels is again plotted against the size of the income, but in this case the vertical scale is arithmetic instead of logarithmic.[13]   The plotting of percents of consumer units on an arithemtic scale has certain visual advantages.   First, it is easy to tell at a glance, from the comparative distances on the vertical scale, the percentage of income receivers above any given level, or conversely the percentage with incomes below any given level.   It is only necessary to look at the center of the vertical scale to find the 50 per cent mark, etc.

---

[13] This type of curve was used very ingeniously by David Durand in his article, "A Simple Method for Estimating the Size Distribution of a Given Aggregate Income," *Rev. Econ. Stat.*, Vol. XXV, No. 4 (Nov., 1943), pp. 227–30.

For the same reason it is easier to determine at a glance the percent of families that fall within any given income range. From this graph it is possible also to derive a simple picture of one aspect of the "degree of inequality" in the distribution of incomes; the steeper the curve in any given income range, the larger is the percent of families that fall within that range. But the most fundamental difference between this semi-logarithmic graph and the

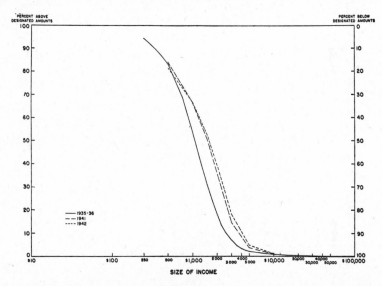

Fig. 4. Semi-logarithmic income curves; percent of consumer units with incomes above and below designated amounts, U. S. incomes, 1935–36, 1941 and 1942. (Source: 1935–36, see Table; 1941 and 1942, unpublished data of the U. S. Bureau of Labor Statistics.)

double logarithmic treatment in the Pareto chart is the increased clarity of the picture for the modal and lower income groups. The chart shows clearly the character of the distribution down to the lowest 5 per cent or even 2 per cent of income receivers. It is at the same time, and for the same reason, inadequate for the presentation of the upper part of the income distribution. The values of this graphic technique will be illustrated further with other sets of income data.

II. Experiments in the Graphic Analysis of Income Distributions by Occupational and by Racial Groups

That the distributions of incomes in various occupational groups are significantly different is generally recognized, but the nature of the differences has received only limited attention.   Such data are

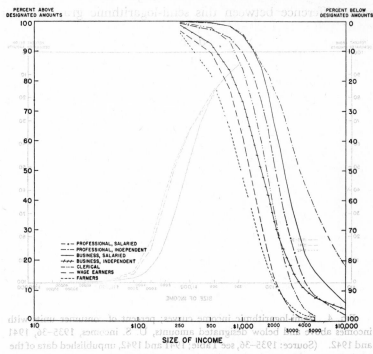

Fig. 5.   Percent of nonrelief families with incomes above and below designated amounts by occupational groups, U. S. incomes, 1935–36. (Source: Derived from U. S. National Resources Committee, *Consumer Incomes in the United States, 1935–36*, Table 10, p. 26.)

plotted here in Figures 5 and 6, for the United States in 1935-36 and for Minnesota in 1938-39 respectively.   For the study of these relationships a Pareto distribution (and to a lesser extent the Gini chart) is clearly unsatisfactory because of its emphasis almost exclusively on the high income tail.   The semi-logarithmic graph introduced in the preceding section has been used, plotting the cumulative percent of households on an arithmetic scale, the size of income attained or surpassed by any given percent of families on the logarithmic scale. For incomes below $250 and above $7,500 the curves are free-hand extrapolations. The results are exceedingly interesting, both in subject matter and as illustrations of the usefulness of this type of chart.

In turning first to the U. S. data (Figure 5), the curves for salaried and independent professional and for salaried and independent business households command our attention. The incomes of independent professionals are the largest of any group and show the greatest spread. Next in order of magnitude in the modal range of the distributions are the incomes of salaried business men; and these incomes are closely paralleled in the form of the distribution by those of salaried professionals, though at a somewhat lower level throughout. Independent business men, like independent professionals, have widely differing incomes; but the modal group is at a very much lower level, even below a large proportion of the clerical group. On the other hand, the distribution for independent business men tails out at a slope that no doubt carries these top incomes well above those of the top group of professional salaried people. The highest frequency of both clerical and independent business incomes is in the range between $1,000 and $3,000; but whereas only 53 per cent of independent business men's families receive incomes between $1,000 and $3,000, 73 per cent of clerical families fall within this income range. Wage earner incomes are almost as concentrated within a limited income range as are those of clerical families, but at a lower average level.

The Minnesota data are given in Figure 6. No distinction is made in these data between salaried and independent professional families, or salaried and independent business families, but it is evident that the spread of incomes at the top is less for these groups in Minnesota than in the whole of the United States. The marked concentration of clerical incomes (and to a less extent of wage-earner incomes) within a limited range is again evident. The chart shows further that low income families (below $1,000) are proportionately less common among the clerical than among the profes-

sional and business groups.   The Minnesota data are of particular
interest, however, because they include a category of "non-earners."
The distribution of incomes in this group is extremely uneven,

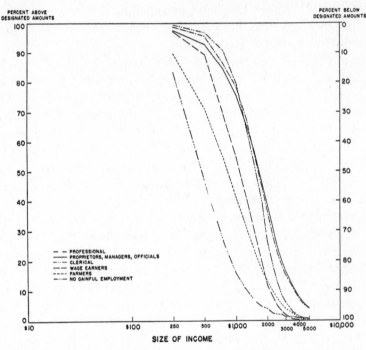

FIG. 6.   Percent of consumer units with incomes above and below desig-
nated amounts by occupational groups, Minnesota incomes, 1938–39.   (Source:
Derived from Minnesota Resources Commission, *Minnesota Incomes 1938–39*,
Table 10, pp. 123–27.)

tailing out indefinitely in the highest income ranges while at the
same time a much larger proportion of consumer units in this group
have total incomes under $500 and even under $250.

Lorenz Curves of Distributions by Occupational Groups

Since no figures on average or aggregate incomes by occupational groups are available for the United States in 1935-36, it is
impossible to present these data in a Lorenz curve form.   Lorenz
distributions for the Minnesota data are, however, given in Figure 7.

A comparison between the picture shown by the Lorenz curves and the semi-logarithmic cumulative distributions reveals some interesting facts concerning the data and the nature of the two graphic techniques. The concentration of clerical incomes in a limited income range, as shown by Figure 6, is reflected in the fact that the Lorenz curve for these income-receiving units lies the closest to the "line of equality." The wage-earner distribution is, consistently, next. The very slight distinction between the professional and business groups as shown in Figure 6 becomes more clear-cut on the Lorenz diagram, reflecting in all probability some differences in the high income tails of the distributions that are not shown in Figure 6. Figure 6 indicates that the distribution of farm incomes is definitely more spread through the modal ranges than are those of business and professional groups; but here a difference in the high income tails (which is evident even on Figure 6) must explain the picture shown on the Lorenz diagram. The Lorenz curve for farm incomes does, in fact, cross that for professional incomes, lying farther from the "line of equality" in the lower part of the distribution, significantly closer to it in the upper ranges.

Most striking of all is the distribution of incomes of households of non-earners. It cuts three of the other Lorenz curves, swinging far to the right at the upper income end. The effect of the high income tail, inadequately shown on Figure 6, is here extremely evident—as is the concentration of a large proportion of non-earner families in the lowest income brackets.

An Illustration of Ambiguity in the Definition of "Inequality"

The Minnesota data on distributions of incomes of farm and of business families provide a useful illustration of ambiguities in the comparison of degrees of "inequality." Which of these two distributions should be regarded as the more unequal will depend on the aspect of inequality that is for any particular purpose of the greatest interest.

Three of the techniques of measurement discussed in this article support the thesis that the distribution of the farm incomes is the more "unequal." (1) On visual inspection of Figure 7, it would appear that the area inside the farmer income curve is slightly greater than that inside the curve of incomes of business families; the Gini concentration ratio should then be larger for the farm group, indicating *greater* "inequality" in the farm than in the busi-

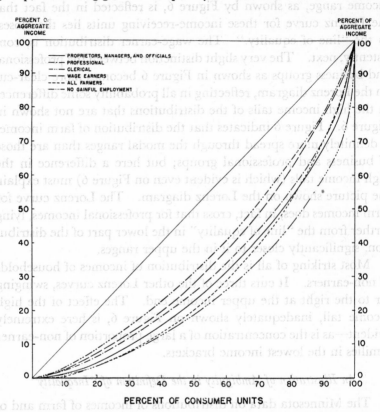

FIG. 7. Lorenz curves of income distributions by occupational groups, Minnesota incomes, 1938–39. (Source: Derived from Minnesota Resources Commission, *Minnesota Incomes, 1938–39*, Table 10, pp. 123–27.)

ness family income distribution. (2) The spread of incomes in the ranges of highest frequency, as shown on Figure 6, is *greater* for the farm families. (3) It is evident from Figure 7 that the reversal of the Gini Chart (as in Figure 2), cumulating aggregates from the lower income end of the distributions, would give a line with a smaller slope, *greater* "inequality" for the farm families than for the business group.

On the other hand, two of the measures and graphic techniques used in this article would lead to the opposite conclusion. (1) It is clear from the combined evidence of Figures 6 and 7 that were Pareto curves to be drawn, the slope of the high income tail would be steeper for the farm than for the business group, indicating that the distribution of farm family incomes is the *less* "unequal." (2) It is evident from the Lorenz curves of Figure 7 that a Gini chart of the distribution of incomes among farm families would show a smaller slope, hence *less* inequality, than the distribution of incomes among the business families.

This conflicting evidence brings out vividly the ambiguity in the concept of "inequality."

Use of the Semilogarithmic Graph for Comparison of the Income Levels of White and Negro Families

Most mathematical and statistical experimentation with personal income distributions has focused on the characteristics of any given distribution rather than on the relation between income distributions among different categories of the population. Concepts of inequality have referred to the characteristics of a given distribution. There is, however, another framework in which inequality may be considered, the inequality between the incomes of distinctive groups of the population. This is illustrated in part by the positions of the curves in Figures 5 and 6; but it is most vividly portrayed by a graphical analysis of incomes of white and Negro families in the South.

Figure 8 presents such a comparison, again as a cumulative distribution on semi-logarithmic paper. The three curves to the right are distributions of incomes of white households in three sizes of cities; those to the left are distributions of incomes of colored households in the same cities. The shapes of these curves are very similar for all groups, except that the incomes of white households tail out at the upper income end to a significantly greater extent. The striking thing about the graph is the great distance between the two sets of curves, white and Negro. Throughout the modal range the horizontal distances between the curves are almost constant. Any given percentile of the white population in large cities is at or above roughly 2.6 times the level attained by the same

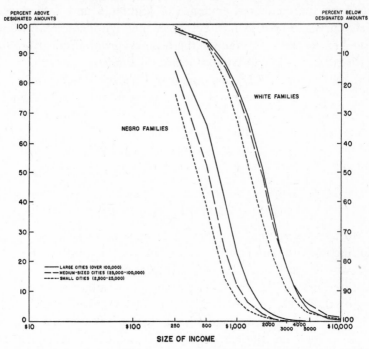

FIG. 8. Percent of nonrelief families with incomes above and below designated amounts, white and colored families in Southern cities, United States incomes, 1935–36. (*Source:* Derived from U. S. National Resources Committee, *Consumer Incomes in the United States, 1935–36,* Table 21-B, p. 100.)

percentile of the Negro population. In the small cities the difference is even greater; the graph indicates ratios of over 3.0.

III. CONCLUSION

Two basic types of information are important in the analysis of personal income distributions: (1) the general level of living that such distributions may indicate, and (2) the shape of the distribution. This question of shape is not merely a matter of "degree of inequality or concentration," however measured, but of the particular character of the disparities in incomes. Allyn Young, in 1917, approached this problem with his usual perspicuity, and his words will bear repeating:

> The degree of departure from absolute equality, however measured or stated, must itself be referred, if not explicitly, then in some vague way, to a standard of normal or justifiable concentration. A dead level of uniformity is neither practicable nor desirable. . . . [14]

And some pages later he argues that:

> The amount of concentration, the amount of departure from a condition of uniform incomes, does not matter so much as does the particular form of the income distribution underlying the concentration. . . .
> The worst thing in the present situation is undoubtedly the extreme skewness of the income frequency curve. . . . The problem of poverty and the problem of great fortunes are the problems of the lower and upper limits of this income curve. . . . . The most serious aspect of the distribution of property and incomes in this and other countries is not the presence of a larger or smaller degree of "concentration," but the general distortion of the whole income scheme, reflecting as it undoubtedly does the presence of a high degree of inequality in the distribution of opportunity.[15]

The methodological import of Young's discussion was simple. He argued that simple frequency distributions are far more useful and much less misleading than any coefficients of inequality or any formulas purporting to describe an income distribution. He went one step further and urged the use of the Pearsonian system of curves and of measures of dispersion.

We cannot go along with Young in his attachment to the Pearsonian system of frequency analysis for the interpretation of persona income distributions. Even when plotted on a semilogarithmic graph, a non-cumulative distribution is a less useful device than the cumulative distributions discussed in this article; this point hardly requires argument at the present date. But in

---

[14] Allyn A. Young, "Do the Statistics of the Concentration of Wealth in the United States Mean What They are Commonly Assumed to Mean?" *Jour. Am. Stat. Assoc.*, Vol. XV, New Series, No. 117 (Mar., 1917), pp. 471–84.

[15] *Jour. Am. Stat. Assoc.*, Vol. XV, New Series, No. 117.

one respect Young was fundamentally sound. A frequency distribution of some type is a far simpler and more complete basis for the interpretation of income data than is any collection of the most commonly used coefficients or formulas.

It is equally true that any single graphic device is incomplete.

A Pareto chart is of distinctly limited usefulness in the middle and lower income ranges, and its meaning is not readily comprehended; yet it has proven an extremely valuable device in the study of income distributions within the higher income ranges. A Gini chart has the special advantage that it permits both extrapolation and interpolation for the upper income ranges starting from a lower point than would be admissible on a Pareto chart. It provides also a picture of the distribution of the aggregate income of a society among its members, an aspect of income distribution that is not revealed by a Pareto chart. On the other hand, the Gini chart is somewhat more complex in the concepts involved; it cannot be translated directly into an ordinary type of frequency distribution; and to plot such a chart it is necessary to have facts concerning the distribution of the aggregate income that are not needed for the construction of a Pareto graph. Finally, the Gini chart shares with the Pareto, though to a less extent, an emphasis on the upper income levels that obscures relationships at the lower end of the income scale. Gini graphs are far more useful when expressed in terms of percents than when given in absolute figures. When the problem under consideration requires special emphasis on the higher income tail of the distribution, the choice between the Gini and the Pareto curves will depend on the character of the data and the particular facts that may be of most interest to the investigator.

A reversal of the Gini approach, cumulating the percents of consumer units and of aggregate incomes from the lower levels upward, was plotted on a double logarithmic scale. This procedure counters the emphasis on the distribution in the high-income ranges with an emphasis on the low-income end of the distribution. Taken in conjunction with a Gini chart, it draws a sharp picture of the characteristics of the distributions at the two ends of the scale.

For most purposes, however, two types of charts of more general usefulness will provide a sufficiently complete analysis.   These are the Lorenz curve and the semi-logarithmic chart used in this article. The Lorenz curve shows the distribution of the aggregate income among the members of the population, and it is a fairly sensitive indicator of inequality in so far as disparities may legitimately be weighted in terms of arithmetic differences.   A careful reading of the Lorenz chart will reveal most of the relationships shown by the combination of the Gini chart and its reversal (Figure 2).   But the Lorenz curve gives no clue as to the general level of incomes or the numbers or proportions of families in different income-size classifications.   These facts are shown by the cumulative distribution on semi-logarithmic paper.   This latter is an extremely versatile device for the description of any given distribution and for a comparison with other distributions, particularly for the middle and lower income groups.   It is a mediocre method of indicating the character of the income distribution at the top; and it takes no account of the aggregate amounts of income held by various percentiles of the population.

PRODUCTION FUNCTION AND MARGINAL PRODUCTIVITY

5

ON THE LAW OF VARIABLE PROPORTIONS*

By John M. Cassels†

Introduction

Among the contributions that have been made in recent years to our better understanding of the fundamental principle of diminishing productivity those of F. H. Knight and J. D. Black are basic to the present article.[1] Professor Knight in his book, *Risk, Uncertainty and Profit*, brought out more clearly than had hitherto been done the logical implications of what we know in a general way about the diminishing returns obtained from successive applications of any variable factor of production to others that are fixed, and stressed particularly the symmetrical character of the law.[2] Professor Black in his work along these lines has consistently emphasized the need for empirical research to give the law greater precision and practical usefulness. Not only has he been instrumental in having specific projects of this sort undertaken but he has also developed the theoretical analysis in such a way as to be more readily applicable to this type of investigation. Among other things he has shown how the problem of dealing with *two* variable factors (*e.g.*, seed and fertilizer) in combination with one factor that is fixed (*e.g.*, land) can be simply presented by means of a cross-classification table.[3] It is the purpose of the present dis-

* *Explorations in Economics*, 1936, pages 223–236. Reprinted by courtesy of the McGraw-Hill Book Co. and the author.

† Formerly, Harvard University.

[1] Among the earlier writers on this subject to whom they acknowledge especial indebtedness are F. M. Taylor, T. N. Carver, and P. H. Wicksteed.

[2] Pp. 97–103.

[3] *Production Economics*, Chaps. XI and XII. Also Analysis 45 in Rice: *Methods in Social Science*, and United States Department of Agriculture Bulletin 1277, *Input as Related to Output in Farm Organization*, H. R. Tolley, J. D. Black, and M. B. Ezekiel.

cussion, first, to bring out by an extension of the type of analysis employed by Knight some of the most significant characteristics of the combinations that are represented in such a table, and, second, to relate the results of this analysis in a non-mathematical way to the more mathematical concepts of production surfaces and isoquants.

A STRICTLY STATIC LAW

It is important to recognize at the outset that productivity depends on the following things:

I. Proportions of factors of production.
II. Methods of production.
    a. Dependent on scale of production.
    b. Dependent on state of the arts.

Although it is true that with large-scale operations a finer adjustment of the proportions of the factors of production is generally possible, a highly significant distinction is nevertheless to be made between the basic principles involved under the two main heads of this classification. As long ago as 1902 Professor C. J. Bullock[4] pointed out that the principle of increasing returns rests on a different basis from the principle of decreasing returns. Decreasing returns arise from the scarcity of some factor of production and the consequent necessity of using greater and greater proportions of the others along with it. Increasing returns, on the other hand, depend on improvements in "organization" made possible by the increase in the scale of operations; division of labor, specialization of machinery, utilization of by-products, and so on.[5] The reference to these as "economies of organization," however, is not entirely satisfactory because there are improvements in organization which come about through the natural progress of the arts and are not

---

[4] "The Variation of Productive Forces," *Quarterly Journal of Economics*, August, 1902.

[5] Some writers attempt to reduce these changes in organization to changes in factoral proportions by identifying them with variations in the quantity of management employed but this does not seem to be an acceptable procedure. A good discussion of this point is to be found in E. H. Chamberlin's *Theory of Monopolistic Competition*, Appendix B.

introduced as a result of an increase in the scale of production. They are of the same character as Marshall's "substantive new inventions." They belong in the fourth period of his analytical scheme and not in the third. On the other hand, he would include in his third period changes following from an increase in scale of output which we would think of more naturally as changes in technique rather than in organization. It is desirable therefore to make one general heading "methods of production" to contrast with "proportions of factors" and to include under it changes both in technique and in organization, but to classify them under two subheadings: (*a*) Those dependent on the scale of production; (*b*) those dependent on the state of the arts.

This general classification has the added advantage of bringing out clearly an important difference between the Marshallian scheme of analysis and that employed by J. A. Schumpeter. Professor Schumpeter denies the validity of the distinction between those economies which follow "automatically" from a change in the scale of production and those which are "spontaneous."[6] The actual realization of the economy in either case depends on "innovation" and innovation of any sort belongs to the realm of dynamics, not to the realm of statics. That is, according to the Schumpeter concept, static analysis can cover only our first main heading (I) while according to Marshall's concept it can include also the first subheading under the second main heading (I and IIa).

It should be noted that even if we are prepared to extend the static analysis as Marshall does to include the long-run normal it is nevertheless perfectly consistent with his general principles of procedure to introduce as a preliminary step in the development of the study a more strictly static concept of the law of variable proportions. The logic of the analysis seems to require not only that we distinguish the effects of changes in the proportions of factors from changes in the state of the arts but also that we distinguish them from the effects (if any) of changes in the scale of production. It is only in this way that we can conceive of a homogeneous pro-

---

[6] "The Instability of Capitalism," *Economic Journal*, 1928, p. 378 n.

duction function such that a doubling or a trebling of the quantities of all the factors will exactly double or treble the output obtained. It is with this strictly static law that the present study is concerned.

A Restatement of the Law

The effects of variations in the proportions of the factors of production are commonly introduced into our economic analyses through a statement of the principle of diminishing productivity in some such terms as the following: *In a given state of the arts, after a certain point is reached, the application of further units of any variable factor to another fixed factor (or fixed combination of factors) will yield less than proportionate returns.*

A statement of this sort, while it has the great merit of calling attention in a very few words to the most important general characteristics of the basic principle involved, is so lacking in precision on certain particular points that it leaves the way open for rather serious misunderstandings. First, it is not clear whether the effects of economies of scale are excluded or not by the proviso that the state of the arts remains unchanged. Second, it is not clear whether the point referred to (commonly called "the point of diminishing returns") is the point where marginal returns begin to decline or where average returns begin to decline. Third, it is uncertain whether the statement about returns being "less than proportionate" means that the return from each successive unit is less than the return from the preceding one or that the percentage rate of increase in total output is less than the percentage rate of increase in the variable factor. And fourth, nothing is said as to whether the total output will continue to increase absolutely as long as the variable factor is increased or whether after another certain point is reached the effects of further additions of the variable factor will actually be negative. Largely because of this last deficiency it fails to bring out as it should the symmetrical character of the interfactoral relations involved. The above statement of the law is not incorrect but it is neither sufficiently precise nor sufficiently complete to afford an adequate foundation for the analysis that must be based upon it.

Although the most important consequence of this law is that, within certain limits, the marginal productivity of any factor which is increased relative to the other factors decreases, it is nevertheless more convenient and more helpful for general analytical purposes to formulate the complete statement of the law in terms of total outputs rather than in terms of either marginal or average outputs. There are advantages also in referring to it as "the law of variable proportions" rather than as "the law of diminishing productivity" or the "law of diminishing returns."

As a statement of the law which would bring out the essential points the following may be suggested:

If, without change in the methods of production (in the sense explained above) successive physical units of one factor of production were added to a fixed physical quantity of another factor (or constant combination of other factors) the *total physical output obtained* would vary in magnitude through three distinct phases:

1. In the first phase, it would *increase*, for a time at an increasing absolute rate and then at a decreasing absolute rate, but always at a percentage rate greater than the rate of increase of the variable factor, until the final point in this phase was reached at which its rate of increase was exactly equal to the rate of increase of that factor.

2. In the second phase, it would continue to *increase*, but at a decreasing absolute rate and at a percentage rate always less than that of the variable factor, until the final point of this phase was reached where the maximum output was attained.

3. In the third phase, it would *decrease*, possibly for a time at an increasing absolute rate but probably through most of this phase at a decreasing rate, until the final point was reached at which the product was reduced to zero.[7]

---

[7] The law could of course be stated in terms of marginal or average outputs obtained from the variable factor but when either of these is used alone it is difficult to distinguish clearly the three important phases. When they are used together, however, this is easily done since the end of the first phase is marked by the point where average outputs attain their maximum and the end of the second is marked by the point where the marginal outputs become zero. It should be

The most important thing to observe about this law is that it is symmetrical[8] and consequently the third phase is simply the converse of the first.   In the third phase the proportion of the variable factor in relation to the fixed factor is so great as to be positively harmful while in the first phase it is the fixed factor which is present in such excess relative to the variable factor that it actually has the effect of reducing the output.   In either case a greater total output could be obtained by discarding enough of the excessive factor to bring the factors into such proportions as they have at one or other limit of the second phase.   The only economically relevant phase in the operation of the law is the second.   Within the limits of this phase the marginal productivity (and the average productivity) of whichever factor is increased relative to the others decreases in absolute amount.

GRAPHIC REPRESENTATION OF THE LAW FOR TWO FACTORS

The curves of total output, marginal output, and average output which are commonly drawn to represent the effects of increasing the applications of a variable factor to a fixed factor have certain characteristics which deserve special attention.   These are indicated in Fig. 1.   The quantity of factor A is taken as constant while increases of factor B are measured along the X-axis and units of output are measured along the Y-axis.[9]   The curves do not begin at the origin but at some point on the X-axis to the right

---

noted that this law besides being strictly static is purely physical, and is applicable only on the assumption that the factors (or at least the variable factor) can be broken up into small separable homogeneous units.   This is admittedly an extreme abstraction as far as most factors and most practical production conditions are concerned but it is thought to be useful as a starting point for our economic analysis provided that these limitations and assumptions are kept clearly in mind.

[8] The word "symmetrical" as used in this discussion is not intended to imply symmetry in the strict mathematical sense of the term.

[9] It should be recognized that the heights of the average marginal curves are dependent on the particular unit of input used and bear no fixed proportion to the total output curve.   If the marginal curve is looked on as a mathematical curve representing changes in the rate of change in total output we must think of the units on the Y-axis as representing ratios or slopes.

of it, because before the ratio of the excessive factor to the deficient one becomes infinite (as it is at the origin) the product is reduced to zero.   All three curves begin by rising.   At the point M the marginal curve reaches its maximum and directly above it on the total-output curve is a point of inflection, S.   Up to this point the total-output curve rises at an increasing rate and beyond it the curve rises only at a decreasing rate.   At the point D the average-output curve reaches its highest point and is intersected by the marginal curve.   Directly above D on the total-output curve is a point N where a tangent to that curve would pass through the origin.   A vertical line through D and N marks the beginning of

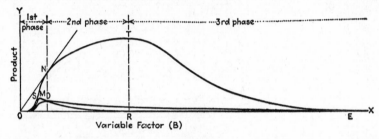

FIG. 1.

the second phase in the operation of the law.   At T the highest total output is reached and directly below this point the marginal-output curve cuts the X-axis at R.   A vertical line through R and T indicates the end of the second phase.   Beyond this point the total-output curve descends continuously till it meets the X-axis along with the average-output curve at E.[10]

By a curve such as this we can represent only the outputs obtained when varying quantities of B are used along with *one*

---

[10] Knight makes the curve descend quite sharply and makes it cut across the X-axis but since the output is measured in physical units the negative product seems illogical and since the *proportions* of the factors are less affected by each additional unit of the variable factor as we move to the right along the X-axis it is clear that *in general* the third phase must be more prolonged than the first.   The typical shape of the curve in this phase will be as if the part in the first phase were reversed and stretched out, with greater stretching effect at the lower end than at the top.

fixed quantity of A, but by means of a cross-classification table (or a surface) we can represent the outputs obtained when any quantity of B is combined with any quantity of A. In this case the quantities of B are measured along the X-axis, the quantities of A are measured along the Y-axis, and the outputs are indicated by the figures in the cells (or by the height of the surface above the basic plane). In Fig. 2 purely hypothetical output figures have been

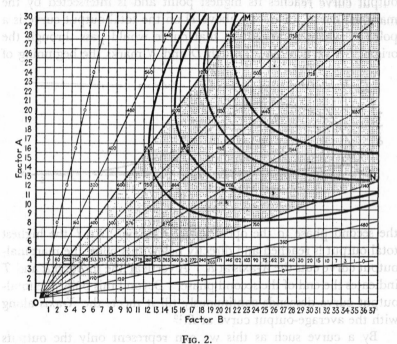

FIG. 2.

inserted to show the results of combining various quantities of B with 4 units of A. The variations in output are in accordance with the law of variable proportions and are, in fact, exactly those represented by the total-output curve in Fig. 1. It follows from the assumption that "methods of production" are unchanged that wherever the factors are combined in the same proportions the outputs obtained will be proportionate to the quantities of the factors used. Further, since the proportions of factors are the same on any straight line from the origin it is evident that when any one row or column is given the whole table is determined. From the row inserted it is seen: (1) that highest average output per unit of B is obtained when the proportions are $3B$ to $4A$, and (2) that the highest total output from A is obtained when the proportions are $12B$ to $4A$. Along the line OM the proportions are $3B$ to $4A$ and along the line ON the proportions are $12B$ to $4A$. Therefore all rational combinations lie between these two lines—i.e., the second phase of the law is represented by the dotted area between them.[11]

It is in connection with such a table as this (or the surface that it represents) that the concept of an "isoquant" can best be introduced. An isoquant is the locus of a point joining equal-output figures and thus corresponds to a contour line on a survey map. In Fig. 2 they are shown as heavy black lines. From the nature of the surface represented it follows: (1) that all isoquants at the points where they intersect the line OM must have tangents which are vertical and that above those points they must curve away from the Y-axis; (2) that all isoquants at the points where they intersect the line ON must have tangents which are horizontal and that beyond those points to the right they curve away from the X-axis; and (3) that within the significant economic area between these lines the isoquants must have a negative inclination and, except where the factors are perfect substitutes, must be convex toward the origin. To illustrate the use which can be made of these isoquants in economic analysis it will suffice to point out here that the least cost combination of factors for producing any quantity of the product may be found by drawing a tangent to the appropriate isoquant at a slope representing inversely the relative cost rates of the factors.

AN APPLICATION OF THE ANALYSIS TO THREE FACTORS

When we go on to apply the reasoning of the foregoing sections to the more realistic cases, in which three or more factors are combined in the productive process, we have to consider the effects of

[11] In the special case where the factors have to be combined in certain definite proportions, as in a chemical compound, the significant area is reduced to a single line.

variations in the quantities of any one of the capacities of all the others to combine with one another.   In what follows an attempt will be made to illustrate the nature of the problems here involved with the simplest of these cases, where only three factors are employed.   Suppose, for example, that the curves in Fig. 1 represent the effects of employing various quantities of seed in the cropping of a given piece of land.   Then suppose that half a dozen scarecrows are added as a third factor in the combination and that in this way the amount of seed lost to the birds was reduced from 10 per cent of what was sown to zero.   In this case the addition of the third factor very definitely affects the mutual combining capacities of the other two.   Nine bushels of seed will now have the effect that ten had before and the curves representing the products obtained with varying amounts of seed under the new conditions will have heights and general characteristics exactly like those in Fig. 1 but will be compressed horizontally to nine-tenths of their former dimensions.   If for a third factor instead of scarecrows we were to take water the interactions to be analyzed would be more complicated.   On the one hand the application of water, by increasing the percentage of seeds that germinated, might tend to have an effect exactly similar to the erection of scarecrows.   But, on the other hand, the presence of moisture in the soil would have the effect of making plant food more readily available to the growing crop and may thus have the effect of increasing the capacity of the land to combine with seed.   In addition to this the water itself is a constituent element of most plant structures and even if it had neither of the above effects it might still contribute directly to an increase in the weight of the product obtained.

When the third factor has an effect, as in the scarecrow example above, of compressing the curves horizontally, we may say that it is *augmentative* to the variable factor (seed) and *attenuative* to the fixed factor (land).   Similarly in the case of the water if in addition to raising the curve it has a tendency to shift the point of highest total returns (and other corresponding points) farther over toward the Y-axis it also would be *augmentative* to the seed and *attenuative* to the land.   On the other hand, if the curve is stretched out horizontally as well as heightened the third factor is *attenuative* to the variable factor and *augmentative* to the fixed one.   Between these cases there will be, theoretically at least, another set in which the third factor is *neutral* in its effects on the mutual combining capacities of the other two and in which, although the curves may be raised, the points of highest total, average, and marginal outputs will merely be shifted to new positions in the same vertical lines. In actual practice the interrelations existing among the factors will ordinarily be far more complicated than this classification would at first sight suggest.   This is due principally to the fact that, although for certain combinations the factor C is augmentative to the factor B, it may for other co ι binations be augmentative to the factor A.   On the other hand the conditions of neutrality are so restrictive that they could not apply to the cross relations between all the factors at the same time.   The distinctions made here do not correspond to the distinctions made by J. R. Hicks and R. G. D. Allen[12] between competitive and complementary goods, nor are they likely to prove as generally useful, but they do serve the particular purpose here of putting in its proper setting the highly implified exposition which follows.

Graphic Representation of the Law for Three Factors

We may begin by making the assumption (admittedly unrealistic) that B is neutral with respect to A and C while C is neutral with respect to A and B.   Suppose then that the total outputs obtained when various quantities of B are applied to the fixed factor (say $10A$) plus 1 unit of C, are as shown in the appropriate row of Fig. 3; and the total outputs when various quantities of C are applied to $10A$ plus $1B$ are as shown in the appropriate column.[13] Given this column and row (or any other column and row), the table can be completely filled in with figures that are mutually con-

---

[12] "A Reconsideration of the Theory of Value," *Economica*, February, 1934, and May, 1934.

[13] The fact that figures in the bottom row are zeros indicates that C is an indispensable factor while the zeros in the left-hand column indicate that B is also indispensable.

sistent with one another and consistent with the essential characteristics of the basic law. In each row from left to right and in
each column from bottom to top, the figures represent total outputs, varying through the three characteristic phases determined
by the law of variable proportions for two factors. The changes
in magnitude from point to point in any row are in the same pro-

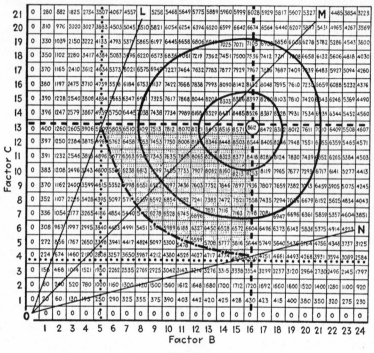

Fig. 3.

portion as between corresponding points vertically above or below
them in all other rows. The same is true of changes between points
in any one column and corresponding points horizontally across
from them in other columns. What concerns us particularly here
are the following facts: (1) the highest average outputs in all the
rows will be obtained with 5 units of B and will lie along the
vertical dotted line; (2) the highest total outputs in all the rows

will be obtained with 16*B* and will lie along the vertical broken line; (3) the highest average outputs in all the columns will be obtained with 4 units of *C* and will lie along the horizontal dotted line; and (4) the highest total outputs in all the columns will be obtained with 13*C* and will lie along the horizontal broken line.

It is our object now to determine which of the factoral combinations represented in this figure are rational economic possibilities and which are not.   That is, we want to mark out the area on this surface which corresponds for the three factors concerned to the second phase in the operation of the law of variable proportions as originally stated for two factors alone.   This is, in fact, the dotted area.   At any point outside this area the proportion of one of the factors relative to the other two is so great as to be positively harmful and to diminish the total output that could be obtained if less of it were used along with the same quantities of the other factors.   It is clear that even if *B* were free, it would never be rational to use more than 16 units along with the 10 units of *A* no matter how many units of *C* were used in the combination.   Consequently the area within which the points represent rational proportions is limited on the right hand by the vertical broken line. Similarly with no quantity of *B* along with the 10 units of *A* would it pay to use more than 13 units of *C*.   Therefore the upper limit of the rational area is marked by the horizontal broken line.   The inner limit of the area marked by the dotted-and-broken line has been located by determining the points beyond which in the direction of the origin the proportion of *A* relative to the other factors is so great as to be positively harmful.   This has been done by applying to the present case with its three factors the same reasoning by which it was shown in the simpler case of two factors that, up to the point where the percentage rate of increase in total output was just equal to the percentage rate of increase in the variable factor, the fixed factor was present in the combination in too great proportion.   Along any diagonal line in Fig. 3 (such as *OL*, *OM*, or *ON*) the curve of total outputs must exhibit the features characteristic of the law (as in Fig. 1), because as we move out from the origin along such a line it is as if successive units of a compound factor B-C (the proportions of B and C in each unit being constant) were being added to the given quantity of A. By locating the points on these diagonals which mark in each case the beginning of the second phase in the operation of the law the inner limit of the dotted area in Fig. 3 has been determined. The exact method used is explained in a footnote below.[14]

In cases where the assumption of neutrality among the factors is not fulfilled the determination of the precise location of this inner

---

[14] Moving from point to point along any of these diagonals the percentage rate of increase of the compound variable factor is the same as the percentage rate of increase in the quantity of B used and the same as the percentage rate of increase in the quantity of C used.   The corresponding increase in output, although it cannot be broken up into definite parts one of which could be attributed to the increase of B and the other to the increase of C, can nevertheless be related to the increases in these factors in the following way.   Let P be any point on the diagonal and Q any other point farther from the origin.   Let R be a point horizontally to the right of P and vertically below Q; and let S be another point horizontally to the left of Q and vertically above the point P.   Then the increase in output between P and Q may be thought of in either of two ways: either (1) as the increase from P to R (due to the increase of B while C is unchanged) plus the increase from R to Q (due to the increase of C with B held constant after its initial increase) or (2) as the increase of output from P to S (due to the increase of C while B was unchanged) plus the increase from S to Q (due to the increase of B with C held constant after its initial increase).

The increase from P to R is not equal in absolute amount to the increase from S to Q nor is the increase from R to Q equal exactly to the increase from P to S, but, under the conditions of neutrality assumed in the present case, the percentage increases would be equal along each pair of lines.   Therefore the increase of output from P to Q may be thought of as a certain percentage increase due to B and a certain percentage increase due to C, taking effect cumulatively in either order.   Suppose, for example, that the increases horizontally were 5 per cent and vertically 2 per cent.   Then the product at Q would be greater than the product at P by $7\frac{1}{10}$ per cent since

$$\frac{105}{100} \times \frac{102}{100} = \frac{107.1}{100}.$$

If it happens that the corresponding increase in the variable factor was also $7\frac{1}{10}$ per cent, then this would be the place where the average output per unit of the variable factor was at its highest and beyond which in the direction of the origin the proportion of A would be too great.   That is, we would have found the point

boundary line would naturally be a matter of greater difficulty, but the fact that it must lie within the area (no longer a rectangle) enclosed by the lines (now sloping, curved, or even irregular) corresponding to the broken and the dotted lines in Fig. 3 can easily be demonstrated. Take any point Q on a diagonal below the horizontal dotted line and to the left of the vertical broken line and any other point P on the same diagonal nearer to the origin. Let S be a point vertically above P and horizontally to the left of Q Then the difference in output between P and Q is equal to the difference in output between P and S plus the difference in output between S and Q. But we know that in this section of the chart, the difference in output between P and S is more than proportionate to the difference in the quantity of the factor C used and (since the percentage rate of increase for C is the same as the percentage rate of increase of the compound factor used along the diagonal) more than proportionate to the increase of the compound variable factor in question. We also know that in this section the

---

for which we were looking. A method for locating such points can be based on the observation that in the above case

$$\frac{105/100}{\sqrt{107.1/100}} \times \frac{102/100}{\sqrt{107.1/100}} = 1.$$

Stated more generally, this means that at the point on any diagonal where the percentage rate of increase of output and the percentage rate of increase of the compound variable factor are equal

$$\frac{\overset{(1)}{\text{Product at } R \text{ as per cent of product at } P}}{\sqrt{\text{Quantity of } B \text{ at } R \text{ as per cent of } B \text{ at } P}} \times$$

$$\frac{\overset{(2)}{\text{Product at } Q \text{ as per cent of product at } R}}{\sqrt{\text{Quantity of } C \text{ at } Q \text{ as per cent of quantity of } C \text{ at } R}} = 1$$

Taking the two parts of this expression separately, figures can be worked out for all quantities of B and all quantities of C. When this has been done it is a comparatively easy matter, given any quantity of B, to find the quantity of C whose coefficient when multiplied with the coefficient worked out for B will give a product of 1. Points so located must be the points of highest average output per unit of the compound variable factors on the diagonals on which they lie.

product at Q is larger than at S.   Therefore the percentage increase of product between P and Q is definitely greater than the percentage increase in the quantity of the variable factor used.   This will be true up to the point where the dotted line is reached and it follows that the points of highest average return per unit of the variable factor on all diagonals running across the central area will lie farther from the origin than the intersections with these dotted lines. The boundary line in this case, it should be noted, need not meet the broken lines at their intersections with the dotted ones but may meet them at points farther toward the point where they intersect with one another.

The isoquants in this case, unlike those in Fig. 2, are closed curves encircling the summit of the surface where the horizontal and vertical broken lines intersect.   At this point the output is the highest that can possibly be obtained from the fixed factor $(10A)$ through applications of B and C.   Where the isoquants cut the vertical broken line their tangents must be horizontal and where they cut the horizontal broken line their tangents must be vertical. Within the relevant economic area, as in Fig. 2, they must be negatively inclined and, with the exception of cases in which B and C are perfect substitutes for one another, they must be convex toward the origin.

6

PRODUCTION AND DISTRIBUTION
IN THE SHORT RUN*

By George Stigler †

In the 1890's perhaps the most disputed question in production theory was whether the coefficients of production should be treated as fixed or variable.[1] Wicksteed, Marshall, Walras, and Wicksell favored the view that these coefficients are variable; Pareto, Barone, and others favored the view that some of the coefficients are fixed. The verdict has since been delivered for the former group: It is almost universal practice at present to treat only with variable production coefficients.

But the triumph was too complete. In rejecting—quite properly, the writer believes—the fixed-coefficient approach in problems of long-run equilibrium, the neoclassical economists overlooked the applications of this approach to short-run problems. One thesis of this paper is, in fact, that the variable-coefficient hypothesis has obscured important problems in the theory of production and distribution in the short run.

The classical theories of fixed coefficients are, however, largely inapplicable to the short-run problem. The *simpliste* doctrine in the earlier editions of Walras' *Eléments*,[2] the formal generality of Pareto's "solution,"[3] and even the admirable theory of Georgescu-

* *Journal of Political Economy*, Volume 47, June 1939, pages 305–327. Reprinted by courtesy of the publisher and author.

† University of Minnesota.

[1] The extensive literature is summarized in my forthcoming book, *Studies in the History of Production and Distribution Theories, 1870–1895*, esp. chap. xii. In this article Walras' definition of production coefficients will be followed, i.e., the production coefficient of productive service X is the amount of X necessary to produce one unit of product.

[2] E.g., *Eléments d'économie politique pure* (1st ed., 1874), Lect. 41.

[3] *Manuel d'économie politique* (2d ed., 1927), pp. 605 ff.

Roegen,[4]—none of these is able to cope fully with the problems in hand. Some of the peculiarities involved in these problems will be discussed in the next section; their significance for cost and distribution theory will then be considered.

I. PRODUCTION AND DISTRIBUTION IN THE SHORT RUN

The short run is generally defined, following Marshall, as the period within which there are fixed or overhead costs. It is patent that there are in general an infinity of different "short runs," in each of which there is a different amount of fixed costs. The short run presumably refers to that period within which the physical plant is fixed: "For short periods the stock of appliances of production are practically fixed, but their employment varies with demand."[5] Fixed costs may include, of course, not only the costs of durable plant, but also the salaries of executives, etc., which by law (contract) or by custom and/or because of "non-economic" factors are not easily varied.

It will be argued subsequently that one cannot uniquely define fixed and variable costs with reference only to time periods. At least two additional circumstances must be considered, the existing cost-price relationships and the anticipated movements of prices and outputs. For the present, however, we shall assume that there is an acceptable division between fixed and variable costs, deferring the explanation of the division to the subsequent discussion.[6]

We may proceed at once to the central problem. The law of diminishing returns and the marginal productivity theory describe the quantitative variations of the output of a product when all

---

[4] "Fixed Coefficients of Production and the Marginal Productivity Theory," *Review of Economic Studies*, III (1935), 40–49.

[5] Marshall, *Principles of Economics* (8th ed., 1920), p. 374, margin. It is probably unnecessary to add that Marshall denies that any sharp division can be drawn between long and short periods (cf. *ibid.*, pp. 378 and 379 n.).

[6] In this paper it will be assumed that there are no changes in the known technology; for the rest, the usual postulates of partial equilibrium analysis will be followed. The discussion is directed primarily to perfect competition, although it is also appropriate, with suitable qualifications, to imperfect competition.

but one of the productive services are held constant in quantity, the remaining one varying in quantity. The law of diminishing returns requires full adaptability of the form, but not the quantity, of the "fixed" productive services to the varying quantity of the other productive service. To use a well-known example, when the ditch-digging crew is increased from ten to eleven, the ten previous shovels must be metamorphosed into eleven smaller or less durable shovels equal in value to the former ten,[7] if the true marginal product of eleven laborers is to be discovered.

In the short run, however, the very existence of fixed costs (representing the return on fixed "plant," etc.) precludes full adaptability to changing amounts of the variable factors (day labor, materials, fuel, etc.). It follows that in the short run the law of diminishing returns need not hold, at least in its conventional form. Numerous writers have therefore been too hasty in asserting that increases of output necessarily entail rising marginal costs, and, as a matter of fact, it will be argued that not only may short-run marginal costs be constant within certain ranges of output, but also that under certain conditions they very probably do behave in some such manner.

The same problem arises in connection with short-run distribution theory. Quasi-rents, the returns to the fixed "plant," are measurable, Marshall suggests, by marginal productivity analysis.[8] But since full adaptability is ruled out by the very circumstances of the short run, it is easily demonstrable that this line of analysis may over- or underestimate the return to the fixed productive services (and, *pari passu*, to the variable productive services).

So much for the problem—what are the major empirical facts that must be considered in a solution? There are obviously very many factors which affect the short-run marginal cost curve (and

---

[7] This value is stated in terms of a *numéraire*, for our purposes; hence no index-number problem is present.

[8] *Op. cit.*, pp. 419–20. Marshall is not specific on this point, and he, of course, adds some interesting qualifications which will be considered in Part III of this paper.

that is what the production problem amounts to), but several may be selected on grounds of importance and theoretical interest. Certain technological considerations will be raised first.

We must differentiate, with respect to technological questions, between operation at outputs less than the optimum and operation at outputs in excess of the optimum.[9] These two cases need not be, and in general will not be, symmetrical. The situation in real life is complicated by the fact that the optimum output may be an optimum through time, i.e., the optimum may be based on anticipated increases or decreases in the output of the firm. The immediate analysis will be restricted primarily to the simpler stationary condition, where the optimum output is also the equilibrium output (under competition) through time.

An additional problem that must be mentioned arises out of the relationship between the control unit (the firm) and the production unit (the plant). Almost universally the firm and the plant are assumed to be in a one-to-one ratio, and certainly no general theory of the relationship between the two has yet been evolved. The present discussion will follow this precedent, although a few rather obvious generalizations will be noted from time to time.

In general, there are two major technical alternatives that may arise in the utilization of fixed "plant": it may be divisible or indivisible. Perfect divisibility can probably be found in some cases; it is approximated wherever there are a large number of identical machines in a plant. Complete indivisibility is the opposite limiting case, suggested, although not perfectly illustrated, by the roadbed of a railroad.

In the case of fixed plant, however, we may also divide the field according to another principle: the unit of plant may be adaptable to changing quantities of the variable productive services, or it may not be adaptable.[10] Almost all observable cases

---

[9] Optimum output is here defined as the rate of production at which average cost is a minimum. This definition is not unambiguous, but it will serve immediate purposes.

[10] For an explicit definition of adaptability cf. below. pp. 314–15.

seem to fall between these limiting concepts, just as they usually fall between perfect divisibility and complete indivisibility. It is instructive, nevertheless, to examine the four possible combinations of divisibility and adaptability for operation both at less-than-optimum and greater-than-optimum outputs.

a) The case of divisible plant that is completely adaptable to changing amounts of the variable productive services will result, of course, in decreases of the marginal productivities of the variable services as their quantities are increased, throughout the whole range of outputs. For in this case the conventional law of diminishing returns is almost fully applicable,[11] and therefore as the ratio of variable to fixed services increases, the marginal productivities of the variable services decline. Each laborer (of the reduced working force), for example, can operate a larger number of machines.[12]

a') The corresponding case for outputs in excess of the optimum is parallel: with increases of the variable services, their marginal productivities will continue to decline, and those of the fixed services will increase.

b) The second possible combination is a divisible but unadaptable fixed plant, e.g., there are numerous identical machines but each machine can be used only with a fixed amount of labor and materials. This is an unrealistic case, but it sheds light on intermediate situations. At less-than-optimum outputs, the "marginal" productivities of the variable services will remain constant. It is difficult to speak of the marginal productivities of either the variable services or the fixed plant, however, since it is not possible, by incremental analysis, to impute productivities when the production coefficients are fixed.

b') The case of outputs in excess of optimum cannot arise

---

[11] Almost fully applicable but not completely so. With full divisibility of the fixed plant there can be no economic significance in the initial stage of increasing marginal returns, as displayed by the "Knightian" curve (cf. F. H. Knight, *Risk, Uncertainty and Profit* [1921], pp. 99 ff.).

[12] This case is usually present where the plant is divisible, if only because unemployed machines can be resorted to when employed machines require repairs.

here—once the fixed plant is fully employed, the output has reached its maximum.   Further units of the variable services would therefore have zero marginal productivities.

c) Third, the fixed plant may be indivisible but completely adaptable to any quantity of the variable service. This is the standard case of the law of diminishing returns, which is applicable without qualification. This situation differs from (*a*) only in that there will be an early stage of increasing marginal productivities of the variable services—a region that could have no significance with a divisible plant.

c') For outputs in excess of the optimum, this case is identical with (*a'*).

d) The final possibility is that the fixed plant is both indivisible and unadaptable.   It is indeed unlikely that this case would ever arise in practice, but its general character may be suggested by a blast furnace.   If there is only one fixed factor, and it is unadaptable, the plant can operate at only one output.   In the more important and interesting case where some adaptability is present, a priori one would expect that the marginal productivities of the variable services would fall very rapidly as the optimum output was approached.   At very small outputs relative to the optimum, however, the marginal productivities would probably also be very small.

d') Similarly, for greater-than-optimum outputs, the marginal productivities of the variable factors will be zero if there is no adaptability, and in the more realistic case, they will decrease faster than they would in (*c'*).

There is no need to labor the point that usually the fixed plant will be imperfectly divisible and partially adaptable, and, indeed, that the fixed plant will consist of numerous parts that differ greatly among themselves. Nevertheless, there is a possibility, at this stage of analysis, that the short-run marginal cost curve will be constant in the range of suboptimum outputs, if there are important divisible parts of plant.   If there is also adaptability, the marginal cost curve will be rising in this range.

So far we have tacitly assumed that technology dictates a

single most desirable arrangement of the fixed plant which is independent of fluctuations in output.   In fact, of course, this is rarely, if ever, true.   Adaptability can also be built into a plant, and entrepreneurs in trades where fluctuations are frequent and great will endeavor to secure flexibility in their operations.   But flexibility will not be a "free good": A plant certain to operate at X units of output per week will surely have lower costs at that output than will a plant designed to be passably efficient from $X/2$ to $2X$ units per week.

It is impossible to generalize, in the present state of our knowledge, whether entrepreneurs make more allowance for rates of production less than or in excess of optimum.   In certain of our capital-goods industries, *Anpassung* to superoptimum rates of production seems to have received most attention; in agriculture very little has been done in planning for either kind of nonoptimum production rate.   It seems plausible to assume that the adaptability of plant to changes in output decreases in both directions from the optimum as the output continues to increase or decrease.

At this point it is convenient to drop the assumption that there is only one short run.   Even after a plant has been built and equipped, it is usually possible to make alterations within short time periods which will better adapt the plant and equipment to contemporary (nonoptimum) rates of output.   The possible extent of such changes is a technological problem which will not be explored.   The profitability of the changes, however, is determined by the anticipated duration of the nonoptimum rate of production and the cost of making the change.   The longer the nonoptimum production rate is anticipated to continue, the greater is the inducement to make the change.   If the common belief that entrepreneurs are essentially optimistic be accepted, one would expect this to be a factor tending to decrease the cost of superoptimum outputs relative to suboptimum outputs.

This line of reasoning leads directly to the conclusion that time must be an implicit variable which affects the form of the production function.   There is not a short run and a long run;

rather there are continuous variations[13] in the marginal cost curve from very short periods to full, long-run equilibrium.[14]

II. The Short-run Marginal Cost Curve

The foregoing list of considerations, incomplete though it be, emphasizes the fact that short-run marginal cost curves form a rather extensive genus, each species of which is appropriate to a particular set of assumptions about technology and anticipations. It may nevertheless be instructive to examine a few of these species, following the procedure of the previous section in introducing complications step by step.

The case of perfect adaptability, with or without divisibility of plant, is so widely used at present, and, if the preceding analysis be accepted, it omits so many important factors in short-run production, that it will be passed over summarily. The cost curves appropriate to complete divisibility and complete indivisibility respectively are illustrated in Figure 1. In this and subsequent figures, AC, MC, and AVC represent average, marginal, and average variable costs, respectively. The difference between the two situations lies, of course, in the fact that the entrepreneur will not operate, under competition, in a region of decreasing average variable costs;[15] hence in case B output must be either zero or in excess of X_0. There cannot be a region of decreasing average

---

[13] This word is used in its literal mathematical sense in the calculus of variations. It properly suggests that the movements in question are from one cost curve to another, rather than along one curve.

[14] Of course there is nothing novel in this conclusion; it is implicit in the *natura non facit saltum* analysis of Marshall. The only explicit application of this approach that the writer knows is that of Professor Knight, who employed it as long ago as 1921 in his neglected article, "Cost of Production and Price over Long and Short Periods," reprinted in *The Ethics of Competition* (1935), pp. 186–216. Most of the phenomena under consideration have been discussed, although not with reference to formal cost theory, by J. M. Clark in *The Economics of Overhead Costs* (1923), esp. chaps. v and vi.

[15] This follows from the fact that in such a region total variable costs are greater than total revenue. Under competition, price will equal marginal costs, but marginal costs are less than average variable costs when the latter are falling.

variable costs with complete divisibility of the fixed plant, since the productivity of variable productive services can always be increased in such a region by using less of the fixed plant.   The subsequent analysis will deal primarily with the marginal and average cost curves, subject to this understanding.[16]

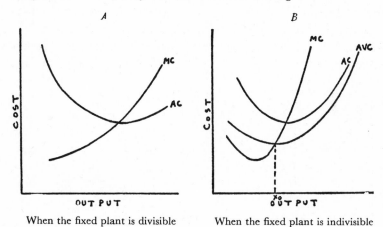

When the fixed plant is divisible   When the fixed plant is indivisible

Fig. 1.

Once we abandon the assumption that the fixed plant is not completely adaptable, the marginal cost curves of Figure 1 are no longer appropriate.   Consider first the case of an unadaptable plant that is completely divisible.   At less-than-optimum outputs, the marginal productivities of the variable services will remain constant.[17]   It follows that if the prices of the variable services remain unchanged, the marginal and average variable cost curves

---

[16] One could draw cost curves on the assumption that the fixed plant was divisible only into a finite number of parts, but that would unduly lengthen this paper. Miss M. F. W. Joseph has ingeniously analyzed one such case in "A Discontinuous Cost Curve and the Tendency to Increasing Returns," *Economic Journal*, XLIII (1933), 390–98.   Despite her assertion to the contrary (*ibid.*, p. 395), however, Miss Joseph is analyzing a long-run situation according to the terminology of this paper, for she excludes only historical change (i.e., there is no fixed plant).

[17] Ignoring such possible elements of adaptability as that arising out of the ability to avoid costs of interruption due to repairs of plant.

(which will coincide) will be horizontal lines. At outputs in excess of optimum, marginal costs will rise sharply. In fact, if there is no adaptability, the output cannot be increased in the short run beyond the point where the fixed plant is fully employed. The cases of zero and partial adaptability with divisible plant are illustrated in Figure 2.

In the case of an indivisible and unadaptable fixed plant, the conclusion has already been indicated: the short-run marginal cost curve is a vertical line. With partial adaptability, increases

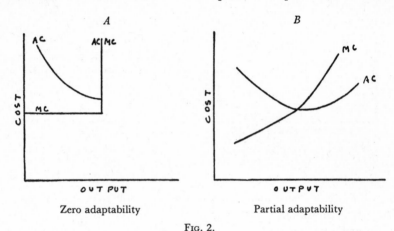

A   B

Zero adaptability   Partial adaptability

Fig. 2.

in the quantities of the variable services may lead to increases or decreases of their marginal productivities, depending on the region of output considered. The permissible range of output (under competition) may be reduced considerably, i.e., it is possible that there will be a considerable region of outputs for which average variable costs are decreasing. Figure 3 illustrates these two situations.

The first complication to be considered is the possibility of building flexibility of operation into the plant, so that it will be passably efficient over the range of probable outputs. Flexibility is not synonymous with adaptability; an example will suggest the difference. If a fixed plant of quantity X can be combined with from a to b units of a variable service, within this range there is complete adaptability if for any combination of the two services, it is possible to use the best-known technology that utilizes the two productive services in these quantities.[18]   But the best technology for combining X with (say) Z units of the variable service, with a product of Y units, need not be, and for non-optimum outputs generally will not be, the same as the technology which (given the prices of the productive services) would minimize the cost of producing a product of Y.   This latter technology will almost certainly require a different quantity of the fixed services.

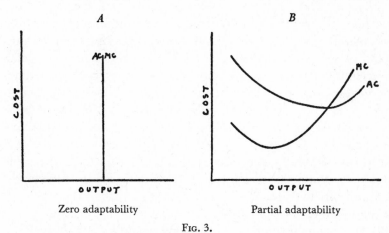

Zero adaptability   Partial adaptability

Fig. 3.

Flexibility permits this best technology for producing Y, and other nonoptimum outputs, to be approximated, but at the cost of not being able to use the best-known technology for any output.

This line of reasoning indicates that flexibility and adaptability differ, but, on the other hand, there is a prima facie case for the proposition that the greater the adaptability, the less the need for flexibility.   This case rests on the fact that with adaptability,

---

[18] By definition, X represents a physical fixed "plant" in the short run.   Illustrations of perfect adaptability are therefore difficult to find, but one might suggest agricultural land, which may be combined with a varying amount of plowing, seed, etc., within fairly wide limits.   The historical connection between agricultural land and the law of diminishing returns may explain in part the failure of economists to recognize the difficulties in short-run applications of the law.

output may be reduced greatly without leading to unemployment of fixed plant or inefficiency of variable factors. Nevertheless, additional flexibility may be desirable even in this limiting case of complete adaptability. A plant may operate at X output half of the time, and at $X/5$ output the remainder of the time.[19] The net profits of such a plant would very probably be increased if the firm adopted a production function that did not absolutely minimize its average costs for any output.

The real need for flexibility, however, clearly arises when there is only partial adaptability. Were it not for the flexibility built into plants, outputs in excess of optimum would involve prohibitive marginal costs, while those at less-than-optimum outputs would be very unprofitable. It is unnecessary to examine in detail the techniques for securing flexibility of operations, but two methods are obviously important. The first is based on divisibility of fixed plant, which will reduce variable costs of suboptimum outputs. The second method is to reduce fixed plant relative to variable services, i.e., to transform fixed into variable costs. The first method is frequently used where much fixed plant is indispensable (e.g., the automobile and steel industries); the second where mechanization is more or less optional (e.g., the sweatshop industries).

The amount of flexibility built into the plant depends on the costs and gains of the flexibility. One would expect, in general, flexibility to be subject to increasing marginal costs and to decreasing marginal returns from such flexibility (since, normally, great fluctuations of output are less frequent than small fluctuations). The three sets of conditions relevant to the entrepreneur's decision are

1. The anticipated rate of output in each period up to the end (if any) of the life of the plant;
2. The anticipated prices of the productive services in each such period of time; and

---

[19] Illustrations could be found in seasonal industries where production is not carried on at a uniform rate because the commodity is perishable—owing either to physical or to economic ("style") factors.

3. The production function relating flexibility to inputs of productive services.

The formal solution is apparent: Flexibility will be added until its "accumulated" marginal cost equals the discounted marginal returns from savings due to that additional flexibility. [20]

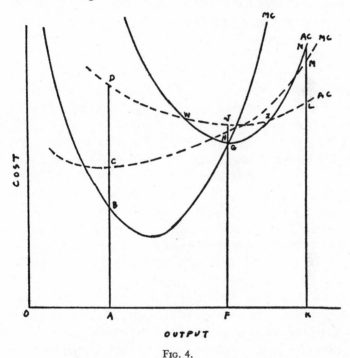

FIG. 4.

The differences between the cost curves of an indivisible and relatively inflexible plant and those of a relatively divisible and flexible plant are illustrated in Figure 4.   The cost curves of the former type are drawn as solid lines; the latter case is represented by the dotted lines.   At optimum output *OF*, the indivisible and unadaptable plant has lower average and marginal costs; the flex-

[20] The problem is complicated when the firm has several plants, for then it is possible, within certain limits, to concentrate the fluctuations of output in certain plants, and to build a maximum of flexibility into these plants only.

ible firm's costs, indeed, are larger by GJ times $OF.$[21] When output is OA, however, the flexible plant has much smaller losses (OA times CD), and the inflexible firm would even have to close down if it were in a competitive market (see n. 15). Similarly, at output OK, the profits of the flexible firm are larger by OK times LN, and the inflexible firm would require a prohibitive price to cover marginal costs at this output. If output were anticipated to fluctuate only between W and Z, clearly a less flexible plant would be desirable.

We have arrived now at the final complication (to be considered here) in the analysis of the short-run cost curves of the firm. That complication lies in the typical possibility of altering the fixed plant, even in the short run, when experience has demonstrated that the forecasts of the entrepreneur have been erroneous. It should be remembered that such alterations are not equivalent to movements along the long-run average cost curve, because they are based on changes in existing plant, not the construction of a completely new plant (except, of course, in the limiting case).

The two fundamental questions involved in short-run alterations of plant are: (1) When should such a change be instituted? and (2) What effect will it have on the firm's cost curves? The answer to the first question is simple enough from a formal viewpoint: The change will be made when the discounted gains (i.e., reduction of costs or increase of receipts) of the alteration exceed the cost of the change. The longer the new situation is expected to continue, the lower the cost of making the change, and the lower the interest rate, the sooner and greater will the alteration of plant be.[22] Aside from questions of technology, the relevant factors are therefore the anticipated prices of productive services and of products. The alterations will be carried to the point where

---

[21] Outputs, rather than selling prices, are selected for analysis, in order to avoid the complications arising out of the question of the slope of the demand curve if imperfect competition is considered.

[22] Not only the time and extent, but also the rate at which the alterations are made, are variables. Given alterations will be cheaper, the more slowly they are carried through, in part because the existing plant can be more fully depreciated.

the marginal "accumulated" cost of the change equals its discounted marginal return.

Certain more explicit factors in this difficult entrepreneurial decision may be indicated briefly. The problem, first of all, is in all probability asymmetrical. Extensions or enlargements of plant are in general much simpler than contractions. The reason, in part, is that a plant cannot always be depreciated completely out of existence, and rarely is this possible within moderate time periods unless the liquidation was anticipated at the time of construction. In the case of a railroad, for instance, current maintenance expenditures which are sufficient to keep the system in operation at all may be sufficient to keep it in operation indefinitely. And even in the general case, it is safe to assert that entrepreneurs usually build with an eye to future expansion and hardly ever with an eye to future contraction.[23] To the extent that such considerations are present, movements are not and cannot be made with equal facility in either direction between short-run cost curves.

It may be noted, secondly, that there is a strong presumption that short-run alterations of plant will affect the final equilibrium position. The received doctrine is that the long-run cost curve is the envelope of the family of short-run curves, each of which represents the ideal combination of resources for that size of plant. This long-run cost curve is the locus of positions that the plant may occupy in the long run, and, in fact, that plant size will be selected where the long-run curve marginal to this envelope intersects the marginal revenue curve.

At a certain level of abstraction all this is certainly true. When building a plant de novo, the long-run average cost curve does present all possible sizes of plant.[24] In stable equlibrium, more-

[23] H. T. Noyes reports that of 132 successful manufacturing firms, 89 considered their greatest error to have been the inadequate allowance for expansion (cf. "A New Manufacturing Plant," *Annals of the American Academy*, LXXXV [September, 1919], 68). This is necessarily a biased sample, however; among failing firms a major cause of distress is the undue provision for expansion.

[24] E. F. M. Durbin has made essentially the same point, apropos of the long-run curve: "There is nothing particularly 'long period' about the problem. . . . It arises when a new plant is to be constructed and all the curves exist at the moment

over, every entrepreneur will choose the size of plant which maximizes net profits, dictated bv this long-run curve, if he is certain that there will not be any changes in cost or demand conditions.

But when price changes take place,[25] what was an equilibrium size of plant at one time will probably become a nonoptimum size. The entrepreneur must then make the best of the situation and usually this involves a short-time alteration of plant. If major changes of output are frequent, relative to the life of the plant, and if they are not perfectly anticipated, then the plant existing at any time is in part determined by what the plant was in preceding periods. In other words, if the plant is at all durable and (what is already partially involved in this assumption) if changes of prices are not fully anticipated, then in general the short-run cost curve will not be the lowest one for that size of plant, and it will not be one of the family of curves on which the conventional long-run curve is based.

Finally, once short-term alterations of plant are admitted, it is impossible to draw short-run cost curves with reference only to time periods. Each such cost curve is now subject to restrictions, not directly of time, but rather of a set of prices. The cost curves are defined for an interrelated range of prices; if prices move outside this range, short-run alterations of plant will ensue, leading to a new set of curves.

It is not difficult to give a formal treatment of this final complication, either graphically or symbolically. The general effect of short-run plant alterations on costs is indicated by Figure 5.[26] Curve *I* represents the marginal cost curve for a given rate of production *OM*. If the rate of production increases, the plant will be enlarged, and curves *II*, *III*, and *IV* represent successive stages

---

when the size of plant is chosen. No long period of time is in question. The envelope is really an 'inter-plant,' not a 'long period' curve. . . . " (cf. "Note on Mr. Lerner's Dynamical Propositions," *Economic Journal*, XLVII [1937], 577 n.).

[25] Technological improvements are excluded from consideration.

[26] Fig. 5 is adapted from Diagram V of Professor Knight's "Cost of Production and Price," *op. cit.*, p. 206. His entire discussion should be consulted on this problem.

in this process.   They are derived, so to speak, from an envelope
of cost curves, not of different plants but of an expanding plant.
Curves *III* and *IV* are drawn through point *B* because there seems
to be no general reason why they might not equally well be above
or below this point; their locations are largely a matter of anticipations.   These are "dynamic" cost curves in the proper sense of
that much-abused word, and in general they are not reversible
within limited time periods.

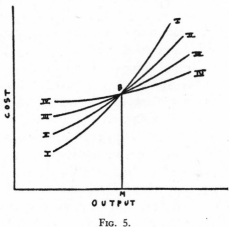

Fig. 5.

It is possible to assume that such changes are continuous, and
then a complete presentation (for any given set of price anticipations) involves a third axis, time, and the marginal and other cost
functions become surfaces.   The assumption of continuity is justifiable if alterations of plant can be made by small increments.[27]
But whether alterations of plant are continuous or discontinuous,

---

[27] This is not to say that alterations will necessarily be made by small increments.   The *minimum sensibile* of the entrepreneur is likely to be rather large.   If
output is falling, he will be loath to alter the plant accordingly, hoping for a return
to "normal" conditions—or for favorable legislation!   If output is expanding, it
is very likely that the plant will be expanded to handle rates of production in
excess of the contemporary level, which may, of course, be the sensible thing to
do.   A crucial factor is the frequency with which anticipations are revised.

it is no longer possible to handle the problem of the rate or extent of alteration by the use of plane geometry, since future prices are now important variables.

The tendencies toward flexibility and short-run alteration of plant are to a certain extent conflicting in nature. The greater the ease with which the plant can be altered in the short run, the less the need for flexibility (unless we include in flexibility ease in making alterations). Where fluctuations of output are regular, however, flexibility is virtually independent of alterability.

Cost curves have received less attention from statistically minded economists than have demand curves, although the data on costs seem much more subject to control and theoretical interpretation than the usual price-consumption figures. For several decades, German engineers have derived statistical total cost curves, but these curves are usually much oversimplified linear relations between total costs and the *Beschäftigungsgrade*.[28] The important pioneer work of Dr. Joel Dean,[29] preliminary though it be, does suggest two major discrepancies between the "facts" and usual short-run cost theory.

The first discrepancy is the relative constancy of marginal costs over the usual range of output;[30] the second is the fact that certain costs behave erratically with respect to variability and fixity.[31] The foregoing discussion contains a rationalization of both of these phenomena. Constancy of marginal costs follows from the building of flexible plants, and it is further supported by short-run alterations of plant, which permit movements between as well as along, short-run cost curves. The alterability of plant

---

[28] The attitude of these studies has all too frequently been that of R. Hildebrandt: "Theoretische Überlegungen haben hierbei keinen Zweck und führen zu nichts. Entscheidend sind ausschliesslich tatsächliche Ergebnisse der Praxis in möglichst grosser Zahl" (cf. "Geschäftspolitik auf mathematischer Grundlage," *Technik und Wirtschaft*, XXIV [1931], 127).

[29] *Statistical Determination of Costs, with Special Reference to Marginal Costs*, printed as Part II of the *Journal of Business*, IX (October, 1936).

[30] *Ibid.*, p. 12, chap. vii; cf. also E. Schneider, *Theorie der Produktion* (Vienna, 1934), pp. 50–51.

[31] Dean, *op. cit.*, chap. ii.

also provides a complete explanation for the fact that there are many costs which need not be completely fixed or completely variable within specified short periods of time.

III. SHORT-RUN DISTRIBUTION THEORY

At the outset it must be emphasized that short-run distribution theory is an important economic problem which is not "solved" by simple rule-of-thumb distributions of gross receipts. The entrepreneur is faced in short, as well as in long, periods with the continuous problem of maximizing net returns. This can be done only if within every relevant economic period he knows the effect on output of each type of productive service. Without this information he cannot intelligently plan for the maintenance, replacement, and alteration of "fixed" plant. The net return must be imputed to each productive service in each short period of time: the explanation of this imputation is the task of short-run distribution theory.

Marshall's doctrine of quasi-rents provides the standard explanation of short-run distribution to "fixed" agents, and therefore deserves immediate attention. Quasi-rents are the returns on temporarily specialized resources, and the costs of these resources are supplementary (or fixed).[32] Quasi-rents are net returns after allowance has been made for maintenance and depreciation,[33] so if a machine does not yield enough to cover these charges, its quasi-rent is negative.

Marshall is concerned almost exclusively with the causal relationship between quasi-rents and prices; he devoted little attention to the measurement of the quasi-rent of any particular temporarily specialized resource. His main discussion implies (but not strongly) that the marginal productivity theory is applicable,[34] and it contains no analysis of the difficulties in applying the theory to short-run phenomena.

Elsewhere, however, Marshall appears to recognize that there

---

[32] *Op. cit.*, pp. viii, 74, 362 n., and 412.
[33] *Ibid.*, p. 426 n.
[34] *Ibid.*, Book V, chaps. viii and ix, esp. pp. 406 ff. and 419 ff.

are difficulties present in the short-run application; the relevant passages deserve rather full quotation:

> The fact is that the incomes derived from the specialized capital and the specialized skill belonging to all the various industrial classes engaged in producing houses, or calico, or anything else, depend very much on the general prosperity of the trade. And in so far as this is the case they may be regarded for short periods as shares of a composite or joint income of the whole trade. . . .
>
> Indeed, in some cases and for some purposes, nearly the whole income of a business may be regarded as a quasi-rent. . . . In other words it is a *composite quasi-rent* divisible among the different persons in the business by bargaining, supplemented by custom and by notions of fairness. . . . [35]

In a footnote to these remarks, Marshall says that the allocation of income among specialized resources is "theoretically arbitrary."

From these considerations it would appear that when there are several quasi-rents, they are indistinguishable. This is also the implication of Marshall's approval of the analogy of "composite rents" to the indeterminacy of duopoly.[36] But the important passage on composite rents (e.g., the rent of "land" and the rent of improvements) is more restrained.[37] Marshall states that if a composite rent is produced by two resources, each of which is freely variable, it is possible to impute to each its separate rent. If the proportions between the two are fixed, there is no unique imputation between the resources.[38] This solution is not fully

---

[35] *Ibid.*, pp. 625 and 626. A footnote appended to *composite quasi-rent* refers the reader to nonexistent Sec. 8 of Book V, chap. x. On the basis of the fourth edition of the *Principles*, the last in which a meaningful cross-reference is given, the reference should be to Book V, chap. xi, Sec. 7, of the eighth edition, which is discussed below in the text.

[36] *Ibid.*, p. 494 n.

[37] *Ibid.*, pp. 453–54.

[38] Marshall goes farther and asserts, apropos of a single water power source: "Even if there were other sites at which the water power could be applied, but not with equal efficiency, there would still be no means of deciding how the owners of the site and the water power should share the excess of the producers' surplus which they got by acting together, over the sum of that which the site would yield for some other purpose, and that which the water power would yield if applied elsewhere" (*ibid.*, p. 454). This argument must rest on the assumption that there are no close substitutes for the best site.

applicable to true quasi-rents, despite Marshall's reference to it, since it relates to long-run equilibrium and to (Ricardian) rents, not to short-run quasi-rents.

We may isolate several different cases implicit in Marshall's analysis: (1) Where there is only one "fixed" factor, its quasi-rent is of course the residual remaining after payments for the variable productive services. Since this quasi-rent is a residual, it is also a marginal product. (2) When two or more "fixed" factors are present, and they are indivisible, their quasi-rents cannot be distinguished. (3) Where two or more "fixed" factors are present, and they are divisible, so their proportions may be varied effectively at the margin, their quasi-rents will be in the same ratio as their marginal products.

There can be no serious disagreement with these conclusions, but they are essentially formal rules and cast no light on the peculiarities of short-run distribution. Following the procedure of the previous sections of this paper, cases of progressive complexity will be taken up in turn.

Completely Unadaptable Fixed Factors

1. ONE FIXED FACTOR: DIVISIBLE. The marginal productivity theory sheds no light on this case, for the fixed factor has a zero marginal product for all outputs less than optimum, and thereafter the marginal product becomes infinite (see Fig. 2, A). In this case quasi-rents are obviously a pure residual.

2. ONE FIXED FACTOR: INDIVISIBLE. Here there can be only one output for the firm (see Fig. 3, A), and at this output quasi-rents are a residual.

3. SEVERAL FIXED FACTORS: DIVISIBLE. With several fixed elements of plant, residual analysis will yield no distribution of quasi-rents among these elements. There appears to be only one possible solution: If the units of fixed plant are mobile, and if there are close substitutes for them in other firms (or plants),[39] it is possible to set minimum rates on the remunerations which will reduce

---

[39] If these other machines are identical, the solution remains indeterminate. since effective proportions will be identical everywhere.

greatly the range of the indeterminacy in the distribution of quasi-rents.   This is of course Böhm-Bawerk's theory of distribution.[40]

Parenthetically, it may be added that Walras' solution, by a system of simultaneous equations, does not seem appropriate to the cases so far considered.   His technique is applicable only where the same resources are utilized in different proportions in different firms or industries.   In the case of unadaptable plant, variability of proportions simply cannot arise.   Georgescu-Roegen's elegant generalization of a mixed case of fixed and variable production coefficients is also inapplicable, at least in its present form, since it deals only with long-run equilibrium with full employment of unadaptable factors.[41]

4. SEVERAL FIXED FACTORS: INDIVISIBLE.   This does not differ greatly from the Case 2, since several unadaptable machines are for all practical purposes one machine.   The distribution of quasi-rents is indeterminate.

Partial Adaptability of Fixed Factors

Once partial adaptability is introduced, indeterminacy is diminished and in certain cases removed, for now the marginal productivities of divisible items of plant are positive and finite, within the relevant range of output.   The marginal productivity curves of these fixed factors will be steeper, the less the adaptability becomes, but it does not seem necessary that they be treated by a fixed-coefficients approach.

In one case, however, a fixed-coefficients approach is indispensable.   If some elements of fixed plant are indivisible (and this situation appears to be common), no form of incremental analysis is possible.   If the elements of plant in question are immobile, only residuals of total quasi-rents will be ascertainable, but if the elements of plant are mobile, Walras' approach is feasible.   Then the plant elements will in all probability be combined with other

---

[40] Cf. *Positive Theory of Capital* (1891), Book III, chap. ix.

[41] *Op. cit.*, p. 42.   In his notation he postulates that $F(a, b, y) = \bar{q}$, where $\bar{q}$ is the maximum product to be secured from y (the unadaptable factor).   In the short run $F(a, b, y)$ may well be less than $\bar{q}$.

productive services in different proportions in different firms (or possibly in different industries), and by "simultaneous equations" analysis, the separate quasi-rents may be isolated.

Flexibility of plant has uncertain effects on the allocation of total quasi-rents. To the extent that flexibility involves divisibility of plant, the solution of the short-run distribution problem continues to turn primarily on adaptability.[42] If flexibility is secured by transferring resources from the fixed to the variable category, to that extent the quasi-rent problem is eliminated. If flexibility involves the ability to combine physical elements of plant with variable amounts of other productive services, the marginal productivities of these plant elements will increase relative to those of the variable services at outputs removed from the optimum. Which of these, or of many other possible, forms of flexibility is generally utilized by entrepreneurs is a question of fact that cannot be answered at present.

Finally, when short-run alterability of plant is recognized, the distributive problem becomes extremely complex. There are then few, if any, truly "fixed" items of plant, but their variability is a function of anticipated prices and of the degree of confidence the entrepreneur has in these anticipations. The discounted anticipated future marginal products of the "fixed" services are decisive in the determination of the maintenance, replacement, and short-run alteration policies of the firm. The nature of the complications in this case has already been carefully analyzed by A. G. Hart,[43] and can be passed over here. Until detailed analysis is made of the determinants of these anticipations, however, distribution theory can make only formal allowance for short-run alterations of plant.

Although one may frequently (but not always) speak of short-run marginal products, if the foregoing analysis be accepted, such marginal products bear no simple or direct relationship to the

---

[42] Schneider believes that only limitational (i.e., unadaptable) productive services are indivisible (cf. *op. cit.*, p. 51).

[43] Cf. "Imputation and the Demand for Productive Resources in Disequilibrium," *Explorations in Economics* (1936), pp. 264–71.

marginal products of "normal value" analysis. A portion of the product will generally be attributable to each element of fixed plant, but this portion will change with time unless the firm is in equilibrium. It is not even possible to say that the short-run marginal product will approach identity with the long-run marginal product with the passage of time, unless specific and to some extent unrealistic assumptions are made concerning the durability of plant and the extent and frequency of revisions of anticipations and concomitant alterations of plant. Once a disequilibrium situation is permitted—and it is the great advantage of partial equilibrium analysis that it is feasible to do this—there is no assurance of unique equilibriums independent of the path of movement of economic phenomena.

7

MONOPOLISTIC COMPETITION AND THE PRODUCTIVITY THEORY OF DISTRIBUTION[*][1]

By Edward H. Chamberlin [†]

A word of explanation as to the nature of monopolistic competition will serve to orient the reader unfamiliar with the concept. Under this approach to value theory, whatever degree of control the individual producer enjoys over his own output, price and product receives full recognition as a monopoly force alongside of the competition to which he is subject in the form of similar products produced by others. The demand curve with which he has to reckon varies in elasticity according to the relative strength of these two elements. It is more elastic the more effectively the products of others may be substituted for his own, but it is never perfectly elastic, *i.e.*, horizontal, as under pure competition. The cost curve for the individual firm (average unit costs) is U-shaped, descending within the range in which a larger output yields economies through the more effective utilization or organization of the factors, until it reaches a minimum point, and rising again thereafter as the optimum output is exceeded. The equilibrium price and output are defined by the requirement that each producer seeks to maximize his profit. The familiar way of representing this is by fitting between the two curves just described a profit rectangle of maximum area. Another method much used recently involves the construction of two new curves, one of marginal revenue and the other of marginal cost. The output yielding the

---

[*] *Explorations in Economics*, 1936, pages 237–249. Reprinted by courtesy of the McGraw-Hill Book Co. and the author.

[†] Harvard University.

[1] A revision of a paper read at a meeting of the American Economic Association in Philadelphia, December, 1933, summarized in part in the *American Economic Review*, Vol. **XXIV**, 1934, sup., p. 23.

maximum profit is indicated by their intersection, and the price is the one at which this output can be sold, discovered by reference to the demand curve.

Under monopolistic competition there may or may not be monopoly profits to any particular individual firm. If the demand curve lies above the cost curve over a part of its length, monopoly profits will be earned. If, however, the competition of substitutes is sufficient to push it back to the point of tangency with the cost curve, there will be no profits above the necessary minimum which is included in the cost curve. In either case, the output per firm is smaller and the price higher than it would be under conditions of pure competition. The individual firm being smaller, it follows also that the number of firms is larger than it would be under pure competition. This condition, I hold, obtains wherever the products of different producers or the conditions surrounding their sale are differentiated from each other in any degree or respect which is significant to the buyers concerned, and this means over almost the entire economic system.

Without raising controversial questions about the productivity theory itself, let it be accepted, for purposes of this argument, as valid under the conditions of pure competition to which it has always (until recently) been implicitly or explicitly related. Its central tenet, that factors of production are paid according to their "marginal productivity" is subject to a variety of interpretations.[2] For our purposes, three possible meanings seem to be important. "Marginal productivity" may refer (a) to the physical product, (b) to the value of the physical product, or (c) to the revenue; which is added, in any case, by the presence of the marginal unit of a factor.

As to the first, it is conceivable that, even in an economic system characterized by a high degree of division of labor, factors of production might be paid literally in their physical product. Farm workers, restaurant employees, and domestic servants are laborers who receive at least a part of their wages in the product which they have helped to produce; and there might be mentioned also the case of a large distilling company which recently paid its stock-

---

[2] *Cf.* Machlup, "On the Meaning of the Marginal Product," in this volume.

holders a dividend in whisky. Ordinarily, however, income receivers consume little or none of the product of the enterprise with which they are associated, and it can be marketed so much more effectively by the enterprise itself than by individuals that it would obviously be absurd (and often impossible, as in the case of services) to pay incomes in product and place the burden of exchange upon the income receivers. For this reason, although "marginal product" has ordinarily meant physical product, the proposition that factors are paid according to their "marginal productivity" has meant that they are paid, not the product itself, but the money obtained from its sale. Thus the second meaning of "marginal productivity," referring to the value of the physical product, merely recognizes the fact of exchange: it is the equivalent of the physical product in money terms, the physical product multiplied by its selling price. It is this meaning which will be adhered to throughout this essay.

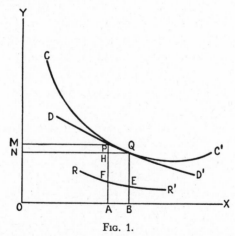

Fig. 1.

The marginal revenue product (or marginal value product, as it has usually been called), on the other hand, is, in general, quite dissociated from the physical product or its money equivalent. It refers to the added *revenue*—the total revenue (price per unit multiplied by the number of units) when the last unit of the factor is used less the total revenue when it is not used. In Fig. 1, if the amount of product is increased from OA to OB by the addition of another laborer, the value of the marginal product is $ABQH$; the marginal revenue product is $OBQN\text{-}OAPM$ (or $ABQH\text{-}NHPM$). The marginal revenue product may be defined most neatly by the use of the marginal revenue curve.   It is the marginal physical product multiplied by the marginal revenue.[3]   If RR' in Fig. 1 is a marginal revenue curve, it is $ABEF$.

Now it is evident that the entrepreneur is always and everywhere, whether under pure or under monopolistic competition, interested only in the marginal revenue products of the factors he employs.   But under pure competition, since he can change his output without appreciable effect upon the price, this will always be identical with the value of the marginal product.   In other words, under pure competition, the demand curve for the product of an individual producer being a horizontal line, his marginal revenue curve coincides with it. Marginal revenue is always equal to selling price.   Hence marginal product and marginal revenue product *to the individual competitor* are always identical.   Thus it is that, interested only in a factor's marginal revenue product, the entrepreneur arrives nevertheless at paying it its marginal product.

This is shown graphically in Figs. 2a and 2b.   Figure 2b is the familiar diagram showing the demand and cost curves (*md* and *cc'*, respectively) for an individual producer under pure competition; Fig. 2a shows the demand and cost curves (*DD'* and *MC*, respectively, constant cost being assumed) for the product of *all* the producers.   The two figures thus show the *same* facts from two different points of view.   It is clear from Fig. 2b that, as I have argued, the value of the marginal product (*abqh*) is equal to the marginal revenue product (*obqm-oahm*) in the eyes of the individual producer. There is an apparent contradiction to this in Fig. 2a, where the value of the marginal product is $ABQH$ and the marginal revenue product is less than this, $ABQH\text{-}MHPN$ (equal to $OBQM\text{-}OAPN$). But it must not be forgotten that the marginal revenue product in which the individual seller is interested is his own, not that for the

---

[3] Strictly speaking, each unit of the marginal product must be multiplied by its own marginal revenue and the sum taken.

market as a whole. If we assume the elasticity of DD' between P and Q in Fig. 2a to be unity, then as an individual seller increases his product by the amount AB, he adds nothing to the value of the whole supply, and therefore nothing to the revenue derived by all producers together from its sale. But he adds proportionately to the value of his own (Fig. 2b), for the sacrifice in price is spread over a large number of producers whereas the greater volume is enjoyed by himself alone. It is for this reason that price will settle

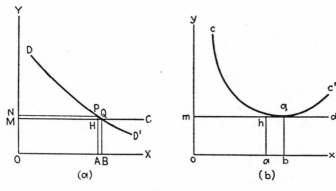

FIG. 2.

at BQ (Fig. 2a) instead of at AP (or at any other point), where the value of the whole supply may be the same. And it is for this reason that each factor will receive the value of its marginal product under pure competition.

Turning to monopolistic competition, let it first be recalled that the number of variables in the problem has increased. Output is now conditioned only in part by price. It is a function also of the "product" in its various phases, and of selling costs.[4] The relation of product variation to the productivity theory will not be taken up in this essay. It is assumed that variations in the proportions of the factors result in different amounts of the *same* product, not in different *kinds* of product. (We may, if we like, suppose that the optimum "product" has been found and that the decisions

---

[4] These matters are discussed more fully in *The Theory of Monopolistic Competition*, pp. 71 *ff*.

to be made have been correspondingly narrowed.)   As for selling costs, they will be put aside only for the time being.   The problems they raise are complex, and will be indicated briefly later on.

Let us look, then, for the moment, at the price-quantity relationships under monopolistic competition.   Because of the sloping demand curve for the product of an individual producer, it appears at once that the marginal revenue product of a factor to him is inevitably smaller than the value of its marginal product.   If DD' in Fig. 1 is the demand curve for the product of one seller under monopolistic competition, and an additional laborer increases the product from OA to OB, the value of his marginal product is $ABQH$, and his marginal revenue product is $ABQH\text{-}NHPM$.   Since, in adding more labor, the entrepreneur is guided by the latter, rather than by the former, it follows that he will never find it profitable and he will often find it impossible to pay to *any* of the factors the value of their marginal products.   It will be impossible if competition has pushed his demand curve to the left until all surplus profit is eliminated, as in Fig. 1.   If the demand curve lies further to the right, the surplus profit obtained may or may not be great enough to permit each factor to be paid its marginal product, but if we assume that entrepreneurs seek to maximize their profits, none of it will be put to this use anyway, and the lot of the other factors is in nowise changed.   There is no escaping the conclusion that even a slight element of monopoly necessarily reduces the remuneration of all factors employed in a given firm below the value of their marginal products.[5]

It should be emphasized that the deviations of the distributive shares from their marginal products are always in one direction—

---

[5] It should be remarked parenthetically that the cost curve which is relevant to variations in one factor while the others are held constant is not the curve (described in *The Theory of Monopolistic Competition* on p. 21, n. 1, and in Appendix B) where resources are most effectively organized with reference to each volume of output.   Assuming them most effectively organized with reference to the output OB, the point Q would lie on this latter curve.   Since a variation in any one factor from this point without changing the others would, in general, involve conditions of production somewhat less effective than the optimum ones for the resulting outputs, the curve here relevant would lie above the curve defined by

the share is always smaller. This fortifies conclusions stressed else-where in the general theory of monopolistic competition, that pure competition is an extreme, a limit, rather than a norm. Actual prices, distributive shares, and conditions of production generally do not tend toward or oscillate about what they would be under pure competition. Rather, they tend toward norms in the definition of which the monopoly elements must be given full recognition. Except where the conditions are actually those of pure competition, competitive theory is a distortion of reality rather than an approxi-mation to it.

Let it be noted that *all* factors (not merely any one, say, labor) receive less than their marginal products; yet it is evident from the figure that this is consistent with a total paid to them which is exactly equal to the total product valued at its selling price. Only minimum profits are included in the cost curve: there is no excess which might be attributed to "exploitation."[6] This requires look-ing into. Apparently each factor produces more than it gets, yet there is nothing left over after all have been paid.

The answer lies in the fact that the sum of the incomes computed on the basis of marginal products is greater than the total product. The two will be equal only when the productivity function is a homogeneous function of the first degree, *i.e.*, when a small pro-portionate change in *all* the factors together will yield a propor-tionate change in product. This will be true only where both average costs and average revenue (price) remain constant with such a change. In other words, it will be true only under pure competition, where, for small deviations from equilibrium (the minimum point on the cost curve) both demand and cost curves are approximately horizontal. At this point the value of the mar-ginal product and the marginal revenue product are equal, and

---

the most efficient organization of factors for each output, at all points except Q, being tangent to it at that point. On the relation between these two sets of cost curves, *cf.* Viner, *Zeitschrift für Nationalökonomie*, Vol. III, p. 23, and Harrod, *Quarterly Journal of Economics*, Vol. XLVIII, p. 442.

[6] *Cf.* Mrs. Robinson, *The Economics of Imperfect Competition*, pp. 283 *ff.* for a different view.

total payments to the factors in terms of either will exactly equal the total income to be distributed.   As the demand curve is tipped more and more from the horizontal, under monopolistic competition, so that its point of tangency with the cost curve lies further and further to the left of this minimum point, the discrepancy between marginal products and marginal revenue products increases.   The sum of the latter continues to exhaust the total product; the sum of the former grows more and more in excess of it.   In the case of firms, the demand curves for whose products lie above the cost curves, there is, of course, a monopoly profit, and it is *possible* that this might be large enough to pay all the factors according to their marginal products.   However, it seems obvious that in such cases it is consumers, not factors, who are being exploited.   To pay labor, for instance, more in such firms, would be to establish uneven rates of pay for the same work in different enterprises.   This would not be returning to labor an exploitative income; rather it would be enlisting labor with the entrepreneur in the exploitation of the consumer wherever demand conditions made it possible.

Evidently the Pigovian definition of exploitation as a wage less than the marginal physical product of labor valued at its selling price[7] is appropriate only to conditions of pure competition, where, if labor receives less than the value of its marginal product, employers are, in fact, pocketing a part of the revenue which the marginal laborer brings in, and where the relation between marginal products and the total product is such that it is possible for labor and all factors to be paid the full value of their marginal products without exceeding the amount to be distributed.   It is not appropriate to monopolistic competition, where these conditions do not hold.   Here *all* factors are necessarily "exploited" in this sense in order that total payments may be brought within the bounds of the amount available to be paid; it would be impossible for employers to avoid the charge of "exploitation" without going into bankruptcy.   Yet Mrs. Robinson adopts such a competitive definition for this field, and even considers how the "exploitation" might be removed, discovering, naturally enough,

[7] *Economics of Welfare*, p. 549.

that, in general, it could not be, except by setting up conditions of "perfect" competition!

I pass now to another phase of the problem. It has been tacitly assumed up to this point that the product added by another laborer in any firm is a net addition to social product, not offset by a lessened product elsewhere in the system. This may well be true. But let us examine briefly at least one case where it is not. There are a number of reasons why prices may rest permanently and normally at some level higher than that to which unrestrained price competition would carry them.[8] This may be true wherever any particular seller is in direct competition with only a few others, a condition which obtains over a large section of industry. It is a possible result, also, wherever there are restraints upon price competition—actual or tacit agreements, business or professional "ethics" which condemn the "price cutter," the imposition of retail prices by the manufacturer or by tradition or custom, and, in general, the expenditure of competitive energy in other directions than that of price competition. If prices are held up by these factors, there can be a larger investment of resources in the general field without diminishing the profits earned by each firm. In so far as it is possible for new firms to set themselves up and secure a part of the business, they will do so, and a condition of general excess capacity may develop disguised by the fact that profits generally are not above the competitive level. Under these circumstances what is the value of the marginal product of any factor of production as more resources are employed? The productivity to society of any factor or of any group of factors composing an enterprise must be considered as the total product it creates less that which its presence prevents others from creating. Let us suppose that three gasoline filling stations are adequately supplying the demands for gasoline at a particular corner at going prices when a fourth company sets itself up in business. What product does the new station add? If the outcome is simply the sharing of the available business by the four at the old prices, as it is very apt to be, it is difficult to see where there has been any appreciable addition at all. The value of the services

[8] Cf. *Monopolistic Competition*, pp. 100–109.

provided by the newcomer less those no longer provided by the three others is approximately zero. To be sure, there may be some additional convenience to those for whom the new station is more advantageously located. The product then will not be zero, but it will be far less than that indicated by regarding the new firm alone. There is a further complication. Since each firm is suffering a reduced volume of sales, average unit costs are higher. It is quite possible that the profits of the first three firms were sufficient before the fourth entered so that all four can now cover their costs including minimum profits without a price adjustment. It is also possible that, faced with higher costs, they will all find it necessary to raise prices, and possible to do so with little fear of undercutting, since each has a strong interest in avoiding a price so low that he cannot cover costs when enjoying his normal share of the available business.[9] Under these circumstances the appearance of the fourth seller has actually diminished (through higher prices) the output of the group. The physical product of the resources he employs being negative, their value at current prices would likewise be negative. Wherever price competition fails to function effectively, complications such as these arise and must be taken into account in defining the net product added by a new firm or by the marginal unit of any factor which it employs. In such cases it appears that the value of the net social marginal product of a factor may even be negative, and, in any event, that it will be far less than its marginal product to an individual firm. Clearly, the value of its net social marginal product bears no relation whatever to its marginal revenue product to the firm, and hence to its income.

What is perhaps the most damaging impact of monopolistic competition upon the productivity theory is in relation to advertising and selling costs. Such costs, it is now generally admitted, are wholly incompatible with pure competition; the productivity theory, on the other hand, is compatible *only* with pure competition. It is not surprising, therefore, that the incomes of factors engaged in selling activity find no explanation whatever under the theory.

Although selling costs, as will be remembered, are directed

---

[9] *Cf. ibid.*, p. 106.

toward altering demands rather than toward producing goods to satisfy them, they may indirectly affect productivity. As the first result of such outlays, whether by a single firm, a group of firms in an "industry," or all firms, a new system of demand curves comes into being. To be sure, producers, pulling in opposite directions, will, to some extent, neutralize each other's efforts, leaving the demands for their products unaffected, and merely raising their costs by the amount of the advertising outlay.[10] In general, however, some spend large amounts, others less, others nothing at all; the results will vary in effectiveness and are bound to be uneven. Thus, although, on the one hand, selling outlays, by definition, contribute nothing toward the satisfaction of the new set of demands which they have created, on the other hand, they may be the indirect cause of a redistribution of productive resources with a consequent increase or decrease in aggregate product.

In attributing such an indirect productivity to selling costs it is evidently necessary, first of all, to deduct the cost of *producing* the goods in question. This being done, the marginal product of additional outlays for factors engaged in selling would be measured by the value of the added product which they had called forth, less the value of the goods which were no longer produced because demand had been shifted away from them.[11] Assuming constant total money incomes, it begins to look as though the positive and negative elements would cancel out exactly, leaving a net marginal product of zero.

There are other complications, however. For example, advertising may, and certainly does, in general, alter the elasticities of the demand curves. In so far as preferences for particular products are created or strengthened, demands are made less elastic, firms are multiplied, and conditions of production become, in general,

---

[10] These higher costs, of course, mean higher prices, different total amounts spent for the general class of goods in question, and thus, indirectly, different demand curves for other goods.

[11] Among these goods no longer produced, there ought to be included leisure if the advertising has induced people to sacrifice leisure in order to produce more goods.

less efficient.   In so far as information about products, prices, and market conditions is spread more effectively, demands may become more elastic, the number of firms may diminish, and output per firm increase with attendant economies.[12]   In defining the marginal productivity of factors applied to selling, it would be necessary to take all such information into account, adding up all the elements in order to arrive at the net product, either positive or negative, valued at market prices (less the cost of production, as distinguished from the cost of selling), for which the selling outlay was responsible. It thus appears that, to *conceive of* a marginal product for factors engaged in selling in terms strictly parallel to the definition as derived from the field of production is perfectly possible.   The difficulties are all in the discovery and measurement of the elements involved.   What is to our purpose, however, is that, even assuming that it *could* be discovered, there would be no connection whatever between such a marginal product and the marginal product to a firm of a factor engaged in altering demands in its favor.   To hold that factors employed in selling activity are paid in accord with the value of their marginal products would be a manifest absurdity.

The leading proposition that a sloping demand curve for the individual firm reduces the remuneration of a factor below the value of its marginal product has now (1936) received some measure of general acceptance.   In view of the fact that it is so readily demonstrable and that it has not, to my knowledge, been contested by anyone, it seems fair to say that its acceptance is general among those who have turned their attention to the problems of monopolistic and imperfect competition in recent years.[13]   Indeed, since

---

[12] It is this latter influence which is most frequently brought forward by the advertising industry itself in its own defense.   Clearly, however, if the social justification of advertising were to be judged on this score, it would be necessary to compare the increment to product obtained indirectly through applying resources toward making demands more elastic with the increment to product obtained by the same resources if they were applied directly to production.

[13] In addition to Mrs. Robinson, who has done more than anyone else in the analysis of problems of distribution as affected by "imperfect" competition, there

Mrs. Robinson has *defined* marginal productivity[14] as what I have here called marginal revenue product, and has been followed by others, the danger now appears that it will be *too* readily accepted. By this I mean that it will be accepted by many without any appreciation of the metamorphosis which has taken place. It was generally held that factors were paid according to their "marginal productivity" under pure competition; it is now held that they are paid according to their "marginal productivity" under monopolistic competition; and so it would appear that the principle involved was at least substantially the same in the two cases—whereas it is evidently not the same at all. True, the rule for monopolistic competition applies also to pure competition, for it is universal.[15] It is universal because, as a moment's reflection reveals, it is little more than a restatement in terms of increments of the axiom from which economic analysis ordinarily proceeds, *viz.*, that producers seek to maximize their profits. But the further rule for competition—that factors are paid according to the value of their marginal products—applies only to competition. As has been shown above, there is no tendency whatever for factors to be paid in this way when monopoly elements are present. Yet, just as value theory has been cast in competitive terms, so with distribution—and the productivity theory of distribution has commonly been taken to mean that the incomes of factors were equal to the value of their marginal products.[16]

---

may be mentioned: N. Kaldor (*Economica*, Vol. I, new series [August, 1934], p. 337); R. F. Kahn (*Economic Journal*, Vol. XLV [March, 1935], p. 3); Fritz Machlup (in this volume, p. 158); and probably others.

[14] *Op. cit.*, p. 237.

[15] Monopsonistic situations excepted.

[16] Lack of space forbids the inclusion of numerous quotations in support of this interpretation of the "productivity" theory. Marshall, although he states the principle in its more general terms of a net addition to the value of the total product of the firm (*Principles*, pp. 406, 521) seems to do so because he holds that definite units of physical product cannot usually be separated (p. 407). On the issues here discussed, he clearly justifies the competitive formulation (Mathematical Appendix, n. XIV). See also Pigou (*Economics of Welfare*, p. 119) and Hicks (*Theory of Wages*, p. 8). Knight's interpretation is doubtful. Although

It is in order to make clear that when monopoly elements are recognized, such interpretations of marginal productivity in terms of the money equivalent of the physical product are no longer possible, that I have introduced in this connection the term "marginal revenue," which Mrs. Robinson has exploited so ingeniously elsewhere.   Certainly the possibility ought to be avoided of carelessly identifying dissimilar concepts by giving them the same name. If the terms "value of marginal product" (for the competitive principle) and "marginal value product" (for the more general principle embracing both pure and monopolistic competition) were strictly adhered to, this would go far toward the desired end.   But they will not be strictly adhered to.   Inevitably, the "value" drops out of one or the other in the hands of different writers[17] and the abbreviated terms "marginal product" and "marginal productivity" acquire a shifting and unstable meaning.   Even if the "value" were always included and put in the right place, the two phrases sound deceptively similar from the fact that they are made up of the identical words in different sequence.

By designating the addition to money income of the firm as a "marginal revenue product" the two concepts receive the necessary sharp contrast.   The term "marginal revenue" may be applied as appropriately to a unit of a factor of production as to a unit of product, and has a well-established meaning with reference to the latter which is readily transferred to the former.   "Revenue" has the further advantage over "value" in the present connection of being a concept closely associated with the individual firm; it therefore serves to emphasize what may easily be missed—that the

---

he defends as productive both monopolistic restriction of output (*Risk, Uncertainty and Profit*, p. 186) and selling costs (p. 339), the competitive formulation is also clearly stated (p. 107 n.).   Illustrations abound in the textbooks.   See, for instance, Garver and Hansen, *Principles*, p. 409.

[17] Thus we speak of the "marginal productivity" theory of distribution, Marshall uses the term "net product," Mrs. Robinson uses "marginal productivity" to mean marginal value product, etc.   Mr. Kahn (*loc. cit.*, p. 3) uses "productivity" in both senses.   His "marginal private productivity" is defined as a value product, whereas, in a footnote a few lines further on, he says that "in what follows . . . (social?) 'productivity' is the 'value of product.'"

principle involved stops short with the individual firm. There is asserted merely that the income of any factor tends to equal its marginal contribution to the revenue (may we say the "profits"?) of the firm employing it. Nothing at all about its contribution to any total outside the firm which is of social, as compared with individual, significance: to such aggregates, for instance, as the total product or value of the product available to the economic community. Only by postulating pure competition may the incomes of factors be related at all to such concepts as these. At any rate, so it now appears. Perhaps the next step in the analysis is the formulation of other than purely competitive criteria by which the results of monopolistic competition may be judged.

8

ON THE MEANING OF THE MARGINAL PRODUCT*

By Fritz Machlup †

The marginal productivity of a "factor of production" is usually
defined as the schedule of the increments in total "product" obtainable through application of additional units of the "factor." As
the quotation marks enclosing "factor" and "product" may indicate, there is no unanimity as to the appropriateness of these words
or as to their meaning and definition. Nothing will be said here
about the comparative advantage of terminologies; the word factor
of production, for example, will be used interchangeably with productive agent, productive service of resources, and the like. It is
with the meaning of the terms employed, especially with the units
in which factor and product are expressed or measured, that we
shall be concerned. Space will not be allocated to the various
problems in proportion to their significance; problems of secondary,
or even minor, importance may be given a greater (unearned) share
of space, partly in order to prove their unimportance, partly because
it is the "small things" that invite the interest of the "disinterested"
student.

I

PHYSICAL UNITS OF FACTORS. The units of services, the application of which leads to a change in "product," are mostly taken
as physical units. They have to be conceived as two-dimensional:
as the services of some physical or natural unit of resource through
some unit of time. The choice both of the unit of *resource* and of
the unit of *time* must be governed by considerations of divisibility

---

 * *Explorations in Economics*, 1936, pages 250–263. Reprinted by courtesy of
the McGraw-Hill Book Co. and the author.
  † University of Buffalo.

and technical or economic relevance, that is to say, it "is not an arbitrary matter of methodology, but a question of fact."[1] We must not take a minute of the labor of an eighth of a man as our unit of labor; nor ordinarily will we take "a year-laborer,"[2] although this may be the smallest unit in which some highly qualified labor services can be bought.   The divisibility with respect to time of highly qualified labor deviates peculiarly from that of the more common types of labor—inasmuch as certain qualified services may be bought by the minute at the one extreme, by five-year contracts only at the other.   Organization and other institutional factors (legal provisions, tradition, rules adopted in collective bargaining) may in some trades or industries make quite ordinary labor indivisible below a week.[3] But differences in the length of the labor-week make the hour a more convenient time dimension and the habit of the market has accepted the labor-hour as the customary physical unit.

The unit of land, of course, is any traditional measure of area—not quite so "natural" a one, thus, as the "human unit."   If some definite size is taken as "the smallest" unit, it is done so, not because of any limited divisibility of land, but because of the limited divisibility of its complementary factors.   The time extension, likewise, depends upon the technique of production—in farming it is a year.

To decide on the unit of capital is to open (or to prolong) a very lively discussion.   What resource, first, is spoken of as capital? Some authors choose to speak in terms of particular capital goods (steam engines, power looms, shovels), others in terms of money capital (dollars, francs), others in terms of "abstract disposal over resources," which last can hardly be considered a physical unit. However capital be defined, its time dimension is perfectly divisible, though rarely is it divided into smaller parts than a day.   The market had adopted the year as the basic time unit ("per annum") for expressing the price but the day as the smallest time unit for actual exchanges.   "Time proper" has been suggested as the only

---

[1] F. H. Knight, *Risk, Uncertainty and Profit*, p. 111.

[2] As does A. C. Pigou, *Economics of Welfare*, 4th ed., p. 772.

[3] J. R. Hicks, *The Theory of Wages*, p. 27.

dimension, and unit, of the factor capital; this has no meaning, it seems to me, unless what is meant is that "waiting time" or "investment period" is to be conceived of as *a third dimension* of any other (otherwise two-dimensional) factor.   This third dimension is, then, the time interval between the application of any productive service, say a labor-hour, and the enjoyment of its product.   It is, for certain purposes, more convenient to take waiting time and the value of productive services invested for this time as the two dimensions of capital.   Capital, in this case, is no longer amenable to expression in terms of physical units.   In the sphere of purely physical units, however, such waiting time can refer only to a concrete physical resource.[4]

"Marginal" productivity of factors has sense only if the units of factors are homogeneous in respect of "efficiency."[5]   This must be taken into account in a puristic definition of "factor" by including only productive services of perfect substitutability (interchangeability), while services which are not perfectly substitutable for one another are considered as different factors.   If this strict definition of factor is employed, the traditional classification, enumerating three or four factors of production, is definitely abandoned; there is a multitude of productive factors.

EFFICIENCY UNITS.   Many theoretical problems can be simplified if one may assume full homogeneity of factors, *e.g.*, equal efficiency of all laborers or uniform grade or quality of land.   (This should not be done for "capital in general" if that is expressed in "physical units.")   But often writers are tempted to proceed from this convenient assumption to such statements as that a labor-hour of a certain efficiency is equal to two labor-hours of half the efficiency or to half an hour of double efficiency.   Such conversion

---

[4] When K. Wicksell discusses "the marginal productivity of waiting" (*Lectures on Political Economy*, p. 177), he assumes, at first, a certain number of physically defined resources which receive their value in a process of capitalization at the rate given by the marginal productivity of waiting.

[5] Hicks (*op. cit.*, p. 28) says: "If the labourers in a given trade are not of equal efficiency, then, strictly speaking, they have no marginal product.   We cannot tell what would be the difference to the product if one man were removed from employment; for it all depends on which man is removed."

of units of different efficiencies into uniform efficiency units sometimes involves the danger of circularity in reasoning.

The efficiency of any physical or natural unit of a factor can
be measured only by its "effect" on the product; if natural units
are then corrected for their different effects on product and, thus,
converted into efficiency units, the further examination of the
relationship between those units and marginal product may be
badly distorted—especially if the different causes of efficiency
disparity are not clearly distinguished, and, still more, if the efficiency in producing value,[6] rather than physical efficiency, is taken
as a base.

Differences in physical efficiency of physical units of factors
may be due to various causes: (a) differences by constitution, i.e.,
natural heterogeneity as to quantity of performance in definite
activities; (b) differences in energy and effort expended on the
work; (c) differences through economies from the larger size of the
productive combination, due to specialization or organization of
lumpy elements (i.e., increasing returns from proportional additions
of all factors); (d) differences through varied proportions in the
factor's cooperation with other factors (i.e., increasing or decreasing
returns with changes in the proportion of factors); (e) differences
due to different techniques.   It seems that only the first two[7] of

---

[6] It is just in this way that Professor Pigou wishes to construct efficiency units.
He makes (op. cit., p. 775) the following suggestion.   "In order to render this procedure legitimate, all that we need do is to select in an arbitrary manner some
particular sort of labor as our fundamental unit, and to express quantities of other
sorts of labor in terms of this unit on the basis of their comparative values in the
market."   Thus, "all the various sorts of labor . . . can be expressed in a single
figure, as the equivalent of so much labor of a particular arbitrarily chosen grade."

[7] Joan Robinson distinguished "corrected natural units," which were the
"natural units of the factors corrected for their idiosyncrasies" (Economics of Imperfect Competition, p. 332), from "efficiency units," which were corrected for variations
in efficiency due to increasing returns.   When the units were corrected for these
differences (type c from above list) only constant physical returns would be got
(op. cit., p. 345).   In a later article on "Euler's Theorem and the Problem of
Distribution" (Economic Journal, Vol. XLIV, [1934], p. 402), Mrs. Robinson
admits "that the device suggested . . . for getting over the difficulty by constructing 'corrected natural units' is completely worthless."

these five causes have been in the mind of recent writers, when they tried, by eliminating them, to construct efficiency units.[8]

Even these two kinds of efficiency disparity could usefully be corrected for by construction of efficiency units only if the differences in efficiency of the natural units of the factors involved were the same in respect of all the various uses to which the units may be put.   (Then, and only then, could one expect wage differences to take exact account of efficiency disparities.)   But if the differences are different in respect of different occupations, then indeed the case is different.

On first thought, one might imagine that labor is grouped in several efficiency classes—each then constituting a group of homogeneous factors—and that degrees of substitutability are established between the various classes.   But this device breaks down when we realize that the members of one group, while uniform within their group and perfectly substitutable with respect to a certain occupation, are not equally suitable for other jobs.   Some members of the group may be almost perfectly substitutable for those of another group, others very little.   In view of the different efficiency in other kinds of work of laborers who are homogeneous only concerning one occupation, it is not possible to express the substitutability of the different groups (factors) for one another by a single definite figure. There would be, instead, a whole range or schedule of figures from almost infinite to almost zero substitutability, and these schedules would be different between the groups F_1 and F_2, F_1 and F_3, F_1 and F_4, . . . F_1 and F_n.   The substitutabilities of factor F_1 for factor F_2 could perhaps be represented as a positive function of the number

---

[8] Marx, of course, got his "homogeneous mass of human labor-power" by correcting all the "innumerable individual units" for their deviations from what he called the labor "socially necessary . . . under the normal conditions of production, and with average degree of skill and intensity prevalent at the time." Thus, after the invention of the power loom, one labor-hour of a hand-loom weaver was "only half an hour's social labor." See *Capital*, Vol. I (ed. Kerr, 1909), p. 46. The great difference between the (however questionable) efficiency units employed by modern writers and those employed by Marx lies in that the former do not try to deduce the value of the products from the quantity of labor after they had deduced the quantity of labor from the value of the products.

of members still working in the F_1 group; for the more units that are still employed as factor F_1, the greater will be the number of the more versatile units included; the greater the number of units from the group F_1 who have been called upon as substitutes for other factors, the smaller will be the "marginal substitutability" for factor F_2 of the rest of factor F_1.

The complications due to the fact that the versatility of a factor is not universal for all types of work but differentiated with respect to different types are bad enough. They are multiplied if one tries to take account of the further fact that the substitutability of services for one another is also an increasing function of time. (Skill is increased, abilities acquired, resistances overcome, etc.) This is true not only of substitutability between different grades of labor, but also between labor and "capital." The very definition of capital, indeed, depends on the length of time allowed for rearrangements to be carried through. If capital is referred to as *one* factor of production, it is because of its efficiency in allowing time-taking processes to be undertaken. This efficiency is different according to the length of time allowed for the forms to be changed.

Apart from these special properties of "the factor" capital, the complications are dire enough to make us well understand how much more convenient it is to assume homogeneity of factors, or to assume a moderate number of non-competing groups, or to reason, with Marshall, about factors of "normal" or "representative" efficiency.[9] Such assumptions are not only more convenient but "realistic" enough to permit of first, and higher, approximations to the solution of most problems. Mr. Hicks's conclusions in his *Theory of Wages* are not appreciably damaged by the fact that he assumed "average unskilled labor" to be of uniform efficiency in all industries.[10]

---

[9] Alfred Marshall, *Principles of Economics*, 8th ed., p. 516. Whether J. B. Clark's "social unit of labor" (*Distribution of Wealth*, p. 63) is an efficiency unit or a value unit, or some still more mythical unit, I have not been able to find out.

[10] *Op. cit.*, p. 33. In drawing marginal productivity curves for a particular firm one need not be disturbed by considerations of whether or not additional units of factors of equal efficiency will be obtainable; the lower quality of additional units

A most peculiar species of efficiency unit is Professor Pigou's "unit of uncertainty-bearing," which is defined as "the exposure of a £ to a given scheme of uncertainty, or . . . to a succession of like schemes of uncertainty during a year . . . by a man of representative temperament and with representative knowledge."[11] Having recognized that uncertainty bearing and waiting were "generally found together" but "analytically quite distinct from" each other, Professor Pigou tries to establish uncertainty bearing as "an independent and elementary factor of production standing on the same level as any of the better-known factors." For want of a natural unit of uncertainty bearing he constructs ingeniously an efficiency unit by reducing the uncertainties involved in different exposures "on the basis of comparative market values" to its equivalent in terms of an arbitrarily selected "fundamental unit" of uncertainty bearing.[12] That through modern developments, especially through the pooling of certain uncertainties, a number of undertakings have become less uncertain than in former times leads Professor Pigou to the statement that "the factor uncertainty-bearing has been made technically more efficient."[13]

As we have said above, efficiency units as natural units corrected for differences in physical performance in well-defined activities are *toto caelo* different from efficiency units with market values taken as the measure of efficiency. These latter are more correctly regarded, and frowned upon, as "value units" of factors.

UNITS OF FACTORS IN TERMS OF VALUE. By measuring units of factors in terms of their market value, marginal productivity analysis is, to my mind, reduced *ad absurdum*. One must bear in mind that marginal productivity analysis as a part of the theory of distribution is to serve as explanation of the market values of factors

---

may be taken care of by a decreased elasticity of the factor supply curve to the firm (Robinson, *Imperfect Competition*, p. 345); that is to say, the slope of the factor supply curve may express the decreasing efficiency of the units which have to be drawn from other groups or grades.

[11] Pigou, *op. cit.*, p. 772.

[12] *Ibid.*, p. 775.

[13] *Ibid.*, p. 778.

or services.   To define these services in terms of their market values is to give up the task of explaining them.   Indeed, to use Professor Knight's words, "we cannot discuss the valuation of things withuot knowing what it is that is being evaluated."[14]   After all, the marginal productivity curve is to be the substance behind, and under certain assumptions the same as, the demand curve for factors, *i.e.*, for definite (physically defined) services, not for units of value.[15]

Value units of factors are what Professor Pigou once called a "Pound Sterling worth of resources."   He used this concept not in the theory of distribution but in an analysis of the national dividend, and he has withdrawn it from the later editions of his *Economics of Welfare*.   One could never explain the exchange ratio between productive services of different kinds, if one measured their units in value terms.   That a hundred dollars worth of labor services equals a hundred dollars worth of uncertainty bearing, and equals a hundred dollars worth of land services would be all our wisdom.

When it has, thus, been made clear that the units of a factor must not be measured in value terms, it becomes twice as difficult to show that "units of capital" in terms of value are of a different stuff from those units which we have just solemnly condemned. Capital, when conceived as associated with waiting time, or investment period, or consumption distance of something, needs, of course, a fuller designation of this "something," be it a commodity or a service of a (human or man-made) resource.   Under quite particular assumptions it is possible to remain in the sphere of purely physical units, but we should have, then, as many different factors as we have different "somethings," and, to be sure, just as many different marginal productivity schedules.   But if we choose to conceive of capital[16] as the total stock of non-permanent resources

---

[14] Knight, *op. cit.*, p. 125.

[15] Mrs. Robinson's "marginal product per unit of outlay" was an attempt at getting a marginal productivity curve which constituted the entrepreneur's demand curve not only under most but under all assumptions.   In these terms, wage will equal "marginal product" even for employers who are monopsonistic buyers of labor.   See "Euler's Theorem," p. 412.

[16] I should like to express my indebtedness to Professor von Hayek, whose

at a given time which enables us to use a part of the available productive services for the production of future outputs, then the aggregate of such resources cannot be expressed but in value terms. They are "homogeneous" only in the one respect that they permit the undertaking of time-consuming methods of production. The value of the resources (bundles of services) is the result of a choice between a great number of alternative uses of their services, of which some are devoted to immediate consumptive satisfaction. The valuation of these services is, therefore, to some extent determined by opportunities other than their use in "capitalistic" (time-taking) production. More about these value units of capital will be said at later points of our analysis.

UNITS OF FACTORS IN TERMS OF MONEY. Measurement in units of value is a highly abstract conception as long as value is thought of "in real terms." To make it more realistic, one may think in terms of money. It is only in the case of one factor that units may properly be measured in terms of money; the case, namely, of capital, or, more appropriately termed, money capital. In a sense, we may regard units of money capital as natural units.[17] It is units of money that are the object of the producers' demand. That money is demanded by entrepreneurs because it gives command over resources does not impair the argument. This demand —for *money to invest*—is not to be confused with the concept of a demand for money—*money to hold*—employed in monetary theory. Observations about the marginal productivity schedule of money capital may be deferred to a later point when we discuss the units of return.

The problem of correcting money units of capital for changes in efficiency (namely in the efficiency to provide command over resources) forces itself on one's mind when one considers that the supply of money capital may originate from credit creation through an elastic banking system or through dishoarding—with ensuing changes of prices. All these price changes would, of course, find

unpublished manuscripts helped me greatly in arriving at my views on capital theory.

[17] *Cf.* Robinson, *Economics of Imperfect Competition*, p. 343.

their expression in changes of the marginal productivity curves. But some writers wish to eliminate certain price changes (of cost elements) by means of corrected units. That is to say, they wish to deflate the money-capital units with reference to particular price indices. Examples of "units of capital in terms of buying-power" so devised are Mr. Keynes's "wage-units" and "cost-units," which relate the money units respectively to the wage level and to the level of all prime-cost factors.[18]

II

PHYSICAL UNITS OF PRODUCT. That the schedule of marginal products in terms of physical units is fundamental for all other productivity schedules can be stated without fear of contradiction. It is also true that serious points of analysis arise in connection with physical productivity: problems such as increasing and diminishing returns as phases of the "law of proportions of the factors," the quite different increasing returns due to specialization of factors and similar "economies," questions concerning divisible, indivisible, limitational factors, and what not. Indeed, the widespread discussion of this range of problems makes it excusable, or even imperative, to leave them aside here in favor of other matters.

VALUE OF THE MARGINAL PHYSICAL PRODUCT. It is only in terms of value that different types and qualities of product become comparable and economic problems arise. But the particular concept of the "value of the marginal physical product" is not the all-important one; it is, in fact, relevant for but two special cases.

The one is the case of a producer who sells his goods on a market so perfectly competitive that he does not expect any price changes to result from an increase or decrease of his output. In such a producer's expectations, the value of an addition to his physical product would be the same as an addition to the total value of his output. This is the meaning of the proposition that, to the competitive seller, the value of the marginal physical product is equal to the marginal product of value.

---

[18] J. M. Keynes, *The General Theory of Employment, Interest and Money*, pp. 40 *et seq.*

The second case is that of an economist, like Professor Pigou, who reflects upon the national dividend and its measurement. For his purpose it is not relevant whether an addition to the physical product of a particular kind does or does not cause the value of all such goods to fall; he considers relevant nothing but the value of the physical marginal (social) net product.[19]

MARGINAL VALUE PRODUCT. "Marginal product" without other adjectival qualification should be understood to mean, not marginal physical product, but marginal value product.[20] Synonyms are marginal product in value, or marginal product of value. Value productivity, and nothing but value productivity, is what matters in distribution theory.

The marginal value product is the composite effect of a number of elements, or changes of elements; how many and which of those elements have to be taken into account in making up the marginal productivity schedule depends entirely on the problem in hand. In an analysis of the equilibrium of the single firm all those "dependent changes" have to be included in the economist's reasoning which are held to be included in the entrepreneur's reasoning. And what these changes are, will depend, of course, on the particular entrepreneur's estimate of his position in the markets in which he deals. The pure competitor will not anticipate any price changes to follow from his actions; a monopolistic competitor will anticipate certain reactions on the part of consumers, and perhaps also certain reactions on the part of his competitors, in framing his own policy of pricing and output; a producer who faces imperfect competition in the markets where he buys will anticipate changes of the factor prices to result from his actions. And this is but a small list of "dependent changes." On another plane, anticipations of more or

---

[19] Pigou, *op. cit.*, p. 135.

[20] It is perhaps worth emphasizing that the founders of modern theory regarded, either implicitly or explicitly, the marginal product as value product. Thus the "marginal contribution to value" in the theory of imputation of Menger and Wieser, Wicksteed's "marginal worth of services," Marshall's "net increase in the money value of total output." These writers, of course, did not see the differences in value product arising out of different degrees of competition.

less future, more or less lasting, price changes, anticipations of political forces, of monetary policy, and the like, may enter.   Turning from the single firm to problems of the industry or the economy as a whole, still more "dependent changes" must be taken into account.[21]

DISCOUNTED MARGINAL PRODUCT.   Just as products of different kinds or qualities can be compared only in terms of value, so products available at different moments of time can be compared only in terms of present or discounted value.   That the rate of discount may depend in turn on the marginal productivity of capital no more invalidates the argument than does the fact that the prices of other factors are data for the productivity schedule of the factor under view.[22]   Thus, it is perfectly correct to explain wages "by the discounted marginal product of labor,"[23] or, in a recent formulation, by the equalization of the "cost of any unit of current labor" to "the discounted value of every alternative output that could be got from it."[24]

UNCERTAIN MARGINAL PRODUCT.   It should be clear that all these marginal products are not realized but expected products, that is to say, they are the resultants of a number of estimates in somebody's mind.   Such estimates are made with more or less confidence in one's own foresight and more or less uncertainty about the probabilities of the anticipated outcomes.   The entrepreneur whose business process is "complicated, long-stretched-out, and uncertain as to its outcome . . . not only discounts, he speculates."[25]   And as has been shown convincingly by Knight, he will, in his demand prices for factors, take account of the uncer-

[21] The problem of selecting those "other things being changed," the reactions of which may be shown by the shape of the curve, and those "other things," the reactions of which may be shown by a shift of the curve, calls for separate treatment.

[22] The discussion of "marginal net productivity" in Section III will dwell upon this point.

[23] F. W. Taussig, *Principles of Economics*, Chap. LII.

[24] Hicks, "Wages and Interest: The Dynamic Problem," *Economic Journal*, Vol. XLV (1935), p. 461.

[25] Taussig, *op. cit.*, Vol. 2, p. 200.

tainty involved in his undertaking—so that, in case his estimates should all be proved right in the course of events, a profit would be left for him.

The marginal productivity schedule for any factor will therefore be in terms of discounted, and more or less "safely" estimated, value. (That is to say, with some "safety margin" because of the uncertainty involved.) Are now these marginal products conceived as value "in real terms" or in terms of money?

MARGINAL PRODUCT IN TERMS OF MONEY. There cannot be any doubt that the marginal productivity schedule within the single firm runs in terms of money and nothing but money. Whether the marginal productivity schedules for factors in the industry or in the economy as a whole are conceived in real terms or in money terms depends on—the economist concerned. Such marginal productivity schedules are nothing but a convenient method of depicting anticipated reactions of the most complicated sort in the form of a simple functional relation. It is a matter of technique, habit, and predilection (of the economist, of course) whether he wishes to lead his train of reasoning in the one way or the other. Logically the two are equally legitimate. Marginal productivity analysis in terms of money has the advantage of appearing more realistic, and of copying more nearly the way of thinking of economic individuals; but it has the disadvantage of requiring allowance for changes in the supply of money and for changes in "price levels." Marginal productivity analysis in real terms has the advantage of yielding more direct results about the factors' shares in the national dividend;[26] the necessary allowance for changes in relative prices is in this case not much less than that in the case of the schedule in money terms; one distinct disadvantage of the schedule in real terms is that it calls for a supply schedule in real terms, which for

---

[26] I suggest that Mr. Hicks's distinction between "labor-saving" and "very labor-saving" inventions (*Theory of Wages*, p. 123) may be represented as follows. Labor-saving inventions may raise the marginal productivity of labor (though relatively less than the marginal productivity of the other factors) in real terms, but must lower it in terms of money. "Very labor-saving inventions" lower it in both real and money terms.

short periods is meaningless. This point has been stressed by
Mr. Keynes on the ground that, owing to the prevalent significance
of money wages in wage bargaining, the labor supply may be
determinate in money terms but not in real terms.[27]

MARGINAL PRODUCT OF CAPITAL IN TERMS OF RATIOS. From
our discussion of the units of the factor "capital," one would rightly
expect that special allowances would have to be made also in the
measurement of its units of product. For certain of its meanings,
we allowed capital to be measured in value terms or money terms
rather than in terms of physical units. If the product, as well as the
factor, is measured in value or money, it will be most convenient to
express the one as a ratio of the other. The most concise definition
of the productivity of capital is Professor Fisher's "rate of return
over cost";[28] cost, in turn, is the value of all invested services with
respect to their alternative uses. In a sense, the ratio or rate in
which the marginal product of capital is expressed is determined by
the "time substitutabilities" between the alternative consumptive
services that can be obtained at different future points of time from
present productive services.[29]

III

The strict definition of the marginal productivity of a factor, as
the schedule of increments in product due to additional units of the

---

[27] Keynes, *op. cit.*, p. 8. Mr. Keynes overemphasizes this point. If money
wages are fixed, the lower and left part of the labor supply curve becomes irrelevant. Changes in employment take place in a range of the graph above and to
the left of the labor supply curve.

[28] Irving Fisher, *The Theory of Interest*, p. 155. Mr. Keynes (*op. cit.*, p. 135)
presents the following definition of the "marginal efficiency of capital in general."
It is defined as equal to the greatest of those rates of discount "which would make
the present value of the series of annuities given by the returns expected from the
capital-asset during its life just equal to its supply price." As I understand it, this
definition is not meant to exclude small investments in working capital, like the
investment in a few labor-hours; such investment is fully covered by the term
"capital-asset."

[29] *Cf.* Hicks's article on "Wages and Interest," in the *Economic Journal*, Vol.
XLV (1935), and my article on "Professor Knight and the Period of Production"
in the *Journal of Political Economy*, Vol. XLIII (1935).

factor *used with a given (unchanged) amount of other factors*, raises problems which we have so far neglected.   To apply the principle of "unchanged amounts of other factors" to the economy as a whole is one thing; to apply it to each single establishment is another. The application to the economy as a whole allows reapportionment of all factors with respect to their combinations in different groups or establishments.   The application to a single establishment breaks down in those cases where the proportion in which the different factors cooperate cannot be varied with continuous and small effects on the amount of product.   Imagine the proportion between all or some of the factors within a group to be rigidly fixed, owing to technical conditions (like the proportion of elements in chemical compounds); then the increase in the amount of one of these factors without accompanying increase in its complementary factors would yield a zero addition to the product, while the decrease in the amount of the same factor would cause a considerable loss of product.   For these reasons, a number of authors (foremost, Wieser and Pareto) raised strong objections against the application of the marginal productivity principle to single groups or single firms, and derived the value of the factors from their alternative uses through transfer of factors between different groups within the economy. Even with rigidly fixed proportions of factors *within* all given groups, an increase (or decrease) in the supply of a certain factor in the economy as a whole can be taken care of through changes in the proportion *of* the different groups, that is to say, through an increase (or decrease) in the number of those groups which employ more of this factor and a decrease (or increase) in the number of those groups which employ less of this factor.

Principle of net productivity is the name by which Mr. Hicks denoted this chain of reasoning.[30]   Its counterpart is the *principle of variation*, which is to give us marginal products through assuming

---

[30] *Theory of Wages*, p. 14; "Marginal Productivity and the Principle of Variation," *Economica*, Vol. XII (1932).   Marshall's "marginal net product" supplied the term, though Marshall himself did not separate it from the marginal product where full variability of factors was given.   Remember the marginal shepherd who did not call for any new complementary factors to be added to the establishment.

variability of the proportion of factors within each combination. It is, as Hicks has shown, the principle appropriate to long-run considerations, while the net productivity principle is that appropriate to the short period, during which some proportions are likely to be rigid.

For the marginal productivity schedules (as substance behind the demand for factors) of single firms or industries, the marginal *net* product is the fundamental concept. "The net product," said Marshall, " . . . is the net increase in the money value of . . . total output after allowing for incidental expenses."[31] The incidental expenses, *i.e.*, the payments to other factors newly employed together with the factor under consideration, are anticipated on the basis of these other factors' prices, which are given for the single firm and determinate for the economy as a whole. It is capital that is nearly always in complementary demand with other factors. If it were possible to employ one more unit of labor in a given plant, with given machinery, given raw materials, and given intermediate products, it still would not be a "given amount of other factors," since the application of more capital is involved in the investment of more labor-hours over a certain period. The net productivity principle may be considered as another support—if it were needed —for the legitimacy of using given rates of interest for finding the marginal net product of labor (the discounted marginal product), and of using given prices of invested services for measuring the units of capital.

The principle of variation and the principle of net productivity yield the same results, if enough time is allowed for the former to come into full play. But also in the short run one may consider the strict marginality principle as fully satisfied[32] by the net productivity principle. For it secures, for the economy as a whole, through factor transfers between different establishments, the perfect variability of proportions which is postulated by the clause that

---

[31] *Op. cit.*, p. 521.

[32] This was recognized by Professor F. M. Taylor, *Principles of Economics*, Chap. IV. See on this point Knight, *op. cit.* pp. 102–114, and Hicks, "Marginal Productivity and the Principle of Variation," *Economica*, Vol. XII (1932).

"additional units of one factor are used with a given (unchanged) amount of other factors." The schedule of a factor's marginal productivity in the economy as a whole will, of course, be quite different from an aggregate of all marginal productivity curves in all single enterprises of the economy. The former will take account of the necessary changes of the latter due to the consecutive changes in prices of the complementary factors in the course of their reapportionment among competing uses.

9

THE CLASSIFICATION OF INVENTIONS*

By Joan Robinson †

In a discussion of the effect of changes in technique upon the position of long-period equilibrium, in my *Essays in the Theory of Employment*,[1] I made use of Mr. Hicks's classification of inventions, according to which an invention is said to be neutral when it raises the marginal productivities of labour and capital in the same proportion, and is said to be labour-saving or capital-saving according as it raises the marginal productivity of capital more or less than that of labour, the amounts of the factors being unchanged. I analysed the effect of an invention upon the relative shares of the factors in the total product, when the amount of capital is adjusted to the new technique (so that full equilibrium is attained, with zero investment), in terms of this classification of inventions and the elasticity of substitution, showing that, with a constant rate of interest, the relative shares are unchanged, in equilibrium, by an invention which is neutral in Mr. Hicks's sense provided that the elasticity of substitution is equal to unity, while if an invention is labour-saving or capital-saving in Mr. Hicks's sense, the relative shares are unchanged (in equilibrium, with a constant rate of interest) if the elasticity of substitution is correspondingly less or greater than unity.

Mr. Harrod[2] made some criticisms of my analysis which lead to the suggestion that it would be more convenient to use a classification in which an invention is said to be neutral when it leaves the relative shares of the factors unchanged, with a constant rate

* *Review of Economic Studies*, Volume V, 1937–1938, pages 139–142. Reprinted by courtesy of the publisher and author.

† Cambridge University.

[1] Pp. 132–6.

[2] *Economic Journal*, June, 1937 p. 329.

of interest, after the stock of capital has been adjusted to the new situation.[3]   A method by which such a classification can be made is put forward in what follows.   The argument is confined to the primitive stage at which it is assumed that there are only two factors of production, labour and capital, and that conditions of constant physical returns prevail.   Draw AP_1 and AP_2, the average productivity curves of capital with a given amount of labour,

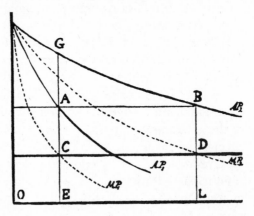

before and after the invention, and the corresponding marginal productivity curves, MP_1 and MP_2.   The amount of capital employed with the constant amount of labour is measured on the x axis, and product per unit of capital on the y axis.   In full equilibrium before the invention, the marginal product of capital,

---

[3] Mr. Harrod's criticisms were mainly concerned with the question of measuring the stock of capital.   For our present purpose capital must be conceived in physical terms, that is, as a stock of capital goods, and it is most conveniently measured in terms of cost units.   Two stocks of capital goods are said to be equal if they would cost the same sum to produce at a given date, in a given state of knowledge.   An invention may introduce the knowledge of new types of capital goods, but it does not destroy the knowledge of the types of capital goods appropriate to the old technique; the date for measuring capital must therefore be chosen after the invention has taken place, and the cost of each stock of capital goods must be measured on the basis of whatever may be the most efficient method of producing it.   By this means the major difficulties presented by the conception of a given stock of capital are evaded, though some ambiguous cases would still remain.

CE, is equal to the rate of interest, the amount of capital employed with the given amount of labour being OE.   The average product of capital is AE.   Total product is equal to OE × AE, the income of capital to OE × CE, and the income of labour to OE × AC.

Now suppose that, when full equilibrium is restored after the invention, the amount of capital employed with the given amount of labour is OL and its marginal product DL, which is equal to CE, both being equal to the constant rate of interest.   The average product of capital is now BL.

In the first position the ratio of the shares of labour and capital in the total product is AC: CE, and in the second position BD: DL. CE is equal to DL.   Therefore the relative share of capital is increased or reduced by the invention according as BD is less or greater than AC.   The relative share of capital is unchanged when, as in the diagram, BD is equal to AC.

Now, the elasticity of the curve AP_1 at A is equal to $\dfrac{AE^4}{AC}$ and the elasticity of the curve AP_2 at B is equal to $\dfrac{BL}{BD}$.   Thus the share of capital is increased or reduced according as elasticity at B is greater or less than elasticity at A.   In the diagram the two elasticities are equal and the share of capital is unchanged.

It thus appears that an invention which is neutral in the sense required by Mr. Harrod, that is, an invention which leaves the ratio of capital to product unchanged if the rate of interest is constant, raises the average productivity curve of capital iso-elastically.[5] A capital-saving invention, which reduces the ratio of capital to product, lowers the elasticity of the average productivity curve (at a given value of y); while a labour-saving, or more properly *capital-using*, invention, which increases the ratio of capital to product, raises the elasticity of the average productivity curve.

This classification of inventions lends itself more easily than that of Mr. Hicks's to realistic interpretation.   An iso-elastic rise in the average productivity curve of capital means that there is a certain

---

[4] See my *Economics of Imperfect Competition*, p. 36.
[5] Ibid., p. 42.

proportion, say k, such that if the amount of capital per unit of labour is increased by k, output also increases by k. Thus an invention which raises the average productivity curve iso-elastically, that is, a neutral invention in Mr. Harrod's sense, has the same effect as an increase in the supply of labour, in the ratio k, with unchanged technique. A neutral invention is thus seen to be equivalent to an all-round increase in the efficiency of labour. A capital-saving invention is one which improves efficiency in the higher stages of production relatively to efficiency at lower stages, and a capital-using invention is one which brings about a relative increase in efficiency in the lower stages. This corresponds to our general notions about the nature of inventions, wireless, for instance, being a capital-saving invention in this sense, and railways a capital-using one.

There is no inconsistency between this and my former method of analysis. The two concepts which I formerly used—the elasticity of substitution and the change, due to an invention, in the ratio of the marginal productivities of given amounts of the factors— merely represent two aspects of the productivity curves, and these aspects are equally well represented by the single concept of the change in the elasticity of the productivity curve brought about by an invention. The manner in which the two methods of analysis dovetail together can easily be seen.

Consider, for instance, the case in which an invention raises the average productivity curve of capital iso-elastically (so that the invention is neutral in Mr. Harrod's sense). In this case (with a constant rate of interest) the relative share of capital in the total product is unchanged by the invention; it follows from my former analysis that if, in this case, the elasticity of substitution with the new technique is equal to unity, then the invention must be neutral in Mr. Hicks's sense, while if the elasticity of substitution is less or greater than unity, the invention must be capital-saving or labour-saving, to a corresponding extent, in Mr Hicks's sense.

These relations can be demonstrated as follows: let GE be the average product of the original amount of capital, OE, with the new technique, and HE its marginal product. Then, with the new

technique and the old amounts of the factors, total product is
GE × OE, and the income of labour is GH × OE.

Now, if the elasticity of substitution is equal to unity over the
relevant range, it follows that the ratio of the income of labour to
the total product is independent of the amount of capital. There-
fore $\frac{GE}{GH}$ is equal to $\frac{BL}{BD}$. Therefore the elasticity of the curve AP_2
at G is equal to its elasticity at B. But the elasticity of the curve
AP_1 at A is also equal to the elasticity of AP_2 at B. Therefore the
elasticity of AP_2 at G is equal to the elasticity of AP_1 at A. Therefore $\frac{GE}{GH}$ is equal to $\frac{AE}{AC}$. It follows that the marginal product of
labour is raised by the invention (with a constant amount of capital)
in the same proportion as total output, and the invention is neutral
in Mr. Hicks's sense. Similarly, if the elasticity of substitution is
less than unity, then $\frac{GE}{GH}$ is correspondingly greater than $\frac{AE}{AC}$ (as in
the diagram) and the invention is labour-saving in Mr. Hicks's
sense, while if the elasticity of substitution is less than unity, the
invention is capital-saving, to a corresponding extent, in Mr.
Hicks's sense.[6]

---

[6] This argument reveals an interesting property of the productivity function.
The magnitude of the elasticity of substitution varies with the rate of change of the
elasticity of the average productivity curve, being greater or less than unity according as the elasticity of the average productivity curve increases or decreases with
an increase in the proportion of capital to labour.

Let $y = f(x)$ be the average productivity curve of capital, the amount of
labour being constant.

The elasticity of the average productivity curve is $\frac{-f(x)}{xf'(x)}$. The rate of change
of this elasticity is $-\dfrac{x[f'(x)]^2 - f(x)[xf''(x) + f'(x)]}{[fx'(x)]^2}$. This is greater or less than
zero, i.e. the elasticity increases or decreases with an increase in the proportion of
capital, according as

$$xf''(x) + f'(x) \gtrless \frac{x[f'(x)]^2}{f(x)},$$

or according as $xf''(x) + 2f'(x) \gtrless \dfrac{f'(x)[f(x) + xf'(x)]}{f(x)}$ (1).

Now, the return per unit of capital is $f(x) + xf'(x)$, and the return per unit of

Thus there is no conflict between the system of analysis followed in my treatment of long-period equilibrium and the system suggested in this note, but the former is somewhat more cumbersome and less susceptible to realistic interpretation.

---

labour is $-\dfrac{x^2}{L}f'(x)$, where L is the constant amount of labour.

It follows that the elasticity of substitution is

$$-x\left[\frac{2f'(x)+xf''(x)}{f(x)+xf'(x)}-\frac{2xf'(x)+x^2f''(x)}{x^2f'(x)}\right]$$
$$=\frac{f(x)[xf''(x)+2f'(x)]}{f'(x)[f(x)+xf'(x)]}$$

The elasticity of substitution is accordingly greater or less than unity according a

$$xf''(x)+2f'(x)\gtrless\frac{f'(x)[f(x)+xf'(x)]}{f(x)}$$

i.e. by (1) above, according as the elasticity of the average productivity curve increases or decreases with an increase in the proportion of capital.

10

A NOTE ON INNOVATIONS*

By Oscar Lange†

The present article is concerned with the concept and some of the implications of innovations which play such a dominant role in Professor Schumpeter's theory of economic development. Our analysis of innovations will be based on the theory of the firm. We shall consider the firm as planning its activities over a certain period of time, with the purpose of maximizing the discounted present value of the profit it expects to make during this period. The period over which the firm plans its activities will be called its economic horizon.[1] The expected profit consists of the sum of the differences between expected receipts and expected expenses at all moments (or intervals) of time within the economic horizon. It also includes the difference between receipts and expenses at the current (i.e., present) moment of time.[2]

As a rule, future receipts and future expenses are expected with a minor or major degree of uncertainty, and this uncertainty is taken into account by the firm when planning its activities. The

* *Review of Economic Statistics*, Volume XXV, 1943, pages 19–25. Reprinted by courtesy of the publisher and author.

† University of Chicago.

[1] This term is due to Dr. J. Tinbergen. See his article, "The Notions of Horizon and Expectancy in Dynamic Economics," *Econometrica* I (1933), p. 247.

[2] Let $R(t)$ be the receipt and $E(t)$ the expense expected at the moment t. Then $S(t)$, the surplus expected at t, is $S(t) \equiv R(t) - E(t)$. Let, further, $i(t)$ be the continuous rate of interest expected at t, and denote by H the length of the economic horizon. The discounted present value of the profit expected during the period H is

$$P = \int_0^H s(t)e^{-\int_0^t i(t)\,dt}\,dt$$

where $t = o$ stands for the "present" moment of time.

uncertainty consists in the fact that the receipts and expenses realized at some future date may take different possible values, and which of the different values they will take cannot possibly be foreseen.   But not all these values appear to the firm as equally probable.   Thus the firm may be considered as being confronted with a (subjective) probability distribution of receipts and of expenses at each future date.   For our purpose, it is sufficient to assume that the firm is aware of only two characteristics of this distribution, namely, of the most probable value (mode) and of the range.[3]   The first indicates the most probable of the receipts or expenses expected; the other expresses the degree of uncertainty of the expectation.[4]   Firms prefer, as a rule, expectations which can be held with little uncertainty to expectations to which a larger degree of uncertainty is attached.[5]   Consequently, two equal, most probable values are not equivalent when the degree of uncertainty (as expressed by the range of possible outcomes) is different.   A firm is ready to "pay" for a reduction in the degree of uncertainty with a reduced most probable value of expected receipts or with an increased most probable value of expected expenses.   In other

---

[3] This assumption seems to us quite realistic.   It merely implies that in making any decision the firm has an idea of the most probable outcome of the decision and of the range within which the actual outcome may deviate from the most probable one.   For instance, it thinks that a certain action will cost, most probably, $1000, but in any case not less than $800 and not more than $1500.

[4] In most cases the firm will not consider the whole range but will disregard the outcomes at both tails of the distribution, the joint probability of which is too small to bother about.   Thus, if the most probable cost of a certain action is $1000, with a practical range of $800–$1500, the firm may be well aware of the fact that the cost may turn out to be below $800 or above $1500, but the joint probability of larger deviations is so small (e.g., less than one per cent) that the firm is ready to take the chances of disregarding them in its planning.   This "practical" range is similar to the concept of a "confidence interval" used in statistical estimation.

[5] Up to a certain point, firms may prefer the opposite because they like to gamble.   However, the great majority of business planning involves such a large degree of uncertainty that there is definitely a readiness to "pay" for its reduction. Cf. on this point A. C. Pigou, *The Economics of Welfare* (London, 1938, 4 ed.), p. 776.

words, an indifference map, as between most probable values and ranges of the probability distributions of receipts and of expenses expected at any future date, can be drawn for the firm. This is done in Chart 1 for receipts, and in Chart 2 for expenses.

The most probable receipt or expense is measured along the axis OY, and the range is measured along the axis OX. For receipts the indifference curves are rising, because greater uncer-

CHART 1

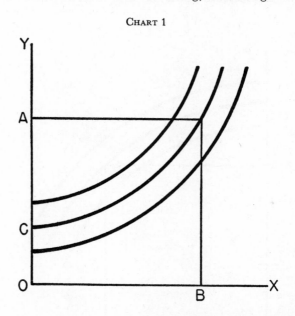

tainty must be compensated by a larger most probable receipt; for expenses, they are falling because greater uncertainty must be compensated by a smaller most probable expense. The concavity or convexity of the curves expresses the increasing unwillingness to bear uncertainty. The indifference curves indicate the reduction in most probable receipts, or the increase in most probable expenses, with which the firm is ready to "pay" in order to get rid of all uncertainty; we shall call it the risk premium. Thus, if the firm expects a most probable receipt, or expense, OA, with a range, OB, of possible outcomes, it is ready to accept instead a receipt or expense, OC, expected with (subjective) certainty, i.e., with a range of possible outcome equal to zero. We shall call OC the *effective* receipt or expense and CA is the risk premium. The effective receipt or expense is thus the most probable value actually expected minus the risk premium (which is positive for receipts and negative for expenses). Taking into account the firm's readiness to "pay" for a reduction in the degree of uncertainty of its expectations, we shall assume that the firm attempts to maximize the

CHART 2

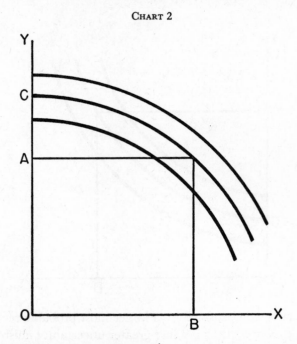

discounted value of its *effective* profit, i.e., the expected profit calculated after risk premiums are deducted from all expected receipts and expenses.

The uncertainty involved in the expectation of future receipts and expenses is due to two causes. One is the uncertainty of the expectation of future prices (or, under imperfect competition, of future demand and supply schedules). We shall call it "uncertainty of the market." The other cause is the uncertainty concerning the quantitative relations between current and future inputs

and future outputs.   We shall call it "technological uncertainty."[6]
Both uncertainty of the market and technological uncertainty are
the greater, the more distant in the future the action planned by the
firm (at least from a certain date on).   Thus the risk premium
increases as the planned receipts and expenses are more distant in
the future.   This imposes a limit upon the dates for which receipts
and expenses are planned.   The firm finds that beyond a certain
date effective receipts are less than effective expenses, and stops
planning receipts and expenses beyond that date.   In this way the
economic horizon of the firm is determined.[7]

*Innovations are such changes in production functions, i.e., in the schedules
indicating the relation between the input of factors of production and the
output of products, which make it possible for the firm to increase the discounted value of the maximum effective profit obtainable under given market
conditions.*[8]   By market conditions we mean the prices and, under

---

[6] Cf. G. Tintner, "The Pure Theory of Production Under Technological Risk
and Uncertainty," *Econometrica*, IX (1941), pp. 305–12.   Technological uncertainty arises either when the production function has to be considered directly
as a stochastic relationship between outputs and inputs (as, for instance, in agriculture), or when, though the production function is not stochastic, the quantitative input-output relationships are subject to changes because of unforeseen
changes in inputs or outputs or of the scale of the operation of the plant (lack of
adaptability and flexibility of the firm's production plan).   On the latter see G.
Stigler, "Production and Distribution in the Short Run," *Journal of Political
Economy*, XLVII (1939), pp. 312 seq., and A. G. Hart, "Imputation and the Demand
for Productive Resources in Disequilibrium," in *Explorations in Economics* (New
York, 1936), pp. 114 seq.   Cf. also A. J. Nichol, "Production and the Probabilities of Cost," *Quarterly Journal of Economics*, LVII (1942–43), pp. 69–89.

[7] Cf. J. R. Hicks, *Value and Capital* (Oxford, 1939), p. 225.   Provision for the
future, however, extends beyond the length of the economic horizon, but it does
not take the form of planning specific receipts and expenses.   Provision for the
future which extends beyond the economic horizon is made by planning to wind
up at the end of this period with a certain amount of assets.   Cf. Hicks, *op. cit.*,
pp. 193–94 and 229–30, and P. N. Rosenstein-Rodan, "The Role of Time in
Economic Theory," *Economica*, I (New Series, 1934), pp. 80–84.

[8] Professor Schumpeter says, "We will simply define an innovation as the
setting up of a new production function."   See his *Business Cycles, A Theoretical,
Historical, and Statistical Analysis of the Capitalist Process* (New York, 1939), Vol. 1,
p. 87.   This definition, however, is too wide.   A large (possibly even infinite)

imperfect competition, the demand and supply schedules, respectively, of the relevant products and factors. Discounted expected prices and schedules as well as current ones are included. An increase in the discounted effective maximum profit means an increase in the sum of the surpluses of effective receipts over effective expenses. This can be achieved either by an increase in the sum of the surpluses unadjusted for risk premiums, or by a decrease of the risk premiums, or by both. The increase in the (discounted) effective profit implied in an innovation may thus result also from a diminution of technological uncertainty. A reduction of uncertainty of the market, however, is excluded from our concept of innovation, because innovation is defined with regard to given market conditions. The economic impact of an innovation depends on the way in which it affects the marginal cost of the output as well as the marginal physical productivity of the input planned for any (current or future) moment of time. This provides a basis for the classification of innovations in terms of their effect upon the firm's supply of products and demand for factors of production.

The marginal cost of any given current output, as well as the expected marginal cost of any output planned for some future date, may be affected by an innovation in either direction, or not affected at all.[9]   If the marginal cost of the current output which maximizes the discounted value of the firm's profit before adoption of the innovation is reduced by the innovation, the current output of the firm increases.   In the opposite case it decreases.   Similarly, with

---

number of ways always exists in which production functions can be changed. But an innovation appears only when there is a possibility of such a change, which increases the (discounted) maximum effective profit the firm is able to make. All other possible changes are disregarded by the firms.

[9] This holds true even in the case where the firm maximizes merely the current profit, as happens when the current profit and the profits expected at later time-intervals are independent of each other (for the profits in two or several sub-intervals of a period are indepedent of each other the total profit over the whole period is maximized by maximizing separately the profit in each sub-interval). The direction of the change of the current marginal cost depends then on how the innovation affects the total cost of the current output and the current "elasticity

regard to the output planned for any future date and the corresponding discounted marginal cost.   An innovation will be called
output-neutral, output-increasing, or output-decreasing, at the date
t according as it increases, leaves unchanged, or decreases the output
planned for that date.

An innovation increases a firm's current demand for a factor
of production, or the demand planned for a certain future date,
when the marginal physical productivity of the quantity of the
factor used on that date, or planned for that date, before the introduction of the innovation is raised.   It diminishes this demand
when the opposite is the case.   This holds under monopoly and

---

of productivity."   Let all factors currently employed be increased in the same
ratio λ, and let x be the current output.   The elasticity of productivity is $\dfrac{Ex}{E\lambda} =$
$\dfrac{dx}{d\lambda} \cdot \dfrac{\lambda}{x}$.   [See R. G. D. Allen, *Mathematical Analysis for Economists* (London, 1938),
p. 263; cf. also S. Carlson, *A Study in the Pure Theory of Production* (London, 1939),
p. 17, and E. Schneider, *Theorie der Produktion* (Vienna, 1934), p. 10.   The concept
was introduced by Dr. Schneider.]   According to a theorem established by Dr.
Schneider (*op. cit.*, pp. 42–43) we have, for any output, x, the relation $k(x) =$
$k'(x) \cdot x$. $\dfrac{Ex}{E\lambda}$, where $k(x)$ is the total cost and $k'(x)$ is the marginal cost of the output
x.   Thus an innovation reduces or increases the marginal cost of the output x
according as it increases or decreases the elasticity of productivity relative to the
change in total cost which it causes.   Clearly, the elasticity of productivity may
be affected by an innovation in either direction, or not at all.   The same holds
for the total cost, $k(x)$, except when x is the output which maximizes the firm's
profit after adoption of the innovation.   In the last mentioned case, $k(x)$ is always
reduced in consequence of an innovation.   This can be seen from the accompanying chart.   *TR* is the total revenue curve, and *TC* is the total cost curve before
introduction of the innovation.   *PQ* is the maximum profit obtainable, and *OA*
is the corresponding output.   After adoption of the innovation, the total cost
curve becomes *TC'*, with *P'Q'* and *OA'* the maximum profit and corresponding
output.   From the definition of an innovation, it follows that $P'Q' > PQ$.   But
$PQ > SQ'$ because *PQ* is the maximum profit before the introduction of the innovation.   Consequently, $P'Q' > SQ'$.   But for any output other than *OA'* (or, if the
cost curves are continuous, for any output not in the neighborhood of *OA'*), total
cost need not be less after adoption of the innovation than before the adoption.
The argument is independent of the shape of the *TR* curve and, therefore, holds
for imperfect competition as well as for perfect competition.   Thus, both the total

monopsony (including monopolistic and monopsonistic competition) just as well as under perfect competition. The marginal
revenues and the marginal expenditures[10] corresponding to the
output and input plan preceding the innovation are all given. A
change in the marginal physical productivity of the corresponding
(current or planned) quantity of a factor thus implies a proportional change of its marginal value productivity.[11] Before intro-

---

cost corresponding to OA and the elasticity of productivity at the output OA may
be affected by the innovation in either direction. In view of Dr. Schneider's
relation, the marginal cost of the output OA may thus be affected in either direction.   In the diagram, A' is at the right of A, and the innovation reduces the marginal cost of OA.   When the marginal cost of OA is increased or left unchanged,
A' is at the left of A or coinciding with A, respectively.

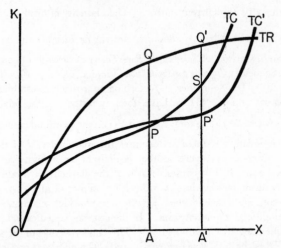

[10] By marginal expenditure for a factor of production we understand the
increment of the firm's total expenditure for the factor resulting from the purchase
of an additional unit of the factor. If p is the price of the factor and ϵ its elasticity
of supply to the firm, the marginal expenditure is $p\left(1 + \dfrac{1}{\epsilon}\right)$. The concept of
marginal expenditure is similar to the concept of marginal revenue which is
$P\left(1 - \dfrac{1}{\eta}\right)$, where P is the price of the product and η is its elasticity of demand.

[11] The marginal value productivity is the marginal physical productivity of
the factor multiplied by the marginal revenue of the product, i.e., by $P\left(1 - \dfrac{1}{\eta}\right)$

duction of the innovation, the marginal value productivity was equal to the marginal expenditure. Now it exceeds it or falls short of it, and the demand for the factor increases or decreases accordingly. An innovation will be called "using" or "saving" a given factor at the date t according as it increases or diminishes the demand planned for that date. Thus innovation will be labeled, e.g., labor-saving after a year, currently steel-using, etc.[12] An innovation which is neither factor-using nor factor-saving will be called factor-neutral.

When an innovation does not "save" any of the factors which the firm employed or planned to employ before its adoption, either it is output-increasing at some (at least) date within the firm's economic horizon, or, instead, it reduces the technological uncertainty attached to the production plan. Under given market conditions an increase, or lack of change, of the quantities of the different factors entering the firm's production plan implies an increase, or at best a lack of change, of the discounted value of the total effective cost planned by the firm.[13] An innovation, however, by definition increases the discounted value of the total effective profit which the firm expects to make during the period covered by its economic

---

[12] The classification of innovation as "using" or "saving" a factor given in the text is in terms of the absolute change in the factor's marginal physical productivity. Professor Pigou (*The Economics of Welfare*, 4th ed., London, 1938, p. 674), Dr. Hicks (*The Theory of Wages*, London, 1932, pp. 121–22), and Mrs. Robinson ("The Classification of Inventions," *Review of Economic Studies*, v, 1938, pp. 139–40) have given other classifications which, though differing among themselves, are all in terms of relative changes in the marginal physical productivity (i.e., in terms of changes of the marginal rate of substitution of factors). The difference between our classification and theirs is due to the fact that whereas we are interested in the effect of innovations upon the demand and the employment of a factor, Professor Pigou is interested in the effect upon the aggregate real income, and Dr. Hicks and Mrs. Robinson in the effect upon the relative shares of the factors under the assumption (common to all three of them) that full employment of all factors is retained or restored after the innovation. Mrs. Robinson's and Dr. Hicks' classifications are related and, with the aid of the concept of the elasticity of substitution, translatable one into the other.

[13] We assume that none of the supply schedules of the relevant factors are negatively sloped.

horizon. Therefore, the discounted value of the total effective revenue must increase by more than the discounted value of the total effective cost. The market conditions being given, any increase in the first requires either an increase in the output planned for (at least) some date,[14] or a reduction of the technological risk-premium. Conversely, an innovation which is not output-increasing at all cannot be all-around factor-using or even factor-neutral, unless it causes a decrease in technological uncertainty. It must "save" at least some factor at some date. Subject to these two restrictions, any combination between the output-increasing or output-decreasing effect and the factor-using or factor-saving nature of an innovation is possible. In particular, an innovation can be at the same time output-increasing at all dates and factor-saving with regard to all factors and dates. Our empirical knowledge seems to indicate that the major part of innovations "use" at least some factors (chiefly investment goods) currently and in the near future and are output-increasing at some more remote future. The economic effects of such innovations can be divided roughly in two periods: a factor-using period of "gestation" and an output-increasing period of "operation" of the innovation.[15]

In order to find the effect of an innovation upon the output of a commodity and the demand for various factors of production in the whole economy, we have to consider, in addition to the points just discussed, its effect upon the number of firms in an industry. When the industry producing the commodity under consideration operates under conditions of perfect competition and, in addition,

---

[14] The discounted marginal revenue corresponding to the output planned for each date is considered as not negative, while for some date at least it is assumed to be positive. Since at each date the planned discounted marginal revenue is equal to the planned discounted marginal cost, the first can be negative only when the latter is so.

[15] This has been pointed out by Professor Schumpeter, who explains on this basis the mechanism of the business cycle, the factor-using period being responsible for the prosperity and the output-increasing period for the recession. Cf. *op. cit.*, Vol. 1, pp. 93 seq.

is subject to free entry,[16] the increase in the discounted value of the effective profit attracts new firms into the industry. The influx of new firms continues until the aggregate output of the industry planned for some or all dates increases[17] sufficiently to reduce the discounted value of the effective profit of the firms to zero level.[18] Thus when free entry is present, any innovation must, with respect to the whole economy, be output-increasing at some date, even though it be exclusively output-decreasing from the point of view of the individual firms.[19] Free entry, by leading to an increase in the number of firms in consequence of an innovation, also exercises a factor-using influence. The net effect of an innovation upon the demand for factors of production by a competitive industry with free entry, however, may be in either direction. When competition is monopolistic or monopsonistic in the Chamberlin sense, the concept of free entry has no meaning,[20] and it is sufficient to analyze the effects of an innovation upon the decisions of the firm. A superficial analogy to free entry exists when the innovation leads to the establishment of new firms producing new commodities. This case, however, can be treated as the extreme case of output-increasing and factor-using innovations.

Some special consideration is due to the nature of innovations in firms which operate under conditions of *oligopoly* and *oligopsony*. Oligopoly or oligopsony occurs when the firm's responses to changes

---

[16] Free entry may be absent even though the competition is perfect in the sense of being atomistic (i.e., no firm being able to influence prices by individual variation of its outputs and inputs).

[17] The demand schedules of the product are all assumed to be negatively sloped.

[18] "Normal" profit is equal to the sum of all the risk premiums. Thus *effective* profit, which is profit after deduction of the risk premiums, is zero when profit unadjusted for uncertainty is "normal."

[19] In the special case where the firms maximize only current profit (see ft. 9, p. 21 above), any innovation increases the current output of the industry.

[20] In this case each firm must be considered as selling a separate product or using separate factors. The concept of an industry thus loses its meaning. Cf. Robert Triffin, *Monopolistic Competition and General Equilibrium Theory* (Cambridge, Mass., 1940), pp. 81–96.

in market conditions are based on conjectures as to how other firms will react to an action of the firm and how this, in turn, will affect the demand or supply schedules confronting the firm which contemplates the response.   As a rule, determinate conjectures are possible only if the firms agree openly or tacitly (often even only subconsciously) upon certain rules of group behavior.   The uncertainty concerning the reaction of other firms makes each firm afraid to change its price and thus to "start the ball rolling."   This leads to the establishment of a conventional price (or price structure) and of conventional patterns of behavior which become endowed with the halo of ethical norms.   Each member of the group is allowed to take actions which do not impinge upon the "rights" of other members, but is penalized for actions which constitute such an infringement.   Thus, when an oligopolistic firm raises the price of its product above the conventional level, the other firms in the group do not react; but when it lowers its price below the conventional level, the others follow suit to "keep their own" or to penalize the transgressor against the social consensus.   In consequence, the demand curve confronting each firm has a kink at the level of the conventionally established price; and the marginal revenue curve is discontinuous at the corresponding output.[21] Under oligopsony the price paid for a factor may be lowered below the conventional level without the other prices reacting, while an increase in this price above the conventional level "spoils the market" and makes the others follow suit.   Thus, at the level of the conventionally established price of the factor, the supply curve has a kink and the marginal expenditure curve is discontinuous at the corresponding input.

The demand under oligopoly and the supply conditions under oligopsony are illustrated in Chart 3 and Chart 4, respectively. In Chart 3, ON is the conventional price and OM is the corresponding output.   The demand curve has a kink at P, and the

---

[21] Cf. Paul M. Sweezy, "Demand Under Conditions of Oligopoly," *Journal of Political Economy*, XLVII (1939), pp. 568–73; and R. L. Hall and C. J. Hicks, "Price Theory and Business Behavior," *Oxford Economic Papers*, No. 2, 1939.   Unlike Dr. Sweezy's article, the kink is here assumed to be real, not merely imaginary.

CHART 3

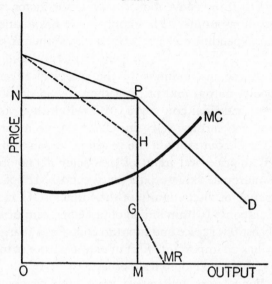

CHART 4

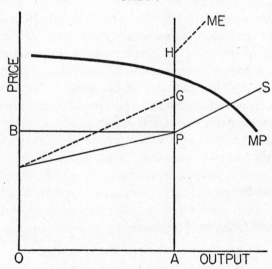

marginal revenue curve, MR, is discontinuous between G and H. In Chart 4, OB is the conventional price of the factor, and OA is the corresponding output. The supply curve has a kink at P and the marginal expenditure curve, ME, is discontinuous between G and H.

Because of the discontinuity of the marginal revenue curve under oligopoly, output and price of the product do not respond to shifts of the marginal cost curve, MC, within the range of discontinuity of the former (GH in Chart 3). Similarly, under oligopsony the discontinuity of the marginal expenditure curve is the reason that price and input of the factor do not respond to shifts of the marginal value productivity curve, MP, of the factor within the range of discontinuity of the former (GH in Chart 4). This lack of response (within limits) of price and output to changes in marginal cost or of price and input to changes in marginal value productivity has an important effect upon the nature of innovations in an oligopolistic or oligopsonistic group.

Under oligopoly an innovation cannot be output-increasing unless the diminution of marginal cost caused by it is sufficiently great to induce the firm to break the "discipline" of the group. The last mentioned case happens when the marginal cost curve shifts to such an extent as to make it move out of the range of discontinuity of the marginal revenue curve.[22]   Thus, only innovations which reduce marginal cost to a great extent can be output-increasing under conditions of oligopoly.   Therefore, under oligopoly, an innovation cannot be all-around factor-using, or even all-around factor neutral, unless it causes a sufficiently large reduction of marginal cost or, instead, a decrease in technological uncertainty; it must "save" at least some factor at some date in the firm's production plan.   Except with regard to *greatly* marginal cost-reducing innovations and to innovations which reduce technological uncertainty, oligopoly exerts a selective action against output-increasing and in favor of factor-saving innovations.

---

[22] Cf. Chart 3.   In order to cause an increase in output, marginal cost must fall below MG.

Oligopsony favors factor-neutral innovations, for the demand for a factor of production changes under oligopsony only when the marginal value productivity curve of the factor is shifted to such an extent as to get out of the range of discontinuity of the marginal expenditure curve.[23]   The demand for factors of production under oligopsony is, therefore, affected only by innovations which produce changes in their marginal physical productivity sufficiently *large* to induce the firm to break the "discipline" of the group.   But innovations which do not affect the quantity of factors entering in the firm's production plan must be output-increasing at some date or, instead, must reduce technological uncertainty.   This type of innovation seems to be favored by oligopsonistic conditions.

The type of competition and the entrepreneurial responses associated with innovations thus exercise an important selective influence upon them.   Under perfect competition with free entry of firms, all innovations are output-increasing at some date at least, with regard to the whole industry, but may be either output-increasing or output-decreasing with regard to single firms.[24] Oligopsony favors innovations which are output-increasing with regard to the firm, as well as the industry,[25] but which at the same time are factor-neutral.   Oligopoly favors output-neutral innova-

---

[23] Cf. Chart 4.   The range of discontinuity is here GH.

[24] When the innovation is output-decreasing with regard to the firm, it causes, in this case, a deconcentration of the industry.

[25] Unlike under monopolistic or monopsonistic competition, the concept of an industry can be applied under conditions of oligopoly or oligopsony.   An industry can be defined in the same way as under perfect competition, i.e., as all the firms which produce the same product (or products) or as all the firms which use the same factor.   A commodity, whether a factor or a product, is defined as all the "objects" (including services) the prices of which vary in the same proportion (equality of prices is a special case of it).   Cf. Triffin, *op. cit.*, p. 138.   Oligopolistic or oligopsonistic group behavior establishes a "price structure," i.e., certain ratios of the prices changed by the various sellers or paid by the various buyers, maintained by the "discipline" of the group.   Thus all the oligopolists can be considered as selling the same commodity and all the oligopsonists as buying the same commodity, i.e., as forming an industry.   As here defined, the extent of an industry coincides with the extent of the oligopolistic or oligopsonistic group. It should be noticed, however, that the industry, defined in terms of sales of

tions which, with regard to the firm as well as the industry, necessarily have factor-saving effects.

---

products is not identical with the industry defined in terms of factor-purchases. A firm may belong to one industry with respect to its product and to a different industry with respect to each of its factors. If it is a multi-product firm it may also belong to a different industry with respect to each of its products. Under perfect competition, however, all firms are alike and belong to the same industry, whether the latter is defined in terms of any of the products or of any of the factors.

11

THE DISTRIBUTION OF THE NATIONAL INCOME*[1]

By Michael Kalecki[†]

Introduction

In this essay we investigate both statistically and analytically the relative share of manual labour in the national income. From the social point of view it would be more interesting to consider the share of labour as a whole: but it is the relative share of *manual* labour which is suitable for theoretical analysis.

For the same reason the national income is here given a slightly unorthodox meaning. First, as we are interested in the *home produced* income alone, we exclude from national income that part which is derived from foreign investments. Further, we shall deal with *gross* income, by which is meant the income before deductions for maintenance and depreciation (gross income = net income + maintenance and depreciation).[2]

It is easy to see that the gross national home-produced income is equal to the value added by all industries of an economy. Usually the Government[3] is treated as an "industry" producing public services, but we shall not adopt this procedure here. Instead we shall mean by national income *the total value added by private enterprises* which we denote below by A.

Essays in the Theory of Economic Fluctuations, 1939, pages 13–41. Reprinted by courtesy of George Allen & Unwin, Ltd., and the author.

† International Labor Office. Formerly, Oxford University.

[1] This essay is an altered version of the article published in *Econometrica*, April 1938. The statistical data differ from those quoted in this article owing either to the slightly altered meaning of some concepts (e.g. of the national income) or to new sources becoming available.

[2] For the sake of brevity we shall speak throughout the essay of "depreciation" instead of "maintenance and depreciation."

[3] We mean here by the Government all public authorities.

THE STATISTICAL DATA

1. The figures for Great Britain are based on Professor Bowley's *Wages and Income in the United Kingdom since 1860*, and Mr. Colin Clark's *National Income and Outlay*.

Using Professor Bowley's data on the distribution of national income (pp. 92, 139) and deducting from the total income the income from overseas (mentioned on p. 96) we obtain the relative share of manual labour[4] in home-produced income: 41.4 per cent in 1880, and 39.4 in 1913.   These figures are for relative shares in *net* income; Professor Bowley does not give data on depreciation and gross income.   The rate of increase of gross income in the period, 1880–1913, is, however, unlikely to differ much from that of net income; for the proportion of depreciation to net income in 1913 was only about 8 per cent, and the changes in the volume of capital equipment and in the national income between 1880 and 1913 were such that this percentage could not have undergone a great proportionate change within this period.[5]   Thus the relative share of manual labour in gross income must have altered within the period in question similarly to that in net income.   Professor Bowley's figures of national income contain also the value of Governmental services, which should strictly be excluded for our present purpose, but this would for similar reasons only slightly alter the trend of the relative shares of manual labour from 1880 to 1913.[6]   Thus it can be concluded from the above that the change in the relative share of manual labour in the national income in our sense (value added by private enterprises) was small.

The figures for 1911 and 1924–35 are obtained from Mr. Colin Clark's data on "Distribution of Income between Factors of Pro-

---

[4] Shop assistants excluded.

[5] The real capital per head increased by about 25 per cent, the real income per head by about 40 per cent (*National Income and Outlay*, pp. 273 and 232), while the rate of depreciation was probably to some extent higher in 1913 than in 1880.

[6] The proportionate rise in expenditure on administration army, navy, etc., in Great Britain in the period considered was not much different from that in national income.   See, e.g., Bernard Mallet, *British Budgets, 1887–1913*, pp. 353 and 407,

duction, 1911 and 1924–35" (*National Income and Outlay*, p. 94), and on depreciation (pp. 86, 169), and expenditure on Governmental services (p. 141) in these years. The relative shares here calculated differ from those given by Mr. Clark (p. 94) in that they are taken in relation to *gross* home-produced income, from which expenditure on public services has been excluded.

TABLE 1. RELATIVE SHARE OF MANUAL LABOUR[7] IN THE NATIONAL INCOME
OF GREAT BRITAIN

1911	40.7	1924	43.0	1928	43.0	1932	43.0
		1925	40.8	1929	42.4	1933	42.7
		1926	42.0	1930	41.1	1934	42.0
		1927	43.0	1931	43.7	1935	41.8

We see that the relative share of manual labour in the national income in Great Britain showed a remarkable stability both in the long run and in the short period.

2. The figures for the U.S.A. are based on Dr. King's *The National Income and Its Purchasing Power, 1909–1928*, and Dr. Kuznets' *National Income and Capital Formation, 1919–1935*.

The relative share of wages[8] in the net national income[9] was, according to Dr. King, 37.9 per cent in 1909 and 40.2 in 1925. The change in the relative share of manual labour in the gross income less "Government produced" services was probably not very different.

For the period 1919–34 Dr. Kuznets' estimates are used. It is easy here to calculate "national income" in our sense. We take "income produced" by private industries including depreciation and maintenance (pp. 14, 80). A difficulty arises, however, in connection with wages being estimated separately only in "selected industries": agriculture, mining, manufacturing, construction, and

---

[7] Shop assistants excluded.

[8] Shop assistants included.

[9] *The National Income*, p. 74. We have excluded from income the services of durable consumption goods which King treats as a part of national income (he calls this part "imputed income").

railways; for other industries they are given jointly with salaries (pp. 62–67).

In 1925 the wage bill in the "selected industries" mentioned above was $17 milliards, while the total wage and salary bill (excluding Governmental employees) was about $44 milliards. But according to Dr. King's estimate the wage bill in trade, services, etc., amounted in 1925 to about $13 milliards, so that if we admit his figure we obtain: wages in "selected industries" 17, in other industries 13, and total salaries $14 milliards. Now as regards the amplitude of fluctuations, the wages in "other industries" keep the middle position between wages in "selected industries" and total salaries. Thus they are likely to fluctuate more or less proportionately to the total wage and salary bill. With this hypothesis it is possible to estimate roughly the wage bill in "other industries" throughout the period considered. Adding the results to the wage bill in "selected industries" as given by Dr. Kuznets, we obtain the hypothetical total wage bill in the period 1919–34 and find its relative share in the national income. The figures obtained are given in the following table.

TABLE 2.   RELATIVE SHARE OF MANUAL LABOUR[10] IN THE NATIONAL INCOME OF U.S..A

1919	34.9	1923	39.3	1927	37.0	1931	34.9
1920	37.4	1924	37.6	1928	35.8	1932	36.0
1921	35.0	1925	37.1	1929	36.1	1933	37.2
1922	37.0	1926	36.7	1930	35.0	1934	35.8

These figures represent of course only a rough estimate, but they are adequate in order to show the stability of the relative share of manual labour in the period considered.

We see that in the U.S.A., as in Great Britain, the relative share of wages in the national income shows but small variations both in the long run and in the short period. We shall now try to explain this "law," and to establish the conditions under which it is valid.

---

[10] Shop assistants included.

The Degree of Monopoly and the Distribution of the Product of Industry

1. Let us consider an enterprise with a given capital equipment which produces at a given moment an output x and sells it at a price p.[11]

If we denote the entrepreneurial income (inclusive of dividends) per unit of output by e_a, the average "overhead" costs (interest, depreciation, and salaries) by o_a and the average wage and raw material cost by w_a and r_a respectively, we have:

$$p = e_a + o_a + w_a + r_a$$

Further, the short-period marginal costs m (i.e. the cost of producing an additional unit of product with a given capital equipment) is made up of the sum of the short-period marginal cost of "overheads" o_m, wages w_m, and raw materials r_m.

$$m = o_m + w_m + r_m$$

We subtract the second equation from the first and obtain:

$$p - m = e_a + (o_a - o_m) + (w_a - w_m) + (r_a - r_m) \qquad (1)$$

Following Mr. Lerner,[12] we shall call the "degree of monopoly" of the enterprise, the ratio of the difference between price and marginal cost to price, or:

$$\mu = \frac{p - m}{p}$$

If marginal cost is equal to marginal revenue, μ is equal to the inverse of the elasticity of demand for the product of the enterprise. Substituting μ for $\dfrac{p - m}{p}$ in the equation (1), and multiplying both sides by the output x we get:

$$x p \mu = x e_a + x(o_a - o_m) + x(w_a - w_m) + x(r_a - r_m)$$

---

[11] We mean here by p the "net price," i.e. the revenue per unit of product after deduction of advertising costs, etc.

[12] "The Concept of Monopoly and the Measurement of Monopoly Power," *Review of Economic Studies*, June 1934.

Such an equation can be written for each enterprise of an economy. Adding the equations for all enterprises we obtain:

$$\Sigma xp\mu = \Sigma xe_a + \Sigma x(o_a - o_m) + \Sigma x(w_a - w_m) + \Sigma x(r_a - r_m) \quad (2)$$

The sum Σxe_a is the aggregate entrepreneurial income (inclusive of dividends). Further, the marginal "overhead" cost is in general small in comparison with the average cost; thus $\Sigma x(o_a - o_m)$ can be represented by $(1 - \beta)O$, where O is the aggregate overhead cost (interest, depreciation, and salaries), and β a small positive fraction. The average cost of raw materials can be supposed approximately constant and consequently the sum $\Sigma x(r_a - r_m)$ can be neglected. Most complicated are the problems connected with the member $\Sigma x(w_a - w_m)$; we must deal with them at some length.

2. The prevailing type of average wage-cost curve seems to have the following shape. It is more or less horizontal up to a point corresponding to the "practical capacity" of the plant, but slopes sharply upwards beyond it. This point is seldom reached—factories, e.g. only exceptionally work in more than two shifts. Thus in enterprises of this type $w_a - w_m$ is small in comparison with w_a.

Of course in some industries the situation is different. Those producing basic raw materials (agriculture and mining) are normally subject to diminishing returns, and $w_a - w_m$ is usually negative and not small as compared with w_a in the enterprises concerned. Other industries have, on the other hand, distinctly falling average wage-costs until "practical capacity" is reached (e.g. railways), and here $w_a - w_m$ is positive and not small in relation to w_a.

It is now easy to see that if wage-cost curves of the first type represent a large part of the aggregate wage bill W the sum $\Sigma x(w_a - w_m)$ is likely to be small in comparison with W. For then in most enterprises $\dfrac{w_a - w_m}{w_a}$ will be small while the rest will be divided between those in which $\dfrac{w_a - w_m}{w_a}$ is positive and those in which it is negative.

We therefore conclude that $\Sigma x(w_a - w_m)$ can be represented by γW where γ is likely to be a small (positive or negative) fraction. In other words: conditions of approximately constant returns prevail, in the short period, in the economy as a whole.

3. On the basis of the above considerations we can now write the equation (2) as follows:

$$\Sigma xp\mu = E + (1 - \beta)O + \gamma W$$

or:

$$\Sigma xp\mu = (E + O) - (\beta O - \gamma W)$$

where β and γ are small fractions.

It is obvious that βO is small in relation to $E + O$; and the same can be said of γW since, as the statistical data quoted above show, W is less than half the gross national income A and thus less than $A - W = E + O$. We can conclude that $\beta O - \gamma W$ is small in comparison with $E + O$, and therefore:

$$\Sigma xp\mu = E + O$$

can be regarded as a good approximation. Now let us divide both sides of this equation by the aggregate turnover $T = \Sigma xp$.

$$\frac{\Sigma xp\mu}{\Sigma xp} = \frac{E + O}{T}$$

The expression on the left-hand side of this equation is the weighted average of the degrees of monopoly μ, which we shall denote by $\bar{\mu}$. The sum $E + O$ is made up of profits, interest, depreciation, and salaries, and thus it is equal to gross capitalist income plus salaries.

We have thus the following proposition: *The relative share of gross capitalist income and salaries in the aggregate turnover is with great approximation equal to the average degree of monopoly:*

$$\bar{\mu} = \frac{E + O}{T} \tag{3}$$

Some remarks are still necessary on the notion of the turnover T. In our above argument by "enterprise" was really meant not the firm but a unit producing marketable goods, e.g. a spinning and weaving mill which belong to the same firm must be considered separate "enterprises." Indeed, such a weaving mill in its pricing would account the yarn from its "own" spinning mill at the market price, and consequently the formation of prices is here much as it would be if the two factories belonged to distinct firms.

Now it is important to stress that with this definition of an "enterprise" the turnover T is *not* dependent on the degree of integration of industry so long as markets for intermediate products are in existence. T is equal to the gross national income plus the aggregate cost of marketable raw materials.

How Is It Possible for the Degree of Monopoly to Determine the Distribution of the Product of Industry?

1. The results obtained in the last section may seem paradoxical. In the case of free competition the average degree of monopoly $\bar{\mu}$ is equal to zero; thus equation (3) seems to show that free competition makes it impossible not only to earn profits and interest, but even to cover depreciation and salaries—all gross income being absorbed by wages. This paradox is, however, only apparent. The formula (3) can be correct only when the assumptions on which it is based are fulfilled. According to these assumptions: (1) The short-period marginal-cost curve does not differ considerably in the majority of enterprises from the short-period average-cost curve of manual labour and raw materials up to a certain point corresponding to "practical capacity." (2) The output in these enterprises is usually below this point. These assumptions are quite realistic, but such a state of affairs is possible only with the existence of monopoly or imperfect competition. If free competition prevails, the second condition cannot be fulfilled; enterprises must close down or maintain such a degree of employment that the marginal cost is higher than the average cost of manual labour and raw materials.

In the real world an enterprise is seldom employed beyond the "practical capacity," a fact which is therefore a demonstration of general market imperfection and widespread monopolies or oligopolies. Our formula though quite realistic is not applicable in the case of free competition.

The second question which may be raised is of a more complex character. According to our formula, the distribution of the product of industry is at every moment determined by the degree of monopoly. Our formula therefore holds both for the short period and in the long run, even though it was deduced on the basis of, so to speak, pure short-period considerations. And contrary to the usual view neither inventions nor the elasticity of substitution between capital and labour have any influence on the distribution of income.

The source of the conflict between our theory and the orthodox view may be explained thus: (1) The long-period analysis of distribution is generally conducted on the basis of oversimplified representation of output as a function of only two variables— capital (taken *in abstracto*) and labour. In this way, the short-period cost curves are, as we shall see at once, excluded artificially from this analysis. (2) On the basis of our assumptions these curves have a special shape which makes for the elimination of factors other than the degree of monopoly from the mechanism of distribution. To clarify the problems concerned we shall now consider the dependence of the long-run distribution of the product of industry on the shape of the short-period cost curves.

2. A particular commodity can be produced with various types of equipment requiring more or less labour and raw materials per unit of product. (A change in the scale of plant is also considered a variation in the type of equipment.) The conditions of production are, however, determined not only by the choice of the type of equipment, but also by the intensity with which it is used. Not only may the kind of machinery be varied, but it is also possible, for example, to work with the same machinery in either one or two shifts.

Let us assume for a moment free competition and draw for each alternative type of equipment which can be applied in the production of the commodity considered a short-period marginal-cost curve and a short-period average-cost curve of manual labour and raw materials (Fig. 1). The shaded area then represents the value of net capitalist's income, depreciation, and salaries, while the unshaded area *LMNO* represents the cost of manual labour and raw materials.

To determine the position of long-period equilibrium we define first for each type of equipment the level of prices at which the shaded area covers salaries, depreciation, interest, and normal profit (i.e., the rate of profit at which the industry in question neither expands nor contracts). We shall call this price the normal

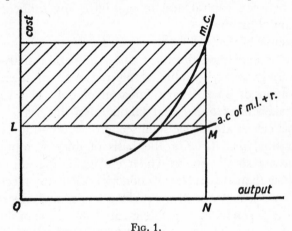

FIG. 1.

price attached to a given type of equipment, and the corresponding use of this equipment, its normal use.[13] We choose of all types of equipment that to which the lowest normal price is attached. It is easy to see that the normal use of this type of equipment represents the long-run equilibrium. It is clear now that the shape of the short-period marginal-cost curves corresponding to various types of equipment influences the formation of long-run equilibrium.

If some change in basic data takes place, e.g. the rate of interest alters or a new invention occurs, the long-run equilibrium is shifted; a new type of equipment is used in a "normal" way, and in general the relation of the shaded and unshaded areas will be different from

---

[13] It is easy to see that with free competition the normal use coincides with the so-called "optimum" use.

that in the initial position. This is quite in accordance with the prevailing long-run theory of distribution. We shall see, however, that such is not the case with the peculiar shape of marginal-cost curves assumed in the deduction of formula (3), and if we admit, instead of free competition, a certain given degree of monopoly.

We take for granted that the short-period marginal-cost curve does not differ appreciably from the average-cost curve of manual labour and raw materials, below the point A (Fig. 2). We represent them therefore by the same thick curve PMB.

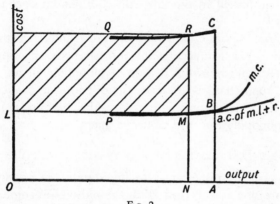

FIG. 2.

With a given degree of monopoly the relation of price to marginal cost is a constant $\frac{1}{1-\mu}$. Thus if output remains below OA the price corresponding to it is represented by the curve QRC, whose ordinates are proportionate to those of the curve PMB. The ratio of the shaded area, representing profits, interest, depreciation, and salaries, to the unshaded area, representing wages and the cost of raw materials, is equal to $\frac{1}{1-\mu}$. We define in exactly the same way as before the normal use for each type of equipment as that at which normal profit is earned. The long-run equilibrium is again represented by the normal use of such a type of equipment that, with a given degree of monopoly, it is impossible to earn profits higher than normal by employing a different type. If the basic data alter the new long-run equilibrium is represented by the normal use of a different type of equipment. The long-run equilibrium price of the product alters too, but not its relation to the average cost of manual labour and raw materials, because for all types of equipment the marginal-cost curve coincides with the average-cost curve of manual labour and raw materials, and the degree of monopoly is supposed to be given. In this way the distribution of the product among factors, as expressed by the relation of the shaded to the unshaded area, remains unaffected by changes of basic data so long as the degree of monopoly is unaltered and the use of equipment in the long-run equilibrium does not reach the point A.[14]

The change of basic data may of course influence the degree of monopoly. For instance, technical progress by affecting the size of enterprises influences the degree of monopoly in an industry. In this case such changes influence the distribution of income, but this is not in contradiction with our results, because it is via the degree of monopoly that the influence operates.

The Distribution of the National Income

1. Our aim in this essay is to investigate the changes of the relative share of the wage bill W in the national income A. The difference $A - W$ is of course equal to the sum of gross capitalist's income and salaries. Thus the equation (3) can be written as

$$\frac{A - W}{T} = \bar{\mu} \tag{3a}$$

In multiplying both sides by $\frac{T}{W}$ we obtain

$$\frac{A - W}{W} = \bar{\mu} \cdot \frac{T}{W}$$

---

[14] It may be asked how is it possible for surplus capacity to exist in the long-run equilibrium without inducing firms to curtail their plant. The answer is that large-scale economies prevent the firms from reducing their plant below a certain limit, a state of affairs described by those writers who have shown that imperfect competition must cause equipment in the long run to be used below the "optimum point." See, e.g., R. F. Harrod, "Doctrines of Imperfect Competition," *The Quarterly Journal of Economics*, May 1934.

From this it follows that the relative share of manual labour in the national income is:

$$\frac{W}{A} = \frac{1}{1 + \bar{\mu} \cdot \frac{T}{W}} \qquad (4)$$

This formula shows at once that the increase in the degree of monopoly reduces the relative share of manual labour. The expression increases not only because of the rise in $\bar{\mu}$, but also because $\frac{T}{W}$ is increased by a rise in the degree of monopoly since this raises prices in relation to wages.

2. Changes in $\frac{T}{W}$ can, of course, be caused by influences other than changes in the degree of monopoly. A change in the price of "basic raw materials," i.e. of the products of agriculture and mining, in relation to wage-costs in other industries, will clearly also have an important influence. It is easy to see that a rise in the prices of "basic raw materials" in relation to wage-cost must result in an increase of *all* prices in relation to wage-cost and consequently in an increase of $\frac{T}{W}$. On the other hand, $\frac{T}{W}$ increases in a much lesser proportion than do "basic raw materials" prices relative to wage-costs. For in each stage of production prices increase (with a given degree of monopoly) proportionately to the sum of raw material- *and wage-costs*.

It is obvious from the formula (4) that with a given degree of monopoly the relative share of manual labour falls when $\frac{T}{W}$ increases, consequently a rise in the prices of "basic raw materials" as compared with wage-costs by raising $\frac{T}{W}$ must lower the relative share of manual labour. (This may be seen also directly from formula (3a) according to which non-wage earners' income $A - W$ changes with a given degree of monopoly proportionately to the turnover T. Thus if the ratio of turnover to wage-bill $\frac{T}{W}$ increases owing to a rise in the prices of basic raw materials as compared with wage-costs, $\dfrac{A - W}{W}$ must also increase.)

It has been noticed already that a rise in the prices of "basic raw materials" relative to wage-costs causes an increase of $\dfrac{T}{W}$ in a *much lesser* proportion.   It is easy to see from formula (4) that the proportionate fall in the relative share of manual labour in the national income is even smaller.

3. We have seen that: (1) A rise of the degree of monopoly causes a decrease in the relative share of manual labour $\dfrac{W}{A}$.   (2) A rise of prices in "basic raw materials" in relation to wage-cost causes a fall in $\dfrac{W}{A}$ but in a much lesser proportion.   We thus have here some reasons for the tendency of the relative share of manual labour in the national income towards stability.   For the degree of monopoly does not undergo violent changes either in the long run or in the short period.   The fluctuations in the prices of "basic raw materials" in relation to wage-costs, though strong, are as stated above only slightly reflected by changes in manual labour's relative share.   But of course if the most unfavourable case of joint action of these factors occurs, the change in manual labour's relative share may be appreciable.   We shall see below that the remarkable stability of the relative share of manual labour which we notice in statistics is the result of these determinants working in opposite directions.   This phenomenon occurred only by chance during the long period considered, and may cease in the future; but in the business cycle there seems to be a steady tendency for the conflict of these two forces to keep the fluctuations in relative share of manual labour within narrow limits.

Changes in the Distribution of the National Income in the Long Run

1. The increasing concentration of industry tends undoubtedly to raise the degree of monopoly in the long run.   Many branches

of industry become "oligopolistic," and oligopolies are often transformed into cartels.

This tendency for the degree of monopoly to increase in the long run may, however, be offset by the diminishing imperfection of the market caused by the fall of transport costs in relation to prices, the standardization of goods, the organization of commodity exchanges, etc.   In the *Spaetkapitalismus*, however, the first tendency has the upper hand, and the degree of monopoly tends to increase.

As concerns the secular trend of the relation of the prices of "basic raw materials" to wage-cost, it is difficult to say anything definite *a priori*.

2. As we have seen in the first section the relative share of manual labour in the national income in Great Britain did not change appreciably between 1880 and 1913.   It can be shown that the relation of the prices of "basic raw materials" to wage-costs also did not alter in this period.   For this purpose we shall compare Sauerbeck's index of wholesale prices with Mr. Clark's index for the deflation of national income.[15]   It is clear that the influence of raw material prices as compared with that of wage-costs is much greater upon the first index than upon the second.   Now between 1880 and 1913 both of these indices changed in the same proportion (increased by 6 per cent), so that we can conclude that the prices of "basic raw materials" relative to wage-cost did not change. Obviously, then, the degree of monopoly could not have undergone a substantial change between 1880 and 1913 since with raw material prices unaltered as compared with wage-costs such a change would have been reflected in the relative share of manual labour in the national income.

Turning to the period 1913 to 1935, Sauerbeck's index fell during that time by 2 per cent while "income prices" rose by about 60 per cent,[16] which shows that there was a considerable fall in the prices of raw materials in relation to wage-costs.   Thus

---

[15] *National Income and Outlay*, p. 231.

[16] *National Income and Outlay*, pp. 235 and 204.

since the relative share of manual labour was stationary between 1913 and 1935, this means that the degree of monopoly must have substantially increased in this period. Had a fall in the prices of basic raw materials not occurred in the last twenty-five years the relative share of manual labour would have tended to fall appreciably and the recent economic and political development of Great Britain would have been quite different.

The course of events in the U.S.A between 1909 and 1925 was similar. The relative share of manual labour was approximately stable. The wholesale all-commodity index increased in this period by about 50 per cent; King's index of "income prices" by about 80 per cent.[17] Thus here again the degree of monopoly must have risen considerably, but its influence on the relative share of manual labour was counterbalanced by the fall of the prices of "basic raw materials" in relation to wage-cost. It is, of course, not at all certain that in the future the rise in the degree of monopoly will continue to be compensated by a fall in the prices of "basic raw materials." If it is not, the relative share of manual labour will tend to decline.

CHANGES IN THE DISTRIBUTION OF THE NATIONAL INCOME DURING THE BUSINESS CYCLE

1. We shall here examine first the cyclical changes in the prices of "basic raw materials" in relation to wage-cost.

The prices of the produce of agriculture and mining fluctuate much more violently than does the cost of labour in other industries. This is due to the fact that marginal-cost curves in agriculture and mining, as distinct from other sectors of the economy, slope steeply upwards. In addition, wages fluctuate much more in agriculture than in other industries during the business cycle. Consequently "basic raw material" prices rise relative to wage-cost in the boom and fall in the slump.

Much more complicated is the question of the change of degree of monopoly during the trade cycle. It has recently been argued

---

[17] *National Income and its Purchasing Power*, pp. 74 and 77.

by Mr. Harrod that the degree of monopoly increases in the boom and falls in the slump.   In the slump consumers "resent and resist the curtailment of their wonted pleasures. . . . Their efforts to find cheapness become strenuous and eager.   Nor are commercial firms exempt from this influence upon their purchase policy; they, too, have received a nasty jolt and must strain every nerve to reduce costs."[18]   Thus the imperfection of the market is reduced and the degree of monopoly diminished.

Mr. Harrod was rightly criticized in that there exist other factors which influence the degree of monopoly in the opposite direction.   For instance, in the slump, cartels are created to save profits,[19] and this, of course, increases the degree of monopoly, but when trade revives they are dissolved because of improving prospects of independent activity and the emergence of outsiders.

More important still is the fact that in spite of the fall of prices of raw materials and wages some prices of finished goods tend to be relatively "sticky" in the slump; this for various reasons: entrepreneurs avoid price cuts because it may induce their competitors to do likewise; cartels are not afraid that outsiders will appear, etc. It can be stated on the basis of data quoted above that the influence of these factors in raising the degree of monopoly during the slump is stronger than that of the diminishing imperfection of the market.

Indeed, if we look at our data on the relative share of manual labour in the national income we see that in general it does not change much during the business cycle.   But the prices of basic raw materials fall in the slump and rise in the boom as compared with wages, and this tends to raise the relative share of manual labour in the slump and reduce it in the boom.   If the relative share of manual labour remains more or less constant it can be concluded that the degree of monopoly tends to increase in the depression and decline in the boom.

We now see that, as has already been mentioned, the apparent stability of manual labour's relative share during the cycle is in

---

[18] *The Trade Cycle*, pp. 86–87.

[19] Joan Robinson, review of R. F. Harrod, *The Trade Cycle, Economic Journal*, December 1936.

reality the effect of the opposite changes in the degree of monopoly and in the relation of the prices of basic raw materials to wages.

2. The stability of the relative share of the wage bill W in the national income A in the short period has far-reaching consequences as regards the formation of the prices of finished goods. Let us divide in the equation:

$$\frac{W}{A} = \text{const.}$$

both the numerator and the denominator of the left-hand side by an index of the volume of output of finished goods. Since the money value of the latter is the national income A we obtain:

$$\frac{\text{index of average wage-costs}}{\text{index of the prices of finished home-produced goods}^{20}} = \text{const.} \quad (5)$$

Now, as stated above, conditions of approximately constant returns prevail in the short period in the economy as a whole. Thus the index of the average cost of manual labour does not depend appreciably on the level of output and employment and with a constant technique and intensity of work does not differ much from the index of wage rates. Consequently the equation (5) shows that with constant technique and intensity of work prices of finished home-produced commodities change approximately in the same proportion as wage rates. This result clearly is of great importance for the theory of real wages, and will be dealt with in more detail and supported statistically in the essay on "Money and Real Wages." We now propose to apply it to the problem of the prices of investment and consumption goods.

3. Let us consider in an economy the sections which produce consumption and investment goods respectively (including in each the corresponding raw material production). Since our argument throughout the essay is not confined to a closed system the formula (5) applies approximately to each of these two sections. Thus if the technique of production and the intensity of work are unaltered,

---

[20] All exported commodities must be here included in "finished" goods. Further "prices" are here, strictly speaking, differences between the actual prices of commodities and the cost of foreign raw materials used in their fabrication.

it may be concluded that the prices of consumption goods will move proportionately to wage rates in consumption goods industries. A similar development may be supposed to take place in the investment goods industries. It therefore follows that the ratio of the price indices of finished investment and consumption goods $\frac{p_i}{p_c}$ is in the short period approximately equal to the ratio of indices of the corresponding wage rates $\frac{r_i}{r_c}$:

$$\frac{p_i}{p_c} = \frac{r_i}{r_c}$$

And since wage rates move more or less proportionately in the two sections[21] marked cyclical fluctuations in $\frac{p_i}{p_c}$ are unlikely. This result is not impaired if we allow for changes in the technique of production. If the increase in productivity due to technical changes is different in consumption goods industries from that in investment goods industries this will, of course, influence the movement of $\frac{p_i}{p_c}$; but this influence can operate only in the long run, and is not of a *cyclical* nature. In order to investigate the movement of $\frac{p_i}{p_c}$ statistically we have constructed indices of the prices of finished consumption and investment goods in the U.S.A. for the period 1919–35. The index of consumption goods prices is a weighted average of the indices of the cost of living and the prices of motor cars,[22] that of investment goods—a weighted average of the building costs and the prices of movable equipment.[23]

---

[21] Wage rates in investment goods industries might be expected to fluctuate more, due to stronger changes in employment. In fact such is not the case, because trade unions are strongest in the heavy industry.

[22] The index of prices of motor cars is obtained from Dr. Kuznets' *National Income and Capital Formation, 1919–35*, by dividing the value of consumers' durable commodities in current prices by their value in 1929 prices (p. 40). The indices of cost of living and prices of motor cars are weighted in the proportion 88:12 according to the "composition of consumers' outlay" in 1929 (ibid., p. 59).

[23] The price index of movable equipment is obtained by dividing the value

The results are computed in the following table:

TABLE 3. PRICES OF CONSUMPTION AND INVESTMENT GOODS IN U.S.A.
1929 = 100

	p_c	p_i	$\dfrac{p_i}{p_c}$		p_c	p_i	$\dfrac{p_i}{p_c}$
1919	102	110	108	1928	100	97	97
1920	119	125	105	1929	100	100	100
1921	105	105	100	1930	96	97	101
1922	98	94	96	1931	87	94	108
1923	101	101	100	1932	78	82	105
1924	101	101	100	1933	76	78	103
1925	104	98	94	1934	80	85	106
1926	103	98	95	1935	83	86	104
1927	101	96	95				

We see that variations in $\dfrac{p_i}{p_c}$ are in general small. At any rate, contrary to prevailing views there was no tendency for $\dfrac{p_i}{p_c}$ to fall in the depression 1930–33.

It is usually supposed that the prices of investment goods fluctuate much more violently than those of consumption goods. This is due to the assumption that increasing marginal-cost curves prevail in the short period; for if such were the case the larger proportionate fluctuations in the output of investment goods as compared with those in the output of consumption goods would lead to correspondingly larger fluctuations in the prices of investment goods. The statistical evidence of approximately proportional changes in the prices of the two types of goods indicates that the assumption of rising marginal-cost curves in the short period is unrealistic, and indirectly supports our assumption about the shape of short-period marginal-cost curves.

---

of "producers' durable commodities" at current prices by their value at 1929 prices (ibid., p. 40).   The indices of building costs and of prices of movable equipment are weighted in proportion of 2:1 according to the amounts spent on these two types of investment (inclusive of maintenance) in 1929 (ibid., pp. 40 and 80).

The important consequence of the above is that since $\dfrac{p_i}{p_c}$ has no marked cyclical fluctuations, changes in the ratio of the prices of investment and consumption goods may be neglected in the theory of the trade cycle.   We make use of this conclusion in the last essay.

FINAL REMARKS

The results arrived at in this essay have a more general aspect. A world in which the degree of monopoly determines the distribution of the national income is a world far removed from the pattern of free competition. Monopoly appears to be deeply rooted in the nature of the capitalist system: free competition, as an assumption, may be useful in the first stage of certain investigations, but as a description of the normal state of capitalist economy it is merely a myth.

WAGES

12

WAGE-GRUMBLES*

By Dennis H. Robertson†

The purpose of this article is primarily to assemble and classify the various complaints that have been made in recent years about the "orthodox" theory of wages, and secondarily to offer some tentative comments on their validity. The phrase "orthodox theory of wages" is obviously a question-begging one; for my purposes it means the proposition that of all the single statements that can be made about wages, the statement that "wages tend to measure the marginal productivity of labour" is at once the most illuminating analytically and the most important practically for the consideration of wage-policy. The objections to this view appear to fall into five classes, of varying degrees of importance.

(1) Some writers appear to object to *any* attempt to express the forces governing wages in terms of an economic law, on the ground that such laws express the action of "natural" forces, whereas the influences determining wages are amenable to "human" action. Thus Messrs. Hamilton and May, in their book *The Control of Wages* (p. 111), write as follows: "There is no such thing as a 'normal wage' or a 'natural rate of wages.' . . . The natural rate of wages, like the 'normal' world to which it belongs, exists only in books and in the minds of men. If wages are not made by 'natural laws,' they are the products of human arrangements. . . . If they are not inevitable, they are subject to control." Thus also Mr. J. W. F. Rowe, in the theoretical chapters which follow the valuable inductive studies contained in his *Wages in Theory and Practice*, writes (p. 178): "Existing wage theory . . . insists that wages are deter-

---

* *Economic Fragments*, 1931, pages 42–57. Reprinted by courtesy of P. S. King & Son, Ltd., and the author.

† Cambridge University.

mined almost exclusively by purely economic causes, and demonstrates how any human efforts will ultimately be brought to nought, if the equilibrium of economic laws is either consciously or unconsciously disturbed." Such objections appear to be based on an entirely imaginary antithesis. Man is part of nature; economic science is a part of the study of human conduct, and its "laws" are generalised statements about the behaviour of human beings.[1]

(2) The second class of objection is based on the misapprehension that the orthodox theory asserts that wages are *determined by* marginal productivity. It does not—it asserts that they *measure* it, and that there is therefore a functional relation between the rate of wages paid and the number of persons employed. It has always been emphasised that to the individual employer it is the wage-rate that is normally the fixed thing, and the number employed that is the variable, just as to the purchaser of tea it is the price which is the given thing, and the number of pounds to be bought which lies within his discretion. It has perhaps been less emphasised, because until recently it has been less important, that the same may be true if we are considering the field of employment for labour as a whole. There is therefore nothing *necessarily* inconsistent between the orthodox theory and the observed fact that wages are nowadays often fixed by outside authority, or as the outcome of a process of collective bargaining in which the factors of bluff and strategic strength play a large part. The operation of

---

[1] Mr. Rowe's main thesis is that Trade Unions, by a "forward policy," can stimulate the efficiency of employers, and so raise the level of payable wages. He successfully convicts Prof. Pigou of error of omission in having confined the application of this principle to cases in which the workpeople are, at the outset, getting less than their marginal net product (see *Economics of Welfare*, 3rd edition, p. 592). As to the quantitative importance of the principle, there is room for great difference of opinion; but Mr. Rowe's statement (*op. cit*, p. 194) that "all existing wage theories appear to ignore a phenomenon which has completely changed the whole conditions of the labour market in the last forty years, namely, the rise to power of trade unionism," fairly takes one's breath away—if only in view of Marshall's careful and elaborate study of trade unions in *Economics of Industry*, which still reads astonishingly freshly.

the normal theory, connecting wages with numbers who can find employment, is one of the factors which the workpeople's organisation presumably takes into account in framing its policy, though it is quite possible that it does not always attach as much weight to it as it should. This point is made perfectly clear by Prof. Pigou in his discussion of the mechanics of collective bargaining. "In view of the fact that a rise in the rate will lessen the amount of employment available, there will be a certain maximum rate above which the workpeople's association will not wish to go" (*Economics of Welfare*, 3rd edition, p. 452). Once this is realised, a vast amount of criticism based on the notion that orthodox theory ignores the existence of collective bargaining, collapses to the ground.

The most amazing blunder of this class is that made by Mrs. E. M. Burns in an attack on orthodox theory entitled *Productivity and the Theory of Wages*, one of the *London Essays in Economics*. She transcribes (*op. cit.*, p. 188) from Marshall's *Principles* (8th edition, p. 517) the following table, intended to illustrate the diminishing marginal productivity of shepherds and the fact that, at a prevailing wage equivalent to 20 sheep, the farmer will hold his hand after taking on the eleventh shepherd.

1	2	3	4	5	6
No. of Shepherds	*No. of Sheep*	*Product Due to Last Man*	*Average Product Per Man*	*Wages Bill*	*Excess of (2) Over (5)*
8	580	..	72½	160	420
9	615	35	68½	180	435
10	640	25	64	200	440
11	660	20	60	220	440
12	676	16	56½	240	436

On this she comments that "if it were really the case that workers tend to receive a wage equal to the net product due to the additional labour of the marginal labourer of their class, columns 5 and 6 should be corrected to read as follows:

5	6
Wages Bill	*Excess of* (2) *Over* (5)
Unknown	*Unknown*
315	300
250	390
220	440
192	484

and there would be no limit to the number of men it would pay an employer to hire, for with every extra worker the total net gain to the employer would increase." It is evident that Mrs. Burns has failed to grasp the elementary notion that while to the individual employer it is the wage that is given, the amount of that wage depends, *ceteris paribus*, on the height of the productivity curve of labour throughout the whole field of employment. After this exhibition, not much attention need perhaps be given to her complaint that the theory assumes "diminishing returns"—she is innocent of the *universal* law of diminishing returns, after a point, from *individual* factors of production; nor to her opinion that the final form of Marshall's theory was dictated by the fact that "if his brain was too good for his theory, his love of form overcame his strength of will." Nor again need we linger over her obscure suggestions that the marginal productivity theory in some way ignores the conception of *value*,—suggestions which culminate in the pronouncement that "a frank recognition of the emptiness of the word 'productivity' and a clearer explanation of the fact that the *value* of the particular work performed is the important factor, would . . . make economics seem nearer to life." The whole article is in truth an almost unique museum of muddle.

(3) The next class of objection is, at its best, of a much solider kind. It is based on the alleged impossibility of disentangling the specific product of the various factors of production, even at the margin of their application. It is true that in the hands of some popular writers this objection seems to be based on sheer ignorance

of the existence of the weapons forged by economic science for performing the process of disentanglement. Thus Mr. Bernard Shaw writes (*Intelligent Woman's Guide to Socialism*, p. 21): "When a farmer and his labourers sow and reap a field of wheat, nobody on earth can say how much of the wheat each of them has grown." Thus also Mr. Bertrand Russell, with less excuse for ignorance of the elements of mathematical economics, writes (*Prospects of Industrial Civilisation*, p. 146): "In an industrial civilisation a man never makes the whole of anything, but makes the thousandth part of a million things. Under these circumstances it is totally absurd to say that a man has the right to the produce of his own labour. Consider a porter on a railway whose business it is to shunt goods trains; what proportion of the goods carried can be said to represent the produce of his labour? The question is wholly insoluble."

But in a subtler form we find a similar objection put forward by eminent economists who are thoroughly conversant with the marginal principle.[2] Thus Taussig (*Principles of Economics*, Vol. II., p. 213) declares: "There is no separate product of the tool on the one hand and of the labour using the tool on the other"; and Cassel (*Theory of Social Economy*, Vol. I., p. 172) reminds us that "if a pit has to be dug, the addition of one more man will make little difference to the day's output unless you give the man a spade." What in effect these distinguished critics are urging is that Marshall has shirked the heart of the problem by assuming that his famous marginal shepherd, with whose product the wages of all shepherds are equated, needs no crook,—or if he does, can cut it for himself in the hedge.

What is the reply of the marginal productivity theory to these objections? The question requires careful consideration, for it is relevant also to the type of objection to which we shall come under (5) below. It seems pretty clear that there is a certain parting of the ways. One of the prophets of marginalism, J. B. Clark, meets this difficulty by taking a long-distance view, and supposing the nature of the capital equipment utilised to be alterable with the

---

[2] In what follows, I am conscious of having been much influenced by Mr. Valk's candid and painstaking essay, *The Principles of Wages*.

number of workers employed. "Any increase or diminution in
the amount of labour that is employed in connection with a given
amount of capital causes that capital to change its forms" (*Distribution of Wealth*, p. 159). It would seem that in this matter Clark
is followed by Pigou, though the latter's statement of the case is
developed in connection with the marginal net product of resources
in general and not of specific factors of production. "Since our
interest is in the difference between the products of two adjacent
flows of resources, it is natural to conceive each of the two flows as
organised in the manner most appropriate to itself" (*Economics of
Welfare*, 3rd edition, p. 135).[3] If ten men are to be set to dig a
hole instead of nine, they will be furnished with ten cheaper spades
instead of nine more expensive ones; or perhaps, if there is no room
for him to dig comfortably, the tenth man will be furnished with a
bucket and sent to fetch beer for the other nine. Once we allow
ourselves this liberty, we can exhibit in the sharpest form the
principle of *variation*,—the principle that you can combine varying
amounts of one factor with a fixed amount of all the others; and
we can draw, for labour or for any other factor, a perfectly definite
descending curve of marginal productivity.

It is not possible, I think, to maintain that Marshall himself
looked at the matter in this way. He asserts, indeed, in a footnote
which has become considerably truncated in later editions, that the
substance of the problem remains unchanged if the shepherd (to
put it briefly) needs a crook; but it is clear that he bases this
assertion not on any assumption about the variability of the forms
which can be taken by an unchanged amount of capital, but on
the quite different principle of *joint demand*. "The net product of
such shepherds [*i.e.* those who need crooks, etc.] cannot be ascertained simply; but it is a case of derived demand and requires us
to take account of the prices which have to be paid for the aid of
all these other agents of production" (*Principles*, 5th edition, p. 517).
And it is this necessity for reliance on the principle of joint demand
which leads him to make the famous qualification of the importance

---

[3] Mr. Valk seems right in suggesting (*op. cit.*, p. 33) that in view of this definition, the word "net" in Pigou's hands becomes otiose.

of the doctrine of marginal productivity which has been such a godsend to critics (*ibid*., p. 518). "This doctrine has sometimes been put forward as a theory of wages. But there is no valid ground for any such pretension. The doctrine that the earnings of the worker tend to be equal to the net product of his work has by itself no real meaning: since in order to estimate net product we have to take for granted all the expenses of production of the commodity on which he works other than his own wages."

Now so long as we are fixing our eyes on a single business or a single industry the assumption that all the other factors of production have clearly defined supply prices is perhaps sufficiently nearly valid to give no great trouble to anyone; but what we are in search of is the principle governing the level of wages *as a whole*, and in this field appeal to the principle of joint demand obliges us to assume that all the factors of production *as a whole* (land presumably excepted) have clearly defined supply schedules. Marshall's presentation of the marginal productivity theory of wages turns out, therefore, to be intimately bound up with his teaching about the real cost of saving; and no one who is not prepared to swallow the latter can be expected to be intellectually satisfied with the former.

Personally I think we must be prepared to follow Clark in setting the theory of marginal productivity on its own legs, so to speak, with the aid of the principle of the variability of the *forms* of the factors of production. But it is important to be alive to the difficulties which this latter principle puts in the way of discerning the operation of the marginal productivity theory in real life.

With an unequivocal curve of the marginal productivity of labour in operation, an artificial raising of the rate of wages will tend, according to ordinary theory, to produce two analytically separable reactions. The first is a movement *along* the existing curve,—a reduction in the numbers employed up to the point at which the product of the marginal man employed equals the artificial wage. The second is a cumulative *lowering* of the curve, caused by the decline in profits and the consequent check to the supply of capital and enterprise, and having the result that the numbers who at any future time can find employment at the artificial wage are even smaller than they would have been had the old curve continued in operation.[4] I return to the practical importance of this distinction in connection with my fifth group of wage-grumbles below. At present it is enough to observe that the first reaction is clearly of a different order of directness and immediacy from the second. It must be expected to occur wherever the employing class consults its own self-interest with regard to the hire and discharge of labour, even though there may be reason to suppose that the amount of the other factors supplied is invariable, so that there is no scope for the second reaction at all.

But if the form of the existing marginal productivity curve of labour itself depends on the assumption of wide possibilities of industrial change, the distinction between the two reactions is apt to become blurred. For the first reaction to occur without the second, we have to assume just so much flexibility, in the way of lapse of time and potentialities of change, as to permit the *forms* of capital and organisation to alter without any alteration in their *amount*. There is no logical absurdity about such an assumption, and it might be the most natural one to make in a socialistic state in which the quantity of capital and organisation was held permanently unchanged by autocratic manipulation. But it must be conceded that there seems to be a certain unreality about the assumption in a capitalistic world. For if the capitalist is to be allowed time and facilities for turning his spades into a steam-plough, it seems unreasonable not to allow him time and facilities for turning them into beer. The notion that, with a defined quantity of capital and a defined quantity of labour, there is, in a certain defined sense, a definite marginal productivity of labour, does not lose its validity; but it seems to become, under certain conditions, less interesting as a proposition and less useful as a guide to conduct,

---

[4] The distinction appears pretty clearly in Pigou's argument about the elasticity of demand for labour, *Economics of Welfare*, 3rd edition, p. 554. It is not, I think, clearly made in language by Marshall, who writes as though the damage done by artificial wage-rates to employment will be effected entirely through the mediation of a check to the supply of capital and enterprise (*Economics of Industry*, pp. 375, 395).

than some expositions of the theory would lead us to hope, or even
than the Marshallian conception of marginal productivity eked out
by joint demand would be, if we could only feel more confidence
in its foundations.

For instance, the tendency to industrial rationalisation is, in one
of its aspects, a tendency to install such elaborate and expensive
and durable plant, and to devise such a close and intimate co-ordi-
nation between it and the labour force required to work it, as to
leave as little room as possible for the operation of the Principle
of Variation. Under such conditions the position and shape of the
true or Clarkian curve of marginal productivity of labour may
well become a matter of somewhat remote interest. We are confronted instead with a kind of bastard compound between a long-
period and a short-period curve,[5] which may well, so far as it can
be conceived of as having any real existence, be of a highly dis-
quieting shape,— nearly flat for part of its length, and then suddenly dropping almost vertically.[6] A completely rationalised
world might turn out to be one in which, if organised so as to
obtain their *de facto* economic worth, a certain proportion of workpeople could find employment at very high wages, while the
remainder could hardly find it on any terms at all.

I pass to comment briefly on the method by which Cassel,
conformably to his objection already quoted to the theory of marginal productivity, believes himself to have relegated the Principle
of Variation to a subsidiary place in the theory of distribution,
and to have solved the main part of the problem without its aid
(*Theory of Social Economy*, Chap. IV). The method consists in
building up a series of equations in which the total supply of each
factor, and the technical combination of factors required to make

[5] This is perhaps one aspect of the truth, of which another aspect is
discussed by Mr. Harrod (*Economic Journal*, 1930, pp. 232 ff.)—the truth that the
"short period" is not the same length at both ends, and that in the case of specially
large and durable instruments—of railways *par excellence*—the long end of the
short period may last for decades.

[6] Very different from the true Clarkian curve—"If capital is freely trans-
mutable in form, labour becomes freely transferable and able to count on an
indefinitely elastic field of employment."

each product, are taken as given. The demand function for each product being also given, it is shown that the price of each factor, and of each product, is unequivocally determined. But how can the first two things *both* be taken as given? If each of 10 industries requires the use of 10 units of labour to every unit of capital, and if there exist 100 units of labour and 100 units of capital, what is to happen? To assume that the whole supply of each factor is used up is to assume tacitly that the Principle of Variation *has* been applied by those whose business it is to apply it.

I claim no originality for this objection, which is made by Mr. Valk in his *Principles of Wages*. At first, indeed, he seems inclined to treat it as of small account: "a few units of some means of production . . . would be left unemployed, but that would not prevent us from calling the situation a state of equilibrium" (*op. cit.*, p. 112). I have suggested above that as regards labour in a rationalised world, for periods of time which the ordinary man would describe as "long," it is not altogether easy to take so optimistic a view. In the next chapter, however, Mr. Valk develops the objection at some length, and ends with a gallant attempt to construct a "synthesis" of the Wieser-Cassel "scarcity" theory on the one hand and the Clark-Marshall "productivity" theory on the other. I venture to doubt whether any such synthesis is needed or helpful. So far as I can see, Cassel's theory, in assuming that the total quantity of each factor *available* is the same as the total quantity of each factor *employed*, *either* tacitly assumes that the Principle of Variation has been in operation *or* assumes what is not likely to be true. At best, therefore, it is identical with the theory of marginal productivity; at worst, the insecurity of its foundations renders it powerless to come to our aid when the theory of marginal productivity leaves us in the lurch.

(4) The next group of objections is based on alleged peculiarities, connected with the poverty of the workman, in the supply curve of labour. In this field it is Marshall himself who has been the first to cast doubts on the adequacy of the theory of marginal productivity (*Principles*, 8th edition, pp. 335–6 and App. F). For he argues that the marginal utility of money to the workman can-

not be taken as constant, and that therefore the relevant analysis is that proper to barter; he tacks on to this argument the celebrated appendix about nuts and apples, in which it is shown that under barter, even though free competition prevails, the rate of exchange is indeterminate; and he thereby unmistakably implies that in certain conditions, even under competition, the theory of marginal productivity fails to give us a solution and the rate of wages is indeterminate. This is an entirely different and much more subversive proposition than that which is universally admitted,— namely, that where, owing to the workman's disabilities in bargaining and for other reasons, some degree of employers' monopoly prevails, the wage-rate may be driven down below the marginal net product of labour by the exercise of monopolistic power. Mr. Hicks has, I think, successfully shown (*Economic Journal*, 1930, pp. 225–6) that Marshall's argument is confused; that "the only situation in the labour market which can possibly correspond exactly to the problem of barter is a bargain between employer and workman for a single day's, or a single week's, work"; and that to explain a continuing divergence between wage-rate and marginal net product it is to the theory of monopoly and not to that of barter that we must have recourse.

It seems then that Mr. Dobb, in the elaborate attack on orthodox theory developed in his book *Wages*, Chaps. IV and V (1928), and in his article "A Sceptical View of the Theory of Wages" (*Economic Journal*, Dec. 1929), is justified in claiming some support from Marshall for his own doctrine of the "indeterminateness" of the wage contract. But his own doctrine does not seem to be quite the same in the two places. In his book, so far as this part of his argument goes, all he desires to prove or succeeds in proving seems to be that if the workpeople possess reserves in the form of money (and *a fortiori* if they possess income-yielding assets), the price at which they will be willing continuously to provide any nth unit of work per week is likely to be higher than if they do not. This is indubitably true and important; but, as Mr. Dobb himself explains, it is not inconsistent with the notion that there exists a defined demand price for this nth unit of work, with which, as well as with the revised supply-price, the wage paid will tend—in the absence of buyers' monopoly—to correspond. Nor is it inconsistent with the proposition that the demand for work is such that the increase in the price *per unit of work* obtained by the workpeople as a result of their acquisition of reserves is incompatible with an increase in the wage received *per head*.[7]

In his article, however, Mr. Dobb seems to come much nearer to endorsing Marshall's argument as it stands; and Marshall's argument as it stands implies that the varying marginal utility of money to the workman may of itself suffice to make the wage-rate diverge from marginal productivity. In one respect indeed, even in this article, Mr. Dobb seems to go less far than Marshall, since I do not think he contends that the asquisition of reserves will of itself enable the workpeople to raise wages *per head* as distinct from wages *per unit* of effort, whereas I can find no such restriction in Marshall's argument. But so far as Mr. Dobb *is* meaning to endorse Marshall's argument, Mr. Hicks' reply seems to be valid as against him also.[8]

Of these two expositions the later and apparently more radical must, I suppose, be taken to represent Mr. Dobb's more considered

---

[7] In point of fact, it is not only in connection with "reserves" that the influence on wages of the varying marginal utility of money to the workman demands consideration. Workpeople will sometimes put forth fewer units of effort in response to a rise in the rate of reward per unit of effort, even though they are not taking advantage of that rise to carry over any savings from one week to the next. Mr. Dobb, instead of making his supply curve of labour slope steadily upwards from left to right, might plausibly have made it bend backwards towards the left. But neither this fact, nor those connected with "reserves," impairs the necessary correspondence between wages and marginal productivity.

[8] Mr. Hicks charges Mr. Dobb with going further than Marshall in one respect. "Marshall spoke of disadvantageous contracts having a tendency to keep wages low: Mr. Dobb speaks of a cumulative fall." I am not sure that this charge can be sustained, in view of a later passage (*Principles*, 8th edition, p. 569) in which Marshall himself speaks of a cumulative fall; though it might be urged that in this later passage he is not relying on the barter analysis, but is taking account of the effects of lowered wages in (i) diminishing efficiency, (ii) diminishing the ability of labour to secure its "normal value" (*i.e.* presumably its marginal net product) under conditions of buyers' monopoly. But this passage, like the

view. But I do not feel sure that he would recognise the depth of the gulf between them. For it sometimes appears as though all he means by the word "indeterminate" is "determined partly by something which happened more than a week ago"; and in *this* sense it can no doubt be said that even the earlier version of the argument is designed to prove that wages are "indeterminate." Whether this is a legitimate use of the word "indeterminate" I must leave to better mathematicians than myself to determine. The point is that Mr. Dobb's earlier version is unlike Marshall's passage in that it contains nothing to throw doubt on the *truth* of the doctrine that wages tend to measure the marginal productivity of labour. Whether it contains anything to detract from the paramount *importance* of that doctrine as a guide to practical policy depends on whether it can fairly be regarded as expedient to raise wages per unit of effort at the cost of lowering wages per head. Where the working day or the working life[9] is inordinately long, it seems clear that it can; but the strenuous attempts which have been made (*e.g.* in the coal trade) to ensure that reductions of hours are accompanied by a compensatory increase in hourly rates suggest that this is not a very common object of working-class policy in Western countries at the present day.

(5) But Mr. Dobb has also another string to his bow. The alleged demand curve for labour, he says, is itself not an "independent" factor in the problem, since its height depends upon the willingness of the capitalists to save, this again upon their con-

---

earlier one, is obscure. In any case I do not expect that Mr. Dobb will be much disturbed by Mr. Hicks' proof that the alleged cumulative fall must come to an end, if not earlier, then, when the workman's reserves are completely used up. The point is rather that neither an absence nor a progressive depletion of reserves can prevent the workman from getting, at each point, the full value of his marginal net product, so long as competition prevails.

[9] *E.g.* if there is labour of young children or nursing mothers. Mr. Dobb also appears to attach much importance to "relative wages," *i.e.* the proportion of the aggregate wage-bill to the national income. In view of the unhappiness caused by envy, it might, I suppose, be expedient to increase relative wages at the cost of a fall in aggregate wages; but I think that to most people this would seem a retrograde step.

ventional standard of comfort, and this again upon the outcome
of the bargains they have made with wage-earners in the past.
Hence if these bargains had been more advantageous to the wage-
earners, the capitalists might never have thought of going to the
Riviera, and might have saved more instead: thus wages would
have been higher to-day.

I am sure that these last pages of Mr. Dobb's article and the
corresponding pages of his book (pp. 101 onwards) deserve careful
reading. I do not feel sure that I have understood them fully or
can criticise them precisely. But I suggest that they raise three
points,—a point of words, a point of analysis, and a point of fact.
The point of words turns again on the meaning of "independent"
and "indeterminate." I am not persuaded that the present normal
level of wages is rightly called "indeterminate" because among the
forces determining it is the whole course of past history, including
the history of wage-contracts. The point of analysis turns on the
relative importance in the theory of wages of the Principle of
Variation and the Principle of Joint Demand respectively. In
Mr. Dobb's hands the latter is exalted to supreme heights, the
former virtually disappears. To take the extreme case, Mr. Dobb
holds that in a Socialist State wages might rise until they swallowed
the whole of the national income, minus necessary capital accumulation. I suggest that this is untrue, unless by "wages" we
merely mean "working-class incomes." Even in such a State there
would (subject to the difficulties mentioned above under (3)) be a
defined marginal productivity curve of labour in existence, its
shape and height depending on technical considerations and on the
magnitude of the State's natural resources and accumulated fund
of crystallised saving. There would be a defined rate of wages
which a State trust, working on business lines, would find it worth
while to pay to a workman; and rents of various sizes would
emerge in the various State industries. Of course it would be open
to the State to distribute these rents among wage-earners on any
principles it chose: but a State which did not distinguish between
these rents and wages proper would soon be in a rare muddle.

The error which leaps to the eye in this extreme case seems to me to permeate also Mr. Dobb's analysis of the wage-determining forces under capitalism. The function of the capitalist in *advancing* wages fills the picture to the exclusion of the forces which motivate the advance—namely, the expected productivity of the labour hired. The supply curve of saving is glorified to such an extent that it almost *becomes* the demand curve for labour turned upside down. [10]

The question of *fact* is how much pressure the employing class will stand without growing sulky and refusing to play. I do not believe there is any fundamental difference between Mr. Dobb and most modern economists on this matter. None of us knows precisely: all of us are prepared to experiment up to a point. In 1927 I shocked some of my progressive friends by suggesting that the Colwyn Committee were too optimistic about the innocuousness of high income taxes; in 1930 I find these same friends much more panicky than myself. Even Mr. Dobb does not expect aristocracies to surrender their privileged standards altogether without a revolution: even Sir Ernest Benn would not really, I feel sure, desire to abolish the system of national education in the interests of the growth of capital.

But it is just here that the distinction drawn in connection with grumble-group (3)—a distinction which Mr. Dobb's analysis ignores altogether—seems to me to be still of practical importance, in spite of the difficulties which we there found in making it precise. I allude to the distinction between a movement along the existing marginal productivity curve of labour and a lowering of the curve. Even if there were no reason to expect the latter reaction, that would give us no excuse for doubting the former. It does not need any remote calculations about the motives of savers to establish the proposition that an over-ambitious wage policy will cause unemployment. And the practical inference seems to be that which

---

[10] I cannot refrain from protesting in passing against Mr. Dobb's assertion that orthodox theory taught that in equilibrium "the disutility involved in the marginal unit of work supplied (when expressed in money) equalled the disutility involved in the marginal unit of the investors' investment." Can he quote any authority for this?

various persons[11] have drawn,—that there is more scope for improving the distribution of wealth along the lines of progressive taxation than along the lines of Trade Union pressure; though (short of Mr. Dobb's revolution) there is not unlimited scope along either.

---

[11] Including Mr. Keynes in the *Political Quarterly*, Jan. 1930.

13

ON THE ELASTICITY OF DEMAND FOR INCOME IN TERMS OF EFFORT*

By Lionel Robbins †

1. It is a generally accepted proposition of theoretical economics that the effects of a change in the terms on which incomes from work can be obtained depend upon the elasticity of demand for income in terms of effort.[1] If the elasticity of demand for income in terms of effort is greater than unity, then the effects of a tax or a fall in wage rates will be a diminution of work done and the effects of a bounty or a rise in wage rates will be an increase in work done. If it is less than unity, then the opposite movements are to be expected.

2. These propositions are capable of demonstration by the familiar geometrical constructions of either (a) unit or (b) integral demand curves. The only difference between the constructions relevant here and those of commodity price analysis is that the prices exhibited will be, not money, but effort prices.

(a) Thus, if we employ the unit demand apparatus, we measure quantity of income demanded along O X and the effort price of income along O Y. The curve d d^1 exhibits the conditions of demand, and the quantity of work done for any given income

---

* *Economica*, Volume X, June 1930, pages 123–129. Reprinted by courtesy of the publisher and author.

† University of London.

[1] See Dalton, *Public Finance*, Second Edition, pp. 100–108, or Robertson, *Banking Policy and the Price Level*, Chapters I and II *passim*. It is possible, of course, to reformulate this proposition in terms of the elasticity of supply of effort, and for some purposes it is convenient to do so. But there is much to be said for exhibiting all psychological variables as phenomena of demand. See Wicksteed, *Commonsense of Political Economy*, Book II, Chapter IV, and "The Scope and Method of Political Economy," *Economic Journal*, 1913, pp. 1 *seq.*

will be shown by a rectangle formed by erecting perpendiculars on O X and O Y to cut any point of equilibrium (P) in d d[1]. If e.g. the effort price of income is $O E_1$ then the quantity of income which will be earned will be $O I_1$, and the amount of work done will be $O E_1 P_1 I_1$.

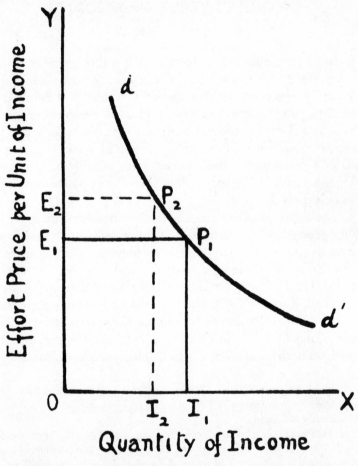

The effects of a change in the terms on which income can be obtained can be shown by shifting E. Let us suppose for instance the imposition of a uniform income-tax which shifts E from E_1 to E_2. Then the quantity of income earned will shift to I_2 and the change in the amount of work done will be shown by the difference between $E_1 P_1 I_1 O$ and $E_2 P_2 I_2 O$.   If in this region d d^1 shows an elasticity greater than one this difference will be negative (i.e. less work will be done).   If it is less than one the difference will be positive (i.e. more work will be done).

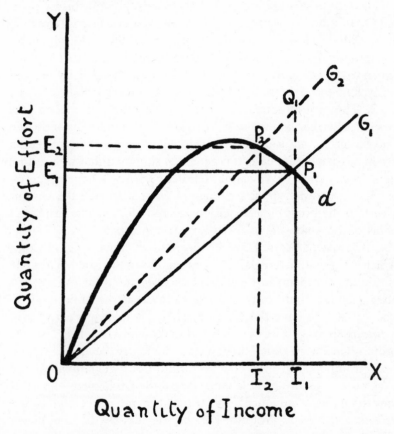

Quantity of Income

(*b*) The integral apparatus shows the same result with even greater clarity.   Along O X we continue to measure quantity of income.   Along O Y, however, we measure the total amounts of effort which will be expended for different quantities of income. (That is to say, what was a rectangle on the unit apparatus has become a line on this apparatus.)   O d is the total demand curve.

The terms on which income can be obtained will evidently be an angular magnitude, the tangent of the angle G_1 O X. Thus in the case depicted if the terms on which income can be obtained are represented by tan G_1 O X we get equilibrium at P_1 with O I_1, income earned for an expenditure of O E_1 effort.

Now suppose a tax imposed.   We may represent this by swinging O G to the left.   (To get O I_1 before, it was necessary to expend I_1 P_1 effort.   Now it is necessary to expend I_1 Q_1.)   Equilibrium is re-established at P_2 with O I_2 income earned and O E_2 income expended.   Since, in this region, O d shows an elasticity less than unity, O E_2 is greater than O E_1 (i.e. more work is done).

3. The propositions thus analysed are purely formal in character.   They explain what will happen if the conditions of demand are of a certain nature.   To discover what the conditions of demand are in any particular case, it is generally supposed that we must rely upon observation.   We cannot predict *a priori* what the effects of a change in taxation or of a change in wage rates will be; we must ascertain the probable elasticity of demand for income in terms of effort of the taxpayers or wage-earners concerned.

4. In recent years, however, propositions have been advanced which suggest that formal analysis enables us to predict that the elasticity of demand in the case of effort demand for income must always be less than unity—that is to say that the imposition of a tax will always have the effect of making a man work more, and a rise in his wage rates will always make him work less.   If these propositions were true, they would obviously be of the highest *practical* importance—the effect on output of higher taxation need have no terrors for needy Chancellors of the Exchequer—and since they have been advanced by authorities no less eminent than Professor Pigou and Professor Knight, they clearly deserve the very closest attention.

5. The arguments of both the authorities mentioned involve in one form or another implicit appeal to the "law" or assumption of the declining marginal utility of units of income.   Now *prima facie* it is difficult to see how this "law" or assumption justifies the inferences which appear to be based on it.   *The assumption that, as*

income increases, the utility to an individual of additional units declines, justifies us indeed in inferring that the curve which exhibits the condition of demand for income in terms of effort will slope downwards, but it does not seem to justify the assumption that this curve must always cut a rectangular hyperbola negatively (i.e. that it must show an elasticity less than one at all reaches). The assumption or "law" lays it down that the final degree of utility diminishes, but it does not *prima facie* say anything about the *rate* of diminution.

6. But let us examine more closely the actual arguments concerned. Professor Knight's is the more general and will be taken first.

Professor Knight's argument concerns the effect of a change in wage rates. "In so far as men act rationally," he argues,[2] ". . . they will at a higher rate divide their time between wage earning and non-industrial uses in such a way as to earn *more money* but to work *fewer hours.*" And he justifies this proposition by the following reasoning. "Suppose that at a higher rate per hour or per piece, a man previously at the perfect equilibrium adjustment works as before and earns a proportionately higher income. When, now, he goes to spend the extra money, he will naturally want to increase his expenditure for many commodities consumed and to take on some new ones. To divide his resources in such a way as to preserve equal importance of equal expenditures in all fields he must evidently lay out part of his new funds for increased leisure; i.e. buy back some of his working time or spend some of his money by the process of not earning it."

At first sight the argument appears overwhelmingly, convincing, sufficient even to overcome the reflection of commonsense that, if it were true, it would follow that it would always be futile to offer rational men permanently higher wages if it was desired to elicit a permanently increased supply of work. But closer inspection seems to reveal a flaw. Professor Knight's argument assumes that the prices of the commodities constituting real income are unaltered. This is presumably true so far as money prices are concerned. But the relevant conception in this connection is not *money price* but

---

[2] *Risk, Uncertainty, and Profit,* pp. 117–18.

effort price, and a change in the rate at which money income can be earned, money prices remaining constant, *constitutes* a change in the effort price of commodities. *The money price is the same but the effort price is diminished.* And, that being the case, the question whether more or less effort is expended on commodities is obviously still an open one. It depends on the elasticity of demand for income in terms of effort.

This may sound abstract, but if it is thought of in concrete terms, it becomes very simple. If real income be conceived as consisting of a flow of one commodity, say, bananas, and the process of producing bananas as an exchange of effort for income, then it is surely clear that, if for some reason the effort price of bananas (real income) diminishes (a change equivalent to a rise in money wage rates), it is entirely a matter of elasticity of demand for bananas (real income) whether more or less effort is given for them, just as, if the money price of bananas changes, it is entirely a matter of elasticity whether more or less money is given for them.

The same objection can be put yet another way. In Professor Knight's example leisure is purchased by sacrificing income. We may therefore conceive—as he does—of a *real income price of leisure.* Now when the money rate of wages rises (commodity prices remaining the same) the real income price of leisure (the cost of leisure in terms of real income sacrificed) rises. And when the price of leisure (or anything else) rises it is not at all clear that more will be bought even out of an increased real income. Again it is all a matter of elasticity.

7. Professor Pigou's proposition[3] relates to the effect of a tax on the willingness to work of an individual. "Since a part of his income is taken away, the last unit of income will be desired more urgently than the last unit of income that would have been left to him if there had been no taxation. But the last unit of energy that he devotes to work will not affect him differently from what it did, consequently there will be a tendency for him to work a little harder. . . . " Elsewhere this is put even more succinctly. "Since income is taken away from taxpayers the marginal utility

---

[3] *Economics of Welfare* (First Edition), p. 593.

of money to them is raised but the marginal disutility of work is unchanged. Hence, unless they are somehow impeded, they will increase the amount of work done."[4]

With very great deference it is submitted that this mode of argument proves much too much. This can be seen very readily if the argument be made completely general.

Suppose a man to be in receipt of a constant flow of exchangeable goods of any sort, say, corn. (The constant flow here is equivalent to the constant flow of disposable time which is assumed when variations in the supply of work are being considered.) Suppose that he is in the habit of exchanging some of this corn for a constant flow of some other kind of goods, say, coal (the constant flow of coal procured is equivalent to the constant flow of real income which can be earned by exchanging time for product). Suppose now that a tax is imposed which makes the price of coal higher (i.e. which makes the effort price of real income higher), would Professor Pigou acquiesce in an argument which ran as follows? The marginal utility of coal (real income) is now greater. But the marginal disutility of parting with corn (time) is unchanged. He will therefore, unless impeded, part with more corn (time). Such an argument seems plainly fallacious: it implies that the elasticity of demand for *any* commodity is less than unity. But in what way is it different from the argument on which Professor Pigou is relying?

Is it not clear that the relevant circumstance in the case of the imposition of a tax or the raising of a price is the change in the terms on which exchange is possible? The marginal utility of real income (or the single good) changes with changes in the quantity possessed as before. It is the terms on which income (or the single good) can be obtained which alter and it is the magnitude of this change together with the rate at which the utility of income diminishes which determines the nature of the new equilibrium. The flaw in Professor Pigou's argument seems to be due to an ambiguity in the expression "marginal utility" used in this connection. If a tax is imposed the utility of the marginal unit of

---

[4] *Public Finance*, pp. 83–4.

income will rise, but the utility of the income derived from a unit of work at the original point of equilibrium may rise or fall, for it depends on the rate of exchange as well as on the utility of the marginal unit.[5]   When the price of anything rises, we are entitled, if we assume diminishing marginal utility, to infer that, in all but exceptional cases, less of the commodity will be bought.   But we are not entitled to infer that more money (or more effort) will necessarily be spent on it.

8. If these considerations are valid we are left with the conclusion, reached earlier, that any attempt to predict the effect of a change in the terms on which income is earned must proceed by inductive investigation of elasticities.   The attempt to narrow the limit of possible elasticities by *a priori* reasoning must be held to have broken down.

---

[5] Mr. Hicks, to whom I am greatly indebted for assistance in framing the above criticism, has formulated the point symbolically thus:

If u = Utility of income earned,
   v = Disutility of work done,
   x = Amount of work done,
   y = Amount of income received,

then in equilibrium $\frac{du}{dx} = \frac{dv}{dx}$. If the same amount of work is done, then $\frac{dv}{dx}$ remains unchanged, but $\frac{du}{dx}$ may vary in either direction; for $\frac{du}{dx} = \frac{du}{dy} \cdot \frac{dy}{dx}$. $\frac{du}{dy}$ must increase but $\frac{dy}{dx}$ must diminish, and the change in $\frac{du}{dx}$ will therefore depend on their relation, i.e. on the elasticity of demand for income.—Q. E. D.

14

A RECONSIDERATION OF THE THEORY OF EXPLOITATION*[1]

By Gordon F. Bloom†

Exploitation, like discrimination and monopoly, has ceased to be a noun and has become a noise. That it has received this emotional content in its non-academic usage is, however, no reason why economists should not consider the problem as scientists and give exploitation the same precise and unbiased treatment as has been accorded discrimination and monopoly. Yet a scrutiny of the literature on the subject, in particular the writings of current "popular" labor economists (who have received a great stimulus from the present wage and hour legislation), reveals that "exploitation" is one of the most misused, ambiguous, and misunderstood terms in the economist's vocabulary. For instance, some economists urge that minimum wage legislation be confined to low wage areas, on the theory that because the laborers therein are being "exploited," an arbitrary rise in wages imposed on these employers will not cause unemployment. Actually, low wages are no indication at all of exploitation; indeed, in its common form, there is rather more basis for presuming it to exist where wages are high.[2] Furthermore, as we shall see later, a minimum wage law at a high level is less likely to cause unemployment to ensue in high wage industries than is a lower minimum in low wage industries. This

* *Quarterly Journal of Economics*, Volume LV, 1940–1941, pages 413–442. Reprinted by courtesy of the publisher and author.

† Formerly, Harvard University.

[1] I wish to express my appreciation to Professors E. H. Chamberlin, S. H. Slichter and Fritz Machlup for their helpful criticism of certain portions of this article.

[2] Since high wages are more likely to be indicative of a rising supply curve for labor. See below, p. 252.

is typical of the confusion which is common in much of the current literature. A re-examination of the theory of exploitation therefore seems justified on grounds of both theoretical interest and practical importance.

In the consideration of the problem of exploitation this paper will pursue the following procedure. We shall begin with a restatement and reconsideration of the definition of "exploitation," "marginal product" and "wage." Thus prepared, we shall inquire into the conditions in which it is likely that labor will receive less than its marginal revenue product—the definition of exploitation which we shall adopt. Lastly, we shall close with an appraisal of the importance in real life of various possible sources of exploitation and with a word about the policies which may be adopted to eliminate certain types of exploitation.

DEFINITIONS AND CLASSIFICATION

EXPLOITATION. The term "exploitation" will be used to denote the payment to labor of a wage less than its marginal revenue product.[3] This is, of course, not the only possible definition of exploitation. We might, for instance, adopt the Pigovian criterion of a wage less than the value of the marginal physical product.[4] But choice of the latter seems to the writer to be unsuited to the purpose in hand. Under monopolistic competition, all factors are "exploited" in this sense,[5] and it is therefore quite uninteresting to examine the conditions under which labor is exploited, since such exploitation will be almost universal.[6] Particularly if we are

---

[3] This term will receive consideration in the next section.

[4] A. C. Pigou, *Economics of Welfare*, 3d ed., London, 1929, p. 551.

[5] E. H. Chamberlin, *The Theory of Monopolistic Competition*, Cambridge, 1938, p. 183.

[6] Some readers, while granting the universality of monopolistic competition, may question the usefulness of the definition which we shall adopt, on the grounds that the slope of demand curves is not sufficiently great in practice to give rise to a significant discrepancy between the value of the marginal product and the marginal revenue product. With this contention, we cannot agree. While it may be true that in some industries demand curves are very elastic, the areas in which this is not so are sufficiently important, and the diversity of types of entre-

attempting to draw some practical conclusions from our study, it is much more fruitful to adopt the marginal revenue product, rather than the value of the marginal physical product, from which to measure the existence of exploitation.[7]   If we adopt the Pigovian definition, the only possibility of removing exploitation is by restoring conditions of perfect competition; by adopting the definition of exploitation as the payment of a wage less than the marginal revenue product of labor, a much wider field is left open for discussion of the possibility of eliminating the discrepancy through the

---

preneurial behavior in the economy as a whole is sufficiently great, to warrant the adoption of a definition of exploitation which takes as its standard the marginal revenue product, rather than the value of the marginal product.

[7] On the other hand, the Pigovian definition has the merit that the absence of exploitation is at the same time a condition of the optimum distribution of resources.   This cannot be said of the Chamberlinian formulation, for in the latter case labor may everywhere be receiving its full marginal revenue product, yet be maldistributed nevertheless.   As long as the wage is equated to the marginal revenue product, the economist is compelled to deny the existence of exploitation, regardless of how low the employer may force down wages.   Thus the definition of exploitation in terms of the marginal revenue product, though in many ways an improvement over the Pigovian definition, is also a retrogression, since the notion of an ideal distribution of resources is lost and in its stead is left a concept which seems, on the face of it, to be faintly justificatory of the existing distribution of resources and inadequate to deal with the problem of improving the allocation of the factors.

The writer does not propose a return to the Pigovian criterion, for such a step would sacrifice "realism for idealism."   But he does suggest (and Professor Chamberlin concurs in this opinion) that there is need for a new definition of exploitation, or at least a supplementary concept, which will take account of monopolistic elements and at the same time relate the wage received by a particular type of labor in a firm to the average remuneration received by that labor in the economy as a whole.   A possible solution would be to define exploitation as *payment to a worker of a wage less than that marginal revenue product which would be attributable to this type of labor in a monopolistic economy in which a perfect market for labor existed.* This indicates the line of approach which might be taken by future study.   Unfortunately, considerations of space make it impossible to give adequate attention to this problem in this paper, since we are here concerned with a reconsideration of the current theory of exploitation, rather than with a re-definition of the concept. Hence the writer wishes only to propose the latter as a worth-while subject for further consideration.

application of the appropriate public or trade-union policy. Therefore, in the following pages, we shall mean by exploitation the latter condition, namely, payment to labor of a wage less than its full marginal revenue equivalent.

MARGINAL PRODUCT.   The marginal product[8] with which we shall be concerned has been variously called the marginal value product, the marginal net product and the marginal revenue product.   Although it does not really matter which expression we adopt, so long as we use it consistently and are aware of what it means, it seems advisable to adopt Chamberlin's term—the marginal revenue product.   As he has pointed out,[9] this designation has the merit that it serves clearly to associate the concept with the individual firm.   The marginal revenue product is the net anticipated addition to the money revenue of the firm attributable to the addition of one more unit of a factor.   The question then arises as to how "long" and how "broad" this concept should be construed.   Not only may we stretch the anticipated addition to revenue over time, but we may also count in it many things which are often not so included.

There are two arguments for preferring a long-period formulation of marginal revenue product to a short-period one.   In the first place, "since the whole conception of marginal productivity depends upon the possibility of variation of industrial methods,"[10] it seems advisable to confine our attention to a period long enough for such variation to be practically feasible.   As Hicks has pointed out, the difference to total production made by the addition of a single man, when form and quantity of coöperating capital are supposed to be unchanged, will be much less than the true marginal product when capital is supposed variable in form and quantity.[11]   In the second place, business men often adopt wage policies

---

[8] The writer assumes that the elements of truth and falsity in the marginal productivity theory are sufficiently well-known, so that we may proceed without going into such details.

[9] Chamberlin, op. cit., p. 189.

[10] J. R. Hicks, *The Theory of Wages*, London, 1932, p. 20.

[11] Ibid., pp. 20–21.

which can only be considered rational if regard is had for their relation to the long-run marginal revenue product of the labor employed. Thus, if a business man pays high wages in the expectation that this will keep out a union, he is thinking in terms of the long-run effect of the high wage policy. If this policy involves payment to labor of a wage greater than its short-run marginal revenue product (though it need not always do so), it does not give a satisfactory explanation of the situation to say that the employer is thereby being "exploited." Rather it would seem more realistic to reason that the latter expects the long-run marginal revenue product of the non-union, as compared with the union, labor to be sufficient to compensate him for the payment of the high wages.

So much for the "length" of the marginal product. The next question is: how "broad" (how wide in scope) shall we make the definition? The marginal revenue product of labor, as we shall use the term, will consist of any additions to the firm's future revenues of any kind which additional units of labor may be expected to make. Ordinarily, the increments in revenue are conceived as arising out of increases in the production of the physical product. This conception must now be broadened to include additions to revenue which accrue from altering the demand for the product. For example, the United States Potters' Association was deterred from pressing for wage reductions in the years 1913–1914 by the realization that this might alienate the Democrats and possibly have unfavorable repercussions on the Administration's attitude toward the tariff duty on pottery.[12] Throughout the history of the agreement between the Union and the Employers' Association in the Pottery Industry, the latter were led to make concessions and pay higher wages than they otherwise would have, largely because they realized that payment of high wages was a valuable bargaining point when demanding further tariff protection from the Committees of the House and Senate.[13] Thus, part of the wage paid labor during this period was a selling cost, in that

---

[12] D. McCabe, *National Collective Bargaining in the Pottery Industry*, Baltimore, 1932, p. 370.

[13] Ibid., p. 371.

it was directed to influencing the demand for the product through preventing encroachment upon the pottery market by foreign sellers.

A similar situation exists when certain companies are pledged to a high wage policy. Insofar as this is based on the belief that high wages attract better workers or get more work out of laborers than lower wages, no problem is raised, so far as marginal productivity is concerned. But in one case which has come to the writer's attention, a company upon building a new plant in a new area immediately offered to pay higher wages than any of its rivals were paying, largely because of the publicity value of this policy. Part of the marginal productivity of the workers thus secured consists of the addition to net revenue they are capable of making, the demand curve being given, and another part is derived from altering and shifting the demand curve for the product itself. Thus the wage paid can be viewed as a composite of selling cost and production cost. As far as the individual entrepreneur is concerned, he is not likely to distinguish these two elements, although analytically they are distinguishable. Ideally, the entrepreneur should discover the optimum amount of wage selling-cost outlay (i.e., that part of the wage which is intended to alter the demand curve for the product) for every price of the product, and then choose the one of these combinations which yields the largest net profit. Actually, he will probably lump the two different kinds of marginal revenue contributions together; the wage set may not be the most advantageous possible with regard to production and selling cost, each taken separately, but whatever it is, the employer will hire labor at that wage until composite marginal revenue product equals the wage.

The marginal revenue product with which we shall be concerned is therefore a long-term one, whose time dimension and scope vary with the individual entrepreneur's calculations, which in turn are influenced by the peculiar conditions which present themselves in the sale of his product.

THE WAGE OF LABOR. The wage paid to labor has generally been assumed to take the form of a money outlay which goes into the worker's weekly pay envelope. Under modern conditions of employment, however, this view gives only an incomplete picture of the nature of labor cost. It seems more realistic, when dealing with problems of wage theory, to state it in terms of employer's total labor cost outlay per man hour,[14] or some similar unit. Wages are, of course, the most important consideration, but the costs of safety and sanitary devices, recreational facilities, pension and hospitalization plans must not be neglected.[15] Indeed, when national or regional wage agreements are in force in piece-rate industries, for example, the standard piece scale may remain largely unchanged for a considerable period, whereas there will be frequent adjustments from time to time in the "conditions" of work. Merely to look at the rigid prices of labor in such an industry during a period in which there had been a considerable increase in the marginal productivity of labor might yield the incorrect conclusion that labor was not sharing in the results of this increased productivity and so was being exploited. Actually, the equation may come about, imperfectly of course, through a gradual improvement in the conditions of work. Therefore, although this paper will continue to use the word "wage," this term should be interpreted to mean employer's outlay on both wages and services.

CLASSIFICATION OF EXPLOITATION. Cases of exploitation may for purposes of discussion be conveniently divided into two categories: non-deliberate and deliberate. Exploitation will be said to be non-deliberate if the discrepancy between marginal revenue product and wage is traceable to conditions which are beyond the employer's control—for example, the existence of discontinuities in the demand curve or of a less than perfectly elastic labor supply curve. Exploitation will be said to be deliberate, if the employer consciously attempts to pay labor less than its marginal revenue product, even

---

[14] This usage was suggested by the article by M. Bronfenbrenner, "The Economics of Collective Bargaining," *Quarterly Journal of Economics*, August, 1939, p. 535.

[15] Of course, the employer may not take full account of these latter costs in his day-to-day hiring, yet in the long-run, which we are considering, they must receive due consideration, if profits are to be maximized.

though conditions are such that he could pay the marginal revenue product if he so desired.   It is with regard to these cases that the greatest confusion prevails.   Our examination will show that the ordinary "sweated industry" argument, which falls in this category, is fallacious, because the cases in point do not usually constitute exploitation, though they may give rise to exploitation under certain circumstances.

Non-Deliberate Exploitation

RISING LABOR SUPPLY CURVE.   Perhaps the most commonly mentioned source of non-deliberate exploitation is the lack of perfect elasticity in the supply curve of labor.[16]   This condition may involve two possibilities: either the employer is faced by a perfectly inelastic supply curve for a considerable range (as, for example, might be the case of an employer having a closed shop where the union pursued a highly restrictive membership policy); or the supply curve is positively inclined, but is not perfectly inelastic (perhaps for skilled labor).   In the former instance, the employer may be compelled to stop adding workers short of the point of equality of marginal revenue product and wage merely because there are no more workers to be had.   In the latter, as Mrs. Robinson has demonstrated,[17] the entrepreneur equates marginal revenue product to the marginal cost of labor.   Since the latter curve is rising, the marginal cost of labor will be higher than the wage, and hence exploitation will exist.   From this argument it seems more likely that exploitation, as we have defined it, will

---

[16] Another source, often mentioned, may be employer ignorance as to the most profitable combination of factors.   However, detailed examination of this possibility would involve a consideration of the validity of the marginal productivity theory per se, and the writer has no intention of undertaking such an inquiry. For the purposes of this discussion, the assumption can be made that, despite the inexactness of the entrepreneur's measurements, the general principle of maximization of profits, one phase of which is equation of marginal revenue product to marginal labor cost, is nevertheless operative.

[17] This case has been so extensively treated that the writer has preferred only to take brief notice of it.   See Joan Robinson, *The Economics of Imperfect Competition*, London, 1933, Ch. 18.

exist where there is a scarcity of labor than where there is a large pool of unemployed labor. It seems certain, at least, that a high price for labor is no evidence of the absence of exploitation.

THE COST OF CHANGE. "Stability of prices," says Professor Burns, "may be sought because it is a simple policy and because the wisest policy is hard to discover."[18] To this we may add that it is often the least expensive policy as well. The fact that there is a cost of change involved in altering prices may give rise to exploitation. This cost may arise from two sources, (1) from the difficulty of ascertaining the best combination of the factors, and (2) from the expense necessary to inform the public of a change in the price of the product.

As an example of the first type, let us suppose that a firm has been maintaining a fairly stable price and then a small fall in wages occurs. In this event, the employer may feel that the trouble and expense of calculating what the new price should be would be so great that it would be cheaper to leave the price as it is. Here he maximizes his profits "by remaining ignorant." As a result, there may be no change in price at all, and marginal revenue and wage need not be equated. Labor would therefore be exploited. If the change in wages occurs in the opposite direction, however, then it is employers who will receive less than their full marginal revenue product. Thus the cost of change cuts both ways, and there is no reason to believe that it is a source of continuing exploitation of labor alone.

What, then, about our second type of cost of change—that which is attributable to increased selling costs accompanying a change in price? If wage rates fall, an employer still may not lower his price, if there is an added cost, such as advertising expense, connected with informing the buying public of the lowered price. The employer would weigh the lower wage against the increased revenue (if any) which would accrue if he lowers his price, and would subtract from the latter the cost of advertising for the additional output.[19] This would mean that the wage is often equated,

---

[18] A. R. Burns, *The Decline of Competition*, New York, 1936, p. 196.

[19] It may be helpful to cite an example at this point. Suppose a clothing house

not to the marginal revenue product, but to marginal revenue product minus the cost of advertising.[20]   Since this is, no doubt, a common case, being a normal consequence of monopolistic competition, we might prefer not to speak of this as exploitation.   Perhaps distribution theory should take account of this phenomenon by recognizing that labor often receives, not its marginal revenue product, but only the latter minus some deduction for selling costs. It might, for example, be argued that just as the recognition of the ubiquity of product differentiation and sloping demand curves has led us to consider as "normal" what formerly would have been considered "abnormal," on the basis of Pigovian standards, so now the acceptance of the prevalence of selling costs in a monopolistic economy compels a redefinition of exploitation to take account of this phenomenon.   Such a redefinition, however, does not seem to the writer to be called for.   The fact is that product differentiation and selling costs have quite different implications for the theory of exploitation.   The existence of sloping demand curves implies that labor (as well as other factors) can never[21]

---

conducts an extensive campaign to impress upon the public that "Hall's Suits sell for $9.99."   The suits are sold at this price for a year; then a small decline in wage costs occurs, which would make possible a reduction in price.   Assuming that there is no question of oligopoly to complicate the picture, the decision of the manufacturer to change his price will depend upon whether or not the additional revenue expected to be derived from the sales at the lower price will be great enough to reimburse not only the costs of producing the added output, but also the cost of an advertising campaign necessary to inform the public that the clothes no longer sell at the conventional price.   In other words, the various points on the demand curve which the economist draws with such ease may in reality be separated, the one from the other, by vigorous advertising campaigns.   The cost of change involved in altering such conventional prices is a factor encouraging continued price inertia.

[20] Of course, marginal revenue product might be defined as net of all expenses which are connected with the increment in employment, in which case the deduction for selling costs would already be included in the concept of marginal revenue product and hence marginal revenue product would be equated to the wage despite the existence of advertising expense.   The writer has preferred not to adopt this "net" definition, because it is less convenient for elucidating the significance of selling costs for exploitation theory.

[21] Except in unusual circumstances, such as that described on page 258 below.

receive remuneration equal to the value of its marginal physical product. But the prevalence of selling costs does not permit us to make a similar statement with regard to the marginal revenue product. Exploitation from this source may, indeed, be general, but it can never be directed at all factors at once, nor is it likely to result in substandard remuneration to any particular factor over a long period of time. In the example cited above, labor was exploited, since it received payment of a wage equal only to its marginal revenue product minus some deduction for the cost of advertising. On the other hand, when wages rise, the employer may not increase his price, if there is a cost connected with informing the public of the change in price policy, and so (unless the employer chooses to deteriorate his product) consumers benefit through the maintenance of the former price despite the higher level of costs. In this instance, the wage is equated to the marginal revenue product plus the cost of advertising, and hence the employer is exploited instead.[22]

Thus the cost of change arising out of selling cost, like the cost of change which arises out of the difficulty of ascertaining the most profitable combination of the factors, is just as likely to make possible the existence of a wage above the marginal revenue product as one below it. The employer is just as likely to be exploited for short periods of time as is labor. Therefore, redefinition of exploitation in terms of a marginal revenue product which

---

[22] Thus, where selling costs are significant, fluctuations of wages, within limits, will be absorbed by altering the size of the shares of the factors, rather than by changes in output. Graphically, this situation implies that the marginal revenue product of labor—in the sense of the value above or below which the wage cannot go without inducing a change in the number of men employed—is not a single line, but rather a band whose width is determined, among other things, by the extent of additional selling costs associated with each output. Thus another distinguishing characteristic of monopolistic as compared with pure competition is the breadth of the marginal revenue productivity curve in the former in contrast to the relative thinness of it in the latter. This is another factor contributing to the result that a wage increase in the individual firm in pure competition will lead to more unemployment than under conditions of monopolistic competition.

would take account of a deduction for selling costs seems neither necessary nor desirable, since any one factor receives the reduced remuneration only part of the time and the rest of the time is just as likely to have its remuneration increased by reason of the existence of selling costs. Indeed, the crucial difference between the exploitation attributable to product differentiation[23] and that due to selling costs is that in the former case all factors are exploited together, whereas in the latter case exploitation of one factor implies an above-normal payment to some other factor. It is evident that we cannot look to selling costs as a source of continuing exploitation of labor.

DISCONTINUOUS PRODUCT DEMAND CURVES. Another possible case in which labor will receive less than its marginal revenue product is the situation of a firm confronted with a discontinuous demand (and marginal revenue) curve for its product. Many articles are sold only at standard intervals such as $1.99, $2.59, and $2.99 (perhaps for dresses), or one cent, five cents, and ten cents (for candy bars).[24] The existence of these "steps," coupled with the utilization of "chunks" of factors, makes *possible* the existence of one type of exploitation. However, such discontinuity is neither a necessary nor a sufficient condition for the emergence of exploitation. That it is not necessary is obvious from the fact that exploitation of the monopsonistic type (p. 268 below) can exist even if the demand curve is of the usual smooth type. It is not a sufficient condition, because even if the demand and marginal revenue curves contain steps, nevertheless the marginal cost curve may be such as to cut the marginal revenue curve on a hori-

---

[23] Note that "the exploitation attributable to product differentiation" is exploitation with regard to Pigovian standards, i.e. payment of a wage which is less than the value of the marginal physical product.

[24] It is to be admitted that the definition of product in these cases is not easy. For example, does the employer see a demand for dresses in general, a different quality being sold at the three different price ranges? Or does he see the demand for a particular quality of dress at the different prices? The latter, the usual type of product demand curve, seems likely to be even more discontinuous in a case such as this than the former type. In either case, however, the demand curve will be discontinuous, and so exploitation is made possible.

zontal portion (as in Figure 1, below); and if we assume, for the sake of simplicity, that marginal cost contains only wages, then in this case there would be no exploitation, since the wage would be equated to the marginal revenue product.

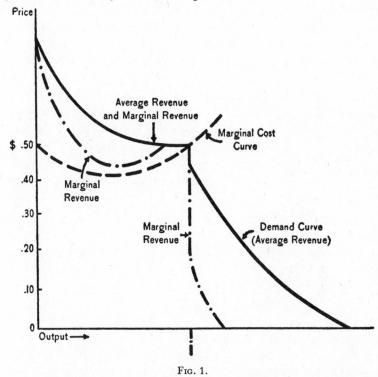

FIG. 1.

An extreme type of discontinuity of demand, characterized by a "kink"[25] at the prevailing price, is liable to exist under oligopoly. With a demand curve of this sort, the marginal revenue curve will be discontinuous, and so a rise in wage rates, and hence in marginal costs, will not affect output and employment, if it changes the position of the marginal cost curve within this discontinuous range.[26] The only effect that it may have is to cause

[25] P. M. Sweezy, "Demand under Conditions of Oligopoly," *Journal of Political Economy*, August 1939, p. 569.

[26] Ibid., p. 570.

more intensive non-price competition, such as advertising, by the firms in order to increase their sales and compensate for the rise in costs.

This condition would seem to be favorable to a discrepancy between wage and marginal revenue product, but it need not be. In fact, it is possible not only that the wage should equal the marginal revenue product, but also that it should equal the value of the marginal physical product, in which case not even exploitation in the Pigovian meaning of the word would exist!

In Figure 1, an extreme case of this oligopolistic condition is illustrated. To show, by means of this diagram, how oligopoly may completely eliminate exploitation *of any kind*, it is only necessary to make four assumptions: (1) the demand curve for the product has a horizontal portion; (2) wage costs are assumed to be all of marginal costs; (3) the marginal cost curve[27] is such that it cuts the demand curve in the horizontal range[28]; (4) the supply of labor over the relevant range is perfectly elastic. (This might easily be the case in depression years, at least within limits, and it is precisely in such times, when business men are particularly fearful of cut-throat price-cutting, that a corner is likely to be found in the demand curve.)

Given these conditions, the oligopolist acts no differently from a pure competitor. A moderate rise in marginal costs will cause a decline in output with no immediate rise in the price charged by the seller. Furthermore, with the given output as pictured above, since marginal revenue equals average revenue at a price of fifty cents, marginal unit wage cost will equal both marginal revenue and price. Therefore, labor will receive not only its marginal revenue product, but also the value of its marginal physical product (the price per unit of the commodity). Here, then, where we

---

[27] The marginal cost curve here rises, not because of a rising labor supply curve (this is ruled out by assumption), but because of the effect of diminishing returns.

[28] If the demand curve has a "kink," but does not become horizontal at any point, then average revenue and marginal revenue must always diverge, and hence the following analysis will not hold.

should least expect it, we find the possibility that the conditions of pure competition may be reproduced.

But of far more theoretical interest and practical importance are those cases in which the marginal cost curve is disturbed from its equilibrium position and cuts the marginal revenue curve on a discontinuous portion. This would be the case in the diagram above, if a fall in wage rates lowered the marginal cost curve so that it no longer cut at the corner but rather on a vertical part of the marginal revenue curve. Or if the discontinuity is not so severe, but more in the nature of a "hump," there will be some range, nevertheless, in the marginal revenue curve which will be discontinuous, and if the marginal cost curve comes to rest in this range, the marginal revenue product and wage will not be equal.

Such discontinuity of demand, and concomitantly such a possibility of an inequality between marginal revenue product and wage, is particularly likely in industries in which prices have been stabilized. The United States Steel Company, for example, announced and maintained a price of twenty-eight dollars a ton for steel rails for one hundred and eighty months.[29] During this period of fifteen years, it is certain that wage rates did not stay constant, yet changing cost relations had no effect upon price. This would seem to indicate that in many of such cases production is not carried to the point where short-run marginal costs equal short-run marginal revenue,[30] and that the wage is not equated to the marginal revenue product.[31] If the rigid price is maintained,

---

[29] Burns, op. cit., p. 205.

[30] P. H. Douglas, "The Effect of Wage Increases upon Employment," *American Economic Review*, Supplement, March, 1939, p. 153.

[31] However, the mere fact that wages change, while prices do not, is no evidence of the existence of exploitation; for equality of wage and marginal revenue product can be maintained with a changed wage rate and an unchanged price through (1) varying the proportions of the factors of production and/or (2) varying the volume of output. For example, if wages rise, but the fixed price is maintained, the equality between marginal revenue product and wage may be reëstablished by bringing old machines into use and otherwise substituting capital for labor. Some such substitution is possible, even in the short-run. Secondly, the firm may refuse to fill all orders immediately at the fixed price and attempt

when wages rise, and conditions of demand remain relatively unchanged, the tendency will be for the employer to be "exploited," for he will be paying labor more than its short-run marginal revenue product. True, he could curtail output and reduce his labor force; but since his price has not changed, such a policy might mean disappointing some of his customers. Consideration of customer goodwill, therefore, may be an important factor deterring him from altering his output. On the other hand, if wages fall, there will be little incentive to hire additional men at the lower wage, so long as the same price is maintained, and thus sales are limited to the given volume, and as a result labor will be exploited, i.e. it will receive less than its marginal revenue product.

Now stability of price under oligopoly may be of different kinds and arise for various reasons. For analytical purposes we may distinguish two different types of stability—the one characteristic of what we shall call "immature oligopoly," and the other typical of what we shall term "mature oligopoly." These are pure concepts and their direct practical applicability may be limited; oligopoly, in reality, is a combination in varying proportions of the two extremes. The proposed classification will, however, be found helpful in elucidating two types of price stability which have somewhat different implications for the theory of exploitation.

(1) "Immature oligopoly" will be said to prevail in situations where the oligopolist is still free to select the price which he intends to maintain thereafter.

(2) "Mature oligopoly" will be said to prevail in situations where the oligopolist finds the price more or less given to him by the convention of the competitive relationships which have grown up in the market.

The reasons for the pursuance of a policy of price stabilization

---

to postpone deliveries and spread commitments over time. Both of these lines of action would reëstablish equality through a displacement of labor, despite the continued maintenance of the fixed price. But both are definitely restricted in scope. Assuming a relatively uniform demand at the stable price, not much leeway is left either to vary output or the combination of the factors as cost-price relations change.

will differ in the two cases.   In both situations a kink is likely to occur in the demand curve, but the discontinuity in the former type will be due primarily to the oligopolist's expectations of consumer reaction to changes in price, whereas in the latter it will be attributable, in the main, to the fear of retaliation by competitors. The latter type of anticipation is likely to induce an expectation on the part of the oligopolist that demand is extremely inelastic below, and very elastic above, the prevailing price, so that the discontinuity will be in the nature of a sharp corner in the demand curve.   In the former case, however, the discontinuity will not be so severe and can more aptly be described as a "hump" or a smooth "kink."

The immature oligopolist may feel that maintenance of a fixed price "stabilizes consumer demand" by avoiding sudden shifts in buying occasioned by the expectation of a change in prices.   He may be convinced that a reduction in price would create in the minds of the buyers a notion of what is a fair price, which later might become an obstacle to attempts to raise the price.   His decision to maintain a stable price may be conditioned by the use of long-term contracts in the industry, or it may simply be the consequence of his belief that it is the policy least likely to provoke opposition from customers or regulatory agencies.   When these are the dominant motives at work, prices come to be stabilized for periods varying from a season to a few years, but generally only for moderate intervals of time.

In mature oligopoly, however, rigid prices are maintained over much longer periods.   Here the primary motive is to maintain the status quo, to prevent fluctuations in price which might unduly strain the delicate relationships existing between the producers in the industry.   Companies in a competitive position such as the United States Steel Corporation, for example, justify their maintenance of price by the argument that a price cut[32] would not add one iota to their total revenue—in economic terms, the marginal revenue of the increased output would be zero or negative.   Any

---

[32] An open price cut.   Often secret price cuts and rebates will be advantageous in a situation such as this.

short-run advantage achieved through a price-cut would soon be offset by the action of other competitors following suit. Mature oligopoly will frequently be associated with leader-follower relationships among the oligopolists, with strong trade associations, and particularly with a history of past losses occasioned by disastrous price wars. The motives enumerated in connection with immature oligopoly will be present here also, just as fear of price-cutting will, in actuality, exert some influence in the choice of policy in our first type; but it does seem that a distinction is possible—which has considerable importance—on the basis of the dominant motive inducing the practice of price stabilization in the two cases.[33] In mature oligopoly, the principal concern of the producers is to prevent competitive price-cutting from nibbling away

---

[33] Examples of immature and mature oligopoly, as strictly defined in this paper, cannot be found in the real world, because actual oligopolistic situations combine the two types in varying proportions. The steel industry, however, may be cited as an approximation to a condition of mature oligopoly as herein envisaged. Immature oligopoly attracts less attention, and hence examples of it are more difficult to find. A hypothetical example would be that of several producers manufacturing the same article, but who in the course of the growth of the industry have tended to become associated with different distribution outlets. Thus one plant may be equipped to produce large orders for chain stores, while another is equipped to turn out small orders (of the same product) intended for small retailers, etc. The point is that there would be some range within which the respective oligopolists could vary their own prices without being in fear that this would evoke retaliation by others in the industry, yet the demand curve of the producer might have a kink for other reasons and price stabilization might be preferred nonetheless.

The distinction between immature and mature oligopoly, as herein defined, does not turn upon the degree of differentiation of the product, although it is true that the more highly differentiated the product, the less the producer need fear price retaliation by his competitors, and hence the more the situation will tend to correspond to what has been called immature oligopoly. The real distinction lies in the fact that the mature oligopolist is rival-conscious, whereas the immature oligopolist is less so, and this difference has an important bearing upon the kind of price stability which results in the two cases. It should be noted that "oligopoly" is used in this paper in the general sense of "a few sellers," rather than in the more restricted sense (to be found in some of the literature) of "sellers conscious of their rivals' reactions."

at the vulnerable item of fixed cost outlay.   Now it seems probable that in such cases there will be a kink, not only in the short-run conventional demand curve, but in the long-run curve as well.   This does not seem to be as likely in the case of immature oligopoly.[34]

In both instances of price stability the oligopolist will hire that quantity of labor at the prevailing wage which is needed to

---

[34] The long-run demand curve may be defined for our purpose as the geometrical representation of the schedule of quantities which the entrepreneur expects customers to take in the long-run at various prices, the respective outputs being capable of being produced by plants of varying size.   The long-run demand curve of the immature oligopolist will tend to be more continuous than the short-run curve, because in the longer period many of the factors responsible for the inelastic stretch below, and the elastic stretch above, the established price in the short-period curve will be absent.   For example, the fact that in the long run long-term contracts can be renewed on different terms, and that consumers will have an opportunity to obtain auxiliary equipment which may be necessary in order to utilize the product, will tend to make the long-run curve more continuous.   Other similar considerations might be listed.   Although the immature oligopolist (like the average business man) prefers to avoid frequent fluctuations in his price in response to short-run changes in costs, in the long-run he is likely to adapt the price of his product to persistent cost tendencies.

On the other hand, it seems probable that the long-run demand curve of the mature oligopolist will contain a sharp kink at the prevailing price.   The rival-conscious producer will fear that, in the long-run, an increase in price will result in a shift in customers not only to competitors who maintain the old price but also to new firms who enter the industry, mistaking the price increase as a sign of high profits to be had.   This will tend to make the curve more elastic above the given price.   The mature oligopolist may expect a more elastic response to a price cut in the long-run, for some of the same reasons as the immature oligopolist; but the increased elasticity flowing from this source will probably not be sufficiently strong to make much impression on the inelasticity which arises out of the expectation of retaliatory price cuts by rivals.   And this expectation will be held, even in regard to the effects of long-run price movements, since excess capacity—and with it vulnerability to price-cutting—tends to become a long-run condition in mature oligopolistic industries.   The demand curve, then, though it may be less inelastic below, will be more elastic above the established price, and hence a sharp change in slope will occur in the long-run demand curve of the mature oligopolist.   All that the analysis to follow requires is that there be a corner in the long-run demand curve sufficient to produce a discontinuous marginal revenue curve, and this possibility seems not unlikely.

produce the output which he expects to sell at the stable price. But while the immature oligopolist is free (within limits) to select his prospective output, and hence will choose one for which the marginal revenue product of labor is equated to the wage, since this is a criterion of a profitable output, the mature oligopolist must accept the price and output which is more or less indicated by the customary market relationships between producers, and which apart from these relationships would *not* be the most profitable output at the prevailing wage level. Thus we see immediately that the possibility of a discrepancy existing between marginal revenue product and wage is much greater in conditions of mature, than in immature, oligopoly.

Let us assume, however, in order to facilitate further inquiry into the problem, that, in both cases, price and output originally are such that marginal revenue product and wage are in equilibrium. Then, if the quantity demanded at the fixed price increases during the period of price stabilization, the oligopolist in both cases merely hires more labor to produce a larger output at the rigid price, thus preserving equilibrium between marginal revenue product and wage. The real problem is raised by changes in wage costs during the period in which the rigid price policy is pursued. It is in this connection that our distinction between price stabilization in immature oligopoly and in mature oligopoly takes on significance. In both cases, a fall in wage costs[35] concurrent with the maintenance of price will result in exploitation; but the exploitation which results has quite different implications for our theory.

Under conditions of immature oligopoly, the entrepreneur would have made a different original adjustment of output and employment, if he had known beforehand that a lower level of wage costs was to prevail. The exploitation which occurs is therefore attributable to a failure of expectations to materialize, since the entrepreneur had assumed that the level of costs existing at the time of his fixing of price would continue into the future. Dis-

---

[35] Marginal wage cost (marginal with respect to output, rather than with respect to employment) may fall, either because of increasing productivity per worker or because of a decline in wage rates.

equilibrium arising out of this source is essentially a consequence of the dynamic element in economic life, and hence pervades the whole economy, for expectations are rarely fulfilled anywhere. Exploitation which arises under conditions of immature oligopoly, therefore, differs in degree rather than in kind from that exploitation which arises similarly in parts of the economy where prices are not rigid.   Moreover, since the long-run demand curve is not likely to be discontinuous under immature oligopoly, in the long-run, the price will be lowered to conform to the lower level of costs, output will be increased (in an enlarged plant, perhaps), and equality will tend to be reëstablished between marginal revenue product and wage.[36]   Hence, even if it is argued that because of increasing productivity marginal wage cost will, on the average, tend to fall more than rise relative to the stable price, the consequent exploitation is no different in kind than that which normally occurs elsewhere in a dynamic system.   Since immature oligopoly does not seriously obstruct the action of long-run equilibrating forces, it cannot be a source of continuing exploitation of labor.

But where oligopoly is mature, the situation is somewhat different.   In this case, even if the oligopolist had known that labor cost in his firm would be lower (or higher) in the future, his decision as to choice of price would not have been altered, since his freedom of action in this matter is considerably restricted (and in the pure case entirely absent), due to the delicate relationship which has developed in the past between the prices charged by the competing oligopolists.   The proximate cause of the exploitation in this instance, as in the former, is a dynamic change—a change in wage costs—but it cannot be said that the exploitation here is fundamentally attributable to a failure of expectations to materialize. Even if the oligopolist had correctly anticipated a fall in wage rates, he might not have been able to do anything about it; for within limits his employment of labor is dictated not so much by the pre-

---

[36] Furthermore, there is much more chance that a substantial change in costs will, itself, induce a change in short-run price in conditions of immature oligopoly, than is true where mature oligopoly occurs, particularly if the change in wages occurs only in one firm.

vailing level of wages as by the quantity of product demanded at the conventional or fixed price indicated by market relationships. The exploitation is therefore analytically of a different kind.

Furthermore, exploitation will tend to persist much longer under conditions of mature oligopoly than under immature oligopoly. For in the case of mature oligopoly, as we have seen, the long-run demand curve also will be discontinuous, and hence maintenance of price becomes desirable as a long-run policy. Despite the fall in wage costs, the mature oligopolist will not be induced to build a larger plant, since the mere fact that his costs have fallen does not make it possible for him to sell a larger output, as long as the fixed price is maintained. He will, however, if he expects the lower level of wage costs to persist, build or alter his plant in such a manner as to make it possible to utilize more labor and less machinery to produce the *same* output at the *same* price.[37] Thus the forces tending to equilibrium are not entirely absent, but they work in a much more restricted fashion under conditions of mature oligopoly than they do otherwise. For ordinarily a fall in wages (though not necessarily a general change) will be followed not only by some substitution of labor for capital, but also by an increase in output from the existing plant, or from a larger plant, or from new firms (attracted by the profits which may temporarily accrue as a result of the fall in costs). In the situation which we are analyzing, however, only the first process—the recombination of the factors—is likely to be of any consequence.[38] Of course, if the

---

[37] This implies that even if the long-run product demand curve has a corner such that the marginal revenue curve is discontinuous (can be drawn vertically) for a certain range, nevertheless it is still possible that the marginal productivity curve of labor (the demand curve for labor) will not be *perfectly* inelastic for this same range. A fall in the wage rate which would lead to no increase in employment due to demand conditions (i.e. marginal revenue is perfectly inelastic over the relevant stretch) may lead to an increase in employment due to technical conditions, through a recombination of the proportions of the factors. But just as the "deepening" of capital is to some extent a function of the "widening" of capital (as Hawtrey has pointed out), similarly, in our problem, the extent to which labor can be substituted for machinery will be limited by the fact that both output and scale of plant are supposed unchanged.

[38] Entrance of new firms cannot be depended upon as an effective equilibrating

wage change is of sufficient magnitude, it may induce all oligopolists together to change their prices, in which case the other
equilibrating tendencies are able to come into play; but there will
be a considerable range of fluctuation in which this will not be so
and in which, as a consequence, changes of wage cost will give
rise to divergences between marginal revenue product and wage
which will persist for long periods.   This would seem particularly
likely if the wage change occurs irregularly throughout the industry
or only in a single firm.

Thus, in mature, as contrasted with immature oligopoly, long-
run equilibrating forces are so restricted in their action that it
seems more realistic to admit that, on the whole, they are largely
ineffective.   As a consequence, the possibility emerges of long-run
exploitation of labor.   This conclusion is based on the premise that
wage cost will ordinarily be below the long-run marginal revenue
product of labor more than it will be above, because, as was
pointed out above, changes in productivity tend to influence wage
cost mainly in one direction.   Now insofar as unions constitute an
agency whose influence is in the direction of raising wages above
the marginal revenue product of labor, they tend to offset this
downward bias of wage cost and to reëstablish a certain *average*
equilibrium.   If wages are as likely to be above as below the marginal revenue product, then the oligopolist is as likely to be exploited

---

factor in industries in which fixed capital investment is high and excess capacity
is large—which are precisely the conditions typical of mature oligopoly.

However, change in output from the existing plant will be operative to
some extent.   When wages fall, the mature oligopolist will not be induced to
increase output at the stable price, since this is impossible as long as demand
remains unchanged.   But when wages rise, there will be some tendency to curtail
output at the fixed price (by postponing deliveries, etc.), although this adjustment
will necessarily be limited in scope, as long as the same volume of orders continues
at the fixed price.   However, a substantial wage increase is more likely to induce
a change in output at the given price than is a fall in wages, and so this will be a
factor contributing to the result that mature oligopoly is more likely to cause
exploitation of labor than of employers.   The asymmetry of the process of adjustment is attributable to the fact that if wages fall and demand remains constant,
reëstablishment of equality between marginal revenue product and wage necessi-
tates a change in price policy, whereas if wages rise, this is not so.

for short periods of time as is labor. Were this the case, economists might be consoled in their search for equilibrium by the comforting thought that there is at least some tendency for the long-run average price of labor and the long-run marginal revenue product of labor to approximate each other, even in conditions of mature oligopoly. But until unions become more strongly entrenched than they are now, movements of wage cost will be biased in a downward direction with respect to the stable price, and hence rigidity of price under conditions of mature oligopoly, by obstructing long-run forces,[39] will give rise to exploitation of labor. It is, however, exploitation of the non-deliberate type. We shall see shortly that oligopoly, *in connection with other conditions*, can give rise to deliberate exploitation. But the exploitation which follows from mature oligopoly, per se, is better classified as of the non-deliberate variety.

DELIBERATE EXPLOITATION

We turn now to those cases of exploitation which may be termed deliberate. Here would be included the case of monopsonistic discrimination in the hiring of labor.[40] Discrimination may be of two kinds: either payment of the same wage to men of different efficiency, or payment at different rates to men of the same efficiency, as would occur if a separate bargain could be made with each man, assuming that the men differed in the minimum wage they were prepared to accept.

In the first case, the marginal revenue product of the least efficient man will be equal to the uniform wage, and so he is not exploited, although all men of higher efficiency are. Exploitation

---

[39] It might be argued that since the forces are only obstructed, and not entirely restricted, the tendency to equilibrium becomes a matter of degree. The writer maintains, however, that at some point differences in degree pass over into differences in kind, and that it gives a much more realistic picture to say that labor working for the United States Steel Company during the fifteen-year period of stable prices was probably exploited, than to deny this because *some* tendency was at work to restore equilibrium between marginal revenue product and wage.

[40] The treatment accorded this must be brief because of dictates of space For a complete discussion, see Robinson, op. cit., pp. 300 et seq.

could only be removed if each grade of labor were paid in proportion to its efficiency, so that the wage of each efficiency group equaled its marginal revenue product. In the second case, wherein different wages are paid to men of equal efficiency, the wages of the most expensive man will be equal to the marginal productivity of the group. Here, again, all but the last man are exploited, but exploitation can be removed merely by imposing a uniform minimum wage equal to the wage paid for the most expensive man.

This discrepancy between marginal revenue product and wage is not, however, the kind that is usually thought of by labor economists when they speak of exploitation. Rather, the argument usually runs in terms of the "sweated industry." In these industries, the greedy employer is pictured as having extracted an extra profit by working his employees long hours at wages far below their contribution to the product. The reasoning involved in reaching this misleading conclusion goes something like this:

The same kind of labor ought to receive equal remuneration for its work in all parts of the economy. Therefore, if wages are sub-standard in certain industries, in the sense that they are lower than those that prevail on the average for a particular type of labor, then, it is argued, the laborers in these industries must be receiving less than their marginal contributions to the product.

This conclusion does not follow from the premises, nor are the premises applicable to an economy in which rigidities of various kinds are not the exception but the rule. The marginal contribution of a worker in a monopolistic economy is associated with the fortunes of the individual firm in which he is employed; this gives rise to differences in the rate of pay for the same kind of labor which could only be eliminated if labor were perfectly mobile. That labor is not perfectly mobile is evident, and hence there is no difficulty in accounting for the co-existence of different wage levels for the same kind of labor. It should be noted, however, that the fact that immobility of labor makes it possible for employers to secure labor at a lower price than would prevail in a fluid labor market does not, at the same time, imply that the underpaid labor is being exploited. The existence of different levels of pay for the same kind of labor is quite consistent with payment to labor in all its employments of its full marginal revenue product.

If wages are low in certain industries, they are low, in the majority of cases, not because the employer is exploiting the workers, but because the marginal productivity of the workers themselves is low. The mistaken views advanced in connection with the "sweated industry" argument rest upon an apparent belief that the employer *wants* to pay less than the marginal revenue product, because it is profitable to do so. This is not so. In fact, it can easily be shown that if the employer has succeeded in forcing down the wage rate, it is in his interest to hire workers at that rate until the wage equals the marginal revenue product of labor. If, for example, we assume that labor is the only variable cost, then marginal cost will consist entirely of wages. Under imperfect competition the entrepreneur attains his maximum profit at the point where marginal cost equals marginal revenue; according to our assumptions, this will also be the point where the wage is equated to the marginal revenue product.

An employer may want to pay his employees a lower wage in order to be able to lower costs sufficiently to add more workers and so to increase output. *For a time* there may be an inequality between the reduced wage and the marginal revenue product, but this is only a transitional state. When production is increased at the lower level of costs, the marginal revenue product will again be equated to the wage paid. The end in view, the goal toward which the employer directs his efforts, is this equilibration, because only this implies maximum profits.

What is more, the motivation is there, whether there is competition among employers or not.[41] This basic fact is often overlooked by economists. Professor Douglas, for example, distinguishes that exploitation which may occur due to the restricted competition for labor[42] and that which is due to the competitive raising of wages.[43]

---

[41] Except, of course, if the monopsonistic buying of labor leads to a rising supply curve for labor, which it need not, however, always do.

[42] P. Douglas, "Wage Theory and Wage Policy," *International Labor Review*, March 1939, p. 340.

[43] Ibid., p. 344.

By the latter he means the case of rising marginal wage cost, which we have already discussed. In the former category, Douglas includes the concerted action of business men to set a wage which is low. This action, however, need not give rise to exploitation,[44] although Douglas assumes that it will. Professor Daugherty reasons in a similar fashion, maintaining that there is no reason to believe that "employers will pay what they can pay."[45] They will pay workers their full marginal value products "only if the competition among employers for labor is as keen as the competition among wage-earners for work."[46]

Now it is quite true that if employers by collective action can set a wage rate without outside interference, they are likely to set it low.[47] But having set the wage, there is, with few exceptions, no reason why they should cease hiring men at this wage until the addition to total revenue added by another laborer is just equal to the wage paid. Therefore, *competition among employers is not needed to assure that labor gets its marginal revenue product*, nor is it necessary that labor be able to migrate away from the particular locality. All that is necessary is that there be a sufficient pool of labor so that increasing amounts of labor can be procured at the same price and that employers pursue a rational course dictated by maximizing profit.

---

[44] That is, not exploitation as we have defined it. The workers will be exploited in terms of the optimum distribution of resources. Likewise, moral and physical degradation may result as a consequence of the payment of sub-standard wages. Yet as long as the wage is equated to the marginal revenue product, the economist is compelled to deny the existence of exploitation, regardless of how low the employer forces down wage rates. It is in dealing with such situations that one comes to realize how inadequately the term exploitation, as herein defined, covers the range of problems which the word has come to connote.

[45] C. Daugherty, *Labor Problems in American Industry*, rev. ed. 1938, p. 172.

[46] Ibid., p. 172.

[47] Even this, however, is a debatable issue, for experience shows that there is no necessary positive relation between the degree of competition among employers and the wage paid. The "sweated" industries are those very industries where competition among employers is often the greatest, yet wages nevertheless are low. Perhaps if there were more "cooperation" among the firms, prices and production might be stabilized and higher wages paid.

If, in this case in which the employer (individually or in combination with other employers) is able to set a low wage, exploitation does occur, then this phenomenon cannot be explained by looking at the conditions of mobility of labor alone, or by observing the relations of the various employers to one another in the buying market. These factors are crucial in determining *the level at which the wage will be set;* they are only incidentally important in the creation of a situation making deliberate exploitation of labor possible. The real clue to the cause of deliberate exploitation lies in *the conditions of sale of the product.*

For *deliberate* exploitation to exist, these requirements must be met:

(1) There must be a body of labor such that the employer can secure the same amount of labor at a lower price as at a higher price. This means that the supply curve of labor over the relevant range must be perfectly inelastic;

(2) The employer must be able to set the wage;

(3) The conditions of sale of the product must be such that there is a kink in the demand curve at the prevailing price.

No one of these requisites, by itself, is sufficient for the existence of deliberate exploitation, nor does any combination of any two guarantee that deliberate exploitation will exist. If all three are present, however, and the employer seeks to maximize his profits, it will be in his interests to pay less than the marginal revenue product.[48]

---

[48] According to our definition, deliberate exploitation exists when the employer consciously attempts to pay labor less than its marginal revenue product, despite the fact that conditions are such that he could profitably pay the marginal revenue product if he so desired. If, however, the labor supply curve has an elasticity greater than zero and less than infinity, the employer could *not* profitably pay a wage equal to the marginal revenue product of labor, for, in these circumstances, the marginal cost of labor will be above the wage, and since the employer equates the marginal revenue product and the marginal cost of labor, labor will be exploited, even if the employer does not attempt to force down the wage. On the other hand, when the supply of labor is perfectly inelastic over a given range, the employer *could* pay a wage equal to the marginal revenue product without incurring losses, but there is no reason to believe that he will, since he can obtain the

To illustrate this situation, it is necessary to find an answer to this question: when would an employer force down wages and *not* continue to hire men at the lower wage until the marginal revenue product was reduced to equality with the wage rate? The answer is to be found in point (3) above: when the increased output could only be sold at a price so low that the marginal revenue for the additional sales would be less than the marginal wage cost (assuming for simplicity that wages are all of marginal costs). This situation of inelasticity of demand below the prevailing price may be found, as was pointed out above, in oligopolistic industries where price maintenance is practiced. It may also be found—and here is the grain of truth in the popular writing on the subject—in "sweated" oligopolistic industries. It seems likely, both where conditions are highly competitive and price changes frequent and also where conditions are non-competitive and prices rigid, that a kink in the demand curve will be common.[49]

---

labor at any price (within limits). This does not mean, however, that a perfectly inelastic labor supply curve is a sufficient condition for the existence of exploitation, for if the employer can reduce his costs by hiring labor at a lower wage, he will ordinarily also reduce the price of his product. The consequent increase in quantity demanded will increase the employer's demand for labor, while the rise in output will reduce the marginal revenue product of labor, so that a movement will be set up which will tend to restore equality between marginal revenue product and wage. Thus, even if the supply of labor is perfectly inelastic (condition 1) and the employer is able to set the wage (condition 2), continuing exploitation of labor will not prevail. It will be only in the nature of a temporary phenomenon, existing during the period of transition from one level of output to another. The kink in the demand curve (condition 3), by removing the incentive to lower prices as wage costs are reduced, prevents this latter adjustment from taking place, and so permits the inequality between wage and marginal revenue product to persist.

[49] Although the "sweated industries" are highly competitive in terms of price changes, they fit in the category of "oligopoly," rather than in that of pure or monopolistic competition, for numbers are ordinarily few and the sellers are aware of their indirect influence on price. The fact that prices change often in the "sweated" oligopolistic industries but infrequently in mature oligopolistic industries (in both of which the seller is conscious of his rivals' reactions) may possibly be attributed to the greater strength of feelings of *esprit de corps* in the latter and the greater ease of entry and greater frequency of fly-by-night competitors and

Suppose that under conditions such as these the entrepreneur is producing at a point where the marginal revenue is equal to marginal cost, and where the wage is equated to the marginal revenue product of labor. If, now, he is able to reduce costs, he will have no incentive to lower his price and increase output, for because of the extreme inelasticity of demand for a considerable range below the prevailing price, he would not increase his total revenue by a price cut, but would instead decrease it by starting a price war. In a situation such as this, if the employer is able to set the wage at will, and if the supply curve of labor is perfectly inelastic over the relevant range, he will increase his profits at the expense of his workers, yet will not be induced to hire more men at that wage. Therefore, deliberate exploitation will exist. Here, in every sense of the word, the workers would be exploited by their employer.

The Importance of Exploitation

Having reviewed the conditions under which exploitation may exist, we are now prepared to inquire how important these instances actually are in the business world. The three most important kinds of exploitation would seem to be (1) the deliberate type just discussed, (2) the non-deliberate type caused by a rising labor supply curve (of less than infinite and more than zero elasticity), and (3) the non-deliberate type attributable to stability of price under mature oligopoly.

Conditions making possible the first may be present, as has been mentioned, in both the competitive oligopolistic industries and in those oligopolistic industries where price competition is largely absent.[50] In the former, the so-called "sweated" trades, the workers are generally not so well organized, so that the employer is better able to force wage rates down. But in these same trades prices change frequently, and this would seem to imply that even

---

wild-cat firms in the former. A fear of price wars will probably be found in both kinds of industries.

[50] Professor Fritz Machlup has suggested that we may distinguish between "oligopolies in fight" and "oligopolies in truce."

if the wages are forced down low, the employer frequently makes changes in output and so is likely to equate labor's marginal revenue product and wage.   Furthermore, since entry is relatively easy in these industries, abnormal profits obtained from exploitation of labor would soon attract new firms into the industry, and this would tend to remove the discrepancy between marginal revenue product and wage.   Thus exploitation is possible, but not very probable, in the "sweated" industries.   The same holds true for oligopolistic industries characterized by price rigidity.   Here there may exist one of the conditions necessary for the practice of exploitation—the lack of incentive on the part of the entrepreneur to lower his price.   But the other necessary factors—the ability of the employer to lower wage rates and still get the same amount of labor—may generally be expected to be absent; for in these semi-monopolistic industries unions are likely to be well-entrenched[51] and will not allow wages to be lowered at the will of the employer. The latter often must accept the wage rate as a datum and adjust output to it.   In so doing, he will attempt to equate marginal revenue product and wage.   Thus exploitation of this type is probably not very common.

Conditions of a supply curve of labor of some elasticity short of infinity are, on the other hand, probably characteristic of a large part of American industry.   The ubiquity of this phenomenon is, however, no reason for believing that exploitation is equally widespread.   A rising supply curve for labor is most typical of skilled wage groups, but these are the very ones that are most likely to be highly unionized.   When a trade union sets a minimum wage rate for work of a particular kind, it in effect makes the supply curve for labor perfectly elastic, thus eradicating any exploitation of this kind.[52]   Therefore, a rising supply curve for labor, although making exploitation possible, does in a sense produce its

---

[51] This is not to say that every oligopolistic industry is strongly unionized.

[52] No unemployment need occur, despite the rise in wages.   In fact, if the union sets the wage at the level at which the former average cost curve of labor cuts the demand curve for labor, both employment and wage will be higher than formerly, if the firm continues in business.   See Douglas, op. cit., p. 347.

own cure—unionism. Thus, again, it would seem that the existence of exploitation is not a common phenomenon, at least as far as this source is concerned.

There remains the third possible source of exploitation—stability of price under mature oligopoly. We have seen that the latter, though it creates a condition making possible a continuing inequality between marginal revenue product and wage, can give rise to exploitation of labor, in particular, only by reason of the tenuous circumstance that marginal unit wage cost tends to be below the long-run marginal revenue product of labor more than above. But as unions grow in strength and in their ability to obtain wage increases in proportion to increases in productivity, this type of exploitation also will tend to disappear.[53]

We are thus led to the interesting conclusion that unions are an important economic institution tending to restore and maintain equality between marginal revenue product and wage. Proponents of unionism are therefore right when they argue that "labor must organize to prevent its exploitation by employers," although these advocates have not used the word exploitation in its precise scientific sense, or been aware of the sophisticated economic analysis upon which a justification of their thesis can be based.

Exploitation, as it exists in the actual economic system, would seem to be scattered throughout the economy, arising in different sectors out of different sources. Insofar as it is general, it must be attributed either to employer ignorance, to the ubiquity of monopolistic elements, or to the dynamic factor in economic life. It does not seem likely that it is so confined to any special sector of industry that this can be referred to as a problem area. If exploitation is

---

[53] Unions are probably strong enough (1) to be an effective agent preventing the arbitrary lowering of wages which is a prelude to deliberate exploitation, and (2) to be able to set wages in many industries so that the supply curve of labor, within limits, becomes perfectly elastic, thus "curing" nondeliberate exploitation caused by a rising labor supply curve. But it will take time before they reach a position so dominant that they are able constantly to press on the share in the product of the employer, himself, so that nondeliberate exploitation occurring in mature oligopolistic industries can be effectively combated.

more common in certain industries, they are probably not the "sweated" industries, but rather the oligopolistic non-competitive ones, since here we have the possibility of exploitation of both the deliberate and the non-deliberate kinds.   Therefore, a minimum wage requirement set at a high rate in these industries is less likely to cause unemployment to ensue than a lower minimum applied to the "sweated" trades.   If a minimum wage does not cause unemployment in the "sweated" industries, this phenomenon is evidence, not of the prior existence of a discrepancy between marginal revenue product and wage, but more likely of the increased efficiency of the employers and workers which was brought about by the rise in wage rates.   If a minimum wage is set in an oligopolistic firm, either by the government or by trade union agency, and if the demand curve for the firm is such that it has a kink at the prevailing price, then if the wage set coincides with the horizontal portion of the demand curve, the conditions of pure competition will be reproduced.   Thus exploitation of the Pigovian type may be lessened, either by making competition more "pure," so that the gap between average revenue and marginal revenue is reduced, or by making competition less perfect and then setting a minimum wage equal to the rigid oligopoly price.   At the same time, of course, this will tend to reduce or eliminate exploitation as we have defined it.[54]

---

[54] Needless to say, the fact that this paper has minimized the importance of exploitation is intended neither as a justification of the marginal productivity theory nor as an apology for the continued payment of low wages.   Under monopolistic competition, there is no necessary correspondence between marginal revenue product and marginal social product; hence payment to labor of a wage equal to the former carries with it no moral implications.

15

THE DISCOUNTED MARGINAL PRODUCTIVITY DOCTRINE*

By Earl Rolph †

I

The purpose of the present discussion is to re-examine the concept of discounted marginal productivity. After many years of neglect, this doctrine has recently been revived.[1] Once more it must be asked whether the proposition that agencies earn and are paid the value of their marginal products should be qualified by the notion of discounting.

Whether production and distribution theory are interpreted in terms of discounting or not may seem to be a small matter—too small, in fact, to be worthy of attention. Yet there are reasons for believing that much larger issues lie behind this seemingly slight variation in terminology. The discounting notion has important ramifications in the field of interest theory. Those using this approach try to explain interest by a time-lag between production

---

* *Journal of Political Economy*, Volume XLVII, 1939, pages 542–556. Reprinted by courtesy of the publisher and author.

† University of California.

[1] Wassily Leontieff, "Interest on Capital and Distribution: A Problem in the Theory of Marginal Productivity," *Quarterly Journal of Economics*, XLIX (November, 1934) 147–61; Arthur Smithies, "The Austrian Theory of Capital in Relation to Partial Equilibrium Theory," *Quarterly Journal of Economics*, L (November, 1935), 117–50; Oskar Lange, "The Place of Interest in the Theory of Production," *Review of Economic Studies*, III (June, 1936), 159–62; John R. Hicks, "Wages and Interest: The Dynamic Problem," *Economic Journal*, XLV (September, 1935), 456–68; Albert G. Hart, "Imputation and the Demand for Productive Resources in Disequilibrium," *Explorations in Economics* (New York, 1936), pp. 264–71; Frederic Benham, *Economics* (London, 1938), pp. 235–36.

For a system of ideas closely associated with the discounting approach, see E. H. Phelps Brown, *The Framework of the Pricing System* (London, 1936).

and product. It is this view which has received the vigorous criticism of F. H. Knight.[2]

A re-examination of the theory of discounted marginal productivity will, I think, go to the heart of this problem. At the same time, the basis will be laid for an alternative interest theory along lines suggested by Knight.

II

The justification of marginal productivity analysis arises from the fact that most agencies are substitutes for one another. If all types of services were used only in fixed proportions, a marginal-productivity theory would be neither necessary nor possible.[3] In the presence of substitution, marginal-productivity analysis explains the relative demand for factors when they can be combined in various proportions to produce a given output. Adherents to the discounting version and to the unqualified version have no quarrel about the need of a theory of imputation.

To crystallize the ideas associated with the discounting approach, one may ask: What distinction is there between the statements (1) that factors receive the value of their marginal products and (2) that they receive the discounted value of their marginal products? An examination of the context in which these two propositions appear in economic discussions reveals that the term "product" does not mean the same thing. In the unqualified productivity statement, product refers to the immediate results of present valuable activities. If the product is consumption, such as electricity for domestic purposes, production and consumption are necessarily simultaneous, since production (the service-flow)

---

[2] "Note on Dr. Lange's Interest Theory," *Review of Economic Studies*, IV (June, 1937), 229. See bibliography of the controversy over the period of production, in an article criticizing Knight's position, "Annual Survey of Economic Theory," by Nicholas Kaldor, in *Econometrica*, July, 1937; also Knight's reply to Kaldor and Kaldor's rejoinder, *ibid.*, January and April, 1938.

[3] With fixed proportions, the demand for an agency in any one use is explained by the demand for the product. Its supply is determined by the possible gain from alternative employments. The price of the service is, of course, determined by the interaction of the two.

and consumption (the enjoyment) are merely different ways of viewing the same composite activity. Furthermore, if the product is an asset, there is likewise no lag in time between the application of resources and the product. To visualize this implication, one must be prepared to define assets as all things which are expected to yield a valuable service flow in the future, whether at the moment they are in "salable" or "unsalable" form. For example, workmen and equipment beginning the construction of a building may have only a few stakes in the ground to show for their work the first day, but this and not the completed structure is their immediate product. Thus the doctrine that a factor receives the value of its marginal product refers to this immediate product. The simultaneity of production and product does not require any simplifying assumptions. It is a direct appeal to the obvious. Every activity has immediate results. The unqualified version of the productivity theory is an economic application of this generalization.[4]

Some conclusions are immediately evident. Because production and the product (in the sense of immediate results) are necessarily simultaneous, the unqualified statement of the productivity theory is formally accurate and general. Under competitive conditions, owners receive the value of the marginal products of their agencies, regardless of how these agencies may be classified. This proposition holds for the case of the production of assets as well as for the case of the production of services for consumption. Thus, the unqualified productivity theory cannot be criticized on

---

[4] This point is commonly misunderstood by those adhering to the discounting approach. E.g., Leontieff asserts: " . . . If production required no time and goods were turned out at once, simultaneous with the productive use of factors involved, no capital would be needed" (*op. cit.*, p. 150). Here he confuses the rather fantastic notion that production is timeless with the idea that production and product are simultaneous. It is obvious, to be sure, that nothing can happen in no time at all and thus it must be true that production proceeds at some rate at any moment. This is no more than saying that production is a kind of activity. But it should be equally obvious that at every moment in the history of an activity it achieves results—i.e., that products emerge simultaneously with the application of factors.

the ground that it is incorrect or even incomplete in the sense of requiring special assumptions.

In contrast, the term "product" in the phrase "discounted value of marginal product" refers to some remote product. At least two meanings of the term are apparent in the writings of those inclined toward the discounting approach. Product sometimes refers only to "consumers' goods." Indeed, this is the meaning of product found in the concept of an average period of production as defined by Boehm-Bawerk.[5] Viewing product in this way, one finds a time interval between the application of resources and the "product," since, in fact, not all results of current activities in an economy are consumers' goods. More recently, product has been identified with those items which firms sell to the public.[6] As long as a business produces anything which it uses itself, it is possible to find a period of time between production and the salable product. Of course, no time interval can be discovered if product is defined in the causal sense as the immediate results of current activities.

When the meanings of the term "product" are made explicit, the discounting theory may be stated as follows: Agencies are paid the discounted value of the future service-flow of the immediate product. Restated in this fashion, there is no great difference between the two versions of the productivity theory. The unqualified version holds simply that agencies receive the value of their marginal product. It contains no direct implication as to how this value is determined. The discounting approach goes one step beyond this. It implies that the present value of a product is found by discounting its anticipated future returns. When products are assets, there is little difference between saying that agencies receive the discounted return and saying that agencies receive the present value of the product. The present value of an item must always be equal to its future yield discounted back to the present

---

[5] *The Positive Theory of Capital*, translated from the German by William Smart, pp. 78–91.

[6] Leontieff, *op. cit.*, pp. 150–51; K. E. Boulding, "Professor Knight's Capital Theory: A Note in Reply," *Quarterly Journal of Economics*, L (May, 1936), 525–26.

if the correct rate of discount is employed. Thus, the only apparent difference between the two views is a choice of words to say virtually the same thing. One must be prepared, then, to admit that the discounting approach, judged purely from a formal point of view, is equally as correct as the unqualified version.

This reasoning reveals at least one possible source of debate. As noted above, the discounting statement conveys the implication that the determination of the value of an immediate product is found by discounting its anticipated yield. Since there are other ways than discounting of determining present values, notably by the costs of producing assets, the view that present values must be determined by discounting may be challenged. This point is considered in some detail below.[7]

The formal identification of the discounting statement with the unqualified statement does not settle a much more profound difference between the two explanations of returns. Without exception, the "time-lag" theorists insist that only some factors receive the discounted value of the service-flow of the immediate product. The use of the concept of discounting is supposed to convey the idea that because some agencies receive a discounted share, other agencies receive a share explained on other grounds. This is the doctrine of the *nonco-ordination of factors*. There would be no logical objection to saying that all agencies receive the discounted value of the future yield of the immediate product, but there are very strong objections to saying that some factors receive a discounted return and that other factors do not. This is the fundamental fallacy of the discounting approach and the issue is not a purely verbal one. The following discussion will aim to demonstrate that the doctrine of the nonco-ordination of factors is erroneous.

III

The idea that not all factors of production are co-ordinate finds its origin in the view that labor is the only factor which is "really" productive. Because laborers receive only the discounted value of their product, something remains for the owners of other agencies.

---

[7] See below, p. 289.

The older wage-fund doctrine and its modern equivalent, the wage-flow concept, are based on the contention that labor is productive in some sense which is not true of other agencies.[8]   Wicksell partly generalizes this doctrine by insisting that owners of land as well as owners of labor receive a discounted value product.[9]   With his usual candor, Wicksell goes on to ask whether the owners of "capital" receive a discounted share, but at this point he retreats, contending, without explanation, that it is absurd to suppose that some one "advances" to the "capitalists."[10]   The separation of labor and land from capital reveals, according to his view, that whereas the former receive a discounted share, the latter receive an undiscounted share.   Labor and land are, in Wicksell's opinion, the only factors that are "really" productive.[11]   What this is supposed to mean is not clear from his discussion, but it forms the foundation for his contention that the earnings of "capital" are explained indirectly through the productivity of land and labor rather than in terms of productivity of capital agencies as such.

A recent version of the asymmetrical view of the factors of production is expounded by O. Lange.[12]   Instead of using the much-criticized distinction between "original factors" and "capital,"[13] he classifies all agencies into "physical factors" and "money capital."[14]   "Money capital," instead of being co-ordinate in production with other agencies, is said to be "superordinate" in the

---

[8] F. W. Taussig, *Wages and Capital* (New York, 1896), p. 20.

[9] *Lectures on Political Economy*, I (New York, 1934), 150.

[10] *Ibid.*, p. 188.   The idea that all earnings received by owners of property and labor are "advanced" is, of course, absurd.   But the remedy is not to suppose as Wicksell does that some owners advance earnings to others, but rather to recognize that all factors receive what they currently earn.

[11] *Ibid.*, p. 150.

[12] *Op. cit.*

[13] F. H. Knight is a severe critic of this distinction (cf. "The Quantity of Capital and the Rate of Interest," *Journal of Political Economy*, XLIV [August, 1936], 453).

[14] Just how Lange's distinction differs from that of Wicksell is not clear.   At times Lange uses the concept of physical factors to mean labor and natural resources—i.e., Wicksell's original factors (cf. "Professor Knight's Note on Interest Theory," *Review of Economic Studies*, IV [June, 1937], 232).

sense that it is " . . . . a *method* of employing the 'physical factors.'" To support this view, Lange analyzes the borrowing process of a business. At the beginning of a period, the firm is assumed to sell its securities (borrow money) to obtain cash, and then, by hiring services, to produce goods which are partly finished. At the end of the assumed "delay-period," the firm is supposed to have used up everything produced during the period except the finished product. The cash realized from the sale of the finished product is compared with the sums spent for the hired services during the period. The condition for the existence of interest is that the cash realized is greater than that spent in the purchase of services. The earnings of the hired services are explained by discounted marginal productivity, in terms of the value of the finished product at the end of the period. The earnings over and above this amount are explained, not by the productivity of "physical factors," but by the shortage of "money capital." This appears to be the only discernible reason for maintaining that "money capital" is superordinate to other factors.

This time-lag approach to production and distribution theory must be analyzed in some detail to reveal its errors. It neglects the productivity of (1) the goods produced and used entirely within the firm, and (2) cash itself. If it can be demonstrated that all agencies, including these two, are co-ordinate in production, Lange's thesis that money capital is superordinate to other factors breaks down.

To prove that all agencies must be treated alike, let us consider a firm operating in a completely competitive environment. The prices of all hired service and the price of the salable product are given for the management of the business. The application of the productivity theory to the goods produced and used within the firm can perhaps be best explained if the functions of a business are separately considered. In one aspect, a business unit is a device to own property. It is impractical and often impossible for a business to rent all the property it uses. The income of the property owned within the business goes to the owners of the firm's securities. Whatever the legal character of the securities, their owners jointly receive whatever income the property of the business earns. The receipt of this income is independent of the dividend policy of the company. If, during any period, the business pays to its security holders less cash than the net value product of its property, it is nevertheless true that the security holders receive these earnings. In this case, the earnings are in the form of an increase in the value of the property owned within the business.

In addition to the function of ownership, a business may be regarded as a collection of productive centers. Each center is a combination of services producing a particular type of product. Many of these centers have a product which is employed in other centers. Only a few centers may yield a product which is sold to the public. For example, an automobile company consists of a large number of centers, each producing an item which when combined with others forms the "finished" product. Only the selling branches of the company have a product which is in the form of cash. A center may be thought of as buying its services from the ownership organization. It pays for these services by the simultaneous sale of its immediate product to the ownership organization. Thus conceived, there is no lag in time between the payment for services and the receipt of the value product with respect to each center, regardless of the character of its product. The unqualified productivity doctrine means not only that production and product are simultaneous, but also that the payment for services and the receipt of the value product are also simultaneous.

The concept of a productive center reveals why the goods-in-process within the business (as well as all other items) have a direct and immediate value product. Each center employs some services hired outside the business (e.g., labor) and the services of various kinds of property, some or all of which may have been previously produced within the enterprise. The yields of all things employed in each center are explained in the same manner. For any assumed set of prices, the quantity employed of each item is the amount which equates its marginal value product to the price of the service to the center. This equalization provides the best combination of resources within each center, since the management could always increase its own gain by employing more of those items which yield a marginal value product greater than their prices and by employing fewer of those which yield less than their prices. Given the assumed set of prices for all services, the condition of equilibrium for each center (and hence for the entire business) is equality between each item's marginal value product and its price.

To make our analysis formally complete, it is necessary to determine the equilibrium set of prices for the services employed in each center. The prices of hired factors present no difficulties, since, under competitive conditions, they are given for the firm. In the absence of explicit market prices for the services of the property owned within the business, we must ask what prices the ownership organization charges the centers for the use of its property. Since the ownership organization presumably attempts to maximize the net earnings of its property, it will so allocate these services among the centers that each item earns a maximum net yield. The best system of allocation satisfies the condition that no gain can be achieved by shifting property from one center to another. Aside from the possibility of renting property, the prices of the services of property and the quantities allocated to each center depend upon the amounts of the various kinds of property owned within the business as a whole.[15] Changes in the quantity owned may occur because of failure to maintain particular depreciating items or through procuring more property. In the light of these possible variations in quantities of particular assets, the prices charged for property services by the ownership organization must also fulfil the condition that no item yields marginally a higher rate of return on its cost of replacement than

---

[15] The concept of ownership requires some explanation. A business may have a property right even in property which it may be renting if the contract is not continually subject to revision. A contract providing for a given rental to endure for a long period may itself become a valuable asset to the business in the sense that the property currently earns more than the rental. Likewise the reverse may be the case. In the present discussion, ownership refers to such assets as well as to the property which the management may dispose of as it sees fit.

the prevailing rate of interest.   Otherwise, an incentive exists to add such property to the enterprise.[16]   The prices of the property services which satisfy these conditions are the theoretically correct costs of using the property owned within the business, and it is the equality between the marginal value product of an item and the price of its services thus determined which decides the amount of the various kinds of property employed within each center.

No reasons have been discovered for the view that the goods-in-process within the firm do not have a productivity in the same sense as hired factors.   On the contrary, once a firm is divided into various centers, the goods-in-process clearly have an immediate value product in the center in which they are employed.   The fact that they are the products of other centers does not in any way qualify this conclusion.   The moment an item is produced, its services co-operate with others to produce a product of some sort. Exclusive attention to the "finished" product makes it easy to overlook this fact.   Thus, we must reject the doctrine that goods-in-process within the firm are nonco-ordinate with other factors.[17]

Since some writers, notably Lange, lay great stress on the difference between money ("money capital") and other things as far as productivity theory is concerned, our theory cannot be complete unless the productivity cash is explained also.   This subject is full of pitfalls.   To avoid confusion, cash must be distinguished from income-yielding securities.   The latter are claims on the earnings of human beings or property.   They are devices to separate the control of property from its ownership.   Likewise, the productivity of cash is not the productivity of what can be bought with cash.   The yield of any physical item acquired by a

---

[16] The function of the rate of return in the economy as a whole is discussed below; see below, p. 289.

[17] From the foregoing analysis, one confusion in the concept of "money capital" becomes apparent.   As this term is used by Lange and others, it includes the cash balance of the business and the value of the various items produced within the business during the period under observation.   Thus "money capital," like the concept of "capital," does not designate a homogeneous factor, but simply the sum of the money values of some factors.

business is explained by its productivity. The earnings of cash arise from the difference a stock of cash makes in the operation of a business.

The cash-balance approach gives the clue to the explanation of the role of cash in a business. A firm may acquire cash by selling its securities, by selling any property owned within the business, including the "finished" product, or by selling some composite service-flow. It releases cash by buying back its own securities (including paying its debts), or by buying property or services. If a business could depend upon releasing cash at the same rate that it acquires cash, it could operate, conceivably, without a cash balance. In this case there would be no productivity of cash within the business, since it would hold no cash, even momentarily.

Since perfect synchronization of money payments and money receipts cannot be relied upon, a cash balance is essential. To release more cash than is currently acquired, a firm must hold a cash balance to begin with. Likewise, to acquire more cash than it releases, a balance must come into existence. A firm may be able to plan its receipts and disbursements to minimize its average balance, but any planning involves costs. Economical arrangement requires adjusting the size of the balance held during each moment of time to make the value of its marginal product equal to its service price. A larger amount would not be worth its cost; a smaller amount would be worth more.

In practice, aside from lack of synchronization, a business finds it necessary to hold some cash. A firm cannot anticipate in detail when it may be required to pay out money. Some minimum balance is usually maintained as a matter of policy in the light of this uncertainty. Furthermore, even though it owns property of a sort that could readily be converted into cash, there may be costs involved in disposing of it or some uncertainty concerning the price it will bring. The idle balance which acts as an insurance fund has a productivity in the same sense as a fire extinguisher. The cost of holding a dollar in cash may be compared with the gain of avoiding the possible loss from events whose occurrence is unpredictable in detail. The usefulness of cash explains its return and we find that cash, too, stands on the same footing as the other factors of production.[18]

Thus all factors are co-ordinate in production whether they are the services of items hired outside or the services of things owned within the business.[19]

IV

One further aspect of the discounting theory remains to be considered. As pointed out above,[20] when restated in terms of immediate product, the discounting approach becomes a theory of capitalization. It is an assertion that the present prices of products (when products are assets) are determined by discounting their future yield. To evaluate this doctrine, a theory of capitalization and of the rate of interest is needed. The scope of this discussion does not permit an adequate development of interest theory, although once all factors are seen to be co-ordinate, this task is greatly simplified. The outlines of a theory of interest will, I think, show that the discounting theory of capital values is correct as far as it goes, but because it assumes the interest rate to be given it is highly incomplete.

The rate of return of an item is its net income divided by its capital value. If any two of the three items, rate of return, net income, and capital value are determined, it follows by arithmetic

---

[18] The proposition that cash is productive is only superficially contradictory to the older view that money is an unproductive form of wealth. The position given above relates to a firm in a given price environment. For the economy as a whole, the productivity of cash is independent of its quantity, since the latter is a purely arbitrary calculation. This is, I think, the proper meaning of the notion that money is unproductive.

[19] In the operation of the present economic system, the fact that property is largely owned by those who use it does make some important differences. The prices of these services are completely flexible, in the sense that any change in their marginal value productivity is automatically reflected in their prices. In the case of hired services a change in marginal value productivity may not be reflected in a price change either immediately or "in the long run," in which case unemployment may arise. Under competitive conditions, this is not a problem, since all prices are automatically flexible.

[20] See above, p. 282.

that the third is determined also.   Thus, a theory of capitalization and a theory of the rate of interest must come to the same thing.

The net yield of an asset is determined by the value of its marginal product minus its calculated maintenance cost.   The latter is that part of an item's gross yield (rental) which must not be consumed if a continuous even flow of income in perpetuity is to be obtained.[21]

The yields and prices of assets (capital values) are explained by the demand and supply conditions surrounding each type of asset.   The demand for assets arises from the desire of property owners to obtain net incomes, either by renting property to others, or by turning over its control to a business unit, or by the owners using the property themselves.   However the earnings arise, people desire assets because of an expected valuable service-flow in the future.   The attempt of investors to maximize net income per dollar's worth of assets owned explains the relative demand for assets.   Those assets which are expected to yield a higher rate of return than others are obviously preferred.   But this preference operates to bring the rate of return of such items into line with others.   Competitive bidding reduces the prices of those yielding low rates and raises the prices of those yielding high rates.   Equilibrium is reached when each item yields the same rate of return as every other.   The demand for assets, like the demand for consumption, is determined by the equalization principle—equalization of gain per dollar's worth.   Applied to assets, the gain is anticipated net income.

The relative or money costs of producing assets finally determines their prices.   The fact that the public desires assets gives entrepreneurs a money-making opportunity.   The entrepreneur's

---

[21] This definition of maintenance cost is independent of whether property owners actually consume more or less than this amount.   It is a point of reference, not a description of how economic agents behave. (Cf. F. H. Knight, "The Quantity of Capital and the Rate of Interest," *Journal of Political Economy*, XLIV [August, 1936], 457.)   This calculation depends upon people's ideas about the future.   For any given moment of time, these expectations are given and are assumed to be definite.   Expected results may, of course, turn out to be wrong.

motivation is that of realizing a return for his own services.   The costs of production are the sum of the prices of all services employed to produce any particular kind of asset.[22]   These prices are explained by two principles: (1) marginal productivity and (2) the allocation of services (both of human beings and of property) to maximize gain.   Marginal productivity explains the demand for services to produce any particular product.   Allocation explains the supply of services for that product.   Equilibrium conditions exist when the price of each type of service is equal to its marginal return in every employment.

The demand and cost schedules of an asset mutually determine its price.   In equilibrium, the price of each currently produced item is equal to its cost, and all rates of return are equal.   This uniform rate is finally determined by the costs of producing assets.[23]   Thus, as F. H. Knight has explained, the cost of producing new assets determines the rate of return at which the future yields of all other assets are discounted.[24]

The objection may be raised that costs can never be said to determine prices unless constant costs prevail.   There is no presumption that this is the case in the production of assets of any particular kind.   Consequently, a theory of the demand for assets is essential to a complete theory of asset-price determination.   Such

---

[22] It should be noted that the prices of the services of partly finished assets are to be included among these costs.   The same result may be achieved by including interest during the period of construction.   This interest cost is the net earnings of the goods-in-process.   The concept of a construction period, unobjectionable in itself, is apt to mislead those accustomed to the time-lag approach, by suggesting that this period is another illustration of a gap in time between production and the product (e.g., O. Lange, "Professor Knight's Note on Interest Theory," *Review of Economic Studies*, IV [June, 1937], 231).   To forestall this possible confusion, the concept of a construction period is avoided in the present discussion.

[23] Marginal cost, if in each firm there is some service which is fixed in quantity with its earnings excluded from costs; average cost, if no earnings are excluded from costs.   When the quantity of all services, including management, is dependent upon earnings in any degree, all earnings must be counted as costs to determine output.

[24] "Interest," *Encyclopedia of the Social Sciences*, VIII, 135.

a theory is provided by the application of the equalization principle to the desire to own property.

The discounting theory of capital values is correct, in the sense that once the future yield of an item and the rate of return are known the capital value is known also. At best, however, it provides only a theory of the demand for assets—namely, that owners will pay that price for an asset which makes its rate of discount equal to that for every other asset. But the marginal costs of producing assets are the final determinants of capital values. Thus, as a theory of capitalization, the discounted productivity doctrine, restated in terms of immediate product, fails because it is incomplete.

V

If the previous analysis is correct, it becomes clear that the discounted marginal-productivity doctrine must be discarded. It is devised to explain some earnings when production is falsely assumed to be separated in time from the product. This erroneous idea gives the discounted product view a certain plausibility, for once a time-lag approach is adopted, the adequacy of the simple productivity analysis to explain all earnings is no longer clear. But the difficulty is an imaginary one, and when this is realized the discounting approach ceases to have an excuse for existence. It explains nothing which cannot be more effectively explained without it.

The doctrine of the nonco-ordination of factors gives the discounting approach its importance and explains why it has persisted in economic thinking. This asymmetrical theory of returns misses the fact that at every moment the services of all agencies, including capital items, co-operate to produce products. No factors are superordinate to others; they must all be treated alike. It follows that the time-lag approach provides no explanation of interest. These earnings are explained by the marginal value productivity of property items in exactly the same manner as the earnings of nonproperty items, such as labor service. The rate of interest, on the other hand, finds its explanation in the mutual relation between the attempts of investors to maximize net earnings per dollar's worth of assets owned and the attempts of entrepreneurs to make money by producing assets. The rate of interest is finally determined by costs. The discounted doctrine, with its implications, obstructs the recognition of this simpler and more direct way of explaining economic processes. Economic analysis will be well served if the theory of discounted marginal productivity is placed among the obsolete doctrines in the development of economic thought.

16

RELATIONS BETWEEN WAGE RATES, COSTS AND PRICES*

By Lloyd G. Reynolds †

The subject of this paper is restricted to cost-price relations within the individual firm under conditions of cyclical change. It is focused on the problem of how changes in cost-price relations occur rather than on the effects of a given change. Discussions of the effect on employment of a general wage increase or decrease usually start from some assumption about the price reactions of individual firms. Beginning a step farther back, let us explore these assumptions. Is it reasonable to suppose that cost increases are reflected immediately in prices and that the price increase will bear a definite relationship to the cost increase? Under what conditions might prices remain unchanged in the face of appreciable cost changes?

It is assumed throughout that the firm in question is an oligopolist selling a differentiated product. The firm is assumed to make only one product and this product is sold directly to a large number of final users. There is no price discrimination among customers. All buyers and sellers of the product are assumed to be located at a single point, so that problems of geographical price structure do not arise. All costs of production are assumed to vary with output; there is no fixed plant and no fixed charges. Raw materials and finished goods are highly perishable and inventory accumulation is impossible. The possibility of product variation and of increasing demand by selling expenditures are ignored.

---

* *American Economic Review*, Volume XXXII, Supplement, 1942, pages 275–289. Reprinted by courtesy of the publisher and author.

† Yale University. Formerly, Johns Hopkins University.

The discussion relates to situations in which business executives have considerable autonomy in deciding on prices and rates of output. It is scarcely necessary to add that business autonomy is at present much reduced and that government control of prices, output, and profit margins is increasing rapidly. Should these central controls prove to be permanent, the type of reasoning employed in this paper may be of little use in explaining future price behavior, though some of the same considerations will be relevant for government price decisions.

The theory of monopolistic competition, like its predecessor, the Marshallian system, defines an equilibrium price and output for the firm under cost and demand conditions which have remained unchanged long enough for full adjustment to be reached. It also defines the direction of movement of price and output when one of the basic variables is changed, all others remaining unchanged. The direction of movement can be predicted, however, only if the firm knows what has happened, if other data have remained unchanged, if the reactions of rival producers are known and stable, and if there is sufficient time for adjustment before some new shift in the data occurs. Where these conditions are not met there can be no certainty that the firm will move toward a new "equilibrium position," and the relevance of the concept of static equilibrium becomes seriously attenuated.[1] In this respect the theory of monopolistic competition stands on all fours with the theory of pure competition. If by a "realistic" theory we mean one which furnishes a close approximation to actual behavior, the theory of monopolistic competition is no more realistic than its predecessors.[2] It does not furnish a basis for predicting the behavior of a firm

---

[1] A careful argument for this view, developed under assumptions of pure competition, will be found in Moses Abramovitz, *Price Theory for a Changing Economy* (New York: Columbia University Press, 1939), Ch. II. This argument can readily be extended to situations of monopolistic competition.

[2] It may even be argued that it is less realistic. The monopolist's economic problem being so much more complicated than that of the producer under pure competition, his calculations are likely to be more seriously upset by cyclical changes, and there is likely to be a wider divergence between actual behavior and hypothetical behavior under static assumptions.

which is attempting, with imperfect knowledge and foresight, to respond to rapid and correlated shifts of economic data associated with cyclical change.

But perhaps the basic tools of the theory of monopolistic competition—the cost and revenue functions—can be used in the analysis of price behavior under cyclical conditions. The main object of the present paper is to suggest some possible applications of these tools. No attempt will be made to elaborate a generalized theory of price determination. It is possible to set up thousands of hypothetical firms, each of which will behave somewhat differently because of differences in the assumptions used, and there is no a priori basis for choosing among these hypotheses. The problem is whether one can construct any hypothesis whose assumptions are varifiable and reasonably complete, and which will therefore furnish a rough approximation to the cyclical behavior of any firm possessing the assumed characteristics. If an affirmative answer can be given to this question, the path of future investigation in this field is clarified.

I. Price and Output Policy with Changing Cost and Revenue Functions

The ordinary "instantaneous" demand curve shows sales as a single-valued function of price. As soon as time is introduced into the system, however, an industry is faced, not with a single demand curve, but with a "pencil" of curves running through the prevailing price, the slopes of the curves depending on the amount of time allowed for adjustment to a price change. The immediate effect of a price change on sales is generally considered by manufacturers to be very slight because of the rigidity of consumers' buying habits and, in the case of producers goods, the short-run rigidity of industrial techniques.

While producers tend to regard aggregate demand as very inelastic in the short-run, they ordinarily regard their own demand curve as elastic upward. If one firm raises its price, no change in data having occurred, other firms are unlikely to follow the increase and the price-raising firm will lose sales. The amount of the loss will depend on the substitutability of competitors' products, and on the period of time taken into account. If the firm cuts its price, it is likely that other producers will follow almost at once. The firm's demand curve below the prevailing price is a replica of the aggregate demand curve, usually conceived as highly inelastic. The two wings of the demand curve may thus meet almost at right angles, with marginal revenue discontinuous and negative at any price below the prevailing price.[3]

Empirical studies of the short-run cost function have usually yielded linear results over medium and high ranges of output.[4] These results are not necessarily in conflict with traditional cost theory, but may mean simply that the "fixed factors" usually assumed indivisible are in fact rather highly divisible. Many plants are made up of batteries of similar machines, each of which can be operated as an independent unit. Provided that the machines are of equal age and efficiency, the setting in motion of successive units need not involve any increase or decrease in marginal cost.[5] Even where the plant is a single producing unit which must be operated as a whole, it may be operated for only a part of each week or month. Again, there need be no marked departure from constant marginal cost up to the limit of one-shift, normal-hour operations. Under existing rules concerning overtime payment, work in excess of forty hours per week involves a discontinuous increase in marginal costs, which may then move

---

[3] See Paul M. Sweezy, "Demand under Conditions of Oligopoly," *Journal of Political Economy*, 1939, pp. 568–575. Even this picture exaggerates the continuity of the demand curve. Where prices are customarily changed by round numbers the curve reduces to a series of points, only two or three of which are relevant to a particular decision.

[4] See, for example, Joel Dean, *Statistical Cost Functions of a Hosiery Mill* (Chicago: University of Chicago Press, 1941).

[5] The marginal cost curve is continuous only if plant is perfectly divisible. If this is not the case, there are two possibilities: if output is varied only by the full product of an additional machine, the cost curve reduces to a series of points running horizontally. If output is varied by smaller amounts, the curve becomes sawtoothed because of partial use of a particular machine, the bottoms of the teeth again lying in a horizontal line.

horizontally on a higher level.   Introduction of a second or third
shift may involve a similar discontinuous increase because of
reduced efficiency and possibly higher wages of the added shift.

While the horizontal marginal cost curve and the "kinked"
demand curve have been generally accepted, the consequences of
combining the two have not been fully explored.   An obvious
consequence is that factor prices may vary over a wide range with
no effect on output and therefore no effect on product prices via
output.   In the extreme case of a right-angled demand curve,
marginal cost could vary between average revenue and zero without affecting output.   It may be suggested that this result is consistent with business behavior.   Current production schedules are
based mainly on anticipated movements of demand, which seem
to be conceived of as horizontal shifts—more or less can be sold at
the prevailing price.   Costs enter as a significant factor only when
there is some question of abandoning the line entirely, i.e., when
variable costs have risen or threaten to rise above the selling price.

As the marginal cost curve rises during a recovery period, prices
eventually rise also, not because of a reduction of output, but
because of a direct revision of price levels.   The common business
explanation that prices have been raised to cover the higher costs
is clearly inadequate.   If the costs of only one firm had increased
it is unlikely that a price increase would follow.   The firm raises
prices when it is able to, and it is able to when the costs of other
producers have risen sufficiently that they will concur in a price
increase.   At this point the firm shifts over to an inelastic demand
curve based on the assumption that price increases will be followed.
The price policy of the firm is mainly determined not by its own
costs but by the costs of other producers as reflected in their price
policies and thus in the firm's own demand curve.   This provides
a means of reconciling the importance which businessmen attach
to cost with the traditional emphasis of economic theory on demand
as the main determinant of short-run price movements.

Once an increase in price has been made, the firm returns to
the lower branch of the demand curve and remains there until
another increase in costs has accumulated.   As a result of rightward

displacement of the demand curve, combined with occasional jumping back and forth between its upper and lower branches, the kink of the demand curve traces a zigzag path upward during recovery and prosperity.[6]

It is now necessary to explain how an increase in costs which is not sufficient to make any one firm raise prices can make producers generally more willing to follow a price increase initiated by any of their number.   To put the matter somewhat differently: if a general price increase would have been profitable before a change in costs occurred, why was it not made earlier?   How can prices remain below the level which would maximize profits in the immediate future?

The price of a product at a given time may be regarded as in some sense a "critical" price.[7]   It represents the opinion of one or more producers concerning the maximum price dictated by wise market strategy.   This opinion is based on an estimate of the volume of sales which can be obtained at a given price over a period of years.   It is recognized that a price increase may lead in time to substitution of rival commodities and possibly to entrance of new producers[8] or more rapid growth of existing small producers. Different firms will of course look ahead for different periods of time, and will make different forecasts even over the same period. The most farsighted and pessimistic members of the group will

---

[6] Changes in the level of demand are probably accompanied also by changes in the elasticity of aggregate demand for the product.   It is doubtful, however, whether producers' estimates of aggregate demand elasticity change sufficiently to have any influence on their price policies.   The dominant factor is almost certainly the jumping back and forth between the two branches of the individual firm's demand curve.

[7] This term was suggested to the writer by Dr. Richard Bissell, of Yale University.

[8] This need not mean creation of a new enterprise, but may arise from expansion of an existing enterprise into new fields.   Large and profitable concerns such as General Motors, General Electric, Du Pont, etc., are in a sense investment trusts with pools of liquid funds, prepared to invade almost any field which appears highly profitable.   This fact not only makes "freedom of entrance" greater than it otherwise might be, but is gradually changing the whole meaning of the concept.

have the lowest estimate of the critical price, and their opinion will tend to set the level for the entire industry.

A cost increase affecting most members of an industry tends to raise their estimates of the critical price. Since the higher costs must be faced by potential producers, product prices can now be raised without setting up an "umbrella" beneath which new producers or existing small producers can grow and flourish. Cost increases which affect producers of rival commodities as well will have a still more powerful effect by rendering intercommodity substitution less probable. A cost increase confined to one industry stimulates price increases by reducing apprehension about leftward shifts of individual firm demand curves. A general cost increase reinforces this by reducing apprehension about leftward shifts of the aggregate demand curve.

How large an increase in variable costs will be necessary to set off a price increase, and how large will the price increase be relative to the preceding cost increase? The answer probably depends mainly on such factors as: the dispersion in the cost increases[9] of individual producers, whether this arises from differences of economic situation or differences of accounting technique; dispersion of demand anticipations, arising either from differences in the period of time considered or from differences in estimates for the same period; the presence or absence of firms which desire to expand their share of the market and therefore embark on aggressive competition; the amount of consultation among producers about prices, and the extent to which the leading producers have been able to arrive at a common pricing policy.[10] The combination of these elements in a particular case will largely determine the movement of the critical price. Cost increases may be reflected

---

[9] Not the dispersion in unit costs themselves, though this will of course have an effect on the critical price prevailing at the beginning of the period studied.

[10] It is necessary to distinguish sharply between the amount of consultation and the effectiveness of consultation. Frequent consultation may not result in homogeneity of opinion about the desirable course of prices, and may indeed indicate that there are major difficulties in the way of arriving at a common course of action. In an industry which has really resolved its differences, very little

in prices rapidly or slowly, more than proportionately or less than proportionately.

It is essential to emphasize that cost increases are responsible for price increases only indirectly via their effect on demand anticipations. The amount of the price increase therefore depends not on the amount of the cost increase but on the behavior of demand anticipations and on the relations existing among the oligopolists. While it may be convenient for purposes of cycle theory to assume that a wage increase will lead to a price increase of the same absolute amount or the same percentage amount, there is no reason to regard these results as more probable than any others. There is undoubtedly the widest variation among industries both as regards the size of the price reaction and the length of the time lag involved.

It should be noted that the explanation developed above for price increases cannot be turned into reverse to explain price decreases, and it is doubtful whether any mechanism can be devised which will operate symmetrically for cyclical downswings and upswings. Under the conditions assumed at the outset, it is not legitimate to resort to the elastic downward "wing" of the demand curve. The firm must ordinarily assume that price cuts will be followed very quickly,[11] and price cuts are thus unprofitable even in the short run. Nor is there great force in the argument that a decline in costs will lower the critical price by making producers more apprehensive of new competition. It is unlikely that new producers would appear during a period of declining sales and profits. They are more likely to appear at the beginning of the next recovery, and prudence would dictate merely that prices be

---

discussion may be necessary. Intensive consultation at one period, resulting perhaps in uniform cost accounting systems, uniform methods of estimating and quoting prices, and uniform methods of changing prices, may greatly reduce the amount of consultation necessary in subsequent periods.

[11] How quickly probably depends on: (1) The size of the firm. Large producers may allow small firms to nibble at the price structure for some time before retaliating. (2) The visibility of price changes. Where visibility is low, it may be possible to follow a "hit and run" policy, cutting prices until competitors find out and are about ready to retaliate, then raising them again to the prevailing level.

reduced some time before recovery begins. A possible reason for earlier reductions would be a decline in prices of competing commodities.

Once the feeling that a price cut is in order has become widespread, there is an advantage in being the first to make the cut. But the development of such a feeling must itself be explained. The fact that price declines are so difficult to explain when price discrimination is assumed absent suggests that actual declines very frequently start with discriminatory reductions to one or more customers, which are later extended to other buyers and taken up by other sellers.

To sum up: It has been argued that the shape of cost and revenue functions is such that marginal cost can change greatly without changing the output at which marginal cost equals marginal revenue; that output and employment are therefore not directly affected by changes in cost-price relations,[12] output being mainly a function of anticipated sales at the prevailing price; that the prevailing price must be explained mainly in terms of long-run market strategy and established relations among producers; and that the considerations relevant to an explanation of price increases are not sufficient to explain price decreases.

II. Some Difficulties in the Concept of "Cost"

1. *Valuation of Materials Used*

It is necessary now to take account of some of the problems which were excluded at the outset by simplifying assumptions. Most of these have to do with the meaning and measurement of cost.

Costing of raw materials may be complicated by the fact that materials are bought at one date and used at another. Consider

---

[12] Output will of course become zero if marginal cost rises above price. Theoretically, output should be reduced whenever marginal cost rises above marginal revenue (which will be below price unless the demand curve is perfectly elastic upward), but it is doubtful whether this qualification is of any practical importance. Little error is involved in taking anticipated sales at the prevailing price as the sole determinant of output for all outputs greater than zero.

the case of a firm which makes heavy purchases of materials at low prices near the beginning of recovery and reduces its purchases as prices rise toward the peak of the cycle. The effect on the firm's cost and profit calculations will depend on the way in which materials are valued for cost accounting purposes. The "first-in-first-out" method, which is still most commonly used, will show lower costs and larger profits than the "last-in-first-out" method. Use of the average cost of inventory on hand yields an intermediate result; material costs will lag behind the market price of materials but the lag is not so great as under first-in-first-out.[13]

Use of one of these methods rather than another, by changing the apparent rate of increase in costs, may well have an effect on price decisions. It is an interesting question how far business executives perceive and make allowance for the tricks played by accounting conventions. Do they realize, for example, that the margins shown by the first-in-first-out method at a particular time may consist largely of inventory profits which will be wiped out in the next recession and that manufacturing margins proper may be much narrower? If they consciously or unconsciously discount the bias of the accounting system it may make little difference what system is used. But if they take accounting results literally, the effect on price policy may be important.

Another consequence may be additional dispersion in the cost changes of rival producers. Different firms may use different methods of costing raw materials, and a firm which uses one method in preparing its record of past earnings may use a different method in making price decisions. This dispersion of cost estimates, by causing increased uncertainty and disagreement concerning the price policy which should be pursued at a particular time, may influence the timing and magnitude of price changes.

It is worth noting that small firms with limited working capital

---

[13] These results hold even if the company merely carries a normal inventory throughout the cycle and does not engage in inventory speculation. Use of the first-in-first-out method allows inventory profits and losses arising from revaluation of the normal inventory to be reflected in profit margins, while the last-in-first-out method reflects manufacturing profits only.

are often unable to carry substantial inventories and are forced to use materials bought at current prices. If the large firms in the industry do carry inventories, and if they use any method of inventory accounting other than last-in-first-out, their material costs will rise more slowly than those of the small firms during recovery and fall more slowly during recession. Unless labor costs are very important and show an opposite tendency, unit variable costs of the large producers will lag throughout the course of the cycle. This may cause small producers to take the initiative in price changes, particularly during recession.

2. *Computation of Unit Overhead*

Manufacturers usually calculate the "trading profit" or "margin" on a product as the difference between price and total unit cost, including overhead. To the extent that price decisions are influenced by the size of the trading profit, the methods used in computing unit overhead become important.

In economic usage, unit overhead varies as the reciprocal of output. If this method were generally used by businessmen the effect of increasing output—factor and product prices remaining unchanged—would be to increase profit margins and *a fortiori* aggregate profits. Margins might well increase even though variable costs were rising relative to prices.[14] Fluctuations in overhead would tend to offset fluctuations in variable costs, and it is conceivable that total unit costs might remain approximately stable over the course of the cycle. The exact pattern traced by

---

[14] If overhead is a large percentage of total cost and if cyclical fluctuations of output are large, no reasonable increase in variable costs can prevent profit margins from rising during recovery, while very drastic cuts in variable costs cannot prevent margins from shrinking during depression. It has been calculated, for example, that a reduction of material prices by 75 per cent between 1929 and 1933 or a reduction of wage rates to zero would not have enabled the International Harvester Company to show a positive trading profit. (*Industrial Wage Rates, Labor Costs and Price Policies*, Washington, Temporary National Economic Committee, 1940, Part II.)

The writer recently had occasion to examine the records of a firm which had granted a 10 per cent wage increase during a period of rapidly rising output.

total unit costs would of course depend on the relative importance of overhead, the relative magnitude of fluctuations in output and in factor prices, and the timing of output and factor price changes.[15]

Two other methods of computing unit overhead are probably used more frequently in business. Some firms calculate standard costs on the assumption of a constant "normal" output over a period of time. The behavior of unit overhead under this system will depend on the method used to calculate normal output and on the period of time for which output is assumed constant. If the period exceeds the length of a business cycle, cyclical fluctuations in unit overhead will be eliminated. Where job costs are used, as in the machinery industry, it is common practice to compute unit overhead as a percentage of unit variable costs. This results in rising unit overhead during prosperity and falling unit overhead during depression,[16] and the movement of variable costs is accentuated rather than offset. In some cases, the effects of this method are mitigated by revising the percentage added for overhead in response to marked changes of output. If these revisions were sufficiently frequent, unit overhead might move in much the way assumed by economists. In practice, revisions are usually infrequent, and it is doubtful whether they prevent a perverse fluctuation of overhead.

The profit margin per unit fell temporarily, but within two months was larger than it had been before the wage increase though prices had remained unchanged. It is not necessary in such a situation to raise prices after a cost increase in order to restore the profit margin, since margins have not fallen.

[15] Stability of total unit cost over the cycle would be unlikely to occur in practice. An increase is likely, for example, during the second half of the upswing; increases in factor prices will probably proceed at least as rapidly as during the first half, while the absolute reduction in unit overhead will necessarily shrink even though the percentage rate of decrease remains constant. Moreover, for increases in output beyond one-shift capacity, unit variable costs will probably rise even though factor prices remain constant.

[16] This result is not as absurd as may appear, because the definition of "shop overhead" includes many items—supervision, maintenance and repairs, light, heat and power, etc.—which do vary with output, though not proportionately, and are thus not overhead in the economic sense.

But is unit overhead, however computed, an important influence on price policy? This amounts to asking whether price decisions are based mainly on changes in average total cost or in average variable cost (which is equal to marginal cost if a linear short-run cost function is accepted as normal). Do sales executives look to the movement of trading profits or to the movement of factor prices? This question can be answered satisfactorily only by investigation. There is some evidence that on the upswing of the cycle businessmen are guided, or think they are guided, by the movement of trading profits; i.e., by total unit costs. One is tempted to conclude that standard costing or use of percentage additions for overhead will result in larger and more rapid price increases than treatment of unit overhead as the reciprocal of output. But again it is necessary to ask whether businessmen do not perceive and make mental allowance for the bias of their accounting system—for example, the fact that standard costs or percentage additions smuggle an element of profit into costs at high rates of output. Perhaps, after all, generous allowances for overhead are simply a way of rationalizing the profits which the state of demand permits.

This suspicion is strengthened by the trend of events on the down-swing of the cycle. The producer may still include unit overhead in his calculation of the price which he should get, but he draws a clear distinction between this price and the price which the market will permit. The fact that trading profits become zero or negative does not lead to abandonment of production. Again, standard costs help to rationalize this behavior by making margins look larger than they actually are. The view that overhead costs are largely irrelevant to short-run price decisions appears to be justified in this phase of the cycle.[17]

---

[17] The greater the importance of overhead in total cost, the greater the reduction in profits associated with a given decline in output, and therefore the greater the incentive to maintain output. But price cutting will be used to maintain output only if it is believed that demand has considerable elasticity in the short run. This belief seems to be relatively rare, and is rarest in the heavy industries where overhead is most important.

Where the firm produces more than one product there is a still stronger case for regarding unit overhead as a consequence rather than a cause of prices. There is a marked tendency to allocate a disproportionate share of overhead to products which are able to carry it because of inelastic aggregate demand and a favorable oligopoly situation. Petroleum refiners, for example, allocate the cost of refining among the various petroleum derivatives on the basis of their market value; to argue that total unit cost is a determinant of gasoline or fuel oil prices would clearly be circular reasoning. Again, large manufacturers of electrical machinery obtain longer margins on very large sizes of equipment which they alone make than on smaller sizes which are made by a considerable number of small manufacturers.

3. *Interdependence of Cost and Revenue Functions*

Use of cost and revenue functions is usually accompanied by the assumption that these functions are independent of each other. It is probably true that changes in the firm's costs usually have a negligible effect on its revenues,[18] but the converse proposition is not at all true. Revenues do influence costs. Larger profits may lead to lax management and a gradual creeping up of unit costs through less efficient use of productive factors. Conversely a decline in revenue may exert pressure on management to reduce unit costs by more efficient use of productive factors.

Prices of the factors may also be subject to bargaining or manipulation. This is notably true of wage rates. A nonunion employer has considerable latitude in wage setting. Whether he raises or cuts wages by 5 per cent or 10 per cent may in the short run make little difference to his ability to hold his working force together. The conditions of labor supply are better represented by a band than a line. The wage rate selected by the firm within this range of indeterminacy will be markedly influenced by the level of prices

---

[18] It is possible to imagine cases in which the effect on revenues might be important—for example, a firm in a company town which derives part of its revenues from a company store—but these cases are probably of slight importance in the economy as a whole.

and earnings. Where wages are regulated by a collective agreement, the union will take prices and earnings into account in formulating its wage demands.

There is therefore a marked tendency for costs and revenues to
rise and fall together, and this quite apart from general cyclical
impulses. Increases and decreases in price usually do not produce
an equal change in the margin between price and unit cost. Determinate results can be obtained for a hypothetical firm only by
assuming some functional relation between net earnings and managerial efficiency and between net earnings and the wage decisions
of company and trade union officials. The conditions of labor
supply must also be specified in some detail.

III. Limitations of Dynamic Price Theory

The foregoing analysis suggests a few observations on the problem of developing a theory of cost-price relations under conditions
of economic change. Hypotheses about the behavior of a particular firm can be developed only under very detailed assumptions
about its economic characteristics,[19] and there is an almost infinite
number of possible combinations of assumptions. Progress requires:
first, setting up of hypothetical firms, each with a set of assumed
characteristics which are believed to occur frequently in practice;
second, deduction of the logical consequences of the conditions
assumed in each case, and comparison with the behavior of actual

---

[19] In addition to the assumptions made at the beginning of the paper, it would
be necessary to make assumptions on at least the following points: nature of the
aggregate demand function for the product; reaction of other large producers to a
price change by one large producer at different points in the cycle; number of
small producers in the industry and peculiarities of their cost and price behavior;
shape of the marginal cost function; efficiency of management and relation
between efficiency and earnings; relative importance of overhead, labor and
material costs; timing and magnitude of changes in output and factor prices
over the cycle; presence or absence of union organization and main features of
the union contract; customary timing of wage and price decisions; policy with
respect to inventories of raw materials and finished goods; methods of accounting
for raw materials and overhead, and the interpretation placed on the results; any
systematic biases in the cyclical anticipations of the firm.

firms operating under somewhat similar conditions;[20] third, correction of the original assumptions on the basis of observation and development of new hypothetical cases.

Not all of the assumptions made in creating a hypothetical firm are equally important for its behavior. The critical assumptions are probably those concerning the anticipated reaction of rival producers to a price change, the shape of the short-run cost function, the timing and magnitude of cyclical changes in output, demand, and factor prices, the accounting conventions used and the attitude of sales executives toward them, and the relative importance of overhead costs. By different combinations of assumptions on these points it is possible to get wide differences of price behavior over the cycle. It is easy to construct situations which would result in stable product prices for a year or more of recovery or recession despite appreciable changes in factor prices.[21]

The practical usefulness of hypotheses obtained in this way is of course seriously limited. A major difficulty is variability in the timing and magnitude of cyclical changes in demand and factor prices. This fact is well recognized by businessmen, who attempt to keep their plans flexible until the last possible moment instead of acting on a rigid set of cyclical expectations. But satisfactory hypotheses can be developed only by assuming a set pattern of "experienced" cyclical change. Different industries and firms vary widely in the regularity of their cyclical experience. The more regular the cyclical changes in data and the more systematic pro-

---

[20] It is of course impossible to set up assumptions detailed and complex enough to match the actual operating conditions of any firm. One can therefore never hope for more than very rough correspondence between theoretical results and concrete behavior.

[21] For example, the following conditions would be conducive to this result: producers are few, large, and "co-operative"; one or more producers regard aggregate demand as elastic upward over a period of years, but all producers regard it as inelastic downward even in the long run; linear short-run cost functions prevail; raw materials are costed by the first-in-first-out method and large inventories are carried; actual unit overhead is used; output fluctuations are large and tend to precede changes in factor prices in both recovery and recession; accounting results are taken literally; close substitutes for the commodity are not available.

ducers' expectations concerning them, the more hope of developing hypotheses which will approximate to actual behavior over a number of cycles. Even at best, there is no way to take account of random events which continually enter in to deflect the course of business decisions.

Another problem arises from the fact that all of the previously discussed functions and changes of data must be anticipated by the firm. They are not known in advance. To assume that managers have perfect foresight, i.e., that the anticipated functions are exact images of the actual functions,[22] is plausible only in a static or quasi-static economy. For dynamic problems it is necessary to introduce expectations as an explicit variable. But expectations are influenced by configurations of economic and political events which never recur in precisely the same form, and by personality characteristics of the individual business executives. It is thus doubtful whether this variable can ever be reduced to the quantitative form necessary for precise analysis.

Similar difficulties arise in connection with the motivation of business executives. It is a commonplace that they are influenced by many considerations other than a desire to maximize the present worth of the firm. Any attempt to reduce these aberrant motives to quantitative form can yield only an appearance of precision. It is better to admit frankly that our present knowledge of social psychology and politics is inadequate for an explanation or prediction of actual behavior.

It is hopeless to expect any dynamic theory of the firm comparable in precision and elegance to the constructions of static theory. It does not follow that it is impossible to construct any useful picture of business decisions over the course of the cycle. Provided that all of the variables noted above are specified, it is

---

[22] This is frequently done implicitly by including anticipations as part of the data of the problem. But it can readily be shown that to take anticipations as given reduces to an assumption of perfect foresight. "A group of individuals can all entertain consistent and correct expectations only if they all know what to expect, i.e., have perfect foresight." Paul M. Sweezy, "Expectations and the Scope of Economics," *Review of Economic Studies*, V, 234.

possible to predict the general drift of events, though not the exact speed and magnitude of reactions.

IV. METHODS OF INVESTIGATION

It is useless to debate whether case studies of particular enterprises can be used to check the adequacy of our assumptions and hypotheses about cost-price relationships, since if this method of investigation be abandoned no other is available.   It is more profitable to ask what research techniques will reveal most about a firm's operations, admitting frankly that the best obtainable results may not be very good.

Full access to the operating records of the firm is essential to an adequate study.   The first step is to determine what fluctuations have occurred in output, inventories, cash balances, wage rates and labor costs, raw material costs, actual and standard overhead costs, net realized prices, trading profits, and other important variables over the period under investigation.[23]   These data can be used for several purposes.   They may be so manipulated as to shed some light on the short-run cost function of the firm.   They will reveal the timing and magnitude of cyclical changes in demand and factor prices; if a sufficient period of time is covered, they may tell something about the stability of the cyclical pattern.   They provide a direct indication of the firm's policies on some points—e.g., inventories of raw materials and finished goods—and may give clues concerning other types of decision.   The frequency and relative timing of wage and price changes, for example, may suggest a connection or absence of connection between wage and price decisions.

A second major object of investigation should be the administrative machinery which has been developed for formulating certain types of decisions, particularly price decisions.   Within what limits may subordinate officials change selling terms or otherwise depart from published price schedules?   Who takes the initiative in pro-

---

[23] A record should also be made of important events in the company's history which are not disclosed by statistical series, such as unionization of plants, changes in methods of wage payment, introduction of new products or major alterations of existing products, changes in distribution channels and methods of price quotation.

posing a major price change, who passes on the proposal at various levels, who has effective veto power? What types of information do these individuals or committees have in front of them, and how are these balanced against each other? What rules-of-thumb have been erected to guide executives to a decision? A particular effort should be made to find out what interpretation is placed on cost information. The accounting techniques by which cost data are prepared will have been disclosed in the course of analyzing the operating records, but the light in which these data are viewed by price committees must also be known before their significance can be appraised. It would be desirable ideally to check the statements of business executives on these matters by tracing in detail the way in which particular decisions were reached. Adequate knowledge could only be obtained, however, if the investigator were "in on" the decision, and this will ordinarily be impossible.[24]

The general strategy should be to place as little reliance as possible on mere interrogation of company officials and to use interviews only as a check on hypotheses which have emerged from examination of the data. It is particularly futile to ask questions of the type, "What is your policy on such-and-such?" Business decisions are probably opportunistic in the great majority of cases. Situations are met as they arise. Even where administrators profess to follow certain principles, these are constantly modified to meet changing circumstances, and the actual decisions are likely to be less consistent than the announced policy. The reasons given for particular decisions are frequently rationalizations after the fact, and the element of rationalization probably increases with the passage of time.

---

[24] The formation of policy within a number of government agencies has been explored by the "capture and recording" method. Research assistants were allowed to sit in at staff meetings, listen to telephone conversations of top administrators, read relevant correspondence, and in general sit at the elbow of the administrator in action. The method is time-consuming and requires intimate co-operation from the persons under observation. The results of one of these studies appear in Arthur W. Macmahon, *et al.*, *The Works Progress Administration*, Public Administration Committee of the Social Science Research Council, New York, 1941.

Even with the best efforts to avoid opinions and rationalizations and to stay close to quantitative records, it is not at all certain that study of many different firms will permit of generalization. The few studies already made suggest that limited generalizations are possible on some points and at a given moment of time.[25] Only by a continuation of careful empirical work can the theory of the firm be kept from wavering between a fruitless search for complete generality and analysis of convenient but unreal special cases.

------

[25] See, for example, TNEC, *op. cit.*; R. L. Hall and C. J. Hitch, "Price Theory and Business Behavior," *Oxford Economic Papers*, Number 2.

17

THE RELATION OF WAGE POLICIES AND PRICE POLICIES *[1]

BY A. P. LERNER †

I shall consider wage policies and price policies from the point of view of the economy as a whole and not from that of either a particular firm or that of any particular section of the economy. The policies are conceived to be directed to the object of achieving and maintaining the prosperity of the economy as a whole. The main difficulty of this problem lies in the danger of taking propositions that have been established as true when applied to sections of the economy and illegitimately applying them to the economy as a whole. What is true of a firm or of a particular industry or of a set of industries need not be true of the economy as a whole. To draw attention continually to such relationships between the parts and the whole is probably the most distinctive function of the economist.

A very crude example of this error would be to argue thus: Depression in a particular industry may be cured by a restriction of output; i.e., a higher price policy which would lead to an increase in the profits made in the industry. Therefore, to cure depression in the economy as a whole all that is necessary is that there should be a general restriction of output or a general policy of raising prices. It is doubtful whether this argument has ever been put forward quite as crudely, even though there have been governmental policies of price recovery that have applied such measures

* *American Economic Review*, Volume XXIX, Supplement, 1939, pages 158–169. Reprinted by courtesy of the publisher and author.

† The New School for Social Sciences and Research. Formerly, London School of Economics.

[1] I am indebted to Professors Oskar Lange, Paul H. Douglas, and Albert G. Hart, of the University of Chicago, for helpful discussions in the course of my preparation of this paper.

to large sections of the economy. It is, however, illustrative of the kind of illegitimate generalization from a section of the economy to the economy as a whole to warn against which economists have correctly applied the principle that came to be known as Say's Law.

Very roughly speaking, Say's Law points out that the demand for the output of any industry (or firm or individual) comes from the supplies of all the other industries (or firms or individuals). This is because these supplies translated into money constitute the demand for the output of the first industry (as well as for each other's output). A general restriction of supply would bring about a general restriction of demand, and, therefore, could not be depended upon to increase prosperity. Total demand is not independent of total supply.

Now there is some plausibility to the argument that a general policy of raising price by restriction of output can increase prosperity in the sense of raising prices or profits. And, indeed, we shall see later the argument has some validity. But it is hardly possible to argue that such a price policy can increase prosperity in the much more fundamental sense of increasing total output or employment. However, a similar generalization is made with respect to wage policy. A cut in wages in one industry can increase both profits and employment in the industry. Similarly, it is argued, a general policy of reduction of wages will lead to an increase in profits and in employment in the whole economy.

The parallel warning for this illegitimate generality from a part of the economy to the whole has been given by Mr. J. M. Keynes.

Again speaking very roughly, what Mr. Keynes has pointed out is that the costs incurred in the production of any commodity constitute the incomes out of which comes the demand for all the other communities. A general reduction of wages would constitute a reduction in costs, in incomes, and in demand; so that it could not be depended upon to increase prosperity. This may be called "Keynes's Law." Total demand is not independent of total cost.

The argument that a reduction of money wages will increase employment is not often presented in the extremely crude form here indicated. It is usually refined and qualified in one of two

ways. Sometimes the qualifications are such as to describe independent conditions under which the results may be expected to
hold, and an attempt will be made below to develop a general
scheme into which such situations will fit. Such a scheme must
be built on the fundamental, independent determinates of the level
of employment, the estimated profitability of investment, the propensity to consume, the liquidity-preferences, and the conditions
governing the supply of money.

Sometimes the qualifications are such as to describe dependent
concomitants which are nothing but logical implications of the
desired results. One example of this is the argument that a reduction in wages will increase output and employment if MV remains
the same. This is indisputable, for if the same amount of money
is spent on goods that are cheaper (because wages and costs are
lower), then it must be true that it is being used to buy a larger
quantity of goods. But this is no solution for it merely shifts the
question to, "Under what condition will MV remain the same?"
Another example is the argument that the extent to which a cut in
money wages will increase employment is governed by the elasticity
of demand for labor. This may mean the elasticity of demand for
labor with respect to the real wage or the elasticity of demand for
labor with respect to the money wage. If the former, the question
is begged in one way, since a reduction in the real wage is a concomitant of an increase in employment with the resultant decline
in the marginal productivity of labor. A correct translation of the
argument is: there will be an increase in employment if such
increase reduces the marginal productivity of labor. If the latter,
the question is begged in another and more direct manner, for the
elasticity of demand for labor with respect to the money wage is
nothing but a measure of the degree to which a cut in money wages
will increase (or decrease) employment. We may, therefore, leave
the refinements of our second form of illegitimate generalization
and concentrate a little more closely on Say's Law and Keynes's
Law. We shall find that these parallel laws meet.

Say's Law is usually found in a more rigid form than the rule
given above. It declares not merely interdependence but equality

between total supply and total demand. If this means that the total quantity of each good actually demanded is equal to the total quantity of it that is actually supplied, it is a true but not very useful identity, since the two phrases represent the same quantity of goods that changes hands in a given period. If it means that a general increase in output in the "right" proportions will increase total money expenditures by exactly as much as the increase in the selling price of the total output, this is again true but not much more useful. For this immediately follows from the identity of the monies paid for the goods with the monies received for them. Furthermore, it is misleading to suggest that this identity depends upon the maintenance of "right" proportions.

But such interpretations of Say's Law in terms of tautological identities will not do. They prevent the law from being used for the purpose for which it was designed. This was to show that although a section of the economy may get into trouble by producing too much relatively to the rest of the economy, a general overproduction is impossible since it creates its own demand. For this it is not sufficient to show that if output in general is increased, the increase in demand in the sense of the amount paid for the output remains equal to the supply in the sense of the amount received for the output—which is what the identities repeat—since this is true also of any particular section of the economy and does not prevent it from getting into trouble through overproduction. What has to be shown is that the increase in demand that accompanies a general increase in output will be equal not merely to the increase in receipts but to the increase in costs, including such real profits as are necessary to maintain the increase in output. The law must say that demand is equal not only to supply but to cost, whatever the level of output and employment. Such a law would be adequate for the purpose. Unfortunately there appears to be no reason for expecting such a law to be true, but this relationship between demand and cost sounds something like Keynes's Law that "demand is not independent of cost." Perhaps the more exact formulation of this will contain some clew.

A more complete formulation of Keynes's Law does indeed say

that under certain circumstances a change in wages and so in total costs including normal profits will bring about an equal change in demand, but this is not applicable at all to our case. For here it was to be applied to the effect of an increase in output while this Keynesian proposition is strictly confined to a simplified case where there is no change in output but only a change in the wage rate which, just because it makes demand increase as much as cost, prevents any change in output. It is the very last thing, therefore, to be used to show that an increase in output would always be validated by a sufficient increase in demand.

There is, however, another rule to which Mr. Keynes has drawn attention, which is connected with what happens to the relationship between total cost and total demand when output increases. This is the rule that as people's real incomes increase they spend on consumption only a part of the increase, saving the rest. (The marginal propensity to consume is less than unity.) If, as Mr. Keynes usually does, we assume the rate of investment as given and determined by factors other than current consumption, then this rule directly contradicts the non-tautological Say's Law that we saw was necessary to show that a general increase in output generated its own demand. An increase in output will always fail to increase demand by as much as cost, because the extra demand is only a part of the extra income and the extra cost is the whole of the extra income, so that demand will fall behind cost as surely as the part is less than the whole.

We may instead follow Dr. Lange and make the more realistic assumption that an increase in consumption increases the marginal efficiency of investment so that as output of consumption goods increases, there is also an increased demand for newly manufactured assets. This would make it possible for demand to increase by exactly as much as cost when output increased; namely, when the marginal propensity to consume, plus the marginal propensity to invest (the increment of investment that resulted from the increment of consumption that resulted from one unit increase in income) were exactly equal to unity. This is not only indefinitely unlikely a priori, but from the degree of short-period stability of employment that we actually experience it would appear that this sum is definitely less than unity. If the marginal propensity to consume plus the marginal propensity to invest were equal to unity, there would be no limit to the rate of expansion or contraction of employment. While if it were at all greater than unity any expansion or contraction of output would be of a self-accelerating or explosive nature. Fluctuations in employment, like those of the trade cycle, might be expected to take several weeks, or perhaps days, instead of years.

What is really implied in Say's Law is that every individual desire to save is in the nature of a desire to buy a newly manufactured asset. Any increase in income from an increase in output would all be spent either on consumption goods or on new investment goods and the increase in demand would be equal to the increase in costs, including profit, so that no losses need be incurred. But in any modern economy where individuals can save and use their savings to demand not only new investment goods but already existing assets, the whole scheme breaks down and—what so many economic theorists still find so surprising—an equilibrium with unemployment is possible where an expansion of output would lead to losses and a return to the previous equilibrium level of employment.

It should be observed that this criticism of Say's Law does not directly mention the existence of money. What is wrong with it is that it makes a real proposition about the effect of an increase in output on profits which is based upon the questionable assumption that every desire to save is a desire for newly manufactured assets, but which acquired great prestige by being confused with the tautologies considered above. The "truth" of these is, of course, above question.

Economists who have felt something to be wrong have, however, tried to find a flaw in the tautologies instead of in the proposition about profits. Consider the tautology that the supplies of n-1 commodities in exchange for the nth is identical with the demand for the nth commodity and so total supply of all the n commodities for each other is identical with the total demand.

This is independent of the size of output or of prices or of anything else. Now let one of the commodities be forgotten in the calculation; this will upset everything for the supply of n-2 commodities for the nth will not be identical with the total demand for the nth commodity, unless none of the n-1th commodity (the forgotten one) is offered against the nth commodity. Now if none of the forgotten commodities is offered against any other commodity and no other commodity is offered against it, it is neutral as it were and it will not matter if it is left out of account. The calculations will still turn out correct.

Money was considered to be such a commodity if there were no change in the total amount of it. For in that case all goods other than money can be conceived of as exchanged only for each other—money acting merely as an intermediary—no money being acquired or given up. Money can therefore be left out of the picture as it was by Say and by other classical economists who regarded money as a "veil" that merely obscured the workings of the economy; so that an increase in the supply of goods other than money would be accompanied by an equal increase in the demand for them. But if there is a change in the amount of money it is no longer "neutral" and leaving it out of the account will upset the calculations. If the amount of money increased, the flow of new money was imagined to constitute a demand for commodities not originating in any supply of commodities and so the demand for commodities became greater than the supply; and vice versa if the amount of money diminished. The existence of money and the possibility of changes in its total amount (as well as changes in the amounts held by particular individuals or desired to be held by them) was thus supposed to overthrow the tautology or at least its applicability to a monetary economy, and so to admit the possibility of unemployment, inflation, dislocation—all the horrors of the real world.

It might be thought that the tautology could be re-established in all its impregnability by simply including money among the commodities and then total supply would equal total demand whatever happened to the amount of money or its distribution or the desire for it. But this would have taken away the basis of the whole concept of "neutral" money and of many a strange mythology about the beauties of a barter economy in which money did not exist, or could be ignored, and where there was always equilibrium with full employment. As soon, however, as it is recognized that the significant part of Say's Law is the real proposition about saving and investment and profits and no supply-equals-demand tautology, this kind of concern with the non-neutrality of money, as the villain of the piece, loses all significance. One can only regret the energy and ingenuity that has been spent by people like Dr. Koopmans in developing the ramifications of monetary neutrality.

Instead of money, one may attempt to introduce labor as one of the items in the tautological checkerboard so that unemployment of labor does not mean that an increase in output would not create its own demand, but that there is a relative oversupply of labor (relatively to commodities). If only more commodities were produced, this would increase the demand for labor. But this is an even more transparent trick than the one with money. It is true that if more commodities were produced there would be more employment, but that is not because the products are offered in exchange for labor, rather, it is because labor is needed to produce the products. And if there were such an increase it would involve losses (because the marginal propensity to consume plus the marginal propensity to invest is less than unity) and so there would be a return to the old position. One cannot get anything out of trying to trick the tautologies. However, we must not let them trick us into taking up too much time with them. We will, therefore, leave them here and go on to consider how we can apply our analysis to the question of the relation of wage policies and price policies.

The first and simplest case to be considered is that which may be called the Keynesian special case. Here it is assumed that all prices other than wages are perfectly flexible and that the monetary supply is infinitely elastic.

From the assumption that all prices other than wages are perfectly flexible, it follows that there can be no unemployment of such factors. All those that have a marginal productivity greater than zero are employed because their price falls as much as is necessary, relatively to wages, to make their employment profitable. The assumption is plausible and in conformity with the assumption of rationality of entrepreneurs and capital owners who would rather get something for the use of their property then let it be idle, while labor has nonrational money-wage demands.

The assumptions of an infinitely elastic supply of money with respect to the rate of interest implies a rigid interest rate. This is not a plausible assumption but only a device that is useful as a preparation for the examinations of the more realistic situations where the monetary supply is not infinitely elastic and the rate of interest consequently is not absolutely rigid; because it enables us to isolate the influences of the rate of interest by first examining situations in which it cannot change.

In this case there can be no such thing as a price policy separate from a wage policy, since the level of wages determines all prices, the level of real output having been determined independently of wages and prices, by the level of real investment (itself determined by the rate of interest and the schedule of the marginal efficiency of investment), and the propensity to consume. Any policy that determines the level of wages would thereby determine all prices, total output and employment, the ratios between all the prices being unaffected by the decision as to the level of wages and so also of prices.

Next let us suppose the wage, too, to be flexible, whether this is because of or in spite of wage policies. Then if the rate of interest, the schedule of the marginal efficiency of investment, and the propensity to consume are such that the equilibrium level of employment is less than full employment, unemployment will cause wages to fall, and prices, as we have seen in the previous case, will move together with wages. But this does nothing to change the situation and so wages and prices would keep on falling indefinitely. We see that if the monetary supply and all other prices are perfectly flexible, then a rigidity of the money wage is necessary to give determinacy or stability to prices. And not only to prices. For if the fall in wages and prices begins to be anticipated the schedule of the marginal efficiency of investment will fall and there will be a decline in output and employment as a result of the wage flexibility.   An expected fall in prices and uncertainty about the maintenance of economic activity will increase the desire to hold cash. This will make no difference in our case because the infinitely elastic supply of money will prevent it from doing any harm, but if the supply of money were less than infinitely elastic this increase in liquidity-preference would raise the rate of interest and in this way again work to diminish investment, output, and employment. But these are arguments about expectations and a little beyond our present scheme.

We may now give up the assumption of infinitely elastic monetary supply so that the rate of interest is no longer rigid while still assuming that all prices other than wages are perfectly flexible. We now have either a fixed amount of money, so that any increase in the desire to hold money will merely raise the rate of interest, or else a flexible monetary policy that increases the amount of money when the rate of interest rises (as a result of an increase in the desire to hold cash) but does not increase the amount of money sufficiently to prevent any rise in the rate of interest.   If it did, the supply of money would be infinitely elastic.   An increase in the desire to hold cash will now raise the rate of interest while a decrease in the desire to hold cash will lower the rate of interest.

The level of money wages will now determine not only prices but the volume of employment and output.   At a lower level of money wages less money would be needed, if the output were the same and all prices (including prices of assets) were lower in the same proportion as wages, so that people would want to hold less money and the rate of interest would fall.   This would tend to increase investment and real output and employment and a new equilibrium would be reached with a lower rate of interest, a smaller amount of money, and a larger volume of economic activity (unless there were full employment to begin with, in which case there would be an inflation that would restore wages to the original level). It should be noted that this is not the reason for arguing that a lower wage must involve more employment, if M or MV is the same. M and MV cannot be the same unless we assume that there is a deliberate and successful monetary policy to make it so. On our assumption, M will be less at the lower rate of interest if there is any flexibility of the monetary supply at all, and V will be less because at a lower rate of interest there is less incentive for economizing the use of cash.

If now, with the rate of interest flexible we assume the wage rate also flexible, we get a tendency toward full employment. As wages and all prices fall there is a decline in the need for cash to fulfill all the purposes for which it was previously held. This will lead to a fall in the rate of interest (unless it is offset by an increase in liquidity-preference on account of an anticipated fall in prices or output). The lower rate of interest will increase the rate of investment (unless the schedule of the marginal efficiency of investment has declined because of expectations of a fall in prices or output) and this will lead to an increase in the output of consumption goods (unless prospects of bad times or falling prices have weakened the propensity to consume). If all the hurdles are crossed, wages keep on falling until full employment is reached. It is important to note that the reduction in the rate of interest is what does the trick and to remember that if the rate of interest is reduced directly, instead of by means of falling wages, the obstacles mentioned, which may be proof against any subsequent further fall in the rate of interest, will not have occasion to arise.

Analytically, there is no difference between wages and the price of any other factor of production. The four cases we have examined so far might be repeated with wages perfectly flexible throughout and, say, rents playing the part that we have attributed to wages. If rents were fixed in money, and wages, as well as all other prices, were perfectly flexible, the level of money rents would determine all prices and if the monetary supply were imperfectly elastic it would also determine the rate of interest and the degree of employment of land. Labor would always be employed and only land could be unemployed.

We may now go on to consider cases where there are two factors the rigidity of whose prices will be considered. We may call them labor and land.   Assume again a rigid rate of interest (infinitely flexible monetary supply).   We now must see that prices depend upon both wages and rents.   The rate of interest determines the level of employment of labor and of land only when we are given the prices of both labor and land.   But if both of these prices are raised or lowered in the same proportion, this will merely change all prices in the same proportion, leaving employment of both labor and land at their previous levels.   With the given rate of interest it is only changes in the ratio between the prices of the rigid factors that can affect the real situation.

The higher one price relatively to the other, the lower will be the degree of its employment and the higher will be its real rate of remuneration, and, consequently, the higher will be the degree of employment of the other factor and the lower its real rate of remuneration.   But we can no longer say that the rate of interest uniquely determines the volume of economic activity.   For the propensity to consume, and even more so the inducement to invest, may be more responsive to the one price than to the other, and if this is the case there will, with the same rate of interest, be a greater rate of investment and/or a greater output of consumption goods if the factor to which the response is greater is cheaper relatively to the other.

Next we may suppose the prices of the two factors to be flexible, while the rate of interest is rigid.   This case has been examined above where we saw that prices fall indefinitely while employment does not change.   We now have an amendment to make to the previous result where it appeared that although there was no stability of prices, there was determinacy of output and employment of labor, while land and all other factors were fully employed. The indefensible asymmetry between labor and land was due to an implicit assumption that while wages were flexible they were not as perfectly flexible as the prices of all these other factors, so that when unemployment made wages fall and keep on falling, other prices always managed to fall as much as necessary relatively to wages to keep fully employed, while wages never fell relatively to other factor prices even enough to cause any shift of unemploy-

ment from labor to the other factors.   Perhaps we should say that
the assumption was that wages were plastic, i.e., they fell and kept
on falling at some finite rate as long as there was unemployment
of labor, but the prices of other factors were perfectly flexible so
that they were always able to catch up with the plastic wage rates.

Now we have wages and rents both plastic, both falling.   With
the qualifications made above the rate of interest determines the
volume of employment of land-*cum*-labor.   How the employment
will be divided between land and labor depends upon their relative
prices and that is indeterminate except in so far as this is given by
some lag in adjustment while prices are perpetually falling.

If we now allow the rate of interest to be flexible, we see that
wages and rents determine both prices and output.   At lower wages
and rents the ratio between them unchanged, all prices will be
lower, less cash will be needed, and there will be a lower rate of
interest and a greater volume of activity (unless there was full
employment to begin with, in which case there will result an inflation which restores wages and rents and all other prices to the
original level).

If, with a flexible interest rate, wages and rents are plastic, then
there is the same tendency toward full employment (of both land
and labor), as stated above, with the same possible obstacles that
can be avoided in the same way; namely, by reducing the rate of
interest directly via an increase in the supply schedule of money,
instead of indirectly, via reduction in wages, rents, and prices.

We have now examined a simplified set of eight different cases
consisting of the combinations of a rigid and a flexible interest rate
with one factor price fixed, one factor price plastic, two factor
prices fixed, and two factor prices plastic, all other prices considered
to be perfectly flexible.   These simple tools enable us to see the
effects and the mechanism of the effects of absolute and relative
changes in factor prices.   We can use them for analyzing more
complex and more realistic cases if we remember that the results
we get about the relative prices of land and labor are just as applicable to any pair of prices—prices of different kinds of land, capital
goods or services, or prices of different kinds or grades of labor.

Even the prices of products can be treated in the same way.   In so far as products are used in the production of further products they are factors and in so far as rigidity of their price relatively to other prices limits the demand for them and so for the factors used in making them, the repercussions on the economy as a whole are just as if these factors had rigid prices (apart from the effects due to the different distribution of the receipts from the sale of the rigidly priced product).   It may sometimes be conveninent to fit such a case into our framework by supposing the rigidity in the product-price to be due to the incorporation of a fictitious rigidly priced factor, supplied by the entrepreneur at the stage of production where the factor in question emerges.

We may conclude by stating as examples some of the more obvious results we can get out of our scheme that have some bearing on wage and price policies.

A policy of general cost reduction amounts to nothing but an inconvenient and roundabout attempt at lowering the rate of interest when that can be done directly by increasing the amount of money.   A general policy of raising prices is even worse.   Its direct effects, just like lowering wages, amount to nothing because they cancel out, while the indirect effect on the rate of interest is to raise it and so to curtail output and employment.

Significant policies must, therefore, be concerned with the ratios between costs or between prices, and not with absolute levels, and there might be a useful purpose served in breaking down some price or cost rigidities while leaving others.   Our examination of rigid rents shows that they are beneficial to the employment of labor though they adversely affect labor's wages.   For the lower one price factor is relatively to the other, the higher will be the degree of its employment for any given rate of interest, and the higher will be the rate of interest that is low enough to give it any given degree of employment (though the lower will be its real remuneration for any given degree of its employment).   But this is so only if we assume the rate of interest, the schedule of the marginal efficiency of investment, and the propensity to consume as given.   This we cannot do.   For in so far as prices other than wages are kept up by rigidities, a larger proportion of income will go to non-wage earners with a lower propensity to consume so that total real income (and output and employment) will be less for any given rate of investment. Further, there will probably be less investment for any given rate of interest because there will be less land and existing equipment available to co-operate with the new equipment—though this effect is uncertain. Finally, there will be a higher rate of interest for any given condition of monetary supply because of the greater demand for cash at higher prices (and possibly also because of the greater demand for cash by property owners compared with workers). Therefore, rent rigidity will almost certainly be harmful to both employment and real wages of labor.

Since rent and wages, both being prices of factors of production, play the same part in our analytical structure, the same argument might be applied to wage rigidities. A particular kind of labor, by keeping up its wage through restricting entry to its craft, may cause employment in general to diminish. The removal of such a rigidity by, say, allowing or encouraging other workers to enter this trade and lowering the wage therein may seem to have the same beneficial effect as the removal of a rigidity in rents or in the price of some other non-labor service or product. But the benefits are much more doubtful. There may not be much difference between the propensity to consume of the different kinds of workers and in so far as the breaking down of the rigid price shows itself in the cheapening of a product consumed by wealthier people the shift of real incomes to them is likely to diminish total output by lowering the social or representative propensity to consume.

In deciding which prices it is desirable to reduce relatively to others, we are thrown back on the criteria developed above as to the effects on employment of the relative prices of labor and land, given the rate of interest. That factor price should be lowered to which the marginal efficiency schedule of investment and the marginal propensity to consume are most responsive. A conspicuous case of this would be the wages in the building trades, a reduction of which would so much increase the marginal efficiency of investment in housing as to swamp any of the offsetting influences. Examples of a price reduction that could considerably increase the propensity to consume seem to be more difficult to think of.

But even in such "ideal" cases as the building trades example, we should be careful to remember that it is only the relative reduction in this wage that is significant, and if it is easier to raise other wages instead this will do the trick just as well as long as monetary policy can maintain the same rate of interest; i.e., as long as the amount of money can be increased so as to satisfy the greater demand for cash at the higher level of prices.

Finally it should be noted that in many instances the adjustment of relative prices is most easily and automatically obtained as a by-product of the more straightforward attempt to increase economic activity by operating on the ultimate determinants; i.e., lowering the rate of interest by an easy money policy, raising the marginal efficiency schedule of investment by public works and subsidies, and increasing the propensity to consume by redistribution of income from savers to spenders.

By this means the prices that would be relatively higher are pulled up by increased demand—which is what is wanted—rather than their being pushed up by price policies. In some cases—like our building trades example—a general expansion may pull up the prices that ought to stay down if there is to be a better use of resources, and it is desirable to discourage these prices from going up or to force them down. But even here we cannot escape from the same fundamental criteria—the ultimate determinants of the level of economic activity. All policies of general or particular, of absolute or relative prices of factors or of products can be decided only in the light of the effects on the rate of interest, the marginal efficiency schedule of investment, and the propensity to consume.

18

CHANGES IN REAL AND MONEY WAGES *

By Lorie Tarshis †

In this note I should like to present certain data which, I believe, amplify some of the conclusions reached by Mr. Dunlop in his article in the ECONOMIC JOURNAL for September 1938.[1] In particular these data relate to the first section of his article and to the citation from Mr. Keynes' *General Theory*, quoted on p. 413: "But in the case of changes in the general level of wages, it will be found, I think, that the change in real wages associated with a change in money wages, so far from being usually in the same direction, is almost always in the opposite direction. When money wages are rising, that is to say, it will be found that real wages are falling; and when money wages are falling real wages are rising."[2]

The materials on which my conclusions are based are these. Series to indicate the level month by month of money earnings per hour and real hourly earnings were prepared.[3] The figures relate to wage-earners and employees in the lower-salary groups in the United States. The series begin with January 1932 and extend to March 1938—75 months in all. The coverage is quite wide: the earnings of employees in manufacturing, mining, public utilities, retail and wholesale trade, laundries, dyeing and cleaning,

---

* *Economic Journal*, Volume XLIX, March 1939, pages 150–154. Reprinted by courtesy of the publisher and author.

† Tufts College.

[1] John T. Dunlop, "The Movement of Real and Money Wages," *Economic Journal*, September 1938, pp. 413–34.

[2] *General Theory of Employment, Interest and Money*, p. 10.

[3] There are advantages in using monthly data, since we can thereby assume the existence of the conditions of the short period. Certainly Mr. Keynes, in writing the paragraph quoted above, assumed such a framework.

hotels, railroads and building construction are provided for in the indices. Some important groups are, due to the lack of data, omitted, the most important of them being employees in the service of the Government—about 3.3 millions in all; wage-earners in agriculture—1.5 millions; employees in the professional services— nearly 1 million; domestic servants numbering about 1.75 millions; and other service industries—nearly 1 million. In all, into the calculation of these figures for money wages and real wages enter materials that relate to more than 16 of the 28 million employees in the United States.[4]

To allow for changes in the purchasing power of money wages, I used for my basic series the index of the cost of living that is published by the Bureau of Labor Statistics of the United States Department of Labor. Since this index covers only four months— or fewer—a year, I secured estimates for the intervening months on the basis of the monthly index of living costs published by the National Industrial Conference Board. Finally, I prepared what I shall in this note identify as the "corrected" index of real wages. The corrections were made to allow for changes in the cost of living that were due to changes in the prices of agricultural products.[5] A table containing the relevant data appears below.

Two scatter diagrams were prepared. In the first I measured along one axis percentage changes in the level of money wages, and along the other axis percentage changes—for the corresponding months—in the level of "uncorrected" real wages. In the second diagram the relations between the percentage changes in money wages and the percentage changes for corresponding months in the "corrected" index of real wages were indicated. The second diagram is presented on p. 334. There is no considerable difference

---

[4] And it is doubtful, in any case, whether we should *for this purpose* take account of the earnings of Government employees and of certain others—for obviously Mr. Keynes' arguments assume that the employing units make their decisions on the basis of profits.

[5] For the United States, changes in the terms of trade between agriculture and industry are of some importance in determining the level of real wages; changes in the terms of trade in the international sense are relatively unimportant, and were here neglected.

MONEY WAGES AND REAL WAGES IN THE UNITED STATES

	Money Hourly Earnings (Actual Figures)	Real Wages Per Hour (Index: 1932 = 100)	
		Uncorrected	"Corrected"
1932 Jan.........	53.0	102.6	104.0
Feb.........	52.2	102.7	103.2
Mar.........	51.0	100.6	101.0
Apr.........	50.6	100.6	100.9
May.........	50.4	101.4	101.1
June........	49.6	100.6	100.1
July.........	49.2	100.1	100.0
Aug.........	48.4	99.2	99.3
Sept.........	47.3	97.4	97.8
Oct.........	47.0	97.7	97.4
Nov.........	46.9	98.0	97.7
Dec.........	46.6	98.4	97.5
1933 Jan.........	46.7	100.3	97.8
Feb.........	46.4	101.6	99.6
Mar.........	46.5	102.6	100.9
Apr.........	46.0	101.6	100.5
May........	45.8	100.5	102.0
June........	45.1	97.9	98.7
July.........	45.9	96.4	99.1
Aug.........	50.5	104.4	106.5
Sept.........	52.2	107.1	109.2
Oct.........	53.3	109.9	111.7
Nov.........	53.2	110.4	112.4
Dec.........	52.6	110.2	111.9
1934 Jan.........	54.7	114.3	117.0
Feb.........	54.6	113.0	116.4
Mar.........	54.4	112.3	115.7
Apr.........	55.2	114.3	117.3
May........	55.7	115.1	118.0
June........	55.9	115.2	119.3
July.........	56.4	116.4	120.6
Aug.........	56.5	116.0	122.0
Sept.........	56.8	115.2	122.0
Oct.........	56.7	115.6	121.6
Nov.........	56.7	115.9	121.9
Dec.........	56.4	115.4	121.8

Money Wages and Real Wages in the United States—*Continued*

		Money Hourly Earnings (*Actual Figures*)	Real Wages Per Hour (*Index: 1932 = 100*)	
			Uncorrected	*"Corrected"*
1935	Jan..........	57.4	116.4	124.3
	Feb.	58.1	116.5	124.8
	Mar.........	57.6	115.6	123.6
	Apr.	58.2	115.9	124.5
	May	58.2	116.4	125.0
	June	58.3	116.9	124.8
	July.........	58.0	116.7	124.4
	Aug.........	57.6	116.0	124.2
	Sept........	57.6	115.7	123.9
	Oct.........	57.6	115.4	123.3
	Nov.........	57.7	115.2	122.8
	Dec.	57.6	114.4	122.3
1936	Jan..........	58.6	116.5	124.5
	Feb.	58.4	116.9	125.4
	Mar.........	58.5	117.5	125.2
	Apr.	58.3	117.0	124.8
	May	58.5	116.9	124.2
	June	58.6	115.6	123.5
	July.........	58.6	115.6	124.4
	Aug.........	58.6	115.1	124.8
	Sept........	58.5	114.7	124.4
	Oct.	58.6	115.4	125.0
	Nov.........	59.2	116.5	126.6
	Dec.	59.2	116.2	127.2
1937	Jan..........	60.1	117.0	128.8
	Feb.	60.5	117.7	129.5
	Mar.........	61.0	117.7	130.4
	Apr.	62.7	120.6	132.9
	May	63.7	121.9	133.5
	June	63.9	122.4	133.7
	July.........	64.5	123.5	135.4
	Aug.........	64.9	124.0	135.2
	Sept........	64.9	123.5	134.5
	Oct.	65.4	124.3	133.5
	Nov.........	65.4	124.8	132.3
	Dec.	64.2	122.9	129.8
1938	Jan..........	64.6	125.0	131.7
	Feb.	64.5	125.6	131.9
	Mar.........	64.2	125.1	131.1

in the results, whether we are concerned with the "corrected" or "uncorrected" index of real wages.

It is obvious that there is a rather high direct or positive association between changes in money wages and changes in real wages. Mr. Keynes appears to be mistaken, for when money wages are rising, it is generally found that real wages are rising, and when money wages are falling, real wages are usually falling. The coefficient of association[6] is +0.86. If we omit from our calcu-

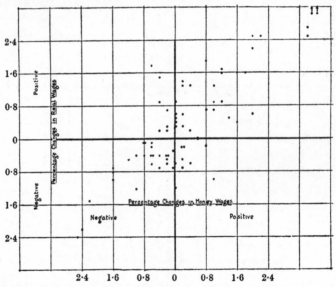

lations those changes for which there were changes of two-tenths of one per cent. or less, the coefficient of association is even higher: +0.96. The coefficient of association between changes in money wages and changes in the "uncorrected" index of real wages on the same basis is +0.94.

Mr. Keynes' conclusions, which are not borne out statistically for this period, are based upon three assumptions which, in my opinion, are not realistic. The first is that money wages only begin to rise after unemployment has fallen to quite a low figure. The second is that increases in output beyond this level—in the

[6] G. Yule, *An Introduction to the Theory of Statistics*, p. 38.

region in which money wages are rising—are associated with rising marginal costs, even in the absence of rises in money wages. Finally, he assumes that the degree of competition does not change appreciably as between slump and boom, and, more important, that price revisions occur frequently.   It is because none of these assumptions truly portrayed conditions in the United States, because there were many wage-goods the prices of which were inflexible, and because marginal cost curves were not inclined positively, that we get a positive association when we should expect, on Mr. Keynes' assumptions, the association to be inverse and negative.

POSTSCRIPT.   Further analysis of the material, undertaken after this note had been set up in proof, brought to light certain results relevant to this inquiry.   These have to do with the relationship between changes in real wages per hour and changes in man-hours of employment.

The data for man-hours are derived from the industries, mentioned above, for which we have wage data.   If changes in man-hours are related to changes in "real hourly wages, uncorrected" a rather high negative association is to be found.   For the period of 75 months, considered above, the coefficient of association is -0.64, and with the exclusion of changes of two-tenths of one per cent. or less, the coefficient stands at -0.75.   That is to say, changes in real hourly wages are in general opposite in direction from changes in man-hours of work.   However, it is surprising that there is a less close association between changes in the "corrected" (cf. above) figures for real wages and man-hours.   In this case, the coefficient stood at only -0.48.

19

WAGE POLICIES OF TRADE UNIONS*

By John T. Dunlop †

The use of the term policy has become a fad in recent years, particularly as applied to industrial price formation.[1] Such popularity is apt to breed ambiguity. The phrase is here used simply to imply that (a) trade unions have some discretion and alternatives in the bargaining process through which terms of the labor bargain are determined, (b) some types of wage strategy and pattern will be found superior to others by a trade union, given its objectives and specific problems, and (c) the mechanism whereby a trade union experiments with tactics and chooses among them need not connote an entirely self-conscious process.

An investigation of trade union wage policy may be thought to be an elucidation of the obvious since the only objectives are more favorable wage structures. As Professor Bakke states, "I guess really what I mean when I say fair wages is more wages."[2] At times, "more wages" has been construed as only higher wage rates. All wage policy by this view is epitomized by the slogan, "push 'em up." A little study will show not only that this view is an unwarranted simplification but that a great deal is to be learned from a study of the manipulation of wage structures for specific objectives. Just as the statement that an enterprise attempts to maximize profits does not preclude fruitful investigation of price policy, so any objective of a trade union does not

---

* *American Economic Review*, Volume XXXII, Supplement, 1942, pages 290–301. Reprinted by courtesy of the publisher and author.

† Harvard University.

[1] E. G. Nourse, "The Meaning of 'Price Policy,'" *Quarterly Journal of Economics*, LV (February, 1941), pp. 175–209.

[2] E. Wight Bakke, *The Unemployed Worker* (New Haven: Yale University Press, 1940), p. 66.

automatically determine the wage structure.[3] The interesting issues arise in examining the formulation of broad wage policies and the selection of detailed wage tactics.

The terms of sale for labor services are typically complex, either designating or implying a great many conditions. Some of these terms directly influence the price, that is the wage, defined as the amount of money exchanged between the buyer and seller per unit of services. This group of terms—designated as the wage structure —ordinarily contains a base rate modified by overtime, bonus arrangements, vacations with pay, minimum guarantees, shift differentials, and other extras. The remaining terms of an agreement of sale—labeled the nonpecuniary structure—specify conditions of work, grievance procedure, seniority, union recognition, working hours, strike limitation, and the duration of the agreement. This latter group of stipulations is not to be regarded as less essential to the total agreement than the wage structure. The contract is made in view of all the conditions of the exchange. At times, bargaining over the total agreement will include some substitution between these two groups of terms. In fact, every provision of the labor contract can be regarded as constituting the price of labor in some fashion. The important implication, for the current discussion, is that discussions of wage policy must always be placed in the context of the total labor bargain with all the terms of sale.

I. Non-Income Objectives of Wage Policy

Aside from the obvious goal of affecting the income of a specified group of wage earners, wage policy may be directed toward a great many other objectives. Both the multidimensional feature of the wage structure and the directness of impact of changes in this structure on costs and incomes render wage changes a highly effective tool. Unless essentially non-income objectives are isolated, the wage policy of many unions will appear incomprehensible and incompetent when appraised from the criterion of

---

[3] The difference between discussing "policy" and "pricing" really involves different levels of abstraction.

maximizing the wage bill. The specific goal of a policy may have been something entirely different.

1. Many changes in wage structure have been intended to promote membership in a trade union. An organizing drive will be more apt to succeed if prospective members can be convinced that they will immediately benefit from affiliation. And there can be no more convincing demonstration of this benefit than a wage increase. Consequently, whether the organizing drive precedes a Labor Board election or is part of a strike, promises of an "increase" will be made. If the union is then to hold its recruits, the "goods must be delivered." In this context, the long-run effects on employment or the future of any specific enterprise are small matters; the principal objective is organization! The trade union is not alone in recognizing the efficacy of changes in wage structure as a means for other objectives. Many enterprises have attempted to prevent or forestall organization by granting an increase. The wage spurt of 1936–37 seems largely a matter of bargaining over organization. Typically, these increases were not successful in their primary objective and a further increase was necessary to the union that had won an election or gone out on strike. In most cases a single wage increase would have been sufficient had not the attempt been made to buy off organization.

2. One of the most complex problems that faces every union is the way in which the available work shall be allocated among prospective wage earners. Wage policy may be used to effectuate this division. The payment of overtime after a standard day is an effective device to encourage the enterprise to hire additional workers rather than incur penalty rates.[4] This feature of overtime rates is most clearly seen in periods of large unemployment when strong pressure is exerted to reduce, if not eliminate, overtime. In seasonal industries, restrictions on overtime rates may be relaxed only at the peak of activity.[5]

---

[4] This explanation is only a part of overtime policy. Overtime may also be regarded as a form of price discrimination.

[5] *The Hosiery Worker*, 16 (December 2, 1938), and the *Eastern Headwear Agreement of the Hat, Cap, and Military Workers*, p. 10.

3. An exceedingly rapid change in wage structure has been made in the last five years with the extension of vacations with pay. Over 25 per cent of all organized wage earners now receive annual vacations with pay under collective bargaining agreements.[6] This spectacular development indicates a wage policy that is directed toward specific elements of the labor bargain: the relative preference for vacations with pay is high as compared to other terms in the wage structure. That vacations with pay should rank so high in wage earners' preference is not unrelated to the experience with "leisure" during the period of prolonged unemployment in the early thirties. For most wage earners leisure had become synonymous with the anxiety of job hunting. Under vacations with pay, "a workingman may have a period of leisure when he is not harassed by unemployment."[7] Furthermore, his vacation is enjoyed, "not as a gratuity of the employer, but as a legally recognized right in return for employment services rendered."[8] Wage policy has been used to achieve in the vacation with pay a social status that had been reserved to other groups. An additional circumstance increasing the relative preference of vacations with pay to a straight wage increase is the automatic character of the saving. The psychic costs of saving may be thought lower since the funds do not pass through the wage earner's hands week by week. For these reasons, then, vacations with pay have been adopted; wage policy has been directed towards achieving a particular type of wage structure.

4. Wage policy has also been used as an effective means of controlling the rate of introduction of technical innovations. The relative wage rates and costs on the new and the old machine or process will significantly influence the rate at which an enterprise will find it profitable to adopt a change. For instance, the flint glass workers apparently attempted to "discourage the use of lamp chimney machines by demanding rates that would equalize the

---

[6] "Vacations with Pay in Union Agreements, 1940," *Monthly Labor Review*, 51 (November, 1940), p. 1070.

[7] *Machinists' Monthly Journal*, 49 (September, 1937), p. 589.

[8] *Loc. cit.*, p. 588.

cost of chimneys produced by machinery and by hand."[9] In 1908 the Glass Bottle Blowers took a reduction of 20 per cent on beer bottles to "protect the manufacturer who was unable to secure one of those machines . . . and to protect ourselves."[10] The international officials of the Glass Bottle Blowers apparently were convinced in 1927 that a basic wage of $6.50 a day in the blown ware departments would lead to a rapid introduction of machinery. For this reason they urged that the proposed increase favored by many locals be voted down.[11]

5. A further non-income objective of wage policy is frequently the attainment of desired working conditions. A wage premium put upon especially unfavorable hours of work or circumstances of employment is intended to remove these conditions. There may be great difficulty in distinguishing between policies directed at preventing undesirable work situations and policies using such conditions simply as a means of increasing income. The more certain that an enterprise cannot avoid the unfavorable situation, the more likely the policy is directed primarily toward higher income. Furthermore, direct action in the form of specific prohibition may be resorted to rather than penalty rates. Nonetheless, there are undoubtedly situations in which differential rates are used to discourage objectionable features of work situations. The provision in many agreements that a minimum daily wage must be paid to any worker required to report for work is intended to remove the inconvenience of persistent unsuccessful reporting.

6. Wage policy may be used to implement the control of entrance to a trade by means of the differential rates paid to apprentices and to learners. Special rates to handicapped and aged workers are also intended to affect entry into and exit from the trade. The way in which rates are graduated during the period of apprenticeship will undoubtedly influence the length of time many apprentices will stay with their training, and, if other

---

[9] Sumner H. Slichter, *Union Policies and Industrial Management* (Washington: The Brookings Institution, 1941), p. 209.

[10] *Report of Proceedings of the 51st Convention of the Glass Bottle Blowers*, 1929, p. 213.

[11] *Idem.*, 1927, pp. 239–247.

regulations are not operative, the number of apprentices, learners, and helpers the enterprise may choose to employ.

The preceding points have indicated ways in which wage policy may be used to attain essentially non-income objectives. The desired consequences are not primarily related to the total volume of employment or the level of pay rolls. The wage rate structure is used in these instances—frequently in conjunction with more direct action—simply because it may be an effective tool to achieve specific objectives. Any appraisal of wage structures that neglects these types of goals will undoubtedly conclude that the wage policy of a union has been inept; the broadest types of objectives must be recognized if wage policy is to be understood. It will be fruitful to examine in every case the possibility that wage structure may be directed towards: union organization, division of work, specific means of remuneration, like vacations with pay, affecting the rate of technical change, desirable working conditions, and partial control over entrance to the trade and quality of training recruits.

II. Elements of Wage Policy

Wage policies might be sought in the pronouncements of leadership. A careful survey of these statements would reveal much talk about no wage reductions, the living wage, the cultural wage, the saving wage, the fair wage, a share in increased productivity, and a larger share in the national income. Too frequently these broad phrases are attacked as meaningless without sufficient appreciation of the role they play in trade union folklore, in building up a case with the public, and in providing a slogan to the membership. An equally grievous error is to suppose that these slogans and epithets (to use Mr. Green's own phrase)[12] exhaust the content of trade union wage policy. Wage policy as practiced by trade unions must be examined in the context of specific situations; individual collective bargaining agreements and wage conferences constitute the basic sources.

A number of common questions and issues respecting the wage

---

[12] *Report of the Proceedings of the 46th Annual Convention of the American Federation of Labor*, 1926, p. 47.

structure can be discerned which face almost every trade union. The specific course of action adopted to deal with these fundamental difficulties varies from one policy-making unit to another. These problematic issues will be designated elements of wage policy; they are suggested as analytically relevant pegs on which to hang studies of wage structure bargaining. At least the following elements can be identified.

1. Every union is faced with the fundamental task of providing a mechanism whereby decisions respecting wage structures are formulated. The policy-determining units must be identified. Shall it be entirely a local affair? To what extent will international veto power be reserved? The resolution of this difficulty will be influenced predominantly by (a) the relative jurisdiction of the bargaining enterprise and (b) the character of competition among firms in the jurisdiction of different locals. Industries like newspapers, book and job printing, construction, building services, theaters, and hotels are apt to see a good deal of local autonomy for these reasons. A number of internationals were formed primarily because of the common dangers of interlocal wage competition.

2. Every union is interested in the differential wage structures among individuals, operations, and occupations—the membership because of social and financial status and the leadership because of additional concern with the prestige of the organization and continued return to office. Each union then will be faced with questions of differential wages. But the importance of the issue will be largely influenced by the structure of the organization. The more narrow a craft union, the fewer the number of differential rates over which to squabble. The issue may then be expected to be most critical in industrial organizations. Several conflicting pressures may be briefly noted. The firm may press in negotiations for a considerable differential between production workers and more highly skilled individuals on the grounds of insuring a labor supply and in order to provide suitable promotion for service well done. The higher paid workers may feel entitled to a customary dollar differential; the production workers frequently con-

stitute a large majority of the union; the union leadership is confronted with the problem of securing a working compromise among these differences. The course of action adopted by a trade union in such a situation constitutes an element of wage policy.

3. Every union faces issues of the method of wage payment. Shall work be compensated for by the piece, by time, or by some combination of the two? The choice among these alternatives has been fully treated by Slichter in his *Union Policies and Industrial Management* (chapters X and XI). Modifying his treatment slightly, two necessary conditions may be identified for the adoption of piece rates by a trade union: (a) that units of output be definable with precision and (b) that conditions of work be not altered in a manner unfavorable to the wage earners over time. Trade unions may be attracted to piece rates for the reasons that small technical changes or increases in effort are automatically reflected in higher earnings, competing firms have equal direct labor costs, older workers need have no special rates, and because an individual worker is frequently permitted his own pace, particularly when this does not interfere with the output of others. The use of piece work also involves a number of possible difficulties: differentiated earnings may be conducive to internal conflicts within the union; conflicts with management will arise over standards of inspection as well as over the condition of equipment, organization of plant, and quality of material; and disputes may arise over the number of workers to be attached to the enterprise.

4. All international unions and many locals are faced with issues arising from the fact that companies in competition with each other differ in their costs and technical efficiency on the one hand and in their market position and control over price on the other.[13] Are equal rates to be charged to low and high cost and to low and high profit firms alike? Shall rates be staggered according to ability to pay? Each alternative is beset with its own difficulties. Equal rates may mean a very low level since high cost enterprises may not be able to pay a higher time rate. This

---

[13] See the discussion of Solomon Barkin, "Industrial Union Wage Policies," *Plan Age*, Vol. I, No. 1, pp. 1–14.

is certain to lead to internal pressure from the membership when some companies are shown to be making high profits. If equal piece rates are established, no firm has a great deal of inducement to make those technical changes that will reduce the wage costs per unit of output. And even more important, the earnings of wage earners in technically inefficient plants will be much below those in the more competent enterprises. Such a condition will certainly lead to internal dissension, resulting in demands for wage increases where they can be least afforded, and raising the serious question of assigning workers to the favored positions. Should rates be staggered among companies dealing with the union, the first issue will be whether highly efficient firms should receive lower piece rates because of the higher hourly and weekly earnings that are possible or be charged higher rates in view of their greater capacity to pay. If time rates are typically chosen, the practical question will be whether the lower cost firms should be asked to pay the same or higher rates. Any system of staggering is certain to raise bothersome questions of administration regarding the merits of individual cases. The range of difficulties that has been presented constitutes an important element in wage policy. The issues will be more important the greater the cost differentials among the competing enterprises, the larger the share of total costs that are wages and salaries, and the more intense the product market competition.

5. A central element of wage policy is involved in formulating some judgment of the effects of alternative wage structures on employment. Trade union leadership, in effect, must make estimates of the elasticity of demand for labor over very short periods, the cycle, and the longer run. Any appraisal must arise from insight on the specific ways in which wage changes have impact on employment. For instance, the independent effects must be appraised of machine substitution, the shift of business through lower product prices to nonunion firms, the birth of nonunion enterprises, the emergence of kickbacks and other arrangements altering the basic rate, the development or expansion of substitute commodities and services, and impact on the rates of busines

mortality. No over-all elasticity of demand is given; the magnitude and speed of these separate effects have to be appraised for alternative wage structures if any intelligent judgment is to be made of the time pattern of the impact of wage changes upon employment. Estimates of the elasticity of demand in these various time periods will vary, not alone with the industrial scope of the wage bargaining unit, but also with the character of competition in product markets.

Economists have been too inclined to believe that trade unions are oblivious to any relationship between wage rates and employment. A few examples of the many forms in which this dependence is thrust upon a trade union may be interesting. The musicians have recognized the relationship between its rules on number of members of a band and the union wage scale; in some instances an employer has agreed on the amount of money he would expend for musicians during a certain time.[14] The photoengravers maintained a high unemployment fund. Complaints were made of inexperienced journeymen who demanded higher rates and then drew unemployment benefits from the union when their demands were refused. The dependence between rates and employment is made vivid by the depletion of the unemployment fund. The hosiery and molders unions have been forced to be concerned with the elasticity of demand for labor through the impact of nonunion competition. The growing number of employment guarantee agreements—for instance, among the machinists—provide for some form of wage rate concessions in return for more employment. The elasticity of demand for labor is recognized in terms of the specific mechanism which impinges on employment.

In the cyclical context, the basic wage rate is probably regarded as a longer-run price, usually set with an eye to noncyclical circumstances. Basic wage increases in the prosperity phase do not exploit every last degree of bargaining power of the union for short-run advantage. Similarly, wage decreases in depression do not represent the total short-run bargaining advantage of enterprises. While an explanation of this condition is beyond the scope of a

[14] *President's Report, Official Proceedings of the 45th Convention,* 1940, p. 72.

brief paper, a comparison of different types of markets, such as an auction, the stock market, a bid system, and markets with designated seasons, would no doubt be suggestive and instructive.

III. Wage Policy and Market Structures

That wages are dependent upon prices received by enterprises in product markets has been no less evident to trade unions than to economists.   But the relations between product and factor markets have been obscured by the particular equilibrium technique. Prices and wages are determined by supply and demand in different chapters in the textbooks.   The thesis is presented here that the study of factor and product markets simultaneously offers a perspective that proves rewarding in the study of price formation. The criticism is not so much with the logic of particular equilibrium as with the habits of mind it has cultivated.   The proposal is to widen the analytical vision from a single market to several related product and factor markets.   Schematically, the point may be presented in the following figure.

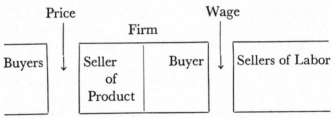

Classically, a trade union is thought of as affecting the wage by restricting the supply of sellers in the factor market.   And yet the above figure shows so clearly that a union may equally well affect the wage by influencing the price of the product.   A surprising amount of trade union activity has been directed toward this end. Attempts to influence the wage through the product market may be classified analytically into: (1) policies designed to shift product demand functions, (2) policies affecting supply conditions in product markets, a form of affecting factor supply conditions, and (3) policies affecting competitive conditions in product markets.

1. The International Ladies' Garment Workers' Union spon-

sored an extensive promotional program for the New York dress industry[15] in negotiations for a renewal of an agreement in early 1941. The proposal was supported by a survey of the industry which examined sales, per capital expenditures, and relative advertising expenditures of competing industries as well as sample costs, earnings, and profits. After ten weeks of conferences, the union's plan was adopted. The promotional campaign was intended to increase demand for the whole industry, not merely in the New York market.

The United Hatters Cap and Millinery Workers have also initiated and supported campaigns to increase the demand for the products of their industries in order to increase the wage bill and increase or protect rates. Local No. 60 initiated the Philadelphia "hat week" and contributed to the campaign. The publicity was apparently so successful that the device of a hat week has spread to other cities. The Millinery Stabilization Commission, Inc., an administrative board created by agreement between the union and several associations of millinery manufacturers, has been concerned with trade promotion and trade practices in the product market.

Lest these cases of activity in the product market be thought rare exceptions, other instances may be briefly mentioned. Many unions have urged higher tariffs to protect the markets of their employers. The Glass Bottle Blowers supported a higher tariff on French perfume bottles, going so far as to send a representative to France to compare costs of manufacturing. The photoengravers made "substantial regular monthly contributions to provide greater distribution of *More Business* being published by the American Photo-Engravers Association for the purpose of further interesting the buyer of engravings of the full possibilities of the process."[16]

---

[15] Julius Hochman, *Industry Planning Through Collective Bargaining*, A Program for Modernizing the New York Dress Industry as Presented in Conference with Employers on Behalf of the Joint Board of the Dressmakers' Union (New York City: January, 1941).

[16] *Official Proceedings of the 39th Convention of the International Photo-Engravers' Union of North America*, 1938, p. 59.

Mention might also be made of the political opposition of the United Mine Workers to the St. Lawrence project; the protest is in part against a possible decrease in the demand for coal.

2. Trade unions may attempt to influence the wage bill or wage rate by acting upon the market supply of the product. The history of both Great Britain and the United States reveals instances where unions have quit work to reduce the stock of coal on hand with employers. Two very early instances may be mentioned. The first miners' union in America, the Bates Union among anthracite miners in Schuylkill County, Pennsylvania, ordered a suspension of work in July, 1849, "for the purpose of reducing the stock of coal on hand, to steady the market and stave off a reduction in wages."[17] The English miners in the *Articles of Regulation of the Operative Collieries of Lanark and Dumbarton* of 1825 provided that "there should never be allowed to be any stock of coals in the hands of any of the masters."[18] The miners have used the same methods on numerous occasions. More recently more sophisticated methods for the same purpose have been adopted in the Bituminous Coal Commission. The relative infrequency of the resort to shut downs to influence product prices and wage rates is probably explained by the specialized conditions that make this technique possible: (a) A highly competitive sector of the system is required, otherwise employers themselves are apt to have curtailed output with reductions in demand. (b) Production for an organized market is essential in which spot prices reflect discounted expectations from day to day. Prices set over longer periods by contract or formal business decision would render the stoppage less useful to affect price. (c) The commodity must be relatively standardized rather than made to order if stocks are to be accumulated.

A number of unions have been concerned with supply conditions in the product market arising from the freedom of entry. The photoengravers, the teamsters, the clothing unions, and the hosiery

---

[17] Edward A. Wieck, *The American Miners' Association* (New York: Russell Sage Foundation, 1940), p. 63.

[18] Sidney and Beatrice Webb, *Industrial Democracy* (London: Longmans, Green, and Company, 1914), pp. 447–448.

union have tended to discourage members from setting up small businesses themselves. These small concerns, usually started on a shoe string, are alleged to undermine the price and wage structure of the industry. Other unions, such as the barbers, electricians, motion picture operators, and stationary engineers, have secured licensing laws which are intended primarily to affect the supply of labor in the factor market. The wage structure may either be affected by direct limitation of supply or by more circuitous impacts on entry.

3. There are a great many ways in which trade unions may influence the wage rate by influencing competitive conditions in the product market. The union label is one of the oldest and most respected techniques through which the elasticity of demand may be affected. The effectiveness of this device in such industries as tobacco, cigars, printing, and garment must not be too easily dismissed. The resort to employer brands and labels has sometimes been encouraged by trade unions. The hosiery union has been active in urging branded names. To quote: " . . . the control of the secondary hosiery market by the manufacturer does allow him to obtain relatively better prices for his goods and a better margin over costs. . . . "[19]

Trade unions have affected wage rates through competitive conditions in the product market by various forms of fairly direct intervention. The photoengravers encouraged the use of cost accounting among employers; one of its agreements provided that the employer "shall not sell engravings or any production upon which members of the union shall have worked . . . at a price which shall be less than the actual cost of production. . . . "[20] The same union was involved in a suit before the Federal Trade Commission over "clause 10" which restricted employment to firms that were members of the Photo-Engravers' Board of Trade.

Much attention has been directed recently to the building trades

---

[19] *Official Proceedings of the 28th Convention of the American Federation of Hosiery Workers*, 1939, p. 18.

[20] *Official Proceedings of the 33rd Convention of the International Photo-Engravers' Union of North America*, 1932, p. 12.

field where unions have used various devices to affect product prices and hence wage rates. Conformity to price scales may be secured by boycott enforced by manufacturers and dealers, by threats of violence and dissemination of misleading statements, or by the strike power of the unions. Slow downs or the assignment of incompetent workmen to "nonco-operating" contractors may be equally effective. The interest here is not in the legal aspects of these methods so much as in the fact that they arise in certain market structures. A relatively large number of contractors with low costs of entry confronted by a union of skilled workers would tend to make for marked price competition. The bid method of pricing may result in shading of estimates since the stakes are usually the whole contract or nothing at all.[21] The union is apprehensive lest contractors attempt to make up their low estimates by speed-ups, kickbacks, or overt rate reductions.

The union's interest in the product market will depend upon a number of considerations, foremost being the relative importance of labor costs and the relative bargaining power of the enterprises hiring labor and the buyers. The less the bargaining power of immediate employers relative to that of the purchasers of their outputs and the greater the importance of labor costs, the more certain that unions will be forced to take some kind of action in the product market to affect wage rates.

The method of factor and product market analysis that has been suggested in this brief paper has wider applications that may be mentioned. The same technique can be applied to any system of related markets.[22] Industrial price policies and agricultural processing prices should be studied in terms of interrelated markets. The various studies of competitive and monopolistic markets that have been stimulated by "monopolistic competition" suffer from the blinders of particular equilibrium analysis. The study of interrelated markets is also revealing as to the jurisdiction of unions and

---

[21] An interesting analytical question arises under these circumstances. What constitutes a rational bid?

[22] See John T. Dunlop and Benjamin Higgins, " 'Bargaining Power' and Market Structures," *Journal of Political Economy* (February, 1942).

the extent of vertical integration among firms. Mr. Lewis, for instance, was interested in the steel industry and automobile industries, not merely because they were unorganized, but also because they were directly related by markets to the coal industry. An appraisal of market interrelations has important implications for antitrust policy. Combination against monopsonistic buyers may result in more competitive prices and wage rates.

The present paper has been intended to survey a range of relatively neglected problems—the wage policies of trade unions. The argument has suggested a number of non-income objectives of wage policy, has listed some elements of wage policy, problems which confront almost every union, and has laid particular emphasis upon the interrelations of product and factor markets in analysis of wage policy.

INTEREST

20

THE MYTHOLOGY OF CAPITAL*

By Friedrich A. v. Hayek†

With every respect for the intellectual qualities of my opponent, I must oppose his doctrine with all possible emphasis, in order to defend a solid and natural theory of capital against a mythology of capital.—E. v. Böhm-Bawerk, *Quarterly Journal of Economics*, vol. xxi/2, February 1907, p. 282.

I

Professor Knight's crusade against the concept of the period of investment[1] revives a controversy which attracted much attention

---

* *Quarterly Journal of Economics*, Volume L, February 1936, pages 199–228. Reprinted by courtesy of the publisher and author.

† University of London.

[1] The following are the main articles in which Professor Knight has recently discussed the problem in question, and to which I shall refer in the course of this article by the numbers given in square brackets []:

[1] Capitalist Production, Time and the Rate of Return. *Economic Essays in Honour of Gustav Cassel*, London 1933, pp. 327–342.

[2] Capital Time, and the Interest Rate. *Economica* (new series), vol. i, No. 3, August 1934, pp. 257–286.

[3] Professor Hayek and the Theory of Investment. *Economic Journal*, vol. xlv, No. 177, March 1935, pp. 77–94.

In addition, certain other articles by Professor Knight which bear closely on the subject and to some of which I may occasionally refer may also be mentioned.

[4] Professor Fisher's Interest Theory: A Case in Point. *Journal of Political Economy*, vol. xxxix, No. 2, April 1931, pp. 176–212.

[5] Article on Interest, *Encyclopaedia of Social Sciences*, vol. viii, 1932, pp. 131–144.

[6] The Ricardian Theory of Production and Distribution. *The Canadian Journal of Economics and Political Science*, vol. i, No. 1, February 1935, pp. 3–25.

The classical "Austrian" position has recently been ably and lucidly restated and defended against Professor Knight's criticism by Professor Fritz Machlup in

thirty and forty years ago but was not satisfactorily settled at that time. In his attack he uses very similar arguments to those which Professor J. B. Clark employed then against Böhm-Bawerk. However, I am not concerned here with a defense of the details of the views of the latter. In my opinion the oversimplified form in which he (and Jevons before him) tried to incorporate the time element into the theory of capital prevented him from cutting himself finally loose from the misleading concept of capital as a definite "fund," and is largely responsible for much of the confusion which exists on the subject; and I have full sympathy with those who see in the concept of a single or average period of production a meaningless abstraction which has little if any relationship to anything in the real world. But Professor Knight, instead of directing his attack against what is undoubtedly wrong or misleading in the traditional statement of this theory, and trying to put a more appropriate treatment of the time element in its place, seems to me to fall back on the much more serious and dangerous error of its opponents of forty years ago. In the place of at least an attempt of analysis of the real phenomena, he evades the problems by the introduction of a pseudo-concept devoid of content and meaning, which threatens to shroud the whole problem in a mist of words.

It is with profound regret that I feel myself compelled to dissent from Professor Knight on this point, and to return his criticism. Quite apart from the great indebtedness which all economists must feel towards Professor Knight for his contributions to economic theory in general, there is no other author with whom I feel myself so much in agreement, even on some of the central questions of the theory of interest, as with Professor Knight. His masterly expositions of the relationship between the productivity and the "time-

---

an article, "Professor Knight and the 'Period of Production,'" which appeared, together with a Comment by Professor Knight, in the *Journal of Political Economy* for October 1935. But this as well as Professor Knight's answer to Mr. Boulding (The Theory of Investment Once More: Mr. Boulding and the Austrians, in the last issue of the *Quarterly Journal of Economics*) reached me too late to refer to them in the body of the article. But one or two references to these latest publications have been added in footnotes where I refer to the Comment and the Reply to Mr. Boulding with the numbers [7] and [8] respectively.

preference" element in the determination of the rate of interest[2] should have removed, for all time I hope, one of the worst misunderstandings which in the past have divided the different camps of theorists. Under these conditions anything which comes from him carries great weight, particularly when he attaches such importance to it that he tries "to force his views on reluctant minds by varied iteration." It is not surprising that he has already gained some adherents to his views.[3] But this only makes it doubly necessary to refute what seems to me to be a series of erroneous conclusions, founded on one basic mistake, which already in the past has constituted a serious bar to theoretical progress, and which would threaten to balk every further advance in this field, if its pronouncement by an authority like Professor Knight were left uncontradicted.

This basic mistake—if the substitution of a meaningless statement for the solution of a problem can be called a mistake—is the idea of capital as a fund which maintains itself automatically, and that, in consequence, once an amount of capital has been brought into existence the necessity of reproducing it presents no economic problem. According to Professor Knight "all capital is normally conceptually, perpetual,"[4] "its replacement has to be taken for granted as a technological detail,"[5] and in consequence "there is

---

[2] Cf. particularly articles [4] and [5] quoted above.

[3] Cf. H. S. Ellis, Die Bedeutung der Produktionsperiode für die Krisentheorie, and P. Joseph and K. Bode, Bemerkungen zur Kapital und Zinstheorie, both articles in *Zeitschrift für Nationalökonomie*, vol. vi, 1935. R. Nurkse, The Schematic Representation of the Structure of Production, *Review of Economic Studies*, vol. ii, 1935. S. Carlson, On the Notion of Equilibrium in Interest Theory, *Economic Studies*, No. 1, Krakow, 1935.

[4] [2], p. 259; a few pages later (p. 266) the treatment of capital once invested as "perpetual" is even described as the "realistic" way of looking at the matter.

[5] [2], p. 264. At one point Professor Knight does indeed say that "the most important fact requiring clarification is the nature of capital maintenance" ([3], p. 84). But instead of the patient analysis of how and why capital is maintained, which after this we feel entitled to expect, we get nothing but a concept of capital as a mystical entity, an "integrated organic conception" which maintains itself automatically. Professor Knight does not actually use the word "automatic" in this connection, but his insistence on the supposed fact that the replacement of

no production process of determinate length, other than zero or 'all history,' "[6] but "in the only sense of timing in terms of which economic analysis is possible, *production and consumption are simultaneous.*"[7] Into the reasons why the capital maintains itself thus automatically we are not to inquire, because under the stationary or progressive conditions, which alone are considered, this is "axiomatic."[8] On the other hand it is asserted that "making an item of wealth more durable" or "using a longer period of construction,"[9] i.e. lengthening the time dimension of investment in either of the two possible ways, is only one among an "accurately speaking, infinite number" of possible ways of investing more capital, which are later even described as "really an infinite number of infinities."[10] According to Professor Knight, "what the Böhm-Bawerk school's position amounts to is simply selecting these two details which are of the same significance as any of an infinity of other details"[11] while in fact "additional capital is involved in very different ways for lengthening the cycle and for increasing production without this lengthening."[12] "Time is one factor or dimension among a practically infinite number, and quantity of capital may and does vary quite independently of either of these time intervals."[13]

---

capital "has to be taken for granted as a technological detail" can hardly have any other meaning but that it needs no explanation in economic terms and is, therefore, from the point of view of the economist "automatic."

[6] [3], p. 78, cf. also [8], p. 64.

[7] [2], p. 275.

[8] [3], p. 84.

[9] [2], p. 268.

[10] [2], p. 270.

[11] [2], p. 268.

[12] [3], p. 81.

[13] [6], p. 82. An attempt to clear up by correspondence at least some of the differences between us has only had the effect of making the gulf which divides our opinion appear wider than ever. In a letter written after reading an earlier draft of the present paper, Professor Knight emphasizes that he "categorically denies that there is any determinate time interval" "which elapses between the time when some product might have been obtained from the available factors and the time the product actually accrues." This can hardly mean anything

Against this I do indeed hold that, firstly, all the problems which are commonly discussed under the general heading of "capital" do arise out of the fact that part of the productive equipment is non-permanent and has to be deliberately replaced on economic grounds, and that there is no meaning in speaking of capital as something permanent which exists apart from the essentially impermanent capital goods of which it consists. Secondly, that an increase of capital will *always* mean an extension of the time dimension of investment, that capital will be required to bring about an increase of output only in so far as the time dimension of investment is increased. This is relevant, not only for the understanding of the transition to more capitalistic methods, but equally if one wants to understand how the limitation of the supply of capital limits the possibilities of increasing output under stationary conditions.

This is not a dispute about words. I shall endeavor to show

---

more than either that no postponement whatever of consumption is possible, or at least that, once such a postponement has taken place, it is impossible to use for current consumption any of the factors which would be needed to maintain or replace the capital goods created by the first investment. I find it difficult to believe that Professor Knight should want to assert either. Quite apart from the fact that such statements would, as it seems to me, stand in flagrant contrast to all empirical evidence, the contrary has been asserted by Professor Knight himself as the first of "the three empirical facts that form the basis of a sound theory of capital." This, in his words ([2], p. 258), "the simple 'technological' fact that it is possible to increase the volume (time rate) of production after any interval by the use during that interval of a part of existing productive resources—in large part the *same* resources previously and subsequently used for producing 'current consumption income'—to produce, *instead* of current consumption income, instruments of agencies of various sorts, tangible or intangible, which when produced become 'productive' of *additional* current income. This activity or process we call *investment*." (In giving permission to quote the above sentence from his letter Professor Knight adds: "It would induce to clearness to add that it is my view that the interval in question approaches determinateness as we impose stationary or given conditions in a sense so rigid that such an expression as 'might have been obtained' loses all meaning." I am afraid this explanation leaves me more perplexed than ever. As I have tried to show in the last section of this paper, all Professor Knight's former argument *against* the concept of a determinate investment period depends exactly on the most rigid static assumptions of this kind.)

that, on the one hand, Professor Knight's approach prevents him from seeing at all how the choice of particular methods of production is dependent on the supply of capital, and from explaining the process by which capital is being maintained or transformed, and that, on the other hand, it leads him to undoubtedly wrong conclusions. Nor does this discussion seem necessary solely because of the objections raised by Professor Knight. In many respects his conclusions are simply a consistent development of ideas which were inherent in much of the traditional treatment of the subject,[14] and which lead to all kinds of pseudo-problems and meaningless distinctions that have played a considerable rôle in recent discussions on the business cycle.

II

Before I can enter upon attempting to refute Professor Knight's assertion, it is necessary to dispose of certain preliminary matters. There are certain ideas which Professor Knight and others seem to associate with the view I hold but which in fact are not relevant to it. I do not want to defend these views but rather to make it quite clear that I regard them as erroneous. Practically all the points to which I now call attention were either implicitly or explicitly contained in that article of mine which Professor Knight attacks.[15] As he has chosen to disregard them, it is necessary to set them out in order.

(1) It should be quite clear that the technical changes involved, when changes in the time structure of production are contemplated, are *not* changes due to changes in technical knowledge. The concept of increasing productivity due to increasing roundaboutness arises only when we have to deal with increases of output which are dependent on a sufficient amount of capital being available, and which were impossible before only because of the insufficient supply

---

[14] For an effective criticism of related earlier views cf. particularly F. W. Taussig, Capital, Interest and Diminishing Returns, in the *Quarterly Journal of Economics*, vol. xxii, May 1908, pp. 339–344.

[15] On the Relationship between Investment and Output, *Economic Journal*, June, 1934, cp. particularly p. 212, note 1, and p. 226 for point (2), p. 217 for (3), p. 210, note 1, and p. 227 for (4), p. 230, note for (5), and p. 228 for (6).

of capital. This assumes in particular that the increase of output is not due to changes of technical knowledge. It *excludes* any changes in the technique of production which are made possible by new inventions.

(2) It is not true that the periods which it is contended are necessarily lengthened when investment is increased are periods involved in the production of a particular type of poduct. They are rather *periods for which particular factors are invested*, and it would be better for this reason if the term "period of production" had never been invented and if only the term "period of investment" were used. To give here only one example: it is not only conceivable, but it is probably a very frequent occurrence that an increase in the supply of capital may lead not to a change in the technique of production in any particular line of industry, but merely to a transfer of factors from industries where they have been invested for shorter periods to industries where they are invested for longer periods. In this case the periods for which one has to wait for any particular type of product have all remained unaltered, but the periods of investment of the factors that have been transferred from one industry to another have been lengthened.[16]

---

[16] A similar case is that where an addition to the supply of capital makes it possible to employ factors (say labor) which before were unemployed. The first question to ask here is how exactly is it that an increase of capital makes their employment possible. We shall have to assume that without this capital the marginal product of this labor would have been lower than the wage at which they would have been willing to work. In what sense can it now be said that an increase of their marginal product is conditional upon more capital becoming available, i.e. why was it impossible, without this increase of capital, to employ them in the more productive processes? I cannot see that the necessity of previous accumulation can mean anything but an increase of the periods for which either the factors immediately concerned, or some other factors employed in providing the former with equipment, are invested.

In the traditional exposition of the theory of roundabout production this case, where only total capital, but not necessarily capital per head of those employed, has been increased, has been taken account of by saying that the average period of production (i.e. the average period for which the labor actually employed is invested) will only increase when capital per head increases, but will remain constant when capital is increased by an extension of its "labor dimension"

(3) *It is not proposed, and is in fact inadmissible, to reduce the description of the range of periods for which the different factors are invested to an expression of the type of a single time dimension such as the average period of production.* Professor Knight seems to hold that to expose the ambiguities and inconsistencies involved in the notion of an average investment period serves to expel the idea of time from capital theory altogether. But it is not so. In general it is sufficient to say that the investment period of some factors has been lengthened, while those of all others have remained unchanged; or that the investment periods of a greater quantity of factors have been lengthened than the quantity of factors whose investment periods have been shortened by an equal amount; or that the investment period of a given quantity of factors has been lengthened by more than the investment period of another equal amount has been shortened. It is true that in some cases (e.g. when the investment period of one factor is shortened, and at the same time the period for which a greater quantity of another factor is invested is lengthened by a smaller interval) the determination of the net effect of the changes of the investment periods of different factors in different directions raises problems which cannot be so easily answered. But the concept of the average period, which was introduced mainly to solve this difficulty, does not really provide a solution. The obstacle here is that the reinvestment of accrued interest has to be counted equally as the investment of an amount of factors of corresponding value for the same period. In consequence the only way in which an aggregate of waiting can be described, and the amount of waiting involved in different investment structures can be compared, is by means of a process of summation, in the form of a double integral over the function describing the rates, at which the factors that contribute to the product of any moment are applied, and at which interest accrues.

It should, however, be especially noted that the assertion that it is conceptually possible to conceive of the aggregate capital of a

---

instead of its "time dimension." Altho this mode of expression is sometimes useful, I think it has to be abandoned together with the concept of the average period of production.

society in terms of possible waiting periods does not mean that *the total period of production* (or the aggregate of all periods of production) of an economic system is necessarily *a phenomenon capable of measurement*. Whether this is the case (and in my opinion it is very unlikely) is altogether irrelevant for the problem at issue. What is essential is solely that whenever a change occurs in any part of the economic system which involves that more (or less) capital is used in the industry or industries concerned, this always means that some of the factors used there will now bring a return only after a longer (or shorter) time interval than was the case in their former use. As Professor Knight himself rightly says, "the rate of interest which determines the value of all existing capital goods is determined exclusively at the *margin of growth*, where men are comparing large, short segments of income flow with thinner streams reaching out to the indefinite future."[17] It is at this margin of growth (of every individual firm and industry) where the extensions of investment occur and where the decisive question arises whether the productivity of investment is a function of time and whether the limitation of investment is a limitation of the time we are willing or able to wait for a return.[18]

---

[17] [2], p. 278. Cp. also [8], p. 45. The disagreement here concerns the question whether it is true that men directly and irrevocably exchange "short segments of income flow" against "thinner streams reaching into the *indefinite future*" or whether it is not essential to take into account that the immediate result of the sacrifice of present income is an equally limited income flow of a different time shape which must be clearly defined as regards size and shape in order to make it possible to decide in the particular case whether the sacrifice is justified. And this limited income stream which is the result of the first investment becomes a permanent income stream only by an infinite series of further decisions when the opportunity of consuming more now and less in the future has to be considered every time. By jumping directly to the desired result, the permanent income stream, Professor Knight slurs over so much that is essential for an understanding of the process that any use of his concept of capital for an analysis of the rôle of this capital in the course of further changes becomes quite impossible.

[18] As Professor Knight now admits "that in so far as any single investment, negligible in size in comparison with the economic system of which it is a part, represents things consumed and reproduced in a regular cycle, the quantity of

(4) It is quite erroneous to regard propositions concerning the greater productivity of roundabout methods as depending upon the possibility of identifying the contribution of the "original" factors of the remote past. In order to be able to give an intelligible description of a continuous stationary process in which factors are invested at any one moment, some of whose products will mature at almost any later moment, one of two methods is possible. Either we can concentrate on all factors invested in any one interval, and relate them to the stream of product derived from it. Or we can concentrate on the product maturing during a short interval, and relate it to the factors which have contributed to it. But whichever of the two methods we select, in all cases *only the future time intervals* between the moments when the factors are, or will be invested, and the moment when the product will mature are relevant, and *never the past periods* which have elapsed since the investment of some "original factors." The theory looks forward, not back.[19]

(5) It is equally erroneous to regard the theory as depending on any distinction between "original" or "primary" and produced means of production. It makes no fundamental difference whether we describe the range of investment periods for *all* factors existing at the beginning of the period,[20] or whether we just describe the

---

capital in that investment does bear a mathematical relation to the length of the cycle" and that in this connection some of his "previously published statements have been too sweeping," there is perhaps some hope that ultimately some sort of agreement can be reached along these lines. (Cf. [7], p. 627.)

[19] In so far as Professor Knight's aim is merely to drive out the remnants of a cost-of-production theory of value which still disfigure many expositions of the theory of capital (cf. [8], p. 45) I am all with him. But while I fully agree that there is no necessary connection between the present value of capital and the volume of past investment, I do maintain that there is a very close connection between the present and anticipated future values of capital on the one hand and the periods for which resources are invested at present on the other.

[20] A peculiar confusion in this respect occurs in the article of Miss Joseph and Mr. Bode quoted above (p. 174) where it is asserted that if all existing productive resources were taken into account, the period of production would "of course" become *zero*. It is true that the impossibility of drawing a fundamental distinction between the "original factors" and the "intermediate products" is one of the considerations which invalidate the construction of an "*average*" period of

range of periods for which those services of the permanent factors are invested that only become available for investment at successive moments as they accrue. I think it is more convenient to use the second method, and to describe the investment structure by what I have called the investment function of the services of these permanent factors. But whether this distinction—which is based on the fact that some of the productive resources have to be deliberately replaced, while others are regarded as not requiring replacement on economic grounds—is accepted or not, in no case is a distinction between "primary" or "original" and "produced" means of production necessary in order to give the concept of the investment function a definite sense.

(6) Last and closely connected with the preceding point, it is not necessarily the case that all "intermediate products" or "produced means of production" are highly specific, and that in consequence any change in the investment structure can only be brought about by investing the "original" factors for longer or shorter periods. This seems frequently to be implied in analysis which follows Böhm-Bawerkian lines. But of course there is no reason why it should be true. The periods for which non-permanent resources are being invested are as likely to be changed as the periods of investment of the services of the permanent resources.[21]

---

production. But whether we describe the investment structure by an expression representing the rate at which the product of all resources existing at any one moment will mature during the future, or by an expression representing the rate at which the marginal additions will mature which are due to the services of the permanent factors applied at that moment, is merely a difference of exposition. As will be easily seen, the former is simply the integral of the latter and can be represented by the area of the figure which is bounded by the investment curve which represents the latter.

[21] It is perhaps necessary, in order to forestall further misunderstandings, to add as point (7) the main conclusion of the article of mine which Professor Knight attacked. It is that the periods of investment are not in all cases given as technical data but can in many instances only be determined by a process of value-imputation. This is particularly true in the case of durable goods, where the technical data only tell us how long we have to wait for a particular unit of its services, but not to what share of the factors invested in it this unit has to be attributed. This attribution, however, involves an imputation purely in value terms.

III

Most of the critical comments in Professor Knight's articles are due to misunderstandings of one or more of these fundamental points. But while each of them seems to be the source of some confusion, probably none was in this respect quite as fertile as number two. The idea that lengthening the process of production must always have the result that a particular kind of product will now be the result of a longer process, or that a person who invests more capital in his enterprise must therefore necessarily lengthen the period of production in this business, seems to be at the root of his assertion that capital can be used otherwise than to lengthen the time dimension of investment, as well as of his statement that I have practically admitted this.

As a proof of the former contention Professor Knight cites a single concrete example, taken from agriculture. "Taking population as given," he writes,[22] "raising *more* plants of the *same* growth period will also require more 'stock,' but *will not* affect the length of the cycle, while the *addition* to total production of varieties of *shorter* growth, say yielding two harvests per year instead of one, will involve an increase of capital while *shortening* the average cycle." Unfortunately Professor Knight only adds that "additional capital is involved in very different ways for lengthening the cycle and for increasing production without this lengthening," but does not tell us how exactly the additional capital is used for increasing production otherwise than by lengthening the period for which some resources are invested. If he had stopped to inquire he would soon have found that even in the cases where his quite irrelevant "cycle" of the particular process remains constant, or is actually shortened, additional capital will be used in order to invest some resources for longer periods than before, and will only be needed if this is the case.

As Professor Knight has not stated why, in his example, either of the two new methods of cultivation will only be possible if new capital becomes available, it will be necessary to review the differ-

---

[22] [3], p. 81.

ent possibilities which exist in this respect. Change in technical knowledge must clearly be excluded and apparently Professor Knight also wants to exclude changes in the amount of labor used, altho it is not quite clear what the assumption "taking population as given" exactly means. If it is to mean that the quantity of all labor which contributes in any way to the product is assumed to be constant, and to be invested for a constant period, it is difficult to see how, with unchanged technical knowledge, they should suddenly be able to raise more plants and to use more capital. There seem to be only three possibilities, and all of them clearly imply a lengthening of the period for which some of the factors are invested.

(1) It may be assumed that the additional capital is used to buy instruments, etc., which are now made by people who were before directly employed in raising the crop;

(2) or it may be used to buy instruments to be made by people who before were employed to produce something else and have been attracted to making instruments, and thereby contributing to the output in question, by the new capital which has become available for the instruments;

(3) or that the additional capital is used to employ additional people.

Case (1) clearly contradicts the assumption that the periods for which the units of the given labor forces are invested are not lengthened, since the amount of time that will elapse between the making of the instrument and the maturing of the crop will clearly be longer than the period which elapses between the direct application of labor in raising the crop and its maturity. Cases (2) and (3) seem to be in conflict with the assumption of constant population. But in these cases, too, an increase of stock in society will only take place if the labor drawn to this particular line of production from elsewhere is now invested for a longer period than before. (I take it for granted here that additional capital means capital newly saved, and not merely transferred from elsewhere, since nobody, of course, wants to contend that a mere transfer of capital from one line of industry to another, which is accompanied by a similar transfer of the labor for whose investment the capital is required, need lead to an extension of the period for which any resources are invested.) Only if the labor which is now drawn to the process in question has before been invested for shorter periods than it will either in producing agriculture implements (case (2)), or in directly raising the crop (case (3)), will its diversion to the new use cause a temporary gap in the stream of consumable income, which will fall short of the value of the current services of the factors of production, and therefore require some saving or "new capital."

In Professor Knight's second case, that of additional production of shorter duration, he has again neglected to state why this should only become possible if additional capital becomes available. For the same reasons it seems to me to follow that this new production can be dependent on a new supply of capital coming forward only if the other factors required have before been invested for shorter periods.[23]

Evidently this example in no way proves that a case is conceivable where additional capital is used without having the effect of lengthening the investment period of some factor. Yet this example is the only thing in Professor Knight's article which even attempts a demonstration of his main thesis.

The same failure to see the point here involved at all leads Professor Knight also to misinterpret completely a statement of my own, and to describe it "as very nearly a 'give away,'" while in fact it simply refers to this case, where the lengthening of the investment structure is brought about not by lengthening any particular process (choosing a more time-consuming technique in the production of a particular product) but by using a greater share of the total factors of production than before in the relatively more time-consuming processes. What I actually said was, that a fall in the rate of interest would lead to the production of a greater quantity of durable goods, and that—explaining this further—"more goods (or, where possible, more durable goods) *of the kind* will be produced simply because the more distant part of the expected services will play a greater rôle in the considerations of the entrepreneur and will lead him to invest more on account of these more

---

[23] I am afraid I am unable to see to what case the sentence in the same paragraph beginning with "in the third case" refers.

distant returns." Even if this statement was not very fortunately phrased[24] it should have been evident to anyone who has ever made an effort to understand the different ways in which extensions in the time dimension of investment may take place that it referred to the case where the periods for which particular factors are invested is being lengthened in consequence of their transfer from a less to a more capitalistic process of production. The production of more goods of the same (relatively durable) kind *does* therefore mean a change in the investment function for society as a whole in the direction of lengthening the time dimension of production.

IV

More serious than these misunderstandings about what the "period of production" analysis implies is the failure to see that without such an analysis no answer whatever can be given to the fundamental question: how the limitation of the available capital limits the choice among the known methods of production. This question is closely connected with the further problem, whether, and in what sense, the non-permanent resources existing at any one moment can be regarded as one homogeneous factor of determinate magnitude, as a "fund" of definite size which can be treated as a given datum in the sense in which the "supply of capital" or simply the "existing capital" is usually treated.

It is necessary first to say a few words about the reason why it is only in connection with the non-permanent resources that the problems which can properly be called problems of capital arise. The very concept of capital arises out of the fact that, where non-permanent resources are used in production, provision for replacement of the resources used up in production must be made, if the same income is to be enjoyed continually, and that in consequence part of the gross produce has to be devoted to their reproduction. But the fact that it may be regarded as the "normal" case that

---

[24] My meaning would have been expressed better if, instead of speaking of the production of more goods of the kind, I had said "a greater quantity of the relatively more durable goods will be produced," or "goods of still greater durability made in place of those produced before."

people will do so, with the aim of obtaining the same income in perpetuity, does not mean that therefore capital itself becomes in any sense perpetual. On the contrary the very problem of capital accounting arises only because, and to the extent that, the component parts of capital are not permanent, and it has no meaning, in economic analysis, to say that apart from the human decision, which we have yet to explain, the aggregate of all the non-permanent resources becomes some permanent entity. The problem is rather to say how the existence of a given stock of non-permanent resources makes possible their replacement by newly produced[25] instruments, and at the same time limits the extent to which this can be done.[26] And this raises the question in what sense these different capital goods can be said to have a common quality, a common characteristic, which entitles us to regard them as parts of one factor, one "fund," or which makes them to some extent

---

[25] I am afraid I feel compelled to disregard the special meaning which Professor Knight wants to attach to the term production. A concept of production which would compel us to say that a man engaged in the production of some instrument which is to replace some similar existing instrument, and which at some time in the future will contribute to the satisfaction of a desire, either produces not at all or produces not the final product in whose manufacture the instrument he makes is actually used, but a similar product which is consumed at the moment when he applies his labor to the instrument, seems to me an absurd abuse of words. But it is on this "concept" and nothing else that the assertion that production and consumption are simultaneous is based (like J. B. Clark's theorem of the "synchronization" of production and consumption).

[26] On the general subject of the amortization of capital Professor Knight is not only rather obscure but his different pronouncements are clearly inconsistent. In [2], p. 273 he writes: "In reality most investments not only begin at a fairly early date to yield their income in consumable services . . . but in addition they begin fairly soon to yield more than interest on cost in this form, and *entirely liquidate themselves in a moderate period of time*. This additional flow of consumable services is ordinarily treated as a replacement fund, but *is available for consumption or for reinvestment* in any form and field of use at the will of the owner." But in [3], p. 83, in order to support his thesis about the perpetuity of capital, this periodic liquidation is denied: "It cannot now escape observation that 'capital' is an integrated, organic conception, and the notion that the investment in a particular instrument comes back periodically in the form of product, giving the owner freedom to choose whether he will re-invest or not, is largely a fiction and a delusion."

substitutable for each other. What creates the identity which makes it possible to say that one capital good has been effectively replaced by another one, or that the existence of the one makes its replacement by another possible? What is that medium thru which the substance, commonly called capital in the abstract, can be said to be transformed from one concrete form into another? Is there such a thing, as is implied in the habitual use of terms by economists? or is it not conceivable that the thing which they all have in mind is that condition affecting the possibilities of production which cannot be expressed in terms of a substantive quantity?

Altho Professor Knight rather overstresses the case where a stock of capital goods is maintained by the preservation or replacement of the same items, his assertion that capital is permanent is of course not based on this assumption. The crucial case on which its meaning must be tested, and the only case where the question arises whether capital as something different from the individual instruments is permanent at all, is the case where capital goods that are worn out are replaced by capital goods of a different kind, which in many cases will not even help to produce the same services to the consumer but will contribute to render altogether different services. What does the assertion that the capital is permanent mean here? It must evidently mean more than that there will always be some capital in existence. If it has any sense it must mean that the quantity of capital is kept constant. But what is the criterion which determines whether the new capital goods intended to replace the old ones are exactly their equivalent, and what assures us that they will always be replaced by such equivalent quantities?

To these questions Professor Knight provides no answer, but, altho admitting that he has no exact answer, postulates that the idea must be treated as if it had a definite meaning if we are to get anywhere. "The notion of maintaining any capital quantitatively intact" he writes,[27] "cannot be given exact definition; but this limitation applies to all quantitative analysis in economics,

---

[27] [3], p. 90. Footnote.

and the notion itself is clear and indispensable, and measurement, even, is fairly accurate."

Now, as I have tried to show in considerable detail in another place,[28] the notion of maintaining capital *quantitatively* intact, far from being either clear or indispensable, presupposes a behavior of the capitalist-entrepreneurs which under dynamic conditions will sometimes be impossible and rarely reasonable for them to adopt. To assume that under changing conditions capital will be maintained constant in any quantitative sense is to assume something which will never happen and any deductions derived from this assumption will therefore have no application to anything in the real world.

In some places[29] Professor Knight does, it is true, come somewhat nearer a realistic assumption by stating that what people aim to maintain constant is not some physical or value dimension of capital, but its "capacity to render service."[30] But even accepting this assumption it proves in no way that people will also always be capable of maintaining this capacity to render service, and, what is more important, it does not in any way help us to explain in what way this "capacity to render service" is limited, why and how it is possible to transfer it from one concrete manifestation in a capital good into another one. It still leaves us with the impression that there is a sort of substance, some fluid of definite magnitude

---

[28] The Maintenance of Capital, *Economica*, August 1935.

[29] [3], p. 86, note: "Wealth, which is identical with capital, can be treated quantitatively only by viewing it as capacity to render service." Also [2], p. 267: "As long as capital is maintained by replacing the capital goods, *if* their life is limited, by others of any form with equal earning capacity in imputed income. . . ."

[30] Professor Knight, however, by no means consistently adheres to this view. The idea that the quantity of capital which is to be regarded as "perpetual" is a quantity of value occurs again and again. He says, for example, that "there is 'of course' no product yielded by an agency until after full provision has been made for maintaining it, or the investment in it, intact, *in the value sense*." ([2], p. 280.) And similarly, a few pages later (p. 283): "New investments represent additions to all the investment previously made in past time. The amount of such investment cannot indeed be stated quantitatively in any other way than as the capitalized value of existing income sources under existing conditions."

which flows from one capital good into another, and it gives us no indication of the set of conditions which actually at any given moment allows us to maintain output at a particular figure.

The fact that we possess at any one moment, in addition to those natural resources which are expected to render services permanently without any deliberate replacement, an amount of non-permanent resources which enable us to consume more than we could if only the former were available, will help us to maintain consumption *permanently* above this level only if by investing some of the services of the permanent resources for some time they will bring a greater return than they would have given if they were used for consumption when they first became available. If this were not the case no existing quantity of "capacity to render service" in a non-permanent form would enable us to replace it by some new instruments with the same capacity to render service. We might spread the use of the services of these non-permanent factors over as long a period as we like, but after the end of this period no more would be available for consumption than could be obtained from the current use of the permanent services.

That actually we are able to replace the "capacity to render service" represented by the non-permanent resources, and by doing so maintain income permanently higher than what could be obtained from the permanent services only, is due to the *two* facts: first, that the existence of the non-permanent resources allows us to forego for the present some of the services of the existing resources without reducing consumption below the level at which it might have been kept with the permanent resources only, *and*, second, that by investing certain factors for some time we get a greater product than we would have otherwise got from them. Both these factors, the extent to which any given stock of non-permanent resources enables us to "wait" and the extent to which investment enables us to increase the product from the factors invested, are variable. And it is for this reason that only a very detailed analysis of the time structure of production, of the relationship between the periods for which individual factors have been invested and the product derived from them, can help us to understand the forces which direct the use of the current resources for the replacement of capital.

By stressing this relationship the period-of-production analysis (and to some extent already the older wage-fund and abstinence theories) introduced an element into the theory of capital without which no understanding of the process of maintenance and transformation of capital is possible.   But the idea was not sufficiently worked out to make it quite clear how exactly the existence of a given stock of capital goods affected the possibilities of renewed investment.   The Böhm-Bawerkian theory in particular went astray in assuming, with the older views that Professor Knight now wants to revive,[31] that the quantity of capital (or the "possibility to wait") was a simple magnitude, a homogeneous fund of clearly determined size.   The particular assumption made by Böhm-Bawerk and his immediate followers, which may have some justification as a first approximation for didactic purposes, but which is certainly misleading if it is maintained beyond the first stage, is that the existing stock of capital goods corresponds to a fixed quantity of consumer's goods and is therefore, on the further assumption of a given rate of consumption, uniquely associated with a definite total or average waiting period which it makes possible. The basis of this assumption was apparently the idea that every existing capital good was completely specific in the sense that it could be turned into only one particular quantity of consumer's goods by a process which could in no way be varied.   On this assumption any present stock of capital could, of course, be regarded as equivalent to one, and only one, quantity of consumers' goods which would become available over a fixed period of time at a predetermined and invariable rate.   This simplified picture of the

---

[31] [8], p. 57: "The basic issue is the old and familiar one of choice between two conceptions of capital.   In one view, it consists of 'things' of limited life which are periodically worn out or used up and reproduced; in the other, it is a 'fund' which is maintained intact tho the things in which it is invested may come and go to any extent.   In the second view, which of course is the one advocated here, the capital 'fund' may be thought of as either a value or a 'capacity' to produce a perpetual flow of value."

existing stock of capital representing a "subsistence fund" of determined magnitude which would provide a support for a definite period and therefore enable us to undertake production processes of a corresponding average length is undoubtedly highly artificial and of little use for the analysis of more complicated processes.

Actually the situation is so much more complicated and requires a much more detailed and careful analysis of the time element because any existing stock of capital goods is not simply equivalent to a single quantity of consumers' goods due to mature at definitely fixed dates, but may be turned by different combinations with the services of the permanent factors into a great many alternative streams of consumers' goods of different size, time-shape and composition. In a sense, of course, capital serves as a "subsistence fund," but it is not a fund in the sense that it provides subsistence for a single uniquely defined period of time. The question which of the many alternative income streams which the existing stock of capital goods potentially represents shall be chosen will depend on which will best combine with the services of the permanent factors which are expected to become available during the future—best in this context meaning that it will combine into a total stream of the most desired time-shape. The rôle of the existing capital goods in this connection is that they fill the gap in the income stream which would otherwise have been caused by the investment of resources which might have been used to satisfy current needs. And it is only by making their investment for these periods possible that those resources will yield a product sufficient to take the place of the products rendered in the meantime by the already existing capital goods. *But there is no other "identity" between the now existing capital goods and those that will take their place than that the results of current investment*, which leads to the creation of the latter, *dovetail with one of the potential income streams*, which the former are capable of producing, into a total income stream of desired shape. And what limits the possibility of increasing output by investing resources which might serve current needs is again nothing but the possibility of providing in the meantime an income "equivalent" to that which will be obtained from the investment of current resources. ("Equivalent," strictly speaking, means here, not equal, but sufficiently large to make it worth while to wait for the increased return that will be obtained from the invested resources because of their investment.)

It should be clear that an analysis of this effect of the existence of capital goods on the direction of the investment of current resources is possible only in terms of the alternative time structures of production which are technically possible with a given equipment. What makes this analysis so particularly difficult, yet the more necessary (and at the same time lets the traditional approach in terms of an average investment period appear so hopelessly inadequate except as a first approach), is the fact that the existing capital goods do not represent a particular income stream of unique shape or size (as would be the case if it consisted of goods which were completely "specific") but a great number of alternative contributions to future income of different magnitude and date. Nothing short of a complete description of these alternative time-shapes can provide a sufficient basis for the explanation of the effect of the existence of the capital goods on current investment and, what means the same thing, of the form and quantity of the new capital goods that will replace the old ones.

In this article no positive attempt can be made to provide the technical apparatus required for a real solution of these problems. Apart from the particular aspect which I have discussed in the article which Professor Knight attacked, this task must be reserved for a more systematic study. I may mention that most of the serious difficulties which this analysis presents are due to the fact that it has to deal largely with joint-product and joint-demand relationships between goods existing at different moments of time. For the present discussion the task has been only to demonstrate why such an analysis of the time structure is necessary and why no description of capital in terms of mere quantity can take its place. The main fault of the traditional analysis in terms of the period of production was that it tried to argue in terms of a single time dimension in order to retain the connection to the conventional but misleading concept of capital as a definite fund. But it has at least the merit of stressing that element in terms of which the real relationship can be explained.

All the other attempts to state the assumptions as regards the supply of capital in terms of a definite fund and without any reference to the time structure, whether this is attempted by postulating given quantities of "waiting," or "capital disposal,"[32] or a "subsistence fund," or "true capital," or "carrying powers," are just so many evasions of the real problem of explaining how the existence of a given stock of capital limits the possibility of current investment. Without such an analysis they are just so many empty words, harmful as the basis of that noxious mythology of capital which by creating the fiction of a non-existing entity leads to statements which refer to nothing in the real world. And the concept of capital conceived as a separate factor of determinate magnitude which is to be treated on the same footing with "land" and "labor" belongs to the same category.[33] It is no better to say, as Professor Knight did at an earlier stage, that "time as such" is a factor of production,[34] since no definite "quantity" of time is given in a way which would enable us to distribute this "fund" of time in alternative ways between the different lines of production so that the total of "time" used will always be the same. But it is certainly much worse to attempt, as Professor Knight does now, to eliminate time entirely from the analysis of the capitalist process of production. This inevitably prevents him from giving any answer to the

---

[32] It is not surprising that Professor G. Cassel, to whom we owe this particular version of the mythology of capital, should now have joined forces with Professor Knight. Cf. his book *On Quantitative Thinking in Economics*, Oxford, Clarendon Press, 1935, p. 20.

[33] If, as seems generally to be the case, one can never be certain that one will not be carried away occasionally by the construction of a quantitatively fixed "fund" which undoubtedly attaches to the term capital, it would probably be advisable to follow Professor Schumpeter's suggestion and avoid the use of the term altogether. (Cf. article Kapital, in *Handwörterbuch der Staatswissenschaften*, 4th ed., 1923, vol. v, p. 582.)

[34] [4], p. 198: "It has long been my contention that the best form of statement to indicate the essential fact on the technical side is simply to say that time as such is a factor of production—the only really distinct, homogeneous 'factor,' as a matter of fact."

question how the limitation of capital limits the possible size of the
product and why and how capital is maintained, and compels him
to treat this as a datum.   And, as we shall see in the next section,
it also leads him into positive errors about the function of interest.

V

How the neglect of the fundamental fact that capital consists
of items which need to be reproduced, and that these serve as
capital only in so far as and to the extent that their existence is a
condition for taking advantage of more productive time-consuming
methods, led to the most erroneous conclusions is well illustrated
by Professor Knight's remarkable assertion that "the rate of interest
could be zero only if all products known, empirically or in imagination, into the creation of which capital in any way enters, were
free goods."[35]   This statement seems to me to be about as plausible
as if it were asserted that the price of air could fall to zero only if
all commodities in the production of which the presence of air
were an indispensable condition were free goods.   Clearly, unless
one of several factors coöperating in the production of a number
of goods can be substituted for the others without limit, the fact
that this one factor becomes a free good will never mean that the
product itself must become a free good.   In the case in question,
however, not even the capital *goods* need become free goods in
order that the rate of interest may fall to zero.   All that is required
is that the value of the services which depend on the existence of a
certain capital good be no higher than the cost of reproduction of
a good that will render the same service or, what amounts to the
same thing, than the value in their alternative current uses of the
services of the factors of production required for this reproduction.
There is no reason why, in order that this may come about, these
services should also become free goods.

I do not, of course, contend that a fall of the rate of interest
to zero is an event in the least likely to occur at any future time in
which we are at all interested.   But, like all questions of what is

---

[35] [2], p. 284.

probable, this is altogether irrelevant for theoretical analysis. What is of importance are the conditions under which this would be possible. Now if a condition were reached in which no further lengthening of the investment periods of individual resources (either by lengthening the process or by increasing the durability of goods in which they are invested) would lead to a further increase of output, new savings could not help to increase output. In the usual terminology the marginal productivity of capital would have fallen to zero because no more satisfaction would depend on a particular capital good ("stored up labor") than would depend on the quantity of labor and other products which are needed to replace it. So long as any of the factors required for this purpose remain scarce, the capital goods themselves and *a fortiori* the final consumers' goods made with their help will also remain scarce. And there can be no doubt that this point where further accumulation of capital would no longer increase the quantity of output obtainable from the factors used in its production, even if almost infinitely distant, would still be reached long before the point where no satisfaction whatever would be dependent on the existence of these factors.

It is not difficult to see how Professor Knight's habit of thinking not only of capital in the abstract but even of particular capital goods as permanent has led him to his peculiar conclusion. Permanent goods which can be produced—if there is such a thing, namely a good which is expected not only to last forever physically, but also to remain permanently useful—stand in this respect in a somewhat exceptional position. The value of such a good expected to render permanently useful services would at a zero rate of interest necessarily be infinite so long as its services have any value at all, and goods of this kind would therefore be produced until the value of the services of one more unit would be zero. And until the services of these goods had become free, there would be a demand for capital for producing more and the rate of interest could not fall to zero. The person making a final investment of this kind, bringing the value of the services down to zero, would of course find that he had made a mistake and lost his investment; and the demand for capital for this purpose would stop when it became known that the investment of one further unit had this effect.

But even if the value of the permanent goods should have to fall to zero in order that the rate of interest may become zero also, this does, as shown above, by no means imply that the value of the non-permanent goods should also have to fall to zero. On each good may depend no more utility than can be had from the current use of the factors required for its reproduction, but the value of such goods will still be equal to that utility.

In concluding this section it may be pointed out that there is, of course, a very important reason why in a changing world the rate of interest will never fall to zero, a reason which Professor Knight's assumption of the permanence of capital would exclude, namely, that in a world of imperfect foresight capital will never be maintained intact in any sense, and every change will always open possibilities for the profitable investment of new capital.

VI

There remain a number of points of not inconsiderable importance which, however, if this article is not to grow to disproportionate size, can be touched upon but shortly. Perhaps the most interesting is the suggestion, which occurs here and there in Professor Knight's articles, that all his deductions about the nature of capital are based on the assumption of perfect foresight.[36] If this is to be taken quite seriously it would represent a main addition to the older Clarkian doctrine of the permanence of capital and to some extent also justify it. It would do so, however, at the expense of restricting its validity to a sphere in which problems of capital in the ordinary sense do not occur at all and certainly deprive it of all relevance to the problems of economic dynamics. But since

---

[36] Cf. particularly [2], pp. 264 (n. 2), 270, 273, and 277. In his latest articles ([7] and [8]) Professor Knight seems however inclined to concede that the period of production analysis has some limited application to static conditions most rigidly defined, and is inapplicable under dynamic conditions! Are we to understand that Professor Knight now wants to abandon all that part of his earlier criticism which was based on the most extreme static assumptions imaginable, i.e., on the assumption of perfect foresight?

Professor Knight's purpose is, *inter alia*, to demonstrate that my analysis of certain types of industrial fluctuations is based on a fallacy in the field of the theory of capital it can evidently not be his intention to base all his argument on this assumption. Hence it seems worth while to explore shortly the question what problems of capital still exist under such an assumption.

If we assume that perfect foresight has existed from the beginning of all things, a question of how to use capital as a separate factor of production would not arise at all. All processes of production would have been definitely determined at the beginning and no further question would arise of how to use any of the instruments created in the course of the process which might be used for other purposes than those for which they were originally intended. If indeed there are natural non-permanent resources in existence at the beginning, a "capital problem" might arise in connection with the original plan.[37] But once this original plan is made and so long as it is adhered to, no problem of maintenance, replacement or redistribution of capital, nor indeed any other economic problem, would occur.

Economic problems of any sort, and in particular the problem how to use a given stock of capital goods most profitably, arise only when it is a question of adjusting the available means to any new situation. In real life such unforeseen changes occur, of course, at every moment and it is in the explanation of the reaction to these changes that the existing "capital" is required as a datum. But the concept of capital as a quantitatively determined self-perpetuating fund does not help us here in any way. In fact, if the justification of this concept lies in the assumption of perfect foresight it becomes clearly inapplicable, since a "factor" which

---

[37] It might be mentioned, incidentally, that this would not be a problem of the preservation of natural resources in the usual sense, i.e., of preservation of the particular resource, but only of its replacement by some produced means of production which will render services of equivalent value. This applies equally to the practical problem of the preservation of exhaustible natural resources where it is by no means necessarily most economical to extend their life as far as possible rather than to use their amortization fund for the creation of some new capital goods.

remains in any sense constant only if complete foresight is assumed cannot possibly represent a "datum" on which new decisions can be based. As has been shown, it would be erroneous to assume that this given "factor" is given as a definite quantity of value, or as any other determinate quantity which can be measured in terms of some common unit. But while the only exact way of stating the supply condition of this factor would be a complete enumeration and description of the individual items, it would be hasty to conclude that they have no common quality at all which entitles us to class them into one group. This common quality of being able to substitute to some extent one item for another is the possibility of providing a temporary income while we wait for the services of other factors invested for longer periods. But, as we have seen, no single item represents a definite quantity of income. How much income it will yield and when it will yield it depends on the use made of all other goods. In consequence the relevant datum which corresponds to what is commonly called the supply of capital and which determines for what period currently factors will be expediently invested is nothing but the alternatively available income streams which the existing capital goods can produce under the new conditions.

It would be difficult to believe that Professor Knight should for a moment have really thought that the concept of capital as a self-maintaining fund of determinate magnitude has any application outside a fictitious stationary state if he had not himself—at least at an earlier date—clearly recognized that the problems of capital fall largely outside the framework of static analysis.[38] In view of these utterances it would seem unlikely that he should now take pains to develop a concept which is valid only on the most rigidly "static" assumptions. The emphasis which he now places on the complete mobility of capital certainly conveys the impression that he wants to apply his concept to dynamic phenomena. It is at

---

[38] [4], p. 206: "The one important difference between price analysis in the case of interest and that of ordinary prices arises from the fact that saving and investment is a cumulative process. It is a phase of economic growth, outside the framework of the conventional 'static' system, unfortunately so called."

least difficult to see what other purpose this emphasis can serve, because certainly nobody has ever doubted that where all the future is correctly foreseen and always has been so no problem of mobility of capital will arise. And altho he qualified his statements about the mobility of capital by the assumption of complete foresight[39] this does not prevent him from disparaging the value of any reasoning based on the limitations of the mobility of captal under dynamic conditions. This attitude is not very far from the assertions sometimes found in the literature that apart from "frictions" invested capital ought to be regarded as completely mobile between different uses (presumably without any loss in value), and that "any theory that is based on partial immobility of invested capital is essentially a frictional one."[40] This clearly assumes the existence of a separate substance of capital apart from its manifestation in concrete capital goods, a "fund" of a mystical quantity which cannot be described or defined but which, if Professor Knight has it his way, is to have a central position in our analytical apparatus. It has the somewhat questionable advantage that there is no way of deciding whether any statement about this quantity is true or false.

[39] [2], p. 270.
[40] H. Neisser, "Monetary Expansion and the Structure of Production," *Social Research*, vol. I/4, November, 1934.

21

CAPITAL AND INTEREST*

By Frank H. Knight†

The concept of capital is peculiarly difficult to explain briefly, because of its intimate relationships with other types of wealth and sources of income, and because of the changes in meaning which all the main concepts used in economic analysis have undergone in the history of the science. Particularly in the past generation or so, this development has made scientific usage quite divergent from that of everyday life.

HISTORICAL BACKGROUND. In the main tradition of "classical" economics, not to go farther back, capital has generally been described as produced wealth used for further production. (The classical and neo-classical schools include the bulk of treatises written in English from Adam Smith's *Wealth of Nations* in 1776 down to the present generation. This definition distinguished capital on the one hand from land or natural resources, supposedly unproduced, and on the other hand "consumption goods." It was also taken for granted that "wealth" should not include human beings, though, in contrast with the later social viewpoint, the earlier writers inclined to treat the working population as a means to political ends or power. Analysis soon came to be built explicitly around the notion of three "factors of production," labor, land, and capital, supposed to correspond with the three recognized forms of income, wages, rent, and "profit." The progress of investigation has tended to make the conception of capital less definite and more inclusive.

The change most sweeping in its implications has been the redefinition of production and consumption, which blurs the dis-

* *Encyclopaedia Brittanica*, Volume IV, 1946, pages 779–801. Reprinted by courtesy of the publisher and author.

† University of Chicago.

tinction between capital and consumers' goods. Adam Smith and his followers for about a century were much under the influence of the immediately preceding French school, the *Économistes* or "Physiocrats" of the third quarter of the 18th century. Both groups viewed production as the creation of a "surplus" of tangible wealth, primarily consumption goods, available for such "unproductive" uses as the support of government and the cultural life, or net growth in the population and wealth of a country. The writers shared the popular belief that agriculture is the only activity which is really productive. At that time, particularly in France, industry was undeveloped and agriculture was in fact the main source of income in excess of the "maintenance" of the employed population. Both schools also accepted the popular notion that all wealth is produced by labor, with land and capital in a merely assisting or supporting role. Capital was viewed as a particular way of using consumption goods, through "advancing" means of subsistence, and raw materials and tools, to support "productive" laborers who reproduced the advances, and something more. This excess was the return on capital, designated as "profit." The typical capitalist, and at the same time the "entrepreneur" (as he later came to be called), was the "farmer" in the British sense, who rented land and hired laborers, received the product at the end of the year, and turned over to the other two claimants their respective shares. The farmers of the poorest land worth using at all paid no rent; others paid the landlord an amount which measured the superiority of their land over that at the margin of cultivation. From the remainder after payment of rent (if any) the capitalist farmer recouped the wages paid the previous year and set aside a more or less arbitrary amount to be advanced to productive laborers the next year. The final remainder he consumed, either directly or in the support of "unproductive" laborers—or paid it as taxes to the state, whose political functionaries were also classed as unproductive labor. The level of wages was determined by subsistence requirements, and all increase in population and wealth (and even maintenance) depended upon the "thrift" of the capitalist, possibly supplemented by saving by landlords and laborers.

These conceptions were carried over into non-agricultural production, with recognition of compound interest on investment in capital which lasted for a term of years; but the role of machinery and durable capital was not effectively incorporated into the distributive analysis. The theory was somewhat systematized by David Ricardo (*Principles of Political Economy and Taxation*, 1817) and his work was largely accepted in England through most of the 19th century. Smith's doctrine was developed along somewhat different lines in France by J. B. Say (*Traité d'économique politique*, 1803) who exerted much influence in the U. S. A. The Americans (notably H. C. Carey in the 1830's and 40's) were particularly critical of the theory of rent, the central feature of Ricardo's system. In capital theory, N. W. Senior (Political Economy, 1836) introduced the notion of "abstinence" as a subjective or sacrifice cost involved in saving, parallel with the irksomeness of labor, and justifying the receipt of profit or interest.

The radical transformation of the classical system may be dated from the promulgation of the "utility" or "subjective" theory of value by a number of writers in the early 1870's (W. S. Jevons, C. Menger, and L. Walras—somewhat later but perhaps independently by the American J. B. Clark). The new theory was gradually popularized by Menger and his followers as the "Austrian" economics. It inverted the causal relation between cost and price, making the former the effect of the latter, and changed its meaning from "real" cost in labor or sacrifice, to the money value of the productive services, paid for their use by the "entrepreneur," the active producer, distinguished from the capitalist. Even more important for economic theory in the long run, this revolution changed the meaning of production and consumption and led to a new theory of distribution as the valuation of productive services of all kinds, derived from product value by "imputation." The subjective-value theorists held various ideas about capital. Most important historically in this connection is E. von Böhm-Bawerk (main works in the late 1880's) who elaborated the "abstinence" theory (in a more or less changed form) and also developed (without reconciling the two) a theory of interest based on a particular conception of the "productivity of capital." This second theory was a development of the Smith-Ricardo view of capital, as consumption goods advanced to laborers to support further production. It treated land and labor as primary factors and added the notion that larger advances not merely support more labor (and possibly bring in more land) but increase production by making it more efficient through increasing the length or "roundaboutness" of the production process. Böhm-Bawerk's work led to a generation of controversy between "productivity" and "psychological" schools of interest theory, and the combination of the two in an "eclectic" theory by Alfred Marshall (*Principles of Economics*, first edition 1890). The issues will be discussed later.

MODERN VIEWS. Contemporary economic thought with respect to capital and its return is still controversial, but the view which seems to be gaining predominance may be sketched out. First of all, production is defined in relation to economic equilibrium, a conception due primarily to J. B. Clark, in the form of a stationary economy. This is a hypothetical society in which capital is maintained without increase or decrease, while population and wants and the "state of the arts" are also unchanging, and all economic adjustments have been carried to a position of stability. Under these conditions, production consists in using "productive agents" of all kinds in a relationship of symmetrical cooperation, to provide an unvarying stream of consumable services or satisfactions as the ultimate product. The production of the services consumed in any period of time includes the maintenance of all productive agents and materials used in the economy, including in turn the replacement of any which are worn out or used up. Thus under equilibrium conditions production and consumption are simultaneous. And where investment or disinvestment intervenes, there is no determinate relation in time between the two. In a progressive economy (in the sense of increased production without change in wants or productive methods), production further includes a net addition to the productive equipment through saving and investment, and exceeds consumption by this amount. In a retrogressive economy (in the same sense) consumption would exceed production, the difference representing a decrease in the total productive equipment, through "dissaving" and disinvestment. Thus the fundamental meaning of "real" capital is simply productive equipment viewed as subject to quantitative increase or decrease. The theory as a whole pictures distribution of the product among different types of productive agents through imputing to each unit of each type, the value of the "increment" of total product which is finally dependent upon the cooperation of any one small unit of that type of agent, or "factor." This is the "marginal productivity" theory of distribution. The theory describes the position of equilibrium for the economy as a whole, which can also be pictured as moving with change in the given conditions.

In this new setting, the problem of the classification of productive agents appears in a different light. The traditional "tripartite" division into three factors, labor, land and capital, loses much of its significance, as does the distinction between producers' and consumers' goods or wealth. As already indicated (and as Professor Irving Fisher in particular has emphasized) the major analytical distinction is that between "income" (q.v.) consumed or saved, and "sources" of (or agents which yield) the services which compose income. All sources are properly productive agents, and are also "capital goods" in the most inclusive meaning. In practice, it is often useful to restrict the notion of capital goods in various directions, and the definition will depend on the problem considered in any particular piece of exposition. Some four or five main lines of restriction may be significant. First, human beings (in "free" society) are not capital in the same sense as property which is regularly bought and sold. Second, "intangibles," including many types of claims upon sources or their earnings, are in a different case from physical sources themselves. Within the class of tangible goods (third) some are used directly for consumption, others indirectly to make other goods. Further, (fourth) some are immediately destroyed in use (food, fuel, chemicals, etc.) while others last and render their services over periods of time of almost any length. Finally, among goods of substantial durability, some are used by those who own them while others are used by a second party, under various contractual arrangements between owner and user. In all these cases there are grounds for restricting the appellation of "capital" to one or the other member of the comparison, and many sub-classes or differences in degree may be recognized.

With respect to the organization of production, and hence for the purpose of general theory, the durability of sources (the fourth distinction) is particularly important, because it largely determines the length of time that will be required to convert an agent of one type into one of another type, suitable for a different mode of use, in response to a change in the demand or in technology. The speed of such transfers also depends on the time required to produce the new form of source. Again, as already indicated, only goods of a minimum durability can be used by parties other than their owners, or their services be bought and sold apart from the sources themselves.

As already observed, the general and fundamental meaning of real capital includes all sources or objects which have productive capacity, the quality of rendering valuable (and scarce) services of any sort. For theoretical analysis, the essential matter is the distinction between such objects or "capital goods," and "capital," i.e., productive capacity, viewed in abstract quantitative terms, as subject to increase or decrease, hence transferable from one use to another through change in form, i.e., decrease of one kind and increase of another. Thus the problem is one of measurement or quantification of productive capacity. This, in turn, is a matter of valuation, since value is the only common denominator between different economic forms. The market enables an individual to change his investment position through changing places with another, and the prices guide the process of real investment and transfer of investment in the economy. Where there is no market for an agent, as in the case of free human beings, or where the price is indeterminate because of imperfect competition, the data which enter into market price may enable computation of a value, or a more accurate one, as the case may be. The economic importance of capital does not depend on exchange, and still less on the borrowing and lending of money, but on the fact that changes in production are effected chiefly through disinvestment and reinvestment. Only to a limited extent can productive agents be moved from one use to another without being changed in form in this way, though in a progressive economy, proportional changes are largely effected through directing new investment into fields where relative expansion is called for.

Reflection upon the process by which production in any line is extended through investment, or contracted through disinvestment, will make clear the reason for the "passing" of the three-factor classification of productive agents. There is no general difference between any two of the three traditional classes—laborers, natural agents and capital goods—with respect to the possibility either of transfer from one use to another "as they stand" or of increase or decrease. We find all degrees of freedom of investment and disinvestment, hence replacement of any kind by any other. And also all degrees of substitutability of one physical kind for others in the production of the same (or an equivalent) consumable service.

CAPITAL-GOODS AND NATURAL AGENTS: EXPLORATION AND INVENTION. Business usage hardly makes a distinction between investment in "natural" and in "artificial" instruments, or materials. This is partly because of their exchangeability in the market, but there are deeper reasons for regarding the business view as sound from the standpoint of general theory. On the historical side, all "natural resources" have at some time been discovered and "developed," at a cost, hence through saving and investment. More important are considerations which look to the future. Most of the resources also require maintenance at a cost, as in the case of agricultural land, or outright replacement, as in that of minerals, etc., which are subject to depletion. And both improvements and increase in supply are constantly being effected through investment in exploration and development, with the expectation of a return. Such operations are not essentially different economically from other production. As long as they are carried out in open competition with other uses of the resources employed, it is to be expected that on the average the outlays will tend to yield the same return that they would yield in more repetitive or routine activities; in other words, the value of the results will tend toward equality with the costs incurred. There may, indeed, be differences. Natural resources may on the whole exceed such things as factory equipment in durability and specialization, making the commitment of investment in the former more permanent, less responsive to changes. And again, the uncertainty which affects explorative activity in any particular case may produce a bias either for or against such investment, depending on the prevalent social attitude toward adventure and risk. Such differences will at most be a matter of degree and will vary enormously from one example or sub-type to another within both general fields; hence they hardly justify a general distinction.

The explorative character of investing in new natural resources brings to mind that improvement in technology is also a field of investment, giving rise to a form of (intangible) capital recognized in business usage. Scientific research and its technical application are carried on at a cost and with the expectation of a return in some form. These activities are also affected with a high degree of uncertainty; but a successful innovation may yield a large income, and there must be a tendency for gains and losses to average out, leaving about the same relation between yield and cost as in fields where the result is predictable in the individual case. However, investment in technology presents one important peculiarity. New knowledge, or a valuable new idea, can usually be copied and diffused at little cost, so that the return would soon fall to zero, in the absence of some artificial restriction upon the extension of its use. Such restrictions bring the value under the theoretical head of monopoly. Such monopolies are good or bad, depending upon whether they are limited in degree and duration to what is reasonably required as an incentive to commit resources to experimentation, and for its rational direction. Any monopoly power is clearly capital to its individual owner, but whether it should be treated as part of the capital of a society or the world depends on complex social conditions.

THE RELATION BETWEEN INTEREST AND RENT. Only historical

accident or "psychology" can explain the fact that "interest" and "rent" have been viewed as coming from different sources, specifically natural agents and capital goods. The difference is clearly one of contractual form, or even of arbitrary "point of view." If one person, A, hires from another, B, the use of any piece of property whatever, the payment will be called a rent. It is quite immaterial whether the property itself is land or anything else, whether it is natural or artificial, tangible or intangible, or is used for production or consumption. Houses, furniture, and even some articles of clothing, are regularly leased for a rental, as well as farms or building sites; and the same is true of patents, though under certain forms of contract the payment is called a "royalty." The lessee in such an arrangement always has the alternative of borrowing money and buying the object, and insofar as competitive conditions prevail, the two forms will be exactly equivalent for both parties. The user may borrow the money from the previous owner, as regularly occurs in the case of real estate; and if the use is wanted for a limited time, the object can be sold and the loan paid off. Thus every lease could be replaced by a sale, and vice versa.

The difference between a lease and a sale mediated by a loan lies in the incidence of changes in value, or rather the "risk" of such changes. If A leases, say, a farm from B, any increase or decrease in its value will accrue to B, while if the transfer is effected by a sale, it will accrue to A. If changes are predictable in advance, or even if both parties have the same expectations of change (and the same psychological attitude toward risk) the competitive terms of lease or sale will again make the two contracts equivalent—or, a sale might be accompanied with a contract for resale at any future date. Even highly perishable goods might be furnished under the form of a lease, the borrower agreeing to return articles identical or equivalent to those received and used up. Further, the owner of any piece of property may arbitrarily view its return as either a rent on the property itself or interest on the investment in it, whether the return is service to himself or a rental paid by some other user. Finally, both lease and sale can be replaced by still other arrangements; in fact, either transaction is equivalent to a partnership agreement, with appropriate provision for dividing the income yield—and any future capital gain or loss—between the two parties. Thus, even in an entrepreneurial economy using money, the relation between capital and its yield, or between rent and interest, has no essential connection with the borrowing and lending of money.

CAPITAL-GOODS AND LABORERS. Similar considerations apply in substance to the laborer and his wages as to land and rent. Though, for "human" reasons, laborers are not usually referred to as "means of production," they are economically similar to other productive agents. The difference is "institutional," in a slave economy laborers of all classes would be merely species of capital goods. This of course was largely the case in parts of the U. S. A. within the lives of people still living. There usually are, indeed, important differences; sentiment and social usage, including religion, cause human slaves to be treated in a somewhat different way than work animals, or machines. Important economic differences arise in the control of reproduction and the rearing of children. However, all these things are matters of detail and of degree, and similar distinctions exist between many categories of capital goods. The procurement of slaves, through raids, or purchase from peoples who themselves recognize slavery, has commonly been hardly more influenced by sentiment than other investment operations.

Even in a free society, human beings are productive agents and are produced at a cost, and this is obviously true of the qualities which give their services economic value. Birth rates, as well as training, are influenced by the expectation of earning power, much as in the case of any investment, which looks beyond the maker's own lifetime. In extreme cases, as when a youth borrows money to secure a technical education, the difference is reduced to a minimum. However, the accepted principle of the sanctity of freedom, embodied in modern law, has the important consequence that an individual cannot be very effectively pledged to secure a debt, since he cannot be sold, or "seized," to enforce payment—since corporal punishment and imprisonment for debt have been abolished. But on the other hand, the law also gives debtors a property exemption and the privilege of bankruptcy. Instead of thinking of a slave economy we may reflect on the method of making human beings and property alike, i.e., converse, legal prohibition of purchase and sale of other property. Since every sale could be replaced by an equivalent lease or other arrangement, even the modern complex organization of production could be carried on without much change if all property were "entailed" as landed estates typically were in the Middle Ages. At that time, too, the prohibition of lending at interest was regularly and easily evaded by recourse to other contractual forms, and was finally dropped because it became ineffective. In short, the meaning of capital and its yield is essentially unconnected with the general organization of the social economy. It would be essentially the same in a Crusoe economy; or, to be more realistic, one may think of an individual or business unit in our own society, which saves and invests directly for its own use. If the role of capital in a situation without exchange or lending is understood, the explanation of the market value of sources, and of their yield as an annual rate per cent of their value, will present no difficulty.

PRESENT-DAY THEORY OF CAPITAL AND ITS RETURN. The essential phenomena of capital center in the necessity for maintenance and replacement of productive agents and the possibility of disinvestment and of further investment in practically any form, old or new. Every economically active person must constantly apportion productive capacity under his control between use to yield a larger current stream of want-satisfying services and the maintenance, improvement or creation of productive agents with a view to a larger flow of such services in the future, or to still further investment. There is little difference among physical classes of resources with respect to this choice. And further, roughly speaking all kinds cooperate in making every kind, including human beings endowed with all varieties of earning power. Accordingly, modern thought is abandoning the distinction between primary and secondary, produced and unproduced, or reproducible and nonreproducible agents. The distinction between human beings and property and that between personal and real property are important in law and human relations, but no fundamental economic differences correspond to them. The original fallacy was probably rooted in the "moral prejudices" that only labor is really productive, and that land is a gift of nature. Realistic economic analysis must avoid any general classifications of productive agents and make distinctions on the basis of the facts that are significant for the problem in hand. For general analysis, it would be desirable to drop also the traditional classification of income forms, and to speak of the yield and "hire" of productive agents, irrespective of kind.

Accurately speaking, investing or disinvesting involves a comparison between consuming income in the immediate and the more remote future, rather than in the "present" versus the future. To avoid technicalities which can only be dealt with by the mathematics of "continuously compounded" interest, we may think of an investment made and completed within an interval short enough to be treated as a moment of time, and which immediately begins to yield a return. The yield itself may of course be either consumed or wholly or partly invested; the latter use corresponds to the facts in a progressive economy or economic unit of any kind, but the same form of choice is involved in deciding between maintenance of the stationary condition and retrogression.

For both simplicity and realism, it is best to approach the rate of return on any income source by considering that the possibility of investment and disinvestment makes any future income, however distributed in time, equivalent to a perpetual and uniform annual flow. What any source actually produces in any interval of time is its imputed yield for that interval, reduced by whatever amount may be necessary to provide for maintaining the source itself intact, including routine maintenance and eventual replacement, thus converting the yield into a perpetuity. (This allowance must be made in identifying the "rent" or "hire" of any productive agent with the "interest" on the investment in it, since rent contracts more commonly make maintenance and replacement the responsibility of the owner and include these costs in the rent paid; in legal language, the property is to be returned in its original condition

except for "ordinary wear and tear and unavoidable accident.")
The annual rate of yield is the ratio between the annual value of
the perpetuity and the investment in the source.   Under conditions
of perfect competition, or in an economic system in the position
of the theoretical equilibrium (stationary or moving), all sources
would yield a uniform rate of return on their cost of production,
which would be equal both to their cost of reproduction and their
market value.   The essential principle is that under ideal conditions—which include perfect knowledge and foresight—existing
resources will be so apportioned between the use to yield current
satisfactions and the investment use, and among all forms of both,
as to make this rate uniform, for the whole economy at the highest
level which can be obtained under existing technical and other
circumstances.   Under real conditions, this rate "tends" to be
approximated at the margin of new investment (or disinvestment),
with allowance for the uncertainties and errors of prediction.   But
existing sources will be valued by "capitalizing" their expected
income yield (or the equivalent perpetuity) at the rate fixed at the
margin of growth (or of disinvestment, in a retrograde society).
In other words, their value will be the market estimation of the
minimum cost of producing any source which will yield the same
income in perpetuity.   The expected yield of any source during its
life may itself be affected by its durability or by the time required
to carry out investment in new forms expected to yield an equal
income at lower cost.

THE RATE OF INTEREST.   It must be evident that if borrowing
and lending of money occurs in a situation where opportunity for
productive investment is open, the rate of interest on loans will
tend to be equal to the theoretical rate of yield on real investment.
An intelligent man will not make a loan at a rate lower than he
could secure by investing his capital himself—with allowance for
uncertainty and for trouble and expense in the two cases; and the
borrower for productive purposes will naturally not pay a higher
rate than his investment is expected to yield.   The lender in this
case becomes in effect the owner of the new assets in the amount
required to produce the income which he receives as interest,

together with additional security. Finally, if loans are made for purposes other than productive investment, i.e., for consumption, competition will tend to fix the same rate on these. If the concepts are carefully defined, loans for consumption purposes are not very different from loans for productive investment, since they involve a lien upon assets,—if the borrower gives security, as he must if the transaction is really a loan. And the case is not essentially changed if the transaction is a means to disinvestment more rapid than the owner could effect through under-maintenance. In a progressive society, particular cases of disinvestment, however carried out, are best viewed as a small deduction from the net growth of capital in the economy as a whole.

THE PSYCHOLOGICAL FACTOR. The argument of the preceding section seems to make the marginal productivity of capital the causal determinant of the rate of yield, and so of the interest rate. This conclusion is essentially correct, but its establishment depends on further argument; what has been said shows merely the necessity of equality, leaving the question open as to which determines the other or whether both are determined by some other cause. We referred earlier to the controversy between productivity theorists and others who have explained the rate of return in "psychological" terms, meaning an alleged general human preference of present over future satisfactions of like kind and amount. (Both groups follow Böhm-Bawerk, who also suggested a third "ground" of interest, but it cannot be explained briefly, and discussion would show it to be unimportant if not unreal. "Time-preference" or "discount of the future" as an independent explanation has been advocated especially by Professor F. A. Fetter in the U. S. A. and Professor L. von Mises in Vienna. Essentially, the theory is the "abstinence" doctrine of Senior and J. S. Mill; but the writers of the British classical school never attempted to use the degree or intensity of abstinence to explain the actual rate of yield or of interest. The neo-classical economists (following Marshall) usually combine productivity and time-preference in an eclectic or equilibrium theory, using the one to yield a demand curve and the other a supply curve. The most elaborate and careful development of this view is found in the work of Professor Irving Fisher.

The issue in interest theory is parallel to that involved in the controversy between "cost of production" and "utility" theories of general price determination, which was also set in motion by the Austrians and other writers of the subjective-value school. It was finally recognized that neither marginal cost nor marginal utility directly determines price. At equilibrium, any two prices must be in the same ratio as both of the other pairs of magnitudes, because the economic behavior of producers and consumers will make all three ratios equal. The process of adjustment must be considered in two steps. First, every consumer buys products, at prices which he finds given, in such proportions as to equalize the marginal satisfaction secured from equal increments of expenditure; and market competition sets the prices that will "clear the market" of the existing or momentarily forthcoming supplies. Second, entrepreneurs and owners of productive agents adjust production, at given prices of both products and productive services, so as to equalize costs and selling prices, and competition fixes the prices of productive services at the levels which will clear the market of the existing or forthcoming supplies of these. Equalization in both fields—prices proportional to utilities and equal to costs—defines the condition of general equilibrium. We must remember that the prices of productive services are at the same time the incomes of consumers, one factor in the effective demand for products. In a still longer view account must be taken of changes in the supply of productive agents and in technology and consumers' tastes, in a theory of historical economic change or progress (Marshall's "secular changes").

Whether we shall say that either relative marginal utility or relative marginal cost predominates over the other in the determination of any price must depend on the relative amounts of change undergone by the two ratios in establishing the equality. As Marshall in particular pointed out, the general rule is that productive adjustments are comparatively slower than those of consumers, but finally much more extensive. In the short run, demand is elastic and supply approximately fixed, hence utility is the determining factor; but in the long run, or "normal price" view, the situation is largely reversed. To the extent that all resources are ultimately transferrable between uses, the investment in them being recoverable, costs will be "constant" (relative to output) in the long run, or supply perfectly elastic. Cost will then determine price, in the sense that equilibrium price will be equal to cost, which is not affected by changes in the shape or position of the demand curve. To the extent that any resources are permanently immobile, because specialized and durable, long run marginal cost will increase with output, and the "eclectic" theory of mutual determination or equilibrium between demand and supply (utility and cost) will be applicable. During the period of adjustment following any important change, when supply is out of line with demand, the productive resources which are relatively immobile will tend to command a premium above interest on their cost in the expanding industry, and a price below the theoretical value in that which is contracting. (These payments are called "quasi-rents" by Marshall.) To the extent that the hire paid by producers themselves lags, the difference will appear as a "profit" (or loss) to the enterprisers concerned. (If there are permanent and unproducible specialized resources, without producible substitutes, they will command a hire which is one-sidedly dependent on the price of the particular product, since it is not affected by the competition of alternative uses; this case fits the classical theory of rent.)

The percentage rate of return on capital is a matter of the price of sources of future income, relative to their (perpetual) annual yield (the reciprocal of the rate itself). The general principles of price fixing apply in this case, but the factual conditions are radically different from those affecting particular consumption services or short-lived and freely reproducible goods. As pointed out earlier, there is little or no permanent specialization of productive agents between the consumption and the investment use, so that the alternative-cost curve for capital goods in terms of sacrificed consumption is practically horizontal—i.e., constant cost—allowing time for adjustment to changes. But in spite of this fact, the total situation is the opposite of constant cost; it is one of fixed supply. The field of investment includes not merely all salable wealth, but the productive capacity of human beings, and in any society at any moment it is the total accumulation made through all past time. Further, under "normal" conditions (apart from disastrous war or depression) the stock of capital must be expected to go on increasing through new saving and investment. It follows that the price theory applicable to the case corresponds to that of short-run or market price in an isolated market where there is a given stock to be disposed of, and not that of equilibrium price, for a consumption good. Typical consumption goods are in fact consumed about as fast as they are produced; and the price in which producers and society are most interested is not that which happens to prevail at the moment (when production may be out of line with demand); it is that which would make the rate of production equal to the rate of consumption and so can be expected to prevail on the average over a substantial period of time. In the case of capital, the normal case is a growing total stock; but this is so large that the net production in a short period of time will not make an appreciable difference in the demand price. ("Historical" changes will be considered presently.)

It is true that a sudden and unexpected change in saving "might" temporarily be so much in excess (or so much short, as the case may be) of what the construction industries are prepared to absorb as to cause a considerable fall or rise in the demand price while construction plans are being changed. But in practice, the important short-run changes are of the opposite sort; high rates of saving go with high interest rates, and conversely. The important short-run changes are connected with the business cycle, and this problem must be considered separately.

Thus the general theory of the yield of capital, to which the rate of interest tends to conform, must conclude that the normal price of capital goods is fixed by the demand for an existing supply. The demand-price will be the cost of a new investment of equal yield. Savers find a certain rate of return obtainable, fixed by the marginal productivity of new investment in the economy, and they save enough of their income to make their "marginal time preference" equal to this rate.   This rate will not be appreciably affected by ordinary changes in the amount saved per unit of time.   This equilibrium rate will, however, respond "permanently" to changes on the side of demand, such as result from an important technological advance opening up a large new field to investment.

CHANGES OVER LONG "HISTORICAL" PERIODS.   The equilibrium just described clearly is not, like the normal price of a reproducible good, a position of permanent stability, defined with reference to given conditions of demand and supply.   In fact, "stationary conditions" of saving and of investment are logically impossible. The facts of history and of human psychology show that capital tends to go on accumulating indefinitely, if general social conditions are stable.   We can "imagine" a stationary or retrogressive society, but it is idle to build theory on the assumption that either the supply of capital or investment opportunity tends to become and to remain stationary.   Accumulation obviously changes the supply of capital, and this must change the conditions which determine both the rate of saving and the demand price, the real rate of return.

With respect to the demand price for the use of capital, if all other things were to remain equal—particularly if progressive accumulation could occur without causing any advance in technology—it would undoubtedly tend gradually to lower the rate of return.   This is because, while investment may increase the supply of most kinds of productive services, and those of any large general class, there are factors in the investment situation, given by nature and economically unalterable, which prevent completely free and uniform growth in all fields.   Consequently, increasing total investment is doubtless subject to "diminishing returns," as a result of the increasing proportion of equipment of types in which investment is more readily expensible, to others where it is less so. But the decline in the rate would be slow, in historical terms.

On the supply side, at the same time, the growth of total income through further accumulation must make saving easier. It is impossible to say on general grounds what would be the net effect of all the inevitable consequences of saving upon the rate of accumulation, or the rate of return. The notion of stationary equilibrium with a zero rate of return is a disputed point among theorists. It rests on the questionable assumption that accumulation could proceed without opening up new demand by occasioning invention and discovery, and in any case is reasonably supposable only as a vague limit at the end of an indefinitely long course of development. During this process any prediction of given conditions tends to become fanciful. The reasonable prediction is that over long periods changes tending to raise the rate of return will more or less predominate during some intervals, and changes of the opposite kind in other intervals. This has been true in the past, as far as we have tolerably reliable statistical records. Professor Taussig fittingly characterized the long-run trend of the interest rate as a race between accumulation and invention.

IRRATIONAL OR "INSTITUTIONAL" FACTORS. The behavior both of savers and of entrepreneur investors is much influenced by social-psychological or "institutional" factors, and by whim and caprice, which resist analysis in terms of rational comparison between present and future enjoyment. Viewing society as a going—and an on-going—entity, the maintenance and accumulation of capital must depend on motives which look beyond the life of the individual. Even within the individual life, analysis which cannot be given here in detail makes it seriously doubtful whether the typical person in such a civilization as ours systematically prefers present to future enjoyments of like kind and amount, or would do so in the absence of opportunity to invest. Further, the attitude toward activity, adventure and risk seems to be a more important influence on saving than the comparison between enjoyment at different dates. If net saving is ever to cease and the supply of capital and the rate of return to become approximately stationary, it will doubtless occur through a balancing of risk and various "costs" against the expected return; and risk may operate on the whole as a stimulus or incentive to action rather than a deterrent or subjective cost.   Even if men on the average were to save all that they could save, without an "impossible" reduction of their standard of living, and if other things were to remain equal, the consequence would be only a more or less rapid decline in the rate through diminishing return.   The course of change would depend on potential investment opportunities, which, like social psychology, are a matter of prophecy rather than predictive knowledge.

Analysis of capital in terms of economically rational behavior and theoretical equilibrium seems unrealistic, and its explanatory and predictive value are rather limited.   In the making of investments, including the lending and borrowing of money, "representing" liquid capital—the consequences of ignorance, error, psychological and institutional factors, and innumerable "prejudices" appear in the enormous variation among actual rates of return.   The "book yield" of a real investment may be anything from total loss almost immediately (or worse, since the result may be a "dead horse") to an increase at an "astronomical" annual percentage.   One may think, for example, of such speculative ventures as prospecting for gold and inventing.   Loans may also be made without interest for accommodation (with varying prospect of loss) or at a rate as high as 25% for a week.   Under special conditions short-term government obligations have been sold for more than their face value at maturity; and a substantial amount of saving is regularly done at a cost, in various ways.

COMPUTATION OF CAPITAL VALUES.   As already observed, where the market for capital goods is highly imperfect, or there is no market at all (as in the case of free human beings), the same data may be found or estimated and used to determine a value, or one supposedly more accurate than that of the market, as the case may be.   There are clearly two main approaches to the problem, which would yield the same result under "theoretical conditions," and are more or less closely related in reality.   The true present value of any future income is found by discounting the calculated expectation as a perpetuity at the "correct" future rate of return.   Allowance must be made for any foreseeable change in this rate itself, as as well in the value or purchasing power of money.   All capitalization is inherently a matter of forecasting, not to say prophecy, rather than of calculation from current or past objective data. The other approach is historical, in terms of cost of production and depreciation. The second is familiar in business and accounting practice, yielding a "book value" of assets. Depreciation is usually computed by some more or less arbitrary rule, in order to give it definite meaning. Where there is enough divergence between this result and the current replacement cost—of a physically similar or an "equivalent" item—and the latter can be definitely ascertained, the stated book value may be modified accordingly in either direction. But it is more usual in corporate statements to add an explanatory note covering this and other sources of error than it is to depart from established rules. In the extreme case, where some unforeseen change or miscalculation makes an asset certainly and permanently worthless, it is likely to be written off. The needs of accounting call primarily for objective definiteness and conservatism—and in fact the rules affecting depreciation and other reserves are largely defined by the income-tax administration.

Computation of a capital value for a human being is much affected by the vagueness of all the factors—prospective life and earnings, historical cost, depreciation, and cost of replacement with allowance for risk. Production of human beings and their useful qualities is governed by a complex mixture of economic and non-economic considerations. With respect to free individuals, no clear or workable distinction can be made between maintenance cost and consumption as an ultimate end. The distinction is valid theoretically, and was stressed by the classical writers, notably J. S. Mill; but modern usage generally treats all the consumption of a laborer as an end. This difficulty is perhaps the strongest objective reason for ignoring the capital aspect of laborers and classifying them apart from (other) capital goods.

CYCLICAL AND MONETARY PHENOMENA. The most important concrete causes of error in anticipation, and hence of divergence between expected and realized rates of return on real investment and on obligations (securities, notes, etc.) center in the business or trade cycle. The Great Depression of the 1930's focussed the atten-

tion of economists on these phenomena and produced a new literature on the theory of capital and interest, under the leadership of
Mr. J. M. (later Lord) Keynes. A school of thought has arisen
which proposes to reverse the previous attitude toward money.
General economic theory had been based on the assumption that
money is "neutral," i.e., that its purchasing power is either unvarying or changes uniformly in all uses, so that money has no effect on
relative prices. Thus money played no causal role in the working
of the theoretical economic system, which was identical with one of
ideal barter. The central idea was formulated in Say's "law of
markets" (*loi des débouchées*) which asserts that the demand for any
good or service is the supply of other things offered in exchange.
The intention was to counteract the older "mercantilist" confusion
between money and wealth, and particularly to show that there
cannot be a "general glut" as commonly believed by the public.
(The Keynes position rehabilitates much of the mercantilist point
of view.) The neglect of monetary and cycle theory in the main
economic tradition (including Marshall) was, indeed, gradually
being corrected by a separate literature beginning in the later 19th
century. Much of this work was of questionable merit, but, the
subject also received increasing attention by conservative writers,
especially in the popular college textbooks.

The new doctrine (his followers often go far beyond Keynes
himself) involves a revolution in general economic theory as well
as that of interest and money. It treats money as an independent
entity in all supply and demand relations, regarding the value of
money itself as determined by the disposition to hold idle cash
("liquidity preference") rather than by its use to purchase other
things. Proceeding from the premise that cash could always be
used for investment in some form, notably for the purchase of
"securities," the theory makes the interest rate a payment for
parting with money instead of holding it. The issue raised is the
relation between the two general grounds of the desirability of
money, its purchasing power over goods and services, and "hoarding"—more especially the motives for holding wealth, or assets, in
the form of money rather than real things which yield an income

in some form, or securities or other claims to money in the future. The theoretical problem may be viewed as that of defining the conditions under which certain assumptions are legitimate. The first is that changes in the value of money, assumed to reflect changes in the disposition to hoard, are immediately expressed through hoarding or dishoarding. Second, the prices of products are assumed to respond (falling or rising) while those that make up costs (particularly wages) do not. Hence (third) the result is a change in profit margins, followed by contraction or expansion of production (and employment) specifically the production of goods for inventory and more durable forms of capital.

The issues and the facts are too complex for discussion in the present connection. Opponents will admit that "liquidity preference" is the main cause of the extremely high short-run interest rate (the bank rate) at the moment of a crisis and the abnormally low rates of deep depression. And it is not questioned that monetary expansion and contraction—whether in consequence of governmental policy or the activities of banks or the public—may bring about a substantial deviation, for a considerable period, in the apparent market loan rate and in general prices, or in the prices of securities or particular classes of goods, in contrast with others or with wages or other services, depending on the nature of the primary change. If any condition creates an anticipation of a rise or fall of general prices, uniformly for all goods and services, loan contracts over long periods (and the price of outstanding long-term securities) will naturally involve an allowance for the expected difference between the purchasing power of the money to be received in the future and that parted with in making the loan or purchase. This is a purely nominal matter, reflecting a change in the unit of measurement and not a difference in the real rate of yield of the loan. What is really most important is the effect of prospective price changes (general or in particular fields) on the disposition to make real investment, creating productive equipment. Rising prices must stimulate, and falling prices inhibit, investment; this is entirely apart from loan rates on money or even the occurrence of money lending in the society in question. As between boom and depression, loan rates seem to vary inversely with liquidity preference, not directly as the theory requires, and the price level for goods also varies with interest rates instead of inversely. It is also to be noted that where the classical equilibrium theory calls for opposite changes in investment and consumption, cyclical variations "swamp" this tendency, and the statistics show a positive correlation, though the production of capital goods fluctuates far more violently. In fact there is heavy net disinvestment in a severe depression such as that of the 1930's in the U. S. A.

MONEY AND CAPITAL. The question whether money should be treated as capital is one of the most difficult aspects of the general problem. It also involves the meaning and role of money, and the forces which determine its value. Money is clearly capital to the individual owner, though its value to living on any theory (except the psychology of the miser) depends on its future purchasing power. Its value may bear nearly any relation to that of the money material, (or metallic "reserve") its cost of production or its utility in non-monetary uses. In the case of a metallic currency, with free and unlimited coinage, these values are equal; but the bulk of a nation's medium of exchange, or even all of it, may consist of paper or bank credit of little cost or intrinsic worth. Money is also capital from the standpoint of the exchange economy as a whole, in the sense that it is one of the vital instrumentalities of organized economic life, virtually a necessity. But the amount of money, or of wealth in that form, that is "required," depends on the conventionally established timing of payments, as well as prices and the volume of economic activity. Hence the amount of money which should be included in an estimate of the aggregate wealth of a society is a question which admits of no definite answer.

THE ETHICS OF INTEREST-TAKING. The scientific treatment of capital and its return (earlier referred to as profit, now usually as interest) has been much influenced—and confused—by ethical controversy over the "justice" of the receipt of interest by individuals. The early classical economics naturally raised the question of the right of the capitalist and landlord to their shares in the product and gave rise to the doctrines of socialism and (later) of "single-tax."

As to interest on loans, the argument given above shows that ethical condemnation rests for the most part on fallacy. The loan at interest could always be replaced by an equivalent agreement of various other forms; its practical significance is a certain redistribution of risk, and the conditions of risk assumption are the only ethical problem which is properly involved—a serious one, to be sure. A general condemnation of interest would be valid only if extended to require the replacement of all sales by gifts. This may well be the intention in the one place in the New Testament (Luke 6:34–35) where interest-taking seems to be explicitly condemned. The prohibition probably applied only between the religious brethren, as in the Old Testament; and rent and equivalent partnership arrangements might also have been condemned if these practices had been familiar—but not too familiar!—to the early Christian and medieval writers. Any custom which is thoroughly established, hoary with age, and accepted as an integral part of the established system of social order is unlikely to be questioned by religious moralists. What is condemned is a threatened innovation, and particularly one which seems to replace an ethic of personal and functional-status relationships with "impersonally rational" norms.

The argument also shows that the sharp distinction, common to popular and reformist thinking, between the ethical claims of property and personal services involves a similar fallacy. The possession of productive capacity in external things and in internal abilities stand in much the same position, particularly with respect to inheritance *versus* effort, foresight and initiative, which seem to be the basis of ethical rights in distribution, according to modern conceptions. Beyond these formal rights lies the moral duty of the strong (or fortunate) to relieve accidental distress and to assist the weak (or unfortunate) through private charity or political action. In such a country as Britain or the U. S. A., personal capacity makes up from three-fifths to three-fourths of all individual earning power. The facts of institutional inheritance, which give individuals vastly different initial advantages in "capacity"—both for production and for appreciation—impose serious limitations on the social-ethical principle of freedom of contract, which modern thought has accepted rather uncritically. The over-emphasis may be more or less explained by reaction against the traditionalism and authoritarianism of the preceding historical epochs. The issue affects all types of economic rights and claims but the borrower-lender relationship is a "mechanical detail" of minor importance.

INVESTMENT AND ITS YIELD: QUANTITATIVE RELATIONS*

In an analytic view of the investment process no quantity of capital or of investment is involved at all. What is really invested is always consumption income, which has the dimensions of intensity and time. A quantity of investment is derived by considering a certain intensity or time-rate for a certain interval of time. But the mere multiplication of intensity by time (the intensity being assumed uniform) does not yield the correct value for the total quantity. This is one aspect of the essential difficulty which creates our problem, especially because Crusoe, or any other investor, may think of his cost in this oversimple way without, in most cases, introducing any serious error. The essential fact which gives rise to the notion of a rate of return is that, if consumption is sacrificed at some rate over some period of time, the subject may begin at the end of the period to draw a larger consumption income in perpetuity. The concrete nature of the process is that of using the productive capacity which would have yielded consumption income over the interval in question to produce instead a new source of income, for current consumption or for further investment. We assume, of course, that in his given situation he acts in such a way, selects the new source and the method of constructing it in such a way, as to make the new income as large as possible for his investment considered as a given rate over a given interval. The rate of

* The following is a section of an article by the same author, on "The Quantity of Capital and the Rate of Interest," *Journal of Political Economy*, August 1936, pages 441–450. Reprinted by courtesy of the publisher and author.

interest may be computed from these data alone, in accord with the simple expression:

$$U_2 = U_1(1 + i)^t. \tag{1}$$

Here U_1 is the intensity magnitude of the income sacrificed (assumed to be uniform); t is the interval of the sacrifice, i.e., the construction period for the new source; U_2 is the intensity magnitude of the new consumption income which begins to flow at the end of t years, consisting of U_1 plus the yield of the new investment, measured after provision for perpetuity at a uniform rate if it is not naturally perpetual and uniform; and i is the rate of interest in the ordinary sense. U_1, U_2, and t are the known or given magnitudes in the expression but may have any value (see below), and i is the unknown. The known magnitudes depend on the conditions under which investment actually takes place, which conditions are assumed to remain unchanged during the course of the investing operation.[1]

There is still a difficulty to be faced, however. This is the fact that in the equation the new income U_2, which begins to come in

---

[1] It is easy to check the correctness of the equation and at the same time to show that this way of looking at the interest relation is identical with treating it as the yield or productivity of a quantity of investment. We simply take note of the amount of investment actually accumulated during t years if one dollar is invested each year. We assume first that the investment is made in a lump sum of one dollar at the beginning of the year, and that the yield takes the same form. Then the principal which will yield its first instalment of interest at the end of the t-th year is the accumulation over $(t - 1)$ years, which is the sum of the series

$$1 + (1 + i) + (1 + i)^2 + \cdots + (1 + i)^{t-1} = \frac{(1 + i)^t - 1}{i}.$$

The yield on this amount of principal at rate i is the numerator of the fraction, and the total new consumption income is obtained by adding the original dollar per year, consumption of which is resumed at the end of the period of investment; this cancels the -1, leaving the expression for the annual yield $= (1 + i)^t$, as given in Equation (1), taking $U_1 = 1$.

The equation is unaffected if both consumption-income streams, U_1 and U_2, are taken as continuous instead of as instantaneous payments. The accumulation at the close of the period of investment, is assumed to be a uniform perpetuity. This, of course, is not in general the immediate result, and this fact itself would force Crusoe to keep capital accounts in order to manage his resources economically. In general the year-to-year yield or rental of a capital good is larger than the true net yield because the instrument will not last always and some deduction must be made each year from its imputed yield in order to provide for its replacement, i.e., for the maintenance of the investment and its yield.

Whether the instrument is actually to be replaced or not (or, if so, with what kind of instrument) has nothing to do with the computation of the rate of return on the investment in it. But the investor must know whether he is receiving more or less than the true net yield (which is the yield on a perpetuity basis) and, if it is more, must treat the excess as disinvestment of capital. (And if he receives less, he must treat the difference as further investment out of yield.) In fact, the phenomenon of replacement is a special case under a special case. The fundamental fact is that the yield of a capital good is irregular and must be converted into an equivalent uniform rate of flow before it can be measured. It might be—and often is—irregular for other reasons than the necessity of periodic replacement which, in turn, means only irregularity in the maintenance outlay. A uniform maintenance cost would not create any problem, being undistinguishable from any other operating expense.

If any particular investment yields its return at an irregular rate, the actual procedure for securing regularity is alternately to

---

at the end of t years, when the new continuous flow of income begins, is then

$$\frac{e^{\rho t} - 1}{\rho},$$

where ρ is the "force of interest" corresponding to rate of simple annual interest i, being $\rho = \log_e (1 + i)$. The annual continuous yield is again the numerator of the fraction, and the argument proceeds as before, $(1 + i)^t$ being replaced by $e^{\rho t}$, which is equal to it. (It is assumed that investment entirely ceases at the end of t years. When the investment is made in instalments, there is in effect an overlap of a year between construction period and earning period.)

invest and disinvest in some other field, investing whenever the primary investment is yielding more than the equivalent uniform rate and disinvesting when it yields less (by more than the current yield on the auxiliary investment). That is, in effect, capital is transferred back and forth between the primary and the auxiliary fields of use. The necessity of this transfer would force the investor to keep capital accounts, i.e., to know the amount of the investment as well as to compare receipts. The computation is fairly simple if it is possible to invest and disinvest at will at the same rate of yield and at any desired "speed"[2] in the auxiliary field. The only simple way in practice for comparing two irregular or time-limited income streams is to find the present worth, the capitalized value, of both; this is, in effect, the mathematical way of converting each into a uniform perpetuity.

There is, however, another and even more fundamental reason for capitalization, i.e., another fact which makes it necessary to know the quantity of capital in order to compare fields or modes of investment and so to secure maximum economy. This is the fact that different investment operations involve different intervals or proceed at different rates, or both. Even if all yields immediately took the form of a uniform perpetual rate of flow (except, perhaps, where otherwise explicitly planned), it would be necessary to "accumulate" the investment during the period of construction, as shown in the explanation of Equation (1). It is only by computing the invested capital, including interest during construction, continuously compounded, and equating the result with the present worth of the anticipated yield, for any two investments, that their relative desirability can be determined and the aim of economy realized. Both sides of the equation express the quantity of capital and involve the rate of interest. The equation is to be solved for the rate, and the investment which yields the highest

---

[2] The ambiguity of the word "rate" is most unfortunate. In expressions such as the "rate of interest" the word is inaccurately used as it combines a time-rate of flow (the correct meaning) with a ratio of this flow to a principal. And in addition there is really involved an instantaneous rate (ratio) of growth with reference to a continuously changing base.

rate is, of course, to be chosen. Thus in most real cases the computation necessary for the perfectly rational directing of investment is far more complex than we have indicated.[3]

The root of the difficulty as regards capital, viewed as the cost of an income-yielding source, is that to make any finite investment necessarily requires time, no matter at what speed it is made. But the instant any investment whatever is made, it must be assumed to begin to yield a return which, since it is not instantly consumed, must be added to the investment itself. That is, if an investor begins to sacrifice (invest) consumption income at a rate U_1 (using the same symbol as before), he is after the first instant really investing it at a higher rate of speed, because he could have had some consumption income by stopping the investment process at the first instant. And the longer the process continues, the greater becomes the rate at which potential consumption is given up. Thus, to find the total amount of investment made in any new source of income, we have to add two elements. One is the investment made from without, as it were—the value of the sacrificed income of the services of previously existing productive agencies

---

[3] The equation may be given in various forms. The following three are for the cases in which the anticipated yield is (A) naturally a perpetuity, (B) time-limited and capitalized as it stands, and (C) time-limited but converted into a perpetuity by deduction of appropriate contributions to a sinking-fund for replacing the source (by a single payment at the end of its life). In all cases the rates of flow—both of income into investment and of yield out of it—are assumed to be uniform. When they are not uniform, the equations will be built around integrals between limits of the expression $f(t)e^{pt}dt$.

Let the cost of a capital good be S dollars per year for c years and its yield R dollars per year for L years. (In (A), $L = \infty$.) All payments are to be in annual sums at the beginning of the year, interest compounded annually. Let $(1 + i) = A$.

$$\frac{S(A^c - 1)}{i} = \frac{R}{i} \qquad \text{or} \qquad S(A^c - 1) = R \qquad\qquad (A)$$

$$\frac{S(A^c - 1)}{i} = \frac{R(A^L - 1)}{iA^L} \qquad \text{or} \qquad SA^L(A^c - 1) = R(A^L - 1) \qquad (B)$$

$$\iota = \left\{ R - \left[\frac{S(A^c - 1)}{i} \cdot \frac{i}{A^L - 1} \right] \right\} \div \frac{S(A^c - 1)}{i}, \qquad (C)$$

which is readily reduced to the same form as (B).

used in creating or constructing the new source. The other element is usually called "interest during construction" and includes not only interest on each infinitesimal investment from without from the instant it is made until the investment is completed, but also interest on each infinitesimal increment of this interest from the instant it is earned until the same point.[4]   In real terms, this interest, and interest on interest, represent the specific product during each instant of the uncompleted capital good as it exists at the beginning of the instant in question.   (Of course an instant has no duration; it is the mathematical limit of a process of taking shorter and shorter intervals to infinity.)

However, as indicated at the outset, it is not necessary to take account of any lapse of time in order to secure the theoretical data for determining the interest rate.   This can be shown by differentiating Equation (1) with respect to time.   The result is

$$\frac{dU_2}{dt} = U_1(1 + i)^t \log_e (1 + i).$$

(It is to be noted that U_1 is a constant in the equation, i.e., is independent of t.)   The new equation gives the rate of change in the individual's income, at any moment, t units of time after the beginning of the investment operation.   But obviously any moment can itself be taken as the beginning, so that t may be made equal to zero.   Then, since $\log_e (1 + i) = \rho$, the right-hand side of the equation reduces to $U_1\rho$.   That is, the instantaneous rate of interest is the rate of growth in income resulting from investment, divided by the rate of investment.

The essential facts of the investment process in a Crusoe economy with uncertainty absent, may be recapitulated as follows.

---

[4] The moment of completion is most realistically taken as the point in time at which outlays cease to exceed return and return begins to exceed outlay, always including in the latter interest on interest as well as interest on expenditure from the outside.   The ordinary rate of simple annual interest, i, is, in fact, the result of continually compounding interest during the year at a somewhat smaller rate, $\rho = \log_e (1 + i)$.

First, investment must take place at some time-rate or speed (really an intensity) over some finite period of time. But each increment of investment must yield its return at the same rate (in the sense of "ratio"), either in consumed service or as an addition to the investment, and *for as long as it remains invested*. It must either yield in perpetuity a return for consumption, or further investment, at this rate, or yield up the original investment. Because the process of investment must be spread over time and because, in general, there is more or less disinvestment in connection with the direct yield of any particular capital good, it is necessary to recognize the separate period of investment, from zero to infinity, of each infinitesimal increment of capital invested in any source or capital good. Only in this way can different investments be made at the same rate and the maximum yield obtained on the whole capital, which is possible under the given economic conditions.

This view of the matter yields a computation form different from that of Equation (1) but does not invalidate the latter or present a different theory. Any one of the equations (1), (A), (B), or (C) expresses the fact that sacrificed income invested yields a return at the annual rate of i dollars per year or the instantaneously compounded rate of ρ dollars per year, which return is itself invested at the same rate of yield whenever it is not instantly drawn out and consumed or reinvested elsewhere. While an investment is being built up, the yield during each infinitesimal interval of time of all the investment previously made is added to principal, along with whatever new investment is added from without during the interval. Summation gives the total invested. Treating this as the present worth of the future yield merely expresses the fact that each infinitesimal increment of capital will continue to yield at the same rate as long as it remains invested, i.e., until it appears in consumable form and is consumed or reinvested under some other account. This is the ordinary view of interest as the ratio between the yield of a capital sum and the capital itself, maintenance of principal being assumed. The rate expresses the marginal productivity of capital in that the investment considered is assumed to represent a negligible addition to the capital of an economic system. The time relations of this fact will be emphasized as we proceed.

The argument as given develops the theory of capital and interest with reference (*a*) to ideal conditions at a given moment in the life of any capitalistic economy (Crusoe or other), and (*b*) to a single increment of investment considered as negligible in comparison with the total amount of capital already invested in the system. By ideal conditions we mean especially that the investor of the small increment of capital under consideration knows everything about the rest of the economy that would in any way affect his conduct in planning this particular investment. This means that he knows the conditions affecting the investment either for all future time or for whatever interval he plans to maintain the investment, i.e., until it is entirely disinvested for consumption or reinvestment under another account.[5]

The theory assumes, as a matter of course, that the investor acts rationally, in the sense of economically, meaning in such a way as to get the maximum yield on his investment, which is mathematically identical with saying that the present worth of the investment is maximized at every moment in the course of the action. The theory has to do only with the relation between income and capital value and assumes that yield itself is a known magnitude. As a matter of fact, the making of an increment of investment would change the composition of real income, and there is no objective common denominator for measuring one income in terms of another of different composition. (The difficulty is especially serious with reference to a Crusoe economy.) Yet incomes are comparable with a fairly narrow margin of error; otherwise no

---

[5] It should be understood that it is impossible for more than one individual in the same human group at the same time to take the rest of the world as given or predictable and act upon his knowledge, unless all those who do so act in complete and express collusion. This is a general limitation on the theory of intelligent behavior as applied to group life. It is a further and much more sweeping limitation, in addition to the impossibility of complete and perfect knowledge of the course of natural events.

behavior which affects any change in conditions could be intelligent at all.

In assuming that the new increment of investment is negligible in size we assume that its addition to the total does not affect the rate of interest. It does not matter how long the construction period is, as the lapse of time is taken into account in the formulas. The moment to which the rate applies refers, then, to any point in time during the interval in which investment is made.

The argument also abstracts from the effect of any anticipated future change in the rate of interest during the life of the invest- ment, which may then be of any duration up to infinity. The effects even of a foreseen change in the rate of interest (the rate obtainable on a small increment of new investment) as well as the bearings of possible changes not accurately foreseeable (the effects of uncertainty) present distinct problems which must be reserved for separate consideration.

This notion of capital quantity as capitalized future yield applies not only to the particular increment of investment being added to a total during any short interval of time, but to all the other items of capital in the system. Of the capital invested up to any given moment, every unit is marginal. Every one is valued by capitaliz- ing its actual yield at the rate yielded by any final infinitesimal increment, which is equal to the yield on the next infinitesimal increment of investment to be effected. The capital represented by any source of yield is the imnimum investment necessary to produce the same yield under the conditions obtaining in the system at the given time. The form which the next increment of invest- ment would take is not in question—specifically the degree in which the new capital good added would resemble any already in existence. The total capital in a system, then, means simply the aggregate of the quantities obtained by capitalizing the future earnings of each item at the rate which is effective at the margin.

22

THE THEORY OF THE RATE OF INTEREST[*][1]

By John Maynard Keynes[†]

Perhaps the following is a useful way of indicating the precise points of departure of the theory of the rate of interest expounded in my *General Theory of Employment, Interest and Money* from what I take to be the orthodox theory. Let us begin with four propositions, which, although they may be unfamiliar in form, are not inconsistent with the orthodox theory and which that theory has no reason, so far as I am aware, to reject.

(1) Interest on money *means* precisely what the books on arithmetic say that it means; that is to say, it is simply the premium obtainable on current cash over deferred cash, so that it measures the marginal preference (for the community as a whole) for holding cash in hand over cash for deferred delivery. No one would pay this premium unless the possession of cash served some purpose, i.e., had some efficiency. Thus we can conveniently say that interest on money measures the marginal efficiency of money measured in terms of itself as a unit.[2]

---

* *The Lessons of Monetary Experience; Essays in Honor of Irving Fisher*, 1937, pages 145–152. Reprinted by courtesy of Farrar and Rinehart and the author.

† Formerly, Kings College, Cambridge.

[1] I have though it suitable to offer a short note on this subject in honor of Irving Fisher, since his earliest and latest contributions have been concerned with it, and since during the whole of the thirty years that I have been studying economics he has been the outstanding authority on this problem.

[2] This implies a slightly different definition of marginal efficiency from that which I have given in my *General Theory* (p. 135), namely the substitution of "market value" for "replacement cost." The meaning of "marginal efficiency of capital" of which I make use—and which is, in my opinion, the only definition of the term which makes good sense—was first introduced into economic theory by Irving Fisher in his *Theory of Interest* (1930), under the designation "the rate of

(2) Money is not peculiar in having a marginal efficiency measured in terms of itself. Surplus stocks of commodities in excess of requirements and other capital assets representing surplus capacity may, indeed, have a negative marginal efficiency in terms of themselves, but normally capital assets of all kinds have a positive marginal efficiency measured in terms of themselves. If we know the relation between the present and expected prices of an asset in terms of money we can convert the measure of its marginal efficiency in terms of itself into a measure of its marginal efficiency in terms of money by means of a formula which I have given in my *General Theory*, p. 227.

(3) The effort to obtain the best advantage from the possession of wealth will set up a tendency for capital assets to exchange, in equilibrium, at values proportionate to their marginal efficiencies in terms of a common unit. That is to say, if r is the money rate of interest (i.e., r is the marginal efficiency of money in terms of itself) and y is the marginal efficiency of a capital asset A in terms of money, then A will exchange in terms of money at a price such as to make $y = r$.

(4) If the demand price of our capital asset A thus determined is not less than its replacement cost, new investment in A will take place, the scale of such investment depending on the capacity available for the production of A, i.e., on its elasticity of supply, and on the rate at which y, its marginal efficiency, declines as the amount of investment in A increases. At a scale of new investment at which the marginal cost of producing A is equal to its demand price as above, we have a position of equilibrium. Thus the price system resulting from the relationships between the marginal efficiencies of different capital assets including money, measured in terms of a common unit, determines the aggreagte rate of investment.

These propositions are not, I think, inconsistent with the orthodox theory, or in any way open to doubt. They establish that

return over cost." This conception of his is, I think, the most important and fruitful of his recent original suggestions.

relative prices (and, under the influence of prices, the scale of output) move until the marginal efficiencies of all kinds of assets are equal when measured in a common unit; and consequently that the marginal efficiency of capital is equal to the rate of interest. But they tell us nothing as to the forces which determine what this common level of marginal efficiency will tend to be. It is when we proceed to this further discussion that my argument diverges from the orthodox argument.

Put shortly, the orthodox theory maintains that the forces which determine the common value of the marginal efficiency of various assets are independent of money, which has, so to speak, no autonomous influence, and that prices move until the marginal efficiency of money, i.e., the rate of interest, falls into line with the common value of the marginal efficiency of other assets as determined by other forces. My theory, on the other hand, maintains that this is a special case and that over a wide range of possible cases almost the opposite is true, namely, that the marginal efficiency of money is determined by forces partly appropriate to itself, and that prices move until the marginal efficiency of other assets fall into line with the rate of interest.

Let me proceed to give the further propositions, which, I suggest, the orthodox theory requires.

(5) The marginal efficiency of money in terms of itself has the peculiarity that it is independent of its quantity. In this respect it differs from other capital assets. This is a consequence of the Quantity Theory of Money strictly stated (a matter to which we shall return later). Thus, unless we import considerations from outside, the money rate of interest is indeterminate, for the demand schedule for money is a function solely of its supply. Nevertheless, a determinate value for r can be derived from the condition that the value of an asset A, of which the marginal efficiency in terms of money is y, must be such that $y = r$. For provided that we know the scale of investment, we know y and the value of A, and hence we can deduce r. In other words, the rate of interest depends on the marginal efficiency of capital assets other than money. This must, however, be supplemented by

another proposition; for it requires that we should already know the scale of investment. This further proposition is as follows.

(6) The scale of investment will not reach its equilibrium level until the point is reached at which the elasticity of supply of output as a whole has fallen to zero.

Hence follows the final synthesis of this theory. The equilibrium rate of aggregate investment, corresponding to the level of output for a further increase in which the elasticity of supply is zero, depends on the readiness of the public to save. But this in turn depends on the rate of interest. Thus for each level of the rate of interest we have a given quantity of saving. This quantity of saving determines the scale of investment. The scale of investment settles the marginal efficiency of capital, to which the rate of interest must be equal. Our system is therefore determinate. To each possible value of the rate of interest there corresponds a given volume of saving; and to each possible value of the marginal efficiency of capital there corresponds a given volume of investment. Now the rate of interest and the marginal efficiency of capital must be equal. Thus the position of equilibrium is given by that common value of the rate of interest and of the marginal efficiency of capital at which the saving determined by the former is equal to the investment determined by the latter.

Now my departure from the orthodox theory takes place, as I have said, at propositions (5) and (6), for which I substitute:

(5)* The marginal efficiency of money in terms of itself is, in general, a function of its quantity (though not of its quantity alone), just as in the case of other capital assets.

(6)* Aggregate investment may reach its equilibrium rate under proposition (4) above, before the elasticity of supply of output as a whole has fallen to zero.

Before we examine the grounds for substituting (5)* and (6)* for (5) and (6), let us stop for a moment to consider more fully the meaning and the practical implications of the special postulates of the orthodox theory.

Let us begin with proposition (5). So far as the active circulation is concerned, it is sufficiently correct as a first approximation to regard the demand for money as proportionate to the effective demand, i.e., to the level of money income; which amounts to saying that the income velocity of the active circulation is independent of the quantity of money. This is, I say, only a first approximation because the demand for money in the active circulation is also to some extent a function of the rate of interest, since a higher rate of interest may lead to a more economical use of active balances, though this only means that the active balances are partially under the same influence as the inactive balances. But we also require the postulate that the amount of the inactive balances is independent of the rate of interest. I do not see, however, how this can be the case, except in conditions of long-period equilibrium, by which I mean a state of expectation which is both definite and constant and has lasted long enough for there to be no hangover from a previous state of expectation.

In ordinary conditions, on the other hand, this postulate would have awkward consequences quite incompatible with experience. It would mean, for example, that "open-market operations" by a central bank would have no effect, other than momentary, on the rate of interest, the price of bonds remaining the same whatever quantity of them the central bank may buy or sell; the effect of the central bank's action on prices being such as to modify the demand for money to just the same extent as that by which the central bank was altering the supply of money.

Let us now turn to proposition (6). A zero elasticity of supply for output as a whole means that an increase of demand in terms of money will lead to no change in output; that is to say, prices will rise in the same proportion as the money demand rises. Inflation will have no effect on output or employment, but only on prices. This is what I mean by saying that the orthodox theory of the rate of interest involves a strict interpretation of the Quantity Theory of Money, namely that P changes in the same proportion as M. This does not, of course, mean that T and V in the equation $PT = MV$ are irrevocably fixed; but the above, in conjunction with proposition (5), does mean that T and V are neither of them a function of M and that they do not change merely as a result of inflation in the quantity of money. Otherwise interpreted, a zero elasticity of supply for output as a whole involves a zero elasticity of supply for employment, i.e., there is, in my terminology, full employment. Indeed the condition in which the elasticity of supply for output as a whole is zero, is, I now think, the most convenient criterion for defining full employment.

It seems, therefore, that the orthodox theory requires (1) that there should be a state of definite and constant expectation and (2) that there should be a state of full employment. These limitations mean that it is a particular theory applicable only to certain conditions; and this is my justification for calling my own theory a *general theory*, of which the orthodox theory is a limiting case. Perhaps I am wrong in making the orthodox theory employ these postulates. For I am under the disadvantage that no one has ever thought it worth while to write down the postulates which the orthodox theory is supposed to require. But I do not at present see any alternative.

If I am right, the orthodox theory is wholly inapplicable to such problems as those of unemployment and the trade cycle, or, indeed, to any of the day-to-day problems of ordinary life. Nevertheless it is often in fact applied to such problems. The postulates which it requires, not having been stated, have escaped notice, with the result that deep-seated inconsistencies have been introduced into economic thought. The orthodox theory of the rate of interest properly belongs to a different stage of economic assumptions and abstractions from that in which any of us are thinking today. For the rate of interest and the marginal efficiency of capital are particularly concerned with the *indefinite* character of actual expectations; they sum up the effect on men's market decisions of all sorts of vague doubts and fluctuating states of confidence and courage. They belong, that is to say, to a stage of our theory where we are no longer assuming a definite and calculable future. The orthodox theory, on the other hand, is concerned with a simplified world where there is always full employment, and where doubt and fluctuations of confidence are ruled out, so that there is no occasion to hold inactive balances, and prices must be constantly at a level which, merely to satisfy the transactions motive and without leaving any surplus to be absorbed by the precautionary and speculative motives, causes the whole stock of money to be worth a rate of interest equal to the marginal efficiency of capital which corresponds to full employment. The orthodox theory is, for example, particularly applicable to the stationary state.[3] For in such conditions, not only is proposition (5) valid for the same reasons that apply in the case of the long period; but the stock of capital being fixed and new investment being zero, the marginal efficiency of capital must depend on the amount of this given stock and prices must be at a level which equates the amount of money, demanded for active balances at a rate of interest equal to this fixed marginal efficiency of capital, to the fixed supply of money in existence.

There is one other comment worth making. It leads to considerable difficulties to regard the marginal efficiency of money as wholly different in character from the marginal efficiency of other assets. Equilibrium requires, as we have seen above (proposition 3), that the prices of different kinds of assets measured in the same unit must move until their marginal efficiencies measured in that unit are equal. But if the marginal efficiency of money in terms of itself is always equal to the marginal efficiency of other assets, irrespective of the price of the latter, the whole price system in terms of money becomes indeterminate. It is the elements of elasticity (a) in the desire to hold inactive balances and (b) in the supply of output as a whole, which permits a reasonable measure of stability in prices. If these elasticities are zero there is a necessity for the whole body of prices and wages to respond immediately to every change in the quantity of money. This assumes a state of affairs very different from that in which we live. For the two elasticities named above are highly characteristic of the real world; and the assumption that both of them are zero assumes away three-quarters of the problems in which we are interested.

---

[3] Unless we suppose that a constant money wage is compatible with a constant level of employment which is less than full employment.

23

MR. KEYNES AND THE RATE OF INTEREST*[1]

By Dennis H. Robertson †

I. Words and Things

§1. The purpose of these lectures is to restate in a more coherent
and positive manner certain criticisms which I have felt impelled
to make of the doctrines regarding the rate of interest put forward
in recent years by Mr. Keynes.

I find it necessary in self-defence to start with a few words on
the distasteful subject of methodology.   In the course of one of our
brushes, Mr. Keynes has suggested that I am a recent and reluctant
convert to the view that the rate of interest is "in some sense a
monetary phenomenon."[2]   This is, I am afraid, a misapprehension.
Obviously in a money-using world the rate of interest, in what
Marshall calls[3] its "strict sense" of the price paid in money for the
use of a sum of money, is "in some sense a monetary phenomenon";
and nobody can ever have supposed otherwise.   The fact is, surely,
that in expounding any branch of economic theory, there are two
courses open to us.   We can start with a situation simplified to
the greatest possible extent by abstraction, and then gradually
build up our theory by introducing successively the complications
of real life.   Or we can start by facing boldly all the complications
of a momentary market situation, and then seek to discard the
accidentals and distil the essentials.   So it is with interest: we can
begin by showing how it would emerge in a Crusoe economy, then
introduce exchange, then money; or we can start with the actual

---

* Essays in Monetary Theory, 1940, pages 1–38.   Reprinted by courtesy of
P. S. King and Son, Ltd., and the author.
† Cambridge University.
[1] See Essays in Monetary Theory, Preface, p. vii.
[2] E.J., June 1938, pp. 318, 323.
[3] Money, Credit and Commerce, p. 73.

world, with its (far from perfect) loan markets and its (far from orderly) monetary systems. The danger of this latter method is that the same motive which leads us to adopt it, namely the desire to show ourselves at all costs "in touch with real life," will tempt us to seek to produce an apparently simple result in circumstances in which simplicity involves the exaggeration of incidentals and the obscuring of fundamentals. So anxious, however, am I to avoid the reproach of "classicality," that I am ready to follow Mr. Keynes by starting the analysis at the most difficult end. Until near its close, however, I propose to allow myself the same simplification as he has frequently done, namely, that of speaking as though there were only *one* rate of interest determined in a single market.

§2. If we start in this way, the natural course seems to be to describe the rate of interest as the market price of the hire of something which Marshall called "free or floating capital," which others have called "capital disposal" or "command over capital," and which recent writers seem to have settled down into calling "loanable" or "investible funds." This price, like other market prices, can be conceived as emerging from the interaction of schedules of supply and demand, showing the amount of loanable funds which, at given hiring-prices, people are respectively willing to put on to, and to take off, the market during the slice of time selected for observation. Since we have decided to start by facing all, or nearly all, the complications of the real world, we must not be surprised to find that these schedules are complicated things. In analysing their constitution, it is to some extent arbitrary whether we enter certain elements as additions to the demand side or deductions from the supply side, and *vice versa*. The classification which follows is no doubt only one of many possible ones; but it seems to bring out the main points requiring attention.

The amount of loanable funds which people are willing to put on the market at any price consists of the following elements, some of which may of course be negative:—

   (i) current savings effected during the period:

  (ii) "disentanglings," *i.e.* savings which have been made in the past and are being currently released from embodiment either in fixed capital (buildings, instruments, etc.) or in working capital (goods in process or in store) and so becoming available for re-embodiment either in the same or in different forms:

(iii) "net dishoardings," *i.e.* previously saved, or previously disentangled, money now being withdrawn from store and placed on the market, less money which is being currently saved, or currently disentangled, and withheld from the market:

(iv) net additional bank loans (including of course investments, since we are not distinguishing at this stage between different markets), *i.e.* the gross amount of new bank loans during the period less repayments to banks out of current disentanglings or current savings.

The amount of loanable funds which people are willing to take off the market at any price may be analysed according to the purposes for which the funds are required, as follows:—

(i) funds destined for expenditure on building up new increments of fixed or working capital:

(ii) funds destined for expenditure on the maintenance or replacement of existing fixed or working capital:

(iii) funds destined to be put into store:

(iv) funds destined for expenditure on consumption, whether individual or collective (*i.e.* through State doles, etc.), in excess of current income.

§3. This analysis, which is substantially identical with that of Professor Ohlin,[4] requires some comments.

(1) To some extent as regards the first, and to a greater extent as regards the second, item on both lists, the demanders and suppliers are likely to be the same persons, *i.e.* they do not appear on the market properly so called, and the assumption that their actions are highly sensitive to the current behaviour of the rate of interest is not entirely realistic. In other words, up to a point

---

[4] *E.J.*, Sept. 1937, pp. 423 ff.

there is probably a measure of automatism, especially as regards the re-entanglement of *working capital* disentanglings, in the conduct of business firms. But it would be a mistake to exaggerate the degree of this automatism, *i.e.* to overlook the extent to which dis-investment even in working capital is an ever-present possibility.

(2) The analysis shows that there is no difficulty, as it has some-times been suggested that there is, in dealing by this market supply and demand method with the phenomenon of the offer of existing money stocks in exchange for securities, or existing security holdings in exchange for money. Still less is there any difficulty in dealing with the case[5] in which no exchanges of this kind are in fact occurring, the rate of interest having already moved sufficiently to prevent them: in this case the relevant elements of the supply and demand schedules are simply equated at zero.[6]

(3) Since the analysis deals in terms of the way in which people are willing to act at a particular time it is evidently necessary to interpret the terms used in a sense which makes it possible to relate them to the choices which are open to people at that time. Thus we must exclude both from "savings" and from "hoardings" (or from their opposite terms) those undesigned increments (or decre-ments) in people's money stocks which occur, as Mr. Lutz has well put it,[7] "after the transactions on the capital market are over," and as an unforeseen result of the behaviour of the flow of total expenditure which is consequential on those transactions. What-ever may be said in other connections for an "expost" definition of money savings which makes them necessarily identical for any period with the money value of the increments of real capital created ("investment"), it is clearly inappropriate to an analysis which seeks to distinguish between the origin of the various streams

---

[5] Specially mentioned by Mr. Keynes (*Q.J.E.*, Feb. 1937, p. 211) and Mr. Townshend (*E.J.*, March 1937, p. 158).

[6] But to ensure the occurrence of this result in any particular market it is usually, I imagine, necessary that dealings should be conducted through a class of middlemen who are in a position to choke off transactions by quoting *different* prices to potential lenders and potential borrowers.

[7] *Q.J.E.*, Aug. 1938, p. 612.

which people choose to place in a given interval upon the capital market. And for a definition of "hoardings" which makes them necessarily identical with the increase in the total stock of money, thus divorcing the concept entirely from the volitional processes of the public, I can see nothing to be said for any purpose whatever.[8]

§4. Since this saving-"investment" identity has played such a large part in the discussions of the last few years, I must be forgiven for a brief digression on it here.   I wish I could feel that its expositors were *continuously* as conscious as at times they profess themselves to be that it is completely nugatory (to use a favourite word of Mr. Hawtrey's) for purposes of causal analysis as distinct from statistical calculation.   But they are, in my view, inclined to forget[9] that these troublesome English words in -ing sometimes denote a process (requiring translation into Latin by an infinitive or gerund) and sometimes denote the object to which the process has been applied (requiring translation by a neuter past participle passive). And thus, since they are conscious that they have not perpetrated the absurdity (of which no one has ever accused them) of portraying the process of saving as identical with the process of "investing," they are tempted to forget that they *have* so defined their terms that aggregate amount saved is irretrievably identical with aggregate amount "invested."   Hence they are enabled to close their eyes to the absurdity of even enquiring what the forces are which "ensure equality" between the two magnitudes which, in Mr. Harrod's words, "are but one magnitude," causing the one to "elicit" the other or the other to "accommodate itself" to the one.   To proceed thus is, I suggest, as though one were to define an elephant's trunk and its proboscis in identical terms, and then to enter upon a complicated discussion of the biological principles which ensure that the trunk is always equal to the proboscis.   This lack of firmness

---

[8] Mr. Lerner, in a recent geometrical fantasia (*E.J.*, June 1938, pp. 211 ff.) appears to me to have overlooked these considerations. Starting with an apparatus designed to register human choices, he proceeds to graft on to it concepts from which choice is excluded, and expects us to share his naïve glee at the confusion which results.

[9] See especially Keynes, *E.J.*, June 1937, p. 249.

in the handling of their own concepts convinces me that Mr. Keynes and his expositors are not altogether comfortable in the terminological garments which they have elected to wear.[10]

In any case I find myself in agreement with Professor Ohlin[11] that in the analysis of the market for loanable funds it is some kind of intentional or "ex-ante" concept of saving that is required. But there is a difficulty here which I must not attempt to conceal.[12] In Professor Ohlin's analysis, "planned saving" is the difference between "expected income" and planned, which can be taken to be identical with actual current, expenditure on consumption. In my own attempts at analysis, "saving" has been identified with the difference between *previously received* income and current expenditure on consumption. Now I am far from denying that people's current expenditure on consumption is influenced by their expectations as regards future income, or from supposing, as Mr. Hawtrey has imagined me to do,[13] that their capacity for present expenditure

---

[10] The *locus classicus* of this two-mindedness is to be found in Mrs. Robinson's exposition of the principle of the "multiplier" (*Introduction in the Theory of Employment*, p. 22). Having a few pages earlier explained the necessary equality of saving and "investment," she proceeds to expound how an act of "investment," *e.g.* an outlay of money on house-building, generates a progressive increase in money income by giving rise to successive "rounds" of expenditure. "If the whole of the outlay on house-building were added to saving at the first round," she writes, "there would be no second round." But according to her own definitions it has inevitably been so added! Again, "the increase in incomes must necessarily continue up to the point at which there is an addition to saving equal to the additional outlay on house-building." But on her definitions this point is reached instantaneously, whether there is any increase in incomes beyond the original outlay on house-building or whether there is none!

[11] *E.J.*, June 1937, p. 237; Sept. 1937, p. 424.

[12] I should like, but am unable, to persuade myself that it is solved by Mr. Lutz, *Q.J.E.*, Aug. 1938, p. 605.

[13] See *E.J.*, Dec. 1933, p. 702, and a welcome defence by Professor Hansen, *Journal of Political Economy*, Oct. 1936, p. 674. Mr. Hawtrey's own position on this matter is highly individual. He speaks of savings over any short period as being supplemented by additional bank loans (*A Century of Bank Rate*, p. 175) — a conception which to the Keynesian is "purely mythical" (Mrs. Robinson, *E.J.*, June 1938, p. 236). Yet he does not appear to feel the need for a definition of savings of my type, and does not even accept Prof. Ohlin's distinction between

is limited by the amount of their immediately preceding income. But I have a twofold difficulty in assimilating my terminology completely to that of Professor Ohlin.   In the first place, as Mr. Hawtrey has insisted,[14] expected income is necessarily a somewhat nebulous concept, since expectations are seldom precise.   Secondly, let us suppose that people expect what is in fact going to occur, *i.e.* intuit rightly the change in the size of the income stream which will eventuate from the current transactions in the capital market. In this event, identity, in Professor Ohlin's terminology, between ex-ante and ex-post saving could coexist with change, indeed with extreme instability, in the stream of money income.   This seems to me inconvenient; though since in this case the amount of the ex-post saving which will be withheld from the market will also be correctly foreseen, and therefore figure as a negative item among "dishoardings," the validity of the supply and demand analysis set forth in §1 is not affected.

§5. I turn to the rival formulation of the immediate determinants of the rate of interest which has been given by Mr. Keynes. Instead of enquiring into what happens on the markets during an *interval* of time, it focuses attention on the position reached, as a result of previous market transactions, at a *moment* of time; and portrays the rate of interest as the child of a marriage between the amount of money which the monetary authority permits to be in existence at that moment and a schedule exhibiting the amounts of money which, in the light of their knowledge of the existence of various rates of interest, people would wish to hold at that moment.   Before examining the relation of this apparatus to

designed and undesigned savings (*E.J.*, Sept. 1937, p. 439).   The explanation appears to be that in his scheme additional bank loans devoted to capital outlay are only to be regarded as a supplement to savings in so far as they lead to a decumulation of stocks of goods.

My own approach, involving as it does the parcelling of time into significant intervals, entails admitted difficulties which may be incapable of a completely tidy solution: but the same, after all, is true of various other concepts, such as the general price-level or "keeping capital intact," which the workaday economist is rightly not willing on that account to abandon.

[14] *E.J.*, Sept. 1937, *loc. cit.*

that which we have just discussed, I must allude briefly to three respects in which, as it seems to me, its author has at various times erected obstacles in the way of its clear comprehension.

(1) In the first place, he shifts about in his book between using the word "money" to *mean* "money" and using it to mean something which in ordinary monetary theory is sharply contrasted with money, namely the real resources over which command is kept in monetary form (whether such resources are better regarded as measured in "wheat," as by Marshall and Pigou, or in "labour," as by Keynes, is a secondary issue). The inconvenience of this latter usage is that if the price of real resources falls, we have to represent the consequence not, as in ordinary monetary theory, as a decrease in the quantity of money demanded, but as an automatic increase in the quantity of "money" supplied—the "supply of money" is no longer something which only the monetary authority can alter. I do not of course contend that this double meaning of the word "money" is illegitimate, but only that it is liable to cause confusion unless very carefully handled.

(2) Secondly, in one of several alternative formulations of the theory given in his book,[15] Mr. Keynes includes among the reasons for the downward slope of the curve by which the demand (in his sense) for money (in the ordinary sense) can be portrayed, the reason that at lower rates of interest the level of output and prices will be higher, and require therefore the holding of larger stocks of money. This is, to my mind, to confuse the amount of money which people will wish to hold in the face of a given rate of interest now existing with the amount of money which they will wish to hold as an indirect consequence of a given rate of interest prevailing at some previous time, and to ignore the overwhelming evidence to the effect that rising output and prices are usually in fact associated with rising rates of interest. This misleading formulation has, however, now been generally discarded[16] in favour of

---

[15] *General Theory of Employment, Interest and Money* (hereafter referred to as *G.T.*), pp. 171–2.

[16] It has, however, been revived by Mr. Lerner, *E.J.*, June 1938, p. 224, without any recognition of the difficulties involved.

one in which the quantity of money demanded at any given moment is regarded as divided into two parts, the one dependent on the level of output and prices and virtually independent of the rate of interest, the other inversely related to the rate of interest.

(3) In certain more recent writings, to which I shall allude further later, Mr. Keynes has again rendered clear discussion difficult by introducing a number of hybrid concepts, such as "the supply of finance" and the "supply of liquidity," which are neither identical with the "supply of money" in his sense, since others than the banks are conceived of as contributing to them, nor identical with the "supply of loanable funds" in my sense, since he attempts to bring them into touch not with a flow of demand during an interval of time but with a state of demand existing at a moment of time.   As in the case of the definition of savings (*supra*, §4), I cannot but regard these verbal monstrosities as evidence that Mr. Keynes is not altogether comfortable in his own suit of clothes.

Nevertheless, when we have picked our way through these verbal tangles we are left, I think, in no doubt about the relation between the two methods of approach.   Essentially they are two different ways of saying the same thing.   Mr. Keynes' long-maintained determination to treat them as "radically opposed"[17] has been to me from the beginning the most baffling feature of this whole controversy.

As regards the relative merits of the two formulations there is doubtless much to be said.   *Prima facie* the main advantages of the method set out in §2 are two in number.   (i) It accords with the ordinary language of the market-place; I do not believe that the bill-broker or the impecunious schoolboy will ever believe that, whatever be the deeper causes of its behaviour, the rate of interest *is* anything other than what people have always supposed it to be—the price of the use of loanable funds.   (ii) It accords with the general tendency of modern theory to emphasise the unity pervading economic phenomena; the rate of interest appears as a special case of the general theory of pricing.   On the other hand

[17] *E.J.*, June 1937, p. 241.

it is quite possible that I have under-rated the merits of Mr. Keynes' formulation, which is apparently found the more convenient to handle by mathematicians. I remain, however, of the opinion that its use entails certain dangers, which can be classified according as we are (1) still taking the momentary market point of view with which we agreed to start, (2) proceeding to examine the course of events in a "short period" of monetary expansion or contraction, (3) proceeding further to examine the development of economic phenomena over long stretches of time. To a consideration of these dangers I will now pass.

II. THE MOMENTARY VIEW

§1. Already, before we leave the momentary market situation, the Keynsian formula, in its quest for an unattainable simplicity, obscures the part played in the determination of the rate of interest by the "classical" forces of productivity and thrift.

It cannot be too clearly stated that there is nothing whatever wrong with the common-sense view that a raising of the schedule of the marginal productivity (in terms of money) of loanable funds, *i,e.* of the net money yields which entrepreneurs expect from using various quantities of them, will raise the demand schedule for such funds in the market and so tend, *ceteris paribus*, to raise the rate of interest. This is true whether the raising of the productivity schedule is due to reasons of physical productivity or to reasons of price. In spite of its temporary concession to the validity of the "loanable funds" concept, elsewhere so emphatically rejected, I still regard as a monument of confusion the sentence in which Mr. Keynes appears to challenge this common-sense conclusion. "The schedule of the marginal efficiency of capital," he writes, "may be said to govern the terms on which loanable funds are demanded for the purpose of new investment; whilst the rate of interest governs the terms on which funds are being currently supplied" (*G.T.*, p. 165). The schedule of the marginal utility of tea may be said to govern the terms on which tea is demanded: whilst the price of tea governs the terms on which tea is being currently supplied! From the fact that to the *individual* borrower the hiring price of loanable funds is a thing to be taken for granted, Mr. Keynes appears to proceed, in a way in which he would never do if he were speaking of an ordinary commodity, to the inference that that price is independent of the level of the collective demands of the *whole body* of borrowers; those who reject this inference are regarded as guilty of some kind of circular reasoning and as the victims of some kind of elementary confusion between a schedule and a price, between a curve and a point on a curve (*ibid.*, p. 184).

Of course Mr. Keynes never really succeeded in banishing the influence of marginal productivity; it crept in again at the back door under the wing of the "demand for money" for purposes connected with the conduct of business and the disbursement of income. Such apparent success as he achieved was due to a strange inconsistency in the scheme of his book, on which I commented at the time.[18] In that scheme "active money" could generally only grow as a result of a previous growth in income, so that the banks could only operate by increasing "idle money": yet at the same time it was apparently contemplated that, even if "idle money" were zero, there would still be some (unexplained) way for total money to be increased and the rate of interest to fall, the growth of incomes following as a consequence.[19] Common sense suggests that the natural way for this to occur is by the banks performing the primary function of banking, *i.e.* lending money to people who want to make productive use of it. But in those days Mr. Keynes was so taken up with the fact that people sometimes acquire money in order to *hold* it that he had apparently all but entirely forgotten the more familiar fact that they often acquire it in order to *use* it.[20]

---

[18] *Q.J.E.*, Nov. 1936, p. 181 *n.* 7.

[19] Cf. *G.T.*, p. 197, with p. 200 (bottom) and p. 209 (top).

[20] Some memory of this familiar fact seems to inspire the curious statement (*ibid.*, p. 195) that some money "is held to bridge the interval between the time of incurring business costs and that of the receipt of the sale-proceeds; cash held by dealers to bridge the interval between purchase and realisation being included under this heading." These are just the intervals during which the persons in question do *not* hold money, but have parted with it!

In later articles[21] Mr. Keynes has regained his memory of this simple truth.   He has recognised that entrepreneurs often desire to be in possession of money which they will subsequently disburse—directly or indirectly—to the factors of production.   He has even recognised that this money, which he calls by the name "finance," is often, though not of course necessarily, obtained from the banks.[22] And he has conceded that if there is an increase in the demand for "finance" there will, other things being equal, be a rise in the rate of interest.   Thus he has not only remedied the inconsistency pointed out above, but also, as it seems to me, made a far longer stride back than he yet realises towards the orthodox view of the status of the schedule of marginal productivity of loanable funds as a principal determinant of the rate of interest.   For it is evidently the height and shape of that schedule—in other words their profit-expectations—which guide the decisions of entrepreneurs as to how much "finance" they shall demand, these decisions in turn helping, as Mr. Keynes admits, to determine the rate of interest.[23]

§2.   The passages in which Mr. Keynes elaborates the concept of "finance" are, in my view, exceedingly confused; since they illustrate well the trouble in which the "demand for money" approach is liable to land those who employ it, unless checked by explicit reference to what is going on in the capital market, I must digress upon them at some length.   My digression is based on the hypothesis that like the Book of Genesis they are an attempt at conflation of the works of two earlier writers, whom, following precedent, I will call by the initials J and E.

"'Finance,'" Mr. Keynes insists (1937, p. 666) "is essentially a revolving fund": the money absorbed by one entrepreneur in preparation for an act of investment is subsequently released and

---

[21] *E.J.*, June 1937, pp. 246–8, Dec. 1937, pp. 663 ff., June 1938, pp. 318 ff. The page references in §2 below are to these articles.

[22] It was a poor reward for adhering religiously to Mr. Keynes' peculiar use of the word "finance," and to his own simplifying assumption that "'finance' is wholly supplied by the banks," to be accused of muddling up the quite distinct concepts of "finance" and bank loans!   (*E.J.*, June 1938, *loc. cit.*).

[23] On this subject I am indebted to writings by, and discussions with, Dr. E. S. Shaw; see his article in *Journal of Political Economy*, Dec. 1938, p. 838.

becomes available for similar employment by another entrepreneur.
Provided therefore that something remains constant the requirements of "finance" have no tendency to make the rate of interest
rise.   What is that something? and what is the act by which money
which has been absorbed by one entrepreneur to serve as "finance"
is released to another for similar employment?   It is to these questions that the writers J and E give conflicting answers.   According
to J the condition for stability in the rate of interest is constancy
in the rate of investment, *i.e.*, in the rate at which the stock of
capital is increasing.   "In the main the flow of new finance
required by current planned investment is provided by the finance
released by current actual investment.   When the flow of investment is at a steady rate, so that the flow of planned investment is
equal to the flow of actual investment, the whole of it can be provided in this way without any change in the liquidity position"
(*ibid.*, p. 666).[24]   Consistently with this approach, the releasing
process is conceived as the purchase of a new issue by some saver
from entrepreneur A which enables the latter to repay the money
which he has borrowed for "finance," thus permitting this money
to become available as "finance" for entrepreneur B.[25]   "There
will always be *exactly* enough actual saving to take up the actual
investment and so release the finance which the latter had been
previously employing" (*ibid.*, p. 669).   Provided this actual saving-
and-investment in any period does not fall short of the planned
investment in that period, there is no reason for the rate of interest
to rise.[26]

---

[24] In this and the following quotation I have ventured, to avoid confusion,
to substitute the words "planned" and "actual" for the words "ex-ante" and
"ex-post," which Mr. Keynes uses, at any rate as applied to investment, in an
entirely different sense from Professor Ohlin.
[25] I continue to adhere to Mr. Keynes' own simplifying assumption that A has
provided himself with "finance" by borrowing from a bank.   The argument can
easily be re-stated for the case in which he has obtained "finance" by selling
securities to the public.
[26] The J theory re-appears in Mr. Keynes' discussion of the problem of Government borrowing, *Times*, July 24, 1939.   "The clue to the solution of the
Treasury problem lies in the Treasury's ability to wait until the new savings

Intertwined with this analysis we have that of the second writer E. According to E the condition for stability in the rate of interest is constancy, not in the rate of investment, but in the outstanding volume of working capital. Here we have to take account of a subsidiary confusion: for two different accounts have been given by E of the date and nature of the releasing process. According to the earlier account, "as soon as 'finance' is used in the sense of being expended, the lack of liquidity is automatically made good and the readiness to become temporarily illiquid is available to be used over again" (*ibid.*, p. 666). This was indeed a hard doctrine; for it is hard to see how the act of parting with money to the factors of production puts the entrepreneur in a position to part with more money in repayment of a loan. And indeed E has been induced to admit that this account of the matter was a mistake (1938, p. 320), since, when the "finance" is expended, the demand for money for "finance" purposes is immediately replaced by a demand for income purposes. Accordingly, in the revised version of E, it is not in the disbursement of money by the entrepreneur, but in its subsequent recapture by the sale of goods to the consumer, that the releasing process consists.

Now taken by itself either J's account or E's (in the revised version) would be quite intelligible. What is not intelligible is the later editor's conflation of the two. For not having clearly perceived that they *are* two, he attempts the impossible task of formulating a conclusion which shall be appropriate to them both. That conclusion is the astonishing one that to afford relief to congestion in the capital market either an act of thrift or an act of consumption will in all circumstances do equally well; the purchase of a new issue and the purchase of consumption goods are indistinguishable in respect of their influence on the rate of interest. The comforting doctrine that an act of investment necessarily breeds equivalent acts of saving by other persons becomes for the moment transmuted

---

have had time to become available in an investable form. If the Treasury waits just long enough for the market to become greedy for stock the weight of savings seeking investment will force the rate of interest downwards." So the rate of interest *does* depend on the volume (or at all events the weight) of savings after all!

into the even more comforting doctrine that it doesn't matter whether it does or not!

Clearly something has gone wrong: Dr. Shaw and I think we know what it is. The purchase of consumption goods from an entrepreneur enables him *either* to maintain his scale of output and the volume of his working capital *or* to repay a loan, *but not both.* If (being perhaps engaged in a seasonal trade such as farming) he elects to repay a loan, thus enabling the lender to provide another entrepreneur with new "finance," it is not indeed the consumer's act of consumption *per se* that has prevented a rise in the rate of interest, but the first entrepreneur's act of temporary disinvestment; nevertheless, in this case as in the other, the act of consumption may perhaps be said to have played a part in maintaining intact a given aggregate stock of capital without a rise in the rate of interest (the kind of stability envisaged by E). The purchase of a new issue from an entrepreneur, on the other hand, enables him to repay a loan *without* performing an act of disinvestment; it thus contributes to maintaining a given rate of increase in the aggregate stock of capital without a rise in the rate of interest (the kind of stability envisaged by J). The two acts are far from being equivalent; on the contrary, in circumstances in which the one will preserve equilibrium, the other will destroy it.

§3. In discussing Mr. Keynes' concept of "finance" I have already been led into my next theme. His formula seems to be apt to lead those who use it into uncertainty as to the part played in the determination of the rate of interest by thrift,[27] *i.e.* by the decisions being currently made to save a certain part of income.

In the first place it seems to be suggested that the proposition that the marginal convenience of holding money is equated with the rate of interest necessarily excludes and invalidates the propo-

---

[27] I prefer this word to Mrs. Robinson's "*thriftiness*" or Mr. Keynes' "propensity to save," partly because it conveys a suggestion of *action*. Changes in -nesses and propensities do not in themselves exercise any effect on the external world. Nor does a decision to get up early necessarily indicate a reduction in the propensity to lie in bed—it may rather indicate an increased determination not to indulge that propensity! Cf. Miss Curtis, *Q.J.E.*, Aug. 1937, pp. 619-20.

sition that the marginal inconvenience of refraining from consumption is equated with the rate of interest. Such phrases as that interest is not the reward of not-spending but the reward of not-hoarding[28] seem to indicate a curious inhibition against visualising more than two margins at once. A small boy at school is told that if he wins a race he may have either an apple or an orange: he wins the race and chooses the orange. When his mother asks him how he got it, must he reply "I got it for not eating an apple"? May he not say proudly "I got it for not losing a race"?

The inhibition just alluded to was not shared by earlier Cambridge writers. "These three uses," writes Pigou,[29] "the production of convenience and security, the production of commodities, and direct consumption, are rival to one another." "The quantity of resources," writes Lavington,[30] "which he holds in the form of money will be such that the unit of resources which is just and only just worth holding in this form yields him a return of convenience and security equal to the yield of satisfaction derived from the marginal unit spent on consumables, and equal also to[31] the net rate of interest." It should be added that my own statement of the matter[32] "decumulation, as well as keeping-hoarded, is an alternative to keeping-invested" is not entirely appropriate to a world in which capital is growing, *i.e.* in which the "representative man" is in fact saving. To such a man the alternatives which present themselves may better be described as adding to hoards, adding to invested resources and (not decumulating but) failing to accumulate. There are inevitable difficulties in expressing in statically-framed terms the situation existing *at a moment of time during a period of change;* it is precisely for this among other reasons that Mr. Keynes' photographic formulation seems to me to need supplementing by a cinematographic one. But that does not affect the validity of the concept of a three-fold as contrasted with a two-fold

---

[28] See *G.T.*, p. 174.

[29] *Essays in Applied Economics*, p. 181.

[30] *The English Capital Market*, p. 30.

[31] Lavington had better, I think, have written "measured also by."

[32] *E.J.*, 1937, p. 431.

margin of preference. Nor would the latter be destroyed, as Mr. Keynes seems to think,[33] if it should be true that on balance a rise in the rate of interest will diminish, and a fall increase, the proportion of a given income which people desire to save. For on the ordinary assumptions it remains true, of those whose response is of this kind, that they so act as to equate the marginal satisfaction derived from consumption with the marginal satisfaction derived from investing resources at the current rate of interest.

§4. I have not succeeded in discovering in Mr. Keynes' book any formal discussion of the effect of an increase or decrease of thrift on the rate of interest; but I do not think the majority of readers can have failed to form, or can be blamed for forming, the impression that, in Mr. Keynes' view, the notion that an increase of thrift will tend to lower the rate of interest or to promote the growth of physical capital is, *except under the rarely-attained condition of full employment,* wholly erroneous.[34] Here too I venture to think there has been a greater change of front than Mr. Keynes himself has yet been able to realise; for it is now agreed that, *whether employment is full or not,* an increase of thrift *will* tend to lower the rate of interest. But, it is urged, this result will only occur to the accompaniment of depression and increased unemployment.[35]

Let me state in my own language what I believe the Keynsian

---

[33] *G.T.*, p. 182. Contrast the interesting quotation from Marshall unearthed by Mr. Guillebaud (*E.J.*, 1937, p. 42): "my reasoning . . . would be valid even if we amused ourselves by supposing that a rise in the rate of interest diminished the supply of capital: provided that we also supposed that it ultimately diminished the demand for capital faster."

[34] Thus it is, I think, suggested that the question posed on *G.T.*, p. 213, namely, why a "fresh act of saving" should affect the factors on which the rate of interest has been asserted to depend, admits of no answer. On p. 185 discredit is cast on the "economic principle" which "has assumed, in effect, that, *cet. par.,* a decrease in spending will tend to lower the rate of interest." At the end of the book (p. 372) we are reminded that "we have seen that, up to the point where full employment prevails, the growth of capital depends not at all on a low propensity to consume but is, on the contrary, held back by it; and only in conditions of full employment is a low propensity to consume conducive to the growth of capital."

[35] For a meticulous statement by Mr. Keynes of his present position, see *E.J.*, Sept. 1938, p. 555.

is trying to convey.   Suppose that I decide to spend £100 of my income on securities, instead of as hitherto on fine clothes.   My action destroys £100 of the income of my tailor and his employees and depletes their money balances by £100.   It also raises the price of securities, *i.e.* lowers the rate of interest.[36]   This fall in the rate of interest tempts some people to sell securities and to hold increased money balances instead.   Thus the fall in the rate of interest is checked, and not all of my £100 succeeds therefore in finding its way, through the markets for old securities and new issues, on to the markets for labour and commodities.   Thus owing to the existence of this siding or trap, my act of thrift does not succeed, as "classical" theory asserts that it will, in creating incomes and money balances for builders and engineers equal to those which it has destroyed for tailors.   The net result of the whole proceeding is a fall in the rate of interest and an increase, perhaps, in capital outlay,[37] but a net decrease in the total of money incomes and (probably) of employment.

The argument is formally perfectly valid; and the practical inference that, if existing money is going to ground in this way, it is *prima facie* the duty of the banking system to create more money, is quite consistent with the arguments of those who have expressed themselves in terms of "neutral" money, or of a "constant effective circulation," or of the maintenance of equality between the market and the "natural" rates of interest.[38]   To the quantitative importance of the factors at work I will return later.   Here I will only say that it seems to me a most misleading way of expressing the

---

[36] Debate on this matter has sometimes been hampered by the ghost of an old argument, dating from the days of the *Treatise on Money*.   According to this argument the loss-making tailor, in order to avoid restricting either his personal consumption or the scale of his business, will sell securities to the same amount as I buy them.   Obviously, so long as such a situation continues, the rate of interest will not fall nor the formation of capital equipment be stimulated; but neither, so far as the mere maintenance of total income (other than the tailor's) and employment goes, is it necessary that they should.   Evidently, however, this can only be a transitional situation and it is not instructive to stop short at it.

[37] Even this is not certain, since the demand of the tailor, weaver, etc., for machines will decline.

[38] Cf. Cassel, *International Labour Review*, Oct. 1937, p. 443.

causal train of events to say, as is sometimes done, that the act of thrift lowers the rate of interest *through* lowering total incomes.   I should say that it lowers the rate of interest quite directly through swelling the money stream of demand for securities; that this fall in the rate of interest increases the proportion of resources over which people wish to keep command in monetary form; and that this increase in turn is a cause of there being a net decline in total money income, *i.e.* of money incomes not expanding in one sector to the extent that they are contracting in the other.

Let us, however, be grateful for such measure of concordance as has been achieved.   We need no longer attempt to believe in a crazy world in which, at some exceedingly elusive point of "full employment," the opposite of all that we have hitherto been saying suddenly becomes true.   We have returned to a rational world, where the outcome of events is a matter of degrees and elasticities— a world which has been so tidily set out by Dr. Lange[39] that Mr. Keynes, at all events, believes it to have been the world of his own book.[40]   And especially we may compliment Mrs. Robinson, who in her *Introduction to the Theory of Employment* has effected the transition within the compass of a few pages.   For having told us quite categorically on p. 12 that "the desire to save does not promote investment," and explained at some length why she believes this to be so, she has decided by p. 47 that "it is thriftiness which makes investment possible" and even that "in an age of expansion, thriftiness appears as a cause of investment."   Only Mr. Kahn remains, apparently, distressed[41] by Dr. Lundberg's desire to "restore to the will to save a determining influence on the rate of interest."

III. LONGER VIEWS

§1.   Further dangers of the Keynsian formulation are brought to light when we pass from considering the situation at a moment of time to considering the behaviour of the rate of interest during a cumulative process of expansion or contraction.

---

[39] *Economica*, Feb. 1938, pp. 12 ff.
[40] *E.J.*, June 1938, p. 321 *n.*
[41] *Ibid.*, p. 267.

According to ordinary doctrine an increase in the quantity of money and an increase in its velocity of circulation, due to a diminished desire on the part of the public to hold command over resources in monetary form, are broadly similar in their effects. But there is this difference, that while the latter need not, the former must normally, operate through a fall in the (*i.e.* in *some*) rate of interest, since banks do not give money away but lend it at interest. This appears to give rise, as already mentioned,[42] to a paradox, since rising prices and activity are commonly found to be associated with rising rates of interest. Marshall's explanation of the paradox is given in a famous sentence[43]: "the increase of currency increases the willingness of lenders to lend in the first instance, and lowers the rate of discount. But it afterwards raises prices and therefore tends to increase discount. This latter movement is cumulative." This result can, no doubt, be reached by shifting the Keynsian schedule with the progressive growth of the demand for money for "finance" and "transaction" purposes. But one at least of Mr. Keynes' expositors seems to have suffered from lack of resolution in applying this process. Mrs. Robinson has formed the view[44] that while in the course of a monetary expansion the rate of interest may be "driven back towards" the level at which it stood before the expansion started, it can never actually reach that level. Interest will always be lower at the end of a period of inflation than at the beginning! Never surely has theory, or pseudo-theory, flown more brazenly in the face of history.

That at one stage of his thought Mr. Keynes himself suffered from a similar inhibition seems to be suggested by his curious misunderstanding of Professor Fisher's celebrated proposition about the influence of price movements on the rate of interest. That proposition may be stated as follows. Owing to the imperfection of markets, and to inequality of foresight and bargaining power between borrower and lender, there is likely during an upswing to arise a divergence between the marginal productivity of investable funds *to the user* and the rate of interest "in the strict sense" which

---

[42] Above, p. 432.

[43] *Money, Credit and Commerce*, p. 257.

[44] *Introduction to the Theory of Employment*, pp. 76–8.

he is compelled to pay in the market. If however the former is rising, it is unlikely that the frictions will be so great as to prevent altogether the competition of borrowers from raising the rate of interest "in the strict sense." "Not only will lenders require, but borrowers can afford to pay higher interest in terms of money, and to some extent competition will gradually force them to do so. Yet . . . we reluctantly yield to this process of adjustment, thus rendering it very slow and imperfect."[45] "The money rate of interest, while it does change somewhat, does not usually change enough to fully compensate for the appreciation or depreciation."[46] Thus there occurs an increase in trade activity; but "as soon as the interest rate becomes adjusted, borrowers can no longer hope to make great profits, and the demand for loans ceases to expand."[47] In view of these passages, it is impossible to agree with Mr. Keynes that Professor Fisher has made "the mistake" of "supposing that it is the rate of interest on which prospective changes in the value of money will directly react, instead of the marginal efficiency of a given stock of capital."[48] Still less is it easy to understand why Mr. Keynes apparently believes him to have argued that it is the rise in the rate of interest "in the strict sense," and not its failure to rise more rapidly, which exercises a stimulating effect on the entrepreneur.[49]

§2. But there is a further point. As stated in §1, according to ordinary theory it is only an increase in the quantity of money, not a decline in the desire to hold money, that need operate on prices and activity through a preliminary dip in the rate of interest. The entrepreneur who holds an idle balance which he desires to activise need not lend it in the market, but can use it directly for the purchase of commodities or the hire of labour: so far therefore as cumulative processes are generated by swings of entrepreneur confidence rather than of bank policy, there is not even a *prima facie* paradox in the positive association of rising interest with rising

---

[45] Fisher, *Purchasing Power of Money*, p. 57.
[46] Fisher, *Theory of Interest*, p. 493.
[47] *Purchasing Power of Money*, p. 64.
[48] *Ibid.*, bottom of page.
[49] *G.T.*, p. 142.

prices. The Keynsian analysis, with its special emphasis on the relation between money and bonds, at first sight appears to cast doubt on this result. Why should the fact that commodities[50] have become more attractive as compared with money lower the attractiveness of bonds as compared with money and thus raise the rate of interest? Indeed, must not the same forces of increased confidence which make some people desire to part with money for commodities make other people desire to part with money for bonds and so *lower* the rate of interest?

These questions can perhaps be answered, at any rate partially,[51] in terms of "finance" or some such concept; or, which I imagine comes to the same thing, in terms of "complementarity"— one cannot do business without some money, but one can without any bonds. The same answer can be arrived at more simply by looking at the bond market and observing that, at a certain stage of revival, the amount of money which people are willing to take off that market in order to reinvest it in commodities exceeds, at the hitherto current rate of interest, the amount which other people are willing to put on to the same market out of their hoards. Let us use what form of expression we please, so long as the right result, namely, that the rate of interest tends to rise, is established.

But having recognised that a rising rate of interest is normally an accompaniment, and indeed a symbol, of an increase of confidence, we must not then proceed to advocate treating such a rise on lines which would only be appropriate if it were a symbol of collapse of confidence. Yet this is precisely the trap into which, on at least one occasion, the Keynsian method of thought has caused its own author to fall. "If the public is deprived of its normal supply of idle balances by the demand for active balances," he wrote during the boom of 1936–7,[52] "or if it gets nervous about the prospects of the giltedged market, then I feel strongly that, unless we deliberately desire to raise the rate of interest, this demand

---

[50] On this whole topic see Hicks, *Value and Capital*, ch. XXII, and Lerner, *E.J.*, June 1938, pp. 227 ff.

[51] This is not, I believe, the whole answer: see below, p. 27 *n.* 1.

[52] *Economist*, Feb. 6, 1937, p. 302.

for idle balances should be satisfied for the time being, the extra
idle balances being subsequently withdrawn as a change in the
atmosphere or the circumstances permits." In other words, the
monetary authority should create money freely during the boom,
and destroy it drastically during the slump! "It is not easy," wrote
Mr. Keynes in a supplementary letter,[53] "to get used to the idea of
trying to avoid booms and slumps": it is not made any easier by
muddling up two possible causes[54] of a rise in the rate of interest
and advocating an inflammatory policy under the guise of a compensatory one.

§3. I have suggested that even from the momentary market
point of view the Keynsian formulation tends to obscure unduly
the parts played by Productivity and Thrift. Much more is this
true when we pass to consider the trend of events over considerable
stretches of time. I remain of opinion that from the long period
point of view the most important things to be said about the rate
of interest are not things about "liquidity preference" and the
supply of money, but things about what Marshall calls productiveness and prospectiveness.[55]

---

[53] *Ibid.*, Feb. 13, 1937, p. 359.

[54] Contrast Marshall, *Money, Credit and Commerce*, p. 254: "The rate of interest
often rises rather high, under the influence of hope, in an ascending phase of
industrial and commercial activity and prosperity: but it seldom rises very high
for that reason. On the other hand, it may be raised to a vast height by fears that
commercial or political disturbances may soon restrict the operations of credit."

[55] *Principles*, pp. 81–2. If this opinion is one of the "past misdeeds" of which
Mr. Keynes wishes me to disembarrass myself (*E.J.*, June 1938, p. 319), I have
made, I am afraid, but little progress towards the light! In riposte I may perhaps
be forgiven for recalling how in 1930 an attempt (even more muddled, I freely
admit, than appears from the printed record) to interest the Macmillan Committee
in the short run relation between the state of confidence and the long term rate of
interest came to grief against the rocks of his sturdy Johnsonian classicalism! See
Committee on Finance and Industry, Minutes of Evidence, vol. I, pp. 334–5, especially
Q. 4834 and Q. 4841. ". . . (*Witness*). What it comes to is this, that a large
part of what appears to be the rate of interest on long-dated securities is now really
a premium for risk, or believed risk, and the long rate of interest remains high
compared with Bank rate because it contains a large element of what are really
profits, the reward for real or imaginary risks. (*Mr. Keynes*) I should have thought

In this connection the first thing to be said is that in one important respect Mr. Keynes has understated his own case.   While there are hints here and there of a broader treatment, in the main his plan is to set the rate of interest in a direct functional relation only with that part of the money stock which is held for what he calls "speculative reasons," *i.e.* because it is expected that the rate of interest will subsequently rise.   Thus the rate of interest is what it is because it is expected to become other than it is; if it is not expected to become other than it is, there is nothing left to tell us why it is what it is.   The organ which secretes it has been amputated, and yet it somehow still exists—a grin without a cat.   Mr. Plumptre of Toronto, in an unpublished paper, has aptly compared the position of the lenders of money under this theory with that of an insurance company which charges its clients a premium, the only risk against which it insures them being the risk that its premium will be raised.   If we ask what ultimately governs the judgments of wealth-owners as to why the rate of interest should be different in the future from what it is to-day, we are surely led straight back to the fundamental phenomena of Productivity and Thrift.

In this respect the older Cambridge theory is kinder to "liquidity preference" than is Mr. Keynes himself.   For it explicitly links up the rate of interest with what Mr. Keynes, including it somewhat paradoxically under the heading of "active" money, calls the money held for "precautionary" purposes—because people do not know what is going to happen, because they are afraid that debts owing to them may not be paid at the due date, because (as Marshall emphasises) they might otherwise miss a sudden chance of making an advantageous purchase.   Thus neo-Marshallian theory elevates the relation between the desire to hold money and the rate of interest to the dignity of a long-period phenomenon, not dependent on the temporary expectation of change in a particular direction, but only on those chronic uncertainties of personal and business life which, while they may find no place in "equilibrium analysis" of

the reason why the bond rate was high in London was that there were rows and rows of foreigners who were very willing to pay extremely high rates for the money. . . . "

the Continental type, have never, I think, been ruled out from the looser Marshallian concept of the long period.

In estimating, however, the long period degree of this dependence of K, the proportion of resources over which people wish to keep command in monetary form, on the rate of interest, there is an important consideration to be borne in mind. The satisfaction derived at the margin by wealth-owners from holding money is equated not directly with a given rate of return from invested resources, but with the satisfaction derived at the margin from that rate of return; and the satisfaction derived from a given rate of

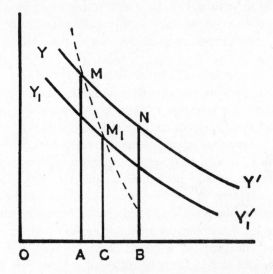

return is not a thing which can plausibly be regarded as remaining eternally fixed while fundamental change is occurring in the whole economic conjuncture. Thus as, with the successful embodiment of thrift in physical capital, the rate of return on invested resources progressively declines, a given nth dose of "convenience and security" derived from holding money may be expected to be balanced up against, and measured by, a progressively lower rate of interest. In geometrical language, the curve connecting the desire to hold resources in monetary form with the rate of interest appears as a highly unstable object, liable to continuous displacement downwards as the volume of invested wealth grows. While a casual fall in the rate of interest from MA to NB may lead to a movement along YY' and an increase in "monetary resources" from OA to OB, a permanent fall will necessitate the re-drawing of YY' as Y_1Y_1' and an increase of "monetary resources" only to OC. And the locus of the points M, M_1, etc., may well exhibit an inclination so steep as to indicate, so far as the influence of this factor goes, virtual constancy in K, whatever the level to which the growth of wealth has attained and the rate of interest fallen. Thus even if we give a more extended interpretation than Mr. Keynes himself has done to the concept of the desire to hold money as a function of the rate of interest, we may well remain reluctant to attach to it any very great importance in determining the secular trend of events.[56]

The most obvious difference between the Keynsian and the neo-Marshallian approaches still remains, however, to be examined. In the former the schedule of liquidity preference is exhibited as one of the determinants of the rate of interest; in the latter the rate of interest is exhibited as one of the determinants of the proportion K, K in turn helping to determine not the rate of interest at all but the general level of prices and money incomes. The instructiveness of this latter approach depends of course on the assumption of the ultimate plasticity of the price and income structure in face of changes in the stream of money demand. It still appears to me that for the purpose of broad comparisons between different societies, or the same society at different stages of its history, this assumption is one that can fruitfully be made. In the making of such comparisons it would be rash indeed to conclude that unemployment of resources is likely to be specially great, or even the rate of interest specially high, in societies where a high estimate

---

[56] It seems to me likely that the solution of the short-period puzzle discussed in III, §2, above, must also be reached partly on these lines. A nominal yield of 4 per cent. on a fixed interest security comes to weigh less heavily in the scales against a given parcel of convenience and security if 8 per cent. can be obtained by direct investment than if only 6 per cent. can be obtained. Even in the short run, YY' may be a tenuous and unstable creature, the ghost rather than the equal partner of the curve of marginal productivity of investable resources.

is placed on the convenience of keeping command over resources in the form of money.[57]   Only if the hunt for liquidity eventuates in the successful devotion of resources to the acquisition of the precious metals will a high "liquidity preference" be inimical to an abundance of income-yielding instruments and therefore to a low rate of interest.   India, for instance, is no doubt less well equipped, and has higher rates of interest, than if she had not dedicated so much of her thrift to the acquisition of gold.[58]   But that conclusion is old-fashioned Ricardo, not new-fashioned Keynes!

IV. Short and Long Rates

§1. I have so far evaded, with an uneasy conscience but with good precedents, one of the most puzzling aspects of the whole problem, namely the relation between the rates of interest on loans of different periods, or (still to simplify unduly) between the short rate and the long.   On this topic I present myself as little more than a *rapporteur* of what has been written by others.   My own understanding of the matter, such as it is, derives rather from the older studies by Lavington, and from a single highly-condensed page of Pigou, than from the more recent discussions by Hawtrey, Hicks, and others; but I have endeavoured to profit from the latter as well.[59]

---

[57] Still less does there seem any reason why a high prestige-value for *land* (*G.T.*, p. 241) should make the rate of interest rule high.   What it does is to keep the purchase price of land high, *i.e.*, the net yield from buying it low, and to make the mortgage rate of interest seem high by comparison; but the mortgage rate (*e.g.* in India) is presumably *lower* than it would be if the land pledged had less prestige-value.   Indirectly, of course, the opportunity to sell land at high prices or to borrow on it at relatively low rates may well encourage extravagant consumption and thus raise interest rates and retard the growth of wealth; but Mr. Keynes cannot be thinking of that, for it is an explanation which he specifically rejects (*ibid.*, p. 242).

[58] Thus from a long period point of view Mr. Keynes' conclusion (*G.T.*, p. 230) that inelasticity in the supply of the money metal helps to keep the rate of interest high seems to be the reverse of the truth.   If the supply of moons is manifestly incapable of increase (*ibid.*, p. 235), no resources can be wasted in their production.

[59] See the following: Lavington, *English Capital Market*, pp. 91–7, and article

If all long lending were really long, *i.e.* if the lender had to part with his money for the full currency of the loan, one would expect the long rate to be, in equilibrium, somewhat above the short; for it is both more convenient to borrow, and less convenient to lend, for long periods than for short. Through the agency of the organised market, however, the long lender can transfer his function to others by the sale of a security, while the long borrower can, to some extent, utilise successive short lengths of lending pieced together for his benefit. Nevertheless, the costs and imperfections of the market are such that we should, in my view, still expect the long rate to stand normally somewhat above the short, even when we have eliminated from the former all risks of total or partial default by finding (if we can) something which really is absolutely gilt-edged.

Lavington, however, concludes that "for many decades up to the end of the war the yield on consols and the three-months bill rate, when averaged over a period of a few years, were substantially identical." He attributes the persistent gap which developed after the war, and which has become more pronounced since he wrote, to a permanent loss of confidence by bankers, etc., in the eligibility of long-term debt, coupled with the emergence of a permanent new supply of eligible short-term investments, namely Treasury Bills.

§2. Given the normal relation between Rate and Yield (as following Lavington we can conveniently call the short and long rates) there is at any moment a further possible reason for divergence between them. The rate is both more spontaneously volatile and more amenable to monetary action than the yield. For any given movement in it there will be an appropriate movement in the yield, depending on how soon and how far the rate is expected to move back again. Thus if the rate falls the yield must theoretically fall enough to establish an appropriate relation between the reward of the man who invests short and that of the man who

in *Economica*, 1923–4, pp. 299 ff.; Pigou, *Industrial Fluctuations*, p. 276; Hawtrey, *A Century of Bank Rate*, chs. V and VI; Hicks, article in *The Manchester School*, 1939; Makower and Marschak, article in *Economica*, 1938, pp. 263 ff.; Kalecki, *Essays in the Theory of Economic Fluctuations*, pp. 107–15.

invests long, facing the depreciation of his bond which will occur when the rate rises again to its normal level. Making some simplifying assumptions, namely simple interest and identity of normal rate and yield, the formula[60] may be given thus:—

Let p = normal rate = normal yield (expressed as a fraction),
$\quad q$ = actual rate,
$\quad n$ = number of years for which the rate is expected to be q before returning to p,
$\quad x$ = actual yield, so that the price of a bond bearing interest p becomes $\frac{p}{x}$ instead of 1.

The net return to be gained by holding such a bond for n years is np interest plus $\left(\frac{1-p}{x}\right)$ capital appreciation. This must equal the return from investing $\frac{p}{x}$ short for n successive years:

i.e.
$$np + 1 - \frac{p}{x} = nq \cdot \frac{p}{x},$$

whence
$$x = p\,\frac{nq+1}{np+1}.$$

Of course this theoretical relation, implying as it does complete mobility of lenders and/or borrowers between the two markets, is not always achieved. But there is a curious lack of unanimity between students as to the direction in which it tends to be departed from during cyclical movements. At the one extreme stands Hicks, who pronounces the yield to be "quite extraordinarily insensitive to the cycle": in this he is joined by Kalecki—in certain circles the doctrine that the yield is infinitely malleable seems to be being rapidly superseded by the doctrine that it never moves at all! Hicks does, however, find a close relation between the movements of the yield and those of the "normal" rate, as represented by the average of the rates of the preceding ten years; this relation fails for recent years, owing (according to Hicks) to the dimming of the

---

[60] Of which Pigou's arithmetic (*loc. cit.*) is an illustration.

conception of a normal during these disturbed times, but is partially restored by reweighting the average of rates so as to give greater importance to the current and quite recent years.

As regards the cyclical relationship, Hawtrey occupies an intermediate position. He finds, in contrast to Hicks, that "there is quite clearly a cyclical movement" in the yield as well as in the rate, but that often when the rate moves the yield does not, or not perceptibly. Lavington, at the other extreme, claims to have established that, at any rate in times of boom, the movements of the yield are *greater* than the theoretical relation would lead us to expect, *i.e.* in boom the price of bonds falls unduly low. This he attributes to the fears of further capital depreciation generated at such a time. Certainly his figures seem to afford little support to those who argue that the yield is virtually immune from cyclical influences.

At any rate, whether over-realised or under-realised in practice, this theoretical relationship between rate and yield serves to show how the yield can stand now below what it is expected to be in future—a fact which is sometimes denied; and to show also that it is to the *difference between*[61] the rate and the yield, and not to the yield as such, that the Keynsian notion is relevant of even the gilt-edged yield being a compensation for a particular sort of "risk," *viz.* not the risk of the yield on the sum invested now varying in future years, but the risk of a bigger yield being obtainable on a given sum invested at a future date than is obtainable by investing it now.

§3. Bearing in mind this analysis of the repercussions of movements in the rate on movements in the yield, let us turn back to the gap, if such there be, between their normal levels. Must we say that this too is due to risk of a peculiar kind, *viz.* the risk of "undis-entanglability"—of having to dispose of an asset on a market which is imperfect? In this event, only the shortest of short rates can be regarded as "the cost of waiting," every other rate containing a larger or smaller element which must be regarded as the cost of some kind or other of risk-bearing. Lavington in the end appears

---

[61] Cf. p. 24, *n.* 4.

to adopt this standpoint; but I do not find it altogether acceptable. It seems to me more reasonable to regard the gilt-edged yield as being *the* rate of interest *par excellence*, the satisfaction of obtaining which is balanced at the margin against the satisfaction enjoyed from consumption; and to regard shorter-dated claims of various kinds as yielding various amounts of a *positive* benefit which can, if we like, be called liquidity, but is perhaps more illuminatingly described as freedom of manœuvre. Lavington's method seems to permit this positive benefit to emerge only in the extreme case, namely that of some kinds of money, in which no interest is paid at all. The alternative method, namely of starting from the gilt-edged rate, brings out that there is a whole range of claims yielding *some* interest and *some* freedom of manœuvre. And this range may well include some kinds of "money"; *i.e.* there is no need (as under both Lavington's method and Keynes') to make the non-yielding of interest the criterion of whether an asset (*e.g.* a current account) is or is not money: the latter term can be defined in the usual way as including anything that is widely or generally acceptable in discharge of business obligations, whether or not it is clever enough to yield its possessor some interest as well.

§4. Two of the writers—namely Lavington and Hawtrey—who have expounded the theoretical impact of changes in the rate on the yield have nevertheless emphasised—as I think rightly—that in the main their movements must be interpreted as the results of a common cause, namely changes in the demand for the use of loanable funds, both for short term purposes and for long. Marshall—again, as I think, rightly—goes further and assigns, from a trend or long term point of view, seniority in the chain of causation to the yield. "It is obvious that the mean rate of discount must be much under the influence of the mean rate of interest for long loans; which is determined by the extent and the richness of the field for capital investment on the one hand, and on the other by the amount of capital seeking investment."[62] Hicks' correlation analysis, which makes the present yield reflect the average rate

---

[62] *Money, Credit and Commerce*, p. 255.

of the last ten years, would, if it is regarded as convincing, cast discredit on Marshall's causal thesis, which is also apparently rejected by Hawtrey.[63]   I must confess that I should myself require very strong inductive evidence to make me abandon what seems to me so plausible an account of the normal relationship, and that I find Hicks' treatment[64] very defective on the side of demand.

V. Conclusion

§1. What is the bearing of the "liquidity preference" view of interest on the problem of the preservation of monetary equilibrium in a progressive world?   What I have to say on this must be much condensed, and itself forms part of a larger story, the earlier chapters of which must be taken as told.   I take for granted that the social function of banking is to procure the effective utilisation of the community's thrift, and that the effective fulfilment of that function requires the execution of a certain policy with regard to the magnitude of the flow of total monetary demand.   Should that policy be to cause that flow to increase in proportion to the increase in production? or in proportion to the increase in population? or in proportion, in some sense, to the increase in the aggregate stock of all factors of production?   On these problems there is much to be said, and I doubt if they are capable of a perfectly clear-cut answer.   But granted we have solved them in theory in some compromise fashion, we can go on to ask the further question, how far is the existence of the liquidity trap for thrift likely to hamper the banking system in its long run task of executing the chosen policy, and so bringing the fruits of thrift to birth?

The question falls conveniently into three parts:—(1) Under what conditions does the effective utilisation of thrift require a progressive fall in the rate of interest?   (2) If such a fall is required, how serious is the influence of the liquidity trap in inhibiting it? (3) How responsive is capital outlay likely to be to such a fall?

(1) Whether a fall in the rate of interest is required depends

---

[63] *Op. cit.*, p. 207.
[64] *Op. cit.*, p. 23.

on whether the rate of invention,[65] including the "invention" of new or resuscitated countries, keeps up with the growth of thrift, accentuated by the coming stagnation and decline of population in the west. On this last subject there is nowadays much anxiety, which I partly share. The excogitation of means to meet new wants requires more initiative than the reduplication of means to meet existing ones; and some of the new wants, *e.g.* for the services of manicurists and mediums, may not be of a very capital-using kind. During the nineteenth century the fundamental deformity of the Marshallian "short period"—the fact that it is not the same length at both ends, since most instruments take longer to wear out than to construct—was largely concealed from view by the growth of population, which increased the chances that the tail of each slump would be bitten off prematurely, as it were, by the head of the next boom. From many points of view the most satisfactory kind of population would doubtless be one which, while never getting any bigger, was always growing; but it is not very easy to see how that is to be achieved.

Nevertheless it is possible, I think, to be too gloomy. At no point has it been possible to divine just *where* the springs of "demand for waiting" would gush forth in the coming years. Marshall, giving evidence in the eighties,[66] set forth, in a striking passage which might almost be mistaken for one of Mr. Keynes' presidential addresses to the National Mutual Assurance Society, the most persuasive reasons why the rate of interest should drop rapidly in the future to 2 per cent.: yet within a few years the tide had turned.

(2) The upshot of our earlier discussion of this point may be conveyed by saying that so far as the desire for liquidity is due to the "speculative" motive, *i.e.* the belief that the rate of interest will rise, it does not seem reasonable to expect it to be proof against a prolonged fall due to a successful accumulation of capital wealth; while so far as it is due to uncertainty in a broader sense, there are

---

[65] See the illuminating discussion by Durbin, *Purchasing Power and Trade Depression,* esp. p. 76 and note.

[66] *Official Papers,* p. 49, Q. 9678.

reasons for supposing the curve representing it to be much more inelastic in the long run than the short. To an enormous extent the contemporary troubles of the world are due to the prolonged prevalence of a state of affairs that is neither peace nor war; real peace would do more than anything—more even than real war— not only to raise the curve of marginal productivity of investable funds, but to rotate and stiffen the roof of the liquidity trap into a straight line as vertical and rigid as Mr. Chamberlain's umbrella.

§2. (3) How responsive will capital outlay be to such fall in the rate of interest as the liquidity trap permits to occur? Can we expect the response to be at all buoyant in a community in which, owing to the rapid growth of wealth, the producers of consumption goods are continually finding their livelihood threatened by the growth of thrift? On this there are three things to be briefly said.

(i) It is as well to remind ourselves, if necessary by an arithmetic example,* that a decline in the *proportion of income consumed* does not necessarily mean a decline in *the rate of growth of consumption*, still less of course in the absolute amount of consumption. It is not mathematically inevitable that, in a progressive society, the producers of consumption goods as a body should live in perpetual fear of extinction.

(ii) Even if particular groups of producers find the demand for their wares sluggish, so that they have no motive to undertake what Mr. Hawtrey has called the "widening" of capital, their best course may yet be to promote its "deepening"—*i.e.* mechanisation may be the best response to a sagging market. From the point of view of labour this is of course a double-edged conclusion.

*Total Income	Consumed	Percentage Growth of Consumption	Percentage of Income Consumed	"Marginal Propensity to Consume"
10,000	8,000	..	80	..
11,000	8,400	5	76	40
12,100	8,820	5	73	38
13,310	9,261	5	70	36

I am in debt to Professor Hansen (*Monetary Policy and Economic Stagnation*, p. 39) on this point.

(iii) As I have said in the course of commentary on Mr. Harrod's exposition of the "principle of acceleration,"[67] some of the quantitatively most important forms of capital outlay in the modern world—the basic instruments of power, transport and business accommodation—are not very closely geared to the demand for particular types of consumption goods, but depend rather on largely and broadly conceived estimates of the potential progress of whole regions. And fortunately it is precisely these forms of capital outlay which, because of their durability, *are* reasonably sensitive to the rate of interest; for while the difference between 5 per cent. and 4 per cent. may make little difference to a manufacturer contemplating the installation of rapidly obsolescent machinery, whose rate of depreciation is large relatively to either rate of interest,[68] nobody really doubts that it does make some difference to a railway company contemplating electrification or an estate company contemplating the development of a seaside resort. It is certainly not impossible to conceive a community devoting a growing proportion of a growing income to such things without reducing the producers of consumption goods to bankruptcy—and that even though our chosen monetary policy should be one which permits the prices of finished goods to fall with the progress of technical efficiency. Indeed it is evident that broadly speaking this is what happened in that remote century which followed Waterloo—a period which even Mr. Keynes seems sometimes ready to treat as an exception to the general law of entropy[69] which he regards as governing human economic affairs.

§ 3. One goes up and down in one's outlook on this matter, as on so many other things. In 1932, between the births of Mr. Keynes' two big books, I find I was taking him to task for expressing in his *Treatise* a view, as I thought, too cyclical and not sufficiently secular of the problem of industrial malaise.[70] I suppose

---

[67] See below, p. 179; and, for a revised statement of Mr. Harrod's position, *E.J.*, March 1939, pp. 14 ff.

[68] For some interesting arithmetic, see article by Bauer and Marrack in *E.J.*, June 1939, p. 237.

[69] See *G.T.*, p. 242.

[70] See the essay on *The Future of Trade Cycle Theory* in this volume, pp. 98 ff.

I am a little hard to please, for I now find myself in reaction against the pessimism as to the future of enterprise which has been spread, especially apparently in certain circles in the United States,[71] by his later book. To me, as I have said, it now seems that our present difficulties are very largely political; and that so far as they are not political, they are largely *institutional* rather than fundamental, and connected above all with the fact that our banking systems grew up in a world in which there seemed to be a natural harmony, which has proved to be illusory, between the desire of the public to keep money easily accessible in a bank and the desire of commerce and industry to borrow for *working* capital purposes. But that is a story for another occasion.

[71] See especially the able *Economic Programme for American Democracy* by a group of Harvard and Tufts economists.

24

MR. KEYNES AND THE "CLASSICS"; A SUGGESTED INTERPRETATION *[1]

By John R. Hicks†

I

It will be admitted by the least charitable reader that the entertainment value of Mr. Keynes' *General Theory of Employment* is considerably enhanced by its satiric aspect. But it is also clear that many readers have been left very bewildered by this Dunciad. Even if they are convinced by Mr. Keynes' arguments and humbly acknowledge themselves to have been "classical economists" in the past, they find it hard to remember that they believed in their unregenerate days the things Mr. Keynes says they believed. And there are no doubt others who find their historic doubts a stumbling block, which prevents them from getting as much illumination from the positive theory as they might otherwise have got.

One of the main reasons for this situation is undoubtedly to be found in the fact that Mr. Keynes takes as typical of "Classical economics" the later writings of Professor Pigou, particularly *The Theory of Unemployment*. Now *The Theory of Unemployment* is a fairly new book, and an exceedingly difficult book; so that it is safe to say that it has not yet made much impression on the ordinary teaching of economics. To most people its doctrines seem quite as strange and novel as the doctrines of Mr. Keynes himself; so

* *Econometrica*, Volume V, 1937, pages 147–159. Reprinted by courtesy of the publisher and author.

† Nuffield College, Oxford University. Formerly, Gonville and Caius College, Cambridge.

[1] Based on a paper which was read at the Oxford meeting of the Econometric Society (September, 1936) and which called forth an interesting discussion. It has been modified subsequently, partly in the light of that discussion, and partly as a result of further discussion in Cambridge.

that to be told that he has believed these things himself leaves the ordinary economist quite bewildered.

For example, Professor Pigou's theory runs, to a quite amazing extent, in real terms. Not only is his theory a theory of real wages and unemployment; but numbers of problems which anyone else would have preferred to investigate in money terms are investigated by Professor Pigou in terms of "wage-goods." The ordinary classical economist has no part in this *tour de force*.

But if, on behalf of the ordinary classical economist, we declare that he would have preferred to investigate many of those problems in money terms, Mr. Keynes will reply that there is no classical theory of money wages and employment. It is quite true that such a theory cannot easily be found in the textbooks. But this is only because most of the textbooks were written at a time when general changes in money wages in a closed system did not present an important problem. There can be little doubt that most economists have thought that they had a pretty fair idea of what the relation between money wages and employment actually was.

In these circumstances, it seems worth while to try to construct a typical "classical" theory, built on an earlier and cruder model than Professor Pigou's. If we can construct such a theory, and show that it does give results which have in fact been commonly taken for granted, but which do not agree with Mr. Keynes' conclusions, then we shall at last have a satisfactory basis of comparison. We may hope to be able to isolate Mr. Keynes' innovations, and so to discover what are the real issues in dispute.

Since our purpose is comparison, I shall try to set out my typical classical theory in a form similar to that in which Mr. Keynes sets out his own theory; and I shall leave out of account all secondary complications which do not bear closely upon this special question in hand. Thus I assume that I am dealing with a short period in which the quantity of physical equipment of all kinds available can be taken as fixed. I assume homogeneous labour. I assume further that depreciation can be neglected, so that the output of investment goods corresponds to new investment. This is a dangerous simplification, but the important issues raised by Mr. Keynes in his chapter on user cost are irrelevant for our purposes.

Let us begin by assuming that w, the rate of money wages per head, can be taken as given.

Let x, y, be the outputs of investment goods and consumption goods respectively, and N_x, N_y, be the numbers of men employed in producing them. Since the amount of physical equipment specialised to each industry is given, $x = f_x(N_x)$ and $y = f_y(N_y)$, where f_x, f_y, are *given* functions.

Let M be the *given* quantity of money.

It is desired to determine N_x and N_y.

First, the price-level of investment goods = their marginal cost = $w(dN_x/dx)$. And the price-level of consumption goods = their marginal cost = $w(dN_y/dy)$.

Income earned in investment trades (value of investment, or simply Investment) = $wx(dN_x/dx)$. Call this I_x.

Income earned in consumption trades = $wy(dN_y/dy)$.

Total Income = $wx(dN_x/dx) + wy(dN_y/dy)$. Call this I.

I_x is therefore a given function of N_x, I of N_x and N_y. Once I and I_x are determined, N_x and N_y can be determined.

Now let us assume the "Cambridge Quantity equation"—that there is some definite relation between Income and the demand for money. Then, approximately, and apart from the fact that the demand for money may depend not only upon total Income, but also upon its distribution between people with relatively large and relatively small demands for balances, we can write

$$M = kI.$$

As soon as k is given, total Income is therefore determined.

In order to determine I_x, we need two equations. One tells us that the amount of investment (looked at as demand for capital) depends upon the rate of interest:

$$I_x = C(i).$$

This is what becomes the marginal-efficiency-of-capital schedule in Mr. Keynes' work.

Further, Investment = Saving. And saving depends upon the rate of interest and, if you like, Income. $\therefore I_x = S(i, I)$. (Since, however, Income is already determined, we do not need to bother about inserting Income here unless we choose.)

Taking them as a system, however, we have three fundamental equations,

$$M = kI, \qquad I_x = C(i), \qquad I_x = S(i, I),$$

to determine three unknowns, I, I_x, i. As we have found earlier, N_x and N_y can be determined from I and I_x. Total employment, $N_x + N_y$, is therefore determined.

Let us consider some properties of this system. It follows directly from the first equation that as soon as k and M are given, I is completely determined; that is to say, total income depends directly upon the quantity of money. Total employment, however, is not necessarily determined at once from income, since it will usually depend to some extent upon the proportion of income saved, and thus upon the way production is divided between investment and consumption-goods trades. (If it so happened that the elasticities of supply were the same in each of these trades, then a shifting of demand between them would produce compensating movements in N_x and N_y, and consequently no change in total employment.)

An increase in the inducement to invest (i.e., a rightward movement of the schedule of the marginal efficiency of capital, which we have written as $C(i)$) will tend to raise the rate of interest, and so to affect saving. If the amount of saving rises, the amount of investment will rise too; labour will be employed more in the investment trades, less in the consumption trades; this will increase total employment if the elasticity of supply in the investment trades is greater than that in the consumption-goods trades—diminish it if *vice versa*.

An increase in the supply of money will necessarily raise total income, for people will increase their spending and lending until incomes have risen sufficiently to restore k to its former level. The rise in income will tend to increase employment, both in making consumption goods and in making investment goods. The total effect on employment depends upon the ratio between the expansions of these industries; and that depends upon the proportion of their increased incomes which people desire to save, which also governs the rate of interest.

So far we have assumed the rate of money wages to be given; but so long as we assume that k is independent of the level of wages, there is no difficulty about this problem either. A rise in the rate of money wages will necessarily diminish employment and raise real wages. For an unchanged money income cannot continue to buy an unchanged quantity of goods at a higher price-level; and, unless the price-level rises, the prices of goods will not cover their marginal costs. There must therefore be a fall in employment; as employment falls, marginal costs in terms of labour will diminish and therefore real wages rise. (Since a change in money wages is always accompanied by a change in real wages in the same direction, if not in the same proportion, no harm will be done, and some advantage will perhaps be secured, if one prefers to work in terms of real wages. Naturally most "classical economists" have taken this line.)

I think it will be agreed that we have here a quite reasonably consistent theory, and a theory which is also consistent with the pronouncements of a recognizable group of economists. Admittedly it follows from this theory that you may be able to increase employment by direct inflation; but whether or not you decide to favour that policy still depends upon your judgment about the probable reaction on wages, and also—in a national area—upon your views about the international standard.

Historically, this theory descends from Ricardo, though it is not actually Ricardian; it is probably more or less the theory that was held by Marshall. But with Marshall it was already beginning to be qualified in important ways; his successors have qualified it still further. What Mr. Keynes has done is to lay enormous emphasis on the qualifications, so that they almost blot out the original theory. Let us follow out this process of development.

II

When a theory like the "classical" theory we have just described is applied to the analysis of industrial fluctuations, it gets into difficulties in several ways. It is evident that total money income experiences great variations in the course of a trade cycle, and the classical theory can only explain these by variations in M or in k, or, as a third and last alternative, by changes in distribution.

(1) Variation in M is simplest and most obvious, and has been relied on to a large extent. But the variations in M that are traceable during a trade cycle are variations that take place through the banks—they are variations in bank loans; if we are to rely on them it is urgently necessary for us to explain the connection between the supply of bank money and the rate of interest. This can be done roughly by thinking of banks as persons who are strongly inclined to pass on money by lending rather than spending it. Their action therefore tends at first to lower interest rates, and only afterwards, when the money passes into the hands of spenders, to raise prices and incomes. "The new currency, or the increase of currency, goes, not to private persons, but to the banking centers; and therefore, it increases the willingness of lenders to lend in the first instance, and lowers the rate of discount. But it afterwards raises prices; and therefore it tends to increase discount."[2] This is superficially satisfactory; but if we endeavoured to give a more precise account of this process we should soon get into difficulties. What determines the amount of money needed to produce a given fall in the rate of interest? What determines the length of time for which the low rate will last? These are not easy questions to answer.

(2) In so far as we rely upon changes in k, we can also do well enough up to a point. Changes in k can be related to changes in confidence, and it is realistic to hold that the rising prices of a boom occur because optimism encourages a reduction in balances; the falling prices of a slump because pessimism and uncertainty dictate an increase. But as soon as we take this step it becomes natural to ask whether k has not abdicated its status as an independent vari-

---

[2] Marshall, *Money, Credit, and Commerce*, p. 257.

able, and has not become liable to be influenced by others among the variables in our fundamental equations.

(3) This last consideration is powerfully supported by another, of more purely theoretical character. On grounds of pure value theory, it is evident that the direct sacrifice made by a person who holds a stock of money is a sacrifice of interest; and it is hard to believe that the marginal principle does not operate at all in this field. As Lavington put it: "The quantity of resources which (an individual) holds in the form of money will· be such that the unit of money which is just and only just worth while holding in this form yields him a return of convenience and security equal to the yield of satisfaction derived from the marginal unit spent on consumables, and equal also to the net rate of interest."[3] The demand for money depends upon the rate of interest! The stage is set for Mr. Keynes.

As against the three equations of the classical theory,

$$M = kI, \qquad I_x = C(i), \qquad I_x = S(i, I),$$

Mr. Keynes begins with three equations,

$$M = L(i), \qquad I_x = C(i), \qquad I_x = S(I).$$

These differ from the classical equations in two ways. On the one hand, the demand for money is conceived as depending upon the rate of interest (Liquidity Preference). On the other hand, any possible influence of the rate of interest on the amount saved out of a given income is neglected. Although it means that the third equation becomes the multiplier equation, which performs such queer tricks, nevertheless this second amendment is a mere simplification, and ultimately insignificant.[4] It is the liquidity preference doctrine which is vital.

---

[3] Lavington, *English Capital Market*, 1921, p. 30. See also Pigou, "The Exchange-value of Legal-tender Money," in *Essays in Applied Economics*, 1922, pp. 179–181.

[4] This can be readily seen if we consider the equations

$$M = kI, \qquad I_x = C(i), \qquad I_x = S(I),$$

which embody Mr. Keynes' second amendment without his first. The third

For it is now the rate of interest, not income, which is determined by the quantity of money.   The rate of interest set against
the schedule of the marginal efficiency of capital determines the
value of investment; that determines income by the multiplier.
Then the volume of employment (at given wage-rates) is determined by the value of investment and of income which is not saved
but spent upon consumption goods.

It is this system of equations which yields the startling conclusion, that an increase in the inducement to invest, or in the propensity to consume, will not tend to raise the rate of interest, but
only to increase employment.   In spite of this, however, and in
spite of the fact that quite a large part of the argument runs in
terms of this system, and this system alone, *it is not the General Theory.*
We may call it, if we like, Mr. Keynes' *special theory.*   The General
Theory is something appreciably more orthodox.

Like Lavington and Professor Pigou, Mr. Keynes does not in
the end believe that the demand for money can be determined by
one variable alone—not even the rate of interest.   He lays more
stress on it than they did, but neither for him nor for them can it
be the only variable to be considered.   The dependence of the
demand for money on interest does not, in the end, do more than
qualify the old dependence on income.   However much stress we
lay upon the "speculative motive," the "transactions" motive must
always come in as well.

Consequently we have for the General Theory

$$M = L(I, i), \qquad I_x = C(i), \qquad I_x = S(I).$$

With this revision, Mr. Keynes takes a big step back to Marshallian
orthodoxy, and his theory becomes hard to distinguish from the
revised and qualified Marshallian theories, which, as we have seen,

---

equation is already the multiplier equation, but the multiplier is shorn of his
wings.   For since I still depends only on M, I_x now depends only on M, and it
is impossible to increase investment without increasing the willingness to save
or the quantity of money.   The system thus generated is therefore identical with
that which, a few years ago, used to be called the "Treasury View."   But Liquidity Preference transports us from the "Treasury View" to the "General Theory
of Employment."

are not new. Is there really any difference between them, or is the whole thing a sham fight? Let us have recourse to a diagram (Figure 1).

Against a given quantity of money, the first equation, $M = L(I, i)$, gives us a relation between Income (I) and the rate of interest (i). This can be drawn out as a curve (LL) which will slope upwards, since an increase in income tends to raise the demand for money, and an increase in the rate of interest tends to lower it. Further, the second two equations taken together give

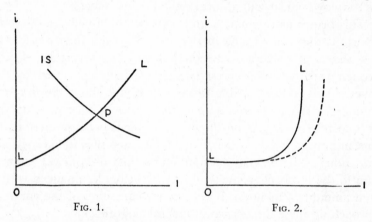

Fig. 1.   Fig. 2.

us another relation between Income and interest. (The marginal-efficiency-of-capital schedule determines the value of investment at any given rate of interest, and the multiplier tells us what level of income will be necessary to make savings equal to that value of investment.) The curve IS can therefore be drawn showing the relation between Income and interest which must be maintained in order to make saving equal to investment.

Income and the rate of interest are now determined together at P, the point of intersection of the curves LL and IS. They are determined together; just as price and output are determined together in the modern theory of demand and supply. Indeed, Mr. Keynes' innovation is closely parallel, in this respect, to the innovation of the marginalists. The quantity theory tries to determine income without interest, just as the labour theory of value tried to determine price without output; each has to give place to a theory recognising a higher degree of interdependence.

III

But if this is the real "General Theory," how does Mr. Keynes come to make his remarks about an increase in the inducement to invest not raising the rate of interest? It would appear from our diagram that a rise in the marginal-efficiency-of-capital schedule must raise the curve *IS*; and, therefore, although it will raise Income and employment, it will also raise the rate of interest.

This brings us to what, from many points of view, is the most important thing in Mr. Keynes' book. It is not only possible to show that a given supply of money determines a certain relation between Income and interest (which we have expressed by the curve *LL*); it is also possible to say something about the shape of the curve. It will probably tend to be nearly horizontal on the left, and nearly vertical on the right. This is because there is (1) some minimum below which the rate of interest is unlikely to go, and (though Mr. Keynes does not stress this) there is (2) a maximum to the level of income which can possibly be financed with a given amount of money. If we like we can think of the curve as approaching these limits asymptotically (Figure 2).

Therefore, if the curve *IS* lies well to the right (either because of a strong inducement to invest or a strong propensity to consume), *P* will lie upon that part of the curve which is decidedly upward sloping, and the classical theory will be a good approximation, needing no more than the qualification which it has in fact received at the hands of the later Marshallians. An increase in the inducement to invest will raise the rate of interest, as in the classical theory, but it will also have some subsidiary effect in raising income, and therefore employment as well. (Mr. Keynes in 1936 is not the first Cambridge economist to have a temperate faith in Public Works.) But if the point *P* lies to the left of the *LL* curve, then the *special* form of Mr. Keynes' theory becomes valid. A rise in the schedule of the marginal efficiency of capital only increases employment, and does not raise the rate of interest at all. We are completely out of touch with the classical world.

The demonstration of this minimum is thus of central importance. It is so important that I shall venture to paraphrase the proof, setting it out in a rather different way from that adopted by Mr. Keynes.[5]

If the costs of holding money can be neglected, it will always be profitable to hold money rather than lend it out, if the rate of interest is not greater than zero. Consequently the rate of interest must always be positive. In an extreme case, the shortest short-term rate may perhaps be nearly zero. But if so, the long-term rate must lie above it, for the long rate has to allow for the risk that the short rate may rise during the currency of the loan, and it should be observed that the short rate can only rise, it cannot fall.[6] This does not only mean that the long rate must be a sort of average of the probable short rates over its duration, and that this average must lie above the current short rate. There is also the more important risk to be considered, that the lender on long term may desire to have cash before the agreed date of repayment, and then, if the short rate has risen meanwhile, he may be involved in a substantial capital loss. It is this last risk which provides Mr. Keynes' "speculative motive" and which ensures that the rate for loans of indefinite duration (which he always has in mind as *the* rate of interest) cannot fall very near zero.[7]

---

[5] Keynes, *General Theory*, pp. 201–202.

[6] It is just conceivable that people might become so used to the idea of very low short rates that they would not be much impressed by this risk; but it is very unlikely. For the short rate may rise, either because trade improves, and income expands; or because trade gets worse, and the desire for liquidity increases. I doubt whether a monetary system so elastic as to rule out both of these possibilities is really thinkable.

[7] Nevertheless something more than the "speculative motive" is needed to account for the system of interest rates. The shortest of all short rates must equal the relative valuation, at the margin, of money and such a bill; and the bill stands at a discount mainly because of the "convenience and security" of holding money—the inconvenience which may possibly be caused by not having cash immediately available. It is the chance that you may want to discount the bill

It should be observed that this minimum to the rate of interest applies not only to one curve *LL* (drawn to correspond to a particular quantity of money) but to any such curve. If the supply of money is increased, the curve *LL* moves to the right (as the dotted curve in Figure 2), but the horizontal parts of the curve are almost the same. Therefore, again, it is this doldrum to the left of the diagram which upsets the classical theory. If *IS* lies to the right, then we can indeed increase employment by increasing the quantity of money; but if *IS* lies to the left, we cannot do so; merely monetary means will not force down the rate of interest any further.

So the General Theory of Employment is the Economics of Depression.

IV

In order to elucidate the relation between Mr. Keynes and the "Classics," we have invented a little apparatus. It does not appear that we have exhausted the uses of that apparatus, so let us conclude by giving it a little run on its own.

With that apparatus at our disposal, we are no longer obliged to make certain simplifications which Mr. Keynes makes in his exposition. We can reinsert the missing i in the third equation, and allow for any possible effect of the rate of interest upon saving; and, what is much more important, we can call in question the sole dependence of investment upon the rate of interest, which looks rather suspicious in the second equation. Mathematical elegance would suggest that we ought to have I and i in all three equations, if the theory is to be really General. Why not have them there like this:

$$M = L(I, i), \qquad I_x = C(I, i), \qquad I_x = S(I, i)?$$

Once we raise the question of Income in the second equation, it is clear that it has a very good claim to be inserted. Mr. Keynes

which matters, not the chance that you will then have to discount it on unfavourable terms. The "precautionary motive," not the "speculative motive," is here dominant. But the prospective terms of rediscounting are vital, when it comes to the *difference* between short and long rates.

is in fact only enabled to leave it out at all plausibly by his device of measuring everything in "wage-units," which means that he allows for changes in the marginal-efficiency-of-capital schedule when there is a change in the level of money wages, but that other changes in Income are deemed not to affect the curve, or at least not in the same immediate manner. But why draw this distinction? Surely there is every reason to suppose that an increase in the demand for consumers' goods, arising from an increase in employment, will often directly stimulate an increase in investment, at least as soon as an expectation develops that the increased demand will continue. If this is so, we ought to include I in the second equation, though it must be confessed that the effect of I on the marginal efficiency of capital will be fitful and irregular.

The Generalized General Theory can then be set out in this way. Assume first of all a given total money Income. Draw a curve CC showing the marginal efficiency of capital (in money terms) at that given Income; a curve SS showing the supply curve of saving at that *given* Income (Figure 3). Their intersection will determine the rate of interest which makes savings equal to investment at that level of income. This we may call the "investment rate."

If Income rises, the curve SS will move to the right; probably CC will move to the right too. If SS moves more than CC, the investment rate of interest will fall; if CC more than SS, it will rise. (How much it rises and falls, however, depends upon the elasticities of the CC and SS curves.)

The IS curve (drawn on a separate diagram) now shows the relation between Income and the corresponding investment rate of interest. It has to be confronted (as in our earlier constructions) with an LL curve showing the relation between Income and the "money" rate of interest; only we can now generalise our LL curve a little. Instead of assuming, as before, that the supply of money is given, we can assume that there is a given monetary system— that up to a point, but only up to a point, monetary authorities will prefer to create new money rather than allow interest rates to rise. Such a generalised LL curve will then slope upwards only gradually—the elasticity of the curve depending on the elasticity of the monetary system (in the ordinary monetary sense).

As before, Income and interest are determined where the *IS* and *LL* curves intersect—where the investment rate of interest equals the money rate. Any change in the inducement to invest or the propensity to consume will shift the *IS* curve; any change in liquidity preference or monetary policy will shift the *LL* curve. If, as the result of such a change, the investment rate is raised above the money rate, Income will tend to rise; in the opposite case,

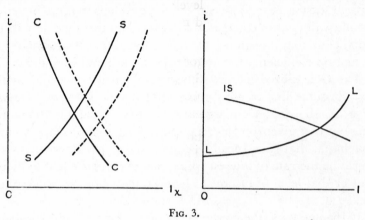

FIG. 3.

Income will tend to fall; the extent to which Income rises or falls depends on the elasticities of the curves.[8]

When generalised in this way, Mr. Keynes' theory begins to look very like Wicksell's; this is of course hardly surprising.[9]   There

---

[8] Since $C(I, i) = S(I, i)$,

$$\frac{dI}{di} = -\frac{\partial S/\partial i - \partial C/\partial i}{\partial S/\partial I - \partial C/\partial I}.$$

The savings investment market will not be stable unless $\partial S/\partial i + (-\partial C/\partial i)$ is positive.   I think we may assume that this condition is fulfilled.

If $\partial S/\partial i$ is positive, $\partial C/\partial i$ negative, $\partial S/\partial I$ and $\partial C/\partial I$ positive (the most probable state of affairs), we can say that the *IS* curve will be more elastic, the greater the elasticities of the *CC* and *SS* curves, and the larger is $\partial C/\partial I$ relatively to $\partial S/\partial I$ When $\partial C/\partial I > \partial S/\partial I$, the *IS* curve is upward sloping.

[9] Cf. Keynes, *General Theory*, p. 242.

is indeed one special case where it fits Wicksell's construction absolutely. If there is "full employment" in the sense that any rise in Income immediately calls forth a rise in money wage rates; then it is *possible* that the CC and SS curves may be moved to the right to exactly the same extent, so that IS is horizontal. (I say possible, because it is not unlikely, in fact, that the rise in the wage level may create a presumption that wages will rise again later on; if so, CC will probably be shifted more than SS, so that IS will be upward sloping.) However that may be, if IS is horizontal, we do have a perfectly Wicksellian construction;[10] the investment rate becomes Wicksell's *natural rate*, for in this case it may be thought of as determined by real causes; if there is a perfectly elastic monetary system, and the money rate is fixed below the natural rate, there is cumulative inflation; cumulative deflation if it is fixed above.

This, however, is now seen to be only one special case; we can use our construction to harbour much wider possibilities. If there is a great deal of unemployment, it is very likely that $\partial C . \partial I$ will be quite small; in that case IS can be relied upon to slope downwards. This is the sort of Slump Economics with which Mr. Keynes is largely concerned. But one cannot escape the impression that there may be other conditions when expectations are tinder, when a slight inflationary tendency lights them up very easily. Then $\partial C . \partial I$ may be large and an increase in Income tend to *raise* the investment rate of interest. In these circumstances, the situation is unstable at *any* given money rate; it is only an imperfectly elastic monetary system—a rising LL curve—that can prevent the situation getting out of hand altogether.

These, then, are a few of the things we can get out of our skeleton apparatus. But even if it may claim to be a slight extension of Mr. Keynes' similar skeleton, it remains a terribly rough and ready sort of affair. In particular, the concept of "Income" is worked monstrously hard; most of our curves are not really determinate unless something is said about the distribution of Income

---

[10] Cf. Myrdal, "Gleichgewichtsbegriff," in *Beiträge zur Geldtheorie*, ed. Hayek.

as well as its magnitude. Indeed, what they express is something like a relation between the price-system and the system of interest rates; and you cannot get that into a curve. Further, all sorts of questions about depreciation have been neglected; and all sorts of questions about the timing of the processes under consideration.

The General Theory of Employment is a useful book; but it is neither the beginning nor the end of Dynamic Economics.

25

MONETARY POLICY AND THE THEORY OF INTEREST *

By Harold M. Somers †

Many issues, both true and false, have been raised and settled since controversy on that time-worn subject, the theory of interest, broke loose anew in 1936, when Mr. Keynes published his General Theory. Few topics in economics, in fact, have received as varied treatment as has the theory of interest. Few topics, moreover, have resulted in as many divisions of opinion, misunderstandings, vigorous attacks and equally vigorous defenses. Before the publication of the General Theory the situation was confused enough. A serious difference of opinion existed between the two non-monetary sets of interest theories. On the one hand, there was the "subjective" non-monetary theory, currently advocated by Professor Fetter and Professor Pigou, which associated the magnitude of the rate of interest with the individual's time preference; on the other, there was the "objective" non-monetary theory, currently advocated by Professor F. H. Knight, which attributed the determination of the rate of interest to the marginal productivity of capital. In between these theories, or, perhaps, over both of them, lay the theory of Professor Irving Fisher and others, which made use of both the subjective and objective elements of the non-monetary explanation of the rate of interest.

Mr. Keynes scrapped the whole non-monetary approach—both the subjective and objective elements—and claimed that the rate of interest was a purely monetary phenomenon. In this he found partial support on the part of students of the business cycle, who felt that monetary factors, although not the only factors affecting

---

* *Quarterly Journal of Economics*, Volume LV, 1940–1941, pages 488–507. Reprinted by courtesy of the publisher and author.

† University of Buffalo. Formerly, Cambridge, Mass.

the rate of interest, were of considerable importance in its determination. The monetary school soon found itself in two camps.
On the one hand, there were Mr. Keynes and his followers, who
claimed that interest was a *purely* monetary phenomenon, the rate
of interest being determined by the demand and supply of money.
Given the amount of money, the magnitude of the rate was held
to be determined by a subjective factor, liquidity preference, the
rate of interest being regarded as the price paid for parting with
liquidity. On the other hand, there were Professors Haberler,
Hicks, Ohlin, Robertson, Viner, and others, who felt that non-
monetary and objective elements as well as monetary and subjective elements determined the rate of interest. At the same time
most of the latter group of writers kept insisting that the two monetary approaches were essentially two different ways of saying the
same thing.

Thus there existed three controversies at one time: between
the subjective and objective non-monetary theories; between the
subjective and objective monetary theories; and between the non-
monetary theories, on the one hand, and the monetary theories on
the other.[1] The first controversy, that between the two sets of
non-monetary theories, is still far from settled. Although most
non-monetary theorists concede the importance of the productivity
of capital, there are some, like Professor Fisher and Professor
Pigou, who still insist upon the importance of psychological time
preference. The second controversy, that between the two monetary theories, has been settled in a somewhat precarious manner by
Mr. Lerner and Professor Hicks, who have given two different, and
somewhat contradictory, explanations of the relationship existing
between the liquidity-preference and the loanable-funds theories.
The third controversy, that between the monetary and non-mone-

---

[1] This classification does, of course, contain a considerable element of arbitrari-
ness and should not be considered to imply an adequate description of the respective theories.

The above references are confined to a few contemporary authors. No
attempt is made here to deal with the history of thought on the subject of interest
theory.

tary sets of theories, had been greatly clarified by Wicksell long before the current controversy, but actually remains as far from settlement as ever. In the words of Professor Hicks, "it is a real dispute, in which one side must be right and the other wrong, even if the rightness or wrongness may ultimately turn out not to be absolute, but only relative to particular problems."[2]

This paper attempts to resolve the controversies described above by setting up a system in which all four variants of interest theory—the two non-monetary and the two monetary variants—have a place. It will then become evident under which assumptions or in what sense each variant of interest theory is valid as such. Aside from this it will be shown that all four variants—with some modifications—play an important part not only in the theory of interest but in any theory purporting to describe economic behavior or to explain economic phenomena. To fulfill this purpose it is necessary to examine the various rates of return on economic resources and study the nature of economic behavior in the face of these rates of return. The method employed draws heavily on the work of Wicksell and Professor Fisher, as well as that of other writers. The greatest direct influence, however, has been that of Professor Knight, to whose persistent emphasis on the "fundamentals" may be traced both the origin and execution of this attempt to evaluate the various theories of interest on the basis of the maximization principle.

I. Rates of Return on Economic Resources

At any point of time an individual has at his disposal (in the sense of "power of allocation to various uses") both his wealth and his income. If we concern ourselves with the income for a finite period, the dimensional difference which exists between wealth (a stock) and income (a flow) need not stand in the way of our considering both together as the resources which the individual has at his disposal for the period. Each purpose to which he may devote his resources—securities, cash, production (including real

---

[2] *Value and Capital* (Oxford, 1939), p. 153.

estate and stocks of goods) and consumption—yields a return to him, either in the form of subjective satisfaction or in the form of goods or money. For each individual these resources are usually in the form of money to begin with, but through the process of purchase and sale may be converted into various forms. The nature of the return on resources devoted to each of these purposes will now be examined.

SECURITIES. Resources may be devoted to the purchase of bonds, shares, promissory notes, mortgages, etc., all of which we group together for convenience and call "securities." There are, of course, a great many rates of return on securities, and the rates of return on various types of securities often fluctuate in divergent directions. Where no organized market exists, even securities of exactly the same term years (if any) and degrees of risk may sell at prices to yield various rates of return. There is, therefore, considerable objection to speaking of *the* rate of interest and changes in *the* rate of interest. Even though for many theoretical purposes no real error arises through the use of this concept, it is highly desirable to find some way of making a valid simplification of the interest-rate structure.

Two ways of approaching this problem suggest themselves. One way is to make use of Professor Hick's analysis of the relation between the long and short rates on fixed interest-bearing claims.[3] This would simplify the interest-structure, as far as the variety of term years is concerned. Then, by making some definite allowance for the risk on each security, measured from some standard security,[4] we could take account of all types of securities. This method, however, cannot readily be applied to shares, which have no term years, and which carry with them immeasurable and non-

[3] Assuming simple interest, "the long rate is the arithmetic average between the current short rate and the relevant forward short rates." (*Value and Capital*, p. 145.)

[4] This may be *any* security, whether "riskless" or not. There is no reason why the "risk allowances" may not be either positive or negative, depending on whether the security under consideration is more or less risky than the security chosen as the standard. Cf. Kaldor, "Speculation and Economic Stability," *Review of Economic Studies*, October, 1939, p. 16, note 1.

economic advantages, such as the power and prestige which accompany ownership of a large equity interest in a corporation.

The other method, although fundamentally the same, is much simpler and, for our purposes, more effective. We again choose any security with a fixed return and consider it the "standard security." Each holder of securities should be able to indicate at what rate of interest on the standard security he would be on the point of indifference as to whether he should sell all his securities and buy a like amount of the standard security. This rate of return may be regarded as an objective indicator of what the holder of the securities considers to be the value to him of all the objective and subjective returns he expects to obtain from the securities he holds. Likewise there would be a certain rate of interest appropriate to each of the *various* possible amounts of securities any individual might be willing to hold, or buy, or sell. The same sort of relation could be established for the total amount of securities in the hands of all holders of securities, as well as for the total amount supplied on the securities market (demand for loanable funds) and demanded on the securities market (supply of loanable funds). Thus we can draw up demand and supply curves of securities in terms of *the* (standard) rate of interest.

CASH. Some of the resources at the disposal of an individual are ordinarily in the form of cash, which may be held for various reasons. These have been classified by Keynes as the Transactions, Precautionary, Financial[5] and Speculative motives. To the individual or organization holding the cash there accrues a definite return, in so far as the cash fulfills one of the above purposes and thus satisfies a need. This return, though subjective and immeasurable in large part, is nevertheless real and important, since it explains why people are willing to hold any cash at all rather than invest it in something yielding an objectively measurable return. So important is this consideration that it is desirable to resort to some sort of expedient to measure the return in units comparable with those in which, for instance, we measure the return on securi-

---

[5] "The 'Ex Ante' Theory of the Rate of Interest," *Economic Journal*, December, 1937, pp. 663–9.

ties, namely, in terms of a certain amount of money per unit of money per period.

For each amount of cash which a person may be willing to hold (above a certain absolutely essential minimum), there is some rate of interest at which he would be on the point of indifference as to whether to hold that amount of cash or purchase an equivalent amount of securities (i.e. the standard security). This rate of return, which when put in marginal terms is closely related to the marginal rate of substitution between cash and securities, may be considered to be an objective indicator of the subjective satisfaction expected to be derived from holding the cash. This indicator we may call the *rate of return on cash*. For different amounts of cash held there would ordinarily be different rates of return on cash. We can, then, draw up a curve showing the various amounts of cash in relation to the appropriate rates of return. As the need for money can be satiated in greater or less degree, this curve has a downward slope. In a similar manner, we may construct an aggregate curve for the economy as a whole.[6]

PRODUCTION. The use of economic resources for purposes of production (including holding real estate and stocks of goods for a rise in value) stems from the fact that a net return over cost is expected. As in the case of the rate of return on cash, we can

---

[6] The line between *cash* and *securities* may arbitrarily be drawn at any reasonable point, as far as the present analysis is concerned. It seems reasonable, for instance, to include demand deposits in cash and time deposits in securities. There necessarily remains a great deal of overlapping, since securities provide liquidity as well as an objective return. This problem may be solved by including in cash only those liquid resources which yield no objective return. We should then regard securities as returning something above the actual interest (or dividends), namely, a liquidity return similar to the return on cash. Since all goods have a certain amount of liquidity, arising out of their salability, we may make a similar adjustment for them, the rate of return on the standard security (now including both the objective interest return and the subjective liquidity return) being used as the base.

The importance of overlapping is emphasized by the fact that securities (and, for that matter, all assets) may be used as collateral for a cash loan. Cf. M. Kalecki, "The Short-Term Rate and the Long-Term Rate," *Oxford Economic Papers*, No. 4, September, 1940, p. 15.

obtain an objective measure of the expected value of the rate of return (all the possible rates of return, weighted by their respective probabilities)[7] by ascertaining the rate of return on the standard security at which the individuals or firms involved would be on the point of indifference as to whether to devote their resources to production or to securities (i.e. the standard security). In this way, for each volume of production per period, we can obtain a money measure of the expected *rate of return on production*. The rates of return on production are thus made dimensionally comparable with the rates of return on securities and cash. On this basis we may draw up a curve[8] showing the relation between the various amounts of production per period and the corresponding rates of return. This may be done both for any line of production and for the economy as a whole.

At this point it is necessary to make the distinction suggested by Mr. Lerner[9] between the *marginal productivity of capital* and the

---

[7] This statement requires many qualifications, which it will not be possible to consider here. Cf. the notes of Messrs. Dow, Kaldor, Hawtrey, Hart and Shackle in the *Review of Economic Studies*, June and October, 1940.

[8] This curve should be considered *net* of an allowance for risk. Whether the risk is an increasing function of the rate of investment, as Dr. Kalecki would have it ("The Principle of Increasing Risk," *Economica*, November, 1937, p. 442), is somewhat doubtful in the case of corporations. (See N. S. Buchanan and R. D. Calkins, "A Comment on Mr. Kalecki's Principle of Increasing Risk," *Economica*, November, 1938, pp. 455–458; and M. Kalecki, ibid., pp. 459–460. Cf. Kalecki, *Essays in the Theory of Economic Fluctuations*, pp. 98–102.)

Related in some ways to the Principle of Increasing Risk is what we may call the "Principle of Increasing Uncertainty" (making the distinction between *uncertainty* and *risk* along the lines suggested by Professor Knight). The greater the rate of increase in the rate of investment, the more difficult it is for a manager to make an accurate estimate of the possible effects which his investment activities will have on his market. After a certain point the manager has so many investment plans under way that he must allow some of them to be carried to completion before becoming involved in new ones. As Dr. Shackle has pointed out (*Expectations, Investment and Income*, Oxford, 1938, pp. 101–102), this results in the deceleration of investments, the operation of the downward Multiplier, the disappointment of expectations, and thus is a contributing factor in the downturn.

[9] "Capital, Investment and Interest," *Transactions of the Manchester Statistical Society*, 1936–37, pp. 26–31. Cf. O. Lange, "The Rate of Interest and the Opti-

marginal efficiency of investment. This may possibly be clarified by considering a finite period of the sort used above. If we take the amount of capital in existence as given, and then consider the prospective additions to capital during the next period, the marginal rate of return on capital measures the increment in return expected from an increment in the amount of capital existing at this moment; whereas the marginal rate of return on investment measures the increment in return expected from an increment in the total amount of capital which will exist after the contemplated investment has taken place. This total amount of capital consists of (1) the amount of capital existing at this moment *plus* (2) the amount of capital to be added by the prospective investment. In this paper the term *marginal rate of return on production* will refer to the marginal efficiency of investment.

CONSUMPTION. When we pass to the "return" on consumption we are in the realm of the same sort of subjectivity and immeasurability as when we consider the return on cash. Again we must resort to some method of obtaining an objective indicator of the subjective satisfaction involved.

If we are at the point of indifference between (1) spending $100 on consumption during the coming year and (2) investing it in securities yielding five per cent and thus providing us with $105 at the end of the year, the rate five per cent must indicate the magnitude of the *extra* satisfaction expected from the consumption of $100 worth of goods this year instead of next. We may call this the *rate of return on consumption.*[10] The return on consumption is thus made dimensionally comparable with the return on securities, cash and production. If there is a diminishing marginal utility of consumption, we may expect a downward sloping curve relating the volume of consumption per period to the various marginal

mum Propensity to Consume," *Economica*, February, 1938, p. 13 n. and T. de Scitovszky, "A Study of Interest and Capital," *Economica*, August, 1940, pp. 308ff.

[10] This may be negative in some special cases. It is understood, of course, that we begin our analysis only after the volume of consumption per period is sufficiently great to permit the possibility of a choice among various uses.

For the relation between the *marginal rate of return on consumption* and the *marginal rate of time preference*, see p. 492.

rates of return.[11]   As in the other cases, we may also have an aggregate curve for the economy as a whole.

Nature of the Rates of Return.   Thus we have rates of return on securities, cash, production and consumption.[12]   Each of these may be expressed in both average and marginal terms (in which form they are related to marginal rates of substitution between the respective resources and the standard security).   Each, moreover, is prospective, and embodies the expected value of the various possible estimates of the community as a whole.   Although, in some cases, the actual subjective return is nebulous and immeasurable, we are dealing here with something objective and measurable, just as the utility derived from a piece of bread is subjective and immeasurable, while the price paid for the bread is both objective and measurable.

II. FUNDAMENTALS OF ECONOMIC BEHAVIOR

We must now pass to the behavior of individuals and organizations confronted with these rates of return.   It is evident that the maximum amount of return would be derived from that distribution of resources which equates the *marginal rate of return* in every use: securities, cash, production and consumption.   As a prelude to the discussion of the theory of interest it is necessary to see to what extent this optimal principle can be, and to what extent it actually is, carried out in the economy by individuals, firms, banks and governments.   Since we are primarily concerned with short-run problems, we are interested mainly in whether or not the short-run marginal rates of return are equalized.

INDIVIDUALS.   The individual has before him all four possible uses to which resources may be put: securities, cash, production and consumption (including charitable contributions).   In order

---

[11] This curve shows that the greater the volume of consumption per period, the lower is the rate of interest at which a marginal unit of resources will be devoted to securities rather than consumption.   This does not imply any assumption regarding the converse relationship, namely, the way in which a change in the rate of interest affects the volume of consumption per period, a subject which is dealt with in Part III.

[12] For most analytical purposes it would be desirable to subdivide these and have rates of return on bonds, shares, inventories, etc.

to maximize the satisfaction he derives from his resources he should devote them to the various uses in such a way that there is equality among all the marginal rates of return.

There are several reasons why this equalization is ordinarily not achieved: the individual may not have the knowledge and experience to estimate some of the rates of return, e.g. the rate of return on production; he may be indifferent to the maximization of his welfare, finding it "rational to be irrational";[13] he may be disinclined to engage in production or to invest in securities, regardless of their rate of return, since he does not wish to gamble, however slightly; he may find the units in which productive resources, securities, and even consumption goods are found to be such that it would, in any case, be impossible for him to equalize the rates of return, even if he wanted to take the trouble; and finally, the organization of markets, with their frictions and other impediments, may be such that it would take a considerable time for him to make the necessary transfers between resources and thus adjust himself to changes in the rates of return.

It need not be assumed, however, that, except in unusual circumstances, the individual would *deliberately* make a transfer among his resources which would reduce the sum total of return derived, i.e. aggravate the discrepancy among the various marginal rates of return. Nevertheless it is true that a discrepancy among the rates may arise and persist without any ameliorative action on the part of the individual.

FIRMS. Business firms, whether incorporated or not, have before them all the above four choices, with the exception of consumption. The alternative of consumption is, however, replaced by that of "drawings"[14] to partners and dividends to shareholders. The question arises, therefore, whether the marginal principle is applied in the payment of "drawings" and dividends.[15]

---

[13] Cf. F. H. Knight, *Risk, Uncertainty and Profit*, p. 62 n.

[14] This term, as used here, is defined *net* of any wage or salary element. Sole ownerships may best be considered in the section on individuals.

[15] Whether the internal distribution of resources is in accordance with the marginal principle is not discussed here, owing to the difficulty of deciding to what

Drawings of partners are usually determined more by the needs of the partners than by the relative rates of return on the various opportunities open to the partnership.   As for dividends, there is some evidence to the effect that their distribution is not based on the marginal principle.[16]   Since drawings and dividends affect the rate of return on securities,[17] it is evident that this rate of return may get out of line (temporarily at least) with the other marginal rates of return.

BANKS.   Ordinary private banks, whether members or non-members of the Federal Reserve System (but excluding the Federal Reserve Banks themselves), may follow the marginal principle in the allocation of their resources between the two alternatives which are ordinarily open to them: (1) holding cash and (2) purchasing securities of various sorts, e.g. making loans to customers, buying industrial and government bonds, etc.   The seriousness of the race between profitability (in the form of a return on securities) and liquidity (which expresses itself in the form of a return on cash, arising largely from the Precautionary motive for holding cash) tends to ensure fulfilment of the marginal principle, whether or not the bank manager is aware of the fact.   If he attempts to maximize the bank's profit, subject to the condition that he does not jeopardize the bank's position by holding too little cash, he is following the marginal principle, for he is attempting to equalize the marginal rates of return on cash and securities.[18]

---

extent "rules of thumb," made necessary by the impossibility of continuous calculation of every conceivable return, are actually conducive to the maximization of profits.

[16] See Norman S. Buchanan, "Theory and Practice in Dividend Distribution," *Quarterly Journal of Economics*, November, 1938, pp. 64–85, or The Economics of Corporate Enterprise (New York, 1940), Ch. IX.

[17] For purposes of this analysis it is best to consider the equity interest of partners in the same category as securities (despite the fundamental legal distinction), since drawings of partners are not necessarily equal to the return on production, and are thus analogous to the return on shares.   A more legalistic classification will not, however, affect the general conclusion.

[18] This gives us the basis for a distinction between "legal excess" reserves and "economic excess" reserves, the latter existing when the bank's marginal rate of

The Federal Reserve Banks, however, do not act on the marginal principle (in the narrow, short-run sense used above), for they are not concerned with maximizing returns. Reserve banks may buy and sell securities for reasons bearing no relation to the marginal principle. Thus the marginal rate of return on securities may fall, through the manipulation of the Federal Reserve Banks, with the result that a discrepancy arises among the marginal rates of return on securities, cash, production and consumption for those individuals and organizations which try to maximize their returns, i.e. follow the marginal principle.

GOVERNMENTS. Governments face even greater difficulties than do individuals in allocating the resources at their disposal in accordance with the marginal principle, particularly because of the difficulty of estimating the rates of return on the various types of (collective) consumption. Sometimes, moreover, there is no desire to maximize the returns to the community, the end being quite different, namely, keeping in power, the marginal principle for which does not interest us here.

In the case of governments important for economic policy, e.g. the Federal Government, a third sort of marginal principle may manifest itself. The government may use its resources to carry out some policy which may only *ultimately* have the effect of maximizing the returns to the community. For instance, the large cash balance of the Federal Government fulfils not only the traditional purposes but also that of monetary manipulation[19] directed towards lowering the cost of new government financing.[20] This has

---

return on cash is below the marginal rate of return on securities. Only the existence of economic excess reserves means that more loans may rationally be granted by the bank.

As banks are usually subject to severe legal limitations in the disposal of their resources, the fulfilment of the marginal principle may be difficult in some cases. This is particularly true with respect to real estate and other physical assets, hence the rate of return on production is not considered above.

[19] Which may, perhaps, be considered a special form of either the Precautionary or Speculative motive.

[20] Cf. Edward C. Simmons, "Treasury Deposits and Excess Reserves," *Journal of Political Economy*, June, 1940, p. 342 n.

the effect of influencing the current rate of return on securities. As a result, individuals and organizations which try to maximize their returns may find that the equality among the marginal rates of return on securities, cash, production and consumption is temporarily upset.

SIGNIFICANCE OF AN ARBITRARY MONETARY POLICY.   The above considerations illustrate the weakness and at the same time the strength of the marginal principle.   In so far as *no* attempt is made to maximize returns, the marginal principle loses significance, and the existence of an "arbitrary" monetary policy[21] has relatively little effect on the various rates of return.   In so far as *some* attempt is made to maximize returns, the existence of an arbitrary monetary policy *increases* rather than diminishes the importance of the marginal principle.   For the existence of a desire to maximize returns (i.e. the conscious or unconscious attempt to apply the marginal principle) means that whenever a change takes place in one of the marginal rates of return, say the marginal rate of return on securities, adjustments[22] tend to be made in the amounts of resources allocated among the various uses, with the result that changes take place in all the marginal rates of return (barring curves of infinite elasticity).   Moreover, that rate of return which is subject to the arbitrary policy assumes unique importance—it sets the pace, or "rules the roost."   This fact is of the utmost importance in a discussion of the theory of interest, to which we now turn.

III. THE THEORY OF INTEREST

The points at issue in the interest-theory controversy have been obscured, and the likelihood of an amicable settlement has been diminished, by the fact that some of the disputants and many of the onlookers have misconceived the nature of the difference of opinion which exists.   One might, for instance, get the impression from some of the literature that Professor Knight and Mr. Keynes

[21] In the sense that allocation of resources is not made with a view to current maximization of returns, narrowly construed.

[22] The actual process of adjustment is complicated by the existence of speculation in stocks of goods and securities.   Cf. Scitovszky, op. cit., and Kaldor, op. cit.

would deny that the term "rate of interest" is correctly defined as the rate of payment for a loan of money per unit of money per unit of time. In actual fact none of the participants in the interest debate has objected to this as a correct *definition* of the rate of interest for a monetary economy.[23] Their sole concern has been with what determines the magnitude of the rate of interest at any time. One group of writers attributes this rôle to time preference, another to the productivity of capital, another to liquidity preference, and another to some or all of these factors combined. The present section proposes to examine each of the interest theories with a view to deciding under what assumptions or for what conditions, if any, each theory may be said to hold true. In this analysis the term "rate of interest" refers to the marginal rate of return on the standard security.

NON-MONETARY THEORIES: THE MARGINAL PRODUCTIVITY THEORY. The marginal productivity theory attributes the determination of the rate of interest to the marginal productivity of capital. As it is not quite clear whether this actually refers to the marginal rate of return on capital or to the marginal rate of return on investment, the validity of the theory will be examined under both conditions.

If the theory refers to the return on investment—our marginal rate of return on production—it would be necessary to show either that this rate is constant or that it sets the pace among all the rates, i.e. when the equality among them is upset it is always because of a change in the marginal rate of return on production. In either case, there would be an adjustment of the other marginal rates of return, including the rate of interest, to the marginal rate of return on production. The first possibility is out of the question, since the marginal rate of return on production is a function of expectations—which are constantly changing. The second possibility could exist only on the very special assumption that all internal and external changes in the economy act first upon the return on

---

[23] Cf. F. H. Knight, "The Quantity of Capital and the Rate of Interest," *Journal of Political Economy*, August, 1936, p. 435; and J. M. Keynes. *General Theory*, p. 186 n.

production and only through it on the other marginal rates of return. Under this assumption it would be impossible for the rate of interest to decline before the return on production declines, because no person acting on the marginal principle would ever be willing to accept a lower marginal rate of return on securities than he could obtain on production. Likewise it would be impossible for the rate of interest to lead a rise in the marginal rate of return on production.

Under more realistic conditions it need not be the marginal rate of return on production which sets the pace. The equality among the rates may be upset by the return on cash (e.g. through a diminished need for cash balances in business) or by the return on consumption (e.g. through an increased consumption) or by the return on securities (e.g. through an arbitrary monetary policy). Where the monetary authority changes the rate of interest, for instance, the marginal rate of return on production must be adjusted to that rate.[24] Under such conditions marginal productivity cannot be considered the only important factor which might affect the rate of interest.[25]

It is often claimed that the marginal productivity theory is perfectly valid for "the long run." If this means that in the long run the marginal rate of return on production is equal to the rate of interest, then the statement is rather empty. In "the long run" (presumably after all adjustments have taken place) all the marginal rates of return are equal to the rate of interest. But if it means that in "the long run" the marginal rate of return on production sets the pace and that all the other rates of return must adjust themselves to it, then the statement holds true only if "the long run" is defined in such a way that independent changes in

---

[24] In the Wicksellian analysis this adjustment would be brought about by a rise in prices. But this is based on several special assumptions, including full employment. Cf. A. P. Lerner, "Some Swedish Stepping Stones in Economic Theory," *Canadian Journal of Economics and Political Science*, November, 1940, p. 582.

[25] Cf. A. E. Monroe, "Investment and Saving: A Genetic Analysis," *Quarterly Journal of Economics*, August, 1929, pp. 594–596, 603.

the other marginal rates of return are ruled out. This would involve the assumption of given tastes, given volume of business, given business habits, etc., for otherwise "long-run" shifts in the curves for consumption and cash could take place, thus causing changes in the respective rates of return.[26]

If the marginal productivity theory refers to the return on capital rather than to the return on investment, then the short-run validity of this theory is more questionable than ever. In the short run it is the marginal rate of return on *investment*, not the marginal rate of return on *capital*, which is kept in adjustment with the other marginal rates of return. The return on capital would be the relevant concept only if the rate of net investment were zero. For the long run, what was said in the previous paragraph about the validity of the theory would still hold. In the long run the marginal rate of return on capital may be considered to be the magnitude which tends to be in adjustment with the other marginal rates of return, and one need not distinguish between the return on capital and the return on investment.

NON-MONETARY THEORIES: THE TIME-PREFERENCE THEORY. The time-preference theory associates the magnitude of the rate of interest with the marginal rate of time preference, which is identical with our marginal rate of return on consumption. For reasons analogous to those given in the case of the marginal productivity theory, a time-preference theory of interest is tenable only if we assume conditions where either the marginal rate of return on consumption is a constant[27] or where it alone initiates changes in the rates of return. Under realistic conditions, as noted above, the latter assumption can certainly not be held. The former assumption requires some examination.

---

[26] Cf. Irving Fisher, *The Theory of Interest* (1930), p. 505.

[27] This is the assumption made by Professor Pigou in "Real and Money Wage Rates in Relation to Unemployment," *Economic Journal*, September, 1937, pp. 405–422. In the *Economics of Stationary States*, Ch. 10, p. 50 ff., the same theory is presented, except that in the latter place the discussion is in terms of a Robinson Crusoe economy, with the result that the expression "rate of interest" refers to the marginal rate of return on production rather than the marginal rate of return on securities.

It was assumed in Part I that the marginal rate of return on consumption is an inverse function of the volume of consumption per period.   This appears reasonable and is supported by Professor Pigou's recent concession that the marginal rate of time preference may be a function of income.[28]   But the satisfaction which an individual—including Professor Pigou's "representative Englishman"—gains from a given rate of consumption also depends in large part upon his ease of mind and freedom from concern over the future.   Some people are relatively "improvident," and their marginal rate of return on consumption (to pass to the objective indicator of the subjective satisfaction) is little affected by the amount of their provision for the future.   Others are relatively "provident" and experience a great change in the satisfaction they gain from a given rate of consumption whenever, for some reason, the amount of their provision for the future is altered.   One way in which the latter can occur is through a change in the rate of interest, since this both changes the rate of compounding of private savings and at the same time affects the capital value of all assets (with opposite effects on private wealth).   Thus the marginal rate of time preference may be considered to be a function of both the volume of consumption per period and the rate of interest.   It obviously cannot be assumed constant.

There is a further point arising from the above analysis.   The time-preference theory has usually been associated with the assumption of a direct relation between the rate of interest and the rate of saving.   Actually, however, the concept of a marginal rate of time preference is independent of this assumption.   If the rate of interest falls, the marginal rate of time preference will also fall, but this may come about through a *shift* in the consumption curve (with no fall, or even with an increase, in the rate of saving) as well as through a movement *along* the curve (with a fall in the rate of saving).   Which of these factors predominates depends on the relative importance of "provident" and "improvident" individuals. Hence the concept of a marginal rate of time preference can be

---

[28] "Money Wages in Relation to Unemployment," *Economic Journal*, March, 1938, pp. 134–138.   Cf. Fisher, op. cit., pp. 66–68.

retained and can be made a useful analytical tool, even though we reject both the time-preference theory of interest and the assumption of a direct relation between interest and the rate of saving.[29]

MONETARY THEORIES: THE LIQUIDITY-PREFERENCE THEORY. According to the liquidity-preference theory the rate of interest is determined by the "demand and supply of money."[30] There are three interpretations[31] which we may make of this theory. The first interpretation, which many people took to be the correct one, is that the demand and supply of idle balances determine the rate of interest. This interpretation must be rejected, however, even if we grant that the *demand* for idle balances is interest-elastic, because there is no such thing as a *supply* of idle balances distinguishable from the total supply of money.

The second interpretation, the one perhaps most widely accepted now, is that adopted by Professor Hicks,[32] namely, that the rate of interest is determined by the *total* demand and supply of money. This is also untenable as a separate theory of interest. Since the total demand for money and the total supply of money obviously determine *all* prices, not only the rate of interest, we can accept this as a theory of interest only if we are willing to take as given all prices other than the rate of interest. But this would leave only the supply and demand of securities as the effective parts of the demand and supply of money in determining the rate of interest. Hence under this interpretation the liquidity-preference theory becomes merely a disguised form of the loanable-funds theory, which says that the demand and supply of securities determine the rate of interest.

---

[29] Conclusions based simply on an observation of the relation between interest and the rate of saving are apt to be misleading, since ceteris paribus conditions do not obtain where changes in the rate of interest affect money incomes. Cf. Dan Throop Smith, *Deficits and Depressions* (New York, Wiley, 1936), pp. 75–76.

[30] Cf. Knut Wicksell, *Interest and Prices* (London, 1936), p. 108: "The money rate of interest depends in the first instance on the excess or scarcity of *money*."

[31] The discussion of the first two is based upon an article by Dr. William Fellner and the present writer, "Alternative Monetary Approaches to Interest Theory," *Review of Economic Statistics*, February, 1941.

[32] *Value and Capital*, Ch. XII.

A third interpretation—and the only one under which the liquidity-preference theory can really be considered a separate theory of interest—arises from the analysis in earlier parts of this paper. The total demand and supply of money determine the marginal rate of return on cash, which, through the purchase and sale of securities, is constantly kept in adjustment with the rate of interest. In this way the demand and supply of money "determine" the rate of interest and the liquidity-preference theory comes into its own once more.

Even under this sympathetic interpretation, however, the liquidity-preference theory has definite limitations. If we assume that adjustments among the rates do take place, then changes in either productivity or thrift can affect the rate of interest *directly* (in the sense that it need not act through the demand for cash) by affecting the marginal rates of return on production and consumption and thus the rate of interest.[33] As was previously pointed out, any change in these will result in a mutual adjustment among all four rates of return (barring infinitely elastic curves).[34] The view that the rate of interest may be affected without an immediate change in the demand for cash is reinforced by the consideration that the business of buying and selling securities requires cash balances, just as does the business of buying and selling goods. Where we have an arbitrary monetary policy as well as various frictions and "irrationalities," the rate of interest may even change without an equal change taking place in the marginal rate of return

---

[33] Mr. Keynes has only agreed that productivity and thrift can affect the rate of interest *indirectly*, i.e. through the demand for money. For an account of this controversy see E. S. Shaw, "False Issues in the Interest Theory Controversy," *Journal of Political Economy*, December, 1938, pp. 838–856; and D. H. Robertson, *Essays in Monetary Theory* (London, 1940), Ch. I. Cf. N. Kaldor, *Review of Economic Studies*, June, 1939, pp. 232–235.

An argument running in terms of utility-maximization and showing how the rate of interest could be affected by a direct transfer from production and/or consumption to securities, without immediately affecting the demand for cash, was pointed out to the writer by Professor Howard S. Ellis.

[34] Cf. O. Lange, op. cit., p. 19, and the writer's paper, *Review of Economic Studies*, February, 1940, pp. 136–137.

on cash for some time.   Under either of these sets of conditions the liquidity-preference theory must be rejected as an explanation of the way in which the rate of interest is determined.

MONETARY THEORIES: THE LOANABLE-FUNDS THEORY.   The loanable-funds theorists make use of productivity, thrift, liquidity preference and changes in the amount of money.   These factors are considered to affect the demand and supply of loanable funds which, by their interaction, determine the rate of interest.   Conclusions derived from their analysis are essentially the same as those obtained above and it is unnecessary to repeat them, particularly since a rather complete description of the theory is readily available elsewhere.[35]

A possible explanation of the relation between the liquidity-preference theory and the loanable-funds theory arises directly from the above discussion.   According to the loanable-funds theory, the rate of interest is determined by the demand and supply of loanable funds.   According to the liquidity-preference theory the rate of interest is determined by the demand and supply of cash.   These statements are mutually consistent, provided that we interpret the liquidity-preference theory, as above, to mean that the demand and supply of cash determine the marginal rate of return on cash, which, through the purchase and sale of securities, is made equal to the

---

[35] See Robertson, op. cit., and Gottfried von Haberler, *Prosperity and Depression* (Geneva, 1939), Ch. 8.   Cf. J. A. Schumpeter, *Business Cycles* (New York and London, 1939), Vol. I, pp. 123–129, Vol. II, pp. 602–607, and earlier writings.

Davenport's loanable-funds theory is similar to the above, except that although it lays stress on the fact that changes in the amount of money affect the supply of loanable-funds and thus the rate of interest, it does not seem to give a place to the demand for liquidity.   Davenport's position among the monetary interest-theorists is secure, however, for he says, "Of only so much as this—which is enough for the present purpose—is the present writer confident: that the problem of the supply of loan fund and of the interest rates paid for loans is, for any given time and situation, rather a banking problem, a question of the volume of circulating medium and the uses for which it is offered, than a question of the aggregate wealth of society, of the source or nature of it, or of the abstinences conditioning the existence of any part of it.   Long-time equilibria are no part of the problem of the current supply of funds or of the current interest rates" (*The Economics of Enterprise*, 1913, p. 350 n.).

rate of interest by a process of mutual adjustment.   This explanation of the relation between the two theories resembles that suggested by Mr. Lerner, whose analysis makes it clear that the rate
of interest equates the demand and supply of cash only at the point
where equilibrium is attained between cash and securities (claims).[36]

VALIDITY OF THE THEORIES OF INTEREST.   From the above
analysis it follows that every one of the "theories" takes account
of factors which must be considered in any discussion of the rate of
interest.   The time-preference theory gives the leading role to the
marginal rate of return on consumption; the marginal-productivity
theory gives it to the marginal rate of return on production; the
liquidity-preference theory gives it to the marginal rate of return
on cash; and the loanable-funds theory deals directly with the rate
of interest, the marginal rate of return on securities.   To the extent
that people act in accordance with the marginal principle, there
tends to be equality among all four marginal rates of return.   None
of them can be ignored, for they all play a part in the adjustment
which takes place when the equality among them is upset.   It is
not difficult to imagine various sets of conditions under which
each of the rates would set the pace, thus giving the corresponding
"theory" the right to be called *the* theory of interest.

Where we have an arbitrary monetary policy, however, only
the loanable-funds theory fully explains changes in the rate of
interest.[37]   By influencing either the demand or supply of loanable
funds the monetary authority can change the rate of interest at
will.[38]   The other marginal rates of return then have to follow along

---

[36] In Figure 3 of his "Alternative Formulations of the Theory of Interest,"
Economic Journal, June, 1938.   For a discussion of other parts of his article, see
Haberler, op. cit.   It should be observed that Mr. Lerner uses the term *claims*
broadly to include all assets other than cash.

In his recent article, "Some Swedish Stepping Stones in Economic Theory"
(cited above), pp. 578–579, Mr. Lerner speaks of changing the rate of interest by
affecting the demand for or supply of "cash and/or debts."

[37] This is true also of the liquidity-preference theory under the second interpretation, whereby it is merely a disguised form of the loanable-funds theory.

[38] Within the limits set by horizontal segments of the cash, production and
consumption curves.

as best they can.   To the extent that the marginal principle is not fulfilled, there is no assurance that these marginal rates of return will ever actually come into equality with the rate of interest.   In such circumstances even the liquidity-preference theory becomes invalid, since the marginal rate of return on cash cannot be assumed to remain in constant adjustment with the rate of interest.[39]

---

[39] This holds only for the liquidity-preference theory under the third interpretation.   The monetary authority may establish a certain rate of interest through security purchases or sales, but the public may fail to buy or sell a sufficient number of securities to change its cash holdings to the point where the marginal rate of return on cash is equal to the given rate of interest.

26

THE STRUCTURE OF INTEREST RATES*
By Friedrich A. Lutz†

It has long been customary in works on the theory of interest to talk about *the* interest rate, and to deal with the problem of the difference between rates on different maturities by adding a footnote to the effect that the author understands by *the* interest rate the whole "family" of interest rates. Although the incompleteness of this kind of treatment was generally recognized, it was not regarded as an essential defect of the theory, because it was assumed that the whole "family" of interest rates moved up and down together, and that furthermore there was a tendency towards equalization of the different rates. The wide discrepancy between long and short rates which is at present observable, and which has existed ever since the middle of 1932 (apart from a short period during the banking crisis), has shown once again that these assumptions are not always borne out by the facts. The last few years have therefore seen new attempts to find out what determines the relationship between long and short interest rates. The present article tries to set out the theory of this relationship and to verify it so far as possible by reference to the facts.

I

In our approach to the problem of the relation between long and short-term rates, we shall start out, in this first section, by making three assumptions: (1) everybody concerned knows what the future short-term rates will be, i.e. there is accurate forecasting in the market; (2) there are no costs of investment, either for lenders or for borrowers; (3) there is complete shiftability for lenders as

---

* *Quarterly Journal of Economics*, Volume LV, 1940–1941, pages 36–63. Reprinted by courtesy of the publisher and author.
† Princeton University.

well as for borrowers. The lender who wants to invest for, say, ten years is equally well prepared to buy a ten-year bond or to lend on a one-year contract and to re-lend ten times. Similarly, a lender who wants to invest for only one year is in principle prepared to buy a ten-year bond or a bond of any other maturity and to sell it again after the first year. The same shiftability is assumed for the borrower.

Under these assumptions we can set out the following propositions as to the relationship between short and long rates:

(1) We can conceive of the long-term rate as a sort of average of the future short-term rates.[1] If we neglected the compound interest factor, it would be a simple arithmetic average. If we take account of that factor, the formula is more complicated.[2] The arithmetic average can, however, be used as a sufficiently close approximation for most purposes. The character of the long rate as an average of the future short rates can also be seen from the table on page 501, which shows short rates for successive years

---

[1] This has been pointed out by many authors. Cf. Irving Fisher, *The Theory of Interest*, 1930, p. 70; W. W. Riefler, *Money Rates and Money Markets in the United States*, 1930, p. 121; F. R. Macaulay, *Some Theoretical Problems Suggested by the Movement of Interest Rates, Bond Yields and Stock Prices in the United States since 1856*, 1938, p. 29; R. G. Hawtrey, *A Century of Bank Rate*, 1938, p. 149; J. B. Williams, *The Theory of Investment Value*, 1938, p. 60; J. R. Hicks, *Value and Capital*, 1939, p. 145.

[2] The exact formula, where Rn stands for the long rate on a loan which is repaid after n unit periods, r_1 for the short rate in period 1, r_2 for the short rate in period 2, etc., is:

$$Rn = \frac{(1 + r_1)(1 + r_2) \cdots (1 + r_n) - 1}{(1 + r_2)(1 + r_3) \cdots (1 + r_n) + (1 + r_3) \cdots (1 + r_n) + \cdots + (1 + r_n) + 1}$$

This formula is based on the assumption that the long term interest payments are made regularly at the same intervals as those at which the short rate is paid.

For a simpler formula, which is exact only for the case where all the interest on the long-term loan is paid out at the end of the loan transaction, see Hicks, op. cit., p. 145. (Cf. also Lindahl, *Money and Capital*, p. 188n. The latter's interpretation of the conditions under which the formula is valid is not quite accurate.)

together with the yields in the same years for bonds with various maturities.

From the property of the long-term rate as the average of the future short rates propositions (2) to (5) below follow:

SHORT AND LONG INTEREST RATES AND BOND PRICES*

I	II	III	IV	V	VI	VII	VIII
Year	"Short" Rates (for One Year) in Years Indicated in Col. I	5% Bond Redeemable at Par at End of Year Indicated in Col. I		Yield on Perpetual 5% Bond (at Beginning of Year Indicated in Col. I)	Prices of Bonds at Beginning of Year Indicated in Col. I		
		Yield to Redemption	Price		Bond with 4 Years or More to Run	3-Year Bond	2-Year Bond
		(at Beginning of First Year)					
	%	%		%			
1	5	5	100	5.22	95.821	96.606	99.101
2	6	5.48	99.10	5.23	95.612	96.436	99.057
3	8	6.23	96.61	5.19	96.349	97.222	(100)
4	6	6.17	95.82	5.05	99.057	(100)	
5	5	5.92	95.82	5.00	100		
All following years	5	5.22†	95.82†	5.00	100		

* The calculations are based on the assumption of *annual* interest payments.
† Perpetual bond.

(2) The long rate can never fluctuate as widely as the short rate. All future changes in the short rate are already reflected in the present long rate, and the lapse of time which makes these changes in the short rate materialize affects the long rate only to the extent to which the average of these short rates becomes higher or lower by the vanishing of one short rate after the other into the past. (Compare, for instance, the movement of the yield of a perpetual bond with the movement of short-term rates, as shown in the table.)

(3) It is possible that the long rate may move temporarily contrariwise to the short rate. The long rate would rise, in spite of a simultaneous fall in the short rate, if the preceding short rate was lower than the average of the succeeding short rates, and *vice versa.* If we use the arithmetic average as a first approximation, it can easily be seen that this is so. If, for instance, the short rates in three successive years are four per cent, three per cent, and eight per cent, respectively, the yield on a bond redeemable at the end of the third year will be five per cent in the first year and will rise to five and one-half per cent in the second year, in spite of the fall in the short rate from the first to the second year.

(4) Turning now from the movement of the rates over time to the structure of the rates at a given moment of time, we see that the current yield to redemption of a long-term bond will be above the current short rate, provided the average of the future short rates up to the maturity date of the bond is above the current short rate (and *vice versa*). Such a situation also indicates that the long rate will rise later on, since the average of the short rates is bound to go up when the prevailing low short rate has passed by.

We can depict the yields to redemption, at a given date, of bonds of different maturities by drawing a graph in which the yields are plotted along the vertical axis and the redemption dates along the horizontal axis. We can, of course, obtain curves of all kinds as we assume different movements of future short-term rates. However, I will list here only a few possible patterns which are of practical significance, as we shall see later.

It is obvious that yields for bonds of different maturities will all be the same, i.e. the curve will be a straight line, if future short rates do not change. If the future short rates move in such a way that each successive short rate is above the average of the preceding ones (this condition, it may be noted, allows the short rate to fall temporarily at some point in the future without bringing about a kink in the curve), we obtain a scale of yields which is steadily ascending. The curve will, of course, flatten out if the short rates settle down at an unchanging level from a certain point onwards. In the reverse case, we obtain a scale which descends with the

increasing length of the maturities and flattens out later.   Finally,
we obtain a scale of yields which first goes up with the increasing
length of the maturities, and then goes down again when the short
rates fall below the average of the preceding short rates.   This is the
case depicted in the table on page 501.   (See columns II and III.)
If we do not know the future short rates, but have a series of yields
for bonds of different maturities, we can calculate from this the
implied future short rates.[3]

(5) It is evident that the return on an investment for a given
time is the same, no matter in what form the investment is made.
The prices of bonds fluctuate in such a way as to make this result
come true.   An investor who wants, for instance, to invest his
money for one year can either invest in the short-term market for
one year, or buy a bond of any maturity and sell it after a year.
For instance, if he buys a perpetual five per cent bond at the beginning of the first year for 95.821 and sells it at the beginning of the
second year for 95.612, he makes exactly five per cent, which is
equal to the short-term rate for one year.   If he holds the bond for
two years and sells it at 96.349 at the beginning of the third year,
he again makes exactly the same as if he had invested short for
five per cent in the first year and six per cent in the second year.
Similarly, a person who bought this bond at the beginning of the
second year at the price of 95.612, and sold it at the beginning of
the third year at the price of 96.349, would make the six per cent
which was the prevailing short rate in the second year.   (A series
of bond prices which move in the manner described may be found
in the table on page 38.)   The formula

$$\frac{\textit{Nominal interest rate} + \textit{capital gain (or} - \textit{capital loss)}}{\textit{purchasing price}}$$

always gives a return which is equivalent to what the investor would
have obtained if he had invested and reinvested at short term for
the same time.   Thus, as long as the long-term rate expresses the
average of the future short-term rates, it does not pay to borrow

---

[3] Cf. Keynes, *General Theory*, p. 168f., and Williams, op. cit., Chap. XX.

---

short and to buy long-term bonds, even though the long-term interest rate (whether this be represented by the running yield or by the yield to redemption) may be above the short-term rate. Whoever engages in such a transaction will discover, when he sells the bond, that he loses on capital account exactly what he thought to gain on interest account. There is, therefore, no mechanism which tends to make short and long rates *equal*. However, there is a mechanism which makes short and long rates *consistent* with each other. Suppose the price of a bond were such that its yield to redemption were above the average of the future short rates for the time for which the bond has to run; then it would pay to borrow short and buy the bond. This process would lower the yield of the bond until it became equal to the "*average*" of the future short rates.[4]

II

The next step in our analysis will be to introduce the costs of investment. We shall proceed on the assumption that the costs of

---

[4] Macaulay in dealing with the same problem reaches a very strange result. Having postulated perfect forecasting in the market, he says, "If in a tight short-term money market in which six-month obligations of the highest grade are selling on a seven per cent per annum basis, a four per cent bond be selling at par, its *price* at the end of the six-month period must have *risen* to $101.50, if it is to show a return of seven per cent per annum for the six-month period. This, of course, means a *fall* in the 'yield' during the six months. To preserve the theoretical relationship between present long-term and future short-term interest rates, the 'yields' of bonds of the highest grade should *fall* during a period in which short-term rates are higher than the yields of the bonds and *rise* during a period in which short-term rates are lower." (Op. cit., p. 33.) Macaulay admits that experience shows more nearly the opposite result, from which he concludes that the actual forecasting done by the market is very bad. It is, however, his own theoretical deductions which are at fault. Under his assumption of correct forecasting, the initial price of 100 for a four per cent bond, when the rate in the short-term market is seven per cent, is only possible if the later short rates are going to be far below seven per cent. That is to say, the opposite movement of short-rate and yield in the example is only temporarily possible. If the short rate is above the yield to redemption on a bond, this yield will fall only under the condition that the average of the future short rates is below the current short rate. Therefore Macaulay's paradoxical conclusion that the yield of a bond has to fall if the short rate is above the yield, and *vice versa*, is not substantiated.

borrowing *per unit of time* are the smaller, the longer the time for which the money is borrowed. This assumption seems on the whole to be justified. As far as bonds are concerned, the absolute costs to be paid to underwriters and other middlemen do not vary with the length of the maturity of the bond, which means that the costs per unit of time are the smaller, the longer the maturity.[5]   In the case of bank loans (where the costs of borrowing are not separated out as such, but are included in the interest rate) the same assumption can be made, since the investigation of the borrower's credit worthiness requires more or less the same procedure, and therefore the same costs, no matter for how long a period the loan is granted.

The question now is: how do these costs of borrowing influence the relation of short to long rates?   In order to answer this question, I shall, as a first approximation, treat these costs (of running the banking business, underwriting, etc.) as a price which has to be paid to a third party (banks, etc.) simply and solely for the service of bringing lenders and borrowers together.   If we are to isolate the influence of the cost factor, we must assume that the rate of interest, once it is established in the market, will not change in the future. This assumption is necessary in order to exclude discrepancies between short and long rates which may arise merely because it is known or expected that the short rates will rise or fall in the future (cf. Section I).

As a starting point, we may think of a situation where there is no shiftability, either on the borrowers' or on the lenders' side. This means that an investor who invests long cannot withdraw his funds before the bond is redeemed, so that a person who has funds

---

[5] The costs of floating bonds do vary, however, according to the amount borrowed. An investigation by the Securities and Exchange Commission shows that they range between 9.2 per cent for issues of less than 250,000 dollars and 2.3 per cent for issues of 25,000,000 dollars and over.   The reader may introduce this factor in the following way: the "costs of borrowing," as we refer to them in the text, may be regarded as the minimum costs of borrowing, to which additions have to be made on the side of the borrower if he borrows in amounts smaller than that to which the minimum applies, just as additions have to be made for increasing degrees of risk.

at his disposal for a shorter time than the bond has to run has no other choice than to invest in the short market. Nor can a borrower finance long-term capital requirements by borrowing short and continually renewing the loan. In such a case the long and short rates (for the time being I assume only two maturities, "long" and "short") are independent on each other. It is very likely that in this situation the long rate will be above the short, because there will be relatively few funds whose owners can part with them irrevocably for a very long time, whereas the demand for long-term funds will be relatively large owing to the importance of fixed capital. By long and short rate in this connection we mean the rate which the lender gets (i.e. exclusive of the costs). The *borrower's* rate, which *includes* these costs, will be higher than this *lender's* rate, and the short rate relatively more so than the long, i.e. the difference between the long and short rates will be smaller for the borrowers than it will for the lenders.

The demand and supply conditions in the two markets which prevail under the conditions assumed above (i.e. where there is no shifting) we shall henceforth call the "original distribution," and we shall generally assume that, for the reasons indicated, this distribution is such as to give a long-term rate which is above the short-term rate.

Let us now introduce shiftability on the lenders' side. Shifting will take place from the short market to the long, since the lender's rate is higher there. In other words, those who have short funds to invest will buy bonds and sell them after a time. This process will bring the long rate down. Moving in and out of the long market, however, entails special costs, consisting of a brokerage fee for the buying transaction and a brokerage fee *plus* a transfer tax for the selling transaction. These costs of shifting, expressed as a percentage per unit of time of the funds lent, vary of course for the different "shifters" according to the length of time for which they have their funds available. Shifting will go on, then, until the lender's long rate has been brought down to a level which is above the lender's short rate by an amount equal to the costs of shifting for what we may call the "marginal shifter," i.e. the person for whom the costs of shifting per unit of time are such that it only just pays to shift into the long market.[6]   For all shifters from the short into the long market we have to distinguish between the gross long rate, which includes the costs of shifting, and the net long rate, which excludes them.   The net rate which the marginal shifter receives in the long market will be the same as he could obtain in the short market.   A long investor who can stay in the long market until the bond is redeemed will, of course, receive the whole of the lender's gross long rate as a net rate, and all those shifters who have their funds available for a longer time than the marginal shifter will receive as a net rate less than the long investor, but more than the marginal shifter, depending on the length of time for which they have their funds available.

As far as the *borrower's* rates are concerned, the long rate as well as the short rate will be above the corresponding lender's rates, owing to the costs of borrowing.   In comparing the borrower's long rate with the borrower's short rate, we have to remember that the costs of borrowing short are higher than the costs of borrowing long.   But to the latter we now have to add the costs of shifting, which, as we have seen, make the lender's gross long rate higher than the lender's short rate.   Whether the net effect will be to make the borrower's long rate higher than the borrower's short rate depends on the magnitude of the costs of shifting and the time over which they have to be spread.   In practice they are not likely to

---

[6] To give an example.   Let us suppose that the marginal shifter has his funds available for three months.   If we assume a brokerage fee of $2 per $1,000 purchase price and a transfer tax of 40 cents, then the total costs of shifting (covering purchase and sale) will be $4.40 on $1,000 for three months, that is, 1.76 per cent per annum, and the lender's gross long rate must be higher than the lender's short rate by that amount.   This figure is not quite accurate since the long investor has also to pay a brokerage fee (for purchasing), which must be reimbursed as part of the interest rate he receives.   Thus, strictly speaking, it is only the *difference* in the costs (per unit of time) of investing for the long lender and investing and disinvesting for the short lender which has to be taken into account in calculating the effect of the costs of shifting on the gap between the lender's long and short rates.   However, if we take the period of long lending long enough we can neglect this refinement.

be such as to raise the borrower's long rate above the borrower's short rate.

The analysis made so far has to be supplemented in two respects.[7] In the first place we do not have only two maturities for which contracts can be made, but many more. This does not invalidate our previous conclusions, but it makes it possible for lenders' rates on some relatively long loans to be above the rates on shorter loans by less than the amount which corresponds to the costs of shifting between the relevant markets. Suppose, for instance, that we have the following three maturities: short, medium and long, and that in the "original distribution" the rates ascend with the increasing length of the maturity. Shifting will then take place from the medium into the long market, and from the short into the medium market, until the lender's long rate is above the medium rate by the marginal cost of shifting from the medium to the long market, and the medium rate above the short rate by the marginal costs of shifting from the short to the medium market. But the lender's long rate need not be sufficiently above the short rate to make it pay to shift from the short into the long market.[8] Thus in the final adjustment the gaps between some of the rates

---

[7] We neglect the possibility that the borrowers too may shift. If, as is most likely, the borrower's short rate is above the borrower's long rate after the shifting on the lender's side has taken place, nothing has to be added to the conclusions reached above. Shifting on the borrower's side from long to short would not pay. Shifting from short to long would not pay either, since the funds, when they were set free in the borrower's enterprise as soon as the need for them had passed, would have to be lent out by him at the lower lender's rate. If, however, the borrower's short rate were below the borrower's long rate, borrowers would shift from the long market to the short provided the costs of so doing were less than the difference between the two rates. The effect of this factor would be to restrict the amount of shifting from the short to the long market on the lender's side to smaller proportions than would obtain in the absence of shifting on the borrower's side.

[8] It is, of course, possible to conceive of an "original distribution" in which the long rate is so high, and/or so few medium-term funds are available, that it pays for the shortest funds to shift into the long market. In this case the long rate would be above the *medium* rate by more than the costs of shifting from the medium into the long market.

may be less than the minimum costs of shifting between the two respective markets.

Secondly, up to this point we have treated the banks as agents, the function of which is simply to bring would-be lenders into direct touch with would-be borrowers. However, the banks do more than that. They change shorter maturities into longer ones. Even though the funds of the depositors may be short funds, they are invested by the banks in commercial loans with longer maturities or even in bonds. How does this shifting activity of the banks affect the rates for different maturities? Suppose that under a direct lending system the funds of the marginal shifter into the long market would be three months funds and that all shorter funds would be lent out in the short market. If these shorter funds are deposited with a bank, the bank can shift part of them into longer maturities without incurring such high costs of shifting as the marginal shifter would incur in the case of direct lending. This is because the bank, since it can rely on the automatic replacement of one depositor by another, does not have to disinvest in three months time. The result will be that the borrower's as well as the lender's rates on longer maturities will be lower, and the discrepancy between the short and long rates smaller, than if the lenders lent directly to borrowers. The owner of three-months funds will in consequence fall below the margin of shifting and will have to become a depositor too. Shifting by lenders on their own account will not pay, unless they have their funds for a much longer time than was needed before the banks intervened.

We may summarize the main points of the analysis as follows:

(1) The costs of borrowing make the borrower's short and long rates higher than the corresponding lender's rates.

(2) The costs of shifting tend to make the lender's long rate somewhat higher than the lender's short rate. There can be no doubt that the costs of shifting alone prevent people with relatively short funds from investing in bonds, and induce them to leave their funds on deposit with a bank where they receive either no interest at all or else a much lower rate than they would receive in the long market.

(3) Within each market the lenders obtain a net rate which is the higher the longer the time for which they have their funds available.

(4) The costs of borrowing make for a higher borrower's short rate than long rate. The costs of shifting for the lender, although they make for a higher long rate than short rate, are not likely to be sufficient to raise the borrower's long rate to equality with, or above, the borrower's short rate. It is not possible to prove this accurately by reference to the facts. For the difference between the rates on bank loans and the long-term rate (say on bonds) is not only dependent on the cost factor, but is also influenced by expectations as to the future course of interest rates. However, it seems safe to say that in "quiet" times, when there is no particular reason for the market to expect changes in interest rates, the customer's rates charged by the banks are considerably above high-grade bond yields,[9] even if we add to these latter a percentage figure expressing the per annum costs of borrowing through the bond market.

III

In this section uncertainty and risk will be introduced, i.e. we shall assume that the future movement of interest rates is unknown, but that people have certain expectations about their movement. Risk of default, however, will be excluded from the discussion; the only risk considered will be that associated with changes in interest rates.

In order to investigate the influence of this risk factor, we shall here analyze the case where all members of the market believe it most likely (i.e. expect) that the interest rate will remain what it is and that the chance of a rise and the chance of a fall are even.

---

[9] Cf. W. W. Riefler, op. cit., p. 67. The chart given there, which shows that the yield on the average high-grade bond was from 1919 to 1928 (with the exception of a few months in 1924) below the average of the rates charged to customers by banks in the larger cities, is not an unimpeachable proof, since the credit risk of the two series may be different. However, the spread seems to be wide enough to warrant our conclusion that the borrower's short rate is higher than the borrower's long rate.

This assumption allows us to isolate the influence of the risk factor, because it excludes discrepancies between the rates which are due solely to the fact that the members of the market *expect* the interest rate to rise or to fall.

How, then, does the risk factor influence the equilibrium relationship between the rates on various maturities? This question has been given two conflicting answers in the literature. Williams,[10] for instance, believes that long and short rates will be equal under these conditions. Hicks[11] thinks that the long rate will be above the short.

Suppose that we have maturities for all the various lengths of time for which different investors think they have their funds available, and suppose further that in the "original distribution" the rates are higher the longer the maturities. Those who move into the latter have a chance that the return on their investment, $\frac{\text{nominal rate} + \text{capital gain or} - \text{capital loss}}{\text{purchase price}}$, may be above what they can obtain in their "original" markets for the same period, but they also run the risk that the return may be below that figure. Consequently, if the attitude of the marginal shifter into the longer market is such that he weights the unfavorable chance more heavily than the favorable one, or in other words that he demands a certain compensation for the risk of disappointment, he will not be satisfied with a rate in the longer market which is above the rate in his own market simply by the cost of shifting. It follows that in equilibrium we shall have a scale of rates which ascends with the length of the maturities more steeply than would be the case if we had the cost of shifting alone to consider. A detailed analysis of what determines the gaps between the yields on different maturities would have to follow the lines of the argument developed in section II, which may be applied to the effect of the risk premium just as well as to the effect of the costs of shifting.

The result just arrived at is, however, entirely dependent on our assumption about the "original distribution." The essence of

[10] J. B. Williams, op. cit., p. 341.
[11] J. R. Hicks, op. cit., p. 166.

the matter is that an investor may ask for a risk premium whenever he moves out of his "original" market, no matter whether he moves into a shorter or longer market, because in either case the return which he will obtain in the market to which he moves is uncertain. Therefore, if we assume an "original distribution" in which the scale of rates descends, or has ups-and-downs, as we pass from the shorter to the longer maturities, we obtain entirely different results. It is not legitimate, therefore, to conclude (with Hicks) that the effect of the risk factor, as such, must necessarily be to make long rates higher than shorter ones. On the other hand, the view (of Williams) that the risk factor will be without effect on the relationship between the rates is correct only provided the investors do not weight the chance of a loss more heavily than the equal chance of a gain.[12]

IV

In section I we laid down certain propositions as to the relationship between interest rates on various maturities under the assumption of complete foresight. If we were content to speak, as is customary, in the vague terms of "expectations of the market," we should now only have to replace the word "foreseen" by the word "expected," and could then repeat the propositions of section I amplified by the application of what has been said on the influence of the cost and the risk factors. However, this would be correct only if it could be assumed that all members of the market have identical expectations. Only then would it make sense to look upon the long rate as being fundamentally the average of the expected future short rates. We know, however, that the different members of the market seldom have identical expectations, and it is the analysis of this aspect to which we shall now turn.

It will be helpful, in the first instance, to set out the method

---

[12] In the analysis in the text we made two unrealistic assumptions, (1) that everybody knows exactly for how long he has his funds available and (2) that there are maturities for all the different lengths of time for which investors think they can invest. However, the main conclusions would not be materially altered, if we dropped these two assumptions.

which a rational investor would have to follow in deciding in which market (short or long) it pays for him to invest. For the time being we assume that there are only two maturities.) An owner of funds will go into the long market if he thinks the return he can make there over the time for which he has his funds available will be above the return he can make in the short market over the same time, and *vice versa*. His estimate of the relative profitability of the two markets will be based on his expectations[13] about future interest rates and bond prices, and will be reflected in the price he is willing to pay for the long-term bond at the present moment. In the simplest case he will determine this price by the following method. He will discount the price at which he expects to sell the bond at the date when he wants to disinvest (this price is dependent on what he anticipates the long rate will be at that date) and all the interest payments up to that time, back to the present moment, using as the discount factor for each year the short rate which he expects to prevail in that year. This procedure gives him a bond valuation which he will compare with the existing bond price in the market. If the latter is higher than the former, he will invest in the short market instead of buying the bond, since this relationship indicates that he can make more in the short market than in the long. If the bond price in the market is lower than his "subjective" bond price, he will invest long. If the two prices are identical he will be indifferent as between the long and short markets, since he expects to make the same in both.[14] In short, he is prepared to pay a price for the bond which is equal to or lower than the price obtained by discounting all the future payments in the fashion described above.

This, however, is not the end of the matter. The fact that

---

[13] In the remainder of the discussion I shall, for brevity's sake, use the expression "expected" interest rate or bond price to denote the rate or price which the person uses in making his calculation. It thus reflects the result both of the probability estimate and of the risk premium.

[14] Since it is possible for a person to adopt a different attitude towards risk with respect to different portions of his funds, it may be that an investor will invest part of his funds in the short market and part in the long.

the discounting procedure just described may give the individual investor a "subjective" bond valuation which diverges from the current price in the market implies that the current long rate does not necessarily reflect the future short rates which that investor expects.   Similarly, his expectations as to the future long rates need not be consistent with his expectations as to the future short rates.   In Section I, where we assumed accurate forecasting for everybody concerned, there was no need to distinguish between the two, since the course of long rates was automatically determined, once we assumed the course of future short rates to be definitely known.   In the present case, however, an investor's personal expectations about the future course of short rates do not necessarily commit him as to his expectations about the long rate, since the latter depends, not on what *he* thinks about the future short rates, but what the "market," i.e. other people, think about them.   The individual investor, therefore, may quite reasonably form an opinion about the future long rate which is inconsistent with his opinion about future short rates.   From this it follows that an investor, if he discounts, as above, the bond price expected at the end of his entire investment period plus the interest payments up to that time, and obtains a "subjective" bond value which is below (or above) the current bond price, will not necessarily go into the short market (or the long market) now.

There are two main possibilities.   First, he may expect that at some intermediate date the yield on the bond (to his personal disinvestment date) will fall below the average of the short rates which he expects to prevail from this intermediate date to the date of his final disinvestment.   This means that he expects the bond price to be relatively *high* at the intermediate date.   If the bond valuation obtained by discounting *this* price, along with the interest payments, exceeds the current bond price in the market, he will go into the long market now (with the intention of shifting into the short market later).   If it is below, he will of course go into the short market from the start.

The second possibility is that the investor may expect the yield on the bond at some intermediate date to exceed the average of the short rates from that date onwards, i.e. he expects the market price of the bond to be relatively *low* at that date.   He will then contemplate going into the short market now and into the long market later.   There will, however, be some price at which it will be worth his while to go into the long market now instead of waiting. In order to calculate this price, he will discount the expected price at the contemplated buying date along with the interest payments up to that date, back to the present moment.   If he were to buy the bond now at this price, he would make just as much as if he went into the short market first and waited till later before buying the bond.   If the current bond price is below this "subjective" bond value, it will pay him to go into the long market now; if it is above, he will invest short now, and go into the long market later.

So we see that for any pattern[15] of expectations the investor arrives at a "subjective" bond value which constitutes the maximum price which he is prepared to bid for the bond in the market. We can now proceed to our main task: the analysis of the effect of differences in expectations among the different members of the market.

(1) We may suppose that, following a situation in which there has been equality between the long and short rates, the expectations of most of the owners of funds change in the direction of *rising* interest rates.   *They change in different degrees for different persons.* On the basis of the analysis given above, all those who expect such a rise will arrive at "subjective" bond values which are below the current price in the market.   We may range the owners of funds in order of the bond prices which they are willing to pay, or, what is the same thing, in order of the yields to redemption (or long rates) which these "subjective" bond prices imply.   All those who now demand "subjective" long rates which are higher than the current long rate in the market will prefer to invest in the short market,

---

[15] More complicated cases such as going into the long market now, getting out later, and going in again still later, etc., can be treated by the same method. They are, however, of minor importance in practice, since investors hardly ever have sufficiently definite ideas to allow them to plan such complicated investment schemes.

their inducement to do so being the greater the wider the gap between their "subjective" long rate and the actual long rate. This will lead to an increase in the volume of funds offered in the short market and a decrease in the volume offered in the long market, as compared with the situation from which we started. The effect will be to lower the short rate and to raise the long, the degree of the movement depending on the elasticities of demand for short and long funds. The rise in the long rate will tend to check the movement from the long into the short market, since the higher long rate will now exceed the "subjective" rates of some investors, thus wiping out their preference for the short market. The long rate will rise until two conditions are fulfilled: (a) the supply of and demand for funds in each market are equal, and (b) all owners of funds whose "subjective" long rates are higher than the current long rate are in the short market. One amendment, however, must be made to the foregoing exposition. We must suppose that the adjustment of the long and short rates in the process of shifting funds from the long into the short market will cause some slight revision of the "subjective" long rates for two reasons: (a) because the current short rate, which is one of the discount factors entering into the calculation of the "subjective" long rates, goes down, thus lowering the "subjective" long rates; and (b) because the expectations about the course of future short (and long) rates are likely to be affected. In which direction this second factor will work we cannot say a priori, and consequently we cannot make any definite statement about the direction in which the "subjective" long rates will be affected by the two factors combined.

The following diagram illustrates the way in which the new equilibrium is reached after expectations have changed. ON is the total volume of funds (assumed fixed) which is available for investment in both markets together. $D^L D^L$ is the demand curve for long funds and $D^s D^s$ (drawn with N as the origin) is the demand curve for short funds. Then in the initial situation, before expectations change, the long rate and short rate are both equal to OB, and OL is invested in the long market and NL in the short. AA is what we shall call the "expectations" curve: it represents the line-up of the "subjective" long rates which correspond to people's expectations after the latter have changed. Now assuming that this curve remains unaltered throughout the process of adjustment, we see that equilibrium will be reëstablished with the long rate OB', the short rate OC', OM invested in the long market, and NM in the short market. And the spread between the long and short rates will have increased from zero to $C'B'$. However, we must suppose

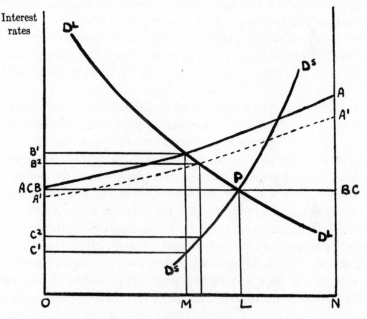

FIG. 1. Volume of funds.

that while the change in the rates is taking place, AA will tend to shift, and the final equilibrium position will give a spread between the rates which is slightly smaller or slightly larger (according to whether the expectations curve shifts to the right or to the left) than that arrived at on the basis of the original expectations curve.[16]

---

[16] The position of the expectations curve corresponding to the rate OC' and OB' would, let us suppose, be $A'A'$. But this curve would again give different interest rates OC^2 and OB^2, and the latter would in turn react back on the expec-

The analysis above shows that the final spread between the two rates will depend on two sets of factors. (1) The more elastic are the demand curves for short and long funds over the relevant range the smaller will be the spread. (2) Broadly speaking, the greater the number of investors (weighted by the volume of their funds) who have high "subjective" long rates, and the higher these rates are, the more funds will be invested in the short market and the greater will be the final spread. More accurately, the spread depends on (a) the shape of the expectations curve (the steeper the curve over the relevant range the greater the spread), and (b) the direction in which and the degree to which this curve shifts in response to changing long and short rates during the process of adjustment.[17]

I can do no more than briefly indicate the results that are obtained if we assume the existence of more than two maturities. An investor will calculate a "subjective" value, on the basis of his expectations, for each of the various maturities, and if he expects a rise in interest rates he will obtain a higher value the shorter the maturity. This will give the result that if most investors expect rising interest rates in the future, the rates on those maturities of which the redemption date lies within the period during which the rising interest rates are expected will ascend with the length of the maturities. In equilibrium all those owners of funds who expect the rates to rise soon and/or to a large extent will have their funds in the shorter maturities, and all those who expect the rates to rise

---

tations curve. All that we can say, then, is that in equilibrium the long rate will be somewhere between OB' and OB^2 and the short rate somewhere between OC' and OC^2.

[17] We have not taken into account the possibility that the borrowers also may shift according to their expectations about future interest rates. However, there is not likely to be much shifting on the borrowers' side in the situation analysed in the text. The borrowers, unless they have opposite ideas from the lenders about the future of interest rates, have no reason to shift. Those who want funds for long-term purposes will, of course, have an additional incentive to borrow in the long market, if they think that the long rate is going to rise. Those, on the other hand, who want short-term funds are not likely to borrow long, no matter what they think about the future rates.

later and/or to a smaller extent will have them in the longer maturities.[18]

(2) There is no need to give a detailed analysis of the case where "the market" expects interest rates to fall. The same sort of analysis could be applied as was used in case (1). In terms of the diagram on page 517 we should have an expectations curve which lay below *BB* over most of its length. With such a state of expectations we obtain a scale of interest rates which descends with the increasing length of the maturities. But two additional remarks are called for. First, borrowers may shift from long to short borrowing, if they too expect a fall in the interest rates. This will tend to accentuate the discrepancy between the short and the long rates which is brought about by the behavior of the lenders. Secondly, it seems likely that the short rate cannot remain above the long for such a lengthy period as the long rate can remain above the short. The reason is that in this case banks will feel more inclined to shift from the long to the short market, because the higher yield will here be combined with compliance with the traditional views about the greater liquidity of short-term paper, whereas the shift from the short to the long market contravenes the liquidity rule.[19]

---

[18] A closer analysis, which is too lengthy to be undertaken here, would also have to take account of the volume of the securities outstanding (or the demand for funds) under each of the various maturities, since this factor will influence the size of the spread between the rates on those maturities.

[19] In more general terms this means that, in addition to costs and uncertainty, certain institutional factors also influence the structure of interest rates. American banks look upon Government bonds and notes with maturities up to five years as eligible for holding in their "secondary reserve." This creates a strong demand for such bonds, and we may presume that this factor by itself makes for lower interest rates on investments with maturities up to five years than on those with longer maturities. (Compare the yields for 1938 on the chart on page 523, where a wide gap is observable between the yield on the five-year maturity and the yield on the next longer maturity.) English banks aim at keeping a certain relatively fixed percentage of their assets (the thirty per cent ratio) in the form of cash and short material. There is therefore a relatively fixed supply of funds whose owners are not prepared to shift them into the long market, even if the rate there is higher. This makes it possible for the Treasury to cause the short rate to fall

(3) The diagram can also be used to show that we may obtain *equal* interest rates, not only if *all* members of the market expect the interest rate to remain stable[20] (I am here neglecting the cost factor), but also if different members have different expectations, provided the distribution of the latter is such as to give an "expectations curve" which goes through the point P in the diagram— an unlikely coincidence.

V

In this section we shall try to verify some of the propositions of Section I as amplified by what has been said in Sections II, III and IV. In order to simplify the terminology, we shall talk in terms of the "expectations of the market." The reader will be aware, from the analysis of Section IV, of the complicated relationships that are hidden behind this term.

(1) We turn first to the *movement* of the interest rates over time. Although the fact that different people in the market hold different opinions about the course of the rates that may be expected to prevail in the future means that there is no precise sense in which we can call the long rate an average of the expected future short rates, it remains nevertheless true that the long rate (or bond yield) is, in the complicated way described in Section IV, the outcome of the whole pattern of expectations of the members of the market as to

---

below the long rate, simply by curtailing the issue of treasury bills. This discrepancy will last as long as the shortage of treasury bills continues, and it is one which cannot be explained in terms of expectations. Furthermore, within each category of short material, the banks, for a variety of institutional reasons, look upon shorter maturities as being more liquid than longer ones. For this reason three-months bills are preferred to six-months bills in the commercial paper and the bankers' acceptances markets, and call loans to time loans to the stock exchange. The result is that the rates are slightly lower on the shorter maturities than on the longer maturities within the same category of short loans. To this rule there are only very rare exceptions. Apparently only if it is practically certain that the rate on the shorter maturities is going to fall (for instance, if bankers are sure that the official discount rate is going to be lowered) will the rate on the longer term bills be below the rate on the shorter term ones (as in England in December, 1929).

[20] Cf. p. 502.

the future short rates during the time the bond has to run. This still gives the result that the long rate cannot fluctuate as widely as the short rate. That the long rate is in practice more stable than the short rate is such a familiar fact as to require no statistical proof.

The long rate can move temporarily contrariwise to the short rate. The long rate may fall while the short rate rises, provided "the market" thinks future short rates will be below the short rate from which the rise starts, and *vice versa*. Considering that "the market" does not form any very definite idea about future short rates which are still a long time ahead, we should not expect this to happen very often. Indeed, as a rule, the long rate is either entirely unaffected by changes in the short rate or else it moves very slightly in the same direction as the latter. A contrary movement of short and long rates is most likely to be found in connection with seasonal fluctuations of the short rate. The market knows that these are temporary, and if, for instance, a seasonal rise in the short rate impinges on a situation in which the general tendency is expected to be a fall in the rates, we may obtain such a contrary movement. This situation seems to have prevailed in the latter half of 1930 in London, when the market rate on three-months bank bills rose from 2.07 per cent in September to 2.18 per cent in November, while during the same time the yield on 2½ per cent Consols fell from 4.52 per cent to 4.27 per cent.[21] Since it was in the early phase of the depression, a general fall in the rates could reasonably be expected, despite the seasonal rise in the short market. Other instances of the same kind can be found.

(2) We turn now to the structure of yields on different maturities at a given date. If nobody concerned has any reason to believe that the future short rates will be higher or lower than the present rates, we shall obtain approximately[22] equal yields for different maturities. Such a situation is likely to occur at a time when busi-

---

[21] The figures cited are the monthly averages.

[22] The risk and cost factors make, as we saw previously, for rates which ascend slightly with the increasing length of the maturity. However, the differences due to these factors are probably so slight in practice that they will always be overshadowed by the expectations factor.

ness is good without, however, showing any sign of a boom. This was approximately the state of affairs in 1927. The chart on p. 523 shows that in May of that year Government bonds and notes, which for purposes of comparison have the advantage of being without default risk, show about the same yields for different maturities.[23] (There seems to be a slight tendency towards lower yields for longer maturities.) Not all yields are exactly in line. There are several reasons for this. First, Government bonds and notes are not all treated alike with respect to tax exemption.[24] Secondly, the impression gained from studying the material is that the "arbitrage" in the bond market does not work as perfectly as it does, for instance, in the foreign exchange market, so that a yield may be out of line for this reason alone.[25] Thirdly, the fact that it is not known for certain that the bond will be redeemed either at the first optional call date or else at the final maturity date (it may be redeemed at some date in between) may account for some irregularities. (Cf. footnote 26 below). But despite the influence of these factors the figures for the date we have chosen in 1927 (as depicted in the chart) are very nearly on the same level.

We shall have a line of yields descending continuously with maturities of increasing lengths and then flattening out, if the short rates are expected to fall in the near future and then to reach a certain level where they will stay. Such a situation is likely to prevail in a financial crisis at the top of a boom, or what is believed

---

[23] In conformity with the generally accepted practice, the yields are calculated to maturity, if the bonds are selling below par, and to the earliest optional call date, if they are selling above par.

[24] For instance, the First Liberty Loan 3½ per cent redeemable 1932–47 shows a yield to the call date 1932 (against which year it is plotted in the chart) of 3.3 per cent, which is below the yields on the other securities redeemable at the same time. This can be explained by reference to the fact that this bond is exempt from all surtax, whereas the others are only partially exempt.

[25] The high yield (3.8 per cent) on the Second Liberty Loan 4 per cent 1927–42 (calculated to the call date and plotted against the year 1927 in the chart) is difficult to explain, considering the fact that the Second Liberty Loan Converted 4¼ per cent 1927–42 with exactly the same tax features has a yield of only 3.4 per cent.

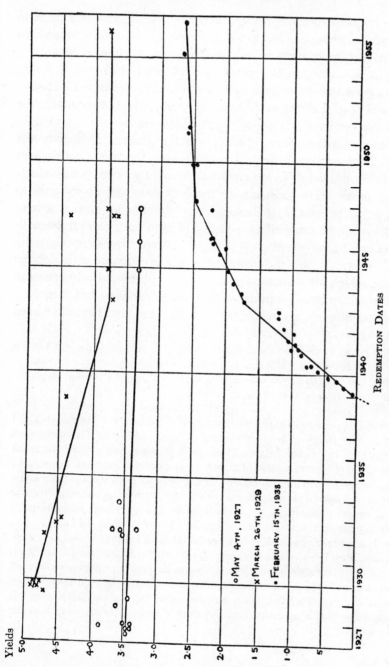

Fig. 2.   Yields on United States government bonds and notes.

to be the top of a boom. On March 26, 1929, there was a crash on the stock exchange. For this date we obtain an almost continuous downward movement in the yields for maturities of increasing lengths, as can again be seen in the chart on p. 523.[26]

In recent years we have had a situation where future short rates (as well as long rates) were expected to rise, which accounts for the fact that we have a series of yields which ascends with the length of the maturities. This is shown in the chart, which gives the yields for Government securities of various maturities on February 15, 1938. Any date in the last seven or eight years gives a similarly rising series. The existence of these expectations at the present time is not proved by this ascending scale of yields alone. Direct evidence to the same effect is to be found in the financial journals, which are full of warnings that present interest rates are unusually low. There is also the evidence of the investment policy of the banks, which are reluctant to invest any substantial proportion of their assets in bonds with distant maturities for fear of a fall in their value resulting from rising interest rates. Finally, there have been

---

[26] A glance at the chart shows that one yield (plotted against the year 1947) is very much out of line. It is the yield on the First Liberty Loan Converted 4¼ per cent bond, call date 1932 and maturity date 1947, which has a yield to maturity of 4.4 per cent, whereas other bonds (plotted against the same year) have a yield of around 3.8 per cent. As this irregularity persisted in the following weeks, it cannot be due merely to imperfect adjustment of the market. The real reason, I think, is this: the bond in question stood at 98⅔₂, and its yield is consequently calculated to the maturity date. However, it is clearly indicated by the whole curve of the yields on securities of different maturities that the market expected a fall in interest rates in the near future. It was therefore likely that the bond would be redeemed *before* 1947 (perhaps as early as 1932), since its price was likely to rise above par before that date. (Much the same is true for the Fourth Liberty Loan 4¼ per cent 1933–38, plotted against the year 1938 in the chart.) The other bonds whose yields are plotted against the same year 1947 (with the exception of the First Liberty Loan 3½ per cent, which is free from all surtax) are bonds which cannot be repaid before 1944 or 1946, so that the same argument does not apply to them. The rule according to which we calculate the yield to the maturity date, if the bond is selling below par, and to the first optional call date, if it is selling above par, is somewhat arbitrary, and in some cases obviously does not make sense.

numerous issues of serial bonds where the bonds which fall due later bear a higher coupon rate than those which fall due earlier.[27]

VI

The analysis of the relationship between long and short rates has a bearing on many problems, practical as well as theoretical. In the remainder of this article we can deal with only four of them.

(1) If it is true that only changes in the *long* rate affect investment, it seems to follow that the discount rate can only influence investment if the discount rate reacts on the long-term rate. Now one of the conclusions which can be drawn from the analysis in this article is that a change in the short rate will bring about a change in the long rate only if a general conviction is created that the short rate will remain low for a considerable time. Therefore the monetary authority has to create such a conviction,[28] if it wants to bring down the long-term rate and to induce more borrowing. Owing, however, to the fact that in the past, particularly under the gold standard, the discount rate was changed very often, partly with an eye to the external situation of the country, the public has become used to frequent changes in the short rate and is not inclined to believe that a low level of short rates is going to persist. This seems to imply that the discount rate should be altered as infrequently as possible. If this is not feasible, the central banks must try to influence the long rate directly, if they want to regulate investment.

(2) An entrepreneur who considers whether to borrow capital or not is said to compare the marginal efficiency of capital with

---

[27] Cases where the market expects the interest rates to rise first and then to fall later can also be found in the empirical material, but I must omit them here for lack of space. I have described the "curves" of the yields on different maturities for only a few selected dates. If we were to trace the movements of these curves continuously through time, they would reveal how quickly, and in response to what events, the expectations of investors change. Such an investigation would thus be a contribution towards obtaining empirical material about the behavior of expectations in a dynamic system. I hope to extend the investigation along these lines at a later date.

[28] Cf. Keynes, *General Theory*, p. 203.

the interest rate. Which interest rate? An entrepreneur who wants to finance long investment has to compare the existing long-term rate with the average of the expected future short-term rates (plus the costs of re-borrowing) or, if he expects the long rate to fall, with the average of the short rates for part of the time and the long rate for the rest of the time for which he wants to borrow. Whichever is the lower will be the one which he will set against the marginal efficiency of his capital or his expected profit rate.[29] As the different entrepreneurs will usually have different expectations, they will base their action with regard to investment on different rates. There is, therefore, no such thing as "the" interest rate which keeps "the" entrepreneurs from expanding, unless we assume very stable conditions in which there is no reason for any entrepreneur to think that the rates will change.

(3) A wide gap between short and long rates may exert a considerable influence on the amount of new borrowing that is undertaken. If the long rate is above the short, which implies an expectation that the long rate will rise, borrowers will try to borrow long in order to take advantage of the particularly low rate. The lenders, among them the banks, have an opposite interest: they prefer shorter maturities in this situation. It may therefore be difficult to float long-term securities. There are, however, several ways out of this difficulty. One way would be for the borrowers to shorten the maturities. Apparently for this reason, the British Treasury did float its Defence Loan of 1937 in the form of bonds with the comparatively short maturity of seven to ten years, and still more recently (January, 1940) a Conversion Loan has been announced with only three to five years to run.

The same problem exists, probably in even greater degree, with regard to flotations by corporations, and the difficulty may possibly be accentuated by the fact that the corporations have to make use of investment houses. The latter may be reluctant to float bond issues, either because they are afraid that the interest rate will have risen before they have sold the whole of the issue, or

---

[29] Cf. Breit, Ein Beitrag zur Theorie des Geld- und Kapitalmarktes, *Zeitschrift für Nationalökonomie*, 1935, p. 644.

because they are anxious to avoid disappointing important customers (e.g. institutional investors), who may suffer a loss because the interest rate rises after the bonds have been sold to them. Here again a shortening of the maturities would facilitate borrowing operations. However, in view of the high costs of borrowing, corporations cannot adopt this procedure so easily as a government can.[30] Corporations have therefore sometimes used different methods to adapt their flotations to the situation where the interest rate is expected to rise.

First, as has been mentioned before, there have been many cases of serial issues where the bonds which fall due later bear higher interest rates than those which are due earlier. By issuing these serial maturities the corporation accommodates lenders who do not want to invest in long-term securities. At the same time it is enabled to take advantage, in some measure, of the low rates prevailing for shorter maturities, and to "spread" the costs of borrowing. Secondly, recourse can be had to the practice, so far not very common, of issuing securities with variable interest rates.[31] Such issues are made attractive to the lender by a rising nominal interest rate which will protect him against a loss (or at least reduce it), if and when the long rate in the market rises.

(4) The analysis of this article has shown that the relationship between interest rates on different maturities is determined in the

---

[30] Before the last war, particularly in the nineteenth century, governments and corporations sometimes floated perpetual bonds or bonds with maturities of a hundred years or longer. Nowadays a government or corporation would hardly issue such bonds. This is no doubt the effect of the increase in uncertainty about future economic developments (including the course of interest rates). Such an increase in uncertainty necessarily makes perpetual bonds, and bonds with very long maturities, unpopular with the investor. The shortening of the maturities is a method by which the capitalistic system adapts itself to the condition of greater uncertainty which has prevailed since the last war.

[31] For instance, R. H. White Co. of Boston recently executed a note for 1.5 million dollars, payable in twenty years, to the Prudential Insurance Co., for which the interest rate was as follows: 4 per cent for the first ten years, $4\frac{1}{4}$ per cent for the next five years, and $4\frac{1}{2}$ per cent for the last five years. (Commercial and Financial Chronicle, Monthly Bank and Quotation Record, March, 1939.)

main by the expectations as to the future course of interest rates. According to the "liquidity theory of interest," it is the degree of liquidity of securities with different maturities which determines this relationship. The most liquid asset, money, does not bear interest. Securities, being less liquid than money, bear an interest rate which is the higher the longer the maturity, since the danger of a capital loss due to a change in the interest rate in the market is supposed to be the greater (and therefore liquidity the smaller) the longer the security has to run. We know, however, that the short-term rate can be *above* the long-term rate, a fact which does not seem to fit in very well with the liquidity theory of interest. It is not possible to get out of this difficulty by calling a situation in which the short rate is above the long an exception, and ascribing it to the "technical conditions of the market" in times of financial crisis. The short rate is too frequently above the long, and often stays above it for too long a time, to warrant such a statement. In London, for instance, the short rate was above the long rate for nineteen months from the end of 1919 to the middle of 1921, and for eleven months in 1929. Before the War of 1914–1918 there are apparently[32] times where the short rate was above the long rate for even longer periods, and the long rate cannot be said to have shown a tendency to stay more often and for longer periods above the short rate than the short rate above the long.

---

[32] The Research Department of the London School of Economics has collected material on short and long rates in London, back to the year 1825. However, in this material the short rate is represented for the period before the War of 1914–1918 only by the rate on the first Friday in the month, whereas the long-term rate is the monthly average of the daily yields on Consols. The reader has to keep this in mind in appraising the following statistics. (In order to reduce the error I have eliminated from the series those months in which the two rates are relatively near to each other.) Between 1825 and 1938 the long rate was above the short in 764 months, whereas the short was above the long in 580 months. If we deduct from the first figure the months of the last years (which have no counterpart in previous times), the long rate was above the short in 677 months. The 580 months can in either case hardly be called an exception. The longest time for which the short rate was without interruption above the long is 42 months, and periods of more than 20 months are not infrequent. If we again exclude the

If we can bring ourselves to adopt a rather unusual yet logical definition of the term liquidity, we can still say, in spite of these facts, that the degree of liquidity determines the relationship between the rates on different maturities.   One asset is said to be less liquid than another because the danger of a loss seems to be greater in case it is sold.   Now if the owner of an asset thinks that he has a good chance of making a gain when he sells it, it seems to be logical to attribute a particularly high degree of liquidity to this asset.   In times, therefore, when an investor expects the interest rate to fall, we should have to say that he regards securities with longer maturities as more liquid than those with shorter maturities, and is consequently prepared to take a lower rate on the long ones than on the short.   Provided we adopt this terminology, we can say that the degree of liquidity of securities of different maturities, as understood by the marginal lenders in the different markets, determines (together with the cost factor) the relationship between the interest rates.[33]

---

current period, we find that the longest time over which the long rate was above the short was 44 months.

[33] However, money then falls out of line.   For, as far as its degree of liquidity is concerned, it would range below securities which give a chance of a capital gain; all the same, the latter bear interest whereas money does not.

PROFIT

27

PROFIT*

By FRANK H. KNIGHT†

Perhaps no term or concept in economic discussion is used with a more bewildering variety of well established meanings than profit. In popular economic usage it is generally associated loosely with either a percentage return on turnover—a "mark-up" of merchandise—or a percentage rate of return on capital. Again, it may mean a gross or a net profit and there are many possible stages between an immediate gross return and an ultimate net return, whether computed on the outlay in a particular transaction or on an investment supposed to be continuously maintained. The question as to what deductions must be made from gross profit to arrive at net profit has so many and such highly controversial answers that the tendency in accounting practise has been to abandon the term profit and to use such expressions as operating revenue or income available for dividends, which if not much less ambiguous in themselves are more amenable to definition according to purpose.

The point most in controversy in this connection leads directly into the theory of profit as regards its relation to other forms of income. The question is whether funds borrowed at a contractual rate, and the interest on them, should be included in calculating the rate of profit or kept entirely separate. This ties up with the question whether profit is properly a return on capital at all, and hence with the general problem of distribution: what are the kinds of income to be recognized and what is the base with which each kind is associated.

* *Encyclopaedia of the Social Sciences*, Volume XII, 1934, pages 480–486, Reprinted by courtesy of The Macmillan Co. and the author.
† University of Chicago.

Modern distribution theory developed out of the treatment of the subject by the classical economists, who viewed the problem as one of the division of the social income among the three socio-economic classes—landlords, laborers and business men or the moneyed class. The share of this last group was called profit. The process of division as they envisaged it took place in two stages: there was first a separation between rent and a kind of gross income of the capitalist, as the business man was then more or less correctly called; subsequently the latter fund was divided between the capitalist and the laboring classes. Wages were supposed to be determined independently, the final share of the capitalist being left as a residuum. The most important commentary on this classical scheme of distribution is the negative statement that it failed completely to "implement" the process of distribution through any discussion of the actual workings of competitive (or monopolistic) principles of price fixing. Fruitful treatment of the distribution problem as a problem in the pricing of productive services, in exchange for which individuals receive their incomes in a competitive economic society, came about gradually as a result of the new treatment of value introduced by the utility theorists.

The classical economists, from Adam Smith onward, had recognized interest as a form of income more or less distinct from profit. Its place in their scheme, however, was quite subordinate. This was in line with the facts of the economic situation in their day, when capital was typically employed in business by its owner, lending at interest for productive purposes being relatively unimportant. In particular the limited liability company, which is the chief borrower at interest in the modern business world, had achieved little development and was assumed to have no large possibilities for the future. All the classical writers recognized at least three elements in the income of the capitalist entrepreneur: one a payment for the bare use of the capital (equal to the interest rate); a second element representing payment for the entrepreneur's activities as manager, and a third connected in a rather vague way with the carrying of the risks or hazards of the enterprise. This distinction was made in an especially clear fashion by J. S. Mill,

who called the second element earnings of management. Mill
did not discuss any possibility of separating the three elements and
continued to use the term profit for the total income of the capitalist
entrepreneur. In contrast with the English school, the expositors
of the classical system in France, beginning with J. B. Say, insisted
from the start on a separation between profit and interest and the
treatment of profit as a species of wage. As early as 1852 a French
writer, Courcelle-Seneuil, advocated treating profit not as a wage
but as due to the assumption of risk.

The view more generally accepted at the present time, particularly among American economists, that profit is a unique form of
income not reducible to remuneration for either capital or labor
of any kind, was early developed by German writers. As early
as 1826, Thünen (*Der isolierte Staat*, Hamburg) defined profit as the
residue after deduction of all three payments, interest, insurance
for risk, and wages of management. An elaborate analysis of
profit was made by H. von Mangoldt in 1855 (*Die Lehre vom Unternehmergewinn*, Leipsic), recognizing the elements of payment for
wages of management and for risk in actual profits, but defining
profit as a surplus above all costs. But the idea of "pure" profit,
as an excess in the income of a business as a whole in comparison
with the income of the productive factors used in it, really worked
its way into economic thought as a result of the efforts of John
Bates Clark.

The classical writers had included several divergent elements
in the concept of profits and had drawn a very loose and questionable distinction between land and capital—in spite of the important
role which rent played in their scheme of distribution. Marx and
later socialists, in taking over and developing the classical economics, seemed justified in dropping this distinction; by merging
land with capital they obtained a concept of profit as including all
non-labor income. Another impulse in this direction was the view,
also abundantly represented in the orthodox economists, that labor
is the real producer of all wealth and all other income a deduction
from what is naturally the remuneration of the laborer. Thus
the socialistic view of profit is one of labor exploitation.

The labor theories of value and of production rest in the first place on a confusion between ethical and economic or scientific explanatory principles. It is obvious that no identification of labor income with ethical income and other incomes with unethical income can be defended; all income represents a mixture of a more or less accurate evaluation of services in the broad sense with force and fraud. Since violence and fraud belong to the sphere of criminology, economic analysis of profit must center around the notion of a more or less accurate evaluation of services. In the perfectly competitive relations of abstract price theory, all services are assumed to be valued correctly and precisely. Under these conditions the entire produce in the form of income would be divided exactly among the various claimants—workers of various sorts and owners of property of various sorts, including the different equities in and claims against tangible property created by financial relationships and ownership of monopoly privileges, such as patents and goodwill. If all payments for personal services are called wages, and all property services are paid for in the primary or natural form of rent, as understood in the business world, only these two forms of income will exist. Interest and rent are differentiated only by the form of equity which the recipient holds in the same concrete source of income and can therefore in such theory be identified. In the idealized society of equilibrium theory, there would be no occasion for assigning the distinctive name of profit to any type of return.

In actual society, however, there is still a third type of ownership besides those involving interest and rent claims—that of the entrepreneur who owns the enterprise itself as distinguished from the productive agencies employed in it. As the classical economists held, profit as a distinct type of income is, to begin with and roughly speaking, the income of the owner of the business. This may include elements due to personal and property services. Even superficially the situation is complicated by the fact that under modern conditions the owner is typically a corporation, and the ownership of the corporation itself is commonly divided up among several forms of equity. Moreover the corporate entrepreneur typically owns outright some of the property used in the enterprise, hires or leases other property for a rental and borrows at interest against part of the assets which it owns directly. As in the case of most general concepts, the definition of profit might run toward either of two extremes. It might strive for the closest possible conformity to empirical fact and general usage or for rigorous differentiation of a theoretically distinct form of income. In a general way the use of the term in British economic literature follows the first of these leads; thus Marshall treats of "profits of capital and business power." In the United States usage in the literature of economic theory has tended toward the other pole: it is a common practise among economists to use the expression pure profit and make it refer to the income of the business after deduction of wages and rent or interest at competitive rates for all the human and property services employed in the enterprise, including both those actually paid for in the market and a virtual wage or interest or rent for the services furnished by the owner himself.

If this second procedure is followed through to its logical end, the result is a definition of profit as the difference between any income as it actually is and what it would be in the theoretical position of general equilibrium of the economic system as a whole. In the case of the owner of the business this difference is the entire income, since under perfect equilibrium the owner as such would have no functions and receive no income. It is evident that in this highly theoretical sense every income, with accidental exceptions, contains an element of profit. This element may be positive or negative in any case. In no case is it possible to determine objectively and accurately the amount of the profit element in an income, since this would involve an accurate determination of every detail of the position of equilibrium corresponding to the given conditions of the society at the given moment.

A compromise position between the realistic and the theoretical extremes starts out from the distinction between contractual and non-contractual income; that is, between the payment for services on a pecuniary basis arranged in advance and the residual income left to the owner of the business after all such payments are made. If the business is a private enterprise, in contrast with a corporation, this residuum will be recognized as containing elements of both interest and wages, since the owner will usually employ both property and labor of his own in the activity. If the enterprise is a corporation, the owners (common stockholders) do not normally furnish an appreciable amount of personal service unless they are also definitely employed by the corporation at a stipulated remuneration. Consequently the wages of management element hardly enters into the profit of a corporation. It must be recognized, however, that the stipulated remuneration or wages of management of corporation officials, whether stockholders or not, is at best most inaccurately adjusted by market competition to the true value of the service rendered, and hence is likely to be largely profit in the analytical sense. Notoriously too officials' salaries in many actual cases represent in large measure a distribution of the revenue alternative in form to stockholders' dividends; the difference is a matter of internal politics of corporations rather than of economic theory. Thus the compromise position is like the realistic, but with recognition of a need for further analysis which can be carried through only in the form of rough estimates.

Either theory, and any theory which recognizes profit as a distinct income at all, must oppose it to all other income, grouped together in a common relationship to profit; profit is either residual income as against contractual payments or a theoretical difference between actual income and the hypothetical level corresponding to general economic equilibrium. In both views the theoretical explanation of profit is the same, if the possibility of a theoretical explanation of any income is admitted. It is of course possible, verbally at least, to deny the relevance of all analysis in terms of price forces and their tendencies and to hold that only a historical explanation in terms of all the conditions at work at any time and place has relevance. It is doubtful, however, whether any writers securing recognition by economists really mean to deny all meaning to statements regarding general conditions which set limits somewhere to fixation of economic magnitudes by more particular, special and accidental circumstances. A sweeping denial of the validity of price mechanics would imply denial of the existence of profit in a theoretical sense, because a divergence between actual costs and prices and theoretical costs and prices would be denied; profit would then have to be defined empirically as the income of the enterprise after costs actually incurred have been met, which is a form of the residual conception of profit.

A theory of profit is inherently a theory of aberrations of actual economic conditions from the theoretical consequences or tendencies of the more general price forces which tend to eliminate them, a theory of the imperfections of competition, supplementary to the theory of perfect competition, defined in a sense which excludes profit. As the conception of perfect competition is admittedly somewhat arbitrary (as well as actually questioned with regard to its usefulness), a brief sketch of profit theory itself may begin with elimination by definition of certain boundary issues. The most important of these are included in the concept of monopoly, which should certainly be dealt with separately under such a caption as monopoly revenue or monopoly income, although economic as well as business usage often calls this profit. The concept of monopoly is here to be taken in the broadest sense, including income from patents, franchises, goodwill and every such source legally recognized as property.

Attempts to present a theory of profit thus restricted in meaning have taken two main directions. The first centers in the effort to identify a peculiar form of service of which profit is the remuneration, a service which can be rendered only by the owner of an enterprise and cannot be paid for in the form of a wage or salary. Since the ordinary managerial activities are in fact frequently hired on a salary basis, there is left the service of "risk bearing" as the basis for such a theory. But again many of the risks of business are familiarly covered, at least in part, by insurance or other organization devices involving the insurance principle, reducing risk by grouping of cases or by applying the law of large numbers. Consequently this line of theory was early forced to specify a peculiar form of uninsurable risk. F. B. Hawley has been perhaps the best known proponent of such a theory in the United States. Among European economists, the importance of the element of risk bearing was recognized by von Mangoldt and later by Mithoff and Diehl among others; more recently a theory of uninsurable risk has been developed by del Vecchio. Discussion of the risk theory, notably by J. B. Clark and his followers, brought about recognition of the fact that the business manager not merely bears risk but estimates risks and selects those to be borne. In fact every detail of business policy both involves the selection and rejection of risks and vitally affects the amount of the risk itself. Thus the risk theory tends to revert to an examination of the functions of management and the nature of business ability, a problem which clearly ties up at the same time with the nature of the risks which cannot be insured and with that of the activities which no one can be hired to perform for anyone else. The conception of profit as remuneration for a unique form of rare human qualities has been advocated recently by Maurice Dobb, although without clear differentiation from wages of management or from Francis A. Walker's rent theory of profit, which was really a wage theory.

J. B. Clark developed the main alternative to a risk theory, one which connects profit with economic change, or in the language which his usage seems to have established, economic dynamics. Profit is emphasized as the lure which induces business men to make improvements in any direction and is depicted as a temporary income as regards any particular improvement, one which is eliminated by competition through transfer to the purchasers of products and to the owners of the labor and capital used in making them. Walras and Cassel also explained profit as resulting from friction in the working of the competitive system. Cassel's theory, like those of Gide, Weber and Alfred Marshall might also be termed a rent theory of profit. More recently Schumpeter, Amonn and Oppenheimer in particular have developed theories of profit as due to the dynamic character of society.

A view of profit combining the conceptions of risk, of economic change and of the role of business ability has been elaborated by F. H. Knight. It begins by pointing out that uninsurable risk is in fact associated chiefly with economic change. When a change results from conscious innovation, the risk affects in different ways both the innovator himself and other competing enterprises. The risk itself is conceived of as error in decisions, sharply contrasted both with chance in gambling devices and with the hazards covered by insurance. It is pointed out that if the manager were completely and accurately informed on every matter connected with his decisions he would never incur losses, and if all competitors were so informed he would have no opportunity to make gains. The connection of profit with change is simply the fact that decisions of a managerial sort either produce changes or involve adaptations to change or both. In a world free from progressive change, no managerial decisions would be called for; fluctuations would cancel out and could be covered by insurance. Moreover changes which could be predicted indefinitely in advance by everyone affected would not give rise to managerial problems or error or profit; many changes, such as the steady growth of population and capital, are fairly predictable and to a corresponding extent do not occasion imperfect competition or profit. This view is a theory of profit only in an indirect sense, as indicating the limits of the theory which explains other incomes and of general principles in determining them. It serves to point out the directions in which price theory is to be supplemented; namely, through a study of the nature of economic changes and of the activity of the human mind, individually and socially, in producing and reacting to change.

Any study of profits must recognize discrepancies between contractual costs and income in both directions; and the explanation of gains and losses will culminate in the question whether profit is on the whole positive or negative. It is possible only to indicate the nature of the issue and certain theoretical presumptions in favor of one answer or the other. In a competitive enterprise economy profit is the difference between the prices paid for productive services and the prices received for products. This formulation assumes a stationary economy, with net saving and investment absent, but may easily be expanded to include the phenomena of growth through investment. If there is on the whole a positive net profit it is because enterprises compete cautiously and do not raise the values of productive services on the average to their full theoretical level; if, on the other hand, enterprises or their managers are rash and overcompete, the prices of productive services will be raised above their theoretical values and profit will be negative. The difference, in case of a negative profit, would be made up from income in the form of wages or of rent or interest accruing to the profit receivers either at the same time at which net losses were incurred or at some other time.

It has been commonly assumed that risk is irksome and that in consequence profit must on the whole be positive. The phenomena of gambling and speculation, where every participant must know that the activity involves a net loss—often large—to the group engaging in it, make any such simple general assertion untenable. On the other hand, the existence of insurance proves that some risks are irksome to some people. The difficulty in reasoning abstractly about profit is that the character of the risk is not known and is moreover peculiarly affected by a human element. The investor-manager is essentially betting upon himself and his ability to meet situations; and other investors almost certainly judge ventures by the management much more than by any direct knowledge of objective conditions. Thus any assertion can be made regarding aggregate net profit, and appropriately rationalized.

Similar reasoning points to negative results from statistical studies of profit. Classifications of ventures with regard to the real risk involved are not much more defensible from the standpoint of objective accuracy if made at any subsequent time than if made when the ventures are initiated—and only those already finally liquidated can be classified even with respect to outcome. Data on investment and return are limited and questionable, even currently, and highly so for any considerable distance into the past. In order that any conclusion may be proved, data which are not exhaustive must be representative, and obtainable data are certainly open to doubt because of various sorts of bias.

Available figures on profit have been brought together by various students, commonly with a view to disproving an alleged theory of a tendency of profits toward a normal level or toward zero after deduction of normal costs. A number of detailed statistical studies were undertaken in Hungary and Germany between 1900 and 1914, the most important work being that of József Kőrösy and Ewald Moll. In all these studies generalizations as to rates of profit over a period of years, or even in any one year, were affected not only by lack of relevant data but by difficulties of classifying logically the various possible types of return upon capital and goods—a difficulty which has never been overcome satisfactorily.

Similar statistical investigation was not developed in the United States until the abnormal profits of the war years and the increasing concentration of industry directed attention toward the importance of such empirical investigation, although earlier experiments with rate regulation had raised the question of normal and fair rates of profit. Among the best known recent studies are those of David Friday, Foster and Catchings, Horace Secrist, Lawrence Sloan, William L. Crum, and those made for the National Bureau of Economic Research by R. C. Epstein. The figures compiled in these various studies show a wide scatter and erratic variation, as would be expected. The reasoning to any negation of price theory is not easy to grasp, since general theory creates no presumption for any particular form of distribution of behavior. It is true that if conditions remained unchanged and transfer of investment were free, competitive theory would call for an approximation of extreme rates of return toward a norm with the passing of time. Secrist's figures reveal such a tendency, while Epstein's later and fuller data from corporation income tax returns, when plotted as a percentage on reported investment, do so only for half the eleven-year period studied. Theory does not call, however, for any particular rate of return on investment; even if investment were known, conditions do not remain constant and transfer of investment is not free. In actual fact the period of relative constancy in the distribution of rates (1924–29) is now known to have been the time of greatest speculation and inflation, even though it was not characterized by a rise in general commodity prices.

The assumption that such profit conditions would continue was largely responsible for what happened in the years following 1929. What the figures prove is that a boom can create enormous profits, on paper and for the time being. Even what would have happened if the legal owners of the profits reported, the holders of common stock of corporations, had secured them and elected to spend them for consumption purposes is itself a matter for speculation.

If it is possible to speak of conclusions indicated by the factual studies, they follow the lines that would be expected from theory or substantiate commonly accepted assumptions. It is none the less an important fact that modern business conditions create enormous amounts of "profit" in the loose sense of the word, although of course they also create enormous incomes from personal services and from property even within what would be called the normal market values of such services. Likewise such conditions create losses which are a problem on their own account. Devices aimed at secure accumulation increase the possible size of other incomes, while uncertainty makes for occasional large profits along with correspondingly large losses. Sloan's figures of the profits of 455 large corporations show an amazing range in the rate of return (from 15 to 181 percent) even for this exceptionally prosperous group. It is to be kept in mind that no objective line can ever be drawn between profit in the theoretical sense and other incomes, and this is especially important with reference to monopoly revenue, itself a broad and rather loose conception. Modern business devices may make it possible to prolong the temporary gains of a quasi-monopolistic sort coming from successful innovations, which play the chief role in J. B. Clark's theory of profit. This observation applies also, and perhaps especially, to the temporary legal monopoly created by patents and trademarks. Certainly modern world wide market organization tends to a greater concentration of the gains from lucky hits in articles of fashion or other new commodities which enjoy a successful run.

The great and overtowering problem, however, in connection with profit, as in economics generally, is that of changes in price levels and in business conditions, generally referred to as the business cycle. As already observed, it is the fact that such changes are not correctly anticipated, in addition to the fact of their occurrence, which makes them a source of gains and losses. Changes in the general price level and in speculative conditions have more than once since the outbreak of the World War transferred a very considerable fraction of the national wealth out of one set of hands and into another set, not merely without regard to desert or justice, but in a way demoralizing to the motivation of normal economic life.

The modern economic order is built around the concept of enterprise, the correlate of which in income is profit, and is often referred to as the profit system. Economic life necessarily involves much uncertainty or risk, in the loose sense, due to the vicissitudes of nature. Not all of this could theoretically be covered by insurance, and for much more insurance is impracticable. Enterprise economy adds to this the far greater uncertainty associated with the almost universal production of goods in anticipation of the wishes of consumers. This latter uncertainty would not be present in a social system controlled by consumers where production went forward only upon responsible orders in advance from consumers or consumer groups. In many cases, however—one may think of the railroads—such a system would be impossible unless the entire population were organized as a consumer unit, presumably through the agency of the state. The only apparent alternative to the whole population acting through the state as a single producer is a system in which the productive decisions are made and its risks assumed by "volunteers." In such an organization the role of entrepreneur appeals to many motives, inevitably including those of the gambler and those of the would be leader. Some of the motives or motive elements are undoubtedly of the sort conventionally called immoral, and opponents of the system as a whole plausibly stigmatize as such "the" profit motive itself, although all or nearly all the motives which ever operate in human life—the noblest as well as the basest—may enter into productive enterprise.

In connection with criticism of the economic system on social and

ethical grounds, it remains to be observed that the notions of fair
return and of profiteering need to be associated with careful analysis. Regarding monopoly gain there has been virtually no difference of opinion, and the only problem has to do with practicable
methods of prevention. Fair rent and interest raise a different
set of problems and should be tied up with a question of fair or
necessary remuneration for personal services at both the higher and
the lower ends of the scale. As concerns fair profit, in the strict
sense, it must be kept in mind that there is serious doubt whether
profit on the whole is actually positive or negative. Profit in one
set of ventures is associated with loss in another set, unless, and in
so far as, there is a biased error one way or the other in the judgment
of those who direct business enterprise. A positive aggregate net
profit above all losses means a bias on the side of caution, while a
preponderance of the spirit of adventure will entail net loss on the
whole. Both in abstract ethics and from the standpoint of social
interest in adequate motivation, a proposal to reduce high profits
raises the question of using the proceeds to reduce losses. It raises
the question; it does not answer it, and no simple categorical answer
can be given. Both profit and loss arise in many cases from circumstances entirely apart from human foresight, and the question then
is one of justice rather than of incentive, but the further question
of the political feasibility of any proposed action also looms large.
In other cases considerations too complex even to be listed here
enter into the issue as to what might be done to secure a wiser
direction of the use of productive resources and a more equitable
distribution of the results than is afforded by individual competitive
choice. Finally, in any judgment of "the profit system," full
weight must be given to questions of the moral value of different
motives, of the qualities of personality and of human relationships
which go with different types of economic constitution and the like,
as well as to more strictly economic issues of efficiency or even
justice

28

RISK, UNCERTAINTY, AND THE UNPROFITABILITY OF COMPOUNDING PROBABILITIES[*][1]

By Albert Gailord Hart[†]

The study of problems of anticipations—especially of the demand for money and the valuation of stocks—has led to intensification of interest in "risk" and "uncertainty." Both risk and uncertainty, in the terminology which now tends to become standard, are *subjective*[2] matters—attributes of anticipations and (by extension) of plans for action. "Risk" is taken to denote the holding of anticipations which are not "single valued" but constitute a probability distribution having known parameters. "Uncertainty" is taken to denote the holding of anticipations under which the parameters of the probability distribution are themselves not single valued.[3]

It is the position of this paper that "risk" has comparatively

---

[*] *Studies in Mathematical Economics and Econometrics*, 1942, pages 110–118. Reprinted by courtesy of the University of Chicago Press and the author.

[†] Committee on Economic Development. Formerly, Iowa State College.

[1] The writer is indebted to his colleagues, Drs. Tintner, Winsor, and Kozlik, for their pains in helping to clarify both the economics and the mathematics of the following paper; but as none of them has seen the final outcome, they cannot be held liable for it.

[2] Following Myrdal, some Swedish economists distinguish between "subjective" and "objective" risks. But they mean by the latter not the "risk" as it would be estimated with full knowledge of all elements of the situation—when, of course, a given outcome would be regarded as either certain or impossible, not merely as likely—but as it would be estimated *from the data available to the actual estimator* by an ideal estimator (see E. Lindahl, *Studies in the Theory of Money and Capital* [London, 1939], pp. 348–49).

[3] On the terminological point see J. Marschak, "Money and the Theory of Assets," *Econometrica*, October, 1938, p. 324; G. Tinter, "A Contribution to the Nonstatic Theory of Production," in *Studies in Mathematical Economics and Econometrics*, pp. 92–109.

little importance in economic analysis in view of the characteristics of the time relations in which we are interested.   It will be shown that, while an uncertainty situation can be described as a risk situation if we apply the rule of compound probabilities, the use of this reduction technique tends to obscure rather than to clarify the economic issues.   In consequence the writer urges that theorists concentrate their attention on uncertainty rather than on risk.

2. The notion that uncertainty exists when the parameters of a probability estimate are not single valued seems to offer two avenues for exploration.   One is to work out the consequences of the assumption that probability estimates are ordinal rather than cardinal: that contingency A is considered more likely than contingency B, but the estimator has no definite notion how much more likely.[4]   The second is to work on the assumption that all probability estimates are cardinal.   This implies that the estimator is sure that some one of a set of alternative probability distributions (having different parameters) is the one by which he should plan, but that he is not sure which one, though he has estimates of their relative likelihood.   That is, if we assume the estimator to make cardinal estimates, uncertainty implies that he has *a probability distribution of probability distributions.*[5]

The assumption of ordinal probabilities, however, seems to the present writer to lead into a blind alley.   If probability estimates are merely ordinal, their expectation value, dispersion, skewness, etc., lack measurability; and for lack of units we are unable to set up preference scales among them.   The economist's normal procedure of breaking up a planning problem into components is thus blocked. Preferences among alternative events and estimates of the relative probability of different events under different courses of action are inextricably intertwined, and we can say only that the individual does what he prefers in view of the whole constellation of circum-

---

[4] Marschak is the writer who has gone farthest in the direction of trying to free himself from the assumption that probability estimates are cardinal (see his article just cited, also the alternative version published in *Economica*, August, 1938).

[5] This is the procedure of Tintner.

stances. In consequence this paper will proceed on the assumption that estimated probabilities are cardinal quantities.

3. At first glance it may appear that an uncertainty situation so conceived is simply a special case of risk. If the planner has a probability distribution of probability distributions for (say) the price of firecrackers next July, all he need do is to multiply each distribution by its probability, and summate (or integrate), and the whole system of anticipations is boiled down into a single probability distribution for the price. Since this is so, why should not theorists content themselves with showing that this sort of reduction is possible and thereafter concern themselves only with risk?

The answer is that the two sorts of probabilities involved—which we may follow Tintner in calling "probabilities" under particular possible probability distributions and "likelihoods" of those distributions occurring—play very different roles in planning. Even though an entrepreneur (say) is interested solely in the expectation value of the distribution of *possible profits*—to the neglect of the standard deviation and higher moments—he must take into account the standard deviation and higher moments of the likelihoods existing in his estimates of *possible prices*, etc. But unless he is interested in the higher moments of the profit distribution, the dispersion of probabilities within the component distributions will be completely indifferent if the number of components distinguished is sufficiently[6] large. The merging of the various contingent probability distributions means merging the likelihoods and the probabilities by multiplication, so that the resulting total distribution conceals some of the data relevant for business or household planning.[7]

***

[6] For the criterion of "sufficiency" see n. 11 below.

[7] That something is lost in the multiplication of likelihoods and probabilities is readily seen from the irreversibility of the merger. While any probability distribution of component probability distributions has but one sum, any total distribution may be the sum of any of an infinity of sets of component distributions. The parameters of the total distribution do not tell us, e.g., whether it is the sum of a large number of components each with a small dispersion, or of a small number of components each with a wide dispersion, or of a large number of com-

4. This difference in the bearing of likelihoods and of probabilities under component distributions turns on two economic considerations: (a) the anticipation of a change in anticipations and (b) the possibility of deferring decisions, with or without special costs. If either one of these elements is lacking in a planner's situation, his affliction is risk rather than uncertainty; nothing is gained by keeping the likelihoods and the probabilities separate. In fact, if he does not expect his anticipations to change, this implies that there is only one component distribution, with a likelihood of unity. If plans once made are to be completely inflexible, there will be no opportunity to make use of later improvements in estimates. In either case, the total distribution contains all the data he is able to use.

Both elements, however, must be assumed to exist in most planning problems. If we are able to form any estimates at all of such future magnitudes as prices, these estimates must be based upon a stock of evidence accumulated in the past. But unless the event in question is imminent, the future must be expected to bring in more relevant evidence. Possibly new evidence will change our outlook and give our estimates a radically different expectation value. More probably new evidence will confirm our impressions and leave the expectation value substantially unchanged. In this case it will almost certainly reduce the dispersion of our estimates. Such a *convergence* of anticipations is normally expected, since we ordinarily think we can estimate the nearer future more accurately than the more remote future.[8] But anticipations, from their very nature,

---

ponents which are very much alike, each with a wide dispersion. Yet for planning purposes these are substantially different cases.

[8] Note that this does *not* necessarily imply that our estimates for very short periods beginning now are more accurate than for longer periods beginning now. On account of random elements affecting particular days, to give an example, a department-store executive can expect to estimate next week's sales with greater relative accuracy than tomorrow's. What *is* implied is that tomorrow's sales can be estimated better than those of day after tomorrow, next week's sales better than those of week after next.

Estimates for very short periods beginning now are inaccurate on account of such random elements; estimates for very long periods beginning now are inaccu-

can scarcely fail to contain an anticipation that they will change.[9]

5. Given the two conditions just described, the pattern of planning may be worked out by projecting ourselves into the situation of the latest date at which decisions affecting output of given date will be taken, and developing the plan backward toward the present.[10] Giving hypothetical values to the inputs to be determined earlier, it is possible to say what will be the input scheme offering the greatest expectation of profit in the light of each price-probability-distribution for output now considered possible; this hypothetical decision will depend merely on the expectation value of each such distribution, not at all on its dispersion or skewness. For each contingency[11] there is thus a profit expectation. Multiplying each expectation by the likelihood ascribed to the corresponding probability distribution at the date of planning gives a combined expectation.

The value of this expectation depends on the setting of the final decision, created largely by the previous inputs. If now we reopen the next-to-last input decision, it is plain that each possible determination of the next-to-last input will create a different situation

rate because they cannot allow properly for the drift of systematic causal elements operating through time. There must thus be some period for which accuracy is a maximum—ranging perhaps from a day to a season according to the kind of business dealing in view.

[9] It is conceivable that the list of component distributions may contain one having all parameters identical with those of the total distribution and that this component may be ascribed a high likelihood; but the case is obviously trivial.

[10] The argument which follows contains an implicit assumption that outputs of different dates are independently adopted in order to save space. The writer has published a sketch of the necessary corrections in ·"Anticipations, Business Planning and the Cycle," *Quarterly Journal of Economics*, February, 1937, and a fuller version in *Anticipations, Uncertainty, and Dynamic Planning* (Chicago, 1940), pp. 60 ff.

[11] The number of component probability distributions which must be factored out of the total distribution before we can neglect the dispersion of probabilities within the components is therefore whatever number is considered now (at the planning date) to be possible for the date when the last decision will be taken (cf. paragraph 3 above).

for the application of the last input. Each of these situations has a corresponding profit expectation (net of outlays for the next-to-last input); and the next-to-last decision is in substance a choice among these situations. Plainly the highest profit expectation should be selected. By a chain process of reasoning along these lines, decision at each stage can be formulated in the light of its effects on the setting of later decisions.[12] This process thus makes it possible to work out a whole plan, though it involves considering an enormous number of variants.

The plan thus arrived at will differ from the plan resulting when all inputs must be definitively planned at the outset in several important respects: (*a*) its expectation value of profit will be higher; (*b*) it must rest not merely on the expectation value of the selling price but on the whole distribution of likelihoods of estimates which may be held at the date of final decision; and (*c*) its dispersion of profit prospects will be different and probably smaller (at least measured by the coefficient of variation).

6. The fact that the expectation value of profit will be higher than under a rigid plan follows from the planner's freedom to make his flexible plan just like the rigid plan if he chooses. Obviously, then, the flexible plan (if chosen) cannot be inferior. But even if the initial input under the flexible plan is just what it would be under the rigid plan, the improvement of estimates by the time of the next input decision will ordinarily show an optimum second input different from the input which would have figured in the rigid plan. That is, by starting along the lines of the rigid plan and then shifting as estimates are modified, the profit can be increased. Over and above this gain, there is a possibility that an initial input different from that figuring in the rigid plan will offer a still more favorable setting for later decisions, however estimates may shift.

7. The importance of the higher moments of the estimate distributions arises from the fact that in a flexible plan the inputs beyond the initial date, as well as the output, will be uncertain—

---

[12] As Lindahl puts it (*op. cit.*, p. 44), "There exists a *mutual* interconnection between the present and future actions included in the plan."

that is, will be planned hypothetically, in several variants corresponding to the different courses it is believed the evolution of estimates may follow. If estimates of the selling price are revised upward, the higher values of later inputs and of outputs will be adopted; if estimates shift downward, the lower values will be adopted. Now the earlier inputs are planned to create a favorable setting for later inputs, in the knowledge that the later inputs are uncertain. It is impossible to judge the appropriateness of planned early inputs without knowing what possible courses the later inputs may follow if a given series of early inputs is adopted. The problem of fixing the early inputs is thus different (and, of course, more simple) if the possible ultimate distributions of selling-price probabilities have similar expectation values than if the likelihood function of their expectation values has a wide dispersion.

8. The writer has not been able to satisfy himself that the relative dispersion of profit expectations must necessarily either rise or fall as flexibility is introduced. It is readily demonstrated that cases *may* arise under which the standard deviation (and a fortiori the coefficient of variation) of the profit distribution is reduced by flexibility; and the conditions governing these cases suggest that this is the normal situation. But the writer has found it possible to concoct special cases under which flexibility raises the standard deviation; and while the downward bias of the coefficient of variation resulting from the rising expectation prevents a rise of relative dispersion in these particular cases, it seems impossible to prove in general that the coefficient of variation cannot rise.

9. In any event, the mere fact that the expectation value is raised by embracing flexibility is enough to overthrow the standard assumption that measures for meeting uncertainty necessarily involve sacrificing part of the income expectation in order to gain security. The more important devices for meeting uncertainty—maintenance of cash balances and inventories, selection of unspecialized equipment, choice of processes under which intermediate products may be shifted to different dates or types of output, etc.—contribute to flexibility and tend to raise income expectations.[13]

---

[13] At least they raise expectation of income if their own costs are zero. If

The device of long-term contracts (since it makes plans rigid) is not quite on the same footing; but it is not plain a priori that it tends to lower expectations.[14]

The economist's instinct that analysis of uncertainty requires consideration of the higher moments of the estimate distributions is sound. But the assumption of "risk aversion" which is ordinarily made at the beginning of the discussion is unnecessary in a first approximation. The fact that the higher moments of the estimate distributions, under flexibility, enter into the expectation value of the profit distributions means that the central problems of uncertainty can be posed and largely solved under the assumptions of "risk neutrality." Dropping this assumption, whose use greatly simplifies the early stages of reasoning, leads only to secondary qualifications.[15]

APPENDIX

A-1. A general mathematical demonstration of the principles of the text is beyond the scope of this note. But this paper is aimed to controvert two opinions: (a) that devices for meeting uncertainty lower profit expectations and (b) that to find a theoretical role for the higher moments of estimate distributions we must suppose the planner to be concerned about the higher moments of the profit distribution. Being essentially negative, these opinions can be overthrown by

---

their costs are high enough (if, e.g., unspecialized equipment which will do given work is more expensive than specialized equipment with like productiveness and operating costs), the *net* effect on income expectations can become unfavorable.

[14] Insurance is also in a special category. It involves rigidity of a certain money-outlay schedule; but in return it guarantees that certain options will not be closed in case of loss, so that it contributes to operating flexibility. Its relation to uncertainty (like that of "liquid" assets) is deeply involved in the problem of *capital rationing*, which cannot be discussed here for lack of space. The writer has gone into the problem in some detail in *Anticipations, Uncertainty, and Dynamic Planning*, pp. 39 ff.

[15] Recognition of the flexibility problem, however, greatly changes the complexion of the conclusions reached by some students of the problem. Since increasing flexibility is likely both to raise the profit expectation and to lower the profit dispersion, a planner with either a neutral attitude or a distaste for danger cannot forego it. If devices of this sort are neglected, it will be by a planner *with a positive liking for danger*—a finding counter to what seems to be the general view.

showing even one special case to the contrary. Such a case will be analyzed in this appendix.

A-2. Suppose a producer is planning to produce a commodity X, to be sold two intervals of time hence, at date t_2. He plans to use an input A applied immediately and an input B to be applied at an intermediate date t_1. Prices of the inputs are considered certain; and, by adopting suitable units, we can make both prices unity. The price of output is uncertain: at t_0 the producer recognizes n possible prices, $P_1, P_2, P_3, \ldots, P_n$, with likelihoods, respectively, of $K_1, K_2, K_3, \ldots, K_n$. He expects that before date t_1 some one of these prices (he does not know which) will become certain. Input and output are bound together by a production function $X \doteq F(A, B)$.

A-3. To begin with, we may assume that institutional pressure makes it necessary to contract in advance for both inputs. In this case, if the price is P_i, the profit will be $N_i = P_i \cdot F(A, B) - A - B$. If the producer wishes to maximize his *expectation of profit*, we have:

$$E(N) = \sum_{j=1}^{j=n} K_i[P_i \cdot F(A, B) - A - B] \qquad (1)$$

$$= \sum_{j=1}^{j=n} [K_i P_i] F(A, B) - A - B = \text{maximum}.$$

In short, if we call the *price expectation*, $\Sigma K_i P_i$, $E(P)$, he should behave as though a price of $E(P)$ were certain. The solution, of course, is found by setting the partial derivatives equal to zero. Then:

$$\sum_{j=1}^{j=n} K_i P_i \cdot \frac{\partial F(A, B)}{\partial A} = 1 \qquad (2)$$

$$\sum_{j=1}^{j=n} K_i P_i \cdot \frac{\partial F(A, B)}{\partial B} = 1.$$

Equations (2) will yield optimum solutions for the inputs A and B and by implication for X; and given A, B, X, and $E(P)$ the profit expectation is determined. No attribute of the price-distribution function except its average $E(P)$ has any effect on the outcome.

A-4. Suppose now that the producer is set free to postpone decision on the input B until the price of X has been ascertained. We may think of him as fixing input A provisionally at a level A_m. He is still free, however, to vary input B and output X. Now for a price P_i, his profit expectation is

$$N_{m,i} = P_i \cdot F(A_m, B) - A_m - B.$$

This may be influenced by his choice of B; plainly if he wants the highest expectation (given the price, his initial decision on A, and the production function), he will set

$$N_{m,i} = P_i \cdot F(A_m, B) - A_m - B = maximum. \tag{3}$$

From this, by differentiation,

$$P_i(\partial F/\partial B) = 1. \tag{4}$$

This gives a solution for the optimum value of B, which we may designate as B^*. Making B^* explicit, we have

$$B^* = G(P_i, A_m). \tag{5}$$

On general economic grounds we may suppose the partial derivatives of G with respect to both P_i and A_m to be positive.

Having determined B^*, we have by implication determined both the optimum output (X^*) and the corresponding profit (N^*). Both these magnitudes will be increasing functions of P_i and A_m. For a given A_m, we may summate over all possible prices, which gives us

$$E_m(N) = \sum_{j=1}^{j=n} K_j N^*_{m,i} = \sum_{j=1}^{j=n} K_j X^*(P_i, A_m) - A_m - \sum_{j=1}^{j=n} K_j B^*. \tag{6}$$

If the maximum expectation is desired, A_m should be so chosen as to maximize this expression. Setting the partial derivative of $E_m(N)$ with respect to A_m equal to zero, we obtain:

$$\sum_{j=1}^{j=n} K_j(\partial X^*/\partial A_m) - 1 - \sum_{j=1}^{j=n} K_j(\partial B^*/\partial A) = 0. \tag{7}$$

Solving this equation will yield an optimum value for A_m, which will depend on the dispersion as well as the expectation value of the price distribution.

A-5. If we express the expectation values of profits in terms of our other magnitudes, we find the profit expectation, in the first case (both inputs determined simultaneously), to be

$$E_0(N) = E(P)X - A - B, \tag{8}$$

and, in the second case (inputs determined successively),

$$E_m(N) = E(PX^*) - A_m - E(B^*). \tag{9}$$

It is readily demonstrated that E_m exceeds E_0. For we might have laid out the flexible plan subject to the restriction that A_m be fixed equal to the equilibrium A of the rigid plan, and that the weighted sum of contemplated possible B's be fixed equal to the equilibrium B of the rigid plan. In this case the last two terms of the expectations would be identical. The expectation of X^* might be somewhat smaller than the equilibrium value of X under the rigid plan if some of the values of B^* greatly exceeded B (owing to the action of diminishing returns to B on the fixed A_m); but by suitably balancing values of B^* in excess of B against values less than B, a plan could be found under which the expectation of X^* would fall short of X by less than any assigned quantity. Since the values of X will be positively correlated with the prices, $E(PX^*)$ must exceed $E(P)X$ when the expectations of X are approximately equal. A fortiori, if the restrictions are removed, the flexible plan is even more clearly the better.

A-6. The fact that higher moments of the price distribution will enter into the expectation of profits under flexibility is plain in the light of the determination of X^*. Obviously, given A_m, the optimum values B^* and X^* must be positively correlated with price. This implies that the function determining X^* must contain a term or terms involving the price with both coefficient and exponent of the same sign. If both coefficient and exponent are positive (as they will be if we adopt any plausible production function), then when X^* is multiplied by the price in obtaining the profit expectation the resulting expression will contain some power of P with an exponent greater than unity.[16]

A-7. The relation between the higher moments of the profit distributions, as was mentioned in the text, is complex. For the case of simultaneous determination, the variance about the expectation is simply X_0^2 times the second moment of the price distribution, when X_0 is the output offering the maximum expectation. The variance with successive determination includes the second moment of PX^*; and by the argument of the previous paragraph it will therefore contain moments of P beyond (or short of) the second. The writer has been unable to discover any proof that the coefficient of variation is necessarily less with flexibility, though he has been equally unable to devise any numerical special case under which it is greater.

A-8. Finally, we may consider the effects of substituting probability distributions with expectation values of P_1, P_2, P_3 . . . , P_n for the supposed certain price estimates anticipated for t_1. So long as it is impossible to defer decision on the input B beyond t_1, there is no effect on the optimum policy either under simultaneous or under successive determination. Furthermore, the expectation of profits under either system of planning will be unaffected. But the variance both of prices and of profits will be increased under both methods, and in the same proportion. Accordingly the fact that estimates are not single valued at the date of final decision will affect planning only if a subsidiary goal of planning is to hold down the profit dispersion.

---

[16] If the expression for X^* contains a negative term with price in the denominator (which will also give a positive correlation of X^* and P_j), then X^*P_j will contain P to some fractional power or even negative power. But in any event moments other than the first will figure in the profit expectation.

29

ENTERPRISE, PROFITS, AND THE MODERN CORPORATION *

By Robert A. Gordon †

Professor Taussig, over forty years ago, referred to profits as "that mixed and vexed income."[1] "Mixed and vexed" that income continues to be; profits theory confessedly remains one of the least satisfactory parts of economic doctrine. To make matters worse, the set of institutional factors out of which profits (as ordinarily defined) arise has become increasingly complex, and statements which were approximately true when applied to the private proprietorship type of enterprise which generally prevailed through most of the nineteenth century become mere anachronisms when considered with reference to the large corporation, with its separation of ownership and control, which characterizes much of industrial organization today.

The analysis of profits has always been characterized by a particular concentration of attention on the manner in which this type of income arises. The fact that profits accrue to the owner of an enterprise after all contractual costs have been met is deeply rooted in the laws of private property and has largely determined the form which the treatment of profits has taken. But this emphasis on the *non-contractual* nature of profits has served to obscure the fact that analyses of the relations between the income and the function for

---

* *Explorations in Economics*, 1936, pages 306–316. Reprinted by courtesy of the McGraw-Hill Book Co. and the author.

The writer is indebted to the Harvard University Committee on Research in the Social Sciences for grants of money to carry on a project of which the present study forms a part.

† University of California. Formerly, Harvard University.

[1] "The Employer's Place in Distribution," *Quarterly Journal of Economics*, vol. X (1895), p. 86.

which it is taken to be the reward have been inadequate. Profits have come to be related to a variety of productive functions—and even to no function at all. Ever present is a confusion, infrequently recognized, between a functional analysis and an analysis which takes its form from the legal institution of ownership.

I

Among English classical writers, profits were at first generally considered a single aggregate income going to the capitalist, who, in the usual type of analysis, was regarded as the owner of the business enterprise to which he supplied capital. No serious and consistent attempt was made to separate and study the various functions performed by the capitalist-owner.[2] Profits were his reward, and they were treated as being residually determined, in contrast to wages and rent, which were not only contractual but each determined by an independent set of factors. Gradually, partly as a result of the sharp demarcation between entrepreneur and capitalist already effected by French economists, the practice arose of subdividing profits into several elements, of which interest—a return for the simple function of supplying capital—was one. Profits, whether interest was included or not, were still thought to be residually determined; and, except for references to "labor of superintendence," no entrepreneur concept developed that could be related to the income being studied.[3]

The literature on profits since the younger Mill (even earlier in France and, to some extent, in Germany) has evolved out of the distinction which now arose between pure capitalist and owner-entrepreneur and has concerned itself with attempts to explain the income and function of the latter. But although enterprise was finally separated from the supplying of resources, the entrepreneur

---

[2] The development in France was along different lines. Say and his followers clearly demarcated between capitalist and entrepreneur and contributed, with some qualifications, a worth-while analysis of the productive functions of the latter.

[3] General comments upon the development of profits theory in English classical economics fail to do justice to some of the minor writers who were in advance of their better known contemporaries in their treatment of this subject.

remained identical with the owner; to a large extent, profits theory remained what it always had been—a study of the income of business ownership.

Later developments in the analysis of profits have been, for the most part, along three different lines.[4] First, a school of profit theorists has developed which has treated profits in excess of interest on invested capital as being over the long run a determinate return for the exercise of a productive function. A second group has developed a concept of "pure" profits as a final residual income accruing to the owners of an enterprise after due allowance has been made for interest on capital and wages of management. It is an income which arises out of the change, uncertainty, and friction inherent in a dynamic world, and which the belated operation of competitive forces tends to eliminate. A third group emphasizes the unearned nature of, if not all, at least a good part of what is termed profits and attributes the existence and allocation of this income to what might be called "institutional monopolies." Since attention has been paid primarily to the peculiar nature of profits, and since the functions of the person receiving this income (the owner) has changed with a changing industrial structure,[5] *functional* concepts have tended to vary not only with the passage of time but also among economists holding to the same method of profit determination.

Consideration of profits as a long-run determinate return is a natural outgrowth of the English classical treatment of distribution, with its systematic analysis of the returns accruing to the several productive factors and its tendency to regard each of these returns as being determinate in the long run. To most of the theorists in this group, profits are determined in some vague way by

---

[4] For a classification of profit theories similar in part to that adopted here, *cf.* Maurice Dobb, *Capitalist Enterprise and Social Progress* (London: 1925), Chap. V. The classification here used is not intended to be all inclusive or to imply that particular theories may not contain elements of more than one of the types of treatment mentioned.

[5] *Cf.* G. E. Barnett, "The Entrepreneur and the Supply of Capital," in *Economic Essays Contributed in Honor of John Bates Clark* (New York: 1927).

the forces of demand and supply operating upon the number of entrepreneurs. A fundamental assumption of this approach is that the operation of market forces over the long run places a "normal" valuation upon the peculiar contribution of the entrepreneur to the productive process. The most advanced type of analysis along these lines has been contributed by Marshall, who, by use of the concept of quasi-rent, distinguished between the long- and short-run aspects of the problem and fitted the long-run determination of profits into his general theory of equilibrium.[6] On the whole, analyses of this type have been most satisfactory on the supply side. The demand side has been inadequately treated, and it is perhaps the difficulty of analyzing in a satisfactory manner the factors of demand at work which points to the fundamental weakness in this, essentially equilibrium, approach to the problem. The entrepreneur himself creates the demand for his services, and the inapplicability of any attempt to measure this demand in terms of the usual marginal productivity analysis is evident.[7] On the supply side, these theorists differ in their treatment of necessary supply prices and in their emphasis upon institutional factors as the latter affect the supply of entrepreneurs and the size of profits, both on the average and as among individual entrepreneurs.

Those economists who, following Walker, have attempted to construct a theory of profits in terms of the Ricardian rent analysis are also to be included in the group looking upon profits as a determinate return for a productive function. This type of theory, which attempts little more than an explanation of differences in profits, inadequately considers both the demand and the supply side of the problem; and it may even be used to explain profits in nonfunctional terms if the differential concept is applied to institutional positions of advantage rather than to productive efficiency.

The nature of the services rendered by the entrepreneur has been variously conceived by this first group of writers. Some have

[6] *Cf.* Dobb, *op. cit.*, pp. 70–71.

[7] In addition to the other problems of imputation here involved, there is the added difficulty of the size and indivisibility of the entrepreneurial unit, which must be taken to be the individual entrepreneur.

termed the entrepreneur but a laborer of a higher type; others have insisted that enterprise is a productive factor distinct from labor. Essentially, these theorists stress the coordination and control by the entrepreneur of the other factors of production and his guidance of the productive process. On occasion, however, the nature of the entrepreneurial service for which profits are a long-run normal return has been taken to be risk-bearing. This, for example, is the approach adopted by Hawley.[8]

Obviously the theorists in this group have in mind the owner-entrepreneur and the private proprietorship type of business enterprise. Contradictory and confusing results have followed upon attempts to apply their analysis to the modern large corporation with its separation of ownership and control. Frequently, in this case, the control function of the entrepreneur is attributed to salaried executives, whose remuneration, despite its contractual form, is taken to be "profits." But this procedure leaves unexplained all or part of what these writers set out to analyze—the residual income of the enterprise, which in this case goes chiefly to stockholders who do not exercise any active control. Other writers, concentrating their attention on the income of the stockholders, which consistently with their original definition they take to be profits, seek to allocate to stockholders some share in the entrepreneurial function. If enterprise is conceived of in terms of active leadership, this procedure seems scarcely applicable where the bulk of corporate ownership is in the hands of passive stockholders.

The second approach to profits theory had its beginnings in the implications of static equilibrium theory and was first made prominent by J. B. Clark in this country and by Walras and his followers of the mathematical school in Europe. In an unchanging frictionless world, "static" laws determine the rewards of the various productive agents. In such a world, all factors get the equivalent of their imputed marginal products; the receipts of every enterprise

---

[8] *Cf.* "Reply to Final Objections to the Risk Theory of Profit," *Quarterly Journal of Economics*, Vol. XV (1901), p. 610, and *Enterprise and the Productive Process* (New York: 1907), Chap. VI. Contrast with this the approach adopted by Knight, who also stresses the risk-bearing nature of enterprise.

exactly equal costs (including imputed wages and interest to the owner); and no surplus accrues to the owner. In the dynamic world of fact, however, a surplus income in excess of contractual costs (and imputed wages and interest to the owner) does arise. It is only imperfectly eliminated by the forces of competition after the passage of time and continually recurs as new changes take place and new frictions arise. Clark and Knight are the best known American exponents of this view. The same view, but with a somewhat different emphasis, forms an integral part of Schumpeter's approach to dynamic economics, and it is also held to a greater or less degree by many other writers on both sides of the Atlantic.

This approach to profits theory has been associated with a variety of entrepreneurial concepts. Clark thought of the entrepreneur sometimes as coordinator, sometimes as merely owner. To Knight, the entrepreneurial function is the dual one of risk-taking and control,[9] although his final concept of control becomes so attenuated as to be of little significance in any analysis of active business leadership. Schumpeter finds the entrepreneurial function to be peculiarly that of carrying through innovations. Other theorists have stressed risk-taking alone, while some others have thought of ownership pure and simple as the essence of entrepreneurship. On the whole, the entrepreneurial concepts of the writers in this group are usually couched in terms of some aspect of "control" or risk-bearing or some combination of the two.[10]

Despite the attempts of these writers to include some concept of enterprise in their analysis of "pure profits," this type of explanation is essentially a non-functional one. Profits are explained in the first instance not as the product of a particular function but rather in terms of change, uncertainty, and friction. In fact, the

---

[9] Throughout this study, "risk-taking" is used for brevity in discussing the views of certain writers whether or not the latter emphasize the distinction, made familiar by Knight, between calculable "risk" and unmeasurable "uncertainty."

[10] Formulation of an entrepreneurial concept is not always considered necessary to a study of profits, the latter sometimes being defined simply in terms of the uncertain nature of the income.

permanence and size of the income is taken to depend upon obstructions to the working out of competitive forces—to a temporarily advantageous position given to the recipient of this income. It is not surprising, therefore, that the writers emphasizing this approach to the problem have been unable to establish any precise relationship between profits and the exercise of an entrepreneurial function, no matter how the latter is conceived. This is particularly true of those holding to a risk-bearing concept of enterprise. Further, the income explained in these terms is a part of the non-contractual income of ownership; conceivably, profits in this sense may go to one class, the owners, while the entrepreneurial function, if it is anything more than passive risk-bearing, is performed by an entirely separate group.

The third type of theory mentioned tends to look upon profits as being wholly or in large part "unearned" and to attribute the origin and size of such unearned income to the existence of monopolistic positions of advantage in the institutional structure which are possessed and exploited by a favored minority. Writers holding to this view range from the Marxians, on the one hand, who level their attack at the "profits of capital" in the English classical sense of the phrase, to such economists as Veblen, Hobson, and C. J. Foreman, on the other, who emphasize the institutional origin of much of the income of the modern business leader or financial magnate. Many other writers, of course, recognize some part of profits as being unearned, but we have in mind here only those who have particularly emphasized this aspect of the problem.

This approach to profits theory is by no means independent of the two others previously mentioned. Rent theories, for example, when differences are those of opportunity rather than ability, fall into this class. Even "functional" theories which treat profits as a long-run determinate return may be "institutional" theories to the extent that the size of the income is related to a scarcity of entrepreneurs (or of entrepreneurs with the requisite capital) originating in the existence of institutional barriers. With respect to the dynamic residual theories, it has already been indicated that the allocation of "pure profits" to particular individuals is based upon the nature and distribution of ownership rights (an institutional phenomenon), whether or not the activities of the owner-recipients are functionally related to the creation of this income.

Some among those who have found the origin of profits in institutional positions of advantage have undoubtedly been too sweeping in their generalizations or insufficiently penetrating in their analysis. Among orthodox economists as a whole, however, more attention needs to be paid to the effects of legal and economic institutions upon business leadership and business income. The bearing of this problem upon the formulation of an adequate theory of enterprise and profits will be briefly indicated in the closing pages of this study.

Although the general nature of the entrepreneurial concepts held by recent profit theorists has already been roughly indicated in the preceding discussion, one feature of these various analyses of enterprise calls for particular comment at this point. For the most part, although admittedly with considerable variation in emphasis and details of treatment, entrepreneur concepts have centered about some aspect of "control" or risk-bearing, or some combination of the two. These two elements, it is to be noted, are implied in the characteristics usually attributed to the ownership of a going business. It is only natural that, since the entrepreneur has always been identified with the owner, the attributes of ownership should have had an important influence not only in the development of profit theory but also in the formulation of a concept of enterprise as a productive function. Unfortunately, the consequences of this identification of entrepreneur with owner have not in general been recognized.

II

One consequence of the emphasis which has been placed on ownership and ownership income is that invariably the analysis tacitly assumes the private proprietorship or close corporation type of enterprise. This method of treatment obviously breaks down when the private proprietorship is replaced by the large corporation in which those who manage and control are altogether or largely distinct from the body of passive stockholders who are the legal owners. The existence and importance of this "separation of ownership and control" in present-day American industry is scarcely to be disputed.[11]

In the modern large corporation, the non-contractual income usually called profits still goes, with some slight qualifications, to the owners. But these owners are for the most part merely passive suppliers of capital, who, though they bear the risks, exercise no real control. Active control is exercised in many cases by executives and "insiders" whose ownership interest is small or negligible. Thus the traditional mode of analysis of "profits" breaks down on two counts. It fails in its attempt to explain ownership income (in so far as there is any income in excess of interest and a risk premium) in functional terms, as the return for entrepreneurial activity. This is certainly true if enterprise be regarded as anything more than merely passive risk-bearing. Secondly, in tacitly identifying owner with entrepreneur, it leaves out of the picture the active and dynamic entrepreneurial function involved in business leadership and fails to explain the income going to those who exercise this leadership.

Emphasis on risk-bearing provides no solution. An analysis of much more than risk-bearing by itself is necessary to explain even ownership income. And an explanation of ownership income, whether attempted in terms of risk-bearing or not, does not tell us much concerning the nature of the entrepreneurial function or the income going to those who perform this function.

No adequate solution of this problem can be attempted in the space here available. Some positive suggestions can be made, however, which may lead to a more satisfactory treatment of business leadership and business income—more satisfactory, at least, in that an analysis along the lines proposed would attempt to meet directly the situation created by the modern large corporation. A modification of the same analysis should make it applicable also to the private proprietorship type of enterprise.

[11] *Cf.* A. A. Berle and G. C. Means, *The Modern Corporation and Private Property* (New York: 1933). See also "Stockholdings of Officers and Directors in American Industrial Corporations," by the present writer, in the *Quarterly Journal of Economics*, Vol. L (1936), pp. 622–655.

In the first place, if our theory is to fit into an analysis of the working of the economic system as a whole, an adequate concept of the entrepreneurial function must be formulated.   This is necessary not merely to explain profits but to take account of the fact that joint production for a market in a dynamic world requires a guiding, integrating, and initiating force.   The exercise of this force toward productive ends is essentially distinct both from routine labor (mental or physical), on the one hand, and from the supplying of resources (with or without contractual guarantees), on the other. It is this type of productive activity which has always called for analysis in our discussions of responsible business and financial leadership; and it is this, it would seem, which may most properly be regarded as the entrepreneurial function.[12]

If this much be accepted, it must be further recognized that the entrepreneur may exercise control without any accompanying ownership—as is in fact the case with many corporate executives and "insiders."   Granted the necessary technological conditions, the entrepreneurial function must be performed, regardless of the legal-economic institutions that may prevail.   These institutions happen at the present time to facilitate the separation of enterprise and ownership.

Since, then, there is an entrepreneurial function which may be exercised without ownership, a theory of functional profit should be formulated that will take in the income of the entrepreneur even when he is not the owner.   Whether the income be called profits or

---

[12] Some readers may question this unqualified identifying of entrepreneurship with "control."   If "entrepreneur," however, is to have any meaning and usefulness as an economic concept, it is difficult to see how it can fail to encompass the *active* exercise of business leadership toward productive ends.   Such leadership is usually, as a matter of fact, tacitly assumed in our use of the term "entrepreneur."   Some may wish to add risk-bearing to control, but risk-bearing is attached fundamentally to ownership of resources that can be risked, and such ownership is not, under modern conditions, a *sine qua non* of control.   Uncertainty enters into the problem not primarily through risk-bearing but through its effects upon the nature of the control needed to meet this uncertainty.   Apart from those attached to the supplying of resources, whatever risks the entrepreneur undergoes (in the possibilities of loss of employment or the reduction of income) are probably more than matched by those borne by ordinary laborers.

not is of no great significance. What is important is that the separate function be recognized and that the income related to the exercise of this function be studied. This income may be received in a contractual or non-contractual form and may arise in a number of different ways. The entrepreneur, furthermore, may receive a total income which is partly non-functional in nature, and it may be difficult to distinguish the functional from the non-functional elements. In any case, the conventional equilibrium analysis will probably prove difficult of application.

The income of the owner as well as that of the entrepreneur must be analyzed in functional terms; and this is necessary even when owner and entrepreneur are the same individual (or individuals). Part of such income represents a functional return for the supplying of resources and, despite its non-contractual nature, may be considered as being determined by the same set of factors as that determining the return to resources supplied under some form of contractual guarantee.[13]

Analysis of the incomes of enterprise and ownership in functional terms alone, however, is not sufficient to account for the total income (in excess of imputed routine wages and interest) either of those who actually exercise the entrepreneurial function or of passive stockholders. The final step necessary is the formulation of a broad concept of "institutional income" or "gains of position." These gains accrue to the persons receiving them not as a result of any productive service performed but rather through their holding or exploiting some favorable institutional position. The analysis here suggested must treat of two types of income.

On the one hand, there are the manipulative and exploitative

---

[13] The term "non-contractual interest" might be used to describe this part of ownership income. Some risk premium, in itself not income, is probably also included; but it is doubtful whether, in view of the optimism which so frequently dictates the purchase of junior securities, any positive return for risk-bearing is received by the average stockholder. It is even less likely, where in individual cases a positive gain in excess of interest does exist, that this return bears any functional relationship to the degree of risk undergone. In many cases, of course, large fortuitous gains—over and above functional rewards—may be contained in ownership income, but this will be discussed below in connection with institutional gains of position.

gains of the business leader which accrue to him because of his strategic position of control. Conceivably, productive activity and functional rewards may become entirely incidental to the pursuit of these "gains of position," and consideration of such gains is frequently essential if the total income going to business leadership is to be explained.

On the other hand, there exists in the income of the passive owner a constantly fluctuating residual element, which may attain large positive or negative proportions over the short run and which may even be a positive or negative sum over the long run. This residual is what the economist terms "pure profits" and includes, in addition to a part of current income, gains arising from the capitalization of ownership income in excess of competitive returns on resources invested. An attempt to account for the origin and fluctuating nature of these gains may run largely in conventional terms, although even here the institutional factors at work may influence the origin and particularly the absolute size of this income. It is important to bear in mind, however, that accounting for the *origin* and *existence* of an income does not in itself explain its *allocation* to particular persons or classes. The way in which a given income accrues to various individuals will depend largely on how those individuals fit into the institutional setting which prevails. Thus, though "pure profits" may be explainable in terms of change, uncertainty, and friction (essentially a non-functional explanation),[14] the fact that these gains go to particular persons is related, not to the exercise of the entrepreneurial function, but rather to the nature and distribution of ownership rights.

These suggestions for an analysis of enterprise and profits have tended to emphasize the situation in which enterprise is separated from ownership, since this aspect of the problem has become increasingly important and is the one most neglected in theoretical discussion. The same type of analysis, however, can also be applied to the case where entrepreneur and owner are one. Here we have to deal with a composite income which must, at least for the purposes of analysis, be broken into its several elements. These com-

[14] See p. 563, above.

ponents may be difficult to separate, and the factors determining their size and variation may be substantially different from those operating when the owner is not also the entrepreneur.   Thus the supply of enterprise, when ownership is also necessary, may be more restricted than when enterprise is not combined with ownership. In the former case, also, the incentive of possible fortuitous gains may be greater that that of purely functional returns, with the result that the nature and intensity of productive activity may be affected. Where entrepreneur is also owner, actively induced gains of position (through unfair trade practices, financial manipulation, etc.) are more likely to go to those taking the action necessary to induce such gains, and from the point of view of the efficient working of the economic system this may result in an undesirable diversion of efforts.   On the other hand, it is also true that there is a greater harmony between the interests of the enterprise (which in some respects are more likely to be those of society as a whole) and those of the entrepreneur.   It is also worth pointing out that theoretical assumptions regarding the working of the price mechanism are more likely to hold where entrepreneur and owner are one.   Where they are not, maximization of individual gain may take precedence over that of the income of the individual firm.   Equilibrium theory, however, has so far been based upon the maximizing of the income of the firm.

A theory of enterprise and profits along the lines here suggested would attempt to explain, then, the income and function of enterprise and the income and position of ownership, and the analysis could be made to apply whether ownership and enterprise were separate or combined in the same group of persons.   It would, further, distinguish between functional and non-functional income and between the existence and allocation of both types of income. Though such a theory is avowedly eclectic, it does offer an explanation in closer accord with the facts of the contemporary economic order than do most theories of profits current today—and it provides at least a partial way out of the confusion into which profits theory has been thrown by the indiscriminate attention which economists have paid to the characteristics of business ownership.

30

CORPORATE EARNINGS ON INVESTED CAPITAL*[1]

BY WILLIAM LEONARD CRUM†

The improvement in the volume of business and in the level of commodity prices, which had been in irregular progress since 1933 and was proceeding by early 1937 at a vigorous pace, was accompanied by a sharp revival in business profits. The subsequent violent contraction in business and decline in prices has undoubtedly depressed profits. In the present business situation, particular interest attaches to precise estimates of the rate of profit because of the great moment of profit anticipations as a factor conditioning the revival of private investment. Unfortunately, current figures on the rate of profit for business enterprise as a whole, even corporate business enterprise, must rest upon estimates constructed from the published statements—usually available only after some delay—of large companies with securities listed on public exchanges. An informed use of such estimates is, however, greatly facilitated by a careful study of the complete record for all corporate enterprise in the aggregate, afforded by U. S. Treasury compilations of corporation tax returns. Although these compilations are inevitably delayed for about two years after the period to which they apply, and are now fully available only through 1934, with partial data through 1935, analysis of them yields immensely helpful base figures for interpreting such current estimates as can be made from published statements.

* *Harvard Business Review*, Volume XVI, 1938, pages 336–350. Reprinted by courtesy of the publisher and author.

† Harvard University.

[1] The analysis reported herein was assisted in its early stages by a grant from the Harvard University Committee on Research in the Social Sciences, during the academic year 1935–1936.

This article undertakes a reconsideration of the Treasury data, with a view to determining on a more refined basis than heretofore the average rate of return on aggregate corporate invested capital during the years 1922–1935. The closing section gives attention to the rough comparison of current estimates based on published corporation statements with the reference period which ends in 1935. The analysis is arranged to bring out important inadequacies in the Treasury data for the purpose indicated, to develop the implications of assumptions made in the course of the calculations, and to state and explore some of the chief theoretical questions raised by the definitions adopted and the results obtained.

The return on invested capital is one of the most significant—in several respects *the* most significant—among possible measures of corporate performance. No entirely satisfactory determination of the average rate of return on invested capital, for corporate industry in the aggregate, can be made; but data accumulated over recent years, and clearer insight into their significance, enable us to prepare a fairly close estimate. The resulting figure pertains to corporate industry in the aggregate; equally accurate estimates for particular types of corporate industry, such as corporations engaged in manufacturing or in trade or in mining, cannot be made. The results pertain, moreover, to a closed period of limited length; *comparable* data are not available before 1922, and the record cannot be brought up to date because of inevitable delays incident to tabulation of the tax data.[2]

A broad picture of the main findings appears in Exhibit I. There the curve of corporate return records the changes in the rate

---

[2] The Treasury's final tabulation for 1934 corporation income tax returns has recently been completed and published: *Statistics of Income for 1934, II, Corporations*. Washington: Bureau of Internal Revenue, 1937. The preliminary tabulation for 1935, *Statistics of Income for 1935, Preliminary Report of Corporation Income and Excess-Profits Tax Returns Filed Dec. 31, 1936*, includes only a selected list of the tables which will appear in the 1935 final report. The 1935 preliminary report is, however, more complete than the preliminary reports for earlier years, which covered only returns received through August 31 of the year following. The final 1935 edition has been completed, and important tables were released to the press on January 19, 21, 24, and 28, 1938.

of return on corporate equity held by outsiders, as defined below and tabulated on page 587. For comparison, the second curve of the chart shows the fluctuations of a very general measure of the gross economic welfare of the entire nation—the national income. This series is in percentage form, with the 1922–1931 average as 100, and is based upon the "net national product" data as given by Simon Kuznets.[3] The national income series affords a helpful basis of reference for the corporate earnings figures, not because there is a necessary close relation between corporate profits and national income, but because national income is an exceptionally general measure of economic conditions.   Although the two curves show similar broad movements, numerous differences in intensity or even direction appear among the year-to-year changes.   Moreover, even as to the broad movements striking contrasts appear: for example, the recovery of 1935, which restored national income well toward the 1922 level, showed a rate of profit far below 1922. Nevertheless, the rate of return had by 1935 recovered more than half the reduction between 1929 and 1932; whereas the recovery in national income from 1933 to 1935 was less than one-third of the reduction, in absolute amount, from 1929 to 1933.

DEFINITION OF RETURN

In determining the rate of return on invested capital, we shall have in mind the capital invested by the owners of corporate enterprise; and we shall therefore define net earnings—the "return"— as the residue of income after all charges.   In order to arrive at the figure for net earnings, we start with statutory net income as defined in the Revenue Act: the residue of gross income—which does not include tax-exempt interest or dividends received from domestic corporations—after subtracting the various deductions allowed by the act.

The statutory net income figure for all corporations in the aggregate is merely the sum of the statutory net income (or deficit) items for all corporations, about a half million of them; and it is

---

[3] *National Income and Capital Formation.* New York: National Bureau of Economic Research, 1937, p. 8.

not strictly the equivalent of a consolidated net income such as would appear if all corporations were operated as one system, and various offsets were made in drawing up the consolidated account.[4] By the law as it stood during most of the period here under observation, 1922–1935, groups of corporations which were closely affiliated were permitted to file consolidated returns, and about half

EXHIBIT I. PERCENTAGE RETURN ON CORPORATE INVESTED CAPITAL, COMPARED WITH NATIONAL INCOME EXPRESSED RELATIVE TO 1922–1931 AVERAGE

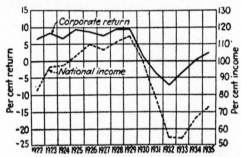

Note: The "corporate return" is the percentage ratio of net earnings to corporate equity held by outsiders (given on page 587). National income is expressed as percentage of 1922–1931 average: 72.34 billions. See text.

the total corporate gross business was in fact reported on consolidated returns.[5] If consolidated returns had not been permitted,

[4] "All" corporations include all corporations subject to income tax. Excluded are certain tax-exempt corporations, which are in the main mutual, charitable, or non-profit concerns. Excluded from the tabulations also are so-called "inactive" corporations, which file returns not showing income data and include numerous concerns in process of liquidation. Inactive corporations, separately counted beginning with 1927, have accounted for somewhat over 10% of the total number of returns filed.

[5] For many years successive revenue acts had, with only slightly varying definitions of an "affiliated group," permitted the filing of consolidated returns of income for each such group. By the Act of 1934, however, the privilege of filing consolidated returns was restricted to railroad corporations. There resulted deep-reaching changes in the 1934 corporate data, and, because the abandonment of the consolidated-return privilege did not occur until 1935 for certain fiscal-year corporations, to a lesser extent in the 1935 data. I propose to discuss in detail these "technical" effects on the 1934 and 1935 data in another place. I have analyzed elsewhere separate tabulations of the consolidated returns for 1928–1930,

really important changes would probably have occurred in certain gross items of the composite account and in certain items reflecting intercorporate transactions.

From statutory net income as tabulated, Federal taxes are deducted in the present study; and this net after taxes is then raised by an item of income not subject to tax. This item is tax-exempt interest; interest on certain government obligations, though income to the corporation, is not a part of statutory net income as defined in the act. The adjustments of statutory net income, described above, are presented in Exhibit II; and the final column of this table shows the resulting figures for the "return," i.e., net earnings available for equity owners.

The foregoing determination of net earnings is not wholly satisfactory. One of the flaws is that statutory net income, as defined by the act, includes net gain (or loss) from the sale of capital assets.[6]

discussing the size and significance of this small number of (mainly) very large enterprises: *Quarterly Journal of Economics*, May, 1933, pp. 414–448.

[6] This was not separately tabulated until recent years; capital gain was first tabulated for 1929, and capital loss for 1930. The sums involved, in millions of dollars, run as follows:

Year	Capital Gain	Capital Loss	Net Figure
1929	1315.4	*	*
1930	645.8	935.7	− 289.9
1931	298.6	1702.3	−1403.7
1932	142.5	1705.2	−1562.7
1933	262.5	1685.9	−1423.4
1934	242.6	297.4	− 54.8
1935	469.9	239.0	230.9

*Not available.

If we may assume the losses (not tabulated) in 1929 were negligible, we can revise the net earnings figures of Exhibit II from 1929 on as follows:

6767.6	−954.6
1665.7	107.0
−1741.1	1443.5
−3812.2	

This "revision" is, however, not complete; for it implies also an adjustment for

576 PROFIT

Theoretical objections arise against the inclusion of such an item
in a definition of net earnings, for purposes of economic or financial
analysis. Such objections have special force against counting gains
and losses "when realized," rather than as accrued; and, although
recent suggestions favor reckoning accrued changes in asset values
as taxable income, only "realized" changes are, and are likely to be,
thus included. If, however, *accrued* capital gains and losses are to
be counted as "earnings," other and more forcible objections
appear. I refrain, in any case, from making what seems an obvious
correction on this account, largely for reasons given in footnote 6.

A suggestion has been made that a further addition, equal to
the two special deductions—amounting to tax relief in whole or in
part on the income needed to afford the legally required additions
to reserve funds—which the act allows to life insurance companies
in computing their statutory net income, be applied to tabulated
statutory net income to arrive at net earnings.[7] The apparent

taxes borne by the capital gains, or obviated by the capital losses. Such adjustment cannot be perfectly made; for, although we have separate capital gain and
loss figures for income and no-income corporations, the revision itself might throw
certain corporations from the income (taxable) class to the no-income class, or
vice versa. For this reason, and because data prior to 1929 are not available anyway, I have decided to let the net earnings stand as in Exhibit II, without this
revision.

[7] The special deductions for life insurance companies are specified as follows
in the Act of 1936:

Sec. 203 (a) (2) "Reserve Funds.—An amount equal to 4 per centum of the
mean of the reserve funds required by law and held at the beginning and end of
the taxable year, except that in the case of any such reserve fund which is computed at a lower interest assumption rate, the rate of $3\frac{3}{4}$ per centum shall be substituted for 4 per centum. Life insurance companies issuing policies covering life,
health, and accident insurance combined in one policy issued on the weekly
premium payment plan, continuing for life and not subject to cancellation, shall
be allowed, in addition to the above, a deduction of $3\frac{3}{4}$ per centum of the mean
of such reserve funds (not required by law) held at the beginning and end of the
taxable year, as the Commissioner finds to be necessary for the protection of the
holders of such policies only"; and (3) "Reserves for Dividends.—An amount
equal to 2 per centum of any sums held at the end of the taxable year as a reserve
for dividends (other than dividends payable during the year following the taxable
year) the payment of which is deferred for a period of not less than five years from

basis for this suggestion is that such deductions are in no sense an expense for insurance corporations. On this basis, the estimated amount thereof, running in recent years around a half billion dollars, should be added to tabulated net income to restore the figure substantially to the level it would have had if the law conferred no such benefits on insurance companies.

EXHIBIT II. RECONSTRUCTION OF NET EARNINGS
(IN MILLIONS OF DOLLARS)

Year	(1)	(2)	(3)	(4)	(5)	(6)
	Statutory Net Income or Deficit		Combined Figure (1) + (2)	Federal Tax	Tax-Exempt Interest	Net Earnings (3) − (4) + (5)
	Income Corporations	No-Income Corporations				
1921	$ 4336.0	−$3878.2	$ 457.8	$ 701.6	$188.8	−$ 55.0
1922	6963.8	− 2193.8	4770.0	783.8	394.0	4380.3
1923	8321.5	− 2013.6	6308.0	937.1	456.2	5827.1
1924	7586.7	− 2223.9	5362.7	881.6	517.2	4998.4
1925	9583.7	− 1962.6	7621.1	1170.3	519.8	6970.6
1926	9673.4	− 2168.7	7504.7	1229.8	499.6	6774.5
1927	8981.9	− 2471.7	6510.1	1130.7	500.8	5880.3
1928	10617.7	− 2391.1	8226.6	1184.1	593.5	7635.9
1929	11653.9	− 2914.1	8739.8	1193.4	536.7	8083.0
1930	6428.8	− 4877.0	1551.2	711.7	536.3	1375.8
1931	3683.4	− 6970.9	− 3287.5	399.0	541.7	− 3144.8
1932	2153.1	− 7796.7	− 5643.6	285.6	554.2	− 5374.9
1933	2986.0	− 5533.3	− 2547.4	423.1	591.6	− 2378.9
1934	4275.2	− 4181.0	94.2	596.0	663.6	161.8
1935	5164.7	− 3468.8	1695.9	735.1	713.5	1674.3

Such an interpretation appears to me unwarranted. The act apparently treats the special interest allowance on required reserves as though it were interest paid to or accrued for account of the creditors, that is, the policyholders, owning the reserve. The adop-

the date of the policy contract"; and these provisions, in substantially similar form, had appeared in the earlier acts pertaining to the period herein studied.

See the discussion by J. Franklin Ebersole, Susan S. Burr, and George M. Peterson, *Review of Economic Statistics*, November, 1929, p. 191, paragraph (45).

tion, in the specific deductions defined in the act, of an interest rate substantially equal to that at which state laws require the reserves to be accumulated for the benefit of policyholders points in this direction. I gladly grant that the case is not clear-cut, particularly in respect of mutual companies for which policyholders may be regarded as equity owners, and in view of the further facts that the rate allowed in the special deductions and the discretion granted the Commissioner in defining certain reserves prevent an exact fit of the tax-free deduction to the legally required rates of addition to reserves. All points considered, however, I remain of the opinion that these special deductions are in the nature of interest paid on indebtedness, and should not be added back into net income.

Another suggestion, made by certain writers, is that compensation of officers be treated as part of corporate net earnings, rather than as a deduction from gross in arriving at net.[8] Considerable force attaches to this notion, especially when we are thinking of corporate earning power in terms of the economic return on management—or, more strictly, entrepreneurship—and capital combined. Data recently collected by the Securities and Exchange Commission and other agencies confirm the long-standing opinion, based on general knowledge, that a very large element in the compensation of officers of large corporations is contingent upon net earnings, and may be regarded as a "distribution" of earnings to management not unlike the distribution to owners in the form of dividends.[9] Moreover, substantial evidence exists that small corporations, many of them presumably closely-held or "family" concerns, pay salaries to executives, whether for tax avoidance or for other reasons, which absorb a large share of what might otherwise be called net earnings.[10]

---

[8] For example, see Lucille Bagwell, *Journal of Business*, October, 1929, pp. 345–360, especially pp. 347 and 351.

[9] See discussion by John C. Baker and William L. Crum, XIII, *Harvard Business Review*, 3, Spring, 1935, pp. 321–333; and John C. Baker, *The Compensation of Executive Officers of Retail Companies, 1928–1935*, Harvard Business School Division of Research, Business Research Studies, No. 17.

[10] For example, for those 1933 returns accompanied by balance sheets—cov-

After considering these points, I have avoided including compensation of officers in my definition herewith of net earnings. One of the chief reasons is that no satisfactory basis appears for separating out that portion of such compensation which might fairly be called a distribution of net earnings. This is especially so because "executives" of corporations do not necessarily exercise the entrepreneur functions in an economic sense; the sober fact is that we do not yet know where the entrepreneur function resides in the modern corporation.[11] Another important reason is that the objective of the present analysis is to measure the return on

ering a very large share of total corporation business, as explained below (p. 589), though only about 88% of all corporations by number—and tabulated according to size of total assets, the following items (in millions of dollars) are significant:

	Corporations Having Total Assets	
	Under $50,000	Over $50,000,000
a. Compensation of officers	483.6	113.8
b. Total compiled receipts	6809.8	26571.2
c. Statutory net income	−382.6	−151.1
d. Same plus tax-exempt interest	−380.1	82.0
e. Same less Federal tax	−389.4	− 68.4
f. Percentage ratio, (a) to (b)	7.1	0.43

The size classes between $50,000 and $50,000,000 show a roughly progressive shift in the percentage of row (f) from the high of 7.1 to the low of 0.43. Some part of the high figure for the small corporations is almost surely ascribable to the use of executive compensation as a means of distributing earnings; but an important part merely reflects a "technical" inadequacy of the data. A small corporation will generally have about the same number of "officers," in the sense of these Treasury statistics, as a large company; but they may be performing duties largely of a wage-earning nature, duties performed in huge companies by official subordinates who may receive high salaries which are nevertheless deducted in the tax returns in the salaries-and-wages items and thus do not appear in the tabulated figure for compensation of officers. The officer of a very small corporation, like a farmer, is frequently at once wage-earner, manager, equity-owner, and entrepreneur in the strict economic sense.

[11] See discussion by R. A. Gordon in the forthcoming issue of the *Quarterly Journal of Economics* (May, 1938).

corporate *capital;* for the owners of capital, pay to officers, on whatever basis reckoned, is generally an expense which does in fact cut down the earnings of capital. That the bargaining position of officers, whether or not enhanced by their ownership of some of the capital, may enable them to secure a portion of the earnings otherwise available to equity owners, admittedly raises questions of great significance concerning the nature of corporate organization, and touching also the meaning of the findings herewith as to the return on corporate capital.

Definition of Invested Capital

In the present analysis, I use in general the approach of Professor S. H. Nerlove.[12] He undertakes to obtain an estimate of the invested capital of the proprietors of corporate enterprise in the aggregate, a figure which, unlike the book value of the equity, does not reflect changes in valuation which themselves represent largely a capitalization of earning power. He says, in fact:

> In obtaining a measure for invested capital, it is necessary to get a figure which does not "capitalize" net incomes. It is evident that the usefulness of the rate secured will be greatly reduced if the base of the ratio reflects the numerator. Obviously, if the changes in the denominator reflect the numerator, the "rate" would always be the same. Accordingly, the base chosen attempts to measure the amount that stockholders have furnished, in a way that will avoid, as far as possible, the capitalization of corporate net incomes.[13]

Although the case is not unequivocally clear for this decision of Mr. Nerlove, much can be said—particularly for certain types of comparisons, including the main comparisons sought in the present analysis—for a base figure, in terms of which the rate of return is to be calculated, which does not respond to variations in that return. So convincing are these reasons that I present in what follows, as my main estimate of the rate of return, a series of percentages resting essentially on the type of analysis which Mr. Nerlove so effectively developed.

---

[12] See his *A Decade of Corporate Incomes, 1920 to 1929*, Studies in Business Administration, II, 4. Chicago: University of Chicago Press, 1932.
[13] *Ibid.*, p. 34.

The essential steps in the Nerlove method are as follows.[14]   The initial figure is that for 1920 (end of the year), obtained by adding to the invested capital at the middle of 1920, shown on 1920 invested-capital returns of corporations (excluding gold-mining concerns) having 1920 net income above $3,000: (1) an allowance for corporations not filing such returns, (2) an allowance for new stock issues during the second half of 1920, and (3) the amount of net earnings reinvested in 1920.[15]   The figures for succeeding years are then obtained by adding to this 1920 base figure successive annual increments representing: (1) net earnings reinvested, (2) stock publicly issued, (3) estimated stock issues for small companies not making "public" offerings of securities Except for variations presently to be noted, I accept and use herein this method.

The net earnings reinvested are the residue of net earnings, as defined above, after distribution of dividends outside the aggregate corporate system.   Not all dividends paid by corporations go outside the system; a substantial portion is received by other corporations.   The difference between dividends paid and dividends received by corporations goes outside the system, and this is the figure to deduct from net earnings to yield the figure for reinvested earnings.[16]   On this basis, reinvested net earnings are calculated in Exhibit III.   These figures for reinvested net differ from those of

[14] *Ibid.*, Chap. VI, and pertinent appendix notes.

[15] The resulting figure, 88.5 billion dollars, may include a substantial margin of error.   The "invested capital" reported to the Treasury, on the 187 odd thousand returns filed, may well have failed to show precisely the capital actually invested by the owners, though the intent of the Treasury regulations was clearly to secure such a figure.   The adjustments applied by Mr. Nerlove, especially (1) and (2), may well have been substantially in error.   Nevertheless, the 88.5 billions for 1920 appears an acceptably close estimate; and, in the rest of the analysis, any error in this figure is propagated horizontally.   This of course means that *ratios* using invested capital as a base, such as those computed below, would contain errors which are *not* horizontal.   I am of the opinion, however, that the error in the 1920 figure is too small to damage seriously these ratios.   So far as time comparisons not involving ratios (involving, for example, amounts of change) are concerned, the 1920 error has no effect.

[16] Separate tabulations for dividends paid and dividends received are available only from 1922 on.   For 1921, I used the estimate of Ebersole, Burr, and Peterson

Mr. Nerlove, falling short of his results by the amount of the special insurance exemption.[17]

The next annual increment, beyond reinvested earnings, is money obtained by publicly offered stock issues. Such issues are made chiefly by large companies having listed securities; and the most acceptable estimate, that used by Mr. Nerlove, is the record published by the *Commercial & Financial Chronicle*. The published figures classify stock issues into "new" and "refunding"; but, as refunding issues of stock are presumably in almost all cases for the purpose of retiring bonds rather than other stock, the total (combined new and refunding) figure is correctly taken. Some unavoidable error exists because no allowance can be made for cost of flotation; the figures published indicate the gross amount issued and not the net funds realized by issuing corporations after payment of bankers' fees and other costs. The amount of this error is influenced by a wide variety of factors, and probably varies

---

(*Review of Economic Statistics*, November, 1929, p. 181) for net dividends paid to outsiders, i.e., 2,630 millions.

[17] *Op. cit.*, p. 72. He has used for reinvested net the figure in line 56 of the table prepared by Ebersole, Burr, and Peterson, *op. cit.*, pp. 180–181. That figure reckons the special deductions allowed to life insurance companies as a part of net earnings; whereas I have not done so, for reasons stated above.

Mr. Nerlove also includes the insurance exemption in the earnings figure (p. 13) which he uses in calculating his rate of return on invested capital (p. 40), but he remarks (p. 69) that "Reserve funds of insurance companies (the net additions to which are deductible from gross income for income tax purposes) were excluded from invested capital" in 1920. As I see it, all hinges upon the question of ownership of the insurance reserves and the legal additions thereto. If the Nerlove treatment requires additions thereto *after* 1920, in the form of specially tax-exempt interest, in order to be regarded as an investment constituting part of the equity, it may fairly be urged that the reserves as stated in 1920 included at least some portion representing such equity interest. On this basis, I regard his treatment as of doubtful consistency. I go further, however, as stated above, and hold that the special exemption because of the legal additions to insurance reserves is in fact mainly an expense, properly chargeable in reckoning net earnings. It is for this reason that I have avoided reckoning legal additions to the life insurance reserves either as a part of net earnings (Exhibit II) or as a part of invested capital (Exhibits III and IV).

EXHIBIT III. DETERMINATION OF REINVESTED NET (IN MILLIONS OF DOLLARS)

Year	(1) Net Earnings	(2) Dividends Paid	(3) Dividends Received	(4) Net Dividends to Outsiders (2) − (3)	(5) Reinvested Net (1) − (4)	(6) Share Paid to Outsiders (4)/(2)
1921	−$ 55.0	*	*	$2630.0†	−$2685.0	*
1922	4380.2	$3436.7	$ 803.1	2633.6	1746.7	76.6%
1923	5827.1	4169.1	870.1	3299.0	2528.0	79.2
1924	4998.5	4338.8	915.2	3423.6	1574.8	78.9
1925	6970.6	5189.5	1175.5	4014.0	2956.6	77.4
1926	6704.5	5945.3	1506.2	4439.1	2265.3	74.7
1927	5880.2	6423.2	1658.1	4765.1	1115.2	74.2
1928	7636.0	7073.7	1916.7	5157.0	2478.9	72.9
1929	8083.1	8355.7	2593.1	5762.6	2320.4	69.0
1930	1375.8	8202.2	2571.2	5631.0	−4255.2	68.7
1931	−3144.8	6151.1	1969.2	4181.9	−7326.7	68.0
1932	−5375.0	3885.6	1260.0	2625.6	−8000.5	67.6
1933	−2378.9	3127.5	1025.7	2101.8	−4480.6	67.2
1934	161.8	4889.4	2217.4	2672.0	−2510.2	54.6‡
1935	1674.3	5940.6	3013.6	2927.0	−1252.7	49.2‡

* Not available.

† Estimate of J. Franklin Ebersole, Susan S. Burr, and George M. Peterson, *Review of Economic Statistics*, November, 1929, p. 181.

‡ Elimination, in the main, of consolidated returns greatly changed reported volume of intercorporate dividends from previous years, and accounts largely for reduced ratios (Column 6) for 1934 and 1935. See note * of Exhibit IV, and note ‡ of Exhibit V.

especially in cases where rights are issued. As no satisfactory means of allowing for the error exists, it is ignored in this analysis.

A third increment comprises stock issues by smaller companies, not floating stock by "public" offerings. I accept Mr. Nerlove's estimate of the average relationship of the volume of such issues to the volume of public issues (discussed above), though he is evidently aware that such an estimate cannot be highly precise. On the average, he finds stock issued by smaller companies run to about one-fourth of the volume publicly offered, that is, one-fifth of the total of all issues. While accepting this estimate of the relationship, I do not agree that issues by smaller companies should be taken at a flat amount over successive years. The Nerlove

Exhibit IV. Calculation of Invested Capital

Year	(In millions of dollars)				(In billions of dollars)		
	(1)	(2)	(3)	(4)	(5)	(6)	(7)
	Reinvested Net	Stock Issues (large companies)	Stock Issues (small) 25% of (2)	Total New Investment (1) + (2) + (3)	Invested Capital, End of Year	Portion Owned Outside Corporations*	Same, Average for Year
1920					$ 88.5	$66.4	
1921	−$2685.0	$ 279.3	$ 69.8	−$2335.9	86.2	64.7	$65.6
1922	1746.7	624.0	156.0	2526.7	88.7	67.9	66.3
1923	2528.0	736.0	184.0	3448.0	92.1	73.0	70.4
1924	1574.8	866.3	216.6	2657.7	94.8	74.8	73.9
1925	2956.6	1311.0	327.8	4595.4	99.4	76.9	75.8
1926	2265.3	1317.8	329.4	3912.5	103.3	77.2	77.0
1927	1115.2	1773.3	443.3	3331.8	106.6	79.1	78.2
1928	2478.9	3627.2	906.8	7012.9	113.6	82.8	81.0
1929	2320.4	6921.4	1730.4	10972.2	124.6	86.0	84.4
1930	− 4255.2	1568.3	392.1	− 2294.8	122.3	84.1	85.0
1931	− 7326.7	343.1	85.8	− 6897.8	115.4	78.5	81.3
1932	− 8000.5	24.0	6.0	− 7970.5	107.4	72.7	75.6
1933	− 4480.6	152.7	38.2	− 4289.7	103.2	69.4	71.0
1934	− 2510.2	34.6	8.6	− 2467.0	100.7	68.6†	69.0
1935	− 1252.7	150.8	37.7	− 1064.2	99.6	67.9†	68.2

* See text for percentage factors applied to Column 5 for securing Column 6; factors for 1920 and 1921 assumed 75%.

† Proportionality factor *assumed* as 68.1 (average of years 1929–1933) because last two items of Column 6 of Table III are distorted by consolidated-return abandonment.

figure for issues by smaller companies is 500 millions in *each* year from 1921 to 1929, and Mr. Nerlove uses the flat figure because he regards these issues as not directly dependent upon the security markets.[18] Although this view has some force, I believe it is

[18] *Op. cit.*, p. 72, note to table: "As capital so obtained is not directly dependent upon the security markets, it cannot be assumed that its amount fluctuated in the same way and to the same degree as that obtained in the security markets. Since no other satisfactory basis was available, it was assumed that such new capital was secured in equal annual amounts each year. This will not result in any serious error, as the amounts are relatively small."

not decisive; and the flat figure seems likely to introduce a greater error than the alternative assumption that the one-to-four relationship between these issues and public issues prevails in each year. No conclusive evidence is available; but though granting that some small companies can sell stock without regard to general financial conditions, much doubt exists whether even small companies can in general secure new funds when security markets are declining or stagnant. Even the owners of closely-held concerns frequently have outside financial interests, and are unlikely to advance new funds readily in times of general stringency. I choose, therefore, to reckon stock issues by small companies in each year as 25% of the current public issues of large companies, but recognize that this basis may introduce a moderate error.

The three annual increments to invested capital, described above, are shown in Exhibit IV; and the fifth column, which adds these increments (as combined in the fourth column) successively by years to the 1920 base figure, gives the final estimate of invested capital at the end of each year.

Average Rate of Return

At this point I again depart from the Nerlove analysis, which uses the estimate of total invested capital as the divisor in obtaining the average rate of return on capital.[19]   The figure thus far obtained is total invested capital, and not the net investment by owners outside the corporate system.   A large share of the invested capital, as determined above, is owned by corporations.   If we are to use for net earnings a figure reflecting the profits available to outside owners, a figure excluding intercorporate dividends, we need for our divisor a figure giving capital invested in the corporate system by outsiders.[20]

Treasury tabulations of balance sheet data do not give cor-

---

[19] *Ibid.*, Chap. VII.

[20] The argument touching upon this point is sufficiently involved to deserve extended treatment, but I note merely that total invested capital cannot be justified as a devisor even by adding intercorporate dividends to net earnings.   Careful examination unmistakably points to the selection made above.

porate holdings of stock in other corporations separately; and even if they did, the very valuation difficulties sought to be avoided by the present analysis would preclude their yielding a precise estimate of the share of total invested capital which is supplied by corporations. In fact, no precise basis for such estimate exists; but, in spite of obvious defects and the danger of substantial error, we can satisfactorily use the dividend figures as an indication. Treasury tabulations give total cash dividends paid and dividends received by corporations. The difference is the net dividends paid to outsiders, and the ratio of this figure to total dividends paid (Column 6 of Exhibit III) may be taken as an estimate of the share of total invested capital owned outside the corporate system. Application of these percentages to the items of Column 5 of Exhibit IV yields the estimate of capital invested by outsiders, given in the sixth column.

This procedure is admittedly open to substantial errors. No clear evidence exists as to whether corporations tend on the average to own relatively more or less dividend-paying stocks than outsiders, or to own stocks paying relatively higher or lower dividends per share, than outsiders. One might suspect that stocks owned by corporations for purposes of control would ordinarily be common rather than preferred; but certain companies, particularly in the finance division, may well lean to preferred stocks in order to obtain income. Moreover, the typical practice may vary from year to year; certain investment trusts, for example, may lean to speculative non-dividend-paying stocks at one stage of the cycle and to steadier issues at another stage. Other considerations bearing on the point will occur to the reader. At best, the dividend ratio is a faulty basis for allocating total invested capital between corporations and outsiders. I use it, despite its imperfections, as affording a result probably less seriously in error than any other allocation which can be made.

The final adjustment of the invested capital estimate consists in shifting from a year-end basis to an average-for-the-year basis; and here also I depart from the Nerlove treatment, which apparently used the year-end figure for invested capital as divisor to be applied to the earnings of the entire year. Average invested capital (owned by outsiders) for each year appears in the final column of Exhibit IV, and is a simple mean of the figures for the end of the current year and the end of the preceding year. This is, of course, only a rough approach to the true average for the year; it takes no account of varying rates during the year at which the three increments to invested capital take place. Net earnings reinvested may develop at a different rate in one part of a given year than in another, and the same applies to stock issues. But the simple mean is a sufficient improvement over mere year-end figures to warrant its use as the divisor.

The ratio of the net earnings (final column of Exhibit II) to this divisor yields the estimated average rate of return on invested capital, and the percentage results are as follows:

1922	6.61	1929	9.58
1923	8.28	1930	1.62
1924	6.76	1931	−3.87
1925	9.20	1932	−7.11
1926	8.79	1933	−3.35
1927	7.52	1934	0.23
1928	9.42	1935	2.46

Figures for 1920 and 1921 are not shown, because tabulated data for those years do not yield comparable figures for net earnings; and the 1935 figure, based on tabulations which do not include all the data essential to the adjustments required by our definitions, is necessarily tentative. The simple average of the fourteen annual percentages is 4.01; and this measures the general average rate of return over one great cycle, as the stage of business revival in 1935 was probably not far from that in 1922.[21]

Year-to-year changes in the percentages, ranging from a peak of 9.58 to a bottom of −7.11, reflect the very high cyclical variability in the rate of return; this is statistical confirmation of the generally recognized fact that profits constitute one of the most volatile of

---

[21] The items for 1934 and 1935 are not strictly comparable with the others, because of the restriction on consolidated returns. See footnote 5, above, p. 574.

economic factors. Variability indicated by these percentages is, moreover, an average manifestation for corporate enterprise in the aggregate, the specific variability in rate of return for many particular corporations must run far higher. From the point of view of the relation of profits to entrepreneurial decisions, this specific variability, rather than the average, is of controlling importance. Corporate enterprise in the aggregate is unmistakably speculative, and numerous specific corporate enterprises are surely far more speculative. In all questions relating to the acquisition of new corporate capital and the determination of the particular use to be made of such new investment, the high degree of variability in return assumes decisive importance. This in itself is a major explanation of the fact that in prosperous times such a large share of new invested capital has been obtained through reinvested earnings, rather than by reliance upon new issues.[22]

RETURN ON BOOK VALUE OF EQUITY

Treasury tabulations of balance sheet data cover a considerably less complete list of corporations than the income tabulations, but yield a fairly close estimate of the book value of aggregate corporate equity. As stated above, this figure contains an element responsive to earning power, and it is therefore a less good divisor for calculating the rate of return than is invested capital. We present, however, the ratios on this basis for comparative purposes, and use the book equity also for other significant steps in the analysis. The tabulated balance sheets show preferred stock, common stock (for issues having a par value, and those non-par issues for which a total value is stated), and surplus and undivided profits less deficit (including total value of common stock equity

---

[22] The portion (percentage) of new invested capital which came from reinvested net earnings in the years 1922–1929, derived from Exhibit IV, is:

1922	69.2	1926	57.8
1923	73.2	1927	33.5
1924	59.2	1928	35.3
1925	64.3	1929	21.2

for those non-par issues of which total value is not stated).[23] The sum of these three items is the book equity. Figures on a substantially comparable basis are available beginning with 1926, and appear in the first column of Exhibit V.

EXHIBIT V. RETURN ON BOOK EQUITY

Year	(In billions of dollars)				Percentages	
	(1)	(2)	(3)	(4)	(5)	(6)
	Tabulated Book Equity, End of Year	Same Stepped Up	Portion Owned Outside Corporations	Same, Average for Year	Rate of Return on Equity*	Rate of Return on Invested Capital†
1926	$119.26	$122.3	$ 91.4			
1927	132.40	135.9	100.9	$ 96.2	6.11%	7.52%
1928	142.89	146.5	106.8	103.8	7.36	9.42
1929	164.97	169.3	116.8	111.8	7.23	9.58
1930	161.08	165.3	113.6	115.2	1.19	1.62
1931	143.26	147.0	100.0	106.8	−2.95	−3.87
1932	133.57	137.0	92.6	96.3	−5.58	−7.11
1933	127.58	130.9	88.0	90.3	−2.63	−3.35
1934	141.59‡	145.3	79.3‡	83.6	0.19	0.23
1935	138.93‡	142.5	70.1‡	74.7	2.24	2.46

* Column 6, Exhibit II, divided by Column 4 herein.

† Column 6, Exhibit II, divided by Column 7, Exhibit IV.

‡ Column 1 items for 1934 and 1935 are elevated by abandonment of consolidated returns. Accordingly, exact ratios of Column 6 of Exhibit III are used to pass from Column 2 to Column 3 herein.

The first adjustment needed allows for the failure of the balance sheet data to cover fully the list of about a half million corporations which file income returns. The deficiency of balance sheets results from various factors, chief of which is the failure to require complete balance sheets from numerous corporations filing income returns. On the basis of number of returns, balance sheets tabulated ran in 1933 about 88% of income returns; but the percentage had been considerably lower in earlier years. This percentage cannot satisfactorily be used to step up the tabulated equity to comparability with the income data; though I, and some other

[23] See, for example, *Statistics of Income*, 1933, pp. 160–171.

writers, have used this method heretofore.[24]   The controlling fact
is that balance sheets are more fully reported for large corporations
than for small, and for income (taxable) corporations than for no-income (non-taxable) corporations.

Beginning with 1931, issues of *Statistics of Income* have included a
special tabulation of income data for those corporations filing
balance sheets.   We have various bases, therefore, among the
income items for comparing all corporations with those filing
balance sheets.   The item selected for the present purpose is total
compiled receipts; and, for 1931–1933, this shows that about 97.5%
of corporate gross business was reported on returns filing balance
sheets.   Although gross business is not necessarily closely correlated with equity, this ratio appears a tolerably precise basis for
stepping up the equity data.   The single ratio is used for every
year of the record, although 1931–1933 data show some variation,
and collateral evidence suggests that the ratio may have been
moderately lower in certain earlier years.   The full extent of
these variations is unknown, and no serious error is introduced by
using the flat ratio.   Application of this ratio, by division, to the
tabulated items of Column 1 of Exhibit V yields the second column.

From this point on, the earlier procedure is followed.   The
share of the equity owned outside the corporate system is estimated
by using the dividend ratios; annual averages are obtained as
simple means of the year-end data, and the resulting figures are
divided into net earnings to give the rate of return on book equity.
To facilitate comparison, the final column of Exhibit V repeats the
rate of return on invested capital, previously found.

The ratios based on book equity necessarily run smaller,
numerically, than those on invested capital, because the book
equity contains an additional element reflecting in the main capitalization of earning power.   The equity ratios thus show less wide
variability, and for the same reason; the equity fluctuates in some
degree in the same direction as net earnings.   These comparisons,

---

[24] See the author's *Corporate Earning Power*.   Stanford University, California:
Stanford University Press, 1929, Chap. VII.

in fact, give point to the argument favoring invested capital above equity, as the divisor.

WRITE-UPS AND WRITE-DOWNS

Direct comparison of figures for book equity and for invested capital throws some light upon corporate practice and policy with respect to writing up or writing down assets. For such comparison also the net year-end figures, representing the share of outsiders (Column 6 of Exhibit IV and Column 3 of Exhibit V), should be used; for otherwise actual changes in valuation might be counted more than once. The differences between invested capital and book equity, absolutely and as percentages of invested capital, appear in Exhibit VI. Not all the 1926 difference can be said to have arisen since 1920; for, if a comparable book equity were available for 1920, it might well run considerably above the basic invested capital of 88.5 billions. *Changes* in the difference after the end of 1926, however, are a significant indication of valuation fluctuations in those years. These changes, actual and cumulated, appear in Columns 3 and 4 of Exhibit VI.

EXHIBIT VI. COMPARISON OF BOOK EQUITY AND INVESTED CAPITAL, 1926–1933 * (IN BILLIONS OF DOLLARS)

Year	(1) Excess of Equity over Invested Capital†	(2) Ratio of Same to Invested Capital	(3) Annual Change in the Excess	(4) Same Cumulated	(5) Same (4) as Percentage of Invested Capital
1926	$14.2	18.4%			
1927	21.8	27.6	$7.6	$ 7.6	9.2%
1928	24.0	29.0	2.2	9.8	10.6
1929	30.8	35.8	6.8	16.6	17.4
1930	29.5	35.1	−1.3	15.3	16.7
1931	21.5	27.4	−8.0	7.3	9.0
1932	19.9	27.4	−1.5	5.7	9.0
1933	18.6	26.8	−1.3	4.4	8.4

* Significance of all items for 1934 and 1935 is greatly in doubt because of abandonment of consolidated returns; those years are therefore excluded from this table.

† Column 3 of Exhibit V less Column 6 of Exhibit IV.

We must avoid the conclusion that these annual changes represent merely and completely write-ups and write-downs, in the sense ordinarily understood in accounting, during those years. In considerable part they result from partially hidden changes in valuation, which arise through intercorporate exchanges of security investments and other assets at prices reflecting more or less imperfectly prevailing market conditions. The case is not clear, for intercorporate sales at enhanced or discounted values presumably give rise to largely equivalent capital gains or losses; these enter into corporate net earnings, and therefore into our invested capital figure used as a basis of reference.

The case is more definite with respect to revaluation of securities held according to market price in order to determine book value. This is an operation more clearly of the write-up or write-down sort, and undoubtedly occurred on a large scale.

So far as revaluation of other types of corporate assets is concerned, little specific knowledge is available, though various helpful qualitative remarks can be made. Changes in valuation of inventories probably bulked large, particularly after 1929; before that date the price movement had for several years been relatively narrow. Here again, some part of the revaluation may have entered our invested capital figure because of the fairly general practice of reckoning inventory at lower of cost or market in determining statutory net income. Valuation of receivables also was subject to important discretionary changes, particularly after 1929. And in this case, too, part at least (but perhaps not a large part) of such changes found its way, through the statutory allowance of bad debts as a deduction, into statutory net income and therefore into reinvested net income and into invested capital.

With respect to fixed assets and such miscellaneous assets as patents, trademarks, and goodwill, direct write-ups and write-downs were not only of large magnitude, but were also not reflected in net income and invested capital. Such revaluations impinged directly on the equity, and must surely enter as a substantial part of the changes shown in Column 3 of Exhibit VI.

The entire case is by no means clear; but, though not all of the annual changes recorded in Exhibit VI reflect deliberate write-ups or write-downs of assets, those changes do broadly represent the aggregate effect upon book equity of write-ups and write-downs plus other less direct revaluations.[25]   The large size of the figures (Column 3, Exhibit VI) indicates that revaluations in the aggregate must have high importance in corporate management, and it is a mistake to speak of them as "mere bookkeeping operations."   That they heavily influence corporate dividend and financing policies, as well as less crucial matters, cannot be doubted.   There may even be some question whether they can be entirely ignored in arriving at a base for reckoning earning power, though the evidence seems overwhelming that the base should be actually invested capital and not book equity.

CURRENT ESTIMATES OF RETURN

No comprehensive data on corporate earning power for dates more recent than the latest Treasury compilation are available; but published statements of individual companies, mainly very large companies with listed securities, are frequently used for compiling approximate figures.   Numerous compilations such as these exist, and I use here those of the National City Bank.[26] The tabulations show, as the percentage profits on net worth:

[25] I have not discussed, in the foregoing, the probable effect of the merger movement—particularly violent during most of the period studied—on the revaluation figures.   The analysis would yield inconclusive results, largely because of the capital gains feature.   Moreover, differences in capital structure of the resultant merged enterprises would assume high importance.

Some part of the "revaluations" were forced; they occurred in consequence of failures and reorganizations.   Although partial evidence on this aspect of the case can be obtained, data are not adequate for even an approximate determination of the amounts involved.   For further discussion of the revaluation problem, see Solomon Fabricant's *Profits, Losses and Business Assets*, Bulletin 55, National Bureau of Economic Research, April, 1935, pp. 7–11.

[26] Appearing annually in the March or April issue of the bank's monthly bulletin on *Economic Conditions, Governmental Finance, United States Securities*.   The compilations cover a somewhat varying list of companies, all of them large, and include data on net profits, net worth, and the ratio between them—classified by industrial groups.   The finance and railroad and public utility divisions are

1928	11.7	1933	3.4
1929	13.3	1934	4.4
1930	7.1	1935	6.7
1931	3.3	1936	10.1
1932	−0.3	1937	10.7

In comparing these figures with those presented above for all corporations, numerous reservations are essential. As observed in footnote 26, they do not cover corporations in the fields of finance or transportation and public utilities. They relate only to large companies, generally very large companies; and detailed examination of earlier Treasury tabulations has abundantly shown that the earnings experience of such companies is very different from that of the vast number of small units which form an important share, in the aggregate, of corporate enterprise. Moreover, the definition of net profits presumably differs, for many of these individual corporation statements, from that derived from the tax data; and even among the several statements wide differences in accounting practice may well exist. Broadly speaking, however, the net profits here reported are designed to cover the same concept of income as the net earnings figure I have defined above. Finally, the net worth figures here not only differ from the invested capital item I have used above, and are in fact closer to the book equity item; but they also (1) include the total net worth rather than the share in the hands of others than corporations within the group tabulated, and (2) apply to the beginning of the year instead of representing an average for the year as a whole.

On the first of these final points, I remark that, in any case, only the intercorporate interest within the group tabulated is at issue; holdings by corporations not in the list tabulated are strictly "outside" holdings. Moreover, the exclusion of finance and transportation and public utilities almost surely cuts down greatly the extent of the intercorporate holdings within the group tabulated. On the second point, I see no means of adjusting the published total

entirely excluded, the latter because of "duplication of profits" resulting from intercorporate holdings (April, 1929, Bulletin).

net worth figures to an average-for-the-year basis, because the list of corporations covered varies somewhat from one year's end to another. I see no satisfactory means of allowing for the non-inclusion of the two great classes—finance, and transportation and public utilities—and tentatively make the assumption that the profit experience for these industrial fields was not greatly different in 1934–1936 from the average experience in the fields covered by the bank's tabulation. On this basis, the bank's percentages for return on net worth given above may be taken as showing roughly the course for all large corporations in the aggregate, in all industrial fields, for the years 1934–1936.

The remaining difficulty is to account for the small corporations, which are in no sense represented by these figures. The return on invested capital (Column 6 of Exhibit V) declined about 83% from 1929 to 1930, and fell far below zero in 1932; whereas the ratio for the large corporations covered in the bank's study dropped only 54% from 1929 to 1930, and barely dipped below zero in 1932. This confirms the conclusion, based upon general knowledge and upon somewhat fragmentary data from various sources, that despite the highly cyclical character of some lines of industry in which large companies predominate, profits of small corporations in the aggregate are more responsive to cyclical variations than profits of large corporations. Taking rough account of the differences, in 1929–1930 and 1934–1935, between the rates of decline and rise in the bank's figures and in my figures for return on invested capital, the 1935–1936 rise in the bank's figures from 6.7 to 10.1 suggests 4% or somewhat higher as a highly provisional estimate of my figure for 1936; and the 1937 figure may well run slightly above that for 1936.

RENT

31

THE HISTORICAL APPROACH TO RENT AND PRICE THEORY*

By Daniel H. Buchanan†

I

After a century and a half of debate over the relation of rent to prices, the principal authorities take up positions which are so divergent as to make harmonisation impossible. One group says with Taussig that:

Rent . . . forms no part of those expenses of production which affect price,[1]

while another equally insistent group replies with Jevons that:

So far as cost of production regulates the values of commodities, wages must enter into the calculation on exactly the same footing as rent.[2]

Looked at from a distance it sometimes appears that opponents in a dispute have been discussing different questions. It is the purpose of this paper to show that this is just what has happened in the case of rent and price. Strange as it may seem, two entirely different questions, starting from different hypotheses and inspired by interest in different aspects of economic theory, have been confused ever since Adam Smith wrote. The two questions were much alike. Both dealt with land rent and with prices: but

---

* *Economica*, Volume IX, June 1929, pages 123–155. Reprinted by courtesy of the publisher and author.

† University of North Carolina. Formerly, Harvard University.

[1] *Principles of Economics*, 3rd ed., ii, p. 63.

[2] *Theory of Political Economy*, 3rd ed., Preface, p. xlvi. A common theory which might seem to harmonise, or compromise between these theories divides rents into marginal and differential elements and says that the latter is not, but the former is, an element in expenses of production. This theory is criticised below, p. 636, n. 72.

at the crucial point their hypotheses were opposite, making it impossible that their answers should be the same.

The essential difference in the two questions is that in one the land was supposed to have an alternative use, while in the other it had none. In the one case a number of uses were sharply competing for the land and whatever use secured it was compelled to pay the competitive rent: in the other case the land had only one annual use and could only accept whatever rental the one use offered, or return to nature and receive nothing. The conclusion therefore followed that in the one case rent was a necessary payment, while in the other it was not. This is the simplest statement of the matter. The more fundamental aspect will come out in the theoretical section at the close of the paper. There it will be shown that equilibrium is formed in different ways in the two cases.

A principal cause of the confusion of these two questions is that the question of rent and price properly lies in two main fields, namely exchange and distribution. In exchange it has been usual to think of the price of particular products and to suppose that the land has many competitive uses: but in distribution it was, especially in the discussions before 1850, common to think of the *group* of commodities which a given *class* produces and to think of the land as taken from nature by one class and having no alternative but to return to nature. Some writers have discussed the question from one point of view at one time and from another at another time. Other writers have confused the two points of view, but have allowed one of them to dominate their discussion. In still other cases a writer has treated the matter exclusively from one point of view. The first of these comments applies to Smith and J. S. Mill, the second to the Ricardians and the third to Jevons.

Our first task is to show that two problems have been confused. After that has been completed we shall undertake to show the result of applying the equilibrium theory of value and distribution to these two problems. We are dealing with only one aspect of rent theory and shall, therefore, deal only with such aspects of its treatment by the most important writers as bear directly upon our task. The two problems are most clearly seen from the writings of the Ricardians, J. S. Mill and Jevons. The reason for their existence, however, goes back to the Physiocrats and Smith. Also they are clearly present in Smith's writings, in spite of less definite statements, and it has seemed best to treat the authors in chronological order.

II

In this section we shall examine the case of the French Physiocrats. This is not because they left any theory as to the relation between rent and price, but because the point of view with which they treated the relation between rent and other incomes was quite similar to the point of view which prevailed later in England. They dealt with a society divided into classes dependent upon economic position. Smith and the Ricardians dealt with a similarly classified society. Also the Physiocratic idea that those occupations which furnished raw produce (the principal of which was agriculture) gave a "surplus" or "net product" while other occupations merely supported the people engaged in them, has close affinity to the English idea that rent is a "surplus" above price-determining expenses of production. We know, too, that Adam Smith was much influenced by their opinions and that other English writers were familiar with their theories.

The principal purpose of this section is to point out the peculiarities of these writers' treatment of the whole question of rent and to note its reasonableness, as well as its affinity to the later English idea. Of these peculiarities we should note three. (*a*) They were concerned with distribution or an explanation of the incomes of the different classes of their society. (*b*) They considered the rent (net product) of rural and not of urban land. (*c*) They looked on the rent (net product) not as from any particular kind of raw produce, but as from raw produce as a whole. They considered agricultural produce as a single commodity. (Their departure from that practice was to consider not the return to a particular kind of agricultural produce but the return to mining and forestry.)

Under mercantilist leadership rural interests had been sacrificed to industrial and commercial interests and the Physiocrats undertook to show that this was a mistaken policy. They hoped to prove that it was not through industry and commerce that a nation became rich, but through agriculture. This meant that they must analyse the conditions upon which the different kinds of incomes depended—that is, they had to develop a theory of incomes, or of distribution.[3] They believed agriculture to be superior to other occupations in that it furnished a net surplus over the costs of carrying it on. The point of view of distribution rather than of price was strictly proper to their problem and purpose.

The same reason accounts for their treating of rural land and its net product rather than of city land. City rents were a small item in the income of the nation. The question of rent for a European nation at that time was of rural rent. But besides this, they were attempting to show the virtues of rural agriculture as against urban industry and commerce. Their usage suited both the facts and their purpose.

Thirdly, it was proper that they should stress the net product from raw produce as a whole rather than from a particular kind of raw produce, and for the same reason. Had they been advocating the production of a particular agricultural crop, then the matter of competing uses for land would have come up: but they were advocating rural as against urban occupations and rural products as a whole, not particular rural products, was their concern. Therefore they could quite logically leave the selection of crops to agriculturists and make a distinction between the group as a whole and the products of industrial and commercial men.[4]

---

[3] Their principal achievement in this direction was, of course, the *tableau économique.*

[4] "The English statisticians of the latter part of the seventeenth century regarded the annual produce of the country with the eyes of a farmer. They thought of the raw produce of a farm, and regarded this as forming the subsistence of the whole of the people. The French économistes, or physiocrats, . . . had the same agricultural standpoint. . . . "—CANNAN, *Wealth,* p. 6.

The class point of view was quite natural to the physiocratic problem. We shall not be surprised if we find similar points of view in the treatment of problems of distribution between classes, or of incomes of classes, in other countries similarly situated.

III

It has been common to pronounce Adam Smith inconsistent in his treatment of rent and price. He stated both that rent was and that it was not an element in determining the price of commodities. The former theory is developed and stated most clearly in Chapter VI of Book I of the *Wealth of Nations*. The latter is set forth in Chapter XI of the same book. In the former he says:

. . . the price of any instrument of husbandry, such as a labouring horse, is itself made up of the same three parts; the rent of the land upon which he is reared, the labour of tending and rearing him, and the profits of the farmer who advances both the rent of this land and the wages of this labour.[5]

He says that corn has the same three elements in its price and that in every improved society:

all the three enter more or less, as component parts, into the price of the far greater part of commodities.[6]

But in Chapter XI the other theory is stated as follows:

Rent . . . enters into the composition of the price of commodities in a different way from wages and profit. High or low wages and profit are the causes of high or low price; high or low rent is the effect of it. It is because high or low wages and profit must be paid in order to bring a particular commodity to market that its price is high or low. But it is because its price is high or low, a great deal more or a very little more, or no more, than what is sufficient to pay those wages and profit, that it affords high rent or a low rent, or no rent at all.[7]

Now Smith allowed these conflicting statements to stand through all the editions of his book and this in spite of the criticism

[5] *Wealth of Nations* (all references to Cannan's edition), i, p. 52.
[6] *Ibid.*
[7] *Ibid.*, p. 147.

of some of his most able friends.[8]   In spite of their seeming inconsistency, Smith believed that both statements were somehow true.[9]

Careful examination reveals a number of facts about Smith's
treatment which, while not making him quite consistent, show
that his inconsistency resulted from the fact that he was discussing
rent from two points of view without clearly distinguishing between
them.   Let us tabulate a few of these main points:

1. Smith discussed rent from the two points of view of price and
   distribution.
2. When he treated of value he considered "particular" commodities "taken separately," but when he treated of distribution he commonly considered "the whole annual produce
   . . . taken complexly."
3. When treating of value and particular commodities "taken
   separately" he looked for the supply of the particular commodity and therefore considered the rent paid for fields
   which had sharply competing uses: but when treating of
   distribution he looked for the supply of "the whole annual
   produce . . . taken complexly" of the land-owning class
   and therefore considered the rent paid for farm land as a
   whole, it having no competing use.

From this it followed that in the former case the rent must be
paid in order to hold the land, while in the latter case rent-payment was not necessary because the land had no alternative but
to accept the rent offered or return to nature and receive nothing.

As Cannan has pointed out, Smith's interests underwent a
decided change on account of his contact with the Physiocrats
during a three-year sojourn in France after considerable work had
already been done on the *Wealth of Nations*.   The earlier chapters
indicate an interest primarily in exchange and prices.   Beginning
with the division of labour, the chapters follow naturally through
exchange, money, price, component parts of price.   Chapters are

[8] See footnote to p. 612, n. 22 below.
[9] As Marshall says: "In many instances he anticipated in one part of his writings truths which in other parts he seemed to deny." *Principles*, 6th ed., p. 439, n.

then given to wages, profits and rent, not because these subjects are interesting in themselves, but because they are the component parts of price and throw light upon that matter.[10] After his sojourn in France, Smith's interest shifts to distribution, which was then the chief subject of study by the Physiocrats. Cannan believes that this led him to make several insertions and modifications in his earlier treatment.[11] Smith appears to have decided that his theory of the component parts of price, that is, of wages, profits and rent, was also a very good theory of distribution of incomes. Wasn't his explanation of what governed the amounts of these shares just what the Physiocrats were striving for? These component parts of price were paid to various persons and seemed to be merely their incomes. The following statement, apparently an insertion, undertakes to make this theory of prices into a theory of distribution[12]:

As the price or exchangeable value of every particular commodity, taken separately, resolves itself into some one or other or all of those three parts: so that of all the commodities which compose the whole annual produce of the labour of every country, taken complexly, must resolve itself into the same three parts, and be parcelled out among different inhabitants of the country either as wages of their labour, the profits of their stock, or the rent of their land: the whole of what is annually either collected or produced by the labour of every society, or, what comes to the same thing, the whole price of it, is in this manner originally distributed among some of its different members. Wages, profit and rent are the three original sources of all revenue, as well as of all exchangeable value.

This statement proves the first and second statements which we have just made about Smith's treatment, namely, that he discussed rent from the two points of view of price and distribution: that when he considered price he considered the price of "particular" commodities "taken separately," but when he considered distribution he thought of the various products "taken complexly" as the "annual produce."

The crucial fact remaining to be determined is whether or not

---

[10] See end of chap. vii.
[11] *Theories of Production and Distribution*, p. 188.
[12] *Wealth of Nations*, p. 54.

the land was supposed to have competing uses in the one case and not in the other. We shall turn to that in a moment, but it will be helpful first to observe (a) the causes of and then (b) the tendencies following the usage thus far pointed out.

It was not unnatural that Smith should look at rent from these two angles. A cost theory of value includes a consideration of the various payments which producers are required to pay: and any theory of distribution, especially in a period in which the dominating class, politically, socially and economically was the landlord class, would have to include rent. It was impossible to treat the two great questions of exchange and distribution without drawing rent into both of them.

It was also not unnatural that when considering value he should think of "particular commodities." The problem of value is the explanation of why the various particular commodities exchange in the ratios at which we find them in the market. That is, the problem of value *always* deals with particular commodities. It is not strange that Smith considered them in his treatment of that subject.

Now when one thinks of rent as an element in the cost of producing a particular commodity and at the same time the income of one of the "classes of society," it is fairly easy to confuse the two. They seemed to be merely opposite sides of the same thing, but in practice they became entirely different. In Smith's two problems rent as a share in distribution became something entirely different from rent as an expense of production of a particular commodity. As an expense of production for a particular commodity it was the competitive amount which that product had to pay in order to take a given field away from other uses. Its payment was necessary, under free competition, if that particular commodity were to be brought to market in the usual amount If the price of that commodity did not allow it to pay a given rental, another commodity took over the field. That is, the land had competitive uses and the competitive rental must be paid in order to secure it for any one particular commodity.

But rent as a share in the distribution of the annual produce of the nation was something different; it was the total income of a "class" of society. This income was received not from the sale of one particular commodity, but from the sale of a large number of these very commodities which in the other case were competing for the use of the different fields. Rent as income became not the amount paid by a particular commodity for a given field, but the amount paid by agricultural, or raw, produce as a whole for "farms" or for the whole of the estates owned by the "landed interest."

This land was in a very different situation from the fields which had sharply competing uses. It had been taken from nature without payment and had no other possible use. It must be used for generalised raw produce or return to nature. Consequently payment to it was not a condition of the furnishing of raw produce. The taking away of a share of particular rent meant that the fields would go to uses which would pay the full rent: but the taking away of this generalised rent meant that the land stayed on in the same use because it had no alternative which would bring it anything. In the former case rent was, in the latter case it was not, a necessary payment.

Let us now take up the matter of the two questions and see whether or not Smith actually considered that the land had a competing use in one case and none in the other. In his earlier treatment of prices he says:

The quantity of every commodity brought to market naturally suits itself to the effectual demand. If at any time it exceeds the effectual demand, some of the component parts of its price must be paid below their natural rate. If it is rent, the interest of the landlords will immediately prompt them to withdraw a part of their land; and if it is wages or profit, the interest of the labourers in the one case, and of their employers in the other, will prompt them to withdraw a part of their labour or stock from this employment.[13]

The important point here is that the owners of land are supposed to be in a position to "withdraw a part of their land" without loss. It is obvious that they put it to other uses which pay a better rental than this low-priced commodity now affords. Unless

---

[13] *Wealth of Nations*, p. 59.

it received the normal rent, that field would not produce that commodity.

Let us now turn to the part of the book in which rent is considered from the point of view of distribution. Although Smith states in the quotation already given[14] that "Wages, profit and rent are the three original sources of all revenue," he gives no part of his work explicitly to a discussion of that aspect of them. His chapter on rent is said to be a continuation of his price discussion and is written supposedly:

> . . . to show what are the circumstances which regulate the rent of land, and which either raise or lower the real price of all the different substances which it produces.[15]

After a short introduction of four pages which contain the above quoted statement to the effect that rent is an effect rather than a cause of high price, and which look more like a postscript after the development of the author's interest in distribution than a part of the discussion of the prices of particular commodities, we have two "parts" which have little bearing upon our problem. It is the "introduction" to which our chief attention should be given, because in it we have the claim that rent is an effect of high price. The central thing in this introductory section is not a field but a farm, and not a "particular commodity" but "the produce of land." At only one place does Smith fall into the use of the other term, and that appears to have been either an oversight or a deliberate attempt to smooth over a matter which he did not quite understand.[16] Here Smith says:

> Such parts of the produce of land can commonly be brought to market, of which the ordinary price is sufficient to replace the stock which must be employed in bringing them thither, together with its ordinary profits. If the ordinary price is more than this, the surplus part of it will naturally go to the rent of land. If it is not more, though the commodity may be brought to market, it can afford

---

[14] See p. 605 above.

[15] *Wealth of Nations*, bk. i, ch. vii, last par.

[16] Cannan has shown that Smith sometimes patched up parts which did not quite fit. *Theories of Production and Distribution*, p. 38.

no rent to the landlord.   Whether the price is or is not more, depends upon the demand.[17]

Now as compared to the statements already quoted from Smith's earlier discussion, the important point to be noted here is that although the rent falls to zero, the landlord is able to do nothing about it.   In the other case the "landlords will immediately . . . withdraw . . . land," and merely because the rent falls.   Here it disappears and the commodity is still "brought to market."

It is obvious that the two cases are different: and equally obvious that in the case of "particular commodities, taken separately" the land is in demand for other uses, while in the case of "produce of land" all the particular commodities are reduced to one and the land must accept what is offered or return to nature and receive nothing.   In the one case it has a competing use and in the other it has not.   The third of our three statements made about Smith's treatment of this subject is shown to be true.   In treating of the value of particular commodities, Smith supposed fields to have competing uses, while in treating of distribution and the value of "Raw Produce," he thought of farm land as a whole, it having no competing use.

There is just one part of his treatment which is not in harmony with this interpretation.   Until the last paragraph but one of the introductory section he speaks of rent in general terms "considered as the price paid for the use of land" and of "the produce of land" giving no hint that he is dealing with the rent paid for producing a "particular commodity, taken separately."   But here, and in the important statement which claims that "rent enters into the composition of the price of commodities in a different way from wages and profit," he uses the term which we should least expect and which is entirely out of harmony with all the balance of the section.   He says not "produce of land," but "a particular commodity."   If he had used the other term the whole treatment would have fitted perfectly with the interpretation

---

[17] *Wealth of Nations*, p. 146.

which we have made and would have been to that extent reasonable. As it is this term is entirely out of place. It cannot be said that Smith *meant* to say "produce of land," but it can be said that he *should* have said it. At any rate it can be affirmed that if he meant to say that rent did not need to be paid in order to bring "a particular commodity" to market, he immediately forgot it: for we only turn the page to find the opposite doctrine again. Here he says:

> A great part of the cultivated lands must be employed in rearing and fattening cattle, of which the price, therefore, must be sufficient to pay, not only the labour necessary for tending them, but the rent which the landlord and the profit which the farmer could have drawn from such land employed in tillage.[18]

This is in strict harmony with his earlier statements regarding rent and the price of a particular commodity; but entirely out of harmony with the last quotation except under the above interpretation, namely, that in that statement, he was actually considering "the produce of farms."

Smith's treatment of taxation bears out the interpretation here given. While not dividing land into that which has and that which has not a competing use, one part of his classification depends upon that fact. His conclusion is that if a general tax is laid on the rent of land,

> the landlord is in all cases the real contributor.[19]

Also, such a tax,

> has no tendency to diminish the quantity . . . and . . . can have none to raise the price of that produce.

This is a tax on land in general and has no relation to the particular crop for which the land is taken. It is assumed that it has no possibility of escape and that it will produce the same quantity of the same goods as before. While containing no reference to marginal produce, this corresponds to the principal case and conclusion of the Ricardians later.

---

[18] *Wealth of Nations*, pp. 149–150.
[19] *Wealth of Nations*, ii, p. 313.

But Smith also considers taxes on some particular products of land. In one of these cases the land is specially fitted for one use which gives it a "monopoly" rent. There is no possibility of avoiding the tax by shifting to another use because there is no effectively competing use for the land. Like the last case, there is thus no tendency to reduce the produce and the tax falls upon the rent-receiver. He says:

A tax upon the produce of those precious vineyards, of which the wine falls so much short of the effectual demand, that its price is always above the natural proportion to that of the produce of other equally fertile and equally well cultivated land, would necessarily reduce the rent and profit of those vineyards. The price of the wines being already the highest that could be got for the quantity commonly sent to market, it could not be raised higher without diminishing that quantity; and the quantity could not be diminished without still greater loss, *because the lands could not be turned to any other equally valuable produce.* The whole weight of the tax, therefore, would fall upon the rent . . . of the vineyards.[20] (The italics are mine.)

The kernel of this matter is that the land *has no alternative use.* The conclusion, as in the above case of a tax on general rent, is inevitable.

But Smith introduces the case of competing uses and here we find the same assumptions and conclusions as in his discussion of price in Chapter VII of Book I. A tax which interferes with the rental which a piece of land can get in one of its competing uses will cause it to be withdrawn from that use and the tax to be paid by the consumer in higher prices. He says:

The rent and profit of barley land . . . must always be nearly equal to those of other equally fertile and equally well cultivated lands. If they were less, some part of the barley land would soon be turned to some other purpose; and if they were greater, more land would soon be turned to the raising of barley.

The different taxes which have been imposed upon malt, beer and ale have never . . . reduced the rent . . . of barley land. The price of malt to the brewer has constantly risen in proportion to the taxes imposed upon it; and those taxes, together with the different duties upon beer and ale, have constantly either raised the price, or what comes to the same thing, reduced the quality of those

---

[20] *Ibid.*, pp. 376–377.

commodities to the consumer.   The final payment of those taxes has fallen constantly upon the consumer and not upon the producer.[21]

It will be observed that the hypothesis is the opposite of what it was in the last quotation.   Here the land has an alternative use—and the conclusion is equally inevitable.   Thus in Book V as in Book I, the rent for one of two or more sharply competing uses is an expense of production; while if the land has only one economical use, the rent payment or non-payment has no effect upon the supply or price of its product.

Hume criticised Smith's findings on rent and price and wrote him:

> I cannot think that the rent of farms makes any part of the price of their produce, but that the price is determined altogether by the quantity and the demand.[22]

Now Smith had not stated that "the rent of farms makes any part of the price of their produce."   When he spoke of rent being an expense of production he had spoken of particular fields and particular commodities.   It appears that neither Hume nor Smith realised that the relation of rent to price was being discussed with two wholly different sets of hypotheses.[23]

---

[21] *Ibid.*, p. 376.

[22] Rae, *Life of Adam Smith*, p. 286.   See also Gide and Rist, *History of Economic Doctrines*, Smart's translation, p. 64 n.

[23] Two recent books furnish good examples of the uncertainty still prevailing between Smith's two points of view.   *The Science of Prices*, by Todd, Oxford, 1925, says (p. 47): "Rent depends on price, not price on rent," but again (p. 49) it says:

"Theoretically, therefore, true economic rent can never enter into cost of production; but there is one case in which it really does do so in effect, namely, that of an established agricultural country where it is proposed to introduce a new crop in competition with those already grown."

Fairchild, Furness and Buck say in their *Elementary Economics* (Macmillan, 1926), p. 129, that "economic rent is not one of the costs which determine the selling price of agricultural products."   But two pages later they state that,

"Costs of the alternate use can in rare circumstances enter into the price." In neither of these books are the two problems distinguished and in both of them two opposing conclusions are reached.

A few writers have mentioned these two questions and Marshall gives a

IV

This section will treat the theories of West, Malthus and Ricardo who developed the so-called Ricardian theory of rent.[24] Its main purpose will be to show that while they treated rent and price in connection with a problem which involved both value and class distribution, their treatment was dominated by the point of view of the latter. They looked on land as having no competing use and grouped all its produce under one commodity which they called variously, "raw produce," "food," "corn."

An outstanding fact about the Ricardian theory is that it was developed in connection with the open discussion of a practical public question. These writers were not cloistered schoolmen, but pamphleteers fighting for definite political policies. Their theories were developed in connection with the English corn-law controversy of 1813–15 and can be understood only in connection with that controversy. As Cannan says:

> . . . We are indebted . . . to the corn law controversy of 1813–15 for the Ricardian theory of rent and distribution in general.[25]

West hurried his publication "before the meeting of Parliament," and Malthus did the same in the hope of influencing the action of that body. Ricardo says that these two publications furnished the world "nearly at the same moment, the true doctrine of rent." His own pamphlet, *Influence of a Low Price of Corn on the Profits of Stock*, was in print within six weeks.[26]

Malthus's pamphlet was practically reprinted in his *Principles*,

---

section of his *Principles* to the case of competing crops and rent. His treatment is criticised below, p. 634, n. 70. Neither Marshall nor any other writer known to the author has pointed out that the two problems involve different hypotheses and different conclusions. For an earlier statement of this position see an article by the present writer in the *Mita Gakkai*, Tokyo, for March, 1921.

[24] Ricardo approves of the rent theory of the other two. *Principles*, author's preface.

[25] *Theories of Production and Distribution*, p. 388.

[26] *Ibid.*, p. 161 n.

and the same ideas were reproduced by Ricardo in his own *Principles*. Speaking of this book, Cannan says:

> Read with the pamphlets which preceded it, Ricardo's *Principles of Political Economy and Taxation* is intelligible enough. Read without them, it is the happy hunting ground of the false interpreter.[27]

Two circumstances were mainly responsible for this great corn-law controversy. First, there was the agricultural situation brought on by the Napoleonic wars. Second, there was the new clash of classes growing out of the industrial revolution.

England had been shut off by the war from her regular supplies of corn from the continent and the prices of farm produce and of land had risen remarkably.[28]   There was a great increase in production, partially through the more intensive cultivation of the old land and partially through the taking in of areas previously uncultivated.   Farms had been purchased and mortgaged with the expectation of paying interest and principal from the sale of these heavy yields at the ruling high prices.   But with renewed access to continental supplies and the fall of prices, agriculture was depressed.   "The landed interest" was agitating for such import duties as would allow the war-prices to continue and had already secured favourable action.[29]

Opposition to these measures was particularly determined because of the changes wrought by the industrial revolution.   The position of the landed aristocracy as the political, economic and

---

[27] *Ibid.*, p. 388.

[28] See Green, *A Short History of the English People*, rev. ed., p. 828.   Cannan shows, *Theories*, p. 151, that some rents were five times as high as in 1790.   A schedule of wheat prices at Windsor market shows that for forty-six of the years of the eighteenth century it was below £2 and that it was below £3 except for two years within the first decade: but that it mounted so high as to range between £5 6s. and £6 8s. in the period from 1808 to 1813.   West, *Application of Capital to Land*, p. 67.

[29] A Corn Committee of the House of Commons proposed in 1813 that the duty on wheat be placed at 24s. 3d. per quarter unless the price were 33⅓ per cent. above the average of the twenty years immediately preceding.   Porter, *Progress of the Nation*, 3rd ed., pp. 153–154.

social dictators of the nation was being challenged by the new urban classes. Labourers had gotten misery rather than affluence from the new conditions and were already demanding "untaxed food." England was rapidly becoming "the work-shop of the world" and the self-made city men whose enterprise was bringing that about were alert to secure and retain every possible advantage. This group was strongly opposed to any measure which might result in higher priced raw materials of any kind. There was a strong belief that if the price of food could be kept low, wages, which were one of the most important items in costs, would also be low. This would mean prosperity for British manufacturers, merchants, shipowners and bankers. Ricardo said:

Corn being one of the chief articles on which the wages of labour are expended, its value to a great extent regulates wages—and there is no other way of keeping profits up but by keeping wages down.[30]

Radicals were also agitating the land question. There were echoes of the French revolution and Thomas Spence and his followers demanded the forcible distribution of the land among the people.[31]   As one writer put it:

The cry of 'no land-lords' stood rubric on the walls.[32]

Everyone knew that the landlords received large rents from the sale of rural produce and it was commonly supposed that these rent payments made the price of rural produce higher in the cities. "Before Ricardo's time most practical men thought that rent was a cause of high price."[33]

It was not only those whose economic interests conflicted with the interests of the landlords who gave impetus to the feeling against them. Leading economists held and published opinions which furthered the idea that landlords were undesirable monopolists.

---

[30] *Protection to Agriculture*, 4th ed., sec. 6.

[31] Shortly before his death, September 1st, 1814, Spence attempted to publish a new periodical, *The Giant-Killer or Anti-Landlord*.   Beer, *History of British Socialism*, i, pp. 107–109.

[32] Cannan, *Theories of Production and Distribution*, p. 223 n.

[33] Toynbee, *Industrial Revolution*, p. 117.

Even Ricardo, who did more than any other person to remove the cause of ill-feeling, said that:

The interest of the landlord is always opposed to that of the consumer and manufacturer.[34]

And J. S. Mill states that:

It was long thought by political economists, among the rest even by Adam Smith, that the produce of land is always at a monopoly value.[35]

But the economist who was most severe upon this class was David Buchanan. He issued an edition of Smith's *Wealth of Nations* in 1814, the very year in which two reports of Parliamentary Committees on the corn question were published,[36] and in his own notes condemned this so-called landlord monopoly in no uncertain terms, saying:[37]

. . . corn always affords a rent, being in no respect influenced by the expenses of its production.

And again:

The neat surplus . . . plainly arises from the high price of produce, which, however advantageous to the landlord who receives it, is surely no advantage to the consumer who pays it. Were the produce of agriculture to be sold for a lower price, the same neat surplus would not remain, after defraying the expenses of cultivation; but agriculture would be still equally productive . . . ; and the only difference would be that, as the landlord was formerly enriched by the high price, at the expense of the community, the community will now profit by the low price, at the expense of the landlord. The high price in which the rent or neat surplus originates, while it enriches the landlord who has the produce of agriculture to sell, diminishes in the same proportion the wealth of those who are its purchasers.[38]

It is clear that Buchanan had no conception of diminishing returns. He appears to have supposed that when corn which requires 70 shillings per quarter in labour and capital to produce

[34] *Principles*, p. 322.
[35] *Principles*, bk. iii, ch. v, sec. 2.
[36] One ordered to be printed on July 26th and the other on November 14th.
[37] Vol. iv, p. 37.
[38] *Ibid.*, vol. iv, p. 134. This was quoted and sharply criticised by Malthus.

is sold in the market at 105 shillings, it is because 50 per cent. has been arbitrarily added for rent.

This appeared when the rent question was already at white heat ·and when those writers who make up the Ricardian group were already deeply interested in it.   Malthus takes up "the cause or causes of the high price of raw produce" and is especially opposed to Buchanan's treatment,[39] saying that Smith, the economists and some "modern writers,"

consider rent as too nearly resembling in its nature and the laws by which it is governed, the excess of price above the cost of production, which is the characteristic of a monopoly.

His main reason for writing his *Nature and Progress of Rent* appears to have been to correct these false ideas.   He considered Ricardo as too hard on the landlords.   In their discussion of this question they developed the theories which were reproduced in their respective *Principles* and which have been the main basis for rent theory until to-day.

It has been stated above that these writers took all raw produce as one and supposed that the land had no competing use: that in this their treatment differs from Smith's first and is similar to his second treatment.   In order to make this clear it is necessary to point out very clearly a number of features which characterise their treatment.

1. These writers considered the question from a point of view which included both value and distribution, but which was dominated by the latter.   The corn law discussion centred about the question as to what determined the price of raw produce to the urban population.   It was to this extent a question of value.   But it was not a question of the value of particular commodities such as must be dealt with in a complete theory of value.   It was a question of the value of the gross produce furnished by one class, the rural class.   It was dominated by the class point of view. Ricardo's chapter on Rent is put in as a sort of appendix to his

---

[39] *The Nature and Progress of Rent*, pp. 12–15.   Ricardo also criticises Buchanan, *Principles*, p. 236.   All references are to Gonner's edition.

chapter on Value, but it contains no reference to any goods save raw produce as a whole which he occasionally contrasted to "manufacturers" as a whole.   It is brought in directly from the corn-law discussion in which its theory was developed.   Also he says that "the principal problem in Political Economy" is "to determine the laws which regulate this distribution" . . . of "the produce of the earth" . . . among "these classes under the names of rent, profit and wages."   Malthus's chapter in his *Principles* was similarly brought in.   There is much in common between the point of view with which they approached the subject and the point of view of the Physiocrats, which also dominated Smith's second treatment.   *Their discussions were dominated by the point of view of distribution between social classes.*

2. These writers therefore considered only rural or agricultural rent.   Urban rents were small and of little importance at the time and had no relation to the corn-laws.   As Cannan says:

> Merchants and manufacturers often owned the land on which shops, counting houses and factories were built, but this was regarded as a small matter which did not suffice to turn them into "landlords," as the rental value of their premises would be generally trifling in proportion to their gains as "monied men."   Land in towns was practically ignored.[40]

Marshall says they supposed

> . . . that all the land will be used for agricultural purposes, with the exception of building sites which are a small and nearly fixed part of the whole.[41]

The quotation just given from Buchanan shows him to have been wholly concerned with agricultural rents.   Rent "enriches the landlord who has the produce of agriculture to sell."   In fact, these writers all place raw produce over against manufacturers and actually suppose that it is only the former that pays rent at all.[42]

---

[40] *Wealth*, pp. 163–164.

[41] *Principles*, 7th ed., p. 434.

[42] This is closely connected with their idea that raw or agricultural produce is furnished under diminishing returns while manufactures are furnished under constant returns.   See Ricardo, *Principles*, p. 51, West, *The Application of Capital to Land*, Hollander's ed., p. 12; Malthus, *The Nature and Progress of Rent*, Hollander's ed., p. 33.

Ricardo says:

> . . . there is always a portion of capital employed on the land which yields
> no rent . . . the result of which, as in manufactures, is divided between profits
> and wages.

And again:

> . . . in the production of manufactured commodities every portion of capital
> is employed with the same results; and as no portion pays rent, every portion is
> equally the regulator of price.[43]

Also:

> Neither the farmer who cultivates that quantity of land, which regulates price,
> nor the manufacturer, who manufactures goods, sacrifice any portion of the prod-
> uct for rent.   The whole value of their commodities is divided into two portions
> only: one constitutes the profits of stock, the other the wages of labour.[44]

The question of rent at that time was wholly a question of rural
rents.   The returns from "raw produce" were divided between
wages, profits and rent and the returns from manufactures
between only wages and profits.   *These writers considered all rent
as agricultural rent.*

3. These writers considered not the rents paid by particular
agricultural products for particular fields but the rent paid by
agricultural (or raw) produce as a whole for agricultural land as a
whole.   They did not place *one kind* of raw produce over against
another, but placed *"raw produce"* over against *"manufactures."*
At no place in West's *Application of Capital to Land*, Malthus's
Nature and Progress of Rent, or in Ricardo's chapter on Rent in the
Principles is there any discussion of the supply of a particular
product or its competition with others for the use of the land.
Buchanan's treatment is similarly concerned.

At only one place does Ricardo intimate that "raw produce"
may be something other than "food" and even here he does not
distinguish between different kinds of raw material or show how
the supplies of particular products, such as bread and cotton

---

[43] *Principles*, pp. 235, 236.   See also p. 87.
[44] Ricardo, *Principles*, ch. vi, sec. 42.

cloth, are in any way dependent upon the production of different particular kinds of raw material. He leaves all kinds of raw material lumped together and takes no note of such facts as that cotton must compete with corn for land. He says:

> Raw material enters into the composition of most commodities, but the value of that raw material, as well as corn, is regulated by the productiveness of the portion of capital last employed on the land, and paying no rent; and therefore rent is not a component part of the price of commodities."[45]

None of these writers recognizes in the discussion of this question the supplies of the different particular kinds of raw produce. Ricardo's treatment makes much of the shifting of labour and capital between raw produce and manufactures, but never comes to the shifting of land, because by his hypothesis land had only one use and did not shift to manufactures. He says:

> . . . when the profits on agricultural stock . . . are 50 per cent. the profits on all other capital, employed either in manufactures or in foreign commerce . . . will be also 50 per cent. If the profits employed in trade were more than 50 per cent., capital would be withdrawn from the land to be employed in trade. If they were less capital would be taken from trade to agriculture . . . the profits on agricultural capital cannot materially vary without occasioning a similar variation in the profits on capital employed on manufactures and commerce.[46]

This is the same principle which Smith applied to land in his early discussion of the relation between rent and prices of particular commodities. Smith supposed that land was withdrawn from one agricultural use to another. Ricardo supposes only labour and capital to be withdrawn and these only as between "the land," manufactures and trade. The reason for this difference is that Smith dealt with particular commodities and supposed that the "fields" had competing uses, while Ricardo dealt with groups of commodities, like raw produce and manufactures, and supposed that "the land" had only one possible use.

But while the Ricardian treatment of rent and price was so dominated by this class point of view that the question of com-

---

[45] *Principles*, p. 55.
[46] *Influence of a Low Price of Corn on the Profits of Stock in Works*, pp. 372–373.

peting commodities did not come into it, this does not mean that Ricardo and the others of the group would have denied the influence of particular rent payments upon the supplies and prices of particular commodities. Indeed, Ricardo specifically agrees to the necessity of land shifting in the same way in which Smith believed it to take place[47] and to the effect which this will have upon the supply of a given product. He quotes with warm approval the statement from Adam Smith's treatment of taxation which we have given above:

> The rent and profits of barley land must always be nearly equal to those of other equally fertile and equally well-cultivated land. If they were less, some part of the barley land would soon be turned to some other purpose; and if they were greater, more land would soon be turned to the raising of barley.[48]

This is just what Smith in his discussion of price had called the withdrawing of land,[49] and what Ricardo called the withdrawing of capital in his discussion of the corn law question.[50] And Ricardo goes on quoting Smith to the effect that any interference with the landlords' receipt of the whole rental for any particular use does affect its supply and price to the consumer. He says:

> The different taxes which have been imposed upon malt, beer and ale have never . . . reduced the rent and profit of barley land. The price of malt to the brewer has constantly risen in proportion to the taxes imposed upon it; and those taxes . . . have constantly either raised the price or . . . reduced the quality of those commodities to the consumer.

It appears that the payment of the *ordinary* land rental was one of the elements determining the supply and price of barley. Land had shifted to uses which paid better. This is the opposite of Ricardo's conclusion when he considers a general tax on land rent for whatever purpose it is used. In that case he says:

---

[47] Both J. S. Mill and Jevons brought this point out later. See below, p. 145 *et seq.* and p. 148 *et seq.*

[48] *Principles*, pp. 237–238.

[49] See quotation above, p. 607, n. 13.

[50] See quotation above, p. 620, n. 46.

A tax on rent would affect rent only; it would fall wholly on landlords, and could not be shifted to any class of consumers.[51]

So also Malthus, although his main treatment is of the relation of rent-payment to the price of raw produce as a whole, introduces the case of competitive rentals and decides that their payment or non-payment *does* affect prices.   He says:

> . . . corn is sold at its natural or necessary price. . . . This price must on an average be at the least equal to the costs of its production on the worst land actually cultivated, together with the rent of such land in its natural state: because, if it falls in any degree below this the . . . land will be left uncultivated.   The rent of land in its natural state is therefore so obviously a necessary part of the price of all cultivated products, that if it be not paid they will not come to market. . . . [52]

This, too, is just the position taken by Smith in his discussion of particular commodities.   It is not inconsistent with Malthus's main position regarding raw produce as a whole because here he is considering corn as a particular commodity and its rental as competing against the rental which the land could earn in pasture or some other non-cultivating use.

Professor Hollander speaks of Malthus's "glaring inconsistency"[53] in this statement, but does not note that a confusing change of hypothesis has been introduced and that this changes the whole situation.   This produce is actually on the margin of not being produced at all and the rent must be paid to secure it.

The Ricardian writers reached their conclusion because they considered the relation of rent payment to the value not of particular products, but to the value of raw produce as a whole.   When they incidentally considered the question of competitive rentals they reached the opposite conclusion.

4. This brings us to the fourth and most important fact about their treatment, namely, that the land had no competing use and

---

[51] *Principles*, ch. x, first statement.

[52] *Principles*, ch. iii, sec. 5.

[53] See Editor's introduction to Ricardo's *Notes on Malthus*, by Hollander and Gregory, p. liv.

must accept the rental which raw produce offered or return to nature and receive nothing.   Ricardo says:

> On the first settling of a country in which there is an abundance of rich and fertile land . . . there will be no rent. . . . When in the progress of society, land of the second degree of fertility is taken into cultivation rent . . . commences . . . on the first . . . with every step in the progress of population, which will oblige a country to have recourse to land of a worse quality, to enable it to raise its supply of food, rent on all the more fertile land will rise. . . . It often . . . happens that capital can be employed more productively on those lands which are already in cultivation. . . . In this case, as well as in the other, the capital last employed pays no rent. . . . When land of an inferior quality is taken into cultivation, the exchangeable value of raw produce will rise. . . . The reason is . . . because more labour is employed to produce it.[54]

The land of a society is taken up *freely* whenever it is needed and is taken, not away from some other rent-paying use, but from non-paying idleness.   It is clear that this is a different situation from that considered by Smith when treating of the value of particular commodities and of the rent on barley land in spite of its commodities being heavily taxed.   It is also a different situation from that mentioned by Ricardo when speaking of the movement of capital between "the land" manufactures and trade.   In those cases the agent was taken from a paying use and could only be taken if that payment were equalled.   In this case it is taken from nature and freely.   So also in those cases it was necessary to keep on paying for the agent because it would go back to another use unless it were paid well.   In this case it is not so.   Ricardo goes on to say:

> Population regulates itself by the funds which are to employ it. . . . Every reduction of capital is therefore necessarily followed by a less effective demand for corn, by a fall of price, and by diminished cultivation.   In the reverse order to that in which the accumulation of capital raises rent, will the diminution of it lower rent.   Land of a less unproductive quality will be in succession relinquished, the exchangeable value of produce will fall, and land of a superior quality will be the land last cultivated, and that which will then pay no rent.

That is, *this land has no rent-paying alternative* to which it can go.

---

[54] Gleaned from secs. 25, 26 and 27 of the *Principles*.

The hypotheses of the Ricardian treatment were natural to the practical problem with which they dealt. They considered only rural rent and reduced all kinds of raw produce to one. They therefore supposed that land had only one use and that rent payment was not necessary to secure its contribution to the product. These hypotheses are essentially the same as those taken by the Physiocrats and by Smith when dealing with rent and "the produce of land." In all three cases the hypotheses depended upon the fact that the writers were interested primarily not in a theory of exchange for particular commodities, but in the incomes of the various classes.

V

It is often said that John Stuart Mill's economic theory represents a period of transition. This applies to his explanation of the relation between rent and price. He was educated in the Ricardian system and the conditions out of which it was moulded continued throughout his young manhood; but a wider set of influences played upon him and a new set of conditions brought new problems and a new point of view. Ricardo was a remarkably able business man who dealt with concrete national problems in a highly abstract manner. Mill considered not so much the practical problem of his own nation as the welfare of mankind. With him the old designation, "political economist," became obsolete, for he was much more, a social philosopher.

Mill's treatment of rent and price contains the two points of view of value and distribution which we have found mixed in Smith's treatment. Like Smith, he fails to distinguish clearly between the two problems. While he reaches Smith's conclusions in both cases, his principal discussion is upon the Ricardian hypothesis that there is no competing use for the land. Here he finds that rent is not a necessary expense of production. In his attempt to formulate a complete theory of value, however, he introduces the case of competing uses and says that in such a case the answer is the opposite. But Mill does not develop this aspect of his theory so fully as he develops the Ricardian aspect and most students of his treatment have pronounced it Ricardian. He did much better in the field through which the Ricardians had blazed the way than in the one in which he had only the dim and devious path of Smith to guide him.[55]

Book II of the *Principles* is on Distribution, and in it Chapter XVI is on Rent. The last section of this chapter is entitled, "Rent does not enter into the cost of production of agricultural produce." Book III treats of Exchange, and Chapter V is entitled, "Of rent in relation to value." It treats of "Commodities which are susceptible of indefinite multiplication, but not without increase of cost" and "The principal of them is agricultural produce." In all this treatment Mill follows strictly Ricardian lines. He supposes a growing community which takes land freely from nature whenever "an increased quantity of produce is required." Like his Ricardian forbears, he lays much stress upon diminishing returns for agriculture and constant returns for manufacture. He says nothing of particular commodities or competing uses and concludes that "rent therefore forms no part of the cost of production which determines the value of agricultural produce."[56]

But Mill does not leave the matter as if it were thus simply and finally settled. He calls this the *pons asinorum* of political economy and says that although it is accepted by "the best political economists," its use is not advisable "even by those who are aware of the restrictions with which" it must be taken. He takes up non-agricultural rents, speaking of mines and fisheries (there being no competing use) and also of rents for residence and trade. It is important to note that in these last two cases he introduces the competitive rental idea and says that the land must receive as much as it could earn in agriculture. He is struck by the high rents in Cheapside, due to "the superior facilities of money-making in the more crowded place."

These wanderings from sole attention to agricultural rent shows

---

[55] As Ricardo himself remarks: "The subject of rent and the laws by which its fall and rise are regulated have been explained since the time of Adam Smith." (*Protection to Agriculture*, 4th ed., sec. 16.)

[56] Bk. iii, ch. v, sec. 2.

that Mill brings into his purview something more than the rent for "raw produce" which came into the corn-law discussion. We should not be surprised, therefore, if we find our safe and sane Ricardian reaching something other than the Ricardian conclusion. In fact, he introduces Smith's first question, the competition of different uses for the same land. In treating it he abandons the so-called Ricardian position and makes rent an expense of production which affects price. Mill says:

> No one can deny that rent sometimes enters into cost of production. If I buy or rent a piece of ground, and build a cloth manufactory on it, the ground rent forms legitimately a part of my expenses of production, which must be repaid by the product. And since all factories are built on ground, and most of them in places where ground is peculiarly valuable, the rent paid for it must, on the average, be compensated in the values of all things made in factories. [57]

And again in the chapter entitled, "Summary of the Theory of Value":

> . . . when land capable of yielding rent in agriculture is applied to some other purpose, the rent which it would have yielded is an element in the cost of production of the commodity which it is employed to produce. [58]

The important thing in these quotations is that there is a *competing use for the land* and that because it is valuable for one use that rental becomes a necessary expense for whatever commodity it furnishes.

Mill's treatment of these questions has considerable significance for the findings of the present study. It indicates that the interpretation of the Ricardian hypotheses put forward in the preceding section is correct. Mill gives no indication that the conclusion that rent "is an element in the cost of production" in the one case is out of harmony with the other conclusion that it is not such for agricultural produce as a whole. Mill learned the Ricardian theory from those who constructed it and used it for half a century before he finally laid his own *Principles* aside. Unless he realised that the

---

[57] *Principles*, bk. iii, ch. iv, sec. 6.
[58] *Ibid.*, bk. iii, ch. vi, sec. 9.

Ricardian theory applied only to a particular set of conditions and with limitations, he would not (a) limit its application to agricultural produce, (b) explain "in what sense it is true that rent does not enter into the cost of production or affect the value of agricultural produce," (c) advise against the use of this statement, and (d) say that when another use takes land from agriculture, the agricultural rent is a cost of production for the commodity produced. The only reasonable explanation of Mill's position is that he knew the hypotheses to be different. Mill was an accomplished logician and it is unbelievable that he, a life-long supporter of the Ricardian position, would publish in the same chapters in which he upheld that theory another theory which, *on the same hypotheses,* upheld the opposite. We have shown that the hypotheses were different and it appears clear that Mill recognized them to be so.

This throws useful light upon what the Ricardian hypothesis really was. There is no question about what Mill's hypothesis is when he concludes that rent is a necessary expense of producing a given commodity. It is that "land capable of yielding rent in agriculture is applied to some other purpose." Now if the rent which land can earn from agricultural produce is a necessary expense of production for another commodity, the rent which it could earn from another commodity is a necessary expense of production for agricultural produce. But this is contrary to both Ricardo's and Mill's conclusions. So also the rent which one kind of agricultural produce would pay is an expense of production for whatever other kind takes possession of the land. Both Mill and Ricardo agree to this. The only possible explanation seems to be that in the case of agricultural produce they supposed that there was no competing use.

Mill discusses rent and price from the two points of view which we have found in Smith's treatment and reaches Smith's conclusions. He agrees with the Ricardians for agricultural produce as a whole, but reaches the opposite conclusion for special commodities competing for the same land. He shows that there were two separate problems with separate hypotheses and that this caused the answers to be different.

VI

Jevons represents the further development of those influences which were apparent in Mill. He lived under different conditions and was interested in a different aspect of economic study. After a thirty-year campaign the corn-law question had been solved and almost forgotten before Jevons reached mature age. The commanding problem of landlord versus urban incomes had passed from the stage. What was more serious, it was practically impossible for Jevons to appreciate the presuppositions with which Ricardo, even Mill, had treated rent and price. Jevons was not concerned with the problem which chiefly concerned men in Ricardo's time, the practical distribution of the annual produce among the different "classes" of the community. He was rather interested in the problem which had first moved Smith and which Mill believed himself to have solved, a theory of exchange.[59] For his purpose,

. . . that able but wrong-headed man, David Ricardo, shunted the car of economic science on to a wrong line—a line, however, on which it was further urged towards confusion by his equally able and wrong-headed admirer, John Stuart Mill.[60]

For Ricardo, and for the Ricardian part of Mill's discussion, the problem of rent had been the relation of rural rent payments to the prosperity of the urban classes. For Jevons it was the relation of *any* rent payment to the supply and price of a particular commodity to whomsoever might buy it. He did not centre his treatment upon the "produce of farms" and the income of the landlord class, but upon particular commodities and the amount which any one of them must pay in order to hold a given parcel of ground from other uses.

Unfortunately Jevons left no elaborate treatment of this question and his theory must be taken from a very few statements. He doesn't even consider a case in which there is no competing use

---

[59] Jevons, *Theory of Political Economy*, p. 75; Mill, *Principles*, bk. iii, ch. i. sec.1.

[60] *Theory of Political Economy*, 4th ed., preface, p. 1.

for the land.   Like Smith, he supposes that there are various competing uses and that any piece of land will be withdrawn from any use which does not pay the competitive rental.   To Jevons, Mill's exceptional case in which land capable of yielding a rent in one use is applied to another "proves to be the rule," and he says that the same principle must apply between different modes of "agricultural employment."   In fact, he was so far removed from the practical contest which presented Ricardo's problem, that he failed to realise its existence.   He says:

> The principle which emerges is that each portion of land should be applied to that culture or use which yields the largest total of utility, as measured by the value of the produce; if otherwise applied, there will be a loss.

And again:

> A potato field should pay as well as a clover field and a clover field as well as a turnip field; and so on. [61]

This is the same analysis which Smith gave when dealing with the supplies and prices of particular commodities.   It differs from the Ricardian analysis in that it brings in another type of shifting. While Ricardo spoke of the shifting of labour and capital between raw produce and manufactures, Jevons adds the shifting of land between different kinds of produce, and insists that this is the rule. He is concerned with the supply not of "raw produce," but of potatoes, of clover and of turnips.   And he takes for granted what the Ricardians did not, that the land had a competing use.

Jevons's treatment bears out the claim of this paper, that two different problems with separate hypotheses have been confused in the treatment of rent and price.   He discussed it from the point of view of exchange, and hence of competing products, and reached the same conclusions which had been reached by Smith and Mill before him.

VII

Having seen that two problems have been confused, let us now see how this affects the equilibrium theory.   The essence of that

---

[61] *Theory of Political Economy*, preface, pp. xlviii–xlix.

theory is that *no expenses determine prices*, but that prices of products and rewards of productive agents are *mutually* determining. As Marshall says:

> The amount of the thing and its price, the amounts of the several factors or agents of production used in making it and their prices . . . all these elements mutually govern one another. . . . [62]

As in the balancing of any forces, the essential thing is the maintenance of equilibrium. A change in either requires a corresponding change in the other.

This equilibrium of commodity-prices and agent-rewards is secured by effecting changes in supplies of the different commodities through the shifting of agents from those uses which pay less to others which pay more. And since expenses and prices are thus kept in equilibrium, all that the theorist can do is to *understand* the machinery by which this equilibrium is maintained and explain it. To quote Marshall again:

> . . . we must go to the margin to study the action of those forces which govern the value of the whole . . . [63]

And again:

> We must do so simply because it is only at the margin that any of those shiftings can occur by which changed relations of supply and demand manifest themselves. [64]

Whenever agents shift from one product to another, the supply of the first is being reduced and of the second increased. This ought to bring a slight change in prices and rewards, and thus result in a new equilibrium. It is the business of the value theorist to know (a) what agents shift in search of higher returns and (b) where this shifting takes place. [65] For our particular problem we

---

[62] *Principles*, 7th ed., p. 526.

[63] *Ibid.*, p. 410.

[64] *Ibid.*, p. 522.

[65] The shifting of non-land agents at the extensive and intensive margins was the heart of the Ricardian analysis. Much has been said and written about land having no supply price, but not by the Ricardians. Their analysis is much closer to the "shifting" analysis developed further by Marshall. Ricardo says:

"I am only desirous of proving that the profits on agricultural capital cannot

are to ask (*a*) whether land is passive in both our problems, or whether it shifts in search of the highest possible returns and therefore aids in adjusting supplies of goods in the market, and (*b*) if it shifts just where this occurs.

In this discussion we shall confine ourselves mainly to our second problem, i.e. to the relation of rent-payment or non-payment to the prices of particular commodities, taking for granted that there are competing uses. This is done because it is believed that with the hypotheses which we have established for the Ricardian theory, no one will seriously question its findings. By hypothesis the land in that problem has no competing use, so it does not shift in search of higher returns. And the Ricardian findings as to the places from which non-land agents are ultimately withdrawn (shifted to manufacturers) is correct. They are withdrawn only from the extensive[66] and intensive margins, that is from land which is so poor as to be only barely worth using and from the last applications on the good land. In that problem labour and capital shift from raw-produce to manufactures and trade, and vice versa, in search of the highest possible returns; but since land has no alternative use, it is passive and remains in its one use regardless of whether rent is paid or not.

Let us now examine the case of particular commodities, accepting the hypothesis of Smith and Jevons that there are sharply competing uses for the land. Both the Ricardian margins are effective for some particular commodities, but not for all. The extensive margin is not effective for such commodities as do not allow of production on the frontier or other poor land: but for

materially vary without occasioning a similar variation in the profits employed on manufactures and commerce." (*Influence of a Low Price of Corn on the Profits of Stock*, in Work, p. 372 n.)

[66] It is only when no-rent land is in use that there is an effective extensive margin. Otherwise we have merely another case of the intensive margin. There is no question of the land going out of use or of all the non-land agents shifting away, but only the shifting of the last or least productive applications of non-land agents. For a particular product it is quite possible that the product-changing margin, soon to be mentioned, be on the poorest land in use for the given commodity.

many commodities, such as wool, meat, wheat, there often are units which come from land which it only barely pays to utilize. On this margin, as we have already seen, land does not shift in search of better returns, so rent-payment or non-payment does not affect the supplies or prices of such commoditities.

The intensive margin is effective for all particular commodities. Economical administration requires that when a given piece of land is devoted to a use it should have sufficient increments of labour, capital and managing ability applied to it, so that the last increments add to the product only enough to reward themselves at what they could earn elsewhere. The units gotten by these applications are "on the margin of not being produced at all" because those agents are always "on the margin of doubt" whether to remain or to go. If the relative price of the commodity is expected to be lower, they will go and it will not be produced at all. The only difference between this case and that for raw produce as a whole is that here the non-land factors may shift to the extensive or intensive margin on other land for another particular product, for instance, another kind of agricultural produce, while there they shift between the two margins for raw produce and manufactures.

But there is also a third margin where units of the supply of a particular commodity are on the margin of not being produced at all because *land* shifts whenever it has a chance, other things being equal, of getting a better return. This margin is best called the *"product-changing margin"* and is made up of all those pieces of land on the margin of doubt whether it is better to continue producing that particular commodity or to change to another product.[67]   For

---

[67] I use the same terminology which I developed in my teaching some years ago and first published in the *Mita Gakkai*, Tokyo, for March, 1921. The same idea of a unified land-shifting margin is presented by Henderson in his *Supply and Demand*, ch. vi, sec. 4, Cambridge University Press, 1922, under the name "Margin of Transference," which may be the neater term.

Considerable attention had been given to the matter of alternative rents by a number of writers, particularly by Davenport and Cassel, but I do not know that the margins had been so definitely reduced to three, adding to the two developed

"raw produce as a whole," there being no competing use for the land, there are only two margins and on them only non-land agents shift. For a particular product, there being competing uses for the land, there are three margins, two of which are the same extensive and intensive margins, and another, the product-changing margin marked by the shifting of non-land agents *and land*. The whole produce from these areas is "on the margin of not being produced at all" because all the factors employed, land, labour, capital and managing ability, are about to change. This is a very considerable area and is the one commonly most effective. Most changes in supplies of products come about through land shifting. It is not easy to detect that fields are worked more or less intensively or that no-rent land goes out of cultivation and returns; but it is easy to see that when the price of cotton bids fair to be high in relation to maize, much land goes to cotton, and vice versa. This is the same for rural and urban land. Both types are commonly useful for any one of several different commodities and they are shifted towards the most remunerative of these. This shifting has been obscured by the fact that land is not "moveable" property: but this does not hinder it from contributing to a variety of different

---

by the Ricardians, and on which non-land agents shift, a third on which land shifts. Professor Marshall separated the problem of rent and price into two, but, as we shall see (below, p. 634, n. 70), he did not apply his theory fully to one of them. Professor Davenport has made much clear but it appears that he did not separate the problem into two or reduce all places where land was on the margin of shifting away from a given commodity, to whatever use, to one unified margin. He supposes Ricardo to be dealing with particular commodities, saying that, "to command a rental for corn a rental possible from some other product must be refused" (*Value and Distribution*, p. 28). And instead of reducing the margins for the production of a particular commodity to three, he says they are "legion." (*Economics of Enterprise*, p. 80). This differs from the theory here presented as polytheism differs from trinitarianism.

In an article in the *American Economic Review* for June, 1927, H. Gordon Hayes presents this unified third margin analysis (under Henderson's terminology) as a substitute for the Ricardian theory. This appears to involve a misinterpretation of the Ricardian analysis. As shown above, it dealt with raw produce as a whole, the land having only one use. Hence there was no place in it for a land-shifting margin.

utilities.[68]   While its range is often not so great, it changes as readily as labour or capital.   Much of capital goods is highly specialised, viz., a cotton gin, a cigarette-making machine, a bleaching factory, etc., and labourers find it more and more difficult to change occupations as they grow older.   Land in a city may be used for groceries, drugs, dry-goods or banking.   At least there is a wide fringe of land in most cities which may be so utilised. Localisation and other influences interfere with this, but perhaps not more than these and other forces hinder the ready shifting of capital and labour.   Rural land may go to cotton, maize, hay, potatoes, meat, etc.

Rent discussions have been so dominated by the Ricardian analysis of the case of raw produce as a whole, in which land could not shift to another use, that it may be well to elucidate this point more.   It is peculiar that in spite of the place which the shifting of land has had in well-established theory, it has not been made a corner-stone of rent theory.   Professor Marshall makes it a central thing in his general theory but not in his explanation of rent.   He says:

> Every agent of production, land, machinery, skilled labour, unskilled labour, etc., tends to be applied in production as far as it profitably can be . . . and equality is maintained between its values for each use by the constant tendency to shift it from uses in which its services are of less value to others in which they are of greater value. . . . [69]

And again:

> . . . each crop strives against others for the possession of the land; and if any one crop shows signs of being more remunerative than before relatively to others, the cultivators will devote more of their land and resources to it.[70]

---

[68] This is not to deny that there are exceptional cases in which land is so peculiarly fitted by nature for one product, such as grapes, that it has no practical alternative and will produce that commodity almost regardless of its price and the consequent rental.   But this is an exceptional case, as is that of a labourer, "marked out from birth for a particular occupation," and should be so treated. In such a case an agent may be forced to accept a very small return (for instance, grape-land in a world gone prohibition) or it may get very much, a monopoly rent.

[69] *Principles*, 7th ed., pp. 521–522.

[70] *Ibid.*, p. 435.   In spite of this clear statement of the very conditions upon

The earnings of land are equalised in various uses and it shifts for higher returns just as non-land agents do and with the same effects for supplies of particular commodities.[71]

---

which the product-changing margin rests, Marshall fails to state that the whole produce from these places is marginal because of the shifting of land.   Marshall makes a great advance in that he recognises the existence of the two problems: but he wholly fails to get away from the Ricardian hypothesis when treating of the case of competing commodities.   He uses the same idea of equilibrium, ignoring the shifting of land, which he had applied in the Ricardian problem, saying (p. 435):

" . . . in equilibrium, oats and hops and every other crop will yield the same net return to that outlay of capital and labour which the cultivator is just induced to apply."

To be in harmony with his general theory this should contain the further truth that all these crops will also yield the same net return to that outlay of *land* which the cultivator is just induced to apply.   His entire treatment proceeds on this partial idea of equilibrium.   Instead of an example in which the person in control of land is "in doubt" as to what use to put his land to we have him able to get 50 per cent. more in one use than in any other.   He says (p. 436 n.):

"If, for instance, he reckoned that he could get a surplus of £30 above expenses (other than rent) . . . by growing hops and a surplus of only £20 above similar expenses by growing any other crop, it could not be truly said that the rent which the field could be made to yield by growing other crops entered into the marginal price of oats."

If the rentals were actually about the same in both cases this would be a fair example.   If so it surely could be said that this was a place at which hops were on the margin of not being produced at all: these hops were marginal: and that the rental was a necessary expense of their production.   Failure to use his theory of land-shifting and earning equalisation caused Marshall to overlook the product-changing margin where units of a particular commodity are on the margin of not being produced at all because land is on the margin of shifting to another use for better rental.   He failed to show the whole machinery by which equilibrium is maintained.

[71] These particular rentals cannot be disregarded in any intelligent administration of land.   It is just as essential to shift land to its best paying uses as it is to shift labour or capital to theirs.   (See Henderson's *Supply and Demand*, ch. vi, sec. 5.)

It should be noted, too, that a tax on the rent paid by a particular commodity will cause land to be shifted to other uses, thus reducing its supply and raising its price.   Ricardo selected the only commodity which "the land" as he saw it could produce and stated correctly that it would be produced even if the rent

This margin is as easily discovered in practice as it is in theory. Every agricultural community shows numerous pieces of good land on the margin of doubt in every production period.   Urban communities have the same.   Often a whole district gradually goes over to another use because of changing circumstances.   This margin is as real and as easily discovered as either of the margins developed by the Ricardians.[72]

---

were taxed away.   But if rent-payment or non-payment has no effect upon the prices of particular commodities, it ought to be possible to tax it away from one while leaving it alone for another without affecting their relative prices.   It is clear that the result differs in this case because the land has a competing use.

[72] A few readers may feel that this good land cannot be "marginal."   But for a particular commodity goodness or badness of land has no effect upon its marginality.   Marginal land for a given use is the land which will shift away from its use with the least fall in the price of its product: and it may be the poorest land in that use or the best land in the use—or any other land.   The good labourers who are about to leave motor-car building to work on aeroplanes are marginal for their industry because they are barely induced to stay by the reward offered, and the motor cars they produce are on the margin of not being produced at all.

Making marginal land the poorest land seems to be the principal fault of the theory referred to on p. 599, n. 2.   Seager (*Principles*, pp. 234, 240) says:

" . . . the wheat farmer pays a marginal rent to cover what the poorest wheat land would be worth for grazing purposes. . . . Rent is thus composed usually of a differential and a marginal element.   The differential element is an expense of production only to enterprisers using superior land for the given purpose, while the marginal element must be paid by all enterprisers engaged in the given branch of production and hence figures as an element in the normal expenses of production." (See also Seligman, *Principles*, 6th ed., pp. 377–378; J. A. Hobson, *The Industrial System*, pp. 94, 95, and *The Economics of Distribution*, pp. 120–121; Patten, *Theory of Dynamic Economics*, p. 58; Chapman, *Political Economy*, pp. 213–218, and *Outlines of Political Economy*, pp. 288 and 298; MacFarlane, *Value and Distribution*, pp. 130, 132.)

The strange thing about this theory is that instead of looking at the supply of wheat and asking which pieces of land are "on the margin" of leaving wheat production, thus affecting its supply, it brings in the "poorest wheat land," although the land pays a considerable rental.   Of course there is no more likelihood that the poorest land in wheat will leave that product than that the best will do so; and the best would affect the supply as much or more than the poorest.   Marginal land for a particular use is not the poorest land, but the land whose alternative use becomes effective with the smallest fall in the price.   In Ricardo's

It frequently happens, especially in these days of Tariff Commissions, that an estimate of the marginal expenses of production of a given goods is required. Now it is a very difficult matter to locate a proper piece of no-rent land and determine what amount of other expenses is required to produce so much upon it. It is even more difficult to measure the additional expense of producing a further one hundred bushels on the intensive margin. It is far simpler to select a good field which might produce equally well this or other commodities, estimate its competitive rental, and add the other expenses of working.

We have found that for the particular problem of the Ricardians, in which the land had no competing use, their analysis holds. Land does not shift in search of better returns and rent-payment or non-payment has no influence upon the supply or price of raw produce. For Smith's first problem, later discussed especially by Jevons, the case is different. Here the land has competing uses and it shifts from use to use in search of its best earnings just as other agents do. This shifting is followed by changes in supplies of various commodities, hence in changes in their marginal utilities and prices.

Two questions have been confused since the time of Adam Smith. Opponents have misunderstood each other, but the principal writers treated in this paper have been in the main correct for the problems which they discussed. The theories of Ricardo and Jevons are not antagonistic, but complementary; they arise from the application of the same *principle* to *two different questions*, and constitute together something like a complete theory of the subject.

---

case the poorest land in use for raw produce had a particular significance; but this was not *because* it was the poorest land in the use. That was a mere *incident* of the problem with which he dealt. Its importance depended upon the fact that the crop from the poorest land was *on the margin of not being produced at all*, because there *agents were shifting to other uses*.

32

THE CONCEPT OF ECONOMIC SURPLUS*

By Kenneth E. Boulding †

Economic surplus may be said to be present whenever a seller makes a sale for a sum greater than the least sum for which he would have been willing to make the sale, or whenever a buyer makes a purchase for a sum smaller than the greatest sum for which the buyer would have been willing to make the purchase. If I am able to sell an article for $10 which I would be willing to sell for $8.00, then $2.00 represents economic surplus. Likewise, if I am able to buy an article for $10 for which I would be willing to pay $13, then $3.00 represents the economic surplus. This concept of an economic surplus has played an important part in economic theory, whether in a simple or in an extended form. It is the basis of the Ricardian theory of economic rent and of the Marshallian theory of consumers' surplus, and is an important concept in welfare economics. It lies at the root also of the Marxian theory of surplus-value.

Economic surplus can arise only where there are differences among the various buyers or sellers of an identical article in respect of their willingness to buy and sell. What is the same thing in other words, it is a phenomenon necessarily associated with less than perfectly elastic demands and supplies. If all the sellers of a given commodity were willing to sell it at a price of $10, the supply would be perfectly elastic within the range of sellers, and no matter what the demand within this range the price would always be $10 and there would be no economic surplus for the sellers. Similarly, if all buyers were willing to buy a commodity at a price of $10, the demand would be perfectly elastic within the relevant range and,

* *American Economic Review*, December 1945, pages 851–869. Reprinted by courtesy of the publisher and author.

† Iowa State College.

no matter what the supply, the price would always be $10 and there would be no economic surplus for the buyers. Suppose, however, that some sellers are willing to sell at $9.00, some at $10, and some at $11. If the demand is such that the $9.00-sellers can supply all that is necessary, the price will be $9.00 and there will be no economic surplus. If, however, the demand rises so that the amount which the $9.00-sellers are willing to supply is insufficient to satisfy the buyers at that price, the price must rise to $10 in order to attract the $10-sellers into the market. Then the $9.00-sellers receive an economic surplus of $1.00, for they would be willing to sell for $9.00, but in fact receive $10. If the demand rose still further, so that the $11-sellers had to be brought into the market, the price would rise to $11, the $9.00-sellers would have an economic surplus of $2.00 and the $10-sellers of $1.00.

Similarly in the case of demand, if there are some buyers willing to buy the commodity for $11, some for $10 and some for $9.00, and if the supply is so small that at a price of $11 all that sellers will offer will be taken by the 11-dollar buyers, the price will be $11 and there will be no economic surplus on the buyers' side. If, however, the supply is larger, so that the price must be brought down to $10 in order to attract the $10-buyers, the $11-buyers will receive an economic surplus of $1.00. If the supply is still larger, so that the price falls to $9.00 in order to bring the $9.00-buyers into the market, the $11-buyers will receive $2.00 economic surplus and the $10-buyers will receive $1.00 economic surplus. Economic surplus on the sellers' side may be called "sellers' surplus" and on the buyers' side, "buyers' surplus."

The principle is illustrated in a familiar diagram in Figure 1. The "buyers' curve," $B_1 \ldots b_n$, shows what quantities buyers are just willing to buy at various prices. Thus, at a price OB_1 there are buyers just willing to buy B_1b_1; at a price ON_2, there are buyers just willing to buy an amount B_2b_2; and so on. The total amount that will be bought at the price ON_2 is, of course, $B_1b_1 + B_2b_2$, or N_2b_2, and, as the same principle applies all the way down the curve, the "buyers' curve" is also the demand curve. The demand curve is essentially the *cumulative frequency distribution* of the amounts that people are just willing to buy at various prices. Similarly the "sellers' curve," $S_1 \ldots \ldots s_n$, shows what quantities the sellers are just willing to sell at various prices. It is the cumulative frequency distribution of the amounts that people are just willing to sell at various prices.

The equilibrium price, ON, is that at which all sellers can find buyers for the amounts desired—*i.e.*, at which the quantity offered is equal to the quantity sold. Then the total buyers' surplus at the equilibrium price is measured by the area NB_1P and the total sellers' surplus by the area S_1NP. The buyers' surplus measures the difference between the total amount actually paid by the buyers ($ONPM$) and the total amount which they would have been willing to pay if perfect price discrimination could have been practiced—(*i.e.*, if each unit had been sold at the highest price that anyone was willing to pay for it)—which would be the area OB_1PM. The sellers' surplus measures the difference between what the sellers actually receive ($ONPM$) and the least sum for which the amount OM could be obtained under perfect price discrimination—*i.e.*, if each quantity were to be paid for at a rate only just sufficient to induce the seller to part with it. This is the area OS_1PM. The sellers' curve is similar to what Marshall called the "particular expenses curve." It is identical with the supply curve only if changes in the willingness to supply due to external economies can be neglected.

This is essentially the "classical" theory of economic surplus. The Ricardian theory of rent appears as a special case: if rent is that which is paid for the "original and inexhaustible powers of the soil," then clearly rent is being paid for something that is perfectly inelastic in supply. In the case of any commodity the supply of which is perfectly inelastic at all prices, the whole payment for the commodity is economic surplus; for the commodity would be supplied even if nothing were paid for it.

Thus in Figure 1, if the sellers' curve were MP, the whole area $ONPM$ would be sellers' surplus—*i.e.*, economic rent. The question of whether any such commodity exists, of course, is a doubtful one: certainly most of the services of land, with the possible exception of the great river-bottoms, are neither original nor inexhaustible. Even the element of *location*, which might seem at first sight to be perfectly inelastic in supply as land cannot be other than where it is, nevertheless is significant only in relation to the location of the human population, which is perfectly capable of shifting. If, however, there exists any commodity with a perfectly inelastic

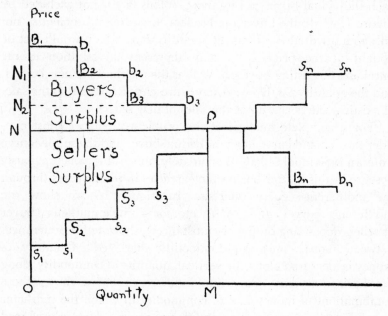

FIG. 1.

supply there can be no doubt that the whole payment received for it by its owners would be economic rent.

The exposition is considerably complicated, although not changed in essence, when we consider that demands or supplies may be less than perfectly elastic for two reasons: first, because *individual* buyers and sellers will buy or sell different quantities in response to different prices; and, secondly, because a change in price may affect the *number* of buyers or sellers.   This is the distinction between what used to be called, rather vaguely, the "intensive" and the "extensive" margins.   In the illustration of the $11, $10 and \$9.00-buyers or sellers, it was assumed that the variation in quantities offered or demanded with change in price came solely from changes in the number of sellers or buyers. In fact, of course, a rise in price may not only attract new sellers, but may also encourage each individual seller to sell more; likewise a fall in price may not only attract new buyers, but may also encourage each individual buyer to buy more. This fact is not excluded by Figure 1, where the buyers and sellers curves refer to *quantities*, not only to individuals.[1] Thus the quantity B_2b_2, which would just be bought at the price ON_2, may represent an addition to the purchases of existing buyers as well as the purchases of new buyers; and the quantity S_2s_2 likewise may represent an addition to the sales of existing sellers as well as the sales of new sellers.

For a complete analysis of the problem, then, we must consider the demand curve of an individual buyer and the supply curve from an individual seller. Fortunately, much that was previously obscure in this matter has been cleared up in recent years through the indifference curve analysis. In Figure 2A we show the indifference curves, M_0I_0, M_1I_1, etc. for a single marketer (buyer or seller, depending on the circumstances), showing his preferences between money and the commodity marketed. Quantity of money is measured along the vertical, quantity of commodity along the horizontal axis. Any one indifference curve shows those combinations of money and of commodity to which the marketer is indifferent. Any point on indifference curve M_1I_1 is preferred to any point on M_0I_0: generally, any point on M_nI_n is preferred to any point on $M_{n-1}I_{n-1}$.

We suppose that the marketer has in his possession a quantity OR_0 of commodity and a quantity R_0P_0 of money. The point P_0, therefore, represents his initial position. The problem is: Given a "market"—*i.e.*, a situation in which he can buy or sell any amount of the commodity at a given price—to what point will he move? The line showing what combinations of money and commodity are open to him through exchange in his "opportunity line." At

---

[1] Marshall does not seem to be quite clear on this point in drawing his particular expenses curve.

FIG. 2A.

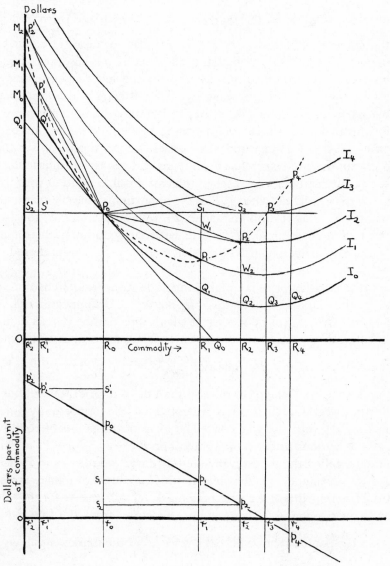

FIG. 2B.

a constant price it is a straight line through the point P_0, the slope of which is equal to the market price. Thus if the price is $\dfrac{P_1S_1}{P_0S_1}$ the opportunity line will be P_0P_1. Moving to the right along an opportunity line means that the marketer is buying—*i.e.*, giving up money for commodity. Moving to the left means selling— giving up commodity for money. The marketer will move along his opportunity line as long as the line is cutting indifference curves, for this means that he is progressing to higher and higher indiffer- ence curves—*i.e.*, more and more preferable positions. When the opportunity line ceases to cut, but instead *touches* an indifference curve, the marketer has reached the best possible position with the given price. Thus, when P_0P_1 is the opportunity line the marketer will move along it until he reaches P_1, where the line P_0P_1 touches the indifference curve M_1I_1. He will not go beyond this point because, if he does, he will be passing to lower—*i.e.*, less preferred— indifference curves.

If the market price is equal to the slope of the indifference curve at P_0, the marketer will neither buy nor sell. His opportunity line will be $Q'_0P_0Q_0$, but no matter in which direction he moved along it from P_0 he would move to lower indifference curves. He will, therefore, sit tight at P_0: the price $\dfrac{OQ'_0}{OQ_0}$ ($= r_0p_0$ in Figure 2B) is his "null price." If the price is lower than the null price, he will buy: if the price is higher, as represented by the opportunity lines $P_0P'_1$, $P_0P'_2$, etc., he will sell. The locus of the points of equilib- rium at various prices is the dotted line $P'_2 - P_0P_1P_2 - P_4$. This may be called the total revenue-outlay curve. From P_0 to P_3 it is a total revenue curve, showing the total amounts of money meas- ured from the line $P_0S_1P_3$, that the marketer will receive for the sale of various amounts of commodity, measured from the line P_0R_0. Thus the point P_1 shows that at a price $\dfrac{P_1S_1}{P_0S_1}$, the marketer will give up an amount S_1P_1 of money and will receive in exchange P_0S_1 of commodity, leaving him with R_1P_1 of money and OR_1 of com- modity. From P_0 to P'_2 the line is a total outlay curve, showing what amounts of money will be received for the sale of various amounts of commodity.

The total outlay-revenue curve can easily be turned into the marketer's demand-supply curve in Figure 2B, where the horizontal axis is identical with that of Figure 2A, and the vertical axis measures the ratio Money/Commodity. For each quantity of commodity represented by r_1, r_2, etc., we calculate the price, $\dfrac{S_1P_1}{P_0S_1}$, $\dfrac{S_2P_2}{P_0S_2}$, ($= r_1p_1$, r_2p_2, etc.) and plot the line $p'_2p_0p_4$ accordingly. The segment p_0r_3 is the marketer's *demand curve:* it shows how much he will buy at each price. The segment p'_2p_0 is the marketer's *supply curve:* it shows how much he will sell at each price. The segment of the outlay-expenditure curve P_3P_4, and of the demand-supply curve r_3p_4 represents a situation (extremely unlikely to occur in a commodity market) where the price is negative—*i.e.*, where the marketer can increase *both* the amount of money he has and the amount of commodity at the same time. In this case the commodity has become a discommodity, as is shown by the positive slope of the indifference curves: at points such as P_4 an increase in the quantity of commodity is so distasteful that it must be compensated for by an increase in the quantity of money.

In Figure 2A the indifference curves have been drawn vertically parallel—*i.e.*, the whole system can be mapped out by moving one of the curves parallel to itself in a vertical direction. It follows that, for each quantity of commodity, the slopes of all the indifference curves are identical. The slope of an indifference curve is called the marginal rate of substitution of money for commodity: it is the amount of money which must be substituted for one unit of commodity if the individual is to feel no gain or loss. Thus, if the marginal rate of substitution (for short, *MRS*) is \$3.00 per bushel, then if a bushel is subtracted from the marketer's stock of commodity, \$3.00 must be added to his stock of money in order to leave him as well satisfied as he was before. If now the indifference curves are parallel, the *MRS* of all the indifference curves at any given quantity of commodity is equal to the price of the commodity. Thus at a quantity of commodity OR_1, the slopes of the indifference curves at Q_1, P_1, W_1, etc., are the same, and are also equal to the slope of the line P_0P_1—i.e., to the price of the commodity—as P_0P_1 is tangent to the indifference curve at P_1. The MRS of all the indifference curves at the quantity OR_1 is therefore equal to r_1p_1 in Figure 2B. That is to say, when the indifference curves are parallel, the MRS curve corresponding to each indifference curve is the same as the demand-supply curve.[2]

There are several concepts of economic surplus which can be derived from this construction. Perhaps the simplest is the "buyer's surplus" and "seller's surplus," analogous to the Marshallian "consumer's surplus." The buyer's surplus is the difference between what the buyer pays for a given quantity of the commodity under the conditions of a uniform price, and what he would have paid under the least favorable conditions of differential pricing. Thus in Figure 2A the curve P_0I_0 shows the path the marketer would follow under perfect differential pricing: at a price just a little less than r_0p_0 he will buy one unit; at a slightly smaller price he will buy another unit; and so on down the curve $P_0Q_1 \ldots I_0$. Under

---

[2] This condition of "parallel indifference curves" is essentially similar to the condition that the marginal utility of money should be constant, assumed by Marshall in his analysis of consumer's surplus. It is, however, somewhat broader than Marshall's assumption. The MRS at any point on an indifference curve is the ratio $\dfrac{\text{Marginal Utility of Commodity}}{\text{Marginal Utility of Money}}$ (see Boulding, *Economic Analysis*, p. 663). Marshall assumed that for a given quantity of commodity the marginal utility of the commodity would be independent of the amount of money, and that the marginal utility of money was likewise independent of the amount of money. This last assumption could only be even approximately true over small ranges. Of these assumptions, of course, the MRS would likewise be independent of the quantity of money for each quantity of commodity. The MRS may also be constant, however, if *both* the marginal utility of commodity and the marginal utility of money change in the same proportion as the quantity of money changes. Thus as we proceed upward along any vertical line in Figure 2A, the marginal utility of money is likely to fall, as the quantity of money increases, following the familiar law of diminishing marginal utility. It is possible that the marginal utility of the commodity will also fall as the quantity of money increases, even though the quantity of commodity is held constant. This will happen if the commodity is "competitive" with money.

perfect differential pricing, therefore, he will pay S_1Q_1 for a quantity R_0R_1; under uniform pricing he would only pay S_1P_1. The buyer's surplus, therefore, is P_1Q_1. Similarly, if the marketer buys an amount R_0R_2 at a uniform price r_2p_2, the buyer's surplus is P_2Q_2. It can easily be shown that the buyer's surplus is also equal to the triangular area under the demand curve. Thus, at a quantity R_0R_1 ($= r_0r_1$) the total amount which the marketer would have to pay under perfect differential pricing is the area $r_0p_0p_1r_1$ in Figure 2B. This is equal to the line S_1Q_1 in Figure 2A. The total amount paid under uniform pricing is the area $r_0s_1p_1r_1$ in Figure 2B ($= S_1P_1$ in Figure 2A). The buyer's surplus in Figure 2B, therefore, is $r_0p_0p_1r_1 - r_0s_1p_1r_1 =$ area $s_1p_0p_1$.

An exactly analogous concept of "seller's surplus" can be derived from the supply curve $p_0p'_2$ in Figure 2B, and the corresponding part of Figure 2A. Thus the marketer will sell an amount $P_0S'_1$ for an amount $S'_1P'_1$ under uniform pricing. Under perfect differential pricing he can be made to sell this amount for only $S'_1Q'_1$. The seller's surplus—the difference between these two amounts—is $P'_1Q'_1$. It can easily be shown that this is also equal to the area $s'_1p_0p'_1$ in Figure 2B.

The next problem is to remove the limitation of parallel indifference curves. Figures 3A and 3B show a situation in which, for each quantity of commodity, the MRS increases as the quantity of money increases: as we move upward along any vertical line in Figure 3A we cut indifference curves of successively steeper slopes. The system of indifference curves do not now reduce to a single MRS curve, but instead each indifference curve has its own MRS curve: in place of the single MRS curve of Figure 2B we now have a system of such curves as in Figure 3B: m_0i_0, m_1i_1, etc., corresponding to the indifference curves M_0, M_1, etc., of Figure 3A. Then at a price equal to the slope of the opportunity line P_0P_1 in Figure 3A ($= r_1p_1$ in Figure 3B) the amount bought will be R_0R_1, P_1 being the point of tangency of P_0P_1 with the indifference curve. If in Figure 3B a perpendicular from r_1 cuts the MRS curve m_1i_1 in p_1, r_1p_1 is the price at which the amount r_0r_1 will be bought—being equal to the slope of the indifference curve at P_1. Similarly r_2p_2,

FIG. 3A.

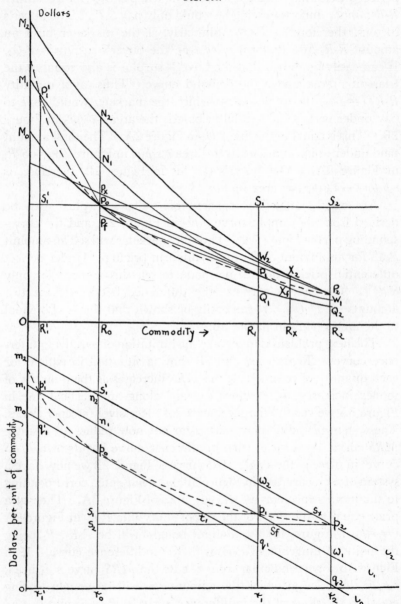

FIG. 3B.

p_2 being on the MRS curve m_2i_2, is the slope of the indifference curve at P_2, and is the price at which r_0r_2 will be bought. The dotted line $p_0p_1p_2$ is, therefore, the demand curve, which is not now identical with any one of the MRS curves, but has a flatter slope. Similarly, $p_0p'_1$ is the supply curve, derived from the outlay curve $P_0P'_1$. The supply curve in this case has a steeper slope than the MRS curves. It is easy to show that if the slopes of the indifference curves at a given quantity of commodity *fall* with increasing quantity of money, the MRS m_1i_1 will lie below m_0i_0, m_2i_2 will lie below m_1i_1, and so on. In this case the demand curve will have a steeper slope than the MRS curves and the supply curve a flatter slope.

The buyer's surplus does not, in this more general case, equal the triangular area under the demand curve. Thus, in Figure 3A the buyer's surplus at the quantity R_0R_1 is P_1Q_1 $(S_1Q_1 - S_1P_1)$. Corresponding to S_1Q_1 in Figure 3A, we have the area $p_0q_1r_1r_0$ under the MRS curve m_0i_0: corresponding to S_1P_1, we have—as before—the rectangle $r_0s_1p_1r_1$. The buyer's surplus, then, is equal to $r_0p_0q_1r_1 - r_0s_1p_1r_1$, which is equal to the triangle $s_1p_0t_1$ minus the triangle $t_1p_1q_1$. This is clearly less than the "demand triangle" $s_1p_0p_1$, which in this case has no meaning whatever. Similarly in the case of supply: the seller's surplus, at a quantity $R_0R'_1$, is equal to the quadrilateral area $s'_1p'_1q'_1p_0$. This is *greater* than the "seller's triangle" $p_0p'_1s'_1$. If the MRS became smaller as the quantity of money increased, the relations would be reversed: the buyer's surplus would be larger than the buyer's triangle, the seller's surplus would be smaller than the seller's triangle.

There is another important concept which is associated with the idea of economic surplus. This is the concept of a "compensating payment": *i.e.*, of the sum of money which would be sufficient to compensate a marketer for a given change in the price of the commodity. Thus, in Figure 3, suppose that there is a rise in price from r_2p_2 to r_1p_1. The opportunity line shifts from P_0P_2 to P_0P_1: the buyer shifts from the position P_2 to the position P_1. P_1 is on a lower indifference curve than P_2—*i.e.*, the buyer is worse off because of the shift in price. The question is, What sum of money, given to the buyer, would just compensate him for the rise in price—*i.e.*, would enable him to get back again to the indifference curve M_2? This is the sum P_0P_x, where P_xX_2 is drawn parallel to P_0P_1 to touch the indifference curve M_2 in X_2. If he had a sum R_0P_x to start with, and if the price were r_1p_1, the opportunity line would be P_xX_2, as the slope of this line is equal to that of P_0P_1: with this sum of money and at this price he will proceed to X_2, where he is just as well off as he was at P_2, X_2 and P_2 being on the same indifference curve. The amount he would buy under these circumstances is in between the amounts he would buy at P_1 and at P_2.

If the indifference curves are parallel it can easily be shown that the compensating payment is equal to the change in the buyer's surplus due to a shift in price: under these circumstances, X_2 coincides with W_2, as the slope of the indifference curve at W_2 is equal to the slope at P_1. The change in buyer's surplus is $P_2Q_2 - P_1Q_1$ $= W_2P_1 = P_0P_x$. If the *MRS* increases with increases in money, as in Figure 3A, the compensating payment is larger than the change in the buyer's surplus[3]. It can be shown that, in terms of Figure 3B, the compensating payment for a change from p_2 to p_1 is the area $s_1s_2p_2s_x$: the change in the buyer's surplus is the area of the complex polygon $s_1s_2p_2q_2q_1p_1$. It should be observed that the compensating payment in the case of a fall in price from r_1p_1 to r_2p_2—*i.e.*, the tax which a buyer would have to pay in order to bring him to the indifference curve I_1 when the price is r_2p_2—is less (in Figure 3A) than the compensating payment in the case of a rise in price. If P_fX_f is drawn parallel to P_0P_2 to touch M_1W_1 in X_f, P_0P_f is the tax which will just balance the gain to the buyer resulting from a fall in price from r_1p_1 to r_2p_2. This is equal to the area $s_1s_2sjp_f$ in Figure 3B. If the indifference curves are parallel, of

---

[3] For a fuller discussion of the "Compensating Payment" concepts see the following:

J. R. Hicks, *Value and Capital* (Oxford, 1939), pp. 38–41; and "The Rehabilitation of Consumer's Surplus," *Rev. Econ. Stud.*, Vol. 8 (Feb., 1941).

A. Henderson, "Consumer's Surplus and the Compensating Variation," *Rev. Econ. Stud.*, Vol. 8 (Feb., 1941), p. 117.

A. Kozlik, "Note on Consumer's Surplus," *Jour. Pol. Econ.*, Vol. XLIX, No. 5 (Oct., 1941), p. 754.

course, the compensating payment is the same whether the movement of price is a rise or a fall.

Consider now what the payment must be to compensate the marketer for the entire loss of the market—*i.e.*, for the prohibition of buying or selling. In that case he will not be able to move from the position P_0. If the original price was r_2p_2, the payment which would be necessary to compensate for the loss of the market would be P_0N_2. This will bring the marketer up to the indifference curve to which he could have attained had he been free to buy at the price r_2p_2. P_0N_2 is equal to the area $p_2s_2n_2$ in Figure 3B. It will be observed that this area is larger than the "demand triangle" $p_2s_2p_0$. In the case of a seller, if the price had originally been $r'_1p'_1$, the sum needed to compensate the seller for the loss of the market is P_0N_1, equal to the area $p'_1s'_1n_1$ in Figure 3B. This area is smaller than the "supply triangle," $p_0p'_1s'_1$.

We can apply this analysis to the consideration of the "gain from trade"—*i.e.*, the total payment which would be necessary to compensate all the marketers for the loss of a market. In Figure 4, a group of individual demand-supply curves is shown, cutting the price axis in S_3, S_2 . . . B_2, B_3. The market demand curve is obtained from these demand-supply curves by summing the total quantity bought at each price—*i.e.*, by adding horizontally that part of the curves to the right of the price axis: it is the curve $B_3H_2H_3N$. Similarly, the market supply curve, $S_3K_2K_1M$, is obtained by adding horizontally those parts of the demand-supply curves which lie to the left of the price axis. The market price is OP, where $PN = PM$ —*i.e.*, the total quantity demanded is equal to the total quantity offered. If now the indifference curves of the marketers are parallel, so that the "demand triangle" measures the compensating payment for each buyer, the total compensating payment to buyers is the area $PN_1B_1 + PN_2B_2 + PN_3B_3$, which is equal to the area PNB_3. Similarly, the total payment which would compensate sellers for the loss of the market is the area PS_3M. If now we draw S_3N the mirror image of S_3M, we get the familiar supply and demand figure, and the total compensating payment is the area S_3NB_3.

It is not difficult to introduce an adjustment to take care of the case where the marketers' indifference curves are not parallel. The curve B_cN is obtained by summing horizontally the MRS curves of each buyer passing through N_1, N_2, N_3, (shown as dotted lines in Figure 4). B_cN is an aggregate MRS curve for the buyers: the total compensating payment is, therefore, the area PB_cN. Similarly, MS_c is the aggregate MRS curve for the sellers: the total compensating payment to sellers is PS_cM. If NS_c is the mirror

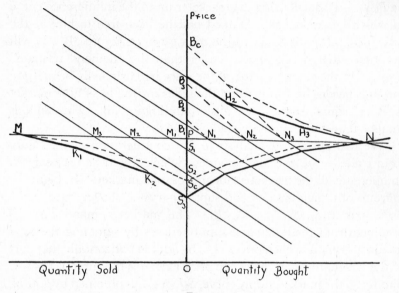

FIG. 4.

image of MS_c, the total payment which would compensate both buyers and sellers for the loss of the market is the area B_cNS_c. Unless conditions are very peculiar, the area B_cNS_c is not likely to differ very greatly from the area B_3NS_3, as the corrections lie in the same direction. While the assumption that the MRS increases with increase in the quantity of money makes the buyers' compensating payment larger, it makes the sellers' compensating payment smaller, so that the total is not much changed. If we assumed that the MRS declined with increase in the quantity of money, the effect would be to diminish the buyers', but to increase the sellers' payment.

We can apply the above analysis to the well-known theorem in the field of taxation, to prove that, if a tax is laid on a commodity, the total tax revenue is less than the "loss" to the marketers, as measured by the compensating payment. That is to say, even if all the revenue from a commodity tax were to be returned as a lump sum to the taxed marketers, the marketers would be worse off than before. This is shown in Figure 5, where BP, SP are the market demand and supply curves. If a tax equal to N_sN_b is placed on each unit of the commodity, when the market is in equilibrium buyers will pay ON_b, sellers will receive ON_s. The

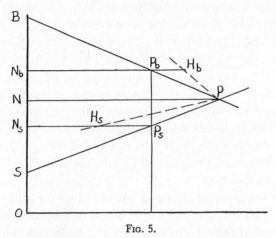

Fig. 5.

total tax revenue is $N_sN_b \times N_sP_s$ = the area $N_sN_bP_bP_s$. If indifference curves are parallel, the sum that would have to be paid to buyers to compensate them for the rise in price is NN_bP_bP: the corresponding sum for sellers is NPP_sN_s. The total payment required to compensate for the tax is $N_sN_bP_bPP_s$: this is greater than the total tax revenues by an amount equal to the area P_sP_bP. If now we introduce a correction for increasing MRS, PH_b and PH_s are the aggregate MRS curves for buyers and for sellers, and the total payment required to compensate for the tax is $N_sN_bH_bPH_s$. This is greater than the total tax revenues by an amount equal to the complex area of the polygon $P_sP_bH_bPH_s$. This area will not differ greatly from the area P_sP_bP.

Up to this point we have considered the concept of economic surplus only in relation to the pure market phenomenon in which there is no production or consumption, only transfers of money and commodity among the marketers. The application of the concept to long-run problems is beset with many difficulties, largely because it is impossible to treat such cases realistically without reference to uncertainty. A distinction can be made between those surpluses (or deficits) which are the results of uncertainty—*i.e.*, the result of the "disappointment" of expectations in a favorable or unfavorable direction—and those which are in some sense part of the permanent structure of economic life. This seems to be the basis for the Marshallian distinction between "true"—*i.e.*, permanent—rents and "quasi-rents." Marshall observed that a supply curve which was highly elastic in the long run might be quite inelastic in the short run. Hence for limited periods the rewards of a factor such as durable equipment might be much diminished, or even completely taken away, without affecting the output of its services. Such a reward has something of the nature of a surplus, or "rent." Because, however, the services of the factor would not be forthcoming indefinitely at low or zero rewards, Marshall called its return a "quasi-rent."

Quasi-rents, however, can exist only because the future is uncertain: if, for instance, the potential owners of a durable good knew at the outset that the returns were going to be lower than the long-run supply price, the good would not be produced. Disappointment, therefore, is of the essence of a quasi-rent. What we know too little about, however, is the relation of a succession of disappointments to the long-run supply price itself. Long-run supply and demand curves are a useful cloak to cover up a vast complexity of inter-temporal relationships and, while they may enable us to perceive the broad shape of these complexities more clearly, they frequently hide the real dynamic structure of the system. Thus the application of the economic surplus concept to long-run demand and supply curves is beset with difficulties, and may not be very fruitful. The concept cannot be used, certainly, to justify the thesis of Marshall and Pigou regarding taxing industries of increas-

ing supply price to subsidize industries of decreasing supply price—
quite apart from the question of whether these categories are
"empty boxes."

Nevertheless, as applied to a particular "industry" or sector of
economic life, the concept has some meaning: in fact, several possible meanings. We may ask ourselves, "What is the greatest
amount that could be extracted from this industry by price discrimination, without change in output?" Thus by price discrimination consumers could be forced to pay more for the present
output, and producers could be forced to receive less. The economic surplus, in this sense, represents that theoretical maximum
which the state might get out of an industry by discriminatory
taxation, without affecting output. Another possible meaning of
economic surplus in this case is the sum of money which would be
just sufficient to compensate the individuals of society for the loss
of the industry. These correspond to the two concepts already
described. There is small likelihood, however, that these concepts will coincide, or that either of them can be measured by the
area between the demand and supply curves.

The problem of applying the economic surplus concept to the
economy as a whole is of the utmost importance, yet tantalizingly
difficult. The "compensatory payment" concept here is quite
meaningless: obviously no sum of money, or purchasing power,
could compensate for the loss of the whole volume of production.
The alternative concept, however, of the amount that might be
extracted from the society without a diminution of output is of
very great importance, for it represents that part of the total
product which is "available"—either for redistribution, or for the
extravagance of the state or for the pursuit of military power. For
Marx, of course, the whole produce of society above the subsistence
of the working class was "economic surplus" (*i.e.*, surplus-value);
for by the labor theory of value the subsistence of the working class
is all that is necessary to call forth the total product. Marx
undoubtedly went too far in this, for the process of production is
not merely a mechanical transformation of acts of labor into product, but is a subtle complex affected by innumerable institutional

and psychological factors. How much can be expropriated from society without destroying productive activity depends a great deal on the manner of the expropriation. Thus the economic surplus of the whole economy is not a very clear concept. There are indications that in modern industrial society it may be very large, and the experience of the war shows what a great proportion of current output can be diverted to "unproductive" uses without any serious impairment of productivity.

The indifference curve analysis used earlier can throw some light on this problem. In Figure 6 we show, for an individual, indifference curves between money and a factor of production. We will suppose, to fix our ideas, that the factor is labor: then OR_0 is the amount of labor at the person's disposal—say, 24 hours per day; R_0P_0 is the amount of money in his possession at the beginning of the day; P_0P_1 is the opportunity line at zero wages (as we have drawn the indifference curve with a positive slope at P_0, indicating that in small quantities labor is positively pleasurable, the individual will give up an amount P_0P_1 of labor even at zero wage). P_0P_2, P_0P_3, etc., are the opportunity lines at successively higher hourly wage rates: the locus of their points of tangency with the indifference curves, $P_0P_1P_2$ . . . is the total receipts curve, measured from the line P_0P_1. From this curve, the supply curve for labor can be derived just as the supply curve was derived in Figure 2. It will be observed that the curve is re-entrant: *i.e.*, above a certain wage, represented by the slope of P_0P_3, an increase in the wage results in a decline in the amount of labor offered. This is the familiar "backward sloping" supply of labor.

Suppose now that a flat-rate income tax is laid on the individual when his wage was equal to the slope of P_0P_4. The result of the tax is simply a reduction in the effective hourly wage: the opportunity line less tax falls to, say, P_0P_3. Because the supply is negatively elastic in this region, there is actually a rise in the amount of work done because of the tax, from R_0R_4 to R_0R_3. The gross income earned is then $S_3P'_4$: the total tax collected is $P_3P'_4$. If the tax were laid in a region where the supply was positively elastic, as between P_3 and P_2, it would cause a fall in the amount of work supplied.

Some interesting conclusions can now be drawn as to the theory of progressive or regressive taxation. A progressive tax is one where the proportion of income paid in taxes rises with rise in

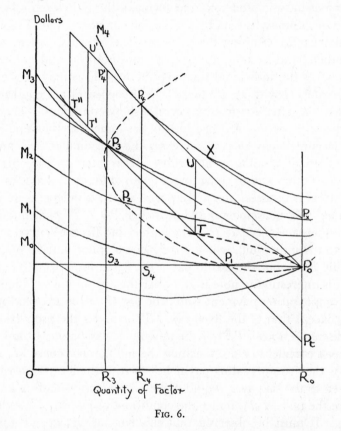

FIG. 6.

income. The opportunity line after tax therefore bends downwards—*i.e.*, its slope becomes less and less with increasing work done. Where the tax rate increases by "brackets" of income, the line will be a series of straight lines of diminishing slope. Thus P_0T represents the opportunity line after a progressive tax is deducted from the income of P_0P_4. It touches an indifference curve at T, and has been drawn so that the total tax paid, TU, is equal to the tax paid under a flat rate tax, $P_3P'_4$. It will be seen that the effect of raising a given revenue from an individual by a progressive rather than a flat-rate tax is to lower the amount of work done, to lower net income after tax, and to make the individual relatively worse off, as may be seen by comparing the position at T with the position at P_3. Raising the same revenue by a regressive tax, on the other hand, results in an expansion of output and of income, and makes the individual relatively better off, as may be seen by comparing T' with P_3, T' being a point where a net opportunity line from P_0 after a regressive tax (not shown on figure) touches an indifference curve. A regressive tax has somewhat the same effect as "overtime" pay—*i.e.*, it increases the marginal return, and so spurs the individual to greater effort. It is interesting to note that an even better way of collecting a given amount of taxes from an individual is to assess him a lump sum which is independent of his income. His net opportunity line is then $P_tTT'T''$, which touches an indifference curve at T''—the highest indifference curve attainable to the individual, whose gross income opportunity is given by the line P_0P_4 and who has to pay a tax equal to P_0P_t.

It is interesting to note that, under the assumptions of Figure 6, the compensating payment would be less than the tax paid in all cases except that of the fixed tax. Thus under the proportionate tax discussed above, $P_3P'_4$ is the amount of tax paid. If now XP_x is drawn parallel to P_0P_3, touching the indifference curve M_4 at X, P_0P_x is the "compensating payment"—*i.e.*, is the lump sum which, if given to the taxpayer, would make him just as well off as he was before the tax. P_0P_x, under the conditions of Figure 6, is less than $P_3P'_4$. It must be observed that this conclusion depends on the assumption that the MRS increases with increase in the quantity of money. The backward-sloping supply curve also can only exist on this assumption.

Some conclusions for tax policy follow from this analysis. If there is no serious unemployment problem we can assume that the objective of policy is to increase production by all possible means.

Then the deleterious effect of progressive taxes on the supply of factors must be taken into consideration. A desirable situation would be one in which taxation was progressive as between individuals, but regressive for each individual. The best system—if it were administratively possible—would be one in which each individual had to pay a lump sum tax based on his "wealth"—i.e., on his earning *power*—but independent of his income—i.e., independent of the degree to which he put his earning power to use. To some extent the property tax is of this nature; and, although one hesitates for political reasons to advocate extending the principle of the property tax to the property that we have in our minds and bodies, real economic benefits might follow.

In the presence of an intractable unemployment problem, however, it is by no means certain that a "property tax" would be even theoretically the most desirable. In such a condition we might wish to repress the labor supply rather than encourage it, and there might then be a case for diminishing the labor force through progressive taxation, even though this might seem a counsel of despair.

The moral of this analysis would seem to be that the concept of economic surplus, while it can be defined to have a good deal of meaning, is not a sufficiently accurate analytical tool for the solution of problems of policy. As an instrument for the analysis of welfare problems it is much inferior to the more general device of indifference curves. It is a concept capable of much ambiguity and, in hands that are not highly skilled, its use can easily lead to false or misleading results. Nevertheless, it is a useful expository device and has a long and interesting history. Even if it occupies a relatively subordinate place in modern economics compared with the central position it once occupied, it is by no means to be discarded. And the student who appreciates its full significance will understand a great deal about the problems which both the classical and the modern economics seek to solve.

CLASSIFIED BIBLIOGRAPHY OF ARTICLES ON NATIONAL INCOME AND DISTRIBUTION

Compiled by

FRANK E. NORTON, JR.

University of California

The purpose of the following classified bibliography is to bring together the theoretical and related statistical literature on national income and distribution appearing in periodical and collected essay form during the period 1920–1945.

Broadly speaking, the bibliography presents the literature in the following order: the social product, its production, its distribution. It is probably unnecessary to point out that any particular classification of the literature on the subject is largely arbitrary. The groups and subgroups adopted are not mutually exclusive, but they should prove helpful providing their limitations are recognized. Recent contributions to the theory of production and empirical studies related thereto have been so extensive that it was believed advisable to have a special division for them. Articles relating in a more general manner to functional distribution and general equilibrium pricing appear separately under the heading general distribution. Also, items concerned with personal distribution are likewise found under the general distribution section.

Under each of the distributive share headings are articles concerned not only with the pricing of the productive service in question, but also the peculiar characteristics of the particular factor market structure leading to a price structure for the factor service.

The bibliography includes articles published in periodicals and essays from collections where the separate essays are the work of different writers. Reviews of books appear only when they are full-length articles or, as in a few instances, when they are of particular interest. Items concerned more or less indirectly with distribution which properly fall under one of the major divisions of economics, such as, labor economics, social reforms, business cycles, monetary theory and policy, public finance, and taxation are excluded. Literature in English on the subject has been rather thoroughly covered for the period 1920–1945. Coverage of literature in foreign languages is much less complete. It should be obvious that the coverage is not intended to be exhaustive and this is true if for no other reason than the inability to determine what items actually should be considered as strictly belonging within the field of distribution proper. An attempt has been made to indicate when a particular item is primarily analytical, statistical, or historical in character by placing an A, S, or H, respectively, immediately after the complete reference. The items are listed alphabetically under each division.

I wish to express my very great indebtedness to Professor William J. Fellner for his continuous assistance and advice in the preparation of this bibliography. The compiler alone, however, is responsible for the classification employed and the inclusion or omission of particular items.

F. E. N., Jr.
Berkeley, California

CLASSIFIED BIBLIOGRAPHY

I. NATIONAL INCOME, NATIONAL WEALTH, AND THEIR MEASUREMENT

I-A. The Concept of National Income and Methods of Measurement

Includes discussions as to what constitutes income, the maintenance of the capital stock and net capital formation, the treatment of inventory valuation, capital gains, and international transactions, the incidence of the activities of the public economy on social income accounting, and problems related to the deflation of money measures of income.

ADAMSON, W. M., Measurement of income in small geographic areas, *Southern Economic Journal*, VIII (1942) 479–492. **A**

ANDERSON, M. D., A formula for total savings, *Quarterly Journal of Economics*, LVIII (1943–1944) 106–119. **A**

BARNA, T., Valuation of stocks and the national income, *Economica*, IX, new series (1942) 349–358. **S**

BENNETT, J. W., National income: a comment, *American Economic Review*, XXI (1931) 283–285. **A.** Reply by W. I. King, 285–286.

BENNETT, R. F., Significance of international transactions in national income, *Studies in Income and Wealth*, Vol. VI, New York, National Bureau of Economic Research, 1943, 142–168. **A**

BLOUGH, R. and W. W. HEWETT, Capital gains in income theory and taxation policy, *Studies in Income and Wealth*, Vol. II, New York, National Bureau of Economic Research, 1938, 191–263. **A**

BOWLEY, A. L., The definition of national income, *Economic Journal*, XXXII (1922) 1–11. **A**

———, The measurement of real income, *Economic Journal*, L (1940) 340–341. **A.** Comment by J. M. Keynes, 341. Further comment by A. L. Bowley, 342.

———, The measurement of real income, *The Manchester School*, XI (1940) 59–86. **A**

———, Note on Mr. Barna's valuation of stocks, *Economica*, X, new series (1943) 64–65. **A**

CANNING, J. B., The income concept and certain of its applications, *Papers and Proceedings of the Pacific Coast Economic Association*, Eleventh Annual Conference (December 1932) 61–65. **A.** Discussion by R. D. Calkins, 66–67.

CHRISTENSON, C. L., Note on national income measurement; a supplement to Professor Whittaker on "Wealth and Welfare," *American Economic Review*, XXXI (1941) 107–108. **A**

COLM, G., Public revenue and public expenditure in national income, *Studies in Income and Wealth*, Vol. I, New York, National Bureau of Economic Research, 1937, 175–248. **A**

COPELAND, M. A., Some problems in the theory of national income, *Journal of Political Economy*, XL (1932) 1–51. **S**

———, Concepts of national income, *Studies in Income and Wealth*, Vol. I, New York, National Bureau of Economic Research, 1937, 3–63. **A**

—— and E. M. MARTIN, The correction of wealth and income for price changes, *Studies in Income and Wealth*, Vol. II, New York, National Bureau of Economic Research, 1938, 85–135. **A**

CRANDELL, W. T., Financial statements of national wealth and national income, *Accounting Review*, XI (1936) 271–290. **A**

CRUM, W. L., On the alleged double taxation of saving, *American Economic Review*, XXIX (1939) 538–548. **A**

DAY, E. E., The measurement of variations in the national real income, *Journal of the American Statistical Association*, XVII (1921) 552–559. **S.**

DE REDIADIS, P., Nuovo methodo di determinazione del reddito nazionale, *Giornale degli Economisti*, LXI (1921) 35–37. **A**

FABRICANT, S., On the treatment of corporate savings in the measurement of national income, *Studies in Income and Wealth*, Vol. I, New York, National Bureau of Economic Research, 1937, 113–142. **A**

FETTER, F. A., Reformulation of the concepts of capital and income in economics and accounting, *Accounting Review*, XII (1937) 3–12. **A**

FISHER, I., Comment on President Plehn's address, *American Economic Review*, XIV (1924) 64–67. **A**

——, Income in theory and income taxation in practice, *Econometrica*, V (1937) 1–55. **A**

——, The concept of income; a rebuttal, *Econometrica*, VII (1939) 357–361. **A**

——, The double taxation of saving, *American Economic Review*, XXIX (1939) 16–33. **A**

——, Paradoxes in taxing savings, *Econometrica*, X (1942) 147–158. **A**

——, Rebuttal to Professor Crum and Mr. Musgrave, *American Economic Review*, XXXII (1942) 111–117. **A**

——, Income tax revision, reply, *Econometrica*, XI (1943) 88–94. **A**

GIBLIN, L. F., F. C. BENHAM, and J. T. SUTCLIFFE, The national dividend—a symposium, I. Review of Sutcliffe: The national dividend by L. F. Giblin, II. The national dividend of Australia by F. C. Benham, III. A rejoinder by J. T. Sutcliffe, *Economic Record*, III (1927) 189–216. **A**

*GILBERT, M. and G. JASZI, National product and income statistics as an aid in economic problems, *Dun's Review*, LII (February 1944). **A**

GOLDSMITH, R. W., Measuring the economic impact of armament expenditure, *Studies in Income and Wealth*, Vol. VI, New York, National Bureau of Economic Research, 1943, 46–92. **A**

GRAVES, C. H., A note on Irving Fisher's concept of income, *Econometrica*, VII (1939) 349–356. **A**

HABERLER, G., National income, saving, and investment, *Studies in Income and Wealth*, Vol. II, New York, National Bureau of Economic Research, 1938, 139–188. **A**

HANSE, W. D., Adequacy of estimates available for computing net capital formation, *Studies in Income and Wealth*, Vol. VI, New York, National Bureau of Economic Research, 1943, 239–276. **A**

HEWETT, W. W., The definition of income, *American Economic Review*, XV (1925) 239–246. **A**

---

* Reprinted in the present volume.

————, Irving Fisher on income, *American Economic Review*, XIX (1929) 217–226. A

HICKS, J. R. and U. K., Public finance in the national income, *Review of Economic Studies*, VI (1938–1939) 147–155. A

————, The valuation of the social income, *Economica*, VII, new series (1940) 105–124. A

HOTELLING, H., Income-tax revision as proposed by Irving Fisher, *Econometrica*, XI (1943) 83–87. A

HOWARD, S. E., Concepts of capital and income, *Accounting Review*, XII (1937) 1–2. A

HUMPHREY, D. D., The relation of surpluses to income and employment during depression, *American Economic Review*, XXVIII (1938) 223–234. A

ISCHBOLDIN, B., Das Problem der nationalen Dividende, *Jahrbücher für Nationalökonomie und Statistik*, CXLIII (1936) Heft 4, 385–404. A

KARVE, D. G., National income: the next step in India, *Indian Journal of Economics*, XIX (1938) 1–17. A

KEYNES, J. M., The concept of national income; a supplementary note, *Economic Journal*, L (1940) 60–65. A

KING, W. I., Income and wealth, *American Economic Review*, XV (1925) 457–474. A

*KUZNETS, S., National income, *Encyclopaedia of the Social Sciences*, (editors E. R. A. Seligman and A. Johnson) XI, New York, The Macmillan Co., 1933, 205–224. S

————, Changing inventory valuations and their effect on business savings and on national income produced, *Studies in Income and Wealth*, Vol. I, New York, National Bureau of Economic Research, 1937, 145–172. A

————, On the measurement of national wealth, *Studies in Income and Wealth*, Vol. II, New York, National Bureau of Economic Research, 1938, 3–82. A

————, National and regional measures of income, *Southern Economic Journal*, VI (1940) 291–313. A

LEWISOHN, S. A., The living wage and the national income, *Political Science Quarterly*, XXXVIII (1923) 219–226. A

LINDAHL, E., The concept of income, *Economic Essays in Honour of Gustav Cassel*, London, Allen & Unwin, Ltd., 1933, 399–407. A

LINDEMAN, J., Income measurement as affected by government operations, *Studies in Income and Wealth*, Vol. VI, New York, National Bureau of Economic Research, 1943, 2–44. A

LITTLETON, A. C., Concepts of income underlying accounting, *Accounting Review*, XII (1937) 13–22. A

MAULDON, F. R. E., L. F. GIBLIN, and C. CLARK, Australia's national income, I. A fresh computation by F. R. E. Mauldon, II. Grumbles and queries by L. F. Giblin, III. Rejoinder by C. Clark, *Economic Record*, XIV (1938) 204–219. A

MAY, G. O., Gross income, *Quarterly Journal of Economics* LV (1940–1941) 521–525. A

MEADE, J. E. and R. STONE, The construction of tables of national income, expenditure, savings and investment, *Economic Journal*, LI (1941) 216–233. A

MEANS, G. C., L. CURRIE, and R. R. NATHAN, Problems in estimating national income arising from production by government, *Studies in Income and Wealth*, Vol. II, New York, National Bureau of Economic Research, 1938, 267–313. A

MUSGRAVE, R. A., A further note on the double taxation of saving, *American Economic Review*, XXIX (1939) 549–550. A

* Reprinted in the present volume.

MYRDAL, G., Sparandets plats i en realinkomstberäkning, *Economisk Tidskrift*, XXXI (1929) 157–169. **A**

PIGOU, A. C., Net income and capital depletion, *Economic Journal*, XLV (1935) 235–241. **A**

———, Measurement of real income, *Economic Journal*, L (1940) 524–525. **A**

———, Comparisons of real income, *Economica*, X, new series (1943) 93–98. **A**

PLEHN, C. C., Income, as recurrent, consumable receipts, *American Economic Review*. XIV (1924) 1–12. **A**

PREST, W., Depreciation and income, *Economic Record*, XV (1939) 17–23. **A**

RORTY, M. C., A national money accounting as the basis for studies of income distribution, *Journal of the American Statistical Association*, XVII (1921) 560–568. **A**

ROTHBARTH, E., Bowley's studies in the national income, 1924–1938, *Economic Journal*, LIII (1943) 55–59. **A**

ROTHSCHILD, K. W., Public expenditure in the national income: a note, *Economica*, XI, new series (1944) 19–22. **A**

RUGGLES, C. G., The relation of corporate surpluses to income and employment, *American Economic Review*, XXIX (1939) 724–733. **A**

STAEHLE, H., Ein Verfahren zur Ermittlung gleichwertiger Einkommen in verschiedenen Ländern, *Archiv für Sozialwissenschaft und Sozialpolitik*, LXVII (1932) Heft 4, 436–446. **S**

STERN, E. H., Public expenditure in the national income, *Economica*, X, new series (1943) 166–175. **A**

———, Public expenditure in the national income: a reply, *Economica*, XI, new series (1944) 23–26. **A**

STONE, R., D. G. CHAMPERNOWNE and J. E. MEADE, The precision of national income, estimates, *Review of Economic Studies*, IX (1941–1942) 111–125. **A**

WARBURTON, C., Accounting methodology in the measurement of national income, *Studies in Income and Wealth*, Vol. I, New York, National Bureau of Economic Research, 1937, 67–110. **A**

WICKSELL, K., Inkomstbegreppet; skattehänseende och därmed sammenhängande skattefragor, *Ekonomisk Tidskrift*, XXIV (1922) 127–154. **A**

WINKLER, W., Einkommen, *Handwörterbuch der Staatswissenschaften*, Vierte Auflage, III, Jena, Gustav Fischer, 1923, 367–400. **A**

I-B. NATIONAL INCOME AND ITS COMPOSITION; NATIONAL WEALTH

Includes statistical estimates of the social income and its elements in various countries, per capita output, and national wealth.

AIRD, J. A., The income method of estimating the national income, *Economic Record*, IV (1928) 270–278. **S**

BOWLEY, A. L., The national income of the United Kingdom in 1924, *Economica*, XII (1933) 138–142. **S**

———, National income in America and the United Kingdom, *Economica*, IX, new series (1942) 227–244. **S**

BUTLIN, S. J., An early estimate of Australian national income, *Economic Record*, XIV (1938) 266–268. **S**

CAMPION, H., Mr. Clark's "national income and outlay," *The Manchester School*, VIII (1937) 170–179. A

CLARK, C. G., Statistical studies of the present economic position of Great Britain, *Economic Journal*, XLI (1931) 343–369. S

——, The national income and the theory of production, *Economic Journal*, XLIII (1933) 205–216. S

CONE, F. M., Revised estimates of monthly income payments in the United States, 1929–1938, *Survey of Current Business*, XVIII (October 1938) 15–20. S

COPELAND, M. A., How large is our national income? *Journal of Political Economy*, XL (1932) 771–795. S

——, National wealth and income—an interpretation, *Journal of the American Statistical Association*, XXX (1935) 377–386. S

CRUM, W. L., National income, 1929–1932, *Quarterly Journal of Economics*, XLIX (1934–1935) 508–517. A

——, The national income and its distribution, *Journal of the American Statistical Association*, XXX (1935) 35–46. S

DEVONS, E., Output per head in Great Britain, 1924–1933, *Economic Journal*, XLV (1935) 577–580. S

EZEKIEL, M., Statistical investigations of savings, consumption, and investment, I, *American Economic Review*, XXXII (1942) 22–49. S

——, Statistical investigations of saving, consumption, and investment, II, *American Economic Review*, XXXII (1942) 272–307. S

FABRICANT, S., Measures of capital consumption, 1919–1933, National Bureau of Economic Research, *Bulletin* 60 (June 30, 1936) 1–15. S

FISK, H. E., New estimates of national incomes, *American Economic Review*, XX (1930) 20–27. S

FRANKEL, E. T., Revised estimates of national income, *Conference Board Bulletin*, VIII (1934) 15–16. S

——, National income and its elements, *Conference Board Bulletin*, VIII (1934) 33–40. S

——, National income produced, 1899–1934, *Conference Board Bulletin*, IX (1935) 29–30. S

FRANKEL, S. H. and S. A. NEUMACK, Note on the national income of the Union of South Africa, 1927/28, 1932/33, 1934/35, *South African Journal of Economics*, VIII (1940) 78–82. S

FRIEND, I., Ezekiel's analysis of saving, consumption, and investment, *American Economic Review*, XXXII (1942) 829–835. A

FULCHER, G. S., Saving of individuals in relation to income, *American Economic Review*, XXXII (1942) 835–840. A

GILBERT, M., Measuring national income as affected by the war, *Journal of the American Statistical Association*, XXXVII (1942) 186–198. S

——, War expenditures and national production, *Survey of Current Business*, XXII (March 1942) 9–16. S

——, U. S. national income statistics, *Economic Journal*, LIII (1943) 76–82. A. Comment by R. Stone, 82–83.

——, and R. B. BANGS, Preliminary estimates of gross national product, 1929–1941, *Survey of Current Business*, XXII (May 1942) 9–13. S

—— and ——, National income and the war effort—first half of 1942, *Survey of Current Business*, XXII (August 1942) 10–17. S

—— and G. JASZI, National income and national product in 1942, *Survey of Current Business*, XXIII (March 1943) 10–26. S

—— and ——, National income and national product in 1943, *Survey of Current Business*, XXIV (April 1944) 6–16. S

——, H. STAEHLE, W. S. WOYTINSKY, and S. KUZNETS, National product, war and prewar: some comments on Professor Kuznets' study and a reply by Professor Kuznets, *Review of Economic Statistics*, XXVI (1944) 109–135. A

——, and D. B. YNTEMA, National income exceeds 76 billion dollars in 1940, *Survey of Current Business*, XXI (June 1941) 11–18. S

GOLDSMITH, R. W., The volume and components of saving in the United States 1933–1937. *Studies in Income and Wealth*, Vol. III, New York, National Bureau of Economic Research, 1939, 217–315. S

GOTTL-OTTLILIENFELD, F. von, Volkseinkommen und Volksvermögen: Kritik in methodologischer Absicht, *Weltwirtschaftliches Archiv*, XXVI (1927) Heft 1, 1–96. A

HAGEN, E. E. and N. B. KIRKPATRICK, The national output at full employment in 1950, *American Economic Review*, XXXIV (1944) 472–500. S

HOUGHTON, H. F., Economic conditions in France and the United States, *Conference Board Bulletin*, XIII (1939) 93–108. S

JASZI, G., National product and income in the first half of 1943, *Survey of Current Business*, XXIII (August 1943) 9–14. S

KNAUTH, O. W., The place of corporate surplus in the national income, *Journal of the American Statistical Association*, XVIII (1922) 157–166. S

KUZNETS, S., National income, 1929–1932, National Bureau of Economic Research, *Bulletin* 49 (January 26, 1934) 1–10. S

——, Gross capital formation, 1919–1933, National Bureau of Economic Research, *Bulletin* 52 (November 15, 1934) 1–19. S

——, Income originating in nine basic industries, 1919–1934, National Bureau of Economic Research, *Bulletin* 59 (May 4, 1936) 1–24. S

——, National income, 1919–1935, National Bureau of Economic Research, *Bulletin* 66 (September 27, 1937) 1–14. S

——, Commodity flow and capital formation in the recent recovery and decline, 1932–1938, National Bureau of Economic Research, *Bulletin* 74 (June 25, 1939) 1–19. S

——, National income, 1919–1938, National Bureau of Economic Research, *Occasional Paper* 2 (April 1941) 1–49. S

——, Uses of national income in peace and war, National Bureau of Economic Research, *Occasional Paper* 6 (March 1942) 3–42. S

LEWIS, C., The trend of savings, 1900–1929, *Journal of Political Economy*, XLIII (1935) 530–547. S

LITOSHENKO, L. N., The national income of the Soviet Union, *Quarterly Journal of Economics*, XLII (1927–1928) 70–93. S

LIVINGSTON, S. M., Postwar manpower and its capacity to produce, *Survey of Current Business*, XXIII (April 1943) 10–16. S

MARSCHAK, J., Annual survey of statistical information: the branches of national spending, *Econometrica*, I (1933) 373–386. S

MARTIN, R. F., The national income, 1933, *Survey of Current Business*, XV (January 1935), 16–18. S

——, National income: realized national income, 1909–1935, *Conference Board Bulletin*, XI (1937) 41–43. S

——, National income, *Conference Board Bulletin*, XII (1938) 9–11. S

MENDERSHAUSEN, H., The relationship between income and saving of American metropolitan families, *American Economic Review*, XXIX (1939) 521–537. S

NATHAN, R. R., National income increased five billion dollars in 1934, *Survey of Current Business*, XV (August 1935) 16–18. S

——, The national income produced, 1929–34, *Survey of Current Business*, XV (November 1935) 16–18. S

——, Expansion in the national income continued in 1935, *Survey of Current Business*, XVI (July 1936) 14–19. S

——, National income gain in 1936 largest of recovery period, *Survey of Current Business*, XVII (June 1937) 11–17. S

—— and CONE, F. M., Monthly income payments in the United States, 1929–1937, *Survey of Current Business*, XVIII (February 1938) 7–13. S

——, National income in 1937 largest since 1929, *Survey of Current Business*, XVIII (June 1938) 11–17. S

——, National income in 1938 at 64 billion dollars, *Survey of Current Business*, XIX (June 1939) 10–16. S

——, National income at nearly 70 billion dollars in 1939, *Survey of Current Business*, XX (June 1940) 6–11. S

NATIONAL INDUSTRIAL CONFERENCE BOARD, Estimates of national wealth and income, *Conference Board Bulletin*, No. 5 (May 1927) 33–40. S

——, Estimates of national income, *Conference Board Bulletin*, No. 40 (April 1930) 317–322. S

——, National wealth and income in 1929, *Conference Board Bulletin*, No. 51 (March 1931) 405–408. S

——, National wealth and national income, *Conference Board Bulletin*, No. 62 (February 1932) 493–500. S

——, National income in 1931 and 1932, *Conference Board Bulletin*, VII (1933) 13–14. S

——, Depression and recovery in the United Kingdom and the United States, *Conference Board Bulletin*, XII (1938) 113–126. S

SCHWARTZ, G. L., Output per head in U. S. A. and United Kingdom, *Economic Journal*, XXXIX (1929) 58–62. S

SHIOMI, S., On Japan's national wealth and income, *Kyoto University Economic Review*, IV (1929) 28–46. S

——, On the form of the distribution of our national incomes, *Kyoto University Economic Review*, VII (1932) 61–75. S

SHIRRAS, G. F., India's national income, *Revue de l'Institut International de Statistique*, IV (1936) 467–483. S

STONE, R., The national income, output, and expenditure of the United States of America, 1929–41, *Economic Journal*, LII (1942) 154–175. S

————, National income in the United Kingdom and the United States of America, *Review of Economic Studies*, X (1942–1943) 1–27. **S**

————, Two studies on income and expenditure in the United States, *Economic Journal*, LIII (1943) 60–75. **A**

SUTCLIFFE, J. T., The Australian national dividend, *Economic Record*, II (1926) 174–179. **S**

THOMSEN, F. L. and P. H. BOLLINGER, Forecasting national income and related measures, *Studies in Income and Wealth*, Vol. VI, New York, National Bureau of Economic Research, 1943, 170–204. **S**

WARBURTON, C., Value of the gross national product and its components, 1919–1929, *Journal of the American Statistical Association*, XXIX (1934) 383–388. **S**

————, How the national income was spent, 1919–29, *Journal of the American Statistical Association*, XXX (1935) 175–182. **S**

————, The trend of savings, 1900–1929, *Journal of Political Economy*, XLIII (1935) 84–101. **S**

————, Three estimates of the value of the nation's output of commodities and services; a comparison, *Studies in Income and Wealth*, Vol. III, New York, National Bureau of Economic Research, 1939, 319–397. **S**

————, Relation of government financing to gross income flow, *Survey of Current Business*, XXIII (April 1943) 17–22. **S**

WINKLER, W., "Volkseinkommens, Statistik des, *Handwörterbuch der Staatswissenschaften*, Vierte Auflage, VIII. Jena, Gustav Fisher, 1923, 746–770. **S**

————, Volksvermögen, *Handwörterbuch der Staatswissenschaften*, Vierte Auflage, VIII, Jena, Gustav Fischer, 1923, 770–786. **A**

WYLER, J., The share of capital in national income—United States, United Kingdom and Germany, *Social Research*, X (1943) 436–454. **S**

II. PRODUCTION THEORY

II-A. THE PRODUCTION FUNCTION AND MARGINAL PRODUCTIVITY

Includes articles dealing with the properties of production relations, the statistical measurement of labor productivity, and cross-section and historical studies involving the Cobb-Douglas function together with appraisals of the significance of these studies.

ASHTON, H., Some considerations in the measurement of productivity of railroad workers, *Journal of Political Economy*, XLVI (1938) 714–720. **S**

BOBER, M. M., Theoretical aspects of the scale of production, *Economics, Sociology and the Modern World*. Essays in Honor of T. N. Carver, Cambridge, Harvard University Press, 1935, 73–91. **A**

BOWDEN, W., The productivity of labor in Great Britain, *Journal of Political Economy*, XLV (1937) 347–369. **S**

————, The productivity of labor in Great Britain: a further note, *Journal of Political Economy*, XLV (1937) 815–816. **S**

————, The productivity of labor: note on terminology and method, *Journal of Political Economy*, XLVI (1938) 857–863. **A**

BRONFENBRENNER, M. and P. H. DOUGLAS, Cross-section studies in the Cobb-Douglas function, *Journal of Political Economy*, XLVII (1939) 761–785. **S**

——, Production functions: Cobb-Douglas, interfirm, intrafirm, *Econometrica*, XII (1944) 35–44. **A**

BROWNE, G. W. G., The production function for South African manufacturing industry, *South African Journal of Economics*, XI (1943) 258–268. **S**

*CASSELS, J. M., On the law of variable proportions, *Explorations in Economics*, New York and London, McGraw-Hill Book Co., 1936, 223–236. **A**

CIRIACY-WANTRUP, S. VON., Economics of joint costs in agriculture, *Journal of Farm Economics*, XXIII (1941) 771–818. **A**

CLARK, C., The marginal productivity of capital, *Economic Record*, XV (1939) 54–59. **S**

——, The marginal productivity of capital, *Economic Record*, Supplement, XV (1939) 110–118. **S**

CLARK, J. M., Inductive evidence on marginal productivity, *American Economic Review*, XVIII (1928) 449–467. **A**

——, Diminishing returns, *Encyclopaedia of the Social Sciences*, (editors, E. R. A. Seligman and A. Johnson), V, New York, The Macmillan Co., 1931, 144–146. **A**

——, Increasing returns, *Encyclopaedia of the Social Sciences*, (editors, E. R. A. Seligman and A. Johnson), VII, New York, The Macmillan Co., 1932, 639–640. **A**

COBB, C. W. and P. H. DOUGLAS, A theory of production, *American Economic Review*, Supplement, XVIII (1928) 139–165. **S**

——, Production in Massachusetts manufacturing, 1890–1928, *Journal of Political Economy*, XXXVIII (1930) 705–707. **S**

——, A regression, *Econometrica*, XI (1943) 265–267. **S**

CROSARA, A., Repartizione del prodotto totale e offerta a costi congiunti, *Giornale degli Economisti*, LXIX (1929) 49–67. **A**

DALY, P., and P. DOUGLAS, The production function for Canadian manufacturing, *Journal of the American Statistical Association*, XXXVIII (1943) 178–186. **S**

——, E. OLSON, and P. H. DOUGLAS, The production function for manufacturing in the United States, 1904, *Journal of Political Economy*, LI (1943) 61–65. **S**

DAS-GUPTA, A. K., Theory of increasing returns under competitive conditions, *Indian Journal of Economics*, XII (1931) 63–72. **A**

DIEHL, K., Zurechnungstheorie und Verteilungslehre, *Jahrbücher für Nationalökonomie und Statistik*, CXXXI (1929) Heft 5, 641–687. **A**

DOUGLAS, P. H., Some new material on the theory of distribution, *Economic Essays in Honour of Gustav Cassel*, London, Allen & Unwin, Ltd., 1933, 105–115. **S**

——, Professor Cassel on the statistical determination of marginal productivity, *Canadian Journal of Economics and Political Science*, IV (1938) 22–33. **S**

DURAND, D., Some thoughts on marginal productivity, with special reference to Professor Douglas' analysis, *Journal of Political Economy*, LXV (1937) 740–758. **S**

FABRICANT, S., The relation between factory employment and output since 1899, National Bureau of Economic Research, *Occasional paper* 4 (December 1941) 3–39. **S**

——, Productivity of labor in peace and war, National Bureau of Economic Research, *Occasional paper* 7 (September 1942) 3–28. **S**

FISHER, I., A three-dimensional representation of the factors of production and their remuneration, marginally and residually, *Econometrica*, VII (1939) 304–311. **A**

---

* Reprinted in the present volume.

————, J. MARSCHAK, and P. A. SAMUELSON, Summaries of papers presented at the annual meeting on the pure theory of production, *American Economic Review*, Supplement, XXIX (1939) 118–120. A

GEORGESCU-ROEGEN, N., Fixed coefficients of production and the marginal productivity theory, *Review of Economic Studies*, III (1935–1936) 40–49. A

GUNN, G. T. and P. H. DOUGLAS, Further measurements of marginal productivity, *Quarterly Journal of Economics*, LIV (1939–1940) 399–428. S

———— and ————, The production function for American manufacturing in 1919, *American Economic Review*, XXXI (1941) 67–80. S

———— and ————, The production function for Australian manufacturing, *Quarterly Journal of Economics*, (1941–1942) 108–129. S

———— and ————, The production function for American manufacturing, *Journal of Political Economy*, L (1942) 595–602. S

HANDSAKER, M. L. and P. H. DOUGLAS, The theory of marginal productivity tested by data for manufacturing in Victoria, I, *Quarterly Journal of Economics*, LII (1937–1938) 1–36. S

———— and ————, The theory of marginal productivity tested by data for manufacturing in Victoria, II, *Quarterly Journal of Economics*, LII (1937–1938) 215–254. S

HAYEK, F. A. VON, Bemerkungen zum Zurechnungsproblem, *Jahrbücher für Nationalökonomie und Statistik*, CXXIV (1926) Heft 1 und 2, 1–18. A

KATSER, L., Die Frage der Zurechnung in der deutschen Volkswirtschaftslehre, *Jahrbücher für Nationalökonomie und Statistik*, CXXVIII (1928) Heft 6, 801–837. A

KLEIN, L. R., The relationship between total output and man-hour output: comment, *Quarterly Journal of Economics*, LVI (1941–1942) 342–343. A

KNIGHT, F. H., A note on Professor Clark's illustration of marginal productivity, *Journal of Political Economy*, XXXIII (1925) 550–553. A. Reply by J. M. Clark, 554–557. Rejoinder by F. H. Knight, 557–561. Concluding note by J. M. Clark, 561–562.

LIEFMANN, R., Zurechnung und Verteilung, *Schmollers Jahrbuch*, LVIII (1924) Heft 3, 35–67. A

*MACHLUP, F., On the meaning of the marginal product, *Explorations in Economics*, New York and London, McGraw-Hill Book Co., 1936, 250–263. A

MAYER, H., Zurechnung, *Handwörterbuch der Staatswissenschaften*, Vierte Auflage, VIII, Jena, Gustav Fischer, 1923, 1206–1228. A

MENDERSHAUSEN, H., On the significance of Professor Douglas' production function, *Econometrica*, VI (1938) 143–153. S

————, On the significance of Professor Douglas' production function: a correction, *Econometrica*, VII (1939) 362. A

————, On the significance of another production function: a comment, *American Economic Review*, XXXI (1941) 563–564. A. Reply by G. T. Gunn and P. H. Douglas, 564–567. Rejoinder by H. Mendershausen, 567–569.

NEISSER, H., A note on Pareto's theory of production, *Econometrica*, VIII (1940) 253–262. A

---

* Reprinted in the present volume.

OLIVER, H. M., JR., The relationship between total output and man-hour output in American manufacturing industry, *Quarterly Journal of Economics*, LV (1940–1941) 239–254. S

PHELPS-BROWN, E. H., The marginal efficacy of a productive factor—first report of the Econometrica Committee on source materials for quantitative production studies, *Econometrica*, IV (1936) 123–137. S

PRESCOTT, J. A., The law of diminishing returns in agricultural experiment, *Economic Record*, IV (1928) 85–89. S

REDER, M. W., An alternative interpretation of the Cobb-Douglas function, *Econometrica*, XI (1943) 259–264. A

ROBBINS, L., Production: theory, *Encyclopaedia of the Social Sciences*, (editors, E. R. A. Seligman and A. Johnson), XII, New York, The Macmillan Co., 1934, 462–467. A

ROBINSON, J., Euler's theorem and the problem of distribution, *Economic Journal*, XLIV (1934) 398–414. A

SCHNEIDER, E., Bemerkungen zur Grenzproduktivitätstheorie, *Zeitschrift für National-ökonomie*, IV (1932–1933) Heft 5, 604–624. A

SLICHTER, S. H. and J. D. BLACK, Economic and social aspects of increased productivity efficiency—discussion, *American Economic Review*, Supplement, XVIII (1928) 166–172. A

SMITHIES, A., The boundaries of the production function and the utility function, *Explorations in Economics*, New York and London, McGraw-Hill Book Co., 326–335. A

*STIGLER, G., Production and distribution in the short run, *Journal of Political Economy*, XLVII (1939) 305–327. A

STRIGL, R., Ertrag, *Handwörterbuch der Staatswissenschaften*, Vierte Auflage, III, Jena, Gustav Fischer, 1923, 840–842. A

TAKATA, Y., On the coefficients of production, *Kyoto University Economic Review*, IV (1929) 47–84. A

THOMPSON, J. G., Mobility of the factors of production as affecting variation in their proportional relation to each other in farm organization, *Journal of Political Economy*, XXIX (1921) 108–137. A

TINTNER, G., A note on the derivation of production functions from farm records, *Econometrica*, XII (1944) 26–34. S

WARBURTON, C. A., Diminishing and increasing returns, *Indian Journal of Economics*, IV (1923) 149–183. A

WEDDIGEN, W., F. Oppenheimer und die Theorie des Ertrages, *Schmollers Jahrbuch*, LXII (1928) Heft 5, 113–138. A

WEISS, F. X., Abnehmender Ertrag, *Handwörterbuch der Staatswissenschaften*, Vierte Auflage, I, Jena, Gustav Fischer, 1923, 11–18. A

WILLIAMS, O. L., Suggestions for constructing a model of a production function, *Review of Economic Studies*, I (1933–1934) 231–235. A

YNTEMA, T. O., Some notes on Black's "Production Economics," *Journal of Political Economy*, XXXVIII (1930) 698–704. A

ZASSENHAUS, H., Dr. Schneider and the theory of production, *Review of Economic Studies*, III (1935–1936) 35–39. A

---

* Reprinted in the present volume.

ZOTOFF, A. W., Notes on the mathematical theory of production, *Economic Journal*, XXXIII (1923) 115–121. **A**

ZUCKERKANDL, R., Zur Produktionslehre, *Schmollers Jahrbuch*, LIX (1925) Heft 6, 1–38. **A**

II-B. THE ELASTICITY OF SUBSTITUTION, INNOVATIONS, AND DISTRIBUTION

Items concerned with the concept of the elasticity of substitution, the various classifications of innovations as factor-using or factor-saving, and technological unemployment are included here.

BIGGE, G. E., Wage rates and use of machinery, *American Economic Review*, XVII (1927) 675–680. **A**

BOUNIATIAN, M., Technical progress and unemployment, *International Labour Review*, XXVII (1933) 327–348. **A**

DOUGLAS, P. H., The effect of wage increases upon employment, *American Economic Review*, Supplement, XXIX (1939) 138–157. **S**

FISHER, A. G. B., Technical improvements, unemployment and reduction of working hours, *Economica*, IV, new series (1937) 371–385. **A**

FISHER, C. O., An issue in economic theory: "The rate of wages and the use of machinery," *American Economic Review*, XIII (1923) 654–655. **A**. Comment by H. G. Hayes, 655–657.

FLAMM, J. H., The problem of technological unemployment in the United States, *International Labour Review*, XXXI (1935) 344–363. **A**

FRIEDMAN, M., J. ROBINSON, A. P. LERNER, and F. MACHLUP, Further notes on elasticity of substitution: I. Note on Dr. Machlup's article, II. Dr. Machlup's commonsense of the elasticity of substitution, III. The question of symmetry, IV Reply, *Review of Economic Studies*, III (1935–1936) 147–152. **A**

GRAHAM, F. D., Relation of wage rates to the use of machinery, *American Economic Review*, XVI (1926) 434–442. **A**

GREGORY, T. E., Rationalisation and technological unemployment, *Economic Journal*, XL (1930) 551–567. **A**

HABERLER, G., Some remarks on Professor Hansen's view on technological unemployment, *Quarterly Journal of Economics*, XLVI (1931–1932) 558–562. **A**. Rejoinder, by A. H. Hansen, 562–565.

HAGEN, E. E., Saving, investment, and technological unemployment, *American Economic Review*, XXXII (1942) 553–555. **A**. Reply by H. Neisser, 555–557.

HANSEN, A. H., Institutional frictions and technological unemployment, *Quarterly Journal of Economics*, XLV (1930–1931) 684–697. **A**

———, The theory of technological progress and the dislocation of employment, *American Economic Review*, Supplement, XXII (1932) 25–31. **A**

HAYES, H. G., The rate of wages and the use of machinery, *American Economic Review*, XIII (1923) 461–465. **A**

HICKS, J. R., Distribution and economic progress: a revised version, *Review of Economic Studies*, IV (1936–1937) 1–12. **A**

JACKSON, D. C., Machinery and unemployment, *Stabilization of Employment*, (edited by C. F. Roos), Bloomington, Indiana, Principia Press, 1933, 33–51. **A**

JEROME, H., The measurement of productivity changes and displacement of labor, *American Economic Review*, Supplement, XXII (1932) 32–40. **A**

KÄHLER, A., The problem of verifying the theory of technological unemployment, *Social Research*, II (1935) 439–460. **A**

KAHN, R. F. and D. G. CHAMPERNOWNE, The elasticity of substitution: I. Two applications of the concept; II. A mathematical note, *Economic Journal*, XLV (1935) 242–258. **A**

KALDOR, N., A case against technical progress, *Economica*, XII (1932) 180–196. **A**

———, Limitational factors and the elasticity of substitution, *Review of Economic Studies*, IV (1936–1937) 162–165. **A**

KALECKI, M., A theorem on technical progress, *Review of Economic Studies*, VIII (1940–1941) 178–184. **A**

KEIRSTEAD, B. S., Technical advance and economic equilibria, *Canadian Journal of Economics and Political Science*, IX (1943) 55–68. **A**

KIMBALL, D. S., The social effects of mass production, *Stabilization of Employment*, (edited by C. F. Roos), Bloomington, Indiana, Principia Press, 1933, 52–69. **A**

*LANGE, O., A note on innovations, *Review of Economic Statistics*, XXV (1943) 19–25. **A**

LEDERER, E., Technical progress and unemployment, *International Labour Review*, XXVIII (1933) 1–25. **A**

LERNER, A. P., The diagrammatical representation of elasticity of substitution, *Review of Economic Studies*, I (1933–1934) 68–71. **A**

LE ROSSIGNOL, J. E., Mill on machinery, *American Economic Review*, XXX (1940) 115–116. **A**

LONIGAN, E., The effect of modern technological conditions upon the employment of labor, *American Economic Review*, XXIX (1939) 246–259. **A**

MACHLUP, F., The commonsense of the elasticity of substitution, *Review of Economic Studies*, II (1934–1935) 202–213. **A**

MORRISON, L. A. and M. A. GEARHART, An issue in economic theory: "The rate of wages and the use of machinery," *American Economic Review*, XIV (1924) 283–286. **A**

MOSAK, J. L., Interrelations of production, price, and derived demand, *Journal of Political Economy*, XLVI (1938) 761–787. **A**

NEISSER, H. P., "Permanent" technological unemployment, *American Economic Review*, XXXII (1942) 50–71. **A**

PIGOU, A. C., A note on Mr. Hicks' distribution formula, *Economica*, XII (1933) 143–146. **A**

———, The elasticity of substitution, *Economic Journal*, XLIV (1934) 232–241. **A**

*ROBINSON, J., The classification of inventions, *Review of Economic Studies*, V (1937–1938) 139–142. **A**

STERNBERG, F., Prolonged unemployment, technical progress and the conquest of new markets, *International Labour Review*, XXXVI (1937) 446–485. **A**

STIER-SOMLO, K., Substitutionsprinzip und Substitutionsgesitz in der Nationalökonomie, *Zeitschrift für die gesamte Staatswissenschaft*, LXXIX (1925) Heft 3, 395–463. **A**

SWEEZY, P. M., Professor Schumpeter's theory of innovation, *Review of Economic Statistics*, XXV (1943) 93–96. **A**

TARSHIS, L., A. P. LERNER, and J. E. MEADE, Notes on the elasticity of substitution, *Review of Economic Studies*, I (1933–1934) 144–153. **A**

TROXEL, C. E., Economic influences of obsolescence, *American Economic Review*, XXVI (1936) 280–290. **A**

---

* Reprinted in the present volume.

WISSLER, W., Note on the effect of wage rates on machine use, *American Economic Review*, XVII (1927) 50–52. **A**

WOLLEY, H. B., The anomalous case of the shifting cost curve, *Quarterly Journal of Economics*, LVII (1942–1943) 646–656. **A**

III. GENERAL DISTRIBUTION

III-A. FUNCTIONAL DISTRIBUTION OF INCOME AND GENERAL EQUILIBRIUM PRICING

Includes articles concerned with the nature and development of classical and neo-classical distribution systems, the concept of opportunity cost, the function of a pricing system, the relation of monopolistic competition to distribution, and the theory of general economic equilibrium.

Several contemporary macro-statical models used in the analysis of the determination of the level of output and employment are included.

ANDERSON, M. D., Marginal productivity versus classical rent, *Southern Journal of Economics*, IV (1937) 38–53. **A**

BAGGE, G., Den aftagande och tilltagande afkastningens lagar, *Ekonomisk Tidskrift*, XX (1920) 193–228. **A**

BALÁS, K. VON, Die Verteilungsvorgänge und die Buchhaltungsbegriffe, *Jahrbücher für Nationalökonomie und Statistik*, CXLVII (1938) Heft 6, 695–705. **A**

BILIMOVIC, A., Zins und Unternehmergewinn im Gleichungssystem der stationären Wirtschaft, *Zeitschrift für Nationalökonomie*, VIII (1937) Heft 3, 297–326. **A**

BRONFENBRENNER, M., The role of money in equilibrium capital theory, *Econometrica*, XI (1943) 35–60. **A**

BROWN, H. G., Opportunity cost: Marshall's criticism of Jevons, *American Economic Review*, XXI (1931) 498–500. **A**

BURCHARDT, F., Die Schemata des stationären Kreislaufs bei Böhm-Bawerk und Marx, I, *Weltwirtschaftliches Archiv*, XXXIV (1931) Heft 2, 525–597. **A**

———, Die Schemata des stationären Kreislaufs bei Böhm-Bawerk und Marx, II, *Weltwirtschaftliches Archiv*, XXXV (1932) Heft 1, 116–176. **A**

BYE, R. T., The nature and fundamental elements of costs, *Quarterly Journal of Economics*, XLI (1926–1927) 30–62. **A**

———, The process of capital formation and its relation to inequality, *American Economic Review*, XXVI (1936) 607–617. **A**. Reply by H. G. Moulton, 617–620.

CASSEL, G., Keynes' General Theory, *International Labour Review*, XXXVI (1937) 437–445. **A**

*CHAMBERLIN, E. H., Monopolistic competition and the productivity theory of distribution, *Explorations in Economics*, New York and London, McGraw-Hill Book Co., 1936, 237–249. **A**

*CLARK, J. M., Distribution, *Encyclopaedia of the Social Sciences*, (editors E. R. A. Seligman and A. Johnson), V, New York, The Macmillan Co., 1931, 167–173. **A**

COHEN, J. L., The incidence of the costs of social insurance, *International Labour Review*, XX (1929) 816–839. **A**

DIEHL, K., The Classical School, *Encyclopaedia of the Social Sciences*, (editors E. R. A. Seligman and A. Johnson), V, New York, The Macmillan Co., 1931, 351–357. **H**

DOBB, M., The Cambridge School, *Encyclopaedia of the Social Sciences*, (editors E. R. A.

---

* Reprinted in the present volume.

Seligman and A. Johnson), V, New York, The Macmillan Co., 1931, 368–371. **H**

DOUGLAS, P. H., Elasticity of supply as a determinant of distribution, *Economic Essays Contributed in Honor of John Bates Clark*, (edited by J. H. Hollander), New York, The Macmillan Co., 1927, 71–118. **A**

EDELBERG, V., An econometric model of production and distribution, *Econometrica*, IV (1936) 210–225. **S**

EZEKIEL, M., Productivity, wage rates and employment, *American Economic Review*, XXX (1940) 507–523. **S**

FRIDAY, D., An extension of value theory, *Quarterly Journal of Economics*, XXXVI (1921–1922) 197–219. **A**

GADOLIN, C. A. J., VON, Cassels Wirtschaftssystem und wirtschaftspolitisches Wirken, *Weltwirtschaftliches Archiv*, LV (1942) Heft 2, 301–320. **A**

GOURVITCH, A., The problem of prices and valuation in the Soviet system, *American Economic Review*, Supplement, XXVI (1936) 267–282. **A**

GRÜNBERG, C., Johann Heinrich von Thünen, *Handwörterbuch der Staatswissenschaften*, Vierte Auflage, VIII, Jena, Gustav Fischer, 1923, 251–257. **H**

HARRIS, A. L., The Marxian right to the whole product, *Economic Essays in Honor of Wesley Clair Mitchell*, New York, Columbia University Press, 1935, 149–198. **A**

HART, A. G., Imputation and the demand for productive resources in disequilibrium, *Explorations in Economics*, New York and London, McGraw-Hill Book Co., 264–271. **A**

HICKS, J. R., Marginal productivity and the principle of variation, *Economica*, XII (1932) 79–88. **A and H**

———, Wages and interest: the dynamic problem, *Economic Journal*, XLV (1935) 456–468. **A**

*———, Mr. Keynes and the "Classics"; A suggested interpretation, *Econometrica*, V (1937) 147–159. **A**

HOOVER, C. B., W. ORTON, and M. T. FLORINSKY, Prices and valuation in the Soviet system—discussion, *American Economic Review*, XXVI (1936) 283–290. **A**

HUANG, P. C., Opportunity cost, *American Economic Review*, XXIII (1933) 82–85. **A**

JAFFÉ, W., Léon Walras' theory of capital accumulation, *Studies in Mathematical Economics and Econometrics: in Memory of Henry Schultz*, (edited by O. Lange, F. McIntyre, and T. O. Yntema), Chicago, University of Chicago Press, 1942, 37–48. **A**

*KALECKI, M., The determinants of distribution of the national income, *Econometrica*, VI (1938) 97–112. **S**. Reprinted in revised form in *Essays in the Theory of Economic Fluctuations*, London, George Allen & Unwin, Ltd., 1931, 13–14.

———, A theory of long-run distribution on the product of industry, *Oxford Economic Papers*, No. 5 (1941) 31–41. **S**

KELBER, M., Die abgeleiteten Einkommen, *Jahrbücher für Nationalökonomie und Statistik*, CXXXVIII (1933) Heft 2, 161–204. **A**

KNIGHT, F. H., Marginal utility economics, *Encyclopaedia of the Social Sciences*, (editors E. R. A. Seligman and A. Johnson), V, New York, The Macmillan Co., 1931, 357–363. **A and H**

———, The place of marginal economics in a collectivist system, *American Economic Review*, Supplement, XXVI (1936) 255–266. **A**

---

* Reprinted in the present volume.

————, The Ricardian theory of production and distribution, *Canadian Journal of Economics and Political Science*, I (1935) 3–25. **A and H**

————, The Ricardian theory of production and distribution (continued), *Canadian Journal of Economics and Political Science*, I (1935) 171–196. **A and H**

————, Some issues in the economics of stationary states, *American Economic Review*, XXVI (1936) 393–411. **A**

KOKKALIS, A., Die Produktionsfaktoren und ihr Verhältnis zueinander, *Jahrbücher für Nationalökonomie und Statistik*, CXXXV (1931) Heft 6, 846–862. **A**

KREPS, T. J., Dividends, interest, profits, wages, 1923–1935, *Quarterly Journal of Economics*, XLIX (1934–1935) 561–599. **S**

LAMPE, A., Schumpeters System und die Ausgestaltung der Verteilungslehre, *Jahrbücher für Nationalökonomie und Statistik*, CXXI (1923) Heft 5, 417–444. **A**

————, Schumpeters System und die Ausgestaltung der Verteilungslehre, *Jahrbücher für Nationalökonomie und Statistik*, CXXI (1923) Heft 6, 513–546. **A**

LANGE, O., The rate of interest and the optimum propensity to consume, *Economica*, V, new series (1938) 12–32. **A**

LAWS, M., The difficulty of imputation, *Economic Journal*, XLIII (1933) 251–258. **A**

LEONTIEF, W. W., Quantitative input and output relations in the economic system of the United States, *Review of Economic Statistics*, XVIII (1936) 105–125. **S**

————, Interrelation of prices, output, savings, and investment, *Review of Economic Statistics*, XIX (1937) 109–132. **S**

————, Output, employment, consumption, and investment, *Quarterly Journal of Economics*, LVIII (1943–1944) 290–314. **S**

LERNER, A. P., Mr. Keynes' General Theory of Employment, Interest and Money, *International Labour Review*, XXIV (1936) 435–454. **A**

————, Keynes' General Theory: a rejoinder to Professor Cassel, *International Labour Review*, XXXVI (1937) 585–590. **A**

LINDAHL, E., Prisbildningsproblemets uppläggning från kapitalteoretisk synpunkt, *Economisk Tidskrift*, XXXI (1929) 31–81. **A**

LUKAS, E., Ricardo und Cassel, *Jahrbücher für Nationalökonomie und Statistik*, CXIX (1922) Heft 5, 369–395. **A**

MARSCHAK, J., Zur Politik und Theorie der Verteilung, *Archiv für Sozialwissenschaft und Sozialpolitik*, LXIV (1930) Heft 1, 1–15. **A**

————, An empirical analysis of the laws of distribution, *Economica*, III, new series (1936) 221–226. **A**

————, and W. H. ANDREWS, JR., Random simultaneous equations and the theory of production, *Econometrica*, XII (1944) 143–205. **A**

MAYER, H., Verteilung, *Handwörterbuch der Staatswissenschaften*, Vierte Auflage, VIII, Jena, Gustav Fischer, 1923, 675–678. **A**

MOELLER, H., Das Problem der Verteilung, *Weltwirtschaftliches Archiv*, LIII (1936) Heft 3, 537–560. **A**

MORSS, N., The distribution equilibrium under the specific productivity theory, *Quarterly Journal of Economics*, XLI (1926–1927) 349–352. **A**

REISSER, H., Gustav Cassels Theoretische Sozialökonomie, *Schmollers Jahrbuch*, LVI (1922) Heft 1, 211–235. **A**

ROBINSON, J., The long-period theory of employment, *Zeitschrift für Nationalökonomie*, VII (1936) Heft 1, 74–93. **A**

*ROLPH, E., The discounted marginal productivity doctrine, *Journal of Political Economy*, XLVII (1939) 542–556. **A**

SCHULTZ, H., Marginal productivity and the general pricing process, *Journal of Political Economy*, XXXVII (1929) 505–551. **A** and **H**

———, Marginal productivity and the Lausanne School, *Economica*, XII (1932) 285–296. **A** and **H**. Reply by J. R. Hicks, 297–300.

———, Comments on Professor Anderson's article, "Marginal productivity versus classical rent," *Southern Economic Journal*, IV (1938) 352–353. **A**. Rejoinder by M. D. Anderson, 353–354.

SOMERS, H. M., Taxes as a share in distribution, *American Economic Review*, XXIX (1939) 349. **A**

SOUTER, R. W., Land, capital, and opportunity cost, *American Economic Review*, XXII (1932) 203–207. **A**

STEPHANS, K. H., Bemerkungen zum Wertaspekt der modernen Verteilungstheorie, *Zeitschrift für Nationalökonomie*, V (1934) Heft 3, 356–371. **A**

TAYLOR, F. M., Guidance of production in a socialist state, *American Economic Review*, XIX (1929) 1–8. **A**

THOMPSON, J. M., Mathematical theory of production stages in economics, *Econometrica*, IV (1936) 67–85. **A**

TINBERGEN, J., Zur Theorie der langfristigen Wirtschaftsentwicklung, *Weltwirtschaftliches Archiv*, LV (1942) Heft 3, 511–549. **A**

TINTNER, G., The pure theory of production under subjective risk and uncertainty, *Econometrica*, IX (1941) 305–312. **A**

———, A contribution to the nonstatic theory of production, *Studies in Mathematical Economics and Econometrics: in Memory of Henry Schultz*, (edited by O. Lange, F. McIntyre, and T. O. Yntema), Chicago, University of Chicago Press, 1942, 92–109. **A**

———, The theory of production under non-static conditions, *Journal of Political Economy*, L (1942) 645–667. **A**

VALK, W. L., Les équations de Walras et de Cassel et la théorie de la productivité marginale, *Revue d'Economie Politique*, XLIII (1929) 34–48. **A**

WARBURTON, C. A., The theory of distribution, *Indian Journal of Economics*, IV (1923) 15–29. **A**

———, Distribution among the factors of production, *Indian Journal of Economics*, V (1924) 38–72. **A**

WASSERMAN, M. J., Taxes as a share in distribution, *American Economic Review*, XXVIII (1938) 103–105. **A**

WEDDIGEN, W., Ertragstheorie und Verteilungstheorie, *Jahrbücher für Nationalökonomie und Statistik*, CXXVIII (1928) Heft 1, 1–37. **A**

WICKSELL, K., Professor Cassels Nationalökonomisches System, *Schmollers Jahrbuch*, LXII (1928) Heft 5, 1–38. **A**

III-B. PERSONAL DISTRIBUTION OF WEALTH AND INCOME

Includes items dealing with the methods of measuring the inequality of incomes, estimates of the distribution of income, and estimates of the distribution of wealth.

---

* Reprinted in the present volume.

ADARKAR, B. P. and S. N. SEN GUPTA, The Pareto law and the distribution of incomes in India, *Economic Journal*, XLVI (1936) 168–171. **A**

ALIMENTI, C., Sulla curva paretiana di distribuzione du redditi; I. Osservazioni critiche, *Giornale degli Economisti*, LXXII (1932) 730–738. **A**

AMES, E., A method for estimating the size distribution of a given aggregate income, *Review of Economic Statistics*, XXIV (1942) 184–189. **S**

AYGANGAR, A. A. K., Inequalities, *Indian Journal of Economics*, XXIV (1943) 65–70. **A**

BACH, G. L., War financing and the distribution of income, *American Economic Review*, XXXII (1942) 352–354. **A**

BAIRD, E. and S. FINE, The use of income tax data in the National Resources Committee estimate of the distribution of income by size, *Studies in Income and Wealth*, Vol. III, New York, National Bureau of Economic Research, 1939, 149–214. **S**

*BOWMAN, M. J., A graphical analysis of personal income distribution in the United States, *American Economic Review*, XXXV (1945) 607–628. **S**

BRADY, D. S., Study of consumer purchases: farm families, *Studies in Income and Wealth*, Vol. V, Part II, Chap. II, New York, National Bureau of Economic Research, 1943, 1–30. **S**

BRESCIANI-TURRONI, C., Su alcune discordanze tra gli indici misuratori della disuguaglianza dei redditi, *Giornale degli Economisti*, LXXVI (1936) 608–616. **S**

——, Annual survey of statistical data: Pareto's law and the index of inequality of incomes, *Econometrica*, VII (1939) 107–133. **S**

BROKATE, L., The Delaware income study, *Studies in Income and Wealth*, Vol. V, Part II, Chap. 4, New York, National Bureau of Economic Research, 1943, 1–45. **S**

BURNS, A. F., The Brookings inquiry into income distribution and progress, *Quarterly Journal of Economics*, L (1935–1936) 476–523. **A**

CANTELLI, F. P., Sulla legge di distribuzione dei redditi, *Giornale degli Economisti*. LXIX (1929) 850–852. **A**

CLAY, H., The authoritarian element in distribution, *Economic Journal*, XXXVII (1927) 1–18. **S**

CRAWFORD, R. H., United States Treasury Department study of 1936 returns, *Studies in Income and Wealth*, Vol. V, Part II, Chap. 3, New York, National Bureau of Economic Research, 1943, 1–45. **S**

CRUM, W. L., Individual shares in the national income, *Review of Economic Statistics*, XVII (1935) 116–130. **S**

——, C. L. HARRISS, and E. G. KEITH, Federal statistics, *Studies in Income and Wealth*, Vol. V, Part II, Chap. 1, New York, National Bureau of Economic Research, 1943, 1–141. **S**

DALTON, H., Measurement of the inequality of incomes, *Economic Journal*, XXX (1920) 348–361. **A**

DENISON, E. F., Incomes in selected professions, *Survey of Current Business*, XXIII (July 1943) 25–28. **S**

——, Incomes in selected professions, *Survey of Current Business*, XXIII (August 1943) 23–27. **S**

——, Incomes in selected professions, *Survey of Current Business*, XXIII (September 1943), 25–28. **S**

---

* Reprinted in the present volume.

————, Incomes in selected professions, *Survey of Current Business*, XXIV (April 1944) 17–20. S

————, Incomes in selected professions, *Survey of Current Business*, XXIV (May 1944) 15–19. S

———— and A. SLATER, Incomes in selected professions, *Survey of Current Business*, XXIII (October 1943) 16–20. S

DURAND, D., A simple method for estimating the size distribution of a given aggregate income, *Review of Economic Statistics*, XXV (1943) 227–230. S

ECKLER, A. R., R. H. CRAWFORD, and S. F. GOLDSMITH, The 1940 population census, *Studies in Income and Wealth*, Vol. V, Part II, Chap. 16, New York, National Bureau of Economic Research, 1943, 1–81. S

FALKNER, R. P., Personal incomes, *Conference Board Bulletin*, X (1936) 41–44. S

GAINSBRUGH, M. R., National and state incomes, 1929–1941, *Conference Board Economic Record*, IV (1942) 221–226. S

GARVY, G., Dr. Rhodes' analysis of the distribution of single incomes in the United States, *Economica*, XI, new series (1944) 104–105. A

GILBOY, E. W., The unemployed: their income and expenditure, *American Economic Review*, XXVII (1937) 309–323. S

GINI, C., Measurement of inequality of incomes, *Economic Journal*, XXXI (1921) 124–126. A

HABER, W. and W. DAUGHERTY, The Michigan unemployment census, *Studies in Income and Wealth*, Vol. V, Part II, Chap. 14, New York, National Bureau of Economic Research, 1943, 1–14. S

HALE, R. L., Coercion and distribution in a supposedly noncoercive state, *Political Science Quarterly*, XXXVIII (1923) 470–494. A

HANNA, F. A., The Wisconsin income tax study, *Studies in Income and Wealth*, Vol. V, Part II, Chap. 5, New York, National Bureau of Economic Research, 1943, 1–106. S

HELLER, W. W. and C. L. HARRISS, State individual income tax data, *Studies in Income and Wealth*, Vol. V, Part II, Chap. 7, New York, National Bureau of Economic Research, 1943, 1–97. S

JOHNSON, N. O., The Brookings report on inequality in income distribution, *Quarterly Journal of Economics*, XLIX (1934–1935) 718–724. S

————, The Pareto law, *Review of Economic Statistics*, XIX (1937) 20–26. S

KARSTEN, K. G., An index of incomes, *Journal of the American Statistical Association*, XVII (1920) 253–276. S

KEYNES, J. M., Mr. Keynes on the distribution of incomes and "propensity to consume": a reply, *Review of Economic Statistics*, XXI (1939) 129. A

KUZNETS, S. and M. FRIEDMAN, Incomes from independent professional practice, National Bureau of Economic Research, *Bulletin* 72–73 (1939) 1–31. S

ANZILLO, A., La curva paretiana di distribuzione dei redditi e le illazioni che suggerisci, *Giornale degli Economisti*, LXXII (1932) 133–143. A

————, Sulla curva paretiana di distribuzione dei redditi, II. Replica, *Giornale degli Economisti*, LXXII (1932) 738–740. A

LESLIE, R., The effect of the abandonment of the gold standard on the distribution of incomes in South Africa, *South African Journal of Economics*, III (1935) 279–280. S

——, The change in the distribution of incomes in South Africa after the abandonment of the gold standard, *South African Journal of Economics*, IV (1936) 122. **S**

——, Distribution of incomes in South Africa, *South African Journal of Economics*, V (1937) 95. **S**

MacGregor, D. H., Pareto's law, *Economic Journal*, XLVI (1936) 80–87. **S**

McGonn, A. F., Inequality and accumulation, *Journal of Political Economy*, XXXII (1924) 648–664. **A**

Marschak, J., Personal and collective budget functions, *Review of Economic Statistics*, XXI (1939) 161–170. **S**

——, Income inequality and demand studies: a note, *Econometrica*, XI (1943) 163–166. **A**

Merwin, C. L., Jr., American studies of the distribution of wealth and income by size, *Studies in Income and Wealth*, Vol. III, New York, National Bureau of Economic Research, 1939, 3–93. **S**

Metzler, L. A., Effects of income redistribution, *Review of Economic Statistics*, XXV (1943) 49–57. **S**

Murray, M. G. and J. R. Arnold, Old-age and survivors insurance records, *Studies in Income and Wealth*, Vol. V, Part II, Chap. 8, New York, National Bureau of Economic Research, 1943, 1–26. **S**

National Industrial Conference Board, Personal incomes, *Conference Board Bulletin* No. 60 (December 1931) 477–483. **S**

Nielsen, O., Survey of family income, *Survey of Current Business*, XVII (December 1937) 12–17. **S**

Palmer, E. Z., Resources and distribution of income in the south, *Southern Economic Journal*, II (1936) 47–60. **S**

Pethick-Lawrence, F. W., Note on the paper by Professor S. N. Procopovitch on the distribution of national income, *Economic Journal*, XXXVI (1926) 302–305. **S**

Procopovitch, S. N., The distribution of national income, *Economic Journal*, XXXVI (1926) 69–82. **S**

Renne, R. R., Income distribution and taxation in Montana, *Studies in Income and Wealth*, Vol. V, Part II, Chap. 6, New York, National Bureau of Economic Research, 1943, 1–28. **S**

Rhodes, E. C., The distribution of incomes in the United States, *Economica*, X, new series (1943) 223–232. **S**

——, Comment on Dr. Garvy's note, *Economica*, XI, new series (1944) 106. **A**

——, The Pareto distribution of incomes, *Economica* XI, new series (1944) 1–11. **A**

Rhodes, R. O., The distribution of incomes, *Economica*, IX, new series (1942) 245–256. **S**

Shiomi, S., Survey of the distribution of the people's incomes in the light of the household rate, *Kyoto University Economic Review*, VIII (1933) 36–67. **S**

Shirras, G. F., The Pareto law and the distribution of income, *Economic Journal*, XLV (1935) 663–681. **S**

Slifer, W. L., Income of independent professional practitioners, *Survey of Current Business*, XVIII (April 1938) 12–16. **S**

Staehle, H., Short-period variations in the distribution of incomes, *Review of Economic Statistics*, XIX (1937) 133–143. **S**

———, A rejoinder, *Review of Economic Statistics*, XXI (1939) 129–130. **A**

STAMP, SIR J., Inheritance as an economic factor, *Economic Journal*, XXXVI (1926) 339–374. **A**

STEWART, C., Income capitalization as a method of estimating the distribution of wealth by size groups, *Studies in Income and Wealth*, Vol. III, New York, National Bureau of Economic Research, 1939, 97–146. **S**

STOCKING, C. and L. LEVINE, Unemployment compensation records, *Studies in Income and Wealth*, Vol. V, Part II, Chap. 9, New York, National Bureau of Economic Research, 1943, 1–28. **S**

SWEEZY, M. Y., Distribution of wealth and income under the Nazi, *Review of Economic Statistics*, XXI (1939) 178–184. **A**

SYDENSTRICKER, E. and W. I. KING, The classification of the population according to income, *Journal of Political Economy*, XXIX (1921) 571–594. **S**

TIBBETTS, C. and H. R. OGBURN, The national health survey, *Studies in Income and Wealth*, Vol. V, Part II, Chap. 13, New York, National Bureau of Economic Research, 1943, 1–43. **S**

TUCKER, R. S., The distribution of income among income taxpayers in the United States, 1863–1935, *Quarterly Journal of Economics*, LII (1937–1938) 547–587. **S**

———, The National Resources Committee's report on distribution of income, *Review of Economic Statistics*, XXII (1940) 165–182. **S**

———, Distribution of income in 1935–36, *Journal of the American Statistical Association*, XXXVII (1942) 489–495. **S**

———, The composition of income and ownership of capital by income classes in the United States in 1936, *Journal of American Statistical Association*, XXXVIII (1943) 187–200. **S**

VINCI, F., Nuovi contributi allo studio della distribuzione dei redditi, *Giornale degli Economisti*, LXI (1921) 365–369. **A**

WARBURTON, C. A., The personal distribution of wealth and income, *Indian Journal of Economics*, V (1924) 161–171. **A**

WASSON, R. C., The Minnesota income study—B. Unemployment compensation data, *Studies in Income and Wealth*, Vol. V, Part II, Chap. 10, New York, National Bureau of Economic Research, 1943, 92–116. **S**

———, The Minnesota income study—C. State income tax returns, *Studies in Income and Wealth*, Vol. V, Part II, Chap. 10, New York, National Bureau of Economic Research, 1943, 117–127. **S**

WEINFELD, W., The Minnesota income study—A. Field survey, *Studies in Income and Wealth*, Vol. V, Part II, Chap. 10, New York, National Bureau of Economic Research, 1943, 1–91. **S**

WICKENS, D. L., The financial survey of urban housing, 1929–1933, *Studies in Income and Wealth*, Vol. V, Part II, Chap. 15, New York, National Bureau of Economic Research, 1943, 1–21. **S**

WILLIAMS, F. M. and M. PARTEN, Study of consumer purchases: City and village families, *Studies in Income and Wealth*, Vol. V, Part II, Chap. 12, New York, National Bureau of Economic Research, 1943, 1–57. **S**

YNTEMA, D. B., Measures of the inequality in the personal distribution of wealth or income, *Journal of the American Statistical Association*, XXVIII (1933) 423–433. **S**

IV. WAGES

IV-A. The Determination of Wages

General issues in wage determination.

ÅKERMAN, G., Teoretiska anmärkningar rörande 8-timmarsdagen, *Ekonomisk Tidskrift*, XXVII (1925) 251–269. A

——, Den industriella utvecklingen och 8-timmarsdagen, *Ekonomisk Tidskrift*, XXVIII (1926) 161–197. S

BRONFENBRENNER, M., The Cobb-Douglas function and trade union policy, *American Economic Review*, XXIX (1939) 793–796. A

BURNS, E. M., Productivity and the theory of wages, *London Essays in Economics: in Honour of Edwin Cannan*, (edited by T. E. Gregory and H. Dalton), London, George Routledge & Sons, Ltd., 1927, 183–209. A

COMMONS, J. R., Wage theories and wage policies, *American Economic Review*, Supplement, XIII (1923) 110–117. A

DICKINSON, Z. C., Recent literature on wage theory, *Quarterly Journal of Economics*, XLIX (1934—1935) 138–146. A

DOBB, M., A sceptical view of the theory of wages, *Economic Journal*, XXXIX (1929) 506–519. A

——, A note concerning Mr. J. R. Hicks on "The indeterminateness of wages," *Economic Journal*, XLI (1931) 142–145. A. Reply by J. R. Hicks, 145–146.

DOUGLAS, P. H. and S. A. LEWISOHN, Factors in wage determination—discussion, *American Economic Review*, Supplement, XIII (1923) 141–146. A

FRAIN, H. L., The relation between normal working time and hourly and weekly earnings, *Quarterly Journal of Economics*, XLIII (1928–1929) 544–550. S

HAMILTON, W. H., A theory of the rate of wages, *Quarterly Journal of Economics*, XXXVI (1921–1922) 581–625. A

HICKS, J. R., Edgeworth, Marshall, and the indeterminateness of wages, *Economic Journal*, XL (1930) 215–231. A

LESTER, R. A., Overtime wage rates, *American Economic Review*, XXIX (1939) 790–792. A

MACLAURIN, W. R., R. E. MONTGOMERY, and S. BARKIN, The determination of wages —discussion, *American Economic Review*, Supplement, XXXI (1942) 302–306. A

MARSCHAK, J., Wages: Theory and policy, *Encyclopaedia of the Social Sciences*, (editors E. R. A. Seligman and A. Johnson), XV, New York, The Macmillan Co., 1935, 291–302. A

MERIAM, R. S., S. H. SLICHTER, J. P. FREY, R. T. BYE, A. B. WOLFE, and G. A. KLEENE, Round table conference: the theory of wages, *American Economic Review*, Supplement, XVI (1926) 240–250. A

MIKESELL, R. F., The possibility of a positively sloped demand curve for labor, *American Economic Review*, XXX (1940) 829–832. A

——, Oligopoly and the short-run demand for labor, *Quarterly Journal of Economics*, LV (1940–1941) 161–166. A

MILLER, J. D., JR., Wages-fund theory and the popular influence of economists, *American Economic Review*, XXX (1940) 108–112. A

Monroe, A. E., The demand for labor, *Quarterly Journal of Economics*, XLVII (1932–1933) 627–646. **A**

Neisser, H., Arbeitszeit und Lohnhöhe, *Zeitschrift für Nationalökonomie*, VI (1935) Heft, 5, 660–664. **A**

Ohlin, B., Åttatimmarsdagens ekonomiska verkningar, *Ekonomisk Tidskrift*, XXVI (1924) 193–218 and XXVII (1925) 65–94. **A**

Riedenauer, O., Grundlagen der Preis- und Lohnbildung, *Jahrbücher für Nationalökonomie und Statistik*, CXXIX (1922) Heft 4, 290–303. **A**

———, Grundlagen der Preis- und Lohnbildung, *Jahrbücher für Nationalökonomie und Statistik*, CXXX (1923) Heft 2, 123–136. **A**

Robbins, L., The economic effects of variations of hours of labour, *Economic Journal*, XXXIX (1929) 25–40. **A**

*———, On the elasticity of demand for income in terms of effort, *Economica*, X (1930) 123–129. **A**

*Robertson, D. H., Wage-grumbles, *Economic Fragments*, by D. H. Robertson, London, P. S. King & Son, Ltd., 1931, 42–57. **A**

Schoenberg, E. H. and P. H. Douglas, Studies in the supply curve of labor, *Journal of Political Economy*, XLV (1937) 45–79. **S**

Schumpeter, J. A., Professor Taussig on wages and capital, *Explorations in Economics*, New York and London, McGraw-Hill Book Co., 1936, 213–222. **A**

Simiand, F., Les théories économiques du salaire, *Revue d'Economie Politique*, XLIV (1930) 1281–1297. **A**

Soule, G., The productivity factor in wage determinations, *American Economic Review*, Supplement, XIII (1923) 129–140. **S**

Strigl, R., Lohn onds und Geldkapital, *Zeitschrift für Nationalökonomie*, V (1934) Heft 5, 18–41. **A**

Stucken, R., Theorie der Lohnsteigerung, *Schmollers Jahrbuch*, LV (1921) Heft 3, 75–102. **A**

Takata, Y., A power theory of wages, *Kyoto University Economic Review*, IV (1929) 14–51. **A**

Turgeon, C., L'homme est-il un capital? *Revue d'Economie Politique*, XXXVIII (1924) 65–86. **A**

Winton, E. M., Wages fund theory and the popular influence of economists: a reply, *American Economic Review*, XXXI (1941) 343–344. **A**

Zwiedineck-Südenhorst, O. von, Arbeitslohn, *Handwörterbuch der Staatswissenschaften*, Vierte Auflag, I, Jena, Gustav Fischer, 1923, 788–790. **A**

———, Lohntheorie und Lohnpolitik, *Handwörterbuch der Staatswissenschaften*, Vierte Auflag, VI, Jena, Gustav Fischer, 1923, 396–426. **A**

IV-B. Regulation and Imperfections of the Labor Market; The Labor Market Structure

Includes discussion of the economic effects of minimum wage and hour legislation and collective bargaining and the significance of the differentiated character of labor services.

Baker, J. C., Fluctuation in executive compensation of selected companies, 1928–36. *Review of Economic Statistics*, XX (1938) 65–75. **S**

---

* Reprinted in the present volume.

BECKWITH, B. P., The relationship of top salaries to profits of manufacturing companies, *Southern Economic Journal*, VI (1939) 178–184. **S**

BENHAM, F. C., The theory of wages in relation to some effects of Australian wage-regulation, *London Essays in Economics: in Honour of Edwin Cannan*, (edited by T. E. Gregory and H. Dalton), London, George Routledge & Sons, Ltd., 1927, 213–247. **S**

*BLOOM, G. F., A reconsideration of the theory of exploitation, *Quarterly Journal of Economics*, LV (1940–1941) 413–442. **A**

———, Wage policies and wage trends in the war boom, *American Economic Review*, XXXIII (1943) 892–897. **A**

BOWDEN, W., Surplus labor and social wage in Great Britain, *American Economic Review*, XXVII (1937) 31–44. **A**

BROWN, H. G., The incidence of compulsory insurance of workmen, *Journal of Political Economy*, XXX (1922) 67–77. **A**

BROWN, W. M., Some effects of a minimum wage upon the economy as a whole, *American Economic Review*, XXX (1940) 98–107. **A**

———, Some effects of a minimum wage upon the economy as a whole—Reply to Messrs. Mikesell, Hagen, and Sufrin, *American Economic Review*, XXX (1940) 578–579. **A**

CAMPBELL, R. M., Family allowances in New Zealand, *Economic Journal*, XXXVII (1927) 369–383. **A**

CARVER, T. N., The theory of the shortened working week, *American Economic Review*, XXVI (1936) 451–462. **A**

COON, S. J., Collective bargaining and productivity, *American Economic Review*, XIX (1929) 419–427. **A**

DAVENPORT, H. J., Non-competing groups, *Quarterly Journal of Economics*, XL (1925–1926) 52–81. **A**

DOUGLAS, P. H., Family allowances and clearing funds in France, *Quarterly Journal of Economics*, XXXVIII (1923–1924) 250–293. **S**

———, Wage theory and wage policy, *International Labour Review*, XXXIX (1939) 319–359. **A**

DUNLOP, J. T., Cyclical variations in wage structure, *Review of Economic Statistics*, XXI (1939) 30–39. **S**

*———, Wage policies of trade unions, *American Economic Review*, Supplement, (1942) 290–301. **A**

FALKNER, R. P. and E. D. LUCAS, JR., Salaries of corporation executives, *Conference Board Bulletin*, XII (1938) 105–107. **S**

FEIS, H., International labour legislation in the light of economic theory, *International Labour Review*, XV (1927) 491–518. **A**

FILENE, E. A., The minimum wage and efficiency, *American Economic Review*, XIII (1923) 411–415. **A**

FISHER, A. G. B., Education and relative wage rates, *International Labour Review*, XXV (1932) 742–764. **A**

FISHER, W. E., Union wage and hour policies and employment, *American Economic Review*, XXX (1940) 290–299. **S**

FLORENCE, P. S., A statistical contribution to the theory of women's wages, *Economic Journal*, XLI (1931) 19–37. **S**

---

* Reprinted in the present volume.

FRAIN, H. LA RUE, Wage levels between firms, *American Economic Review*, XXI (1931) 620–635. S

GARRETT, S. S., Wages and the collective wage bargain, *American Economic Review*, XVIII (1928) 670–683. A

GRIER, L., The meaning of wages, *Economic Journal*, XXXV (1925) 519–535. A

HAGEN, E. E., Elasticity of demand and a minimum wage, *American Economic Review*, XXX (1940) 574–576. A

HEIMANN, E., The family wage controversy in Germany, *Economic Journal*, XXXIII (1923) 509–515. A

HOHMAN, E. P., Wages, risk, and profits in the whaling industry, *Quarterly Journal of Economics*, XL (1925–1926) 644–671. A

JOHNSON, A., Real wages and the control of industry, *American Economic Review*, Supplement, XVI (1926) 54–58. A

JOY, A., Washington's minimum wage law and its operation, *Journal of Political Economy*, XXXIV (1926) 691–716. S

KIDNER, F. L., The variation in wage ratios: comment, *Quarterly Journal of Economics*, LV (1940–1941) 314–318. A

KLOSS, H., Sozialpolitik, Lohnergänzung, Gewinnbeteiligung, *Archiv für Sozialwissenschaft und Sozialpolitik*, LXI (1929) Heft 3, 626–637. A

LEDERER, E., Labor, *Encyclopaedia of the Social Sciences*, (editors, E. R. A. Seligman and A. Johnson), VIII, New York, The Macmillan Co., 1932, 615–620. A

LUFFT, H., Die gleitende Produktivitätslohnskala, *Zeitschrift für die gesamte Staatswissenschaft*, LXXXIV (1928) Heft 3, 596–603. S

MACGREGOR, D. H., Family allowances, *Economic Journal*, XXXVI (1926) 1–10. A

MACMILLAN, J. W., Minimum wage legislation in Canada and its economic effects, *International Labour Review*, IX (1924) 507–537. S

MACLAURIN, W. R. and C. A. MYERS, Wages and the movement of factory labor, *Quarterly Journal of Economics*, LVII (1942–1943) 241–264. S

——, Wages and profits in the paper industry, 1929–1939, *Quarterly Journal of Economics*, LVIII (1943–1944) 196–228. S

MAURETTE, F., Is unemployment insurance a cause of permanent unemployment? *International Labour Review*, XXIV (1931) 663–684. A

MERIAM, R. S., Unemployment reserves: some questions of principle, *Quarterly Journal of Economics*, XLVII (1932–1933) 312–336. A

MIKESELL, R. F., A note on the effects of minimum wages on the propensity to consume, *American Economic Review*, XXX (1940) 574. A

MUHS, K., Zur gleitenden Lohnskala, *Zeitschrift für die gesamte Staatswissenschaft*, LXXVIII (1924) Heft 1, 151–176. A

OGBURN, W. F., The standard-of-living factor in wages, *American Economic Review*, Supplement, XIII (1923) 118–128. A

ORTON, W., Wages and the collective wage bargain, *American Economic Review*, XIX (1929) 251–254. A. Comment by S. S. Garrett, 254–256.

ROBERTS, D. R., A limitation upon the differential wage doctrine, *Quarterly Journal of Economics*, LVII (1942–1943) 314–322. S

ROBERTSON, D. H., "Fair wages" and "net advantages," *Economic Journal*, XXXIX (1929) 643–645. A

ROSEWATER, V., Theory of the shortened working week: comment, *American Economic Review*, XXVI (1936) 714–715. **A.** Reply by T. N. Carver, 715.

SARKAR, B. K., The theory of wages in the light of social insurance and public finance, *Indian Journal of Economics*, XVII (1936–1937) 1–22. **A**

SHISTER, J., The theory of union wage rigidity, *Quarterly Journal of Economics*, LVII (1942–1943) 522–542. **A**

———, A note on cyclical wage rigidity, *American Economic Review*, XXXIV (1944) 111–116. **S**

SLICHTER, S. H., Notes on collective bargaining, *Explorations in Economics*, New York and London, McGraw-Hill Book Co., 1936, 280–291. **A**

STAEHLE, H., Ability, wages, and income, *Review of Economic Statistics*, XXV (1943) 77–87. **S**

SUFRIN, S. C., Monopolies and labor regulations, *American Economic Review*, XXIX (1939) 551–552. **A**

———, The effect of minimum wages, *American Economic Review*, XXX (1940) 576–578. **A**

SUTCLIFFE, J. T., Wages and production, *Economic Record*, I (1925) 63–72. **A**

THORNDIKE, E. L., The variation in wage-ratios, *Quarterly Journal of Economics*, LIV (1939–1940) 369–383. **S**

VLASTO, O., Family allowances and the skilled worker, *Economic Journal*, XXXVI (1926) 577–585. **A**

WALSH, J. R., Capital concept applied to man, *Quarterly Journal of Economics*, XLIX (1934–1935) 255–285. **S**

WILSON, E. C., Unemployment insurance and the stability of wages in Great Britain, *International Labour Review*, XXX (1934) 767–796. **S**

WOLFE, F. E., A survey of profit-sharing and bonuses in Chicago printing plants, *Journal of Political Economy*, XXIX (1921) 521–542. **S**

WOLMAN, L., Wages and hours under the codes of fair competition, National Bureau of Economic Research, *Bulletin* 54 (March 15, 1935) 1–8. **S**

———, Wage rates, *American Economic Review*, Supplement, XXVIII (1938) 126–131. **A**

YODER, D., The structure of the demand for labor, *American Economic Review*, Supplement, (1942) 261–274. **A**

IV-C. GENERAL WAGE CHANGES AND EMPLOYMENT

Includes articles concerned with cyclical real and money wage behavior, price-cost relations, and the relation between changes in money wages and employment. Relevant statistical studies of real and money wages are included.

ANDERSON, M. D., Dynamic theory of wages, *Southern Economic Journal*, VI (1939–1940) 43–55. **S**

BANGS, R. B., Wage reductions and employment, *Journal of Political Economy*, L (1942) 251–271. **A**

BELLERBY, J. R. and K. S. ISLES, Wages policy and the gold standard in Great Britain, *International Labour Review*, XXII (1930) 137–154. **A**

BERGSON, A., Prices, wages, and income theory, *Econometrica*, X (1942) 275–289. **A**

BERNSTEIN, E. M., Wage-rates, investment, and employment, *Journal of Political Economy*, XLVII (1939) 218–231. A

BISSELL, R. M., Price and wage policies and the theory of employment, *Econometrica*, VIII (1940) 199–239. A

BORTKIEWICZ, L. v., Zum Problem der Lohnbemessung, *Schmollers Jahrbuch*, LIV (1920) Heft 4, 53–72. A

BOWDEN, W., E. LONIGAN, and M. G. MURRAY, Summaries of papers on wages and hours in relation to innovations and capital formation, *American Economic Review*, Supplement, XXIX (1939) 237–242. A

BRATT, E. C. and C. H. DANHOF, Components of wartime wage changes, *Survey of Current Business*, XXIV (September 1944) 17–20. S

BRAUN, M. S., Lohnhöhe, Rationalisierung und Arbeitslosigkeit, *Zeitschrift für National-ökonomie*, III (1931–1932) Heft 2, 266–271. A

DAUGHERTY, C. R., P. M. SWEEZY, and L. TARSHIS, Summaries of papers and discussion on wage policies, *American Economic Review*, Supplement, XXVIII (1938) 155–158. A

DUNLOP, J. T., The movement of real and money wage rates, *Economic Journal*, XLVIII (1938) 413–434. S

———, Real and money wage rates—a reply, *Quarterly Journal of Economics*, LV (1940–1941) 683–691. S. Further comment by L. Tarshis, 691–697. Rejoinder by R. F. Ruggles, 697–700.

GIRETTI, E., Crisi Economica, Protezionismo ed Alti Salari, *Riforma Sociale*, XLII (1931) 138–145. A

KALDOR, N., Wage subsidies as a remedy for unemployment, *Journal of Political Economy*, XLIV (1936) 721–742. A

———, Prof. Pigou on money wages in relation to unemployment, *Economic Journal*, XLVII (1937) 745–753. A

———, Money wage cuts in relation to unemployment: a reply to Mr. Somers, *Review of Economic Studies*, VI (1938–1939) 232–235. A

KALECKI, M., The lesson of the Blum experiment, *Economic Journal*, XLVIII (1938) 26–41. S

KEIM, W. G., Prices and wages, *Journal of the American Statistical Association*, XXXVII (1942) 377–382. S

KEYNES, J. M., Prof. Pigou on money wages in relation to unemployment, *Economic Journal*, XLVII (1937) 743–745. A

———, Relative movements of real wages and output, *Economic Journal*, XLIX (1939) 34–51. S

LEDERER, E., Industrial fluctuations and wage policy: some unsettled points, *International Labour Review*, XXIX (1939) 1–33. A

LERNER, A. P., Ex-ante analysis and wage theory, *Economica*, VI, new series (1939) 436–449. A

*———, The relation of wage policies and price policies, *American Economic Review*, Supplement, XXIX (1939) 158–169. A

LONG, C. D., The concept of unemployment, *Quarterly Journal of Economics*, LVII (1942–1943) 1–30. S

* Reprinted in the present volume.

MARJOLIN, R., Reflections on the Blum experiment, *Economica*, V, new series (1938) 177–191. **S**

MARTIN, P. W., The technique of balance: its place in American prosperity, *International Labour Review*, XX (1929) 494–511. **S**

MITNITZKY, M., Wage policy today and tomorrow, *International Labour Review*, XXXII (1935) 344–373. **A**

MOSAK, J. L., Wage increases and employment, *American Economic Review*, XXXI (1941) 330–332. **A**

OLIVER, H. M., JR., Wage reductions and employment, *Southern Economic Journal*, V (1939) 302–318. **A and H**

——, Does wage reduction aid employment by lowering prices? *Southern Economic Journal*, VI (1940) 333–343. **A**

PAGNI, C., Keynes E Gli Alti Salari, *Riforma Sociale*, XLI (1930) 351–355. **A**

PIGOU, A. C., Real and money wage rates in relation to unemployment, *Economic Journal*, XLVII (1937) 405–422. **A**

——, Money wages in relation to unemployment, *Economic Journal*, XLVIII (1938) 134–138. **A**

REYBURN, H. A., Wage and price movements, *South African Journal of Economics*, VIII (1940) 183–184. **A**

*REYNOLDS, L. G., Relations between wage rates, costs, and prices, *American Economic Review*, Supplement, (1942) 275–289. **A**

RICHARDSON, J. H., The doctrine of high wages, *International Labour Review*, XX (1929) 797–816. **A**

———, Real wage movements, *Economic Journal*, XLIX (1939) 425–441. **S**

RUGGLES, R., The relative movements of real and money wage rates, *Quarterly Journal of Economics*, LV (1940–1941) 130–149. **A**

SMITHIES, A., Wage policy in the depression, *Economic Record*, XI (1935) 249–268. **A**

——, Theory of wage fixation, *Economic Record*, XIII (1937) 201–215. **A**

SOMERS, H. M., Money wage cuts in relation to unemployment, *Review of Economic Studies*, VI (1938–1939) 161–163. **A**

——, Money wage cuts in relation to unemployment: a rejoinder to Mr. Kaldor, *Review of Economic Studies*, VII (1939–1940) 136–137. **A**. Comment by N. Kaldor, 137.

SUFRIN, S. C., Wage increases and employment, *American Economic Review*, XXXI (1941) 838. **A**

SWEEZY, A., Wages and investment, *Journal of Political Economy*, L (1942) 117–129. **A**

TAKATA, Y., Unemployment and wages: a critical review of Mr. Keynes' theory of unemployment, *Kyoto University Economic Review*, XII (1937) 1–18. **A**

*TARSHIS, L., Changes in real and money wages, *Economic Journal*, XLIX (1939) 150–154. **S**

TOBIN, J., A note on the money wage problem, *Quarterly Journal of Economics*, LV (1940–1941) 508–516. **A**

TROXEL, C. E., H. OLIVER, JR., and G. W. TAYLOR, Summaries of papers on relation of wage policies and price policies, *American Economic Review*, Supplement, XXIX (1939) 243–248. **A**

---

* Reprinted in the present volume.

Tsiang, S. C., Prof. Pigou on the relative movements of real wages and employment, *Economic Journal*, LIV (1944) 352–365. **A**

Walker, E. R., Mathematics and wages policy, *Economic Record*, XII (1936) 99–101. **A.** Rejoinder by A. Smithies, 101–102.

——, Wages policy and business cycles, *International Labour Review*, XXXVIII (1938) 758–793. **A**

Warming, J., A theory of prices and wages, *International Labour Review*, XXIV (1931) 24–54. **A**

IV-D. Real Wages and Secular Developments; Population

Includes statistical analyses of the trend of real and money wages and the share of labor in national income. A few items are included dealing with changes in population and their economic significance for the standard of living.

Åkerman, G., Den industriella arbetslönens utoeckling och återeverknengar, *Economisk Tidskrift*, XXIX (1927) 31–86. **A**

Anonymous, Zur Lohnstatistik, *Zeitschrift für die gesamte Staatswissenschaft*, LXXVI (1921) Heft 1 und 2, 360–368. **S**

Black, J. D., Agricultural wage relationships: historical changes, *Review of Economic Statistics*, XVIII (1936) 8–15. **S**

Bowley, A. L., Earnings and prices, 1904, 1914, 1937–38, *Review of Economic Studies*, VIII (1940–1941) 129–142. **S**

Cobb, C. W., Some statistical relations between wages and prices, *Journal of Political Economy*, XXXVII (1929) 728–736. **S**

Douglas, P. H. and F. Lamberson, The movement of real wages, 1890–1918, *American Economic Review*, XI (1921) 409–426. **S**

——, The movement of real wages and its economic significance, *American Economic Review*, Supplement, XVI (1926) 17–53. **S**

——, Wages, *American Journal of Sociology*, XXXIV (1928–1929) 1021–1029. **S**

Gainsbrugh, M. R., Wages and salaries in national income, *Conference Board Economic Record*, III (1941) 104. **S**

Gilboy, E. W., The cost of living and real wages in eighteenth century England, *Review of Economic Statistics*, XVIII (1936) 134–143. **S**

Hankins, F. H., Dynamics of population in the United States, *Quarterly Journal of Economics*, L (1935–1936) 164–173. **A**

Hansen, A. H., Factors affecting the trend of real wages, *American Economic Review*, XV (1925) 27–42. **A**

——, The best measure of real wages, *American Economic Review*, Supplement, XVI (1926) 5–16. **A**

King, W. I., Wage rates, wage costs, employment, wage income and the general welfare, *American Economic Review*, XXIX (1939) 34–47. **A**

Kuznets, S., Some problems in measuring per capita labor income, *Studies in Income and Wealth*, Vol. I, New York, National Bureau of Economic Research, 1937, 305–324. **A**

Lewisohn, S. A., Wage policies and national productivity, *Political Science Quarterly*, XXXIX (1924) 97–105. **A**

LIVCHEN, R., Wage trends in Germany from 1929 to 1942, *International Labour Review*, XLVIII (1943) 714–732. **S**

——, Net wages and real wages in Germany, *International Labour Review*, L (1944) 65–72. **S**

MITNITZKY, M., Lohn und Konjunktur vor dem Kriege, *Archiv für Sozialwissenschaft und Sozialpolitik*, LXVIII (1932–1933) Heft 3, 318–350. **S**

PALYI, M., Ein Jahrhundert Preise und Reallöhne, *Archiv für Sozialwissenschaft und Sozialpolitik*, LX (1928) Heft 2, 410–417. **A**

PARRISH, J. B., Changes in the nation's labor supply 1930–1937, *American Economic Review*, XXIX (1939) 325–336. **S**

PIGOU, A. C., Prices and wages from 1896–1914, *Economic Journal*, XXXIII (1923) 163–171. **A**

——, Limiting factors in wage rates, *Economic Essays and Addresses*, by A. C. Pigou and D. H. Robertson, London, P. S. King & Son, Ltd., 1931, 20–33. **A**

RICHARDSON, J. H., Some aspects of recent wage movements and tendencies in various countries, *International Labour Review*, XVII (1928) 179–203. **S**

ROBBINS, L., The optimum theory of population, *Essays in Economics: in Honour of Edwin Cannan*, (edited by T. E. Gregory and H. Dalton), London, George Routledge & Sons, Ltd., 1927, 103–134. **A**

SAYRE, R. A., Wages, hours, and employment in the United States, 1934–1939, *Conference Board Economic Record*, II (1940) 115–151. **S**

SOULE, G., D. A. McCABE, M. W. ALEXANDER, and P. F. BRESSINDEN, The movement of real wages—discussion, *American Economic Review*, Supplement, XVI (1926) 59–70. **A**

TARSHIS, L., Real wages in the United States and Great Britain, *Canadian Journal of Economics and Political Science*, IV (1938) 362–375. **A**

TRIVANOVITCH, V., Purchasing power of wages in the Soviet Union, *Conference Board Bulletin*, XII (1938) 25–28. **S**

TUCKER, R. S., Real wages of artisans in London, 1729–1935, *Journal of the American Statistical Association*, XXXI (1936) 73–84.

WEDDIGEN, W., Lohn und Leistung, *Jahrbücher für Nationalökonomie und Statistik*, CXVIII (1922) Heft 4, 303–332. **S**

WOLMAN, L., Wages, *American Journal of Sociology*, XXXIV (1928–1929) 87–91. **S**

——, American Wages, *Quarterly Journal of Economics*, XLVI (1931–1932) 398–406. **A**

——, Wages during the depression, National Bureau of Economic Research, *Bulletin* 47 (May 1, 1933) 1–5. **S**

——, The recovery in wages and employment, National Bureau of Economic Research, *Bulletin* 63 (December 21, 1936) 1–12. **S**

WOYTINSKY, W., Wages: History and statistics, *Encyclopaedia of the Social Sciences*, (editors, E. R. A. Seligman and A. Johnson), XV, New York, The Macmillan Co., 1935, 302–318. **S**

ZINGALI, G., La bilancia alimentare prebellica, bellica e postbellica di alcuni Stati di Europa, *Giornale degli Economisti*, LXV (1925) 517–532. **S**

ZWIEDINECK-SÜDENHORST, O. VON, Lohnstatistik, *Handwörterbuch der Staatswissenschaften*, Vierte Auflage, VI, Jena, Gustav Fischer, 1923, 375–396. **A**

V. INTEREST

V-A. The Concept of Capital and Its Measurement

Includes discussion of the use of the term capital, the meaning of the maintenance of capital, the mobility of capital, and the valuation of capital.

BAUER, P. T., Interest and quasi-rent, *Economic Journal*, XLIX (1939) 154–157. **A** and **H**

BÖHM-BAWERK, E. VON, Kapital, *Handwörterbuch der Staatswissenschaften*, Vierte Auflage, V, Jena, Gustav Fischer, 1923, 576–584. **A**

BROWN, H. G., Capital valuation and the "psychological school," *American Economic Review*, XIX (1929) 357–362. **A**

CANNAN, E., Early history of the term capital, *Quarterly Journal of Economics*, XXXV (1920–1921) 469–481. **H**

CAZIOT, P., Le capital foncier et les capitaux d'exploitation, *Revue d'Economie Politique*, XLIV (1930) 8–19. **A**

DAS-GUPTA, A. K., The concept of capital, *Indian Journal of Economics*, XIV (1934) 627–640. **A**

FETTER, F. A., Clark's reformulation of the capital concept, *Economic Essays Contributed in Honor of John Bates Clark*, (edited by J. H. Hollander), New York, The Macmillan Co., 1927, 136–156. **A**

——, Capital, *Encyclopaedia of the Social Sciences*, (editors, E. R. A. Seligman and A Johnson), III, New York, The Macmillan Co., 1930, 187–190. **A**

FOSSATI, E., Zum Begriff des Kapitals, *Zeitschrift für Nationalökonomie*, V (1934) Heft 5, 708–709. **A**

HATFIELD, H. R., The earliest use in English of the term capital, *Quarterly Journal of Economics*, XL (1925–1926) 547–548. **H**

——, The early use of "capital," *Quarterly Journal of Economics*, XLIX (1934–1935) 162–163. **H**

HAYEK, F. A. VON, The maintenance of capital, *Economica*, II, new series (1935) 241–276. **A**

——, Maintaining capital intact: a reply, *Economica*, VIII, new series (1941) 276–280. **A**

HEWETT, W. W., Capital value once more, *American Economic Review*, XIX (1929) 646–648. **A**

HICKS, J. R., Maintaining capital intact: a further suggestion, *Economica*, IX, new series (1942) 174–179. **A**

LACHMANN, L. M., On the measurement of capital, *Economica*, VIII, new series (1941) 361–377. **A**

MACHLUP, F., Begriffliches und Terminologisches zur Kapitalstheorie, *Zeitschrift für Nationalökonomie*, II (1930–1931) Heft 4, 632–639. **A**

——, The consumption of capital in Austria, *Review of Economic Statistics*, XVII (1935) 13–19. **S**

PIGOU, A. C., Maintaining capital intact, *Economica*, VIII, new series (1941) 271–275. **A**

RICHARDS, R. D., Early history of the term capital, *Quarterly Journal of Economics*, XL (1925–1926) 329–338. **H**

SELTZER, L. H., The mobility of capital, *Quarterly Journal of Economics*, XLVI (1931–1932) 496–508. **A**

V-B. "REAL" INTEREST THEORY

Includes articles dealing with the marginal productivity theory, the time-preference theory, and Austrian capital theory.

BIRCK, L. V., Moderne Scholastik: Eine kritische Darstellung der Böhm-Bawerkschen Theorie, *Weltwirtschaftliches Archiv*, XXIV, (1926) Heft 2, 198–227. **A**

BISSING, W M. Frhr. von, Zu Cassels Kapitaltheorie, *Jahrbücher für Nationalökonomie und Statistik*, CXXXIII (1930) Heft 1, 22–32. **A**

BLOCK, V., Zur Methode und Problemstellung der Zinstheorie, *Jahrbücher für Nationalökonomie und Statistik*, CXXXV (1931) Heft 4, 504–523. **A**

BÖHM-BAWERK, E., VON, with appendix of F. X. Weiss, Zins, *Handwörterbuch der Staatswissenschaften*, Vierte Auflage, VIII, Jena, Gustav Fischer, 1923, 1130–1157. **A**

BOULDING, K. E., The application of the pure theory of population change to the theory of capital, *Quarterly Journal of Economics*, XLVIII (1933–1934) 645–666. **A**

———, The theory of a single investment, *Quarterly Journal of Economics*, XLIX (1934–1935) 475–494. **A**

———, Professor Knight's capital theory: a note in reply, *Quarterly Journal of Economics*, L (1935–1936) 524–531. **A**

———, Time and investment, *Economica*, III, new series (1936) 196–220. **A**

———, Time and investment: a reply, *Economica*, III, new series (1936) 440–442. **A**

BROCK, F., Kapital, Kapitalzins und Investitionsspanne: Einige Betrachtungen zur neueren Diskussion über Böhm-Bawerks Kapitalbegriff, *Weltwirtschaftliches Archiv*, LVII (1938) Heft 3, 472–496. **A**

CARELL, E., Kann der Zins ein Preis für "Warten" sein? *Zeitschrift für Nationalökonomie*, III (1931–1932) Heft 5, 756–764. **A**

CARVER, T. N., Automatic saving and the rate of accumulation, *Quarterly Journal of Economics*, XXXVIII (1923–1924) 347–351. **A**

CASSEL, G., The rate of interest, the bank rate, and the stabilization of prices, *Quarterly Journal of Economics*, XLII (1927–1928) 511–529. **A**

CLOWER, F. W., Note on the supply curve for capital, *American Economic Review*, XVIII (1928) 272–274. **A**

EDELBERG, V., Elements of capital theory: a note, *Economica*, III, new series (1936) 314–322. **A**

EUCKEN, W., Vom Hauptproblem der Kapitaltheorie, *Jahrbücher für Nationalökonomie und Statistik*, CXLV (1937) Heft 5, 533–564. **A**

FELLNER, W., and H. S. ELLIS, Hicks and the time-period controversy, *Journal of Political Economy*, XLVIII (1940) 563–578. **A**

FISHER, A. G. B., Capital and the growth of knowledge, *Economic Journal*, XLIII (1933) 379–389. **A**

FLEMING, J. M., The period of production and derived concepts, *Review of Economic Studies*, III (1935–1936) 1–17. **A**

FUBINI, R., Nuove note sulla teoria dell'interesse, *Giornale degli Economisti*, LXX (1930) 146–159. **A**

GADOLIN, C. A. J. VON, Bemerkungen zur Diskussion über die Zeitkonzeption des Kapitals, *Zeitschrift für Nationalökonomie*, VIII (1937) Heft 1, 61–77. A

GIFFORD, C. H. P., The concept of the length of the period of production, *Economic Journal*, XLIII (1933) 611–618. A

——, The period of production under continuous input and point output in an unprogressive community, *Econometrica*, III (1935) 199–212. A

GOCHT, R., Der zeitliche Aufbau der Produktion und das "Gesetz von der Mehrergiebigkeit zeitraubender Produktionsumwege," *Jahrbücher für Nationalökonomie und Statistik*, CXLIX (1939) Heft 4, 385–406. A

HAGEN, E. E., Capital theory in a system with no agents fixed in quantity, *Journal of Political Economy*, L (1942) 837–859. A

HALM, G., "Warten" und "Kapitaldisposition," *Jahrbücher für Nationalökonomie und Statistik*, CXXXV (1931) Heft 6, 831–845. A

HAWTREY, R. G., Professor Hayek's Pure Theory of Capital, *Economic Journal*, LI (1941) 281–290. A

HAYEK, F. A. VON, Zur Problemstellung der Zinstheorie, *Archiv für Sozialwissenschaft und Sozialpolitik*, LXVIII (1927) Heft 3, 517–532. A

——, On the relationship between investment and output, *Economic Journal*, XLIV (1934) 207–231. A

*——, The mythology of capital, *Quarterly Journal of Economics*, L (1935–1936) 199–228. A

——, Utility analysis and interest, *Economic Journal*, XLVI (1936) 44–60. A

——, Einleitung zu einer Kapitaltheorie, *Zeitschrift für Nationalökonomie*, VIII (1937) Heft 1, 1–9. A

HILL, M., The period of production and industrial fluctuations, *Economic Journal*, XLIII (1933) 599–610. A

HOLDEN, G. R., Mr. Keynes' consumption function and the time-preference postulate, *Quarterly Journal of Economics*, LII (1937–1938) 281–296. A

INGRAHAM, O., Interest rate and diminishing utility, *American Economic Review*, XX (1930) 480–481. A

IVERSON, C., Die Probleme des festen Realkapitals, *Zeitschrift für Nationalökonomie*, VII (1936) Heft 2, 145–160. A

JOSEPH, P. and K. BODE, Bemerkungen zur Kapital- und Zinstheorie, *Zeitschrift für Nationalökonomie*, VI (1935) Heft 2, 170–195. A

KALDOR, N., Annual survey of economic theory: the recent controversy on the theory of capital, *Econometrica*, V (1937) 201–233. A

——, On the theory of capital: a rejoinder to Professor Knight, *Econometrica*, VI (1938) 163–176. A

KEYNES, J. M., Mr. Keynes' consumption function: reply, *Quarterly Journal of Economics*, LII (1937–1938) 708–709. A. Rejoinder by G. R. Holden, 709–712.

——, Mr. Keynes' consumption function, *Quarterly Journal of Economics*, LIII (1938–1939) 160. A

KLEENE, G. A., Productive apparatus and the capitalist, *Journal of Political Economy*, XXXI (1923) 1–20. A

KNIGHT, F. H., Professor Fisher's interest theory: a case in point, *Journal of Political Economy*, XXXIX (1931) 176–212. A

---

* Reprinted in the present volume.

————, Interest, *Encyclopaedia of the Social Sciences*, (editors, E. R. A. Seligman and A. Johnson), VIII. New York, The Macmillan Co., 1932, 131–143. **A**

————, Capitalistic production, time and the rate of return, *Economic Essays in Honour of Gustav Cassel*, London, Allen & Unwin, Ltd., 1933, 327–342. **A**

————, Capital, time, and the interest rate, *Economica*, I, new series (1934) 257–286. **A**

————, Professor Hayek and the theory of investment, *Economic Journal*, XLV (1935) 77–94. **A**

————, The theory of investment once more: Mr. Boulding and the Austrians, *Quarterly Journal of Economics*, L (1935–1936) 36–67. **A**

————, The quantity of capital and the rate of interest, I, *Journal of Political Economy*, XLIV (1936) 433–463. **A**

————, The quantity of capital and the rate of interest, II, *Journal of Political Economy*, XLIV (1936) 612–642. **A**

————, Note on Dr. Lange's interest theory, *Review of Economic Studies*, IV (1936–1937) 223–230. **A**

————, On the theory of capital: in reply to Mr. Kaldor, *Econometrica*, VI (1983) 63–82. **A**

————, Diminishing returns from investment, *Journal of Political Economy*, LII (1944) 26–47. **A**

*————, Capital and interest, *Encyclopaedia Brittanica*, IV (1946) 779–801. **A**

Kokkalis, A., Kapitalbildung und Kapitalgütervermehrung, *Jahrbücher für National-ökonomie und Statistik*, CXLVIII (1938) Heft 2, 129–154. **A**

Lange, O. The place of interest in the theory of production, *Review of Economic Studies*, III (1935–1936) 159–192. **A**

————, Professor Knight's note on interest theory, *Review of Economic Studies*, IV (1936–1937) 231–235. **A**

Leontief, W., Interest on capital and distribution: a problem in the theory of marginal productivity, *Quarterly Journal of Economics*, XLIX (1934–1935) 147–161. **A**

Lindberg, J. K., Die Kapitalzinstheorie Böhm-Bawerks, *Zeitschrift für Nationalökonomie*, IV (1932–1933) Heft 4, 501–514. **A**

Lutz, F. A., Professor Hayek's theory of interest, *Economica*, X, new series (1943) 302–310. **A**. Comment by F. A. von Hayek, 311.

Machlup, F., Professor Knight and the "period of production," *Journal of Political Economy*, XLIII (1935) 577–624. **A**. Comment by F. H. Knight, 625–627.

————, The "period of production": a further word, *Journal of Political Economy*, XLIII (1935) 808. **A**. A final word by F. H. Knight, 808.

Mackenroth, G., Period of production, durability, and the rate of interest in economic equilibrium, *Journal of Political Economy*, XXXVIII (1930) 629–659. **A**

Mahr, A. von, Zur Kritik der Zinstheorie, *Zeitschrift für Nationalökonomie*, IV (1932–1933) Heft 2, 243–253. **A**

————, Das Zeitmoment in der Theorie des Produktivzinses, *Zeitschrift für National-ökonomie*, VII (1936) Heft 1, 57–73. **A**

Mainz, K., Kann der Zins ein Preis für "Warten" sein? *Zeitschrift für Nationalökonomie*, IV (1932–1933) Heft 5, 651–658. **A**

Marschak, J., A note on the period of production, *Economic Journal*, XLIV (1934) 146–151. **A**

* Reprinted in the present volume.

698 CLASSIFIED BIBLIOGRAPHY OF ARTICLES

MEHTA, J. K., The negative rate of interest, *Indian Journal of Economics*, XXI (1941) 301–306. A

MERIAM, R. S., Some propositions on interest, *Economics, Sociology, and the Modern World*, Essays in Honor of T. N. Carver, Cambridge, Harvard University Press, 1935, 157–170. A

MONROE, A. E., Investment and saving: a genetic analysis, *Quarterly Journal of Economics*, XLIII (1928–1929) 567–603.

MORGENSTERN, O., Zur Theorie der Produktionsperiode, *Zeitschrift für Nationalökonomie*, VI (1935) Heft 2, 196–208. A

NANAVATI, M. H., Equity in distribution and interest of capital, *Indian Journal of Economics*, XIX (1939) 509–513. A

NEUBAUER, J., Kapital und Zeitverlauf, *Jahrbücher für Nationalökonomie und Statistik*, CXLVI (1937) Heft 3, 257–284. A

NURKSE, R., The schematic representation of the structure of production, *Review o, Economic Studies*, II (1934–1935) 232–244. A

PETER, H., Studien zur Kapitalzins- oder Profittheorie und ihrer Methode, *Jahrbücher für Nationalökonomie und Statistik*, CXLII (1935) Heft 6, 641–669. A

SAMUELSON, P. A., Some aspects of the pure theory of capital, *Quarterly Journal of Economics*, LI (1936–1937) 469–496. A

———, The rate of interest under ideal conditions, *Quarterly Journal of Economics*, LIII (1938–1939) 286–297. A

SCHÄFER, T., Kapitalbildung und Zinshöhe, *Archiv für Sozialwissenschaft und Sozialpolitik*, LXV (1931) Hett 2, 297–308. A

SCHNEIDER, E., Das Zeitmoment in der Theorie der Produktion, *Jahrbücher für Nationalökonomie und Statistik*, CXLII (1935) Heft 3, 271–281. A

———, Das Zeitmoment in der Theorie der Produktion, *Jahrbücher für Nationalökonomie und Statistik*, CXLIII (1936) Heft 1, 45–67. A

———, Das Zeitmoment in der Theorie der Produktion, *Jahrbücher für Nationalökonomie und Statistik*, CXLIV, (1936) Heft 2, 129–151. A

———, Bemerkungen zum Hauptproblem der Kapitaltheorie, *Jahrbücher für Nationalökonomie und Statistik*, CXLVII (1938) Heft 2, 183–188. A

———, "Kapital" und "Warten," *Jahrbücher für Nationalökonomie und Statistik*, CXL (1934) Heft 2, 129–165. A

SHIBATA, K., Capital and the subsistence fund, *Kyoto University Economic Review*, XIII (1938) 55–74. A

SMITH, J. G., The measurement of time valuation, *American Economic Review*, XVIII (1928) 227–247. S

SMITHIES, A., The Austrian theory of capital in relation to partial equilibrium theory, *Quarterly Journal of Economics*, L, (1935–1936) 117–150. A

———, Professor Hayek on the pure theory of capital, *American Economic Review*, XXXI (1941) 767–779. A

STEINDL, J., Der historische Regress in der Theorie der Produktionsumwege, *Jahrbücher für Nationalökonomie und Statistik*, CXLV (1937) Heft 2, 143–157. A

STEPHANS, K. H., Zur Problematik der Zinstheorie, *Zeitschrift für Nationalökonomie*, VII (1936) Heft 3, 326–359. A

STRIGL, R. VON, Der Kapitalzins als Residual-Rente, *Archiv für Sozialwissenschaft und Sozialpolitik*, LVII (1920–21) 833–865. A

——, Zeit und Produktion, *Zeitschrift für Nationalökonomie*, VI (1935) Heft 2, 209–229. **A**

TAKATA, Y., Determination of the rate of interest, *Kyoto University Economic Review*, XII (1937) 1–20. **A**

THEISS, E., Time and capitalistic production, *Journal of Political Economy*, XL (1932) 513–531. **A**

VAN DORP, E. C., Löhne und Kapitalzins, *Zeitschrift für Nationalökonomie*, IV (1932–1933) Heft 2, 254–266. **A**

VAN GENECHTEN, R., Über das Verhältnis zwischen der Produktivität des Kapitals und den Löhnen und Zinsen, *Zeitschrift für Nationalökonomie*, II (1930–1931) Heft 2, 200–220. **A**

——, Kritische Anmerkungen zur Zinstheorie, *Zeitschrift für Nationalökonomie*, III (1931–1932) Heft 3, 410–426. **A**

——, Zur Lohn- und Zinstheorie, *Zeitschrift für Nationalökonomie*, V (1934) Heft 2, 227–240. **A**

VARGA, G., Zwei ungarische Kapitaltheorien, *Schmollers Jahrbuch*, LIX (1925) Heft 4, 83–110. **A**

WEISS, F. X., Abstinenz Theorie, *Handwörterbuch der Staatswissenschaften*, Vierte Auflage, I, Jena, Gustav Fischer, 1923, 20–22. **A**

WICKSELL, K., Realkapital och Kapitalränta, *Ekonomisk Tidskrift*, XXV (1923) 145–180. **A**

WIDEN, L. G., Åkermans Kapital- och Kapitalränteteori, *Economisk Tidskrift*, XXXIX (1937) 63–76. **A**

WOLFE, A. B., Savers' surplus and the interest rate, *Quarterly Journal of Economics*, XXXV (1920–1921) 1–35. **A**

——, Three-dimensional diagrams in illustration of consumers' demand and of interest rates and savers' surpluses, *American Economic Review*, XV (1925) 228–238. **A**

WRIGHT, C. A., A note on "time and investment," *Economica*, III, new series (1936) 436–440. **A**

WRIGHT, D. McC., Professor Knight on limits to the use of capital, *Quarterly Journal of Economics*, LVIII (1943–1944) 331–358. **A**

V-C. MONETARY INTEREST THEORY

Includes articles dealing with the liquidity-preference theory and the loanable-funds theory and related material.

ADARKAR, B. P., and D. GHOSH, Mr. Keynes' theory of interest, *Indian Journal of Economics*, XXI (1941) 285–300. **A**

ALEXANDER, S. S., Mr. Keynes and Mr. Marx, *Review of Economic Studies*, VII (1939–1940) 123–135. **A**

BODIN, C., Contribution aux theories du capital et du revenu, *Revue d'Economie Politique*, XXXVI (1922) 157–180 and 465–480. **A**

BÓER, A., Kapitaltheorie und Kapitalbildung, *Jahrbücher für Nationalökonomie und Statistik*, CXLVII (1938) Heft 1, 28–54. **A**

BROWN, A. J., The liquidity-preference schedules of the London clearing banks, *Oxford Economic Papers*, No. 1 (1938) 49–82. **S**

————, Interest, prices and the demand schedule for idle money, *Oxford Economic Papers*, No. 2 (1939) 46–69. **S**

CANNAN, E., P. ADARKAR, B. K. SANDWELL, and J. M. KEYNES, Saving and usury: a symposium, I. Saving on and saving up: the ambiguity of "saving"; II. Mr. Keynes and the Canonists (i); II. Mr. Keynes and the Canonists (ii); IV. Saving and usury, *Economic Journal*, XLII (1932) 123–137. **A** and **H**

DATTA, B., Interest and the complex of preferences, *Indian Journal of Economics*, XIX (1939) 491–499. **A**

DAVENPORT, H. J., Interest theory and theories, *American Economic Review*, XVII (1927) 636–656. **A**

DAVIES, G. R., Factors determining the interest rate, *Quarterly Journal of Economics*, XXXIV (1919–1920) 445–461. **A**

DENNIS, L. and H. SOMERVILLE, Usury and the Canonists: continued; I. Usury; II. Usury and standstill, *Economic Journal*, XLII (1932) 312–323. **A** and **H**

D'SOUZA, V. L., Theory of interest reconsidered, *Indian Journal of Economics*, XIX (1939) 473–481. **A**

ELLSWORTH, P. T., Mr. Keynes on the rate of interest and the marginal efficiency of capital, *Journal of Political Economy*, XLIV (1936) 767–790. **A**

FAN-HUNG, Keynes and Marx on the theory of capital accumulation, money, and interest, *Review of Economic Studies*, VII (1939–1940) 28–41. **A**

FELLNER, W. and H. M. SOMERS, Alternative monetary approaches to interest theory, *Review of Economic Statistics*, XXIII (1941) 43–48. **A**

FETTER, F. A., Interest theory and price movements, *American Economic Review*, Supplement, XVII (1927) 62–105. **A**

FISHER, I., W. C. MITCHELL, M. PALYI, W. F. MITCHELL, F. H. KNIGHT and K. G. KARSTEN, Interest theory and price movements—discussion, *American Economic Review*, Supplement, XVII (1927) 106–122. **A**

FLEMING, J. M., The determination of the rate of interest, *Economica*, V, new series (1938) 333–341. **A**

GOODWIN, R. M., Keynesian and other interest theories, *Review of Economic Statistics*, XXV (1943) 6–12. **A**

HIGGINS, B., A diagrammatic analysis of the supply of loan funds, *Econometrica*, IX (1941) 231–240. **A**

JUDD, P. R., Indifference curves and the rate of interest, *Economic Record*, XVII (1941) 232–239. **A**

KAFKA, A., Professor Hicks' theory of money interest, *American Economic Review*, XXXI (1941) 327–329. **A**

KEYNES, J. M., Alternative theories of the rate of interest, *Economic Journal*, XLVII (1937) 241–252. **A**

————, The "ex ante" theory of the rate of interest, *Economic Journal*, XLVII (1937) 663–669. **A**

*————, The theory of the rate of interest, *The Lessons of Monetary Experience; Essays in Honor of Irving Fisher*, (edited by A. D. Gayer), New York, Farrar & Rinehart Inc., 1937, 145–152. **A**

---

* Reprinted in the present volume.

KRISHNASWAMY, A., Marshall's theory of money and interest, *Indian Journal of Economics,* XXII (1941) 121–143. **A**

LACHMANN, L. M., Uncertainty and liquidity-preference, *Economica,* IV, new series (1937) 295–308. **A**

LANDAUER, C., Staat und Zins, *Archiv für Sozialwissenschaft und Sozialpolitik* LXI (1929) Heft 3, 449–464. **A**

———, A break in Keynes' theory of interest, *American Economic Review,* XXVII (1937) 260–266. **A**

LAUTENBACH, W., Zur Zinstheorie von John Maynard Keynes, *Weltwirtschaftliches Archiv.,* LV (1937) Heft 3, 493–525.

LERNER, A. P., Alternative formulations of the theory of interest, *Economic Journal,* XLVIII (1938) 211–230. **A**

———, Interest theory: supply and demand for loans or supply and demand for cash, *Review of Economic Statistics,* XXVI (1944) 88–91. **A.** Comment by W. J. Fellner and H. M. Somers, 92.

LOKANATHAN, P. S., Interest and investment, *Indian Journal of Economics,* XIX (1939) 483–490. **A**

MEHTA, J. K., Coordination of the theories of interest, *Indian Journal of Economics,* XIX (1938) 251–263. **A**

MELVILLE, L. G., The theory of interest, *Economic Record,* XIV (1938) 1–13 and 161–175. **A**

MILLIKAN, M. F., The liquidity-preference theory of interest, *American Economic Review,* XXVIII (1938) 247–260. **A**

———, P. T. ELLSWORTH, W. A. MORTON and A. W. MARGET, Summaries of papers on general interest theory, *American Economic Review,* Supplement, XXVIII (1938) 69–72. **A**

MODIGLIANI, F., Liquidity preference and the theory of interest and money, *Econometrica,* XII (1944) 45–88. **A**

OHLIN, B., D. H. ROBERTSON, and R. G. HAWTREY, Alternative theories of the rate of interest: three rejoinders, *Economic Journal,* XLVII (1937) 423–443. **A**

OU, PAO-SAN, Ex-ante saving and liquidity-preferences, *Review of Economic Studies,* XI (1943–1944) 52–56. **A**

REDDAWAY, W. B. and R. I. DOWNING, Zero rates of interest, *Economic Record,* XV (1939) 94–97. **A.** Comment by L. G. Melville, 97–98.

RILEY, R. H., A note on "a break in Keynes' theory of interest," *American Economic Review,* XXVIII (1938) 312–314. **A.** Reply by C. Landauer, 314–318, and Rejoinder by R. H. Riley, 318–319.

ROBERTSON, D. H., Mr. Keynes and "finance": a note, *Economic Journal,* XLVIII (1938) 314–318. **A**

———, Mr. Keynes and "finance," *Economic Journal,* XLVIII (1938) 555–556. **A.** Comment by J. M. Keynes, 318–322.

*———, Mr. Keynes and the rate of interest, *Essays in Monetary Theory by* D. H. Robertson, London, P. S. King & Son, Ltd., 1940, 1–38. **A**

---

* Reprinted in the present volume.

702 CLASSIFIED BIBLIOGRAPHY OF ARTICLES

Roos, C. F. and V. von Szeliski, The determination of interest rates, *Journal of Political Economy*, L (1942) 501–535. S

Shaw, E. S., False issues in the interest-theory controversy, *Journal of Political Economy*, XLVI (1938) 838–856. A

Smithies, A., The quantity of money and the rate of interest, *Review of Economic Statistics*, XXV (1943) 69–76. A

*Somers, H. M., Monetary policy and the theory of interest, *Quarterly Journal of Economics*, LV (1940–1941) 488–507. A

Somerville, H., Interest and usury in a new light, *Economic Journal*, XLI (1931) 646–649. A and H

Swan, T. W., Some notes on the interest controversy, *Economic Record*, XVII (1941) 153–165. A

Thirlby, G. F., The rate of interest, *South African Journal of Economics*, VII (1939) 1–17. A

Townshend, H., Liquidity-premium and the theory of value, *Economic Journal*, XLVII (1937) 157–169. A

Tucker, D. S., The interest rate and saving, *Journal of the American Statistical Association*, XXXVIII (1943) 101–102. A

Valk, W. L., Die dynamische Bedeutung des Böhmschen Verlustprinzips und die volkswirtschaftliche Liquiditätsfrage, *Weltwirtschaftliches Archiv*, LVI (1937) Heft 2, 466–475. A

V-D. The Rate of Interest, Investment, and Employment; Monetary Policy

Includes only a small part of the literature dealing with these topics since the literature is beyond the scope of the present compilation.

Bissell, R. M., Jr., The rate of interest, *American Economic Review*, Supplement, XXVIII (1938) 23–40. A

Canning, J. B., J. F. Ebersole, and D. Woodward, Summaries of papers and discussion on the rate of interest, *American Economic Review*, Supplement, XXVIII (1938) 73–76. A

Caplan, B., Reinvestment and the rate of interest, *American Economic Review*, XXX (1940) 561–568. A

Das-Gupta, A. K., The rate of interest, employment, and economic welfare, *Indian Journal of Economics*, XIX (1939) 503–508. A

de Scitovszky, T., Capital accumulation employment, and price rigidity, *Review of Economic Studies*, VIII (1940–1941) 69–88. A

Haberler, G., The interest rate and capital formation, *Capital Formation and Its Elements*, New York, National Industrial Conference Board, Inc., 1939, 119–133. A

Hayek, F. A. von, The Ricardo effect, *Economica*, IX, new series (1942) 127–152. A

Henderson, H. D., The significance of the rate of interest, *Oxford Economic Papers*, No. 1 (1938) 1–13. A

Kaldor, N., Professor Hayek and the concertina-effect, *Economica*, IX, new series (1942) 359–382. A. Comment by F. A. von Hayek, 383–385.

Machlup, F., Interest as cost and capitalization factor, *American Economic Review*, XXV (1935) 459–465. A

---

* Reprinted in the present volume.

MARSCHAK, J., Wicksell's two interest rates, *Social Research*, VIII (1941) 469–478. **A**

MEADE, J. E. and P. W. S. ANDREWS, Summary of replies to questions on effects of interest rates, *Oxford Economic Papers*, No. 1 (1938) 14–31. **A**

NEISSER, H., Monetary equilibrium and the natural rate of interest, *Social Research*, VIII (1941) 454–468. **A**

SCHNEIDER, E., Die wirtschaftliche Lebensdauer industrieller Anlagen, *Weltwirtschaftliches Archiv*, LV (1942) Heft 1, 90–130. **A**

SEIDEL, H., Zur Theorie der Kapitalbildung, *Jahrbücher für Nationalökonomie und Statistik*, CXLIX (1939) Heft 4, 407–443. **A**

———, Zur Theorie der Kapitalbildung, *Jahrbücher für Nationalökonomie und Statistik*, CXLIX (1939) Heft 5, 513–539. **A**

STRIGL, R. VON, Der Wicksellsche Prozess, *Weltwirtschaftliches Archiv*, LV (1942) Heft 3, 443–464. **A**

WELINDER, C., Hayek och "Ricardo Effectin," *Economisk Tidskrift*, XLII (1940) 33–39. **A**

V-E. THE STRUCTURE OF INTEREST RATES

Deals with long and short rate relationships and historical movements of interest rates.

BURGESS, W. R., Factors affecting changes in short term interest rates, *Journal of the American Statistical Association*, XXII (1927) 195–201. **S**

DANIEL, J. L., Interest rates: long-term vs. short-term, *Econometrica*, VIII (1940) 272-278. **S**

DE SCITOVSZKY, T., A study of interest and capital, *Economica*, VII, new series (1940) 293–317. **A**

HAWTREY, R. G., Interest and bank rate, *The Manchester School*, X (1939) 144–152. **S**. Reply by J. R. Hicks, 152–156. Rejoinder by R. G. Hawtrey, 155–156.

HICKS, J. R., Mr. Hawtrey on bank rate and the long-term rate of interest, *The Manchester School*, X (1939) 21–37. **S**

HUTT, W. H., The significance of state interference with interest rates, *South African Journal of Economics*, I (1933) 365–368. **A**

KALECKI, M., The short-term rate and the long-term rate, *Oxford Economic Papers*, No. 4 (1940) 15–22. **S**

LAVINGTON, F., Short and long rates of interest, *Economica*, IV (1924) 291–303. **S**

LUSHER, DAVID W., The structure of interest rates and the Keynesian theory of interest, *Journal of Political Economy*, L (1942) 272–279. **A**

*LUTZ, F. A., The structure of interest rates, *Quarterly Journal of Economics*, LV (1940–1941) 36–63. **A**

MARX, D. JR., The structure of interest rates: comment, *Quarterly Journal of Economics*, LVI (1941–1942) 152–156. **A**

MORGAN, E. V., The future of interest rates, *Economic Journal*, LIV (1944) 340–351. **A**

NIXON, S. E., J. T. BRYDEN, and W. T. G. HACKETT, Interest rates in Canada, *Canadian Journal of Economics and Political Science*, III (1937) 421–448. **S**

SPENGLER, J. J., Economic opinion and the future of the interest rate, *Southern Economic Journal*, III (1936) 7–28. **A**

---

* Reprinted in the present volume.

STAFFORD, J., The future of the rate of interest, *The Manchester School*, VIII (1937) 125–146. **A**

WESTERFIELD, R. B., (chairman), Abstracts of discussions on the future of interest rates, *American Economic Review*, Supplement, XXXII (1942) 217–226. **A**

VI. PROFIT

VI-A. THE THEORY OF PROFIT

General issues relating to profits.

ANDERSON, M. D., Fundamental principles of profit, *Southern Economic Journal*, III (1936) 161–174. **A**

BECKERDIKE, C. F., Essay III, *Essays on Foster and Catchings: "Profits,"* Newton, Massachusetts, Pollak Foundation for Economic Research, 1927, 72-88. **A**

BORNEMANN, A., Accounting profits: an institution, *Journal of Political Economy*, LI (1943) 166–168. **A**

BOULDING, K. E., The incidence of a profits tax, *American Economic Review*, XXXIV (1944) 567–572. **A**

DE SCITOVSZKY, T., A note on profit maximization and its implications, *Review of Economic Studies*, XI (1943–1944) 57–60. **A**

EDELBERG, V., The Ricardian theory of profits, *Economica*, XIII (1933) 51–74. **A** and **H**

ENGLÄNDER, O., Böhm-Bawerk und Marx, *Archiv für Sozialwissenschaft und Sozialpolitik*, LX (1928) Heft 2, 368–381. **A**

FOSTER, W. T. and W. CATCHINGS, Comments on the Essays by the Authors of *"Profits," Essays on Foster and Catchings: "Profits,"* Newton, Massachusetts, Pollak Foundation for Economic Research, 1927, 5–18. **A**

FRITZSCHING, L., Der Profit als eine nichtwirtschaftliche Kategorie, *Jahrbücher für Nationalökonomie und Statistik*, CXXXIII (1930) Heft 4, 481–526. **A**

HASAN, M. A., Enterprise and profit, *Indian Journal of Economics*, XVIII (1937) 193–197. **A**

KALECKI, M., A theory of profits, *Economic Journal*, LII (1942) 258–267. **A**

*KNIGHT, F. H., Profit, *Encyclopaedia of the Social Sciences*, (editors, E. R. A. Seligman and A. Johnson) XII, New York, The Macmillan Co., 1934, 480–486. **A**

KOTANY, L., A theory of profit and interest, *Quarterly Journal of Economics*, XXXVI (1921–1922) 413–453. **S**

LEHFELDT, R. A., Analysis of profit, *Journal of Political Economy*, XXXIII (1925) 278–292. **A**

LITTLETON, A., Contrasting theories of profit, *Accounting Review*, XI (1936) 10–18. **A**

NOVOGILOV, V. V., Essay IV, *Essays on Foster and Catchings: "Profits,"* Newton, Massachusetts, Pollak Foundation for Economic Research, 1927, 89–131. **A**

OLMSTED, F. L., Essay II, *Essays on Foster and Catchings: "Profits,"* Newton, Massachusetts, Pollak Foundation for Economic Research, 1927, 56–71. **A**

SCOTT, H. R., Where do money profits come from? *Indian Journal of Economics*, XVI (1935) 197–202. **A**

---

* Reprinted in the present volume.

SENSINI, G., I "benefici" del produttore, *Giornale degli Economisti*, LXII–LXIII (1922) 101–110. **A**

———, Intorno ai "benefici" del produttore, *Giornale degli Economisti*, LXII–LXIII (1922) 621–629. **A**

SHIBATA, K., On the general profit rate, *Kyoto University Economic Review*, XIV (1939) 40–66. **A**

SMALL, A. W., The sociology of profits, *American Journal of Sociology*, XXX (1924–1925) 439–461. **A**

SOUTER, R. W., Essay I, *Essays on Foster and Catchings: "Profits,"* Newton, Massachusetts, Pollak Foundation for Economic Research, 1927, 19–55. **A**

TUTTLE, C. A., A functional theory of economic profit, *Economic Essays Contributed in Honor of John Bates Clark*, (edited by J. H. Hollander) New York, The Macmillan Co., 1927, 321–336. **A**

WAGNER, K., Brechung der Zinsknechtschaft? *Jahrbücher für Nationalökonomie und Statistik*, CXXXIV (1931) Heft 5, 790–832. **A**

VI-B. UNCERTAINTY; ECONOMIC CHANGE

BELSHAW, H., The profit cycle in agriculture, *Economic Journal*, XXXVI (1926) 29–49. **A**

BUCHANAN, N. S., Toward a theory of fluctuations in business profits, *American Economic Review*, XXXI (1941) 731–753. **A**

CHENAULT, L. R., Buchanan's theory of fluctuations in business profits, *American Economic Review*, XXXII (1942) 840–842. **A**

CRUM, W. L., Cyclical changes in corporate profits, *Review of Economic Statistics*, XXI (1939) 49–61. **S**

*HART, A. G., Risk, uncertainty, and the unprofitability of compounding probabilities, *Studies in Mathematical Economics and Econometrics in Memory of Henry Schultz*, (edited by O. Lange, F. McIntyre, and T. O. Yntema), Chicago, University of Chicago Press, 1942, 110–118. **A**

HICKS, J. R., The theory of uncertainty and profit, *Economica*, XI (1931) 170–189. **A**

KNIGHT, F. H., Risk, *Encyclopaedia of the Social Sciences*, (editors, E. R. A. Seligman and A. Johnson) XIII, New York, The Macmillan Co., 1934, 392–394. **A**

VI-C THE ENTREPRENEUR, CORPORATE ENTERPRISE, AND DIVIDEND DISTRIBUTION

Includes articles dealing with the nexus of problems relating to the concept of the entrepreneur and the organization of contemporary economic enterprise and the distribution of the net earnings of corporate enterprises.

BARNETT, G. E., The entrepreneur and the supply of capital, *Economic Essays Contributed in Honor of John Bates Clark*, (edited by J. H. Hollander), New York, The Macmillan Co., 1927, 14–21. **A**

BECKERATH, H. VON, MacGregor's enterprise purpose and profit, *Quarterly Journal of Economics*, L (1935–1936) 367–371. **A**

BUCHANAN, N. S., Theory and practice in dividend distribution, *Quarterly Journal of Economics*, LIII (1938–1939) 64–85. **S**

---

* Reprinted in the present volume.

COLE, A. H., F. H. KNIGHT, J. M. CLARK, and G. H. EVANS, JR., Symposium on profits and the entrepreneur, *Journal of Economic History*, Supplement (1942) 118–146.

DOBB, M., Entrepreneur, *Encyclopaedia of the Social Sciences*, (editors, E. R. A. Seligman and A. Johnson), V, New York, The Macmillan Co., 1931, 558–560.   A

ENGLÄNDER, O., Unternehmergewinn, *Handwörterbuch der Staatswissenschaften*, Vierte Auflage, VIII, Jena, Gustav Fischer, 1923, 488–498.   A

FORD, J., Profit-sharing in Great Britain, *Quarterly Journal of Economics*, XXXIV (1919–1920) 777–780.   A

GORDON, R. A., Stockholdings of officers and directors in American industrial corporations, *Quarterly Journal of Economics*, L (1935–1936) 622–657.   S

*——, Enterprise, profits, and the modern corporation, *Explorations in Economics*, New York and London, McGraw-Hill Book Co., 1937, 306–316.   A

——, Ownership by management and control groups in the large corporation *Quarterly Journal of Economics*, LII (1937–1938) 367–400.   S

———, Ownership and compensation as incentives to corporation executives, *Quarterly Journal of Economics*, LIV (1939–1940) 455–473.   S

GUTHMANN, H. G., The effect of the undistributed profits tax upon the distribution of corporate earnings: a note, *Econometrica*, VIII (1940) 354–356.   S

HAWLEY, F. B., Orientation of economics on enterprise, *American Economic Review*, XVII (1927) 409–428.   A

LEWIS, B. W., The corporate entrepreneur, *Quarterly Journal of Economics*, LI (1936–1937) 535–544.   A

McINTYRE, F., The effect of the undistributed profits tax upon the distribution of corporate earnings—a statistical appraisal, *Econometrica*, VII (1939) 336–348.   S

——, The effect of the undistributed profits tax: a reply, *Econometrica*, VIII (1940) 357–360.   S

MOLL, B., Unternehmergewinn und Arbeitslohn, *Zeitschrift für die gesamte Staatswissenschaft*, LXXXI (1928) Heft 2, 280–314.   A

OTTE, G., Bemerkungen zum Unternehmerbegriff, *Zeitschrift für Nationalökonomie*, I (1929–30) Heft 4, 610–613.   A

QUANTE, P., Unternehmergewinn und Kapitalprofit als einheitliches Einkommen, *Jahrbücher für Nationalökonomie und Statistik*, CXLI (1935) Heft 2, 129–158.   A

SCHUMPETER, J., Unternehmer, *Handwörterbuch der Staatswissenschaften*, Vierte Auflage, VIII, Jena, Gustav Fischer, 1923, 476–487.   A

SETH, H. C., Interest, wages, and profit-sharing, *Indian Journal of Economics*, XIX (1939) 501–502.   A

SMITH, J. G., Economic significance of the undistributed profits tax, *American Economic Review*, XXVIII (1938) 305–310.   A

STAUSS, J. H., The entrepreneur: the firm, *Journal of Political Economy*, LII (1944) 112–127.   A

STRELLER, R., Zur Lehre vom Unternehmergewinn, *Schmollers Jahrbuch*, LX (1926) Heft 2, 1–21.   A

TAUSSIG, F. W. and W. S. BARKER, American corporations and their executives: a statistical inquiry, *Quarterly Journal of Economics*, XL (1925–1926) 1–51.   S

---

* Reprinted in the present volume.

TUTTLE, C. A., The entrepreneur in economic literature, *Journal of Political Economy*, XXXV (1927) 501–521. **A**

TUTTLE, C. W., Function of the entrepreneur, *American Economic Review*, XVII (1927) 13–25. **A**

VAN ARSDELL, P. M., Note on economic significance of the undistributed profits tax, *American Economic Review*, XXVIII (1938) 737–740. **A.** Reply by J. G. Smith, 740–741.

WOLFE, A. B., "Competitive" costs and the rent of business ability, *Quarterly Journal of Economics*, XXXIX (1924–1925) 39–69. **A**

VI-D. IMPEDIMENTS TO ENTRY

BAIN, J. S., The profit rate as a measure of monopoly power, *Quarterly Journal of Economics*, LV (1940–1941) 271–293. **A**

FOREMAN, C. J., Economies and profits of good-will, *American Economic Review*, XIII (1923) 209–224. **A**

——, Computation of good-will profits, *American Economic Review*, XV (1925) 652–664. **A**

HAWTREY, R. G., Competition from newcomers, *Economica*, X, new series (1943) 219–222. **A**

MACHLUP, F., Competition, pliopoly and profit, I, *Economica*, IX, new series (1942) 1–23. **A**

——, Competition, pliopoly and profit, II, *Economica*, IX, new series (1942) 153–173. **A**

VI-E. THE TREND OF PROFITS; PROFIT RATES

Articles included here deal primarily with the statistical measurement of profits and the rate of return.

BILLING, G. C., Manufacturing profit in New Zealand, *Economic Record*, XI (1935) 35–44. **S**

CRUM, W. L., Large-scale enterprise in the light of income tax returns, *Quarterly Journal of Economics*, XLVII (1932–1933) 414–448. **S**

——, The course of corporation profits, *Review of Economic Statistics*, XVI (1934) 61–64. **S**

*——, Corporate earnings on invested capital, *Harvard Business Review*, XVI (1938) 336–350. **S**

DUNLOP, W. R., Retail profits, *Economic Journal*, XXXIX (1929) 357–370. **S**

EPSTEIN, E. I., Profits of selected American industrial corporations, 1900–1914, *Review of Economic Statistics*, XXI (1939) 122–128. **S**

EPSTEIN, R. C., Industrial profits in 1917, *Quarterly Journal of Economics*, XXXIX (1924–1925) 241–266. **S**

——, Statistical light on profits, as analyzed in recent literature, *Quarterly Journal of Economics*, XLIV (1929–1930) 320–344. **S**

——, Profits and size of firm in the automobile industry, *American Economic Review*, XXI (1931) 636–647. **S**

---

* Reprinted in the present volume.

————, Industrial profits in prosperity and depression 1919–1932, National Bureau of Economic Research, *Bulletin* 44 (January 27, 1933) 1–4. **S**

FABRICANT, S., Recent corporate profits in the United States, National Bureau of Economic Research, *Bulletin* 50 (April 18, 1934) 1–11. **S**

————, Corporate earnings, 1929–1931: subgroups in non-manufacturing industries, *Journal of the American Statistical Association*, XXX (1935) 662–670. **S**

————, Profits, losses, and business assets, 1929–1934, National Bureau of Economic Research, *Bulletin* 55 (April 11, 1935), 1–11. **S**

GAINSBRUGH, M. R. and R. HOFFMAN, Invested capital and earnings in manufacturing, 1925–1940, *Conference Board Economic Record*, III, (1941) 209–213. **S**

————, Capital invested and rate of return in manufacturing, 1925–1941, *Conference Board Economic Record*, IV (1942) 262–266. **S**

————, Long-term trends in corporate earnings on sales, *Conference Board Economic Record*, IV (1942) 373–396. **S**

————, Ratios of corporate earnings to sales, 1936–1941, *Conference Board Economic Record*, IV (1942) 328–340. **S**

HOSKINS, G. O., A quarterly profits index, *Economic Journal*, XLIX (1939) 553–558. **S**

KLEENE, G. A., Rate of return to capital, *American Economic Review*, XXV (1935) 59–72. **A**

KREPS, T. J., Profits and prices in prosperity and depression: Paton, Epstein, Mills, *Quarterly Journal of Economics*, LI (1936–1937) 681–698. **A**

McDOUGALL, J. L., The earning power of Canadian corporate capital, 1934–40, *Canadian Journal of Economics and Political Science*, VIII (1942) 557–565. **S**

McNAIR, M. P., Margins, expenses and profits in retail trade in the United States as studied by the Harvard University Bureau of Business Research, *Economic Journal*, XL (1930) 599–632. **S**

NATIONAL INDUSTRIAL CONFERENCE BOARD, Corporations without net income, *Conference Board Bulletin*, No. 14, (February 15, 1928) 109–115. **S**

————, Profit and loss statements for manufacturing corporations, *Conference Board Bulletin*, No. 24, (December 15, 1928) 189–192. **S**

————, Corporations and their income, *Conference Board Bulletin*, VII (1933) 17–21. **S**

————, The income of manufacturing corporations, *Conference Board Bulletin*, VIII (1934) 17–20. **S**

ROBINSON, L. R., Corporate earnings on share and borrowed capital in ratios of gross income, *Journal of the American Statistical Association*, XXIX (1934) 39–50. **S**

————, Corporate earnings on share and borrowed capital in ratios of gross income 1918–1935, *Journal of the American Statistical Association*, XXXI (1936) 481–490. **S**

————, Corporate earnings on share and borrowed capital in percentages of gross income 1918–1940, *Journal of the American Statistical Association*, XXXVI (1941) 253–264. **S**

RYLAH, M., National income and company profits in Australia, *Economic Record*, XIV (1938) 98–104. **S**

SIMPSON, K., A statistical analysis of the relation between cost and price, *Quarterly Journal of Economics*, XXXV (1920–1921) 264–287. **S**

————, Further evidence on the relation between price, cost, and profit, *Quarterly Journal of Economics*, XXXVII (1922–1923) 476–490. **S**

SMITH, T. and C. MERWIN, Corporate profits and national income estimates, quarterly, 1938–42, *Survey of Current Business*, XXII (June 1942) 13–18. S

———, Monthly dividend payments, 1941–1942, *Survey of Current Business*, XXII (November 1942) 26–28. S

———, and R. SHERMAN, Recent trends in corporate profits, *Survey of Current Business*, XXII (June 1943) 23–28. S

SUMMERS, H. B., A comparison of the rates of earning of large-scale and small-scale industries, *Quarterly Journal of Economics*, XLVI (1931–1932) 465–479. S

SWEEZY, M. Y., German corporate profits: 1926–1938, *Quarterly Journal of Economics*, LIV (1939–1940) 384–398. S

TUCKER, R. S., Is there a tendency for profits to equalize? *American Economic Review*, XXVII (1937) 519–524. A

YNTEMA, D. B., Corporate Profits and national income, *Survey of Current Business*, XXIV (September 1944) 9–16. S

VII. RENT

VII-A. RENT DOCTRINE IN GENERAL

BLOOM, G. F., Technical progress, costs and rent, *Economica*, IX, new series (1942) 40–52. A

*BOULDING, K. E., The concept of economic surplus, *American Economic Review*, XXXV (1945) 851–869. A

BROWN, H. G., Is a tax on site values never shifted? *Journal of Political Economy*, XXXII (1924) 375–382. A

———, Land rent as a function of population growth, *Journal of Political Economy*, XXXIV (1926) 274–288. A

FETTER, F. A., Comment on rent under increasing returns, *American Economic Review*, XX (1930) 72–76. A. Further comment by A. B. Wolfe, 76–77.

———, Rent, *Encyclopaedia of the Social Sciences*, (editors, E. R. A. Seligman and A. Johnson), XIII, New York, The Macmillan Co., 1934, 289–292. A

HOLLOND, M. T., Marshall on rent: a reply to Professor Ogilvie, *Economic Journal*, XL (1930) 369–383. A

MEHTA, J. K., Rent in economic theory, *Indian Journal of Economics*, XXIII (1942) 59–67. A

MERIAM, R. S., Quasi-rent, *Explorations in Economics*, New York and London, McGraw-Hill Book Co., 1937, 317–325. A

NAVRATIL, A. VON, Rentenprinzip und Grundrente, *Zeitschrift für die gesamte Staatswissenschaft*, LXXXXIV (1933) Heft 3, 385–401. A

OGILVIE, F. W., Marshall on rent, *Economic Journal*, XL (1930) 1–24. A

OHLIN, B., Some aspects of the theory of rent: von Thünen vs. Ricardo, *Economics, Sociology and the Modern World*, Essays in Honour of T. N. Carver, Cambridge, Harvard University Press, 1935, 171–183. A and H

PRIBRAM, K., Residual, differential, and absolute urban ground rents and their cyclical fluctuations, *Econometrica*, VIII (1940) 62–78. A

SANDWELL, B. K., Comment on "rent under increasing returns," *American Economic Review*, XX (1930) 252–255. A

* Reprinted in the present volume.

WEINBERGER, O., Grundrente, *Handwörterbuch der Staatswissenschaften*, Vierte Auflage, IV, Jena, Gustav Fischer, 1923, 1223–1242. **A**

WOLFE, A. B., Rent under increasing returns, *American Economic Review*, XIX (1929) 580–604. **A**

ZWIEDINECK-SÜDENHORST, O., Rentenprinzip oder Rentenstellung, *Zeitschrift für die gesamte Staatswissenschaft*, LXXXXII (1932) Heft 2, 193–211. **A**

VII-B. RENT AND THE PRICES OF COMMODITIES

BROWN, H. G., Land, capital and opportunity cost: a reply, *American Economic Review*, XIX (1930) 248–251. **A.** Further comment on capital value by W. W. Hewett, 251–252.

———, Economic rent; in what sense a surplus? *American Economic Review*, XXXI (1941) 833–835. **A**

*BUCHANAN, D. H., The historical approach to rent and price theory, *Economica*, IX (1929) 123–155. **H**

———, Land rent and prices, *Indian Journal of Economics*, XII (1931) 171–177. **A**

DAS-GUPTA, K., Land rent in relation to the pricing process, *Indian Journal of Economics*, XI (1930) 166–173. **A**

———, Some remarks on value and cost, with special reference to their relation to rent, *Indian Journal of Economics*, XII (1932) 520–541. **A**

FRANKLIN, F., Economic theory and economic criticism—Cassel on rent and on interest, *Political Science Quarterly*, XLI (1926) 240–270. **A**

HAYES, H. G., Land rent and the prices of commodities, *American Economic Review*, XVII (1927) 219–229. **A**

SAHA, K. B., Rent in relation to price, *Indian Journal of Economics*, XII (1932) 507–519. **A**

SANDWELL, B. K., Rent, *American Economic Review*, XVIII (1928) 702–703. **A**

SECRIST, H., Commercial rent as an expense and its relation to profits, *American Economic Review*, Supplement, XIII (1923) 60–89. **S**

VII-C. LAND VALUATION AND INCOME; MONOPOLY ELEMENTS IN RENT

ANDERSON, T. J., JR., Competition and monopoly in land markets, *American Economic Review*, XXXI (1941) 341–343. **A**

CANNAN, E., Land and capital, *American Economic Review*, XIX (1930) 78–79. **A**

CHAMBERS, C. R., Relation of farm land income to farm land value, *American Economic Review*, XIV (1924) 673–698. **S**

ELY, R. F., Land income, *Political Science Quarterly*, XLIII (1928) 408–427. **A**

GHOSH, J. C., Rent and land-revenue in Bengal, *Indian Journal of Economics*, X (1929) 59–80. **S**

ISE, J., Monopoly elements in rent, *American Economic Review*, XXX (1940) 33–45. **A**

MOREHOUSE, E. W., Land valuation, *Encyclopaedia of the Social Sciences*, (editors E. R. A. Seligman and A. Johnson), IX, New York, The Macmillan Co., 1933, 137–139. **A**

ORCHARD, J. E., The rent of mineral lands, *Quarterly Journal of Economics*, XXXVI (1921–1922) 290–318. **A**

SINGER, H. W., An index of urban land rents and house rents in England and Wales, 1845–1913, *Econometrica*, IX (1941) 221–230. **S**

---

*Reprinted in the present volume.

INDEX OF AUTHORS
CITED IN THE BIBLIOGRAPHY

711

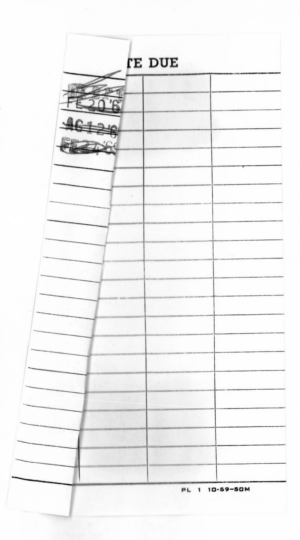

TE DUE

FE 20 '6
AG 12'6
FE 2 '6

PL 1 10-59-50M